ARTIFICIAL INTELLIGENCE:

Methodology, Systems, Applications

Proceedings of the
Sixth International Conference on Artificial Intelligence:
Methodology, Systems, Applications
(AIMSA '94)

ARTIFICIAL
INTELLIGENCE:

Methodology, Systems,
Applications

Sofia, Bulgaria 21 – 24 September, 1994

①
334
I554
1994

Editors

Philippe Jorrand

Centre National de la Recherche Scientifique
Laboratoire d'Informatique Fondamentale et d'Intelligence Artificielle
Grenoble, France

Vassil Sgurev

Bulgarian Academy of Sciences
Institute of Information Technologies
Sofia, Bulgaria

World Scientific
Singapore • New Jersey • London • Hong Kong

Published by

World Scientific Publishing Co. Pte. Ltd.
P O Box 128, Farrer Road, Singapore 9128
USA office: Suite 1B, 1060 Main Street, River Edge, NJ 07661
UK office: 73 Lynton Mead, Totteridge, London N20 8DH

ARTIFICIAL INTELLIGENCE: Methodology, Systems, Applications
Proceedings of the Sixth International Conference on
Artificial Intelligence: Methodology, Systems, Applications (AIMSA '94)

ISBN 981-02-1853-2

Printed in Singapore by Utopia Press.

FOREWORD

Automated reasoning is a central topic in Artificial Intelligence research. Historically, the mechanization of logic has always been a way to implement well founded automated reasoning systems. A large part of this book is devoted to such logical and computational foundations for Artificial Intelligence : automated theorem proving in standard logic, extensions to logic programming, constraint solving, modal logics, reasoning about action and change, machine learning. For most of these topics, this book addresses theoretical bases, algorithms and implementations. Various approaches to object-oriented knowledge representation are presented, with their corresponding forms of reasoning and concrete applications. Several ways to design and apply hybrid systems are also described, where the symbolic and connectionist approaches cooperate, each technique being exploited for the style of reasoning that it can perform better than the other.

Nevertheless, however essential, rich and efficient automated reasoning may be, it cannot, alone, make an Artificial Intelligence system. The actual purpose of such systems is indeed to behave as partners of humans in solving complex problems. In such partnership situations, humans wish to stay with forms and contents of dialog which are as close as possible to their own way of expressing what the problem is and what the steps are towards a solution. Natural language is obviously the most "natural" channel for this bi-directional communication. This book addresses several important topics in natural language processing : parsing, extraction of knowledge from text, modelling of time and space, discourse representation, dialog processing.

The search for foundational roots is becoming a major trend among the Artificial Intelligence community. After decades of pionneering works which have explored new alleys of research, which have led to countless implementations of experimental systems and have considered a vast collection of application domains, Artificial Intelligence is still much in need of a more explicit body of theoretical bases. This is indeed the price to pay for understanding what the relevant questions are, for designing and implementing sound experiments, for building trustable application systems. In short, this is the way to become a mature branch of science and technology. The editors of this book, which emphasises fundamental questions in several key areas of Artificial Intelligence, hope to contribute to this aim.

May, 1994   *Philippe Jorrand, Grenoble, France*
                              Vassil Sgurev, Sofia, Bulgaria

AIMSA'94

is sponsored by

ECCAI
European Coordinating Committee for Artificial Intelligence

and organised by

Bulgarian Artificial Intelligence Association
Foundation "Eureka"
Institute of Information Technology, Bulgarian Academy of Sciences
Laboratoire d'Informatique Fondamentale et d'Intelligence Artificielle, France
Union of Bulgarian Mathematicians

with the support of

Association pour la Promotion de l'Informatique Avancée, France
Bulgarian Association for Pattern Recognition
Bulgarian Society for Cognitive Science

PROGRAM COMMITTEE

Philippe Jorrand, Chairman (France)

Benedict du Boulay (United Kingdom)
Peter Braspenning (The Netherlands)
Jacques Cohen (USA)
Christo Dichev (Ireland)
Danail Dochev (Bulgaria)
Luis Fariñas del Cerro (France)
Les Gasser (USA)
Malik Ghallab (France)
Eva Hajicova (Czech Republic)
Steffen Hölldobler (Germany)
Alberto Martelli (Italy)
Pedro Messeguer (Spain)
Peter Mikulecky (Czech Republic)
Ewa Orlowska (Poland)
Ivan Popchev (Bulgaria)
François Rechenmann (France)
Vassil Sgurev (Bulgaria)
Tibor Vamos (Hungary)

ORGANIZING COMMITTEE

Vassil Sgurev, Chairman (Bulgaria)

Mirella Bello, Secretary (France)
Danail Dochev, Secretary (Bulgaria)

CONTENTS

IX – NATURAL LANGUAGE PROCESSING

I - AUTOMATED THEOREM PROVING

1 - AUTOMATED THEOREM PROVING

Towards a Better Understanding of SL-Resolution

Laurent Oxusoff
LIM, Université de Provence, case 9
2, place Victor Hugo
13000 Marseille cedex – FRANCE
oxusoff@gyptis.univ-mrs.fr

Antoine Rauzy
LaBRI, CNRS, Université Bordeaux I
351, cours de la Libération
33405 Talence Cedex – FRANCE
rauzy@labri.u-bordeaux.fr

Abstract

This paper is an attempt to have a constructive view of the Kowalski and Kuehner's SL-Resolution. More precisely, we show that an intelligent backtracking principle allows the redefinition of the SL-Resolution without the B-ancestor mechanism in terms of an enumerative algorithm, i.e. an algorithm that works by assigning Boolean values to variables. We also study the full SL-resolution and we show that the same construction can almost but not completely be done for this algorithm.

Key words: Automated Reasoning, Linear Resolution.

1 Introduction

Twenty three years ago, R. Kowalski and D. Kuehner published a wonderful paper [1] that was a state of the art on linear resolution and that proposed an new linear resolution algorithm which was more efficient than the previously proposed ones : the linear resolution with selection function (abbreviated in SL-Resolution). Nowadays, SL-Resolution is still considered as one of the most efficient variation of linear resolution and actually outperforms most of the other resolution based methods. This is the reason why it has been chosen to implement the Boolean solver of PrologIII [2].

Nevertheless, the success of linear resolution is mostly due to the success of Prolog. The SLD-Resolution, which is the core of the Prolog inference engine, is a very weak form of linear resolution. It is uncomplete, even when restricted to propositional formulae. On the contrary, SL-Resolution is complete for propositional formulae. However, the proof of completeness of SL-Resolution is hard to understand. It requires a quite unatural induction on the size of the SL-Refutation.

The main difference between SLD-Resolution and SL-Resolution is that the latter includes an ancestor mechanism that permits to avoid many redundant computations. This ancestor mechanism is not clearly applicable on predicate calculus formulae. This is the reason why only few efforts have been done to include it in automated theorem provers.

This paper is an attempt to have a more constructive view of this algorithm, at least for the propositional case. More precisely, we show that an intelligent backtracking principle – the model separation lemma – we have proposed in [3], allows the redefinition of the SL-Resolution without the B-ancestor mechanism in terms of an enumerative algorithm, i.e. an algorithm that works by assigning Boolean values to variables.

The model separation lemma permits also to improve significantly the method and to compare it with variations classical enumerative algorithms.

We show also why it is almost but not completely possible to interpret the full SL-Resolution as an enumerative algorithm.

The remaining of this paper is organized as follows : we begin by presenting the SL-Resolution at section 2. Then, we study the SL-Resolution without B-Ancestor at section 3 and the full SL-Resolution at section 4.

2 SL-Resolution

In this section, we first describe the SL-Resolution as done in the Kowalski and Kuehner's paper, then we give a recursive presentation of the algorithm which is more suitable for our comparison purpose.

2.1 Formal Definition

Let $S = C_1 \wedge C_2 \wedge \ldots \wedge C_m$ be a Boolean in expression in conjunctive normal form, i.e. where each *clause* C_i is a disjunction of literals and each *literal* is either a variable p_i or its negation $\neg p_i$ $(1 \leq i \leq n)$. In what follows, S will be assimilated to a set of clauses and each clause to a set of literals.

A *support set* for S is a subset T of S such that $S - T$ is satisfiable. A typical support set for S is the subset T of its positive clauses (clauses containing only positive literals), since it is clear that $S - T$ is satisfied by assigning the value false to all the variables.

A *chain* is any sequence of literals, each of which is assigned a status of either A- or a *B-literal*. As a notation convention, A-literals are put in boxes. Here follows an example of chain:

$$a \quad \neg b \quad \boxed{c} \quad \boxed{\neg d} \quad e \quad \boxed{f} \quad \neg g \quad h$$

Two B-literals of a chain belong to the same *cell* if they are not separated by an A-literal.

A *selection function* is a function ϕ from chains to chains such that $\phi(C^\star)$ is $C^\star$ or can be obtained from $C^\star$ by interchanging the B-literals of the rightmost cell. The rightmost literal in $\phi(C^\star)$ is the *selected literal* of $C^\star$.

Now, for each clause C_i of S one builds the chain $C_i^\star$ formed with the literals of C_i considered as B-literals. The $C_i^\star$ are called *input chains*.

For a given set of clauses S, support set T and selection function ϕ, a *SL-Derivation* from S is a sequence of chains $D^\star = R_1^\star \ldots R_n^\star$ satisfying (1)–(3).

1. $R_1^\star$ is an input chain from T.

2. $R_{i+1}^\star$ is obtained from $R_i^\star$ by one of extension, reduction or truncation.

3. Unless $R_{i+1}^\star$ is obtained from $R_i^\star$ by reduction, no two literals occurring at distinct positions in $R_i^\star$ have the same atom (*admissibility restriction*).

$R_{i+1}^\star$ is obtained from $R_i^\star$ by *truncation* if (1) and (2).

1. The rightmost literal in $R_i^\star$ is an A-literal.

2. $R_{i+1}^\star$ is the longest initial subsequence of $R_i^\star$ whose rightmost literal is a B-literal.

$R_{i+1}^\star$ is obtained from $R_i^\star$ by *reduction* if (1)–(4).

1. The rightmost literal in $R_i^\star$ is a B-literal.

2. $R_i^\star$ is not obtained form $R_{i-1}^\star$ by truncation.

3. The rightmost cell of $R_i^\star$ contains at least a literal l such that either $R_i^\star$ contains the B-literal l elsewhere than in its rightmost cell (*basic factoring*), or $R_i^\star$ contains the A-literal $\neg l$ (*ancestor resolution*).

4. $R_{i+1}^\star$ is obtained by deleting such a literal l.

$R_{i+1}^\star$ is obtained from $R_i^\star$ by *extension* with an input chain $C^\star$ if (1)–(3).

1. The rightmost literal in $R_i^\star$ is a B-literal.

2. $C^\star$ contains the opposite of the rightmost literal l of $R_i^\star$.

3. Let $C^{\star\star}$ the chain obtained by deleting the literal $\neg l$ from $C^\star$. Then, $R_{i+1}^\star$ is the chain $\phi(R_i^\star.C^{\star\star})$, where . denotes the concatenation and where l has changed of status to become an A-literal.

A SL-Derivation $D^\star = R_1^\star \ldots R_n^\star$ such that R_n is the empty chain (denoted by Λ) is called a *SL-Refutation*.

Example 1 A SL-Refutation

Let $S = (a \lor b \lor c) \land (\neg a \lor b) \land (\neg b \lor c) \land (a \lor \neg c) \land (\neg a \lor \neg b \lor \neg c)$, $T = \{(a \lor b \lor c)\}$, and ϕ be the selection function that arranges literals in alphabetic order. Then, the following sequence is a SL-Refutation :

$R_1^\star$:	c	b	a			
$R_2^\star$:	c	b	$\boxed{a}$	b		extension with $(\neg a \lor b)$
$R_3^\star$:	c	b	$\boxed{a}$			reduction (basic factoring)
$R_4^\star$:	c	b				truncation
$R_5^\star$:	c	$\boxed{b}$	c			extension with $(\neg b \lor c)$
$R_6^\star$:	c	$\boxed{b}$				reduction (basic factoring)
$R_7^\star$:	c					truncation
$R_8^\star$:	$\boxed{c}$	a				extension with $(a \lor \neg c)$
$R_9^\star$:	$\boxed{c}$	$\boxed{a}$	b			extension with $(\neg a \lor b)$
$R_{10}^\star$:	$\boxed{c}$	$\boxed{a}$	$\boxed{b}$	$\neg c$	$\neg a$	extension with $(\neg a \lor \neg b \lor \neg c)$
$R_{11}^\star$:	$\boxed{c}$	$\boxed{a}$	$\boxed{b}$			reduction (ancestor resolution)
$R_{12}^\star$:	Λ					truncation

Theorem 1 Kowalski, Kuehner

A set of clauses S is unsatisfiable if and only if is there exists a SL-Refutation for S.

The proof of this theorem is not easy and requires an induction on the size of the SL-Refutation.

Several remarks can be done on the presented algorithm :

– The admissibility restriction ensures that no extension is performed with a chain $C^\star$ that contains either a literal which occurs as an A-literal in the current resolvent or the opposite of literal which occurs as a B-literal in the current resolvent.

– The condition (2) of reduction ensures that this operation is performed before any further extension.

– In order to be complete, the algorithm must try all possible extensions.

This three remarks lead to a new presentation of the SL-Resolution which is closer to what the algorithm actually does.

2.2 A Recursive Presentation

Let S be a non empty set of clauses and A and B be two sets of literals that don't share any variable and that don't contain both a literal and its opposite.

A clause C is *SL-Deletable* in $< S, A, B >$ if (1) and (2).

1. C contains no literal from A and no opposite of a literal from B.

2. Let $\phi(C) = l_1 l_2 \ldots l_k$ be the sequence obtained by choosing an order on literals of C. Then, each literal l_i of C is SL-Deletable in $< S, A, B \cup \{l_{i+1}, \ldots, l_k\} >$.

A literal l is SL-Deletable in $< S, A, B >$ if one of (1)–(3) is verified.

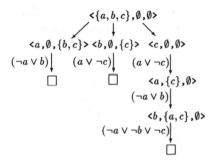

Figure 1: a SL-Refutation tree

1. A contains $\neg l$.

2. B contains l.

3. There exists a clause C in S containing $\neg l$ and SL-Deletable in $< S, A \cup \{l\}, B >$.

The theorem 1 can be rephrased as follows :

Theorem 2 SL-Deletion
Let S be a set of clauses and T be a support set for S. Then, S is unsatisfiable if and only if there exists a clause C in T such that C is SL-Deletable in $< S, \emptyset, \emptyset >$.

In what follows, literals belonging to sets A and B are called respectively A- and B-*ancestors* of the literal or the clause to be deleted.

This new presentation is clearly equivalent to the previous one and induces a tree representation of SL-Derivation. The tree corresponding to the SL-Refutation of example 1 is pictured Fig. 1. On this picture, the set S is omitted and the first member of each triple represents either the clause or the literal to be deleted. Second and third members of a triple denotes respectively the sets A and B.

3   SL-Resolution without B-Ancestor

3.1   Variation

The first step towards a better understanding of the SL-Resolution consists in considering the algorithm without operation and restriction on B-ancestors. We call this variation SLA-Resolution.

The SL-Resolution incorporates one operation on B-ancestors, the basic factoring, which consists in merging, in the current resolvent, different occurrences of the same literal. It is easy to see that the algorithm remains sound and complete and still always terminates if this operation is not performed.

It uses also one restriction on B-ancestors : the condition that no extension is performed with an input chain that contains the opposite of a B-literal of the current resolvent (indeed excepted the selected literal). This condition stands to eliminate tautological resolvents. Once again, soundness, completeness and termination of the algorithm are preserved if this condition is not checked anymore.

The recursive presentation of the SLA-Resolution is as follows :

Let S be a non empty set of clauses and A be a set of literals that doesn't contain both a literal and its opposite.

A clause C is *SLA-Deletable* in $< S, A >$ if (1) and (2).

1. C contains no literal of A.

2. Each literal l of C is SLA-Deletable in $< S, A >$.

A literal l is SLA-Deletable in $< S, A >$ if one of (1) and (2) is verified.

1. A contains $\neg l$.

2. There exists a clause C in S containing $\neg l$ and SLA-Deletable in $< S, A >$.

For the reasons given above, the following result holds :

Theorem 3 SLA-Deletion
Let S be a set of clauses and T be a support set for S. Then, S is unsatisfiable if and only if there exists a clause C in T that is SLA-Deletable in $< S, \emptyset >$.

3.2   Assignments

Let S be a set of clauses, $p_1, \ldots p_k$ be variables and $v_1, \ldots v_k$ be Boolean values. We denote by $S_{p_1 \leftarrow v_1, \ldots, p_k \leftarrow v_k}$, the set S in which the value v_i is assigned to p_i ($1 \leq i \leq k$), i.e. the set of clauses obtained from S by deleting clauses that contain a satisfied literal and suppressing the occurrences of falsified literals from the other clauses. For sake of simplicity, we abbreviate the notations $S_{p \leftarrow 1}$ and $S_{p \leftarrow 0}$ in S_p and $S_{\neg p}$.

Presented as in the previous subsection, the A-ancestor mechanism clearly looks like an assignment of the value true to A-literals. This is formalized by the following property:

Property 4 SLA-Deletion (bis)
Let S be a set of clauses and A be a set of literals that doesn't contain both a literal and its opposite. Then,

- A clause C is SLA-Deletable in $< S, A >$ if and only if A doesn't satisfy C and each literal of C_A is SLA-Deletable in $< S_A, \emptyset >$.

- A literal l is SLA-deletable in $< S, A >$ if either $\neg l \in A$ or there exists a clause containing $\neg l$ in S_A that is deletable in $< S_{A \cup \{l\}}, \emptyset >$.

In what follows, we will simply say that a clause C (resp. a literal l) is SLA-Deletable in S_A.

3.3 Model Partition Lemma, Closed Subsets

Let us now introduce the intelligent backtracking principle that makes the SLA-Resolution comparable with enumerative methods.

Lemma 5 Model Separation [3]
Let S be a set of clauses and A be a set of literals that doesn't contain both a literal and its opposite and such that each clause of S containing the opposite of a literal from A contains also a literal from A. Then, S is satisfiable if and only if S_A is satisfiable.

Proof : it suffices to remark that S_A is a subset of S and that every model of S_A can be extended (with A) into a model of S.

It will appear latter why model separation lemma is a typical intelligent backtracking principle.

Let S be a set of clauses, $H \subseteq S$. We say that H is a *closed subset* of S if there exists a set A of literals that doesn't contain both a literal and its opposite such that (1) and (2).

1. Each clause of S containing the opposite of a literal from A contains also a literal from A.

2. $S_A = S - H$.

We say that A is a character of H.

Example 2 Closed Subset
Let $S = (a \lor b \lor c) \land (\neg a \lor b \lor d) \land (a \lor \neg b \lor \neg c) \land (\neg c \lor d)$. $H = (a \lor b \lor c) \land (\neg a \lor b \lor d) \land (a \lor \neg b \lor \neg c)$ is a closed subset of S, and $\{a, b\}$ is a character for H.

Lemma 6 Union of Closed Subsets
Let S be a set of clauses and H_1 and H_2 be two closed subsets of S. Then, $H_1 \cup H_2$ is a closed subset of S.

Proof : Let A_1 and A_2 be characters for H_1 and H_2. Let A be the set of literals obtained by adding to A_1 the literals l of A_2 such that $\neg l \notin A_1$. It is easy to verify that A is a character for $H_1 \cup H_2$.

Example 3 Union of Closed Subsets
Let S be the set of the previous example (2), H_1 be the subset formed with its first three clauses and H_2 be the subset formed with its three last clauses. $A_1 = \{a, b\}$ is a character for H_1, $A_2 = \{\neg b, d\}$ is a character for H_2. $A = A_1 \cup \{d\}$ is a character for S.

Theorem 7 Covering

Let S be a set of clauses and T be a support set for S. Then, S is satisfiable if and only if there exists a *covering* of T in S, i.e. a set $H = \{H_1, \ldots, H_k\}$ of closed subsets of S such that $T \subseteq H_1 \cup \ldots \cup H_k$.

The theorem 7 has the flavor of an algorithm : in order to verify that a given set of clauses S is satisfiable, it suffices to find, for each clause C belonging to a support set for S, a closed subset that contains C.

Let us now establish the following lemma that gives a constructive way to determine whether there exists a closed subset containing a given clause.

Lemma 8 Finding a Closed Subset

Let S be a set of clauses and $C \in S$. There exists a closed subset H of S containing C if either (1) or (2).

1. C contains a *monotone* literal l (i.e. such that $\neg l$ doesn't occur in S).

2. There exists a literal $l \in C$ such that each clause D of S containing $\neg l$ is such that there exists a closed subset containing D_l in S_l.

Proof : if l is monotone then the subset of clauses containing l is clearly closed and has $\{l\}$ as a character. Now, let $D^1, \ldots, D^k$ be the clauses of S containing $\neg l$. Assume that for each D^i there exists a closed subset H_l^i of S_l containing D^i. By lemma 6, $H_l^1 \cup \ldots \cup H_l^k$ is a closed subset of S_l. It is easy to verify that $H^1 \cup \ldots H^k \cup \{C \in S; l \in C\}$ is a closed subset of S of character $A \cup \{l\}$, where A is any character of $H_l^1 \cup \ldots \cup H_l^k$.

Now, dear reader, please compare the definition of SLA-Deletion with the lemma 8. They are actually dual !

Theorem 9 SLA-Deletion versus Closed Subset

Let S be a set of clauses and $C \in S$. Then C is SLA-Deletable in S if and only if there doesn't exist a closed subset of S containing C.

It follows that SLA-Resolution does nothing but searching for a closed subset containing its root clause.

3.4 Improvement and Comparison

The property 4 permits in some sense the elimination of A-ancestors : at each step, the algorithm works on a given set of clauses $\{D_1, \ldots, D_k\}$ and tries to find a closed subset H_i that contains D_i for $1 \leq i \leq k$. At the first step the D_i's are the clauses of the support set. At a latter step, the D_i's are the clauses of a set $S_{A \cup \{l\}}$ that contained $\neg l$ in S_A.

Several remarks must be pointed out :

- Assume to be found a closed subset H_1 containing D_1. It could be the case that H_1 contains D_2 as well. Nevertheless, the SLA-Resolution "forgets" the closed subsets it finds. Moreover, memorizing a closed subset is very easy since it suffices to memorize one of its character.

- Assume to be found closed subsets H_1 and H_2 of characters A_1 and A_2 and containing D_1 and D_2. Then, by lemma 6, one knows how to build the character A of the closed subset $H_1 \cup H_2$. Thus, it suffices to maintain a single closed subset H (or more exactly its character) that grows step by step until all the D_i's belong to H or that a D_i is found that cannot belong to any closed subset.

- Lemma 8 gives a bottom-up way to build closed subsets. As a consequence, we can consider globally all the clauses to be cover by a closed subset.

Now, consider the following algorithm :
Let S be a set of clauses and A be a set of literals that doesn't contain both a literal and its opposite. Then,

- If S_A is empty, then it is satisfiable.

- If S_A contains an empty clause, then it is unsatisfiable.

- Otherwise, choose a clause $C = l_1 \vee \ldots \vee l_k$ from S_A, then S_A is satisfiable if and only if $S_{A \cup \{l_1\}}$ is satisfiable or $S_{A \cup \{l_2\}}$ is satisfiable or ...or $S_{A \cup \{l_k\}}$ is satisfiable.

This algorithm consists in going through a search tree whose vertices are labeled with clauses and whose outedges are labeled with literals (belonging to the clauses labeling the vertices they leave).

Assume that at a given node n, the studied set of clauses was S_A and that at the node n' the studied set is $S_{A \cup B}$. Assume in addition that $S_{A \cup B} \subset S_A$, i.e. that each clause from S_A that contains an opposite of a literal from B contains also a literal from B. Then, by model separation lemma, S_A is satisfiable if and only if $S_{A \cup B}$ is satisfiable. As a consequence, if $S_{A \cup B}$ is shown to be unsatisfiable, it is useless to explore the remaining alternatives of choice points created between the nodes n and n'.

This the reason why the model separation lemma is actually an intelligent backtracking principle.

Note that the above algorithm is compatible with the support set refinement : the first point can be replaced by the following one:

- If $T \subseteq S_A \subset S$ where T is a support set for S, then S is satisfiable.

Moreover, the clause C can be chosen in the last shortened clauses (as done by SLA-Resolution). In [4], we called the above algorithm augmented with the model separation lemma "weak semantic evaluation".

The following result can be establish by means of a stepwise comparison (that we do not do here, due to space limitation) :

Theorem 10 Comparison
The search tree of weak semantic evaluation is always include into the SLA-Resolution tree.

And thus, this algorithm is always faster than the SLA-Resolution.

Weak semantic evaluation is clearly an enumerative algorithm. It can be seen as a variation of the Davis and Putnam's procedure [5]. However, it is even closer to the Bibel's connections matrix [6]. This method consists in finding a path through the set of clauses considered as a matrix. Such a path cannot contain both a literal and its opposite and must contain at least a literal per clause. Up to the model separation lemma, it is what weak semantic evaluation actually does.

4 Full SL-Resolution

Let us go back to the full SL-Resolution. B-literals play a symmetrical role than A-literals : they are immediately deletable and a clause that contain an opposite of B-literal cannot be used for an extension.

The theorem 4 can be actually extended as follows :

Property 11 SL-Deletion
Let S be a set of clauses and A and B be two sets of literals that don't share any variable and that don't contain both a literal and its opposite. Let us denote by $\neg B$ the set of opposite literals of literals from B. Then, a clause C is SL-Deletable in $< S, A, B >$ if and only if $A \cup \neg B$ doesn't satisfy C and $C_{A \cup \neg B}$ is SL-Deletable in $< S_{A \cup \neg B}, \emptyset, \emptyset >$.

In addition, the weak semantic evaluation can be extended as follows :
Let S be a set of clauses and A be a set of literals that doesn't contain both a literal and its opposite. Then,

- If S_A is empty, then it is satisfiable.

- If S_A contains an empty clause, then it is unsatisfiable.

- Otherwise, choose a clause $C = l_1 \vee \ldots \vee l_k$ from S_A, then S_A is satisfiable if and only if $S_{A \cup \{l_1, \neg l_2, \ldots, \neg l_k\}}$ is satisfiable or $S_{A \cup \{l_2, \neg l_3, \ldots, \neg l_k\}}$ is satisfiable or $\ldots$ or $S_{A \cup \{l_k\}}$ is satisfiable.

The set A contains both A- and B-Ancestors. Note, that this algorithm is close to the Davis and Putnam's procedure, up to the heuristic used to choose the next literal to assign. The model separation lemma can be applied on this algorithm as well.

Alas, it is not possible to generalized the notion of covering by closed sets. Let us consider the following example :

Example 4 SL-Resolution Let $S = (a \lor b) \land (\neg a \lor c \lor \neg d) \land (\neg c \lor d) \land (b \lor \neg d)$. $T = (a \lor b)$ is a support set for S. A possible SL-Derivation is :

$R_1^\star$: b a

$R_2^\star$: $b \boxed{a} \neg d$ c extension with $(\neg a \lor c \lor \neg d)$

failure

The SL-Derivation fails since the only clause containing $\neg c$ ($\neg c \lor d$) contains the opposite of the B-literal $\neg d$ and no other clause contains $\neg a$. But $S_{\{a, \neg b, c, d\}}$ is unsatisfiable !

If it is not possible to interpret the full SL-Resolution as an enumerative algorithm, it is nevertheless possible to simplify its completeness proof by adopting, as for SLA-Resolution, a dual point of view.

Let S be a set of clauses and $C = l_1 \lor \ldots \lor l_k$ be a clause from S. There exists an *halo* around C in S if there exists l_i ($1 \leq i \leq k$) such that either (1) or (2).

1. l_i is monotone in $S_{\{\neg l_{i+1}, \ldots, \neg l_k\}}$.

2. There exists an halo around each clause of $S_{\{l_i, \neg l_{i+1}, \ldots, \neg l_k\}}$ that was containing $\neg l_i$ in S.

It is clear that the notions of SL-Deletion and Halo are dual. Soundness and completeness of SL-Resolution are justified by the following theorem :

Theorem 12 Halos

Let S be a set of clauses and C be a clause from S. If there exists an halo around C in S, then S is satisfiable if and only if $S - C$ is satisfiable.

Proof : By induction on the number of clauses in S.

5   Conclusion

In this paper, we provide a new presentation of the SL-Resolution. We show that, by taking a dual point of view, one can improve this algorithm or at least have a more constructive completeness proof for it. The relationship established with enumerative algorithms is interesting as well, for it permits to have a better feeling to design accurate heuristics and improvements.

It would be very interesting to study whether it is possible to extend these results to predicate calculus formulae, or for instance for resolution based algorithms in modal logic.

References

[1] R. Kowalski and D. Kuehner. Linear Resolution with Selection Function. *Artificial Intelligence*, pages 227–259, 1971.

[2] J.M. Boï and A. Rauzy. Two algorithms for constraints system solving in propositional calculus and their implementation in prologIII. In P. Jorrand and V. Sugrev, editors, *Proceedings Artificial Intelligence IV Methodology, Systems, Applications (AIMSA '90)*. North-Holand, september 1990. Alba-Varna bulgarie.

[3] S. Jeannicot, L. Oxusoff, and A. Rauzy. Évaluation Sémantique en Calcul Proposition-nel. *Revue d'Intelligence Artificielle*, 2:41–60, 1988.

[4] L. Oxusoff and A. Rauzy. *L'Évaluation Sémantique en Calcul Propositionnel*. PhD thesis, GIA – Université de Aix-Marseille II, 1989.

[5] M. Davis and H. Putnam. A Computing Procedure for Quantification Theory. *JACM*, 7:201–215, 1960.

[6] W. Bibel. On Matrix with Connections. *JACM*, 28(4), october 1981.

DECOMPOSITION TECHNIQUES AND THEIR APPLICATIONS IN AUTOMATED THEOREM PROVING

ERICA MELIS*

School of Computer Science

Carnegie Mellon University

Pittsburgh, PA 15213

email: melis@cs.cmu.edu

ABSTRACT

This paper addresses the decomposition of proofs as a means of constructing methods in plan-based automated theorem proving. It shows also, how decomposition can beneficially be applied in theorem proving by analogy. Decomposition is also useful for human-style proof presentation. We propose several decomposition techniques that were found to be useful in automated theorem proving and give examples of their application.

1 Introduction

The way human experts solve problems often differs from the way computers solve the same problem. For instance, among other differences, human experts can take larger steps [8], while automated systems perform well-defined basic steps towards a solution. This is particularly the case in automated theorem proving systems. These systems usually apply fixed proof calculus rules, e.g., resolution, as basic steps. However, some automated theorem provers have in-built procedures that are specialized to deal with particular subproblems [3],[15], and some employ well-defined larger chunks of steps to search more efficiently for a proof.

These chunks have to be defined by the user or system designer and built into the system, or they are created by the system. Since the design and implementation of complex user-defined chunks is laborious, researchers considered alternatives: Some systems are enriched with a few complex methods which are widely applicable, such as rippling. For instance, Nuprl uses tactics, OYSTER/CLAM [16] employs

---

*On leave from University of Saarbrücken, Germany. This work was supported by the Max Kade Foundation

methods, and INKA [1] works with partial plans. Some interactive approaches tackle the building of complex methods by **method synthesis**, i.e., by combining less complex methods via "high level components". But still, these alternatives do not in general yield all methods used by mathematicians nor all those methods that are generated and needed in theorem proving by analogy. We suggest an **analysis** by decomposing methods as an additional means of constructing methods from other methods.

As the decomposed proof in figure 1 shows, structuring is a very natural activity in finding and understanding proofs: level1 of the proof represents the proof idea, whereas the level2 subproofs supply proofs for statements in level1, specific constructions of objects etc. If one of these subproofs is itself complicated, then the details may be pushed further down to lower levels.

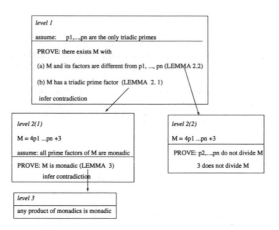

Figure 1: structured proof of theorem1: There exist infinitely many *triadic* primes

This paper addresses heuristically justified break downs of given (partial) proofs into appropriate parts. We introduce techniques for decomposing proofs, and discuss applications in theorem proving by analogy, in debugging of failed analogies, and in proof presentation[a].

---

[a]Denotational notes: We rely on Natural Deduction proofs applying ∧D-rule etc. For our purpose, we use the notion "method" and "(partial) subproof" interchangeable. A problem is defined as a pair (ass, thm) of a set of assumptions and a theorem. A problem is proved by proving $ass \vdash thm$.

2 Decomposition Techniques

We shall now present several general purpose techniques which are widely applicable for decomposing mathematical proofs. These techniques work not just for proofs but also for partially specified (henceforth partial) proofs.

- The decomposition of proofs by user-supplied *motivations* is introduced in [4]. The range of a motivation is a subproof. Brock et al. give the following example:

```
...(motive (Eliminate X in 2)
      (chain 1 and 2)
      (eliminate variable X in 3))...
```

  This motivation specifies that the purpose of the chaining step is to do variable elimination, which means that the steps included in the range of the motivation form a method that can be treated separately.

- A well known technique in theorem proving is decomposing a proof into subproofs when the theorem is a conjunction or an equivalence (see [2]). It provides a subproof for each conjunct and one consisting of a ∧-introduction step.

- The straightforward decomposition of inductive proofs is well known.

- A decomposition of a case analysis yields $n + 1$ methods, which can be identified in a Natural Deduction proof, namely one for each of the n cases and one for the rest of the proof.

- The decomposition techniques which identify key steps in a proof presume that the proof parts leading from one key step to another constitute subproofs. The following two heuristics for finding key steps were proposed by Stephen Owen in [14]:
  - The application of certain assumptions, such as definitions and axioms, are key steps of a proof.
  - A proof step, where temporarily introduced symbols are removed, often represents the completion of a part of a proof. Hence, the step immediately following the removal is usually a key step.

- The applications of a definition or an axioms forms a subproof M_1 itself, such that a proof M can be decomposed into M_1 and the rest of M. This is particularly useful, if the definition or axiom is applied at the beginning or the end of a proof, since you may just cut the first or the last part of the proof.

- A simple decomposition heuristic is to look for a statement that is used several times in a proof. The derivation of such a statement, which is a well defined part of the proof tree, can likely be considered as a subproof.

- Deduction-Theorem Splitting
  If a hypothesis[b] is introduced into a proof P and eliminated later, then

---

[b] which corresponds to "let..." in mathematical proofs

that part of the proof tree which is situated in between (and includes) this introduction and elemination, forms a subproof M_1. M_1 itself can be split into two subproofs M_{11} and M_{12}, where M_{12} consists of the application of the Deduction theorem ($\rightarrow$introduction) and M_{11} contains the rest. In case $\forall$-introductions follow the application of the Deduction theorem, they belong to M_{12} as well. In the example below the decomposition yields just two subproofs, as $P = M_1$.

Example-1

Proof of $\emptyset \vdash \forall x, y((Qxy \rightarrow \forall z(Pxz \rightarrow Pyz)) \land Qab \land (Paa \lor Pbb) \rightarrow \exists x Pbx)$

NNo	S;D	Formula	Reason
		M_{11}	
1.	; 1	$\vdash \ \forall x, y(Qxy \rightarrow \forall z(Pxz \rightarrow Pyz)) \land Qab \land (Paa \lor Pbb)$	(HYP)
$\vdots$	$\vdots$	$\vdots$	$\vdots$
11.	;1;	$\vdash \ \exists z Pbz$	($\lor D$;8,3,1)
		M_{12}	
12.	;	$\vdash \ \forall x, y((Qxy \rightarrow \forall z(Pxz \rightarrow$ $Pyz)) \land Qab \land (Paa \lor Pbb) \rightarrow \exists z Pbz)$	($\rightarrow I$;9)

- ## Several Splittings for Relevant Assumptions
  Our analysis [11] of the proofs by analogy in a mathematical textbook [5] provided evidence for the fact that only *relevant* proof assumptions are used for analogous proofs. For instance, often just common parts of definitions of the source and the target problem create an analogy. These commonalities are sometimes hidden in the assumptions. For example, the definitions of *left-congruence*(R) and *equivalence-relation*(R) have, among others, the common component *symmetric*(R) which is employed in the example below. Relevant-Assumption splitting decomposes a proof into one subproof that extracts it relevant assumptions from the proof assumptions and another subproof that uses the extracted assumptions. As a result, assumptions of different proofs may become comparable.
  The strongest Relevant-Assumptions-decomposition splits a proof M into two subproofs M_1 and M_2, such that M_1 contains all lines with proof assumptions (lines 1 - 4 in example-2) and those lines of M which result from rules that are applied just to lines of M_1 but not to others[c]. M_2 is the rest of the proof. In most cases such a decomposition is far too strong. The weakest Relevant-Assumptions decomposition splits M into M_1 and M_2 such that all assumption lines are in M_1, and all lines of M resulting by applying $\land$-deletion to lines of M_1 are in M_1 and the rest is in M_2. In general, several Relevant-Assumptions splittings exist between the strongest and the weakest decomposition.

---

[c]this seems to be similar to the attempts in [18]

A rather practical and well-suited Relevant-Assumptions technique yields an M_1 that contains all lines with proof assumptions and lines of M which result from applying definitions and $\wedge$-deletion to lines of M_1. Again, this technique can yield several options of splittings, as shown in the examples below. The choice of alternatives can be controlled, e.g., in the analogy procedure, by considering the target problem.

Examples-2
Theorem 4[d]: Let ρ and σ be two equivalence relations, then $(\rho \cap \sigma)$ is symmetric.

Option (1) for Relevant-Assumptions splitting of the proof of theorem 4

NNo	S;D		Formula	Reason
			M_1	
1.	; 1	$\vdash$	$\forall R(equivrel(R) \leftrightarrow refl(R) \wedge symm(R) \wedge trans(R))$	(DEF)
2.	; 2	$\vdash$	$\forall R(symm(R) \leftrightarrow \forall x_1, x_2((x_1, x_2) \in R \to (x_2, x_1) \in R))$	(DEF)
3.	; 3	$\vdash$	$\forall R_1, R_2, x((x \in (R_1 \cap R_2) \leftrightarrow (x \in R_1 \wedge x \in R_2))$	(DEF)
4.	; 4	$\vdash$	$equivrel(\rho)$	(ASS)
5.	; 5	$\vdash$	$equivrel(\sigma)$	(ASS)
6.	; 4	$\vdash$	$refl(\rho) \wedge symm(\rho) \wedge trans(\rho)$	(appl-def 4)
7.	; 4	$\vdash$	$refl(\sigma) \wedge symm(\sigma) \wedge trans(\sigma)$	(appl-def 5)
8.	; 4	$\vdash$	$symm(\rho)$	($\wedge$D 6)
9.	; 5	$\vdash$	$symm(\sigma)$	($\wedge$D 7)
			M_2	
10.	; 2, 8	$\vdash$	$\forall x_1, x_2((x_1, x_2) \in \rho \to (x_2, x_1) \in \rho)$	(appl-def 8)
11.	; 2, 9	$\vdash$	$\forall x_1, x_2((x_1, x_2) \in \sigma \to (x_2, x_1) \in \sigma)$	(appl-def 9)
12.	12;	$\vdash$	$(f_1, f_2) \in (\sigma \cap \rho)$	(HYP)
$\vdots$	$\vdots$		$\vdots$	$\vdots$
24.	;3,2,9,8	$\vdash$	$symm(\sigma \cap \rho)$	($\forall$D,$\leftrightarrow$D,$\to$D)

Option (2) for Relevant-Assumptions splitting of the proof of theorem 4

NNo	S;D		Formula	Reason
			M_1	
1.	; 1	$\vdash$	$\forall R(equivrel(R) \leftrightarrow refl(R) \wedge symm(R) \wedge trans(R))$	(DEF)
2.	; 2	$\vdash$	$\forall R(symm(R) \leftrightarrow \forall x_1, x_2((x_1, x_2) \in R \to (x_2, x_1) \in R))$	(DEF)
3.	; 3	$\vdash$	$\forall R_1, R_2, x((x \in (R_1 \cap R_2) \leftrightarrow (x \in R_1 \wedge x \in R_2))$	(DEF)
4.	; 4	$\vdash$	$equivrel(\rho)$	(ASS)
5.	; 5	$\vdash$	$equivrel(\sigma)$	(ASS)
6.	; 4	$\vdash$	$refl(\rho) \wedge symm(\rho) \wedge trans(\rho)$	(appl-def 4)
7.	; 4	$\vdash$	$refl(\sigma) \wedge symm(\sigma) \wedge trans(\sigma)$	(appl-def 5)
8.	; 4	$\vdash$	$symm(\rho)$	($\wedge$D 6)
9.	; 5	$\vdash$	$symm(\sigma)$	($\wedge$D 7)
10.	; 2, 8	$\vdash$	$\forall x_1, x_2((x_1, x_2) \in \rho \to (x_2, x_1) \in \rho)$	(appl-def 8)
11.	; 2, 9	$\vdash$	$\forall x_1, x_2((x_1, x_2) \in \sigma \to (x_2, x_1) \in \sigma)$	(appl-def 9)

[d]Example from [5].

$$\underline{\hspace{4cm}\text{M}_2\hspace{4cm}}$$

12.	12;	$\vdash \quad (f_1, f_2) \in (\sigma \cap \rho)$	(HYP)
	$\vdots$	$\vdots$	$\vdots$
24.	;3,2,9,8	$\vdash \quad symm(\sigma \cap \rho)$	$(\forall D, \leftrightarrow D, \rightarrow D)$

- **A Rule-independent Heuristic**
  Our experience with analogy-driven proof plan construction so far suggests that the backward reasoning part of a proof constitutes the proof idea. This heuristic can be used for structurings required for analogy of proof ideas.

3 Applications

3.1 *Obtaining New Methods*

Most obviously, the above decomposition techniques provide new chunks or methods for theorem provers as discussed in the introduction. Methods which resulted from a decomposition might be stored (maybe generalized), if they appear frequently.

3.2 *Theorem Proving by Analogy*

Theorem proving by analogy means to find a proof of a target problem, which is supposed to be similar to a source problem, guided by the known proof of the source problem. Empirical evidence indicates that analogies can best be handled appropriately in a proof planning framework (see [12]). There are at least three reasons why methods have to be restructured within the analogy procedure:

1. Analogies exist at different levels of granularity, such that only some submethods can be transferred appropriately to the target. Consider, for instance, theorem1' which results from exchanging "triadic" by "monadic" in the theorem1: There exist infinitely many *triadic* primes. of figure 1. The proofs of theorem1 and theorem1' are similar on "top-level", which means that the level1-method, but not the lower level methods, can be transferred, from proof1 to proof1'. In other proofs by analogy the similarity goes deeper and then lower level methods can be transferred successfully.

2. A condition for the analogical transfer of methods to target proof plan methods is that the problem they prove matches a goal (a problem) of the partial target proof plan. There are, however, different formulations of essentially the same problem. As shown in the examples below, restructuring is one means to make the assumptions and the theorems of the source and the target problem comparable and thus matching (e.g., by extracting common assumptions).

3. The reformulation of methods which perform the analogical transfer of source methods to target methods may be different for different submethods.

Technically, the frame-like planning-operators, called *methods*, contain a slot with the (partial) subproof scheme they produce. Hence, these methods can be restructured by decomposing partial proofs. The restructuring of methods is done by *meta-methods*, which correspond to the decomposition techniques above[e]. For instance, the meta-method Deduction-Theorem-Splitting is applied to a source method S in order to be able to compare (and finally to match) theorems and assumptions of S and a target method T.

Example-3

Assume you like to prove P_T by analogy to the source proof of P_S, where:
P_S: $(\emptyset \vdash \forall x, y((Qxy \rightarrow \forall z(Pxz \rightarrow Pyz)) \wedge Qab \wedge (Paa \vee Pbb) \rightarrow \exists x Pbx)$ and
P_T: $(\{\forall x, y((Qxy \rightarrow \forall z(Pxz \rightarrow Pyz)), Qab, Qbc, (Paa \vee Pcc)\} \vdash \exists x Pcx)$.

As neither the assumptions nor the conclusions of P_S and P_T can be compared directly, even after some reformulation, the source method is restructured by Deduction-Theorem-Splitting. It yields two methods S_2 with the postcondition P_S and S_1 with the postcondition $\{\forall x, y((Qxy \rightarrow \forall z(Pxz \rightarrow Pyz)) \wedge Qab \wedge (Paa \vee Pbb)\} \vdash \exists x Pbx$. In the subsequent analogy process, S_1 can be reformulated to a method the postcondition of which matches P_T.

Example-4

Theorem proving by analogy often requires the application of Relevant-Assumptions splittings in order to compare the actual assumptions of a problem. The actual splitting may depend on the target problem:
Assume you like to prove theorem 3.1 by analogy to theorem4, where:
Theorem 3.1 Let ρ and σ be two leftcongruences, then $(\rho \cap \sigma)$ is symmetric.
Theorem 4 Let ρ and σ be two equivalence relations, then $(\rho \cap \sigma)$ is symmetric.

An appropriate Relevant-Assumptions meta-method splits the proof of theorem4, which can be considered as a method, according to option (1) in example-2.

Assume you like to prove theorem3.2 by analogy to theorem4, where:
Theorem 3.2 Let ρ and σ be two leftcongruences, then
$\forall f(f \in F \rightarrow \forall x_1, x_2((x_1 x_2) \in (\rho \cap \sigma) \rightarrow (fx_1 fx_2) \in (\rho \cap \sigma)))$.
Theorem 4 Let ρ and σ be two equivalence relations, then $(\rho \cap \sigma)$ is symmetric.

An appropriate Relevant-Assumptions meta-method splits the proof of theorem 4, which can be considered as a method, according to option (2) in example-2.

Debugging Analogies

The analysis of failed analogies is an important activity in automated theorem proving by analogy. One necessary component of any such analysis is to find those methods that cannot be transferred adequately to the target proof. Since there are

---

[e]For a more detailed description see [11].

analogies at different levels of granularity (see [9]), the restructuring meta-methods support the debugging process. They isolate those submethods where the failure is located, and which have to be replaced. In the triadic prime number proof (figure 1), for instance, one has to modify all but the level1-methods to get a correct proof plan for the analogous monadic primes proof. In other cases, there is a deeper similarity between the source and the target proof, such that just lower level submethods have to be adjusted.

3.3 *Proof Presentation*

Often automated theorem provers generate proofs that are difficult to understand. Usually they differ considerably from human-style mathematical proofs. Even Natural Deduction proofs are far too detailed and hardly readable. In [7] a presentation of proofs similar to proofs in textbooks is investigated. For such a presentation, proofs that were originally generated by an automated theorem prover are reconstructed. One component of the reconstruction is to find appropriate chunks in a proof. This can be done inter alia by decomposition.

Here is a typical example, where steps of the problem rewriting correspond to the application of decomposition techniques yielding subproofs that prove the rewritten problem[f].

Theorem Let $E \subset F$ and let ρ be a leftcongruence in the semi-group F which is compatible with E, then $\rho \subset \pi_E$.

The problem which is to prove is $\Delta \vdash \rho \subset \pi_E$ with
$\Delta = \{leftcongruence(\rho), compatible(\rho, E), (E \subset F), semigroup(F)\}$.
    The problem is reformulated:
1. **Expanding the definition of** $\subset$ yields the subproblem
   $\Delta \vdash \forall x, y((x, y) \in \rho \rightarrow (x, y) \in \pi_E)$.
2. **Two applications of the Deduction Theorem** yield the subproblem
   $\Delta \cup \{(x_0, y_0) \in \rho\} \vdash (x_0 \in E \leftrightarrow y_0 \in E) \wedge \forall f(f \in F \rightarrow fx_0 \in E \leftrightarrow fy_0 \in E)$.
3. **Expanding the definition of** π_E yields the subproblem
   $\Delta \vdash ((x_0, y_0) \in \rho \rightarrow (x_0 \in E \leftrightarrow y_0 \in E) \wedge \forall f(f \in F \rightarrow fx_0 \in E \leftrightarrow fy_0 \in E))$.
4. **Equivalences splitting** yields the subproblems
   - $\Delta \cup \{(x_0, y_0) \in \rho\} \vdash (x_0 \in E \leftrightarrow y_0 \in E) \wedge \forall f(f \in F \rightarrow fx_0 \in E \rightarrow fy_0 \in E)$
   - $\Delta \cup \{(x_0, y_0) \in \rho\} \vdash (x_0 \in E \leftrightarrow y_0 \in E) \wedge \forall f(f \in F \rightarrow fy_0 \in E \rightarrow fx_0 \in E)$.
5. **Conjunctive Splitting** yields the subproblems
   - $\Delta \cup \{(x_0, y_0) \in \rho\} \vdash \forall f(f \in F \rightarrow fx_0 \in E \rightarrow fy_0 \in E)$
   - $\Delta \cup \{(x_0, y_0) \in \rho\} \vdash \forall f(f \in F \rightarrow fy_0 \in E \rightarrow fx_0 \in E)$.
   - $\Delta \cup \{(x_0, y_0) \in \rho\} \vdash (x_0 \in E \leftrightarrow y_0 \in E)$

---

[f] The next theorem is theorem 17.6.3 is examined in a case-study on a mathematical textbook [10]

6. **Application of the Deduction Theorem** yields the subproblems

  1. $\Delta \cup \{(x_0, y_0) \in \rho\} \cup \{f_0 \in F, f_0 x_0 \in E\} \vdash f_0 y_0 \in E$
  2. $\Delta \cup \{(x_0, y_0) \in \rho\} \cup \{f_0 \in F, f_0 y_0 \in E\} \vdash f_0 x_0 \in E$

Some of the subproofs which are produced by decomposition are likely to be omitted in a human-style presentation, since usually they are not even mentioned in a mathematician's proofs. Actually, the proof of the theorem is presented in [5] as follows (note the reverse order of steps):

Let $(x_0, y_0) \in \rho$.
Let $f x_0 \in E$, then $f y_0 \in E$ is shown,
therefore we have, $\forall f (f x_0 \in E \rightarrow f y_0 \in E)$.
The inverse direction $(f y_0 \in E \rightarrow f x_0 \in E)$ is shown analogously and also $(x_0 \in E \leftrightarrow y_0 \in E)$.
Then $(x_0 y_0) \in \pi_E$.
Hence we get $\rho \subset \pi_E$, since x_0, y_0 were arbitrary elements of F.
The steps 2, 4, and 6 are not mentioned in the textbook.

As shown in [9] different levels of proof presentation may be appropriate depending on the presentation purpose. For a general understanding of a proof, a high level presentation is most useful. For such a presentation you have to find the part of the proof that encodes the proof idea. This is again a question of decomposition. For instance, the level1-partial proof in figure 1 encodes the global view of the proof, while level1 together with level2 provides a lower level presentation.

4   Conclusion

The use of decomposition is not limited to theorem proving. Basically the same necessity of restructuring solutions as in our analogy-driven proof plan construction appears, e.g., in merging multiple cases in the analogical replay of the problem solving system Prodigy, as described by Manuela Veloso in [17]. We claim that often **temporary** macro-operators are sufficient to handle the commonly encountered cases of analogy in problem solving. This is contrary to the common view in planning, (see [13]), which regards macro-operators as repeatedly used sequences of operators and suggests to keep them permanently. The idea behind decomposition is to introduce temporary macro-operators regardless of whether they are repeatedly employed.

This paper has focused on applications in automated theorem proving and in particular on the analogy of proofs. The decomposition techniques presented have been tailored for theorem proving and contribute to analogy, discovery of methods, and presentation of mathematical proofs. The techniques have been tested on exapmles from [5] and applied in the analogy-driven proof plan construction of the pumping lemma for cfl.

Related work was reported in [6] where outlines of proofs, which are somehow comparable to proof ideas, are constructed by abstractions. An open problem is the control of the application of decompositions, as well as of abstractions.

5 References

1. S. Biundo, B. Hummel, D. Hutter, and Ch. Walther. The Karlsruhe Induction Theorem Proving System. In *Proc. 8th International Conference on Automated Deduction (CADE)*, LNCS 230. Springer, 1986.

2. W. Bledsoe. Splitting heuristics in automatic theorem proving. *Artificial Intelligence*, 2:55–77, 1971.

3. R.S. Boyer and J.S. Moore. Integrating decision procedures into heuristic theorem provers: A case study of linear arithmetic. *Machine Intelligence*, 11:83–124, 1988.

4. B. Brock, S. Cooper, and W. Pierce. Some experiments with analogy in proof discovery. Tech.Rep. AI-347-86, Microelectronics and Computer Technology Corporation, Austin, TX, 1986.

5. P. Deussen. *Halbgruppen und Automaten*, volume 99 of *Heidelberger Taschenbücher*. Springer, 1971.

6. F. Giunchiglia and T. Walsh. Tree subsumption: Reasoning with outlines. In *Proceedings of 11th ECAI*, pages 77–81, Vienna, 1992.

7. X. Huang. Reconstructing proofs at the assertion level. In *Proc. 12th International Conference on Automated Deduction (CADE)*, Nancy, 1994.

8. J.Larkin, J. McDermott, D. Simon, and H. Simon. Expert and novice performance in solving physics problems. *Science*, 208:1335–1342, 1980.

9. U. Leron. Structuring mathematical proofs. *The American Mathematical Monthly*, 90:174–185, 1983.

10. E. Melis. Analogies between proofs – a case study. SEKI-Report SR-93-12, Universität des Saarlandes, Saarbrücken, 1993.

11. E. Melis. Change of representation in theorem proving by analogy. SEKI-Report SR-93-07, Universität des Saarlandes, Saarbrücken, 1993.

12. E. Melis. How mathematicians prove theorems. In *Proceedings of the Sixteenth Annual Conference of the Cognitive Science Society*, Atlanta, Georgia U.S.A., 1994.

13. S Minton. Selectively generalizing plans for problem solving. In *Proceedings of AAAI-85*, 1985.

14. S. Owen. *Analogy for Automated Reasoning*. Academic Press, 1990.

15. M.K. Stickel. Automated deduction by theory resolution. In *Proceedings of the 9th IJCAI*, pages 1181–1186, 1985.

16. F. van Harmelen, A. Ireland, S.Negrete, A. Stevens, and A. Smail. The CLAM proof planner, user manual and programmers manual. Technical Report version 2.0, University of Edinburgh, Edinburgh, 1993.

17. M.M. Veloso. *Learning by Analogical Reasoning in General Problem Solving*. PhD thesis, Carnegie Mellon University, CMU, Pittsburgh, USA, 1992. CMU-CS-92-174.

18. Ch. Walther and Th. Kolbe. Optimizing proof search by machine learning techniques. In *Workshop on Automated Theorem Proving IJCAI-93*, Chambery, 1993.

A Polynomial Method for Sub-Clauses Production

R. GÉNISSON and **P. SIEGEL**
Laboratoire d'Informatique de Marseille
URA CNRS 1787
Université Aix-Marseille I, UFR MIM
3 place Victor Hugo - Case 72
13331 Marseille Cedex 3 France

E-mail genisson@gyptis.univ-mrs.fr

ABSTRACT

We introduce a polynomial algorithm whose goal is to simplify the SAT problem resolution. It is a production method which achieves a simplification of a set of clauses by producing some sub-clauses this set implies. The complexity of this algorithm is polynomial and we show that it is complete on the actually known polynomial classes of the SAT problem. The main goal of this method is to perform in polynomial time what is polynomially feasible to concentrate on the hard part of the problems.

1 Introduction

In the following, we shall assume the reader is familiar with propositional calculus. Well-formed formulae will simply be called formulae. Literals are propositional variables with an assigned parity (positive or negative literals). If F is a formula, $v(F)$ stands for the set of propositional variables which occur in F. An interpretation of F is a map from $v(f)$ to $\{0, 1\}$. A formula is said *satisfaiable* if for some interpretation it is true, it is said *unsatisfiable* otherwise. A formula is in conjunctive normal form *(CNF)* if it is written as a conjunction of disjunctions of literals. Disjuncts in CNF are called *clauses*.

The SAT problem is the decision problem of the satisfiability of a boolean formula. We study here the equivalent problem on the CNF expression of the formula. All decision algotithms actually known are exponential, since the problem is NP-complete. On the other hand, practically, the sets of clauses we study often present a sub-set which can be easily simplified. With resolution methods, this simplification can be polynomially achieved essentially by unit-resolution, binary resolution and, more generally, by computing only the resolvents which are not longer than the initial clauses.

This kind of simplification can be useful in particular in random problems and also in the sets of clauses issued from the constraints satisfaction problems. Many constraints satisfaction problems can effectively be written as a small set of first order formulae. In the finite domains case, these formulae can, instanciating variables on domains, be seen as a set of propositional clauses which can be easily simpified.

We introduce here such a simplification algorithm. It is based on a coding of a set of clauses by a set of logical implications and on an inference rule based on the transitivity of logical implication. We show how this method allows us to decide the consistency of a set of clauses among the polynomial classes[1] actually known, e.g. binary clauses, Horn clauses, and problems the inconsistency of which can be proved without going thru an exponential resolution phase. One of the interests of this method is to be insensitive to propositional variables renamings : if the method is complete on a problem, then it is complete whatever variables renaming we should do on this problem.

Although this method is incomplete in general, it can be seen as a quick pre-processing designed to simplify the resolution of hard problems by a complete method (Davis-Putnam[3],SL-Resolution[5] ...). This method is dedicated to *wash* a problem from all the noisy information it contains, and to give a problem we expect to be symmetric[2].

2 Presentation of the method

2.1 Coding

The basic idea is to rewrite a set of clauses as a set of logical implications. For example, the clause $a \vee b \vee c$ can be seen as any of the three following implications :

$$\neg a \vee b \vee c \rightarrow b \vee c$$
$$a \vee \neg b \vee c \rightarrow a \vee c$$
$$a \vee b \vee \neg c \rightarrow a \vee b$$

In the following, we shall call each of these rewritings *rule*. To obtain these rules from a clause C of length n, we isolate in right part the n sub-clauses of C which lengths are $n - 1$. The left parts are the right parts augmented with the complement of the literal we deleted to obtain the right parts. We shall call *coding* of a clause C the set of the n rules obtained in this fashion. The *coding* of a set of clauses is the union of the codings of the clauses in the set. Let's remark here the particular case of a unit-clause l which is coded :

$$\neg l \rightarrow empty.$$

Common parts coding

Let $A \rightarrow B$ and $C \rightarrow D$ be two rules, if $B = D$, then these two rules are semantically equivalent to the rules $AC \rightarrow B$. This property introduces a common parts coding notion. This coding is practically useful to limit the number of produced rules and like this the complexity of the underlying algorithm.

Property 1 *These ones are obvious.*

- *each rule is semantically equivalent to the clause it codes for.*
- *each clause is semantically equivalent to its coding.*
- *each set of clauses is semantically equivalent to its coding.*

2.2 Inference rules and derivation

The simplification of a set of clauses C consists of coding C and of saturating this coding with the two following rules :

Transitivity rule

Let X,Y,Z and T be clauses considered as sets of literals, XZ representing the union of the sets X and Z.

$$\frac{X \rightarrow Y, Z \rightarrow T}{XZ \rightarrow T} \quad \text{if } Y \subseteq Z$$

The purpose of this inference rule is to increase the left parts of the rules. Practically, the initial rule $Z \rightarrow T$ will be replaced by the new rule $XZ \rightarrow T$ which subsumes the previous. The new left part can become a tautology, this leads us to introduce a production inference rule.

Production rule

$$\frac{X \to Y}{Y} \quad \text{if } X \text{ contains a literal and its complement}$$

Example

Let's consider the set of clauses $\{a \vee b \vee c, \neg a \vee b\}$, the coding gives :

$$\neg a \vee b \vee c \to b \vee c \tag{1}$$
$$a \vee \neg b \vee c \to a \vee c \tag{2}$$
$$a \vee b \vee \neg c \to a \vee b \tag{3}$$
$$\neg a \vee \neg b \to \neg a \tag{4}$$
$$a \vee b \to b \tag{5}$$

By applying the rules 5) and 1) and the transitivity rule, we infer the rule :

$$\neg a \vee b \vee c \vee a \vee b \to b \vee c$$

As the left part of this rule contains the literal a and its complement, we infer the clause $b \vee c$ applying the production rule. We have in this way produced the resolvent of the two initial clauses.

From now on, the notation $E = (C, R_C)$ designates a pair in which C is a set of clauses and R_C its coding.

Derivation method

We say that $E' = (C', R'_C)$ is derived from $E = (C, R_C)$ iff one of the three following conditions is satisfied :

- $E' = (C \cup \{c\}, R_C)$ c being a clause obtained applying the production rule on a rule of R_C
- $E' = (C, R_C \cup \{r\})$ r being a rule obtained applying the transitivity rule on two rules of R_C
- $(C, R_C \cup \{r_1, \cdots, rn\})$ $\{r_1, \cdots, rn\}$ being the coding of a clause of C

Saturation

We say that $E = (C, R_C)$ is *saturated* if for each pair $E' = (C', R'_C)$ derived from E, we have $E = E'$ (E is a fixed point for the derivation operation defined above).

Production algorithm (method)

The algorithm produces some sub-clauses implied by the initial set of clauses C. In order to produce these sub-clauses, we first consider the pair $E = (C, R_C)$ and we apply the above derivation until saturation. If $E^* = (C^*, R_C^*)$ is the final obtained pair, then C^* is the union of C whith the set of produced sub-clauses.

Property 2 *These ones are obvious*

- *The algorithm is sound (it only produces theorems from the initial set).*
- *The algorithm terminates.*

Soundness is obvious since the inference rules are sound and the coding preserves semantics. Termination is obvious since we are in a finite propositional case.

3   Some remarkable properties

We establish here some properties which will allow us to show the completeness of the method on the actually identified polynomial classes of the SAT problem.

We call R_C^* the set of rules associated to the set of clauses C after saturation and C^* the set C increased with all the produced sub-clauses after saturation.

We call *classical resolvent* a resolvent obtained by the canonical resolution method.

Property 3 C^* *is saturated for unit-resolution (if C^* contains a unit-clause, it contains all the possible resolvents with this clause).*

Proof :

let $c_1 = l$ be a unit-clause of C^*,
let $c_2 = \neg l \vee X$ be a clause of C^* producing the resolvent X with this clause.
By construction, R_C^* contains :

$$\begin{aligned} &\qquad\qquad \neg l \to empty \quad &&\text{(coding of the clause l)}\\ &\text{and} \qquad l \vee X \to X \quad &&\text{(one of the rules of the coding of } \neg l \vee X)\\ &\text{and so} \quad \neg l \vee l \vee X \to X \quad &&\text{(by the transitivity rule)} \end{aligned}$$

X is then inferred by the production rule. $\square$

Definition 1 *Let C be a set of clauses, let p be a propositional variable of C, we call renaming of p in C the substitution of the occurrences in C of the literal p by the literal $\neg p$ and of the occurrences of $\neg p$ by p.*

Property 4 *If the method is complete on a given problem, then it is complete whatever variable renaming we should do on this problem.*

This is obvious since this method doesn't distinguish positive literals from negative ones. This property allows us in particular to obtain by the same arguments the completeness on Horn and Horn-renamable sets of clauses for example.

Property 5 *Let C be a set of binary clauses. If $a \vee b$ is a clause which can be produced in i classical resolution steps, then R_C^* contains two rules like :*

$$a \vee \neg b \vee L_1 \to a$$
$$and \quad \neg a \vee b \vee L_2 \to b \quad L_1 \text{ and } L_2 \text{ being clauses}$$

Proof :

Let's make a recurrence on the number n of resolvents. If $n = 0$, the clause $a \vee b$ is in C and the coding of this clause gives these two rules. Otherwise, there exists x, such that it is possible to show $a \vee x$ and $\neg x \vee b$ in less than n resolvents. By the recurrence hypothesis, we have then in R_C^*, the rules :

$$a \vee \neg x \vee L_a \to a \tag{6}$$
$$\neg a \vee x \vee L_x \to x \tag{7}$$
$$b \vee x \vee L_b \to b \tag{8}$$
$$\neg b \vee \neg x \vee L_x' \to \neg x \tag{9}$$

the rules 9) and 6) give by transitivity :

$$a \vee \neg b \vee L_1 \to a \quad \text{with } L_1 = L_x' \cup \{\neg x\} \cup L_a$$

the rules 7) and 8) give by transitivity :

$$\neg a \vee b \vee L_2 \to b \quad \text{with } L_2 = L_b \cup \{x\} \cup L_x$$

$\square$

4 Completeness of the method

A method is complete on a given problem (a set of formulae) if it allows to decide the problem consistency; it is complete on a class (a set of problems) if it is complete on all the problems in this class. Resolution for example is complete on all the problems, but it is of course exponential since it computes all the possible resolvents. Here, it is clear that we do not compute all the resolvents, we shall see that in fact, we consider a resolvent only if its length is not longer than the lengths of the clauses which produced it. Like this, we show that we produce all the sub-clauses (even the empty clause in case of inconsistency) which are implied by a set of clauses since this set verifies some algorithmic properties.

The above properties will allow us to show the completeness of the method on the polynomial classes of SAT. By polynomial class, we mean a class of problems for which there exists a polynomial decision algorithm. The classes are few, they are essentially binary clauses, Horn clauses, and problems the inconsistency of which can be proved without dealing with an exponential resolution phase in the logical demonstration.

4.1 Completeness of the method on binary clauses

Property 6 *If C is a set of binary clauses, then C^* contains all the sub-clauses implied by C.*

Proof :

If C gives l by unit resolution, it is obvious by property 3.

If C gives l by binary resolution, then there exists a such that C gives $l \vee a$ and $l \vee \neg a$ by binary resolution. By property 5, R_C^* contains then :

$$a \vee \neg l \vee L_a \to a \quad and \quad a \vee l \vee L_l \to l$$

the transitivity rule gives then :

$$a \vee \neg l \vee l \vee L \to l \quad with \quad L = L_a \cup L_l$$

and l is infered by the production rule.

If C gives the empty clause, then C gives two opposite literals l and $\neg l$. The empty clause is therefore produced by unit resolution. □

4.2 Method's completeness on Horn clauses

A Horn clause contains at most one positive literal. One can decide such a problem consistency by unit-resolution[1].

Property 7 *The method is complete on Horn clauses.*

The proof is obvious since, according to property 3, the method achieves unit-resolution.

Definition 2 *We say that a set of clauses C is* Horn-renamable, *if for some horn-renaming, C is a set of Horn clauses.*

Property 8 *The method is complete on Horn-renamable problems.*

Obvious with properties 3 and 7.

4.3 Completeness when the lengths of the resolvents don't increase

The two previous classes are well known and easily characterizable, even syntactically[4]. Now, we consider the problems the inconsistency of which can be found by resolution only by considering the resolvents which lengths are not longer than the initial clauses lengths.

The resolution we study here extends classical resolution by the following clash :

$$
\begin{aligned}
&\neg y \vee P(l_1 \vee l_2 \cdots l_n \vee X) \\
&\neg l_1 \vee X \\
&\neg l_2 \vee X \\
&\quad \vdots \\
&\underline{\neg l_n \vee X} \\
&\quad \neg y \vee X
\end{aligned}
$$

The notation $P(L)$ stands for a possibly empty sub-set of the clause L. We immediately remark that any resolvent of two clauses whose length is not longer than these two clauses lengths is a particular case of this clash. On the other hand, in general, the intermediate resolvents of this clash can increase their lengths, this clash is so more powerful than classical resolution with no length augmentation.

Property 9 *Let $l \vee X$ be a clause of C, any sub-clause like $a \vee X$ which can be produced in i applications of this clash is coded in the set rules of the form :*

$$\neg a \vee X \vee L \rightarrow L \quad (L \text{ being a clause})$$

Proof :

Let's proceed by recurrence on the number n of clashes. If $n = 0$, the clause $a \vee X$ is in C and this clause gives the rule $\neg a \vee X \rightarrow X$.

If any clause produced after n clashes is coded, let's consider a clause $\neg y \vee X$ obtained in $n + 1$ clashes, we have then the $n + 1^{th}$ clash :

$$\begin{array}{l} \neg y \vee P(l_1 \vee l_2 \cdots \vee l_k \vee X) \\ \neg l_1 \vee X \\ \neg l_2 \vee X \\ \vdots \\ \underline{\neg l_k \vee X} \\ \hphantom{xxxxxx} \neg y \vee X \end{array}$$

The clauses $\neg l_i \vee X$ are obtained after at most n clashes, and by the recurrence hypothesis, they are coded :

$$\begin{array}{l} l_1 \vee X \vee L_x \rightarrow X \\ l_2 \vee X \vee L_x \rightarrow X \\ \vdots \\ l_k \vee X \vee L_x \rightarrow X \end{array}$$

By transitivity, these k previous rules give the rule :

$$l_1 \vee l_2 \vee \cdots \vee l_n \vee L_X \vee X \rightarrow X$$

The clause $\neg y \vee P(l_1 \vee l_2 \cdots \vee l_n \vee X)$ is obtained after at most n clashes, and the coding gives :

$$y \vee P(l_1 \vee l_2 \cdots \vee l_n \vee X) \vee L_P \rightarrow P(l_1 \vee l_2 \cdots \vee l_n \vee X)$$

The transitivity rule gives :

$$y \vee l_1 \vee l_2 \vee \cdots \vee l_n \vee X \vee L \rightarrow X \quad \text{with} \quad L = L_x \cup L_p$$

which is well the expected coding of $\neg y \vee X$. $\square$

Property 10 *The method produces all the sub-clauses (even the empty clause in case of inconsistency) one can produce without increasing the lengths of the resolvents by this clash.*

Proof :

If C contains the clause $a \vee X$ and C gives X with no length augmentation, then there exists l such that C gives $l \vee X$ and C gives $\neg l \vee X$. According to property 9, R_C^* contains then :

$$\begin{array}{ll} l \vee X \vee L_1 \rightarrow X & (\text{coding of } \neg l \vee X) \\ \text{and} & \\ \neg l \vee X \vee L_2 \rightarrow X & (\text{coding of } l \vee X) \end{array}$$

and applying the transitivity rule, we obtain :

$$L_1 \vee L_2 \vee l \vee \neg l \vee X \to X$$

X is then produced applying the production rule on this rule. $\square$

5 Implementation - Complexity

In this section, we introduce the algorithm and analyse its complexity.

5.1 Implementation

The data stucture we use is the following :

- a set of clauses C (the clauses of the problem), they are implemented as ordered lists of literals with no repetition to improve the fusion and inclusion search.
- a set of rules R (the coding of C)
- a set of marked rules R_m (the rules to study), we have of course $R_m \subseteq R$, this set is implemented as an array of booleans indexed by the right parts of the rules in order to avoid repetitions in a very efficient fashion.

```
procedure main
    C = the problem
    R = ∅
    R_m = ∅
    while C ≠ ∅ do
        begin
            while C ≠ ∅ do
                begin
                    choose c in C
                    C = C \ {c}
                    rewrite(c)
                end
            while R_m ≠ ∅ do
                begin
                    choose LP → RP in R_m
                    R_m = R_m \ {LP → RP}
                    study(LP → RP)
                end
        end

procedure rewrite( c : clause )
    forall l ∈ C do
        begin
            consider the rule C \ {l} ∪ {¬l} → C \ {l}
            if there exists in R a rule LP → C \ {l} then
                if ¬l ∉ LP then
                    begin
                        LP = LP ∪ {¬l}
                        R_m = R_m ∪ {LP → C \ {l}}
                    end
                else
                    begin
                        R = R ∪ {C \ {l} ∪ {¬l} → C \ {¬l}}
                        R_m = R_m ∪ {C \ {l} ∪ {¬l} → C \ {¬l}} (here we can subsume...)
                    end
        end
```

```
procedure study( LP → RP : rule )
    if LP contains a tautology then
        C = C ∪ {RP}
    else
        forall LP' → RP' such that RP ⊆ LP' and LP ⊄ LP' do
            begin
                LP' = LP' ∪ LP
                Rm = Rm ∪ {LP' → RP'}
            end
```

5.2 Complexity

The previous algorithm is an iterative algorithm which reaches a fixed point. As each procedure increases the size of the data structure, we can overestimate the complexity by the number of times that each procedure is called which is equal to the size of the coding.

In the following, we consider that the problem has c clauses and p propositions. The clauses length is bounded by k, we have of course $k \leq n$. Our purpose is not to characterize the complexity very finely, but to show that it is bounded by a polynomial.

Number of producible clauses

This algorithm only produces sub-clauses. A clause of size n can potentially produce 2^n sub-clauses. If the clauses size is bounded by k, the number of clauses one can consider is bounded by $c*2^k$.

Coding size

As the rules are distinguished by their right parts, there are as many producible rules as producible sub-clauses. The right part of a rule is of course strictly bounded by k, and the left part can not exceed p propositions for it would be tautological otherwise. The coding size is then overestimated by $c*2^k*(k+p)$.

We asssume that the procedures *rewrite* and *study* have a polynomial complexity. For the procedure *rewrite* it's obvious, and for the procedure *study* we recognize a classical propagation algorithm which is well known to be polynomial as long as we use direct accesses to search for inclusions.

It is clear that this analysys is very rough, since it doesn't take account either of the common parts coding or of the subsumption simplification.

6 Experiments

In this section we present the results we obtained on random instances of the SAT problem. The random problems generator we use is the one described in[6], we study random instances on two hundred variables and clauses of length three. In this paper, the authors show that these random problems have a maximum difficulty when the ratio of the number of clauses to the number of variables is about 4.3. Figure 1 shows the average number of assignments of the Davis and Putnam procedure in function of the ratio with and without the simplification. We see that the gain is maximum at the hardest point. About the third of the assignments are avoided at this point.

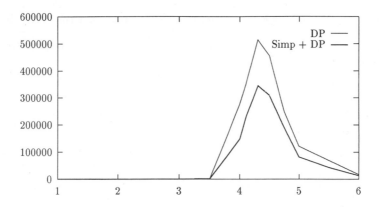

Figure 1: assignments / ratio

7 Conclusion

The introduced algorithm allows to simplify a set of propositional clauses by producing some implied sub-clauses. One of its interests is to allow with a single algorithm to treat the polynomial classes actually known of the SAT problem, whereas one often considers that each class should be treated by a dedicated algorithm.

This method must be seen as a simplification method, the simplified problem being then treated by a complete classic method (Davis-Putnam, resolution ...). Of course, after each step of the complete method, the simplification can be performed in order to concentrate our efforts on the hard part of the problem.

There are three types of problems : the solved problems, the partially solved problems (some sub-clauses have been produced) and the unchanged problems (no clause has been produced). Experimentally, we remarked that the remaining set of clauses after saturation presented some interesting structural properties (symmetries). This kind of problems can be treated using algorithms to detect and use these symmetries.

8 Acknowledgements

This paper is supported by the PRC-GDR Intelligence Artificielle, the project *BAHIA* and the MRE-INTER-PRC project *CLASSES POLYNOMIALES*

References

1. BAHIA. *Booléens, Algorithmes et Heuristiques pour l'IA*. In **Actes des 4èmes journées nationales**. teknea, 1992.

2. B. Benhamou and L. Sais. *Theoretical Study of Symmetries in Propositional Calculus and Applications*. In *Proceedings of the 11th Conference on Automatic Deduction (CADE-11)*, **volume 607**. LNAI, Springer Verlag, 1992.

3. M. Davis and H. Putnam. *A Computing Procedure for Quantification Theory. JACM*, **7:201–215**, 1960.

34

4. J.J. Hébrard. *Un Algorithme Efficace de Horn Renommage.* Technical report, LIUC, Université de Caen, 1991.

5. R. Kowalski and D. Kuehner. *Linear resolution with selection function. Artificial Intelligence,* **2:227–260**, 1971.

6. D. Mitchell, B. Selman, and H. Levesque. *Hard and Easy Distributions of SAT Problems.* In *Proceedings AAAI'92,* 1992.

A Representation of the Set of Models by Means of Symmetries

Lakhdar Sais

Laboratoire d'Informatique de Marseille
URA CNRS 1787
Université de Provence, UFR-MIM
3, place Victor Hugo
13331 Marseille Cedex 3 FRANCE
E-mail: sais@gyptis.univ-mrs.fr

ABSTRACT

Many classes of propositional calculus problems display a large amount of symmetries, i.e. the set of clauses representing such problems remains invariant under certain permutations of variable names. In[1,2] we have shown how such symmetries can be detected and used to simplify satisfiability checking.

The problem of finding all models of a given CNF propositional theory is known to be hard. More generally, we need to explore a complete proof tree and, in some cases, the set of models is much too large to be represented explicitly.

In this paper, we show how symmetries can be used to represent a large set of models by a subset of characteristic models(non symmetric models). The other models can be obtained by applying the computed symmetries.

We present an algorithm for enumerating non symmetric models, and we show results obtained on some known problems, such as the pigeon-hole, queens and some other problems derived from mathematical theorems.

Key words. Theorem proving, propositional calculus, symmetries.

1 Introduction

Finding all satisfying models for a formula in conjonctive normal form (CNF), or even deciding whether a satisfying model exits (Sat), is known to be NP hard. There are, however, a large classes of propositional problems which contains several symmetries. The principle of symmetry originaly suggested by Krishnamurty[8] can lead in many cases to a shorter proof of the problems. Indeed, for a set S of clauses with n propositional variables, there are 2^n possible interpretations (i.e. mapings from the variables to the set {True, False}). If S contains symmetries, then the interpretations can be partioned into equivalence classes. Satisfiability checking can be reduced to the problem of testing one interpretation from each such equivalence class. The number of such classes give us an estimate of the usefulness of a set of symmetries.

We have explained[1,2] how symmetries are detected and used in some automated deduction methods such as Sl-Resolution algorithm and Davis and Putnam procedure. Good results have been obtained on some known hard propositional problems.

Enumerating all the models of CNF propositional theory is an interesting and difficult task[4]. The difficulty is that we generally need to explore a complete proof tree and in some cases the set of models is much too large to be represented explicitly. The interest of this, is that for certain kind of information the model-based representation is much more compact and enable much faster reasoning than the traditional representation using logical formulas[6,7].

In this paper, we show how symmetries can be used to represent the set of models by a subset of characteristic models(non symmetric models), from which all others can be generated. We present an algorithm for enumerating all non symmetric models, and we show results obtained on some known problems.

2 Preliminaries

We shall assume that the reader is familiar with propositional calculus. For a propositional variable p there are two literals p the positive literal and $\neg p$ the negative one. A clause is a disjunction of literals such that no literal appears more than once, a clause containing no literals is called the empty clause. A set S of clauses is a conjunction of clauses. In other words we say that S is in the conjunctive normal form. A truth assignment to a set of clauses S is a map I from the set of variables occurring in S to the set {True, False}. The value of S under the truth assignment will be defined in the usual sense. We say that a set of clauses S is satisfiable if there exists some truth assignments in which S takes the value True; it is unsatisfiable otherwise. In the first case I is called a model of S. Also, if ℓ is true in a model of S, we say that ℓ has a model in S. We identify $\neg \ell$ to the opposite of ℓ.

3 Symmetries

We recall some definitions and property of symmetry, for more details see[1,2].

A bijective map $\sigma : V \rightarrow V$ is called a permutation of variables. If S is a set of clauses, c a clause of S and σ a permutation of variables occurring in S, then $\sigma(c)$ is the clause obtained by applying σ to each variable of c and $\sigma(S) = \{\sigma(c)/c \in S\}$.

In the following we define a permutation on literals.

Definition 3.1 *A set P of literals is called* complete *if $\forall \ell \in P$, $\neg \ell \in P$*

Definition 3.2 *Let P be a complete set of literals and S a set of clauses of which all literals are in P.*
A permutation σ defined on P ($\sigma : P \rightarrow P$) is called a symmetry *of S if it satisfies the following conditions :*

1. $\forall \ell \in P, \sigma(\neg \ell) = \neg \sigma(\ell)$
2. $\sigma(S) = S$

Definition 3.3 *Two literals (variables) ℓ and ℓ' are* symmetric *in S notation ($\ell \sim \ell'$) if there exists a symmetry σ of S such that $\sigma(\ell) = \ell'$. A tuple $(\ell_1, \ell_2, \ldots, \ell_n)$ of literals is called a* cycle of symmetry *in S if there exist a symmetry σ defined on S, such that $\sigma(\ell_1) = \ell_2, \ldots \sigma(\ell_{n-1}) = \ell_n, \sigma(\ell_n) = \ell_1$.*

Example 3.4 *Let S be the following set of clauses : $S = \{a \vee \neg b, c\}$*
and σ the map defined on the complete set P of literals occurring in S :
$\sigma(a) = \neg b$, $\sigma(\neg a) = b$, $\sigma(b) = \neg a$, $\sigma(\neg b) = a$, $\sigma(c) = c$ and $\sigma(\neg c) = \neg c$
σ is a symmetry of S , a and $\neg b$ are symmetric in S ($a \sim \neg b$).
$\sigma(S) = \{\neg b \vee a, c\} = S$.

Definition 3.5 *Let P be a complete set of literals, σ a symmetry, I a truth assignment of P and S a set of clauses then, $\sigma(I)$ is the truth assignment obtained by substituting every literal ℓ in I by $\sigma(\ell)$.*

Proposition 3.6 *I is a model of S iff $\sigma(I)$ is a model of S .*

Proof : cf.[1,2]

From the poposition above, one can define an equivalence relation on the set of interpretations by : $I_1 \sim I_2$ iff there exists a symmetry σ on S such that $I_1 = \sigma(I_2)$.
In the previous example, the set of possible interpretations can be partioned into six distinct classes : $\{[000], [110]\}$, $\{[001], [111]\}$, $\{[010]\}, \{[011]\}$, $\{[100]\}$ and $\{[101]\}$. Also we can easily distinguish two distinct classes of models : $\{[001], [111]\}$ and $\{[101]\}$ ([101] should be read as [a=True, b=False and c=True]).

Theorem 3.7 *Let ℓ and ℓ' be two literals of S.*
if $\ell \sim \ell'$ in S, then ℓ has a model in S iff ℓ' has a model in S .

Proof : direct consequence of proposition 3.6

Let us define $S_{\ell_1, \ell_2, \ldots, \ell_n}$ the set of clauses obtained after assigning to the literals $\ell_1, \ell_2, \ldots, \ell_n$ the value true, consequently,

Corollary 3.8 *Let $(\ell, \ell_1, \ell_2, \ldots, \ell_n)$ be a cycle of symetry of ℓ in S then, S is satisfiable iff S_ℓ or $S_{\neg \ell, \neg \ell_1, \neg \ell_2, \ldots, \neg \ell_n}$ is satisfiable.*

The previous theorem is very usefull to make prune the proof trees. Indeed, if ℓ has no model in S and $\ell \sim \ell'$, then ℓ' will have no model in S, thus we prune the branch which corresponds to the assignment of ℓ' in the proof tree. Therefore, if there are n symmetric literals we can cut $n - 1$ branches.

In[1,2], we have explained how symmetries are detected and used in different automated deduction algorithms such as SL-Resolution and the Davis and Putnam procedure. It should be noted that in our previous work[1,2], we search for symmetries at each level of the proof tree : on the set of clauses simplified by the current assignment, we call these symmetries local, in opposition to symmetries of the original set of clauses (global symmetries).

Local symmetries must be very usefull, when the problem holds some symmetric kernels. This kind of symmetries can't be used, if we adress the problem of computing non symmetric solutions of the problem. In some other problems, the symmetries appear on the original problem (global), but they can disapear after assignment of some variables.

4 A characterization of the set of models

In the sequel, We show how the principle of symmetry can lead to a short representation of the set of models.

Definition 4.1 *Two models m_1 and m_2 of a set S of clauses are symmetric if there exists a symmetry σ of S such that $\sigma(m_1) = m_2$*

Remark 4.2 *If $\ell \sim \ell'$ on S, then ℓ and ℓ' have the same number of models.*

Definition 4.3 *Let S be a set of clauses and A a set of literals occurring in S which don't contain a literal and its opposite.*
We define $M(S, A)$ as a set of models of S which contain the literals of A. and $M(S, \emptyset)$ is the set of all models of S.

Definition 4.4 *Let S be a set of clauses and $A = \{\ell_1, \ell_2, \ldots, \ell_n\}$ a set of literals of S which don't contain a literal and its opposite.*
We define $M(S, \emptyset)/A$ as a partition of all the models of S on A :
$$M(S, \emptyset)/A = \{M(S, \ell_1), M(S, \neg\ell_1\ell_2), M(S, \neg\ell_1\neg\ell_2\ell_3) \ldots$$
$$M(S, \neg\ell_1\neg\ell_2 \ldots \neg\ell_{n-1}\ell_n), M(S, \neg\ell_1\neg\ell_2 \ldots \neg\ell_n)\}$$

Theorem 4.5 *Let S be a set of clauses and σ a symmetry on S such that $(\ell_1, \ell_2, \ell_3, \ldots, \ell_n)$ is a cycle of symmetry, then,*

1. *$\forall i$ such that $2 \leq i \leq n$,*
   $M(S, \neg\ell_1 \ldots \neg\ell_{i-1}\ell_i) = \sigma^{i-1}(M(S, \ell_1\neg\ell_{n-(i-2)} \ldots \neg\ell_n))$ [1] and;

2. *The models $M(S, \ell_1)$ and $M(S, \neg\ell_1 \ldots \neg\ell_n)$ are not symmetric.*

Proof :
1)- Obvious. By the definition of a cycle of symmetry, one can easily write $\sigma^{i-1}(M(S, \ell_1\neg\ell_{n-(i-2)} \ldots \neg\ell_n))$ as $M(S, \neg\ell_1 \ldots \neg\ell_{i-1}\ell_i)$

2)- Suppose that there exists $m_1 \in M(S, \ell_1)$ and $m_2 \in M(S, \neg\ell_1 \ldots \neg\ell_n)$ such that $\sigma^i(m_1) = m_2$ with $1 \leq i < n$.
$\ell_1 \in m_1$, then $\sigma^i(\ell_1) \in m_2$ and $o^i(\ell_1) \in \{\ell_1, \ell_2, \ldots, \ell_n\}$. m_2 contain the literals $\neg\ell_1, \neg\ell_2, \ldots, \neg\ell_n$, one can see that m_2 contain a literal and its opposite (contradiction).

This theorem shows that, for a cycle of symmetry $\rho = (\ell_1, \ldots, \ell_n)$ on S, the set of models of S can be partitioned into three subsets :
$M_1 = M(S, \ell_1), M_2 = \cup_{i=2}^{n}\sigma^{i-1}(M(S, \ell_1\neg\ell_{n-(i-2)} \ldots \neg\ell_n))$ and
$M_3 = M(S, \neg\ell_1 \ldots \neg\ell_n)$.
The models M_2 are included in M_1 up to symmetry. The models M_1 and M_3 are non symmetric.

4.1 Use of symmetries

We will show an algorithm *Find_Non_Symmetric_Models(S)*(Figure 1), for enumerating all non symmetric models of S, this algorithm uses as its basic subroutine *Solve(S)*. If S is satisfiable, then it

---

[1] σ^i : application of σ i times

returns a satisfying truth assignment; otherwise, it returns nil. The notation $Solve(S, \phi)$ is a shorthand for $Solve(S \cup \phi)$, ϕ is the set of literals in the current assignment.

In order to find all the solution, we use the Davis and Putnam procedure without monotone (pure) literal rule.

Let $\phi = \{\ell_1 \ldots \ell_k\}$ be the current set of literals assigned the value true. Suppose we have found all the models of $S \cup \phi$. Before searching for the models of $S \cup \{\ell_1 \ldots \ell_{k-1}, \neg \ell_k\}$, we search for a cycle of symmetry ρ of the literal ℓ_k on S(global symmetry), with the condition that $\{\ell_1, \ell_2 \ldots \ell_{k-1}\}$ is invariant under the symmetry[2]. This additional condition allows us to avoid symmetric models to the models found at the current level of the proof tree. Now, we search for the models of $S \cup \{\ell_1 \ldots \ell_{k-1} \neg \ell_k\} \cup \{\neg \ell, \forall \ell \in \rho\}$.

As shown in Figure 1, in subroutine *Find_Next_Model* we search for global symmetries to avoid symmetric models, and in *Solve* we search for local symmetries in case of contradiction.

Find_Non_Symmetric_Models(S)
```
{
φ ← ∅
model←Solve(S,φ)
while model≠ nil
do { print model
     model←Find_Next_Model(S, model)
     }
}
```

Find_Next_Model(S,$\{\ell_1, \ell_2 \ldots \ell_n\}$)
```
{
for i=n downto 1
do {
     /* global symmetry */
     compute a cycle of symmetry ψ of ℓ_i on S such that {ℓ_1, ℓ_2 ... ℓ_{i-1}} is invariant
     model←Solve(S,{ℓ_1, ℓ_2 ... ℓ_{i-1}¬ℓ_i} ∪ {¬ℓ, ∀ℓ ∈ ψ})
     if model≠nil then return(model)
     }
return(nil)
}
```

Solve(S,ϕ)
```
{
unit_propagate(S,φ) /* repeated application of unit-literal rule */
if contradiction discovered then return(nil)
else if all clauses are satisfied then return(φ)
       else {
             x ← some unvalued variable
             if Solve(S,φ ∪ {x})=nil
             then {
                  compute a cycle of symmetry ψ of x on S ∪ φ /* local symmetry */
                  return(Solve(S,φ ∪ {¬x} ∪ {¬ℓ, ∀ℓ ∈ ψ}))
             else return(Solve(S,φ ∪ {x}))
             }
}
```

Figure 1: Algorithm Find_Non_Symmetric_Models

5 Results

We now present some results on the algorithm (Figure 1) with and without symmetry. For each problem, we give the total number of models(NM) and the number of non symmetric models(NSM). Also in the case of unsatisfiability we show also how symmetries affect the size of the proof tree.

---

[2]A set of literals ϕ is invariant under a symmetry σ iff $\forall \ell \in \phi, \sigma(\ell) \in \phi$

5.1 Description of the benchmarks

- Queens. Placing N queens in $N \times N$ chessboard such that there is no couple of queens attacking each other. Notation Queen(N)

- Erdös's theorem. Find the permutation σ of N first numbers such that for each 4-tuple $1 \leq i < j < k < l \leq$ N none of the two relations $\sigma(i) < \sigma(j) < \sigma(k) < \sigma(l)$ and $\sigma(l) < \sigma(k) < \sigma(j) < \sigma(i)$ is verified.
  This problem is modeled by creating for each couple (i,j) a variable $f_{i,j}$ which means $\sigma(i) < \sigma(j)$. The rules express the associativity of the relation $<$, and prohibit the misplaced 4-tuples. For $N \leq 9$ the problem admits solutions, beyond it doesn't.Notation Erdos(N)

- Pigeon Hole: Put n pigeon in $n - 1$ pigeon-holes such that each pigeon-hole holds at most one pigeon. The problem is unsatisfiable, for n pigeon and n holes the problem have $n!$ solutions. Notation Pigeon(P,H)

- Schur's lemma: How to distribute N counters numbered from 1 to N into 3 boxes A, B, C in accordance with the following rules:
  1) A box can't contain both the counters numbered i and $2 * i$
  2) A box can't contain the counters numbered i, j and $i + j$
  For $N \leq 13$ the problem admits solutions, beyond it doesn't. Notation Schur(N)

- Ramsey problem's: Color the edges of a complete graph on N vertices with k different colors such that no monochromatic triangle appears. Notation Ramsey(N,K)

Problems	SAT	Without symmetry			With symmetry		
		NM	Steps	Times	NSM	Steps	Times
Pigeon(10,10)	Y	10!	-	-	1	156	4.11"
Queen(4)	Y	2	76	0.53"	1	28	0.150"
Queen(6)	Y	4	1066	4.13"	2	278	2.150"
Queen(8)	Y	92	17304	1'21"	23	7321	30.53"
Erdős(9)	Y	1356	35732	3'57"	125	16328	2'.17"
Erdős(10)	N	0	2332	6.213"	0	1166	4.56"
Schur(13)	Y	18	2029	5.83"	1	148	1.96"
Schur(14)	N	0	1878	4.17"	0	374	1.517"
Ramsey(5,2)	Y	2	231	0.200"	1	43	0.01"

Table 1 : Schur's Lemma and Ramsey's problem,etc.

Number of pigeons	Clauses	Variables	With symmetries	
			Steps	Times
14	1197	182	193	3.21"
16	1816	240	253	6.83"
18	2619	306	321	13.11"
20	3630	380	397	23.04"
22	4873	462	481	35.29"
24	6372	552	573	54.73"
26	8150	650	673	1'20"
28	10234	756	781	2'15"
30	12645	870	897	3'34"

Table 2 : Pigeon-hole problems

6 Related Work

Krishnamurty[8] discuses the idea of using symmetries to reduce the length of resolution proofs, he uses a rule of symmetry to avoid repeated independent derivations of intermediate formulas that are permutations of others. His work does not adress the problem of detecting symmetries or of using them in search problems.

Benhamou and Sais[1,2] discusses the detection and the use of symmetries in automated deduction methods.

40

Freuder[5] discusses the elimination of interchangeable value in constraint satisfaction problem. Also, a theoritical analysis of reasoning by symmetry in first-order logic have been presented in Crawford[3].

7 Conclusion

In this paper, we have shown how global symmetries can be used to obtain a new characterization of the set of models of a given CNF propositional theory. For some problems symmetries give us a way to represent large sets of models.

Also, the results obtained in this paper, shows the usefulness of global symmetries in case of checking satisfiability. There are, however, some problems which possesses abundant local symmetry. Consequently, in order to increase the tractable classes of problems by using symmetries, it is necessary to combine the two kinds of symmetries.

In special case of Horn and 2-CNF formulas, computing all models, although counting is #P-complete, we intend to experiment our algorithm on this kind of formulas.

8 Acknowledgements

This paper is supported by the PRC-GDR Intelligence Artificielle, the project *BAHIA* and the MRE-INTER-PRC project *CLASSES POLYNOMIALES*

References

1. B. Benhamou and L. Sais. *Theoretical study of symmetries in propositional calculus and application.* Eleventh International Conference on Automated Deduction, Saratoga Springs,NY, USA, 1992.

2. B. Benhamou and L. Sais. *Tractability through symmetries in propositional calculus.* To appear in Journal of Automated Reasoning, 1994.

3. J. M. Crawford. *Theoritical analysis of reasoning by symmetry in first-order logic.* Workshop on Tractable Resonning, AAAI-92, San Jose, pages 17–22, July 1992.

4. R. Dechter and A. Itai. *Finding all solutions if you can find one.* Workshop on Tractable Resonning, AAAI-92, San Jose, pages 35–40, July 1992.

5. E. C. Freuder. *Eliminating interchangeable values in constraint satisfaction problems.* In proceedings of AAAI-91, pages 227–233, 1991.

6. H. A. Kautz, M. J. Kearns, and B. Selman. *Reasoning with characteristic models.* In procedings of AAAI-93, pages 34–39, 1993.

7. J. L. Kolodner. *Improving human decision making through casebased decision aiding.* AI Magazine, **12(2)**:52–68, 1992.

8. B. Krishnamurty. *Short proofs for tricky formulas.* Acta informatica, **(22)**:253–275, 1985.

A NETWORK FLOW APPROACH
TO CLAUSE INFERENCE

V. SGUREV and E. MILANOV

Bulgarian Academy of Sciences
Institute of Informatics
Bl. 29A, Acad. G. Bonchev Str.
Sofia 1113, Bulgaria

ABSTRACT

Network flows are a powerful mechanism, a specific case of linear programming, for describing and solving hard combinatorial problems. For this reason they may be worth for approaching logical inference. The present paper suggests an approach for representing propositional formulaes in clausal form using their syntactical structure, as a network flow problem, and for representing the inference as the calculation of a feasable flow over the network. An example with Horn clauses is given.

II - EXTENSIONS TO LOGIC PROGRAMMING

STABLE MODELS FOR THEORIES WITH REFUTATION RULES

MARION MIRCHEVA*

Dept. of Logic, Institute of Mathematics and Computer Science,
Bulgarian Academy of Sciences
"Acad. G.Bonchev" str. bl. 8, Sofia 1113 , Bulgaria
e-mail: marion@bgearn.bitnet

ABSTRACT

We extend logic programming to deal with theories that include both ordinary clauses and new *refutation rules*. While the ordinary rules are supposed to add knowledge, when they are activated, the refutation rules are supposed to remove knowledge. To adapt logic programming to manage with such kind of mixed reasoning we extend Stable Model Semantics introduced by Gelfond and Lifschitz by giving a higher priority to refutation rules.

We also propose a transformation which eliminates refutation rules by using negation by failure over the initial language augmented with a new *test operator*. To prove that the proposed transformation preserves the original meaning of the program and the refutation rules we prolong Stable Model Semantics to programs that include *test sentences*.

We extend our results to programs that include *explicit* negation in addition to default one and to disjunctive logic programs. The transformed programs can be implemented by logic programming methods suitable for stable models.

1. Introduction

In this paper we extend logic programming to include explicit representation of refutation rules. We can use both general rules such as

$$fly(x) \leftarrow bird(x)$$

and refutation rules such as

$$\sim fly(x) \Leftarrow ostrich(x)$$

$$\sim fly(x) \Leftarrow penguin(x).$$

*This work has been partially supported by Bulgarian Ministry of Science and Education, Research Branch, under grant number U-303/93.

If Tweety is both an ostrich and a bird, we conclude that Tweety does not fly, because the refutation instance

$$\sim fly(x) \Leftarrow ostrich(x)$$

overrides the general rule.

Here, and throughout the paper, "$\sim$" denotes default negation and "$\neg$" denotes explicit negation. We consider reasoning with refutation rules based on the background on two valued stable model semantics[4]. Such kind of rules are important in the areas which provide reasoning with mixed rules is advocated. We mean both kinds of rules, the ones that add things (to attain knowledge) and rules that remove things (to attain wisdom). For example default logic[10] can be considered as a system that operates with rules that have the form: if δ_i are accepted and σ_j are not accepted ($\neg\sigma_j$ are consistent with the current state) then l is accepted. Default rules could be considered as rules that add knowledge, even on the ground of default premises. Loosely this is also the meaning of a clause $l \leftarrow \delta_i, \sim \sigma_j$ according to stable model semantics. In fact there is one-one correspondence between maximal consistent sets of rules from a given default system or from a normal logic program and *extensions* in default logic or *stable models* in Stable Model Semantics correspondingly. That kind of rules extend the knowledge base, even in nonmonotonic setting. What we propose is to extend logic programming to deal with rules that explicitly state which sentences to be removed if some others are accepted. We also insist that after removing certain sentences, the reasons for these changes should remain valid. Refutation rules provide alternative reasoning mode as they remove knowledge when they are activated. This kind of reasoning is useful not only when exceptions have to be presented as in the example above. In dynamic domains, such as legal contexts, selfeducated systems and open expert systems, inconsistent rules have to be included on the bases of some priority ordering. The fact that refutation rules have higher priority to the ordinary rules is extremely natural. We mean that the use of theories with refutation rules makes sense only if the later have higher priority than the program rules, otherwise we can simply withdraw them.

The intended procedural meaning of a refutation rule like $\sim l \Leftarrow \Delta, \sim \Sigma$ above is to block the activation of all program rules with head l if Δ is true and Σ is false and let them proceed if that is not the case. It is clear that refutation rules modify the original meaning of a default negation. Thus there exist two reasons that could verify for instance $\sim l$: either failure of l or some extra evidence (refutation rules) that require l to be refuted. In fact $\sim fly(x) \Leftarrow ostrich(x)$ presents an instruction: if x is an *ostrich* according to an outgoing model, then revise it to a situation in which x *doesn't fly* and still would be an *ostrich* otherwise keep the initial model.

The contribution of this paper is three-fold.

- We describe semantics for logic programming with clauses and refutation rules. We call it R-Stable semantics (R stands for a set of refutation rule). The syntactic difference between ordinary rules and refutation rules is that clauses have literals in the conclusions, whereas refutation rules have *default* negated literals in the conclusions. The semantics for clauses and refutation rules is a modification of the stable model semantics[4].

- We present a transformation which encodes the refutation rules into the program rules by using negation as failure over the so called *test operators*. This translation is easy to understand and it fits the proposed semantics perfectly. This transformation yields the stable model semantics defined over programs with *test sentences*.

  The program obtained after the transformation has the same semantics as the original theory (program and refutation rules), thus the theory and the program are equivalent. To formalise this equivalence we prolong stable semantics to programs with *test expressions*. Therefore we get:

  $$R\text{-}Stable(P) = Stable(P_{transformed})$$

- We extend our results to theories that include explicit negation and to disjunctive programs. We also show that refutation rules are equivalent to certain forms of integrity constraints. Our transformation presents a method that eliminates integrity constraints from program databases.

The paper is organized as follows. Section 2 introduces the syntax of the theories with refutation rules. In Section 3 we formally describe semantics for clauses and refutation rules. Section 4 extends stable model semantics to include programs with *test* sentences. Section 5 describes the transformation and proves that it preserves r-stable semantics of the original program. Section 6 discusses related works and gives some conclusive remarks.

2. Theories with Refutation Rules

A normal logic program is a set of formulae of the form

$$c \leftarrow a_1, \cdots, a_m, \sim b_1, \cdots, \sim b_n$$

where $n \geq 0$, $m \geq 0$[1] and all c, a_i and b_j are atoms. The sign $\sim$ stands for default negation and $\sim a$ is read as "default atom". A clause containing variables is treated as standing for the set of all ground instances of that clauses. The premises of any clause are either atoms or default atoms.

An extended logic program is a set of formulae of the form

$$l_0 \leftarrow l_1, \cdots, l_m, \sim s_1, \cdots, \sim s_n$$

---

[1]If $n = m = 0$ we mean the rule $c \leftarrow$ and when $m = 0$ or $n = 0$ we mean $c \leftarrow \sim b_1, \cdots, \sim b_n$ or $c \leftarrow a_1, \cdots, a_m$ correspondingly.

where $n \geq 0$, $m \geq 0$ and all l_i and s_j are literals. The sign $\neg$ stands for classical (explicit) negation and $\sim$ stands for default negation. A literal is a formula of the form a or $\neg a$, where a is an atom. By default literal we mean $\sim l$ where l is a literal. The premises of any clause are either literals or default literals.

A disjunctive logic program is a set of formulae of the form

$$p_1 \vee \cdots \vee p_k \leftarrow l_1, \cdots, l_m, \sim s_1, \cdots, \sim s_n$$

where all p_r, l_i and s_j are literals.

Definition 2.1. A refutation rule is a rule of the form:

$$\sim l \Leftarrow \delta_1, \cdots, \delta_m, \sim \sigma_1, \cdots, \sim \sigma_n$$

The only syntactic difference between ordinary clauses and refutation rules is that the head of a refutation rule is a default atom (literal).

A theory is a logic program augmented with a set of refutation rules. For the aim of simplicity we restrict our considerations to theories that include a single refutation rule.

3. Stable Models for Programs and Refutation Rules: r-Stable Models

As we already mentioned, the intuition behind reasoning with refutation rules is that such rules have a higher priority than ordinary rules. If a contradiction arises between a program clause and a refutation rule the later overrides the ordinary rule. That is the contradictions are avoided by preferring the refutation of the literals $\sim l$ to their counterparts l.

To get intended models for theories with refutation rules we modify the original definition of Stable Model Semantics introduced by Gelfond and Lifschitz.

For all definitions below: let P be a normal program with clauses of the form

$$c \leftarrow a_1, \cdots, a_m, \sim b_1, \cdots, \sim b_n$$

and r be a single refutation rule: (r): $\sim l \Leftarrow \delta_1, \cdots, \delta_k \sim \sigma_1, \cdots, \sim \sigma_s$ where l, δ_i, σ_j are atoms. Usually instead of (r) we write $\sim l \Leftarrow \Delta, \sim \Sigma$ where $\Delta = \{\delta_1, \cdots, \delta_k\}$ and $\Sigma = \{\sigma_1, \cdots, \sigma_s\}$. We include in the language of P all atoms of the rule r.

We begin by providing a definition of r-interpretation which incorporates the refutation rule from the beginning.

Definition 3.1 (r-interpretation). A two-valued interpretation I (a set of atoms) is called an r-interpretation iff from $\Delta \subseteq I$ (Δ is true in I) and $\sim \Sigma \subseteq I$ [2] (Σ is false in I) follows $l \notin I$.

---

[2]Instead of $\Sigma \cap I = \emptyset$ we write $\sim \Sigma \subseteq I$, where $\sim \Sigma = \{\sim \sigma_1, \cdots, \sim \sigma_s\}$.

We next extend with an additional provision GL-transformation of $P \, modulo \, I$ (P/I) to account for the refutation rule.

Definition 3.2 $(P/^r I)$. By $P/^r I$ we mean a new program obtained from P by performing the following three reductions:

1. Remove from P all clauses which contain a default premise $\sim x$ such that $x \in I$.

2. Remove from P all clauses with head l if $\Delta \subseteq I$ and $\sim \Sigma \subseteq I$.

3. Remove from all remaining clauses those default premises $\sim x$ which satisfy $x \notin I$.

Since the resulting program $P/^r I$ is by definition positive, it has a unique least model J. We define $\Gamma^r(I) = J$.

We changed the original P/I definition by adding extra condition (2) for deleting any clause in P having conclusion l, with $\Delta \cup \sim \Sigma \subseteq I$ (remind (r): $\sim l \Longleftarrow \Delta, \sim \Sigma$).

Definition 3.3. An r-interpretation I of the language of P is called a r-Stable3 model iff $\Gamma^r(I) = I$. Two valued r-Stable semantics is determined by the set of all r-Stable models of P.

Note that we could get r-Stable semantics by considering arbitrary interpretations of the language of P, instead of r-interpretations. Then it is easy to prove that each model is an r-interpretation.

Example 1. Consider a theory $P_1 \cup r$.

$$P_1 : \quad a \leftarrow \sim b$$
$$b \leftarrow \sim a$$
$$r : \quad \sim b \Longleftarrow \sim c, \sim a$$

Obviously c must be false (there is no rule with head c). Then there are three candidates for r-stable models, namely the sets $\{a, b\}$, $\{b\}$, $\{a\}$. The first two however are not even r-interpretations. Then let us check whether $I = \{a\}$ is an r-stable model. $I = \{a\}$ is indeed an r-interpretation as it satisfies the refutation rule r. It is easy to calculate that $P_1/^r I = \{a \leftarrow \}$. The least fixpoint of Γ^r of this positive program is I. Therefore I is an r-stable model.

Remark:

- For a theory with more then one refutation rules $P \cup R$ we have to define an R-interpretation as one that satisfies all rules from R. Then the definition of $P/^R I$ goes as before taking into account all instances from R. The point 2 from definition 3.2 must be replaced with

  2° For every refutation rule $\sim l_i \Longleftarrow \Delta_i, \sim \Sigma_i$ from R remove from P all rules with head l_i if $\Delta_i \cup \sim \Sigma_i \subseteq I$.

It is easy to extend our approach to programs that permit both default $\sim$ and explicit $\neg$ negation. Instead of stable model semantics we have to modify answer set semantics[5] by adding extra condition 2) to the correspondent *transformation of P modulo I* in order to get answer sets.

We can also adapt our framework to deal with disjunctive programs. We follow Przymusinski's[9] extension of answer set semantics for programs with explicit negation to the class of disjunctive logic programs. The only difference with the original answer sets definition for disjunctive programs is that the resulting program P^M after *transformation of P modulo M* is *positive* disjunctive and therefore, applying the generalized closed world assumption (GCWA), its semantics is determined by the set of all *minimal* models of P^M. Then we have to add the following extra condition to the correspondent *transformation of P modulo M* and after that to apply GCWA.

> Remove from all disjunctive heads of clauses of P the literal l if $\Delta \subseteq I$ and $\sim \Sigma \subseteq I$. If l is the only literal in the head of that clause then remove that clause.

Consider a disjunctive program P_2 and a refutation rule r.

$P_2: \quad a \vee b \vee q \quad \leftarrow \quad \sim c$
$r: \qquad \sim a \quad \Leftarrow \quad \sim d$

Let $M = \{b\}$. After applying the *transformation of P_2 modulo M* we get the program P_2^M

$P_2^M: \quad b \vee q \quad \leftarrow \quad \sim c$

As M is a minimal model of P_2^M it is also an r-stable model for P_2. Similarly the set $\{q\}$ is an r-stable model of P_2.

4. Stable Models for Programs with Tests

In this section we extend the propositional logic programming to deal with programs that include a new truth functional connective, called *test* operators[3].

Definition 4.1. We extend ordinary language of logic programs to include a new truth functional connective called *test*, such that $t(x_1, \cdots, x_n)$ are new formulas, where x_i are atoms (literals) or default atoms (literals). The meaning of test formulae is defined as follows:

$$t(x_1, \cdots, x_n) = true \text{ if all } x_i = true, \text{ otherwise } t(x_1, \cdots, x_n) = false^4.$$

In fact $t(x_1, \cdots, x_n) = x_1 \wedge \cdots \wedge x_n$ where $\wedge$ stands for classical conjunction. It is clear that $t(x) = x$.

---

[3]A general study of programs with variety of test connectives is presented in [8]

[4]Three valued variant of this test connective (according to strong three valued Kleene logic) is used in[8] where a framework for restoring consistency in extended logic programs is presented. Similar connective in three valued setting has been used by Fitting[3] in connection with logic programming languages based on billatices. In a sense t is external connective that is applied over the underground logic. A gallery of similar "external" connectives has been considered by Finn et al.[2] in connection with implementation of systems based on plausible reasoning in style of G.S.Mill.

Definition 4.2. A program with *test* is a set of clauses such that some rules may have default negated test formulae in addition to the other premises. Thus it might contain rules with test:

$$c \leftarrow a_1, \cdots, a_m, \sim b_1, \cdots, \sim b_n, \sim t(\Delta, \sim \Sigma)$$

where $t(\Delta, \sim \Sigma)$ stands for $t(\delta_1, \cdots, \delta_m, \sim \sigma_1, \cdots, \sim \sigma_n)$, that is $(\delta_1 \wedge \cdots \wedge \delta_m \wedge \sim \sigma_1 \wedge \cdots \wedge \sim \sigma_n)$.

We slightly modify Two Valued Stable Model Semantics to deal with programs with test formulae. As we have already explained, $t(\Delta, \sim \Sigma) = (\delta_1 \wedge \cdots \wedge \delta_m \wedge \sim \sigma_1 \wedge \cdots \wedge \sim \sigma_n)$ on two valued domain. In fact we prolong stable semantics to programs with test connective. This is done according with the meaning of a test operator.

For the presentation below let us assume t-P be a logic program with test. The clauses of such programs might have in addition to ordinary premises only default negated test sentences.

Definition 4.3 (I_t interpretation). Given a program t-P with a test, let I be an ordinary 2-valued interpretation of t-P (set of atoms). I_t is obtained from I by adding $t(\Delta, \sim \Sigma)$ to I for any test formula $t(\Delta, \sim \Sigma) \in Lang(t$-$P)$ if $t(\Delta, \sim \Sigma) = true$ for the current value of δ_i and σ_j in I. Thus I_t contains atoms and eventually some test formulae $t(\Delta, \sim \Sigma)$.

I_t extends ordinary interpretation I in a natural way to interpretations over the language with a test and this extension conforms with the semantics for test connective.

Definition 4.4 (t-P/I_t program). By t-P/I_t transformation we mean a new program obtained from t-P by performing the following two operations that concern each default negated atom or *default negated test formula* in the bodies of the program rules.

1. Remove from t-P all rules containing $\sim X$, if $X \in I_t$;

2. Remove from all remaining rules their default premises $\sim X$.

The only difference compared to the original *modulo transformation* is the new concern with *default negated test formulae*. The resulting program t-P/I_t is by definition positive and it has a unique least 2-valued model.

Definition 4.5. An interpretation I is called a Stable model iff *least model* $(t$-$P/I_t) = I$. Stable semantics for a program t-P with a test is determined by the set of all stable models of t-P.

There is no syntactic difference between stable models for programs with tests and ordinary programs. In both cases any stable model is a set of atoms. Moreover t-interpretations play only an auxiliary role during the calculation.

Example 2 Consider a program a with test t-P_1.

$$t\text{-}P_1 : \quad a \leftarrow \sim b$$
$$b \leftarrow \sim a, \sim t(\sim c, \sim a)$$

Consider $I = \{a\}$. Then $I_t = \{a)\}$ as $t(\sim c, \sim a) = \sim c \wedge \sim a = false$ as $\sim a$ is *false* in I. It is easy to calculate that $t\text{-}P_1/I_t = \{a \leftarrow\}$. Then *least model* $(t\text{-}P_1/I_t) = \{a\} = I$.

5. The Transformation

We have already given some hints about how to transform a theory $P \cup r$ into a new program with a test $t\text{-}P$ (t depends from r) such that r-Stable(P) = Stable($t\text{-}P$).

Definition 5.1 (The Transformation). Let $P \cup r :\sim l \Leftarrow \Delta, \sim \Sigma$ be a theory. We define a new program with a test $t\text{-}P$, obtained from this theory:

> For any rule in P with a conclusion l add $\sim t(\Delta, \sim \Sigma)$ to the premises of that rule.

Theories containing a set of refutation rules R are naturally transformed into programs with test sentences:

> For the general case with a set R of refutation rules the transformation is obtained by applying the previous transformation taking into account each refutation rule from R in turn.

For instance after applying the transformation above the theory $P_1 \cup r$ (example 1) turns into $t\text{-}P_1$ (example 2):

$$
\begin{array}{llll}
P_1: & a \leftarrow \sim b & & t\text{-}P_1: \quad a \leftarrow \sim b \\
& b \leftarrow \sim a & \Rightarrow & \qquad\quad b \leftarrow \sim a, \sim t(\sim c, \sim a) \\
r: & \sim b \Leftarrow \sim c, \sim a & &
\end{array}
$$

Lemma 1. Let $P \cup r :\sim l \Leftarrow \Delta, \sim \Sigma$ be a theory and let $t\text{-}P$ be the program with a test obtained after the transformation. If M is a stable model of $t\text{-}P$ then M satisfies the refutation rule r.

Proof. Assume the opposite, namely Δ and $\sim \Sigma$ and l are true in M. Then each rule in $t\text{-}P$ with a head l has among its premises the formula $\sim t(\Delta, \sim \Sigma) = \sim t(\Delta \wedge \sim \Sigma)$. Since Δ and $\sim \Sigma$ are true in M the formula $\sim t(\Delta \wedge \sim \Sigma)$ is false, so l must be false too. #

The following theorem shows that the transformation preserves the meaning of the original theory.

Theorem 1. Let $P \cup r :\sim l \Leftarrow \Delta, \sim \Sigma$ be a theory and let $t\text{-}P$ be the program with a test obtained after the transformation. Then: r-Stable(P)=Stable($t\text{-}P$).

Proof.

1) We show more generally that for any r-interpretation I of P

$$P/^r I = t\text{-}P/I_t \text{ (these are positive programs)}$$

From here immediately follows that any least model of P is also a least model of $(t\text{-}P)$ and the vice verse. Therefore r-stable models of P coincide with stable models of $t\text{-}P$.

There are two subcases:

1. Let $\Delta \cup \sim \Sigma \subseteq I$. Since I is an r-interpretation , $\sim l \in I$. From the definition of I_t, we get $t(\Delta, \sim \Sigma) \in I_t$, therefore $I_t = I \cup t(\Delta, \sim \Sigma)$. The only difference after applying the reductions (def.3.2, def.4.4) concerns the rules with head l. However according to point 2, def.3.2 these rules are discarded from the program P. The rules with head L are also discarded from the program $t\text{-}P$ since all such rules have a premise $\sim t(\Delta, \sim \Sigma)$ which is false in I.

2. If $\Delta \cup \sim \Sigma \nsubseteq I$ then def.3.2 and def. 4.4 coincide since $\sim t(\Delta, \sim \Sigma)$ is true in I.

6. Discussion

We presented an adaptation of Stable Model Semantics to theories with refutation rules. To obtain suitable models that conform with the intended meaning of the refutation rules we revised some of the stable models of the original program by giving a preference to those default negated literals that are conclusions of the refutation rules.

Partly our treatment of rules and refutation rules is in the spirit of Kowalski and Sadri's[6] distinctions between ordinary rules and negative conclusions of the exceptions. Their semantics however is an adaptation of the answer set semantics of Gelfond and Lifschitz, so they avoid contradictions by deriving the classically negative conclusions. They allow explicit representation of exceptions, that are rules with heads of the form $\neg x$, in addition to the original program. They restrict the syntax of the original program, so that explicit negation does not appear in the heads of ordinary clauses. Kowalski and Sadri use a transformation that calculates their intended meaning in terms of answer sets. For that aim they propose a *cancellation technique* that is different from ours.

We don't explore classically negative conclusions to represent refutation rules. Restricted to two-valued stable models our approach can incorporate the presentation of exceptions without need of explicit negation. However in our case $\sim x$ is true either by default or because it is an exception. In the approach of Kowalski and Sadri, exceptions are always of the form $\neg x$ and all the derivable literals of the form $\neg x$ are exceptions. Given the canonical example, $bird(Tweety) \leftarrow$, default rule $fly(x) \leftarrow bird(x)$ and the refutation rule

$$\sim fly(Tweety) \Leftarrow bird(Tweety)$$

we would be able to derive $\sim fly(Tweety)$ by the simple transformation

$fly(Tweety) \leftarrow bird(Tweety), \sim bird(Tweety)$
$bird(Tweety) \leftarrow$

Thus there is an alternative possibility to express exceptions (even over 2-valued interpreted language) using normal logic programs and exceptions without classical negation.

54

Our models are not deductively closed in a sense that it is possible to have $a \leftarrow \sim b$ in a program, b false and a not true. This holds also for the models of *Logic Programs with Exceptions* of Kowalski and Sardi and for some semantics for inconsistent databases[7].

The idea to use a transformation between programs was widely explored in different contexts. Besides the other advantages this idea is useful as the transformation usually facilitates implementation. A transformation that can eliminate certain restricted forms of integrity constraints from definite clause databases is proposed in the work of Asirelli et al[1].

Refutation rules can be also viewed as a particular case of integrity constraints. Our transformation presents a way of eliminating integrity constraints from program databases. Instead of the general form of integrity constraints

$$\longleftarrow \underbrace{\delta_1, \cdots \delta_k}_{\Delta}, l, \underbrace{\sim \sigma_1, \cdots, \sim \sigma_s}_{\sim \Sigma}$$

our refutation rules present a particular case of constraints

$$\sim l \Longleftarrow \underbrace{\delta_1, \cdots \delta_k}_{\Delta}, \underbrace{\sim \sigma_1, \cdots, \sim \sigma_s}_{\sim \Sigma}$$

that explicitly indicate which sentences are to be removed from the database.

References

1. P. Asirelli, M. De Santis and M. Martelli, *J. Logic Programming* **3**, (1985) p. 221-233.
2. V. K. Finn and S. M. Gusakova, *in Russian, Technical Cybernetics,* **5** (Moscow, VINITI, 1987).
3. M. Fitting, *Kleene's Three Valued Logics and Their Children*, (August, 1993, Manuscript).
4. M. Gelfond and V. Lifschitz, in *Proc. of 5th ICLP*, eds. R. A. Kowalski and K. A. Bowen (MIT Press, 1988) p. 1070-1080.
5. M. Gelfond and V. Lifschitz, in *Proc. of 7th ICLP*, eds. D. Warren and P. Szeredi (MIT Press, 1990) p. 579-597.
6. R.A. Kowalski and F. Sadri, in *Proc. of 7th ICLP*, eds. D. Warren and P. Szeredi (MIT Press, 1990) p. 588-613.
7. M. Mircheva, in *Proc. of JELIA '92, LNCS* **663** eds. D. Pearce and H. Wansing (Springer-Verlag, 1992) p. 252- 263.
8. M. Mircheva, in *Proc. of META '94, LNCS*, (1994, in press).
9. T. Przymusinski, in *Proc. of 7th ICLP*, eds. D. Warren and P. Szeredi (MIT Press, 1990) p. 459-477.
10. R.A. Reiter, *J. Artificial Intelligence* **13(1,2)** (1981) p. 81-132.

A FRAMEWORK FOR KNOWLEDGE STRUCTURING [1]

CHRISTO DICHEV

Department of Computer Science, University College Dublin
Dublin 4, Ireland

E-mail. cdichev@ccvax.ucd.ie

ABSTRACT

This paper presents a knowledge representation framework, based on a logic programming approach. By extending logic programming with theory relations, this framework provides a means for expressing structural concepts. Instead of being restricted to one global knowledge base, this framework allows segmentation into separate theories, which through theory relations can be composed into compound structures. The framework provides a number of theory relations for composing new knowledge fragments out of predefined components. Throughout the paper compositional properties of the framework are illustrated by examples.

1. Introduction

A computational system with multiple theories and theory relations can be studied from two aspects: the representational aspect[3,4,5,6,8] and the logic programming aspect.[1,2,7,9,10,11] From a logic programming point of view, in such a system separate theories can be handled as first order objects and might be dynamically combined into compound theories. From a representational point of view, being able to treat theories as first-class objects enables us to reason about them, modify and interrelate them. Theories provide a way to structure a knowledge by splitting it into smaller, more manageable units, while the theory relations provide a way to build "compound knowledge" by relating existing fragments. As a result, logic programming with multiple theories and theory relations can be used as a computational model in some AI tasks.

In the next sections we present a language framework, an extension to the logic programming computation model with theory relations. Each program in the multiple theory logic programming framework is a collection of a finite set of named theories, linked by theory relations. The theories defined by a finite set of clauses, called *units*, are used as basic components for building the other theories. Each theory therefore is either a unit or *compound theory* - defined by application of theory relations to existing theories. Throughout this paper the expressive power of the framework is illustrated by examples.

---

[1]This work is supported by IBM under a Newman Scholarship

2. Background

2.1. Motivation

The first logic programming languages were developed based on a single theory approach. The need for a modular and structured logic programming has given rise to many proposals.[1,2,7,8,9,10,11] An unifying framework for structuring logic programs has been proposed recently.[1,2] In general, a program in logic programming languages provided with means for program structuring, is composed of a set of separate programs called units or modules. Each unit consists of a set of clauses and is provided with a unique name for reference. The relations allowed between units in these type of languages are restricted to a fixed number of structural links. Thus a structured logic program is conceived as a collection of units with fixed structural links between them.

In this paper we suggest a more general view of structuring logic programs based on *theory relations* rather than on fixed unit links. Assume that $u_1, u_2, ..., u_n$, are n units. A straightforward way to combine them into a program P, is just by unifying the units: $P = u_1 \cup u_2 \cup ... \cup u_n$. We will use the symbol "+" to name the union relation, i.e. $P = u_1 + u_2 + ... + u_n \equiv u_1 \cup u_2 \cup ... \cup u_n$.

However when composing a program P, we may not want to include all clauses from each unit but rather to select from each unit u_i, a specified subset $v_i \subseteq u_i$. For instance when two units define predicates with the same name and arity, we may want to ignore the definitions of the common predicates in some of the units. In such cases we can extend the existing list of relations between units by the following relation: $P = \{C \mid C \in u_2 \vee (C \in u_1 \rightarrow \forall D \in u_2(\hat{C} \neq \hat{D}))\}$, where $\hat{C}$ denotes the name of the predicate $p(X_1, ..., X_k)$ defined by the clause C, i.e. p/k. To distinguish these two relations we denote the latter one by the pair of symbols "+'", thus: $P = u_1 +' u_2 \equiv \{C \mid C \in u_2 \vee (C \in u_1 \rightarrow \forall D \in u_2(\hat{C} \neq \hat{D}))\}$

When we define a set S containing all even natural numbers less than 10, we do this either by listing all members of the set, i.e. $S = \{2, 4, 6, 8\}$ or alternatively we may define $S = \{x \mid x \in N, x \bmod 2 = 0, x < 10\}$, where N is the set of the natural numbers. The latter definition can be interpreted as a relation R between the set S and the set of the natural numbers N. The relation $S = R(N)$ defines the properties of the natural numbers belonging to S, and thus selects a subset with a specified property out of N. Although the set S is defined by imposing certain constraints on the set N, we do not refer to the latter set when we perform any operations with S.

If we look at the program units as collections of clauses, a similar approach may be applied when we define a new program out of existing *components*. A logic program P can be defined in an *intensional way* either by explicitly listing the corresponding subsets of clauses out of the composing units, or by defining a relation $P = R(u_1, u_2, ..., u_n)$ which specifies the properties of the clauses in units $u_1, u_2, ..., u_n$ that belong to P. The concept of unit relations can be used as an abstraction for describing a program in terms of other programs. In the following, with abuse of notation we will write $P = R(u_1, u_2, ..., u_n)$ to indicate the relation $R(P, u_1, u_2, ..., u_n)$.

Moving from units to theories, the unit relations can be generalized to *theory relations*. Theory relation R applied to $u_1, u_2, ..., u_n$ interpreted as theories, defines an expression $t = R(u_1, u_2, ..., u_n)$, which we call a *compound theory*. Theory relations are a generalization of unit relations in the sense that one theory can cooperate with others in terms of a specified set of provable sentences, without accessing the definitions generating them. For instance we can define a relation $enc/1$, such that when applied to a unit u, interpreted as a theory, it results in a compound theory $enc(u)$ defined as a set of all atomic formulae derivable from u. The application of the theory relation $enc/1$ to u makes the unit u visible to other units only in terms of its logical consequences. Since $enc(u)$ encapsulates the clauses defining the unit u, it enables us to make a conceptual separation between a computation and the output of a computation.

With set theory operations we can write complex expressions for defining particular sets. In a similar fashion, having defined a collection of basic theory relations we can write complex expressions describing compound theories. For instance, the expression $T = t_1 +' (t_2 + t_3)$ defines a theory T containing the same clauses as theories t_1, t_2 and t_3 except for the clauses in t_1 using the same names as some of the clauses in t_2 or t_3.

There are situations in which it is useful to view a program as an incomplete description of some knowledge domain. The composition of such programs may increase the degree of completeness of the description. For example the definitions of given predicates can be modified by composing one program with some other programs. On the other hand in some cases it might be useful to limit the level of interactions between certain programs. Since theory relations are entailment extensions to unit relations, they enable us to integrate in a new theory specified fragments of derivable propositions from the composing theories supporting different knowledge composition techniques.

2.2. Basic concepts

In the following the term theory will be used as a synonym for a logic program. In a structural context a theory $R(t_1, t_2, ..., t_n)$ is viewed as a part of the structure yielded from the relation R applied to components $t_1, t_2, ..., t_n$. Put in another way, a theory can be viewed as a $n + 1$ tuple of theories $\langle R(t_1, t_2, ..., t_n), t_1, t_2, ..., t_n \rangle$. The syntax structure of $R(t_1, t_2, ..., t_n)$ is visible from the external environment and can be exploited when combining it with other theories. On the other hand, the components (arguments) $t_1, t_2, ..., t_n$ are not directly accessible by the other theories. With respect to theory $R(t_1, t_2, ..., t_n)$ its components are defined in an *extensional* way: the set of formulae provable in components $t_1, t_2, ..., t_n$ can only be referred by the visible part $R(t_1, t_2, ..., t_n)$ of the theory. In the following when referring to a theory, we will mean its visible part.

In our logic programming framework as in contextual[10]*andmodularlogicprogramming*[7] the basic building elements forming any theory are called *units*. Each unit is a collection of clauses denoted by a unique name. In conventional logic programming there is no need to indicate a program in which a goal must be solved. By default all goals are solved in a single program. However in a multi-theory setting, pointing to the theory where a goal must be solved becomes relevant. Our language provides several options for directing a prove of a goal into a fixed theory. Each option corresponds to either a static or a specific dynamic theory formation. For instance the goal G in E forces the proof of the goal in the theory (possibly compound) denoted by the expression E. A program clause is an expression of the form $A \leftarrow G_1, G_2, ..., G_n$ with precisely one positive literal. Some of the goals $G_i, i = 1, 2, ..., n$ may include an expression indicating explicitly to the theory, where the proof of the goal must be directed. If B is an atomic formula, which does not include any of the predicates: $in/2$, $if/2$, $if'/2$, then a goal G is defined as follows:

$$G ::= B \mid G \ in \ E \mid G \ if \ E \mid G \ if' \ E$$

If the unit expression is omitted in the goal specification (the goal has the form B), such type of goal can be interpreted as an abbreviation of the unit expression: B in u, where u is the name of the unit in which the goal B currently occurs.

Definitions.

(i.) With every theory t is associated a finite collection $||t||$ of all predicate names defined in t.

(ii.) If A denotes a predicate $p(x_1, x_2, ..., x_k)$ we will use $\hat{A}$ to denote the name of A.

(iii.) If t is a theory by $comp(t)$ we denote the set of all its components.

3. A language framework with theory relations

In the next few sections we define a fixed set of theory relations and a set of predicates dealing with theories of a multiple theory logic programming framework $\mathcal{L}_T$. The operational semantics of the framework, defined in terms of a sequence of inference rules in the form $\frac{Assumptions}{Conclusions}$ if $Conditions$ is introduced in our previous work[4]. In the following sections the same type of rules will be used to explain the operational behavior of some of the constructs of the framework.

3.1. Compound theories

Encapsulation. If t is a theory then $enc(t)$ is a theory called *encapsulated theory*.

$$enc(t) = \{g \mid t \vdash g \land atomic(g)\}$$

The encapsulated theory $enc(t)$ can be viewed as a denotation of the set of all atomic consequences derivable from the theory t. Note that if u is an unit, then $enc(u)$ does not include the set of clauses defining u. The qualification *encapsulated* is used here to emphasize the fact that $enc(u)$ makes accessible only the "extensional knowledge" hiding the "intensional knowledge", defined by the set of definitions u. Notice, that the necessity of such a separation becomes obvious, when combining compound theories into a structure of interacting components.

Union. If t_1 and t_2 are theories then $t_1 + t_2$ obtained by unifying t_1 and t_2 is a theory called *union* of t_1 and t_2.

The union $t_1 + t_2$ preserves the "extensibility" structure in a sense that t_1 and t_2 cooperate with each other wile exploiting their components separately. Therefore in general the meaning of the compound theory $t_1 + t_2$ is different from the meaning of $t_1 + enc(t_2)$. Assuming that u_1 and u_2 are primitive units, then the union $u_1 + enc(u_2)$ can be interpreted as feeding the output of u_2 to u_1 as input, while $u_1 \mid u_2$ denotes the collection of clauses obtained by unifying the sets of clauses u_1 and u_2.

Predicate overriding. If t_1 and t_2 are two theories then $t_1 +' t_2$ is a theory called *overriding union*.

In general two different units could provide both definitions for common predicates. There are occasions when it is desirable for the most recent predicate definition to override the previous ones. The overriding union $t_1 +' t_2$ is a theory obtained by unifying t_1 and t_2, excluding the common predicates in t_1. Note that the overriding union is a *non-monotonic theory relation*. Operationally it means that an evaluation of a goal g can progress through some of the components of theory t_1 provided that no definition for g can be found in t_2.

Intersection of theories. If t_1 and t_2 are theories, then $t_1 \& t_2$ is compound theory called *intersection* of t_1 and t_2.

$$\frac{t_1 \vdash g[\theta] \qquad t_2 \vdash g[\theta]}{t_1 \ \& \ t_2 \vdash g[\theta]}$$

Assume we wish to specify the "visible" fragment of a theory t, assuming that the theory v_t defines "what is to be visible" in t. One way to represent the notion of "visibility" used in modular logic programming systems is by introducing a new copy of the theory t under the name t_{aux}, while t is redefined as $t = t_{aux} \& v_t$. Obviously in theory $t = \{g \mid (t_{aux} \vdash g) \wedge (v_t \vdash g) \wedge atomic(g)\}$ derivable are only those formulae of t_{aux} that satisfy the corresponding constraints imposed by v_t.

Subtraction of theories. If t_1 and t_2 are theories then $t_1 \backslash t_2$ is a theory called *subtraction*.

$$t_1 \backslash t_2 = \{g \mid (t_1 \vdash g) \wedge (t_2 \nvdash g) \wedge atomic(g) \}$$

Notice that the subtraction is a *non-monotonic* theory relation. Suppose from theory $t = R(t_1, t_2, ..., t_n)$ we want to create a new one, where some of the goals derivable in t are to be invalidated[8]. It might be rather difficult to redefine the corresponding predicate definitions in t, for we might have to look for such definitions in all components t_i. Goal invalidation in our approach is handled in a way similar to the "visibility". Therefore definitions specifying a conceptual fragment "Not to be derivable" are provided in a separate theory. The latter theory can be combined with appropriate theories applying a theory *subtraction* relation.

3.2. Theory switching

From the viewpoint of a goal evaluation, each theory determines an environment (context) of proof, dependent on its components and applied relation. For switching to a new theory t, proving a goal G, a *theory-switching* operator G *in* t is provided. The meaning of the operator G *in* t is that the goal G is proved in the new theory t regardless of the theory in which the current theory-switching operator occurs:

$$\frac{t \vdash g[\theta]}{t_1 \vdash g[\theta] \text{ in } t}$$

One interpretation of the expression $t_1 + enc(t_2)$ is as union of t_1 and the unit $u_t = \{P \leftarrow P \text{ in } t_2 \mid \hat{P} \in \|t_2\|\}$ defining a collection of transmission clauses to the predicates in t_2.

In the following examples, expressions of the type $R(t_1, t_2, ..., t_n) \vdash g$ will be used to denote: "a goal g with respect to theory $R(t_1, t_2, ..., t_n)$". Consider the following three units:

unit (cat)	unit (food)	unit (pet)
$eats\_cat(X) \leftarrow food(X)$	$food(meat)$	$eats\_pet(X) \leftarrow eats\_cat(X)$

The top goal *eats_pet(X) in (cat+enc(food)+enc(pet))* switches the derivation of the goal *eats_pet(X)* to the theory *cat+enc(food)+enc(pet)*.

> $\vdash$ *eats_pet(X) in* (`cat+enc(food)+enc(pet)`)
> `cat+enc(food)+enc(pet)` $\vdash$ *eats_pet(X)*
> **pet** $\vdash$ *eats_pet(X)*
> **pet** $\vdash$ *eats_cat(X)*
> $\sqrt{}$ `failure`

3.3. Dynamic theory formation

Theory relations allow different forms of a dynamic theory formation. The term dynamic is used to emphasize that the theory composition depends on the history of computation and on the current theory configuration where the call for a dynamic theory formation occurs.

The predicate for a *dynamic theory formation* G *if* $R(X, t_1, ..., t_{n-1})[X/t]$, where X stands for the current theory t, forces the proof of G in a new theory $R(t, t_1, ..., t_{n-1})$, obtained by applying the theory relation R to the current theory t and the theories $t_i, i = 1, 2, ..., n - 1$. Thus the current theory can be combined dynamically with new components applying one of the predefined theory relations.

$$\frac{R(t, t_1, ..., t_{n-1}) \vdash g(\theta)}{u \vdash g[\theta] \text{ if } R(t, t_1, ..., t_{n-1})}$$

In the following example a dynamic theory formation predicate is used in the second clause of the unit **pet**. Therefore the goal *eats_pet(X)* will be evaluated in a new unit generated after applying the $+$ operation to the *current theory* and *cat*.

unit (pet)   **unit (cat)**

$eats\_pet(X) \leftarrow eats\_animal(X)$
$eats\_my\_pet(X) \leftarrow eats\_pet(X)$ if $T + cat$ $eats\_animal(X) \leftarrow food(X)$
$food(canned\_food)$ $food(meat)$

$\vdash eats\_my\_pet(canned\_food)$ in pet
pet $\vdash eats\_my\_pet(canned\_food)$
pet $\vdash eats\_pet(canned\_food)$ if pet + cat
pet+cat $\vdash eats\_pet(canned\_food)$
pet+cat $\vdash eats\_animal(canned\_food)$
pet +cat $\vdash food(canned\_food)$
$\checkmark$

Goal if $X + Assumptions$ can be interpreted as proving the *Goal* provided that
the current theory X is extended with *Assumptions(Hypothesis)*[6,9].

3.4. Global dynamic theory formation

In applications merging object-oriented and logic programming, compound theories
can be used to define objects. Assume that *tweety* is an object inheriting properties
from *bird* and *animal* objects[8]:

unit (animal)   **unit (bird)**   **unit (tweety)**

$mode(walk)$ $mode(fly)$
$mode(run) \leftarrow no\_of\_legs(2)$ $no\_of\_legs(2)$ $no\_of\_wings(2)$
$mode(gallop) \leftarrow no\_of\_legs(4)$

$$tweety \leftarrow^{isa} bird \leftarrow^{isa} animal$$

The structural relations between the theories *tweety + enc(bird + enc(animal))* and
bird + enc(animal) reflects the inheritance defined between the corresponding objects.
If we want to know "How many legs does Tweety have" we will try to derive the
goal *no_of_legs(X)* in the theory *tweety + enc(bird + enc(animal))*. Although initially
directed to the latter theory the derivation of the goal *no_of_legs(X)* will be redirected
to the theory *bird + enc(animal)*. Note that in this case we do not specify how to
switch between classes within a superclass during the proof of a goal. The switching
between classes is done implicitly as a result of the predefined inheritance relation
between them, expressed in terms of theory relations.

$\vdash$ *no_of_legs(X)* in *tweety + enc(bird + enc(animal))*.
tweety + enc(bird + enc(animal)) $\vdash$ *no_of_legs(X)*
bird + enc(animal) $\vdash$ *no_of_legs(X)*
$\checkmark$ $X = 2$

Since operations over theories are a generalization of the above type of structural relations, when a proof of a goal is initiated in a compound theory $R(t_1, t_2, ..., t_n)$, the proof process may in a similar way be switched to certain components t_i of the later theory. Similarly to object-oriented systems a theory t_i is to be understood as part of structured context. To make a distinction between a theory and the most general structure in which the former theory is a component of, we will call the the latter *original theory*.

Assume that the current goal referring to a global dynamic theory formation occurs in the unit u, which is possibly a component of a compound theory. Then with respect to the proof history and the current theory u the *original compound theory* t_{org} is defined as the compound theory with the most general structure, where u is one of its components, i.e. $u \in comp(t_{org})$, such that $\neg\exists t$ in the immediate proof history satisfying the relation $comp(t_{org}) \subset comp(t)$.

Global dynamic theory formation is handled by the operator $g \; if' \; R(X, t_1, ..., t_{n-1})$ $[X/t_{org}]$, which forces the proof of the goal g in a new theory $R(t_{org}, t_1, ..., t_{n-1})$, by applying the theory operation R to the current original theory t_{org} and the theories $t_i, i = 1, 2, ..., n - 1$. Thus the original theory can be combined dynamically with new components applying one of the predefined theory relations.

$$\frac{R(t_{org}, t_1, ..., t_{n-1}) \vdash g(\theta)}{u \vdash g[\theta] \; if' \; R(t_{org}, t_1, ..., t_{n-1})}$$

As an illustration of a global dynamic theory formation, consider the following hierarchical system:

unit (person)   **unit (entertainer)**   **unit (thief)**

$activity(work)$ $like(X) \leftarrow activity(X) \; if' \; self$ $activity(stealing)$

$artist ::= entertainer + enc(person)$
$pickpocket ::= thief + enc(artist)$

$$pickpoket \leftarrow^{isa} artist \leftarrow^{isa} person$$

This example illustrates a particular application of the global dynamic theory formation rule, where if' applies an union operation to the current original theory and the empty set. The application of the predicate $activity(X) \; if' \; Y$ $(activity(X) \; if' \; (Y + \emptyset))$ results in switching the proof of the goal $activity(X)$ from $artist$ to the class on whose behalf a proof is being initiated. This corresponds to proving the latter goal in the compound theory $pickpocket$ in which the chain of reasoning leading to the goal $activity(X) \; if' \; Y$ has been initiated. This particular case of a global dynamic theory formation can be interpreted as a version of $self$ used in object oriented systems.

$\vdash like(X)$ in $thief+enc(entertainer+enc(person))$
thief+enc(entertainer+enc(person)) $\vdash like(X)$

thief + enc(artist) ⊢ *like(X)*
artist ⊢ *like(X)*
entertainer + enc(person) ⊢ *like(X)*
entertainer + enc(person) ⊢ *activity(X) if' thief+enc(entertainer+enc(person))*
thief | enc(entertainer | enc(person)) ⊢ *activity(X)*
√ X = stealing

3.5. Parameterized theories

Parameterized modules are also interpretable in terms of theory relations. To handle parameterized theories the set of unit names, defined initially as the set of atomic names, is extended to sets of *general terms*. If $u(X_1, ..., X_m)$ denotes a parameterized unit, then the variables X_i pass terms $x_i, i = 1, 2, ..., m$ unified with them to the clauses defining the unit. Consider a "parameterized version" of the **pet** example, where the set of the primitive units is extended with one more, defining a new pet - **monkey**. The name of the first unit is now a term $pet(A)$ rather than an atom. Once the variable A is instantiated to a term, it is propagated to the clauses defining $pet(A)$.

$$\text{unit (pet(A))}$$

$$eats\_pet(X) \leftarrow eats\_animal(X) \text{ if } T + A$$
$$food(canned\_food)$$

unit (cat)	**unit (monkey)**
$eats\_animal(X) \leftarrow food(X)$	$eats\_animal(X) \leftarrow food(X)$
$food(meat)$	$food(nuts)$

⊢ *eats_pet(nuts)* in *pet(monkey)*
pet(monkey) ⊢ *eats_pet(nuts)*
pet(monkey) ⊢ *eats_animal(nuts) if pet(monkey) +' monkey*
pet(monkey) +' monkey ⊢ *eats_animal(nuts)*
pet(monkey) +' monkey ⊢ *food(nuts)*
√

4. Conclusion

From a practical point of view providing structural concepts are recognized as fundamental to extending the application domain of logic programming languages. Logic programming with multiple theories and theory relations allows an integral view on different notions such as modules, information sharing, information hiding and dynamic theory formation. On the other hand such an approach provides a basis for dealing more directly with reasoning mechanisms such as hierarchical, hypothetical, contextual and abductive reasoning. The framework presented here provides a conceptual basis for implementation and a further development of a prototype theory configuration language[3,4,5]

5. Acknowledgments

Many thanks to Allan Ramsay for stimulating discussions. Thanks also to Fergus Fletcher for proofreading this paper. I also gratefully acknowledge the support of the IBM Newman Scholarship.

REFERENCES

1. A. Brogi, P. Mancarella, D. Pedreschi and F. Turini *Modular logic programming*, Journal of the ACM (to appear).

2. M. Bugliesi, E. Lamma and P. Mello *Modularity in logic programming*, J. Logic Programming **12**: 1-199, 1993.

3. C. Dichev *Knowledge representation with W-Prolog*, SPIE Vol. **1963** Applications of Artificial Intelligence, 1993, pp. 316-327.

4. C. Dichev *Knowledge bases as compound theories*, Proceedings of the 6th Irish Conference on Artificial Intelligence and Cognitive Science - AICS'93, Belfast, 1993, pp. 155-164.

5. C. Dichev *Theory relations and context dependencies*, Proceedings of the 6th Conference on Artificial Intelligence, Melbourne, Australia, 1993, pp. 266-272.

6. D.M. Gabbay and U. Reyle *N-Prolog: an extension of prolog with hypothetical implications*, J. Logic Programming, 1:319-356, 1984, 2:251-284 1985.

7. E. Lamma, P. Mello and A. Natali *An extended Warren Abstract Machine for the execution of structured logic programs*, J. Logic Programming **14**: 187-222, 1992.

8. F.G. McCabe *L&O: Logic and Objects*, International series in Computer Science, Prentice-Hall International, 1992.

9. D. Miller *A logical analysis of modules in logic programming*, J. Logic programming **6**:79-108 (1989).

10. L. Monteiro and A. Porto *Contextual logic programming*, Proceedings of the 6th ICLP, Lisbon, Portugal, 1989, MIT Press, pp. 284-299.

11. R.A. O'Keefe *Towards an algebra for constructing logic programs*, Proceedings of the IEEE Symposium on Logic Programming, 1985, pp. 152-160.

A DISTRIBUTED ARCHITECTURE FOR LOGIC AGENTS

A. CIAMPOLINI, E. LAMMA, P. MELLO, C. STEFANELLI

DEIS, Università di Bologna
Viale Risorgimento 2, 40136 Bologna, Italy
{anna,evelina,paola,cesare}@deis33.cineca.it

ABSTRACT

We present an architecture, based on a concurrent logic language that can be suitably used for supporting and integrating multi-agent models both blackboard- and object-based. The logic language is characterised by multi-head clauses with committed-choice behaviour and restricted AND parallelism. Thanks to the parallel nature of the language, we obtain a distributed implementation on a Transputer-based architecture both for blackboard- and object-based systems where parallelism is highly exploited.

1. Introduction

The procedural interpretation of logic, first proposed in [1], has led to the use of logic as a programming language. The main features of logic programming are the expressive power of logic, together with the sound and clean semantics. Moreover, logic programming, thanks to its computational model which is intrinsically parallel, seems to be very attractive for parallel and distributed implementations. Distributed computing is acknowledged to be one of the key components of future systems. Following these considerations, and in attempt to broaden the application area of logic programming toward artificial intelligence applications, it would be of interest to investigate how to build and support distributed multi-agent systems in a logic programming framework.

This paper addresses this issue. The resulting system is based upon a two level architecture. The highest level supports the multi-agent model and interaction between agents. The lowest level supports distributed logic programming abstractions for concurrency, communication and synchronisation, and is built upon an extended logic programming language.

Two main choices have to be done in designing the two architectural levels: selecting which multi-agent models to support (*level 2*); selecting a concurrent logic language expressive enough to support different communication models and suitable for a distributed implementation (*level 1*).

With respect to the selection of the logic language (*level 1*), we argue that the use of stream-based logic languages[2,3], the most widely adopted approach in the literature for introducing concurrency in logic programming, is not the best for our purpose. Streams, in fact, behave like shared variables and thus introduce a centralisation point in the resulting computational model. In the language we consider, instead (called Rose [4]), no sharing of variables is allowed and communication is performed via multi-head clauses as in [5,6]. The communication by means of multi-head clauses maps easily to the communication in a distributed system.

We show that Rose, if extended with read-only atoms, is expressive enough to easily support both blackboard and object-based models in a uniform manner. In particular, multi-head clauses are very similar to the activation patterns of a blackboard, while the computation can be interpreted as the sending and receiving of goals (messages) to/from a blackboard-like structure representing the multi-set of current goals.

Just the adding of some syntactic sugar allows us to build, starting from Rose, an extended logic language, inspired by Conery's seminal paper[7], supporting all the peculiar features of object-oriented programming. The language is characterised by active, possibly asynchronously executing agents which communicate through message passing. State change is cleanly obtained by mapping logic objects into processes and by using unification and recursion.

Since both blackboard and object-oriented systems are built on top of a fine-grained parallel logic language, the degree of real parallelism achieved is very high. Logic agents are rule instances in the case of the blackboard architecture, and objects instances in the case of objects. Both the access to the blackboard and the message send are mapped into goals to be solved. In the resulting system not only agents execute in parallel (*inter-agent parallelism*) but also the evaluation of the same agent can generate parallel threads of control (*intra-agent parallelism*). The distributed implementation for the blackboard and the object-based models exploits the implementation of Rose on a distributed memory architecture based on Transputer technology [8,9].

2. Level 1: The Logic Language

Stream-based concurrent logic programming languages (see [2,3]) have been proposed in the literature to address parallel applications. Communication and synchronisation between processes is supported via read-only variables. However, logical variables for process communication fail as soon as one consider the possibility of having distributed implementations, where processes are allocated on several computational elements with no shared memory.

To better fit with distribution, other concurrent logic languages perform inter-process communication via message-passing primitives (events) [10] and multi-head clauses [5]. Inspired by the latter proposal, we ground our multi-agent architecture on a concurrent logic language with multi-head clauses (Rose, [4]).

2.1. Rose

We briefly overview the main features of Rose. We concentrate ourselves on the concurrent aspects of the language while omitting the description of the sequential part. Rose is a proper extension of Horn Clause Logic. Its complete definition is reported in [4] along with its semantics and some programming examples.

In order to make the language more suitable for a distributed implementation, variable sharing between goals in the body of a clause is not allowed. Communication is performed only via multi-head clauses.

We extend the original definition of the language by introducing the concept of *read-only* atom in multi-head clauses. As will be made clear in the following, this concept makes a blackboard-based interpretation possible (see section 3.1) and allows an object to avoid the cumbersome and expensive recursive calls to itself when no state change is present (see section 3.2). A Rose program now consists of a finite set of multi-head clauses with committed-choice behaviour, of the form:

$$A_1,...,A_m,*R_1,...,*R_k \leftarrow \quad G \mid B_1,B_2,...,B_n \qquad (1)$$

where $m,k,n >= 0$, and A_i, B_i and R_i are atomic literals. An atomic literal has the form $p(t_1,...,t_k)$ where p is a predicate name and each t_i is a term. In the following, a Prolog-like syntax is adopted for terms and atoms. In particular, atoms may contain variables, which are identifiers starting with an uppercase letter.

The atoms occurring in the head of a clause can be of two different kinds: *read-only* or *consumable*. The former (*Rs*, prefixed by *) correspond to atoms which are simply inspected when the clause is applied. The latter (*As*), instead, correspond to atoms which disappear because of the clause application.

The guard G consists of a set of built-in predicates. When the guard is empty, the commit operator "|" can be omitted. The "," operator is a parallel composition operator and may occur both in the left- and right-hand side of a clause.

Operationally, a guarded multi-head clause functions as an alternative in a guarded command. In particular, a multi-head clause like (1) applies to a parallel composition of atoms, $A_1',...,A_m',R_1',...,R_k'$ say, if there exists a substitution ϑ such that:

$$\vartheta = mgu((A_1,...,A_m,R_1,...,R_k),(A_1',...,A_m',R_1',...,R_k'))$$

If $G\vartheta$ is satisfied (yielding a substitution γ), commit to the clause and reduce the parallel composition of processes $A_1',...,A_m'$ to the parallel composition of (new) processes $(B_1,...,B_n)\vartheta\gamma$, while living unchanged the atoms $R_1',...,R_k'$.

Rose operational semantics has been given according to the true concurrent model (see [4]). Here, we extend it to deal with read-only atoms too. The initial goal is denoted by a multiset of atomic formulae, and one rewriting rule suffices to describe the behaviour of any Rose program P:

$$\frac{A_1,...,A_m,*R_1,...,*R_k \leftarrow G \mid B_1,B_2,...,B_n \in P}{\lfloor A_1',...,A_m' \rfloor \cup \lfloor R_1',...,R_k' \rfloor \rightarrow \lfloor B_1,...,B_n \rfloor \vartheta\gamma \cup \lfloor R_1',...,R_k' \rfloor}$$

where $\vartheta = mgu((A_1,...,A_m,R_1,...,R_k),(A_1',...,A_m',R_1',...,R_k'))$ and γ is the substitution computed during the evaluation of guard G (Eval(Gϑ)=γ). Notice that the application of substitutions is component-wise. A derivation is a (possibly infinite) sequence of goals each one represented by a multiset of atoms obtained by starting with the initial goal and applying the previous rewriting rule.

The computation can be defined in terms of applications of rewriting rules to disjoint sub-parts of the current state. Concurrency emerges from the fact that more than one rewriting rule is applied at each step of the computation. The condition to be satisfied in order to simultaneously apply several rewriting rules is that their left-hand sides do not apply to the same elements of the current state trying to read and consume them at the same time. Therefore, mutual exclusion on the global state is automatically guaranteed since parallel reduction of clauses is allowed only if they do not compete for consuming the same data structure in the current state of the computation.

68

3. Level 2: Multi-Agent Models

In this section, we show how to support multi-agent models such as blackboards and objects by using the concurrent logic language described in section 2. Roughly speaking, agents (i.e., rule instances in a blackboard model, and objects instances in an object-based model) are represented by multi-head clauses. In the multi-head of a clause, some atoms carry the agent state as arguments and others represent communication items to be read or consumed. In the body of a clause, atomic goals are used for modifying the state of an agent and for creating new communication items.

3.1. Blackboard-based Systems

The blackboard architecture and paradigm have been used for many different purposes [11]. The blackboard model of problem solving consists of partitioning the knowledge about a particular problem into several subsets, in order to keep domain knowledge separate from control knowledge and to organise the communications via a central data structure, named blackboard.

The blackboard model is well-suited for expressing the cooperation of concurrent agents. The use of multiple, independent sources of knowledge raises the possibility of exploiting parallel programming techniques. In particular, the control module can select several knowledge sources to be activated in parallel. A control mechanism is then needed in order to organise and rule concurrent accesses to the shared memory.

According to [12], we can give a blackboard interpretation of the extended Rose language, and thus use it as underlying support for concurrent logic agents communicating via a blackboard. The key idea is to interpret sets of (multi-head) clauses as logic agents communicating via a common working memory. Synchronisation and communication is ruled by the committed-choice nature of Rose clauses, thus the control component is not a separate entity but is distributed among the agents, in the guard.

A blackboard-based application is composed of a set of Rose clauses (knowledge sources), each one representing the knowledge of an agent, and a blackboard, that is a (possibly empty) multi-set of atoms. Both the state of the agents and communication items are stored in the blackboard.

Example 3.1 *Let us consider the following example, inspired to [12], representing a reservation system. The system is specified by a database stored in the blackboard, a set of theories corresponding to the agencies, and a theory corresponding to the airline company. The blackboard initially contains the number of free seats for each flight. This is obtained, in Rose, by the (AND parallel) goal:*

←flight(az503,100), flight(az504,200), flight(az505,150), flight(az506,200)

The blackboard is therefore represented by a multiset of (ground) atoms, which are created by an (AND parallel) goal and exist as independent entities until an agent consumes them. The agents can modify the blackboard by adding or removing atoms to or from it. In this respect, the (asynchronous) communication between two agents takes place through the blackboard, one agent adding an atom to the blackboard and another agent consuming or simply reading this atom from the blackboard.
The following multi-head clauses represent the knowledge of an agency:

book(Flight,N_book), flight(Flight,N_free) ←
     N_free >= N_book, N_new is N_free - N_book | flight(Flight,N_new)
inspect(Flight,N_free), *flight(Flight,N_free) ←

When an agency wants to book some seats (N) on a flight (F), it raises the request:
    ←book(F,N)
Only if the number of free seats on the flight is greater than N and no other agency is currently changing the state of the flight, the reservation request will be served. The committed-choice nature of Rose ensures that knowledge sources trying to consume the same atom from the blackboard are synchronised.

In the example above, several agencies, each one raising a request for inspecting the state of a flight (← inspect(F,N)), are served in parallel since they simply read the state of the flight without modifying the corresponding atom in blackboard. However, even if two rule instances cannot be executed in parallel, both multi-head unification and guard evaluation can be processed in parallel. This corresponds to introduce parallelism inside the *match* phase of the control cycle (see [11]) since multi-head unifications for different rules can execute in parallel, and between the *match* and the *select* phase since multi-head unification for a rule instance can execute in parallel with the guard evaluation of a different rule instance. Moreover, the body execution for each rule instance can be performed in parallel, by exploiting the (restricted) AND parallelism peculiar of Rose. This corresponds to introduce parallelism inside the *act* phase of the control cycle.

3.2. Object-based systems

The framework of multi-head clauses can also be used for supporting objects communicating via message passing, such as *Distributed Logic Objects (DLO)* (see [13]) inspired by Conerys seminal paper [7].

A *DLO* class is a set of multi-head clauses, each one serving some method invocation. *DLO* clauses are multi-head clauses of the kind:

$$M_1,...,M_n,{}^*R_1,...,{}^*R_k,S_1,...,S_m \leftarrow \quad G \mid O_1':M_1',...,O_k':M_k',S_1',...,S_m'$$

where the guard G is a conjunction of system predicates. In the multi-head of a clause, some atoms (Ms) represent method names and arguments, and other atoms carry the object state as arguments.

In the body of a clause explicit method invocations occur through message passing primitives. A goal of the kind $O: M$ corresponds to sending a message M (which is an atom) to the object instance with name O. *self*-method invocations have the form *self: M*.

Atomic goals in the body of a clause (Ss) are used for modifying the state of an object. In particular, a rule with a consumable atom in the head and another atom with the same name in the body is a rule for modifying the state of the object. Thus, state changing is obtained through recursive calls to the state of an object.

Example 3.2 *Let us consider the following example, inspired to* [14]:
    class point::
    projx, y(Y) ← true | y(0)
    projy, x(X) ← true | x(0)

trans(Dx,Dy), x(X), y(Y) ← X1 is X+Dx, Y1 is Y+Dy | x(X1), y(Y1)

print, *x(X), *y(Y) ← true | printer:print_values(X,Y)

It represents the code of class point *of bi-dimensional points. The first clause projects a point on the x-axis. The second clause projects the target point on the y-axis. The third clause applies a rectilinear translation of vector* (Dx,Dy) *to the target point.*

Notice that to obtain the state change (e.g., setting to zero the y coordinate of the target point), the state variables of the target point (e.g., y(Y)*) to be modified by the method (e.g.,* projx*) must occur both in the head (as consumable atom) and in the body of the clause. The (recursive) occurrence of the state variables in the body thus plays the role of the* become *primitive of Actor languages* [15].

The last clause serves a print *request by raising, in turn, a* print_values *request to the* printer *object. Notice that the coordinates* X *and* Y *of the target point are simply read in the (multi-)head but not consumed, therefore they do not need to be restored in the body of the clause.*

Thanks to the intrinsic non-determinism of logic programming languages, different clauses can be written for the same method. At run-time, the adoption of the committed-choice behaviour for clause applications will ensure that only one of the definitions is used to serve a method request. For instance, suppose the following clause is added to the class point:

print, *x(X), *y(Y) ← true | laser_printer:print_values(X,Y)

When a print message is sent to a target point, a print_values message will be raised to either object printer or laser_printer. Only one of the two will non-deterministically serve the request.

In *DLO, intensional messages* can easily be supported. A message of the kind O:print, where O is an unbound variable, is sent to each object of the system (*broadcasting*).

DLO classes can be connected into hierarchies in order to obtain non-replication of behaviour. For the lack of space, we omit the discussion about inheritance in *DLO*. For details see [13].

Thanks to the underlying computational model different forms of parallelism are exploited in *DLO*. In particular:

- *inter-object parallelism*: object instances (belonging to the same or to different classes) can execute in parallel since they apply to disjoint sets of atoms.
- *intra-object parallelism*: different threads of control can be simultaneously active on the same object. In particular, different methods or several applications of the same method for different requests can be executed in parallel if they do not involve changing the same state variables. This is always the case if the object we consider is non-mutable. If the object we consider is mutable, i.e., it changes its state, the commit operator can be used to ensure that only one method at a time changes the state of the object. Therefore, an object in *DLO* can execute a method while, in parallel, accepting a new request for it.

The mapping of *DLO* into the Rose support is obtained via translation by considering two issues. First, we have to maintain the link between the object instance and its class. Moreover, we have to relate instance variables to the specific object and suitably transform the message sent.

Each *DLO* clause in class *C* must be transformed properly. In particular, each atom occurring in the head is transformed into a new (Rose) atom having the same predicate symbol name but an additional argument (variable *O*) which represents the object instance name. In practice, we map objects into logic variables. The *instance_of* relationship between objects and classes is implemented through an explicit predicate relating each object instance to its parent class. A new read-only head (with predicate symbol equal to the name of the class and argument set to the object name) is therefore added to represent the *instance_of* relationship between an object and its class.

The body of each *DLO* clause is a (parallel) conjunction of messages. Each message of type O: $p(T_1,...,T_n)$ is mapped into a (parallel) Rose goal of type $p(O,T_1,...,T_n)$. Each state variable $q(V_1,...,V_m)$ occurring in the body is mapped into a Rose atomic goal of type: $q(O,V_1,...,V_m)$.

Therefore, we map objects' names into logic variables, a technique used in most implementations of logic objects. However, as pointed out in [16], there is an efficiency problem with this approach: the concept of message sending is quite far from message passing in traditional object-oriented languages. From the implementation point of view a sender does not really send the message to the receiver, but rather includes the identifier of the receiver in the message and posts the message to a blackboard-like structure (the set of current goals) from which the receiver picks it up using unification. The advantage is that the resulting communication mechanism is more flexible, since no explicit communication pattern has to be established. Moreover, intensional messages can be directly supported by using, in messages, logical variables in place of constants for objects identifiers.

Example 3.3 *Let us consider the class* point *of example 3.2. Its clauses are transformed into the following Rose program:*

*point(O), projx(O), y(O,Y) ← true l y(O,0)

*point(O), projy(O), x(O,X) ← true l x(O,0)

*point(O), trans(O,Dx,Dy), x(O,X), y(O,Y)← X1 is X+Dx, Y1 is Y+Dy l
$$x(O,X1), y(O,Y1)$$

*point(O), print(O), *x(O,X), *y(O,Y)← true l print_values(printer,X,Y)

Notice that state change is achieved by consuming state variables and re-instantiating them by a recursive call. If, instead, a method simply accesses the state of an object for reading values but not modifying them, it is sufficient to use read-only atoms. In this way, we avoid to re-instantiate explicitly the state by a recursive call when the state does not change. The object state can be partitioned into several atoms, each one handling some instance variable. At run-time each (Rose) atom is mapped on a different *AND* process (see section 4). Therefore, by allocating these processes on different nodes we get the distribution of the object state over several nodes.

4. The Distributed Implementation

The multi-agent systems presented in the paper, both blackboard and object-based, are transformed in sets of Rose clauses. In this way, the execution of an agent is performed through the creation of a set of Rose processes interacting via message passing. Parallel composition of goals (either top-level goals or body of clauses) are mapped into *AND* parallel processes while clause applications are mapped into *OR* processes. *OR* processes that have completed the multi-head unification start the guard evaluation and if this evaluation succeeds commit.

The potential parallelism of the multi-agent systems can be transformed into real parallelism at the run-time support level by properly distributing Rose processes on the available physical resources. The distribution degree of processes is driven by both architectural features (e.g., the number of processing elements and the communication cost) and the application program.

In our implementation, logic agents are transparent with regard to parallelism and location. In fact, on the one hand, the decomposition of an application into Rose clauses is not influenced by the degree of real parallelism exploited by the run-time support. On the other hand, it is not necessary to be aware of the physical location of an agent in order to send it a message.

Since communication between agents and local and remote invocations are treated in a uniform way, it is possible to move agents at run-time among the nodes of the distributed system, thus allowing for dynamic load balancing and enhancing the degree of parallelism between agents.

The multi-agent architecture has been tested in [13], pointing out the major problem of the implementation, represented by the overhead due to communication, which is increasing with the degree of real distribution. For instance, the translation of *DLO* into Rose implies, at the run-time support level, performing multicasting (i.e., sending a message to a selected group of machines) or even broadcasting communications (i.e., sending a message to all machines) even if *DLO* messages are point-to-point. Notice that broadcasting communication is very expensive on a Transputer architecture, where point-to-point hardware links interconnect processors. This communication overhead is lower on architectures where multicast/broadcast communication is directly implemented in hardware.

The overhead deriving from broadcast communication and distributed unification can be also reduced as pointed out in [17,18] by applying static analysis techniques based on abstract interpretation. In particular, they can be suitable in order to avoid some unification operations which are subject to failure and unuseful communications.

5. Related Work

Multi-head clauses are very similar to the activation patterns of a blackboard, while the evolution of the computation can be interpreted as the addition and deletion of goals (messages) to/from a blackboard-like structure representing the multiset of current goals.

For this reason, our system is very similar to systems such as Linda [19], Shared Prolog [12] and CPU [20].

The RETE algorithm [21] is generally considered the best evaluation strategy for production and blackboard-based systems. Our implementation can be considered a parallel and distributed implementation of RETE. The committed-choice behaviour of our language avoids to propagate negative elements through the network to remove elements from the memories as in RETE. The analysis of all possible sources for parallelism in RETE reveals that our system supports all of them. Moreover, we provide a parallel distributed implementation, whereas most work on implementing parallel execution of production systems is done only by simulation.

With respect to objects, our system can be considered as a natural extension of Conery's work. In [7] the implementation of *Logical Objects* is obtained in a sequential environment following both a meta-interpretation approach and a translation into Prolog code. More recently, an implementation on top of the concurrent logic programming language Andorra has been provided [??]. The architectural support is a multi-processor environment with shared-memory. We address, instead, an implementation of logic objects in a distributed environment.

In [14], Andreoli and Pareschi introduce *Linear Objects* as an extension of logic programming grounded on linear logic. The approach is similar to our logic objects since the basic extension is the presence of multiple literals in the head of program clauses to implement methods. However, some differences can be pointed out with respect to *DLO*. As in [7], *don't know* non-determinism is adopted in *Linear Objects*. An interesting feature of *Linear Objects*, not present in our system, is the possibility of having multiple contexts, i.e. several multisets of atoms at a time. Our implementation could be considered as a basis for the distributed implementation of *Linear Objects*, provided it is suitably extended with multiple contexts.

6. Conclusions

We have presented a multi-agent architecture that provides both the high and the low level concepts necessary for distribution and parallelism in an artificial intelligence environment based on logic programming. The architecture supports and possibly integrate the two main communication models for multi-agent systems, i.e. blackboard and objects, and is based on a concurrent logic language with committed-choice multi-head clauses and restricted *AND* parallelism. One distinguishing feature of our work is that we address a real parallel implementation of the resulting system in a distributed environment exploiting different forms of parallelism.

The use of static analysis techniques to reduce the overhead due to distributed unification and broadcast communications is scope for future work.

7. Acknowledgements

This work has been partially supported by M.U.R.S.T. 60% and by C.N.R. "Progetto Finalizzato Sistemi Informatici e Calcolo Parallelo" under grants n. 93.01627.PF69.

8. References

1. M.H. van Emden and R.A. Kowalski. *The semantics of predicate logic as a programming language.* Journal of the ACM, 23(4):733-742, 1976.
2. E. Shapiro. *The family of concurrent logic programming languages.* ACM Computing Surveys, 21(3):412-510, 1989.
3. E. Shapiro and A. Takeuchi. *Object oriented programming in Concurrent Prolog.* New Generation Computing, 1:25-48, 1983.
4. A. Brogi. *AND-parallelism without Shared Variables.* In D.H.D. Warren and Peter Szeredi, editors, Proc. Seventh International Conference on Logic Programming, pages 306-324. The MIT Press, 1990.

5. M. Falaschi, G. Levi, and C. Palamidessi. *A Synchronization Logic: Axiomatic and Formal Semantics of Generalized Horn Clauses*. Information and Control, **60**:36-69, 1984.

6. L. Monteiro. *Distributed Logic: A Theory of Distributed Programming in Logic*. Technical report, Universidade Nova de Lisboa, 1986.

7. J.S. Conery. *Logical objects*. In R. A. Kowalski and K. A. Bowen, editors, Proc. Fifth International Conference on Logic Programming, pages 420-434. The MIT Press, 1988.

8. A. Brogi, A.Ciampolini, E.Lamma, and P.Mello. *A Distributed Implementation for Parallel Logic Programming*. In R. Negrini and V.A. Monaco, editors, COMPEURO91 Proceedings, pages 118-122. IEEE Computer Soc. Press, Bologna, May 1991.

9. A. Brogi, A.Ciampolini, E.Lamma, and P.Mello. *The Implementation of a Distributed Model for Logic Programming based on Multiple-headed Clauses*. Information Processing Letters, **42**:331-338, 1992.

10. L. Monteiro. *A proposal for distributed programming in logic*. Implementations of Prolog, pages 329-340. Ellis Horwood, 1984.

11. R. Engelmore and T. Morgan. *Blackboard Systems*. Addison-Wesley, 1988.

12. A. Brogi and P. Ciancarini. *The Concurrent Language Shared Prolog*.ACM Transactions on Programming Languages and Systems, **1**(1), 1991.

13. A.Ciampolini, E.Lamma, P.Mello, and C. Stefanelli. *A Distributed Implementation of Logic Objects*. Technical Report TR-4-100, CNR Progetto Finalizzato Sistemi Informatici e Calcolo Parallelo, 1993.

14. J.M. Andreoli and R. Pareschi. *Linear objects: logical processes with built-in inheritance*. In D.H.D. Warren and P. Szeredi, editors, Proc. Seventh International Conference on Logic Programming, pages 495-510. The MIT Press, 1990.

15. G. Agha. *Actors: A Model of Concurrent Computation in Distributed Systems*.The MIT Press, 1986.

16 V. Alexiev. *Mutable Object State for Object-Oriented Programming: A Survey*. Technical Report TR 93-15, Department of Computing Science, University of Alberta, 1993.

17. M. Bourgois, J.M. Andreoli, and R. Pareschi. *Extending Objects with Rules, Composition and Concurrency: The LO Experience*. Technical Report TR-92-26, ECRC, 1992.

18. J.M. Andreoli, T. Castagnetti, and R. Pareschi. *Abstract Interpretation of Linear Logic Programming*. In D. Miller, editor, Proceedings of IEEE Symposium on Logic Programming ILPS93. The MIT Press, 1993.

19. D. Gelernter. *Generative Communication in Linda*. ACM Transactions on Programming Languages and Systems, **7**(1):80-112, 1985.

20. P. Mello, A. Natali. *Extending Prolog with Modularity*. Concurrency and Meta-Rules. New Generation Computing, Vol. **10**/4 August 1992, Springer-Verlag, Tokyo, Japan.

21. C. Forgy. *RETE: a fast algorithm for the many pattern/many object pattern match problem*. Journal of Artificial Intelligence, **19**:17-37, 1982.

22. J.S. Conery and S. Haridi. *Eudorra: An Object-Oriented Andorra*. In ICLP91 Workshop on Object-Oriented Logic Programming Proceedings, 1991.

III - CONSTRAINT SOLVING

SOLVED FORMS FOR LINEAR CONSTRAINTS IN CLP LANGUAGES.

Jean-Louis J. IMBERT

Laboratoire d'Informatique de Clermont–Ferrand
Les Cezeaux
F-63177 AUBIERE Cedex (France)
Email: imbert@gia.univ-mrs.fr

ABSTRACT
Linear constraint solving in Constraint logic programming languages rests on rewriting constraints under syntaxic forms. These syntaxic forms are generally called solved forms, since a satisfiable linear constraint system can be rewritten under one of these forms, and reciprocally, a linear constraint system of one of these forms is satisfiable. This paper aims to present three different solved forms two of which are used in the main CLP languages with linear constraints CHIP, CLP($\Re$) and Prolog III. The third form was proposed by JL. Imbert and P. Van Hentenryck in 1993. We discuss the advantages and disadvantages of each and present the results of some comparative tests.

Keywords: Solved Forms, Constraint Logic Programming.

1 Introduction

Constraint Logic Programming (CLP) is the combination of two programming paradigms: Logic programming and Constraint Programming. The power of Logic Programming rests on its relational form, and on non-determinism and unification. Unification is an equational theory. The pioneers are A. Robinson [15] and R. Kowalski & D. Kuehner [8] for the automatic deduction, and A. Colmerauer & P. Roussel [1], and R. Kowalski [9, 10] for the specific part of Logic Programming. Constraint Programming makes it possible to formulate problems in a declarative way. Constraints express relations between objects. The pioneers are D. Waltz [21], A. Mackworth [14], J.L. Laurière [12, 13], G.L. Steele, G.J.Sussman [17, 18]. Constraint Logic Programming aims at generalizing Logic Programming in order to extend it to domains distinct from herbrand universe, using more efficient computation mechanisms. Unification is replaced by Constraint Solving. From this, we need to find Constraint Solvers which on the one hand are able to incrementally process constraints, on the other hand fit with backtracking techniques. In 1986, J. Jaffar & JL. Lassez [6] proposed a general theoretical structure for this type of language. In this article, we are interested in linear constraints. The main languages ensuing from this approach and processing linear constraints are CHIP [3], CLP($\Re$) [7] and Prolog III [2].

This paper presents and to compares three solved forms for linear constraint systems. These forms fit the incremental objective very well, and fit the efficiency and backtracking objectives to different degrees. Each of them has some advantages and some drawbacks. A *solved form* is a syntactic form such that if a constraint or a constraint system is satisfiable, then it can be rewritten under this form, and reciprocally, a constraint or a constraint system under this form is satisfiable. We are interested in constraints of the three following forms: $0 = t$ (equation), $0 \leq t$ (inequation) and $0 \neq t$ (disequation), or equivalent forms, where t is for $a_n x_n + \ldots + a_1 x_1 + a_0$. In practice, each inequation is replaced by an equation with a new variable s called *slack variable* as follows: $s = t$ and $0 \leq s$. Generally, $0 \leq s$ is left understood. Since the slack variable s represents the inequation $0 \leq a_n x_n + \ldots + a_1 x_1 + a_0$, there are as many slack variables as there are inequations in the system. Now, we have only two types of constraints ($=$ and $\neq$), but we have two types of variables: *arbitrary variables* denoted by x_i which can take any value, and slack variables denoted by s_j which can take only non-negative values. Section 2 presents the three solved forms for the equations. Section 3 tackles the problems of disequations. Finally, in Section 4, the results of some comparisons between these organisations are given along with general remarks on the advantages of each of them.

In the sequel, a variable is said *to be in* a linear constraint if its coefficient is non-zero in this constraint. It is said to be k times in a linear constraint system when it exactly appears in k distinct constraints of this system. It is in a system if k is non-zero. We assume that each variable occurs at most once in each constraint. An equation is in *solved form* if it is written in one of the following two forms:

$$\text{or} \begin{cases} x_j = \sum_{i \neq j} a_i x_i + \sum_k b_k s_k + a_0 \\ \\ s_j = \sum_{k \neq j} b_k s_k + a_0 \qquad (0 \leq a_0). \end{cases}$$

The lefthand side (lhs) variable is said *defined*. Variables in the equation rhs member are called *parameters*. It is evident that a solution is obtained as soon as the parameter values are known. The solved form for a disequation is

$$0 \neq \sum_i a_i x_i + \sum_k b_k s_k + a_0$$

with $a_0 \neq 0$ when no variable is in the rhs member of the disequation.

2 Equations

2.1 Gauss-Jordan Solved Form

Let a constraint system in a solved form and let a new constraint. The objective of a Constraint Solver is to produce a new constraint system in the same solved form. An equation system is in *Gauss-Jordan Solved Form* denoted by GJSF, if its constraints are all in solved form and each defined variable appears only once in the whole system. In practice, the system is divided into two sub-systems E and S. E is the sub-system of equations with

> Input: (E, S), an equation system in GJSF form. And C, an equation in solved form.
> Output: A flag *Satisfiable* which indicates whether the system is or is not satisfiable.
>   And if so, the new system in FST form.
> **begin**
>   0. Put the flag *Satisfiable* to *true*.
>   1. In C, substitute for each variable defined in E its rhs member and simplify.
>   2. If C is trivially satisfied, go to end.
>   If C is trivially unsatisfied, put *Satisfiable* to *false* and go to end.
>   3. If there is an arbitrary variable in C, rewrite C in solved form with an arbitrary variable as lhs member, then insert it into E and go to end.
>   4. If there are only slack variables in C.
>   Insert C into S using *simplex* procedure.
>   If S is unsatisfiable, put *Satisfiable* to *false*,
>   Else, replace in E each occurrence of a defined variable in S with its rhs member, and each occurrence of a fixed variable output by the *simplex* procedure with the value to which it is fixed.
> **end**

Figure 1: GJSF Algorithm to introduce a new equation

at least one arbitrary variable in each. In this case, the defined variable must be an arbitrary variable. S is the sub-system of other equations. Hence, there are only slack variables in S. We will not speak about the S system. We assume that there exists a procedure named *simplex* which verifies that S is satisfiable, and when it is, outputs the system S in GJSF form and all the slack variables which are fixed. An arbitrary or slack variable is *fixed* if in every solution of the system, it has the same value. For more details on such a *simplex* procedure the reader is referred to [19]. It can be shown that the GJSF form is a solved form. In practice, constraints are assumed to be inputed one after another. Let (E, S) [1] be a satisfiable system. We want to know if by adding in the new equation C, the new system is satisfiable. If it is, the new system must be in GJSF form. An algorithm adding a new equation in a system in GJSF form is given in Figure 1. This type of solved form is used in CLP-languages such as CHIP and CLP($\Re$).

Example 1 Consider the initial system

$$(1) \quad 0 = -x_5 + x_4 + x_3 + 3$$
$$(2) \quad 0 = -x_5 + 2x_3 - x_1 + 1$$
$$(3) \quad 0 = x_3 - x_1 - 3$$
$$(4) \quad 2 \leq x_3$$

At the start E and S are empty. The equations (1), (2), (3) and the inequation (4) rewritten $s_1 = x_3 - 2$ are incrementally added to E. The final system E is:

---
[1] comma is for the juxtaposition of constraints.

$$\begin{cases} x_5 = s_1 + 6 \\ x_4 = 1 \\ x_3 = s_1 + 2 \\ x_1 = s_1 - 1 \end{cases}$$

One of the advantages of the GJSF form is that each fixed variable (arbitrary or slack[2]) is automatically detected. We are interested in detecting fixed variables, firstly for arbitrary variables: on the one hand to simplify the constraint system, on the other hand, in systems which integrate non-linear delayed constraints to make their progressive linearisation possible, and secondly for slack variables: if the value is zero, to detect implicit equations and then the affine hull of the solution set, else, when the value is non-zero, the inequation associated with that slack variable is redundant. Among the drawbacks are the constant updating of constraints already processed in E. This makes the process heavy both in progress and in backtracking.

2.2 Gaussian Solved Form

To overcome the drawbacks of the previous solved form, a triangular form is chosen. As a result, some variables are now both defined in one constraint and parameters in others. The objective is to work as little as possible while backtracking. This solved form is called *Gaussian Solved Form* and is denoted GSF. It is based on a total ordering of the variables. In this ordering, each slack variable is less than each arbitrary variable. In these problems, this variable will be the least variable. In the sequel, to complete our variable ordering, if $\ll$ denotes the order relation, then we choose: $i \leq j$ implies $x_i \ll x_j$ and $s_i \ll s_j$. In an equation in GSF form, the defined variable is the greatest for the ordering $\ll$. It follows that when only slack variables appear in, $0 \leq a_0$ can be unsatisfied. An equation system is in GSF form if each of its equations is in GSF form and each defined variable is defined only once in the whole system. In practice, not as in the GJSF form, the equation system is kept as a whole in E. However, to determine the satisfiability of the sub-system of equations in which only slack variables appear, it is necessary to duplicate this sub-system in another sub-system S, and to verify the satisfiability of S using the *simplex* procedure. It is easy to show that the GSF form is a solved form when S is satisfiable. Figure 2 gives an algorithm which adds a new equation to a system in GSF form. The Prolog III language uses this type of organisation.

Example 2 Consider the initial system of Example 1 At the start E is empty. By incrementally adding in E the constraints (1), (2), (3) and (4), the system E becomes

$$\begin{cases} x_5 = x_4 + x_3 + 3 \\ x_4 = x_3 - x_1 - 2 \\ x_3 = x_1 + 3 \\ x_1 = s_1 - 1 \end{cases}$$

---

[2]these last ones by the *simplex* procedure

> Input: An equation system E in GSF form. A system S in GJSF form equivalent to the sub-system of equations of E in which only slack variables appear. An new equation C in solved form.
>
> Output: A flag named *Satisfiable* which indicates whether the system is satisfiable or not. And if so, the new system E in GSF form, and the new system S in GJSF form.
>
> **begin**
>
> 0. Put flag *Satisfiable* to *true*.
> 1. **while** the greatest variable of C is defined in E, replace it, then simplify and order C.
> 2. If C is trivially satisfiable, go to end.
>   If C is trivially unsatisfiable, put *false* in *Satisfiable* and go to end.
> 3. Rewrite C in GSF form, then insert it in E.
> 4. If only slack variables occur in,
>   Duplicate C in C' and Insert C' in S using *simplex* procedure.
>   If S is unsatisfiable, put *false* in *Satisfiable*,
>   Else, for each fixed variable s found by the *simplex* procedure, insert the equation $0 = -s + c$ in E, only using steps 1 to 3. c is value to which s is fixed. (If s is already defined, the two constraints are exchanged)
>
> **end**

Figure 2: GSF Algorithm to introduce a new equation

Now, introduce the new constraint (5) $0 = -x_3 + x_2 - 1$. It is transformed into $0 = x_2 - x_1 - 4$. The variable x_1 is not replaced because it is not the greatest. Hence, the new system is

$$
\begin{cases}
x_5 = x_4 + x_3 + 3 \\
x_4 = x_3 - x_1 - 2 \\
x_3 = x_1 + 3 \\
x_2 = x_1 + 4 \\
x_1 = s_1 - 1
\end{cases}
$$

The uncontestable advantage of such an organisation in GSF is to minimize the work to be done while backtracking. We might think that a number of substitutions are avoided when the process is in progress, but sometimes this is misleading as shown in Example 3. Among the drawbacks are, firstly, that each fixed arbitrary variable is not detected, secondly, the same substitution can be repeatedly done, lastly it will be necessary to process some substitutions to output the final results. The first drawback can be overcome with a good ordering on variables, and with a daemon to supervise some variables.

eq	GSF system	Nc	Sum	GJSF system	Nc	Updt	Sum
1	$x_5 = x_4 + x_3 - x_1 + 1$	0	0	$x_5 = x_4 + x_3 - x_1 + 1$	0	0	0
2	$x_5 = x_4 + x_3 - x_1 + 1$ $x_4 = x_3 + x_1 + 1$	4	4	$x_5 = 2x_3 + 2$ $x_4 = x_3 + x_1 + 1$	4	3	7
3	$x_5 = x_4 + x_3 - x_1 + 1$ $x_4 = x_3 + x_1 + 1$ $x_3 = -x_1 + 1$	7	11	$x_5 = -2x_1 + 4$ $x_4 = 2$ $x_3 = -x_1 + 1$	5	4	16
4	$x_5 = x_4 + x_3 - x_1 + 1$ $x_4 = x_3 + x_1 + 1$ $x_3 = -x_1 + 1$ $x_1 = 1$	9	20	$x_5 = 2$ $x_4 = 2$ $x_3 = 0$ $x_1 = 1$	5	2	23
5	$x_5 = x_4 + x_3 - x_1 + 1$ $x_4 = x_3 + x_1 + 1$ $x_3 = -x_1 + 1$ $x_2 = -3x_1 + 5$ $x_1 = 1$	9	29	$x_5 = 2$ $x_4 = 2$ $x_3 = 0$ $x_2 = 2$ $x_1 = 1$	2	0	25

Figure 3:

Example 3 Consider the initial system

$$(1) \quad 0 = -x_5 + x_4 + x_3 - x_1 + 1$$
$$(2) \quad 0 = +x_5 - 2x_4 + 2x_1$$
$$(3) \quad 0 = +x_5 + x_4 - 4x_3 - 2x_1 - 2$$
$$(4) \quad 0 = -x_5 + 2x_4 + x_3 - 2$$
$$(5) \quad 0 = +x_5 + x_3 - x_2$$

The table of Figure 3 indicates the state of the system after the incremental introduction of constraints (1), (2), (3), (4) and (5). The first column indicates the number of the introduced constraint. Column Nc gives the number of additions to be computed on the new constraint and column Updt gives the number of additions to be computed to update the GJSF system. Column Sum gives the sum of the additions computed so far. We see that for this particular example, the advantage had at the beginning with the GSF method disappears by the end. This example has no proof value, it just indicates that it is not clear that one method is better than another.

2.3 Classification

The *Classification Solved form* [5] denoted CSF aims at detecting all (arbitrary or slack) fixed variables, and to compute as few substitutions as possible. It divides the constraints into classes. As for the GJSF form, the equation system is composed of two sub-systems E and S. E is the sub-system of equations with at least one arbitrary variable in each. The defined variable must be an arbitrary variable. S is the sub-system of other equations in which appear only slack variables. The sub-system S is processed by the *simplex* procedure.

Class	Form of the equation	invariants
E_0	$x_j = a_0$	fixed variable
E_1	$x_j = a_i x_i + a_0$	E_1 must be in GSF or in GJSF. x_i can be defined in (E_2, E_4) but not in (E_0, E_3).
E_2	$x_j = \sum_{i \neq j} a_i x_i + \sum_k b_k s_k + a_0$ rhs : *at least one i and at least two variables*	E_2 must be in GJSF. The x_i's cannot be defined in E. The s_k's can be defined in S.
E_3	$x_j = b_k s_k + a_0$	E_3 must be in GJSF. s_k can be defined in S.
E_4	$x_j = \sum_{k \neq j} b_k s_k + a_0$ *at least two k*	(E_4, S) must be in GJSF.

general invariant: the variables can be defined at most once in the whole system (E, S).

Figure 4: Classification of the equations

In this solved form, E is divided into five classes $E_0, \ldots, E_4$ as defined in Figure 4. It can be shown that it is a solved form. Figure 5 gives an algorithm which adds a new equation to a system in CSF form. The technique used is to maintain the constraints in the simplest form, without losing sight of the fact that we want to detect all the fixed variables. For example, let the equation be $x_j = a_i x_i + a_0$. Then, the variable x_j is fixed if and only if the variable x_i is fixed. The same reasoning holds for equations of the form $x_j = a_i s_i + a_0$. As a result, as soon as an equation can be put into one of these forms, the substitution for the variables defined in E has not to be pushed beyond those defined in the classes E_0, E_1 and E_3 (substitutions from theses classes do not increase the number of variables in the new constraint). Then, if at least one of the variables defined in the new constraint is already defined in E, its definition being more complex than the new, it is temporarily removed. The new constraint is inserted in its class. Then the removed constraint is added to the new system as if it is a new constraint. For more details on this solved form, the reader is referred to [5].

3 Disequations

Let (F, D) be a linear constraint system, where F is the sub-system of the equations and D the sub-system of the disequations. According to [11], such a system is satisfiable if and only if, for each disequation d, the system $(F, \{d\})$ is satisfiable. Moreover, if F is satisfiable, the system $(F, \{d\})$ is unsatisfiable if and only if by replacing in d every variable defined in F, by its rhs member, the disequation $0 \neq 0$ is obtained.

Input: (E, S), an equation system in CSF. C a new equation in solved form.
Output: A flag *Satisfiable* which indicates whether the system is satisfiable or not.
        And if so, the system increased by the new constraint, in CSF form.
begin
    0. Put the flag *Satisfiable* to *true*.
    1. Replace in C each variable defined in (E_0, E_1, E_3) by its rhs, and simplify.
    2. **While** it is possible and the constraint is not in a form of E_0, E_1 or E_3, replace
         in C each variable defined in E_2 and E_4 by its rhs, and simplify.
    3. If C is trivially satisfied, go to end.
       If C is trivially unsatisfied, put *false* in *Satisfiable* and go to end.
    4. If C can be put in one of the forms of E_0, E_1 or E_3, and if in C occurs a
         variable x_i defined in a constraint C' of E_2 or E_4,
        4.1.   Remove C' from E,
        4.2.   Rewrite C in solved form with x_i as lhs member,
        4.3.   Insert C in its class and update if necessary,
        4.4.   Insert C' in the system using CSF algorithm. Then, go to end.
    5. If an arbitrary variable still occurs in C, rewrite C in solved form with that
         variable as lhs member, then insert it into E and go to end.
    6. If only slack variables occur in C.
       Insert C in S using *simplex* procedure.
       If S is unsatisfiable, put *false* in *Satisfiable*,
       Else, replace in E_4 each slack variable defined in S by its rhs member, and
       replace in E each fixed variable given by the *simplex* procedure, by the
       value to which it is fixed. If necessary, change the constraints of classes.
end

Figure 5: CSF Algorithm to introduce a new equation

3.1 Disequations and GJSF Form

Let (E, S, D) be a linear constraint system, where (E, S) is an equation system, and D a disequation set. The system (E, S, D) is in GJSF form if the three following conditions are met: (E, S) is in GJSF form, each disequation of D is in solved form, and no variable defined in (E, S) occurs in D. In the GJSF form, the disequations are systematically updated, which implies a significant cost. Figure 6 gives an algorithm which adds a new disequation to a system in GJSF form. To take into account disequations when a new equation is added to the system, the algorithm of Figure 1 must be modified as follows: The system (E, S, D) is input in place of the system (E, S). The output system is of the same type of (E, S, D), and step 3 and 4 are modified as indicated in Figure 7.

Input: (E, S, D), a constraint system in GJSF, where (E, S) is the set of equations, and D is the set of disequations. A new disequation d in solved form.

Output: A flag named *Satisfiable* which indicates whether the system is satisfiable or not. If it is, the system increased by the new constraint in GJSF form.

begin

0. Put the flag *Satisfiable* to *true*.
1. Replace in d each defined variable of (E, S) by its rhs member, and simplify.
2. If d is trivially satisfiable, go to end.
   If d is trivially unsatisfiable, put *false* in *Satisfiable*,
   Else insert d so modified in D.

end

Figure 6: GJSF Algorithm to introduce a new disequation

3. If there is an arbitrary variable in C,
   3.1. Rewrite C in solved form with an arbitrary variable as lhs member,
   3.2. Replace in D the new defined variable of C, and simplify.
        If during the substitution, a disequation becomes trivially satisfied, remove it.
        If during the substitution, a disequation becomes trivially unsatisfied, put *false* in *Satisfiable*, and go to end.
   3.3. Insert C into E, and go to end.
4. If there are only slack variables in C.
   Insert C into S using *simplex* procedure.
   If S is unsatisfiable, put *false* in *Satisfiable*,
   Else, replace in E and D each occurrence of a defined variable in S with its rhs member, and each occurrence of a fixed variable output by the *simplex* procedure with the value to which it is fixed. If during the substitution a disequation becomes trivially satisfiable, remove it, else if during the substitution a disequation becomes trivially unsatisfiable, put *false* in *Satisfiable*.

Figure 7: Modifications in the GJSF equation Algorithm

Example 4 Let E be the following system:

$$\begin{cases} x_8 = x_3 + 2x_2 + 6 \\ x_7 = 1 \\ x_6 = x_3 - x_2 + 2 \\ x_4 = x_1 - 1 \end{cases}$$

Input: (E, D), a constraint system in GSF form, where E is the set of equations, and
D the set of disequations. A new disequation d in solved form.
Output: A flag named *Satisfiable* which indicates whether the system is satisfiable
or not. And if so, the system increased by the new constraint in GSF form.
begin
   0. Put the flag *Satisfiable* to *true*.
   1. **while** the greatest variable of d is defined in E, replace it, simplify
      and order d.
   2. If d is trivially satisfiable, go to end.
      If d is trivially unsatisfiable, put *false* in *Satisfiable*,
      Else insert d as modified in D.
end

Figure 8: GSF Algorithm to introduce a new disequation

Let $0 \neq x_8 + x_5 + x_4$ be the new disequation to be introduced. Eliminate the variables x_8 and x_4. This disequation becomes $0 \neq x_5 + x_3 + 2x_2 + x_1 + 5$, and is inserted in D.

Now, let $0 = 2x_8 - x_3 - 1$ be a new equation to be introduced. Eliminate the variable x_8 from the equation, and rewrite it in solved form: $x_3 = -4x_2 - 11$. The previous disequation then becomes $0 \neq x_5 - 2x_2 + x_1 - 6$, and the equation $x_3 = -4x_2 - 11$ is inserted in E.

3.2 Disequations and GSF Form

Let (E, D) be a linear constraint system, where E is an equation system, and D is a disequation set. The system (E, D) is in GSF form if the following three conditions are met: E is in GSF form, each disequation of D is in solved form and the greatest variable of each disequation is not defined in E. The objective is to do work only when necessary. Since when a variable is not defined it can take an infinite number of values giving a solution of E, there are an infinite number of solutions of a disequation having it as greatest variable. As a result, it suffices to put a device in place which makes it possible to supervise the moment when this variable becomes fixed. This device is called a daemon. Figure 8 gives an algorithm which introduces a new disequation d into (E, D). The algorithm of Figure 2 must be modified: the input system is (E, D), the output system is of the same type, and step 3 is modified as indicated in Figure 9.

Example 5 Take again Example 4: Let $0 \neq x_8 + x_5 + x_4$ be the disequation to be introduced. Eliminate the variable x_8. This disequation becomes $0 \neq x_5 + x_4 + x_3 + 2x_2 + 6$, and is inserted in D, since x_5 is not defined in E.

Now, let $0 = 2x_8 - x_3 - 1$ be the equation to be introduced. Eliminate the variable x_8 from this equation. and rewrite it: $x_3 = -4x_2 - 11$. Unlike the GJSF form, here, the previous disequation is not modified, and the equation $x_3 = -4x_2 - 11$ is inserted in E.

3.3 Disequations and CSF Form

The CSF solved form aims at avoiding unnecessary substitutions. For example, let a constraint of D of the form $0 \neq a_i x_i + a_0$. While the variable x_i is not fixed, this constraint

> 3. 3.1. Rewrite C in GSF form, then insert it into E.
>
>   3.2. Replace in D the defined variable of C each time it is the greatest variable of a disequation of D, and simplify.
>
>   For each modified disequation, continue to eliminate the greatest variable while it is defined in E.
>
>   If during the substitution, a disequation becomes trivially satisfied, remove it.
>
>   If during the substitution, a disequation becomes trivially unsatisfied, put $false$ in $Satisfiable$, and go to end.

Figure 9: Modifications of the GSF equation Algorithm

Class	Form of the disequation	invariants
D_0	$0 \neq a_0$	Trivial constraint
D_1	$0 \neq a_i x_i + a_0$	x_i must not be defined in E_0. It can be defined anywhere else.
D_2	$0 \neq \sum_i a_i x_i + \sum_k b_k s_k + a_0$ *at least one i and* *at least two variables*	The x_i's cannot be defined in E. The s_k's can be defined in S.
D_3	$0 \neq b_k s_k + a_0$	s_k can be defined in S, but cannot be fixed.
D_4	$0 \neq \sum_k b_k s_k + a_0$ *at least two k*	The s_k's cannot be defined in S.

Figure 10: Classification of the disequations

is satisfiable. Since this solved form detects all fixed variables, this type of disequation does not have to be modified while x_i is not fixed, even if x_i is defined. The same reasoning holds for constraints of the form $0 \neq a_i s_i + a_0$. Moreover, for constraints of the form $0 \neq \sum_i a_i x_i + \sum_k b_k s_k + a_0$ it is useless to substitute for slack variables while at least one arbitrary variable occurs in it. With the same definitions and notations as Figure 4, the table of Figure 10 completes the classification for the disequations. The set D is divided into five classes $D_0, \ldots, D_4$ of which only the last four are kept. The algorithm of Figure 11 describes the operations to be realized in order to introduce a new disequation d into (E, S, D). When a new equation is inserted in one of the classes E_1 to E_4, only class D_2 is checked. If a constraint is inserted in E_0, then D_1 and D_2 are checked. When an equation changes class, there is no check except if it is in E_0. In this last case, only class D_1 is checked. Now, if a constraint is inserted in the system S, after its insertion using the

88

Input: (E, S, D), a constraint system in CSF, where (E, S) is a set of equations as
      defined in the CSF equation Algorithm, and D is the set of disequations. A
      disequation d in solved form.
Output: A flag named *Satisfiable* which indicates whether the system is satisfiable
      or not. And if so, the system increased by the new constraint, in CSF form.
begin
  0. Put the flag *Satisfiable* to *true*.
  1. Replace in d each defined variable of E_0 by its rhs member, and simplify.
  2. **while** it is possible, and the disequation is not in a form of D_1 or D_3, replace
     in d each defined variable of (E_1, E_2, E_3, E_4) with its rhs member, and
     simplify.
  3. If d is of the form of D_4, and while it is possible and the disequation is not of
     the form of D_3, replace in d each defined variable of S by its rhs member.
  4. If d is trivially unsatisfiable, put *false* in *Satisfiable*,
     Else if not trivially satisfiable insert d so modified in its class.
fin

Figure 11: CSF Algorithm to introduce a new disequation

simplex algorithm, class D_4 is updated, and each fixed variable is replaced in the whole system (E, D), by the value to which it is fixed. This can lead to new class changes. The modifications of Algorithm 5 implied by these considerations are evident and are found in the operations 4.4, 4.5, 5 and 6. For a precise example too long for this short paper, the reader is referred to [4]. Note that for this form there exist improvements using the *simplex* procedure, which are detailed in [5]. These improvements make it possible to divide in half the cost of updating in the disequations at the output of the *simplex* Algorithm.

4 Final Remarks

We have tested these solved forms [20, 16]. We have used three meta-interpretors similar to that presented in [4], one for each solved form. The *simplex* procedure used was the same for the three interpretors [19], and the ordering over variables, also the same: the defined variable, when we have this choice, is always the greatest one. We have not taken into account the improvements proposed in [5]: "Lazy dereferencing" and "Early detection of failure". The efficiency is measured by the number of additions processed in the substitutions, updatings included. The time to restore the system when backtracking has not been taken into account. In each case, the number of additions processed on the equations and the number of additions processed on the disequations have been counted separately. The tests have been carried out over sixteen small examples. We have brought the results together in the table of Figure 12. Even if the number of tests is not great, and the examples rather small, we can see that

- The CSF form often seems better than the GSF form. The scores are: for the disequations, 6 to 1, and for the general constraints, 11 to 5.

	GJSF			GSF			CSF		
	Equa	Diseq	Total	Equa	Diseq	Total	Equa	Diseq	Total
Badex	25743	22312	48055	5039	10040	15079	22640	5890	28530
Puzzle4	1354	0	1354	680	0	680	831	0	831
Puzzle8	327723	18931	346654	1232075	18931	1251006	329066	18931	347997
Fibonacci14	0000	0	0000	00000	0	00000	0000	0	0000
queens4	2262	531	2793	1043	631	1674	806	531	1337
queens8	275100	125379	400479	1078727	454356	1533083	348642	125379	474021
mortgage1	337	0	337	69	0	69	126	0	126
mortgage2	391	0	391	141	0	141	269	0	269
sequence	32	2	34	34	2	36	25	2	27
sendmory1	1050	822	1872	1039	2014	3053	1697	206	1903
sendmory2	12460	12641	25102	25930	37550	63480	10466	10351	20817
magicsquare1	35017	23348	58365	49650	40546	90196	24911	12516	37427
magicsquare2	14817	0	14817	28982	0	28982	14817	0	14817
affectation	1974	0	1974	1737	0	1737	1452	0	1452
list	180	94	274	142	69	211	200	88	288
sort	9436	435	9871	91275	435	91710	9436	435	9871

Figure 12: Test results

- The GJSF form is more often less efficient than the CSF form. The scores are for the disequations, 0 to 5, and for the general constraints, 4 to 9. In this last case, 3 out of 4 give next to the same total).

- In each method, if we look proportionnally at the times (which are not in the table) to the number of additions, it can be noticed that when the number of backtracking increases, the GSF form becomes more efficient than the other methods.

It would be good to continue these tests with more numerous and bigger examples. These tests are not significant enough to draw general and definitive conclusions. However, they provide some interesting indications.

Of course, the GJSF form in CLP($\Re$) and CHIP, and the GSF form in Prolog III, are used with a certain number of fittings which we have not taken into account here. These fittings again improve the efficiency of these forms. In the same way, the CSF form which does not work in any well known programming language can be fitted efficiently. Our goal has been simply to make comparisons between the various solved forms, and to draw attention to the different qualities of each of them.

References

1. A. Colmerauer, H. Kanoui, R. Pasero and P. Roussel. "Un système de communication en français". Rapport préliminaire de fin de contrat IRIA, Groupe Intelligence Artificielle, Faculté des Sciences de Luminy, Université Aix-Marseille II, France, October 1972.

2. A. Colmerauer. "Opening the Prolog III Universe". In *BYTE*, August 1987, p177–182.

3. M. Dincbas, P. Van Hentenryck, H. Simonis, A. Aggoun, T. Graf and F. Berthier. "The Constraint Logic Programming Language CHIP". In *Proceedings of the International Conference on Fifth Generation Computer Systems*, Tokyo, Japan, December 1988.

4. JL. Imbert, J. Cohen and MD. Weeger. "An Algorithm for Linear Constraint Solving: Its Incorporation in a Prolog Meta-Interpreter for CLP". In *Journal of Logic Programming. Special issue on Constraint Logic Programming.* Vol. 16, Nos 3 and 4, July–August 1993.

5. JL. Imbert and P. Van Hentenryck. "On the Handling of Disequations in CLP over Linear Rational Arithmetic". In F. Benhamou and A. Colmerauer, editors, *Constraint Logic Programming: Selected Research*, p 49–71, MIT Press, Cambridge, USA. Sept 1993.

6. J.Jaffar, JL. Lassez. "Constraint Logic Programming". Technical Report 86/73. Dept. of computer science. Monash University (June 1986).

7. J.Jaffar, S. Michaylov. "Methodology and Implementation of a CLP System". In *Proceedings of the Logic Programming Conference.* Melbourne, 1987. M.I.T. Press.

8. R.A. Kowalski and D. Kuehner. "Linear Resolution with Selection Function". Memo 78, University of Edinburgh, School of Artificial Intelligence, 1971.

9. R.A. Kowalski. "Predicate Logic as Programming Language". in *Proceedings of IFIP 1974*, North Holland Publishing Company, Amsterdam, pp. 569-574, 1974.

10. R.A. Kowalski and M. Van Emden. "The Semantic of Predicate Logic as Programming Language". in JACM 22, 1976, pp. 733-742.

11. JL. Lassez and K. McAloon. "Independance of Negative Constraints". In *TAPSOFT 89, Advanced seminar on Foundations of innovative Software development*, Lecture Notes in Computer Science 351, springer Verlag 1989.

12. JL. Laurière. "Un langage et un problème pour énoncer et résoudre des problèmes combinatoires". Ph.D. Thesis, University Pierre et Marie Curie, Paris, May 1976.

13. JL. Laurière. "A Language and a Program for Stating and Solving Combinatorial Problems". In *Artificial Intelligence*, 10(1): p 29–127, 1978.

14. A.K. Mackworth. "Consistency in Networks of Relations". In *AI Jour* 8(1): p 99–118, 1977.

15. J.A. Robinson. "A Machine-Oriented Logic Based on the Resolution Principle". Journal of the ACM 12, 1, pp. 23-41, January 1965.

16. N. Singer. "Résolutions incrémentale de contraintes linéaires sur les nombres rationnels". mémoire de DEA, GIA, Faculté des sciences de Luminy, Marseille, 1993.

17. G.L. Steele. "The Definition and Implementation of a Computer programming Language based on Constraints". Ph.D. Thesis, MIT, USA. August 1980.

18. G.J. Sussman and G.L. Steele. "CONSTRAINTS. A language for Expressing Almost-Hierarchical Descriptions" In *AI Journal*, 14(1), 1980.

19. P. Van Hentenryck and T. Graf. Standard Forms for Rational Linear Arithmetics in Constraint Logic Programming. *Annals of Mathematics and Artificial Intelligence*, 1992.

20. JF. Verrier. "Résolutions numériques en programmation logique par contraintes". mémoire de DEA, GIA, Faculté des sciences de Luminy, Marseille, 1992.

21. D. Waltz. "Generating Semantic Descriptions from Drawings of Scenes with Shadows". Technical Report AI271, MIT, MA, USA. November 1972.

Theoretical Study of Dominance in Constraint Satisfaction Problems

Delaid Denhamou

Laboratoire d'Informatique de Marseille
URA CNRS 1787
Université de Provence,
3,Place Victor Hugo - F13331 Marseille cedex 3, France
phone number : 91.10.61.08
e-mail : Benhamou@gyptis.univ-mrs.fr

ABSTRACT

Constraint satisfaction problems (CSP's) involve finding values for variables subject to constraints on which combinations of values are permitted. Symmetrical values of a CSP variable are values which have the same chance to fit into solutions of the CSP. They are in a sense redundant, their removal will simplify the problem space. However, CSP values are not always equally in chance to participate in solutions of the CSP. Thus, in this paper we study both symmetry and the notion of *dominance* to characterize values which *dominate* (i.e. which have more chances to participate in solutions) other values in order to considere them in prior. Of course values dominating each others will be symmetrical. The concept of interchangeability introduced by Freuder, is a particular case of symmetry. Some dominant resp. symmetrical values can be computed efficiently thanks to the structure of the problem, a detection method is studied. Theoritical analysis indicate that our proposed approach is an improvment for the principle of interchangeability.

Content areas: Automated reasoning, Constraint satisfaction.

1 Introduction

The finite domain constraint satisfaction problem (CSP)[1] is well known in Artificial Intelligence. It has been investigated in the past by a number of researchers in different contexts; and steal a well-studied research area of recent years (refer to Kumar[8]). A CSP involves, (1) a (finite) set $V = \{v_1, v_2, \ldots, v_n\}$ of variables, (2) a finite set $D = \{D_1, D_2, \ldots, D_n\}$ of discret domain values in which D_i is the finite discrete domain associated whith the variable v_i; to avoid confusions between values of different domains, d_i will denote the fact that it belonges to the domain D_i, (3) a finite set $C = \{c_1, c_2, \ldots, c_n\}$ of constraints, a k-ary constraint c_i is defined on a subset $V_k \subseteq V$ of variables which we denote $var(c_i)$, (4) and a finite set $R = \{R_1, R_2, \ldots, R_n\}$ of relations corresponding to the constants in C, R_i represents the list of tuples (notation $tuples(R_i)$) form in which the tuples of values satisfying the constraint c_i are enumerated. Thus, a CSP can be seen as a quadriplet $\mathcal{P}(V, D, C, R)$.

A value assignment is a mapping which specifies a value for each variable: formally a value assignment I can be seen as: $I : V \longrightarrow \cup_{i \in [1,n]} D_i$ such that $I[v_i] \in D_i$, $\forall i \in [1, n]$. A value assignment satisfies a constraint if it gives a combination of values to variables that is permitted by the constraint; otherwise it falsifies it. Thus a constraint satisfaction problem is the task of finding one or all value assignments for the constraints network such that all the constraints are satisfied together.

As beeing expected, various techniques for solving CSP's have been developed; these include backtraking, arc consistency (Mackworth[9]), path consistency (Freuder[5]). Good description can also

---

[1]Through out this paper, we use CSP to refer to the finite domain constraint satisfaction problem.

be found in (Mackworth[10], Haralick and Elliott[7], Dechter[4]). Backtracking algorithms enumerate the entire universe of tuples possible, to costruct a list of tuples satisfying all the constraints (Nadel[11]).

On other hand, symmetries for boolean constraints are well studied in (Benhamou and Sais[2,3]). They showed that it is a real improvment for efficiency of several automated deduction algorithms. Symmetrical values of a CSP variable are values which have the same chance to feet into solutions of the CSP, they are in a sense redundant, their removal will simplify the problem search space. However, CSP values are not always equally in chance to participate in solutions of the CSP. This is why, in this paper we study both symmetry and the notion of *dominance* to caracterize values which *dominate*(i.e. which have more chance to participate in solutions) other values in order to considere them in prior. Of course values dominatting each others will be symmetrical. The paper is organized as following :

Two levels of *semantic dominance* resp. *semantic symmetry* are defined in Section 2, the principle of Interchangeability[6] is shown to be a particular case of *symmetry*. Section 3 discusses *syntactical symmetry* which is a form of semantic symmetry that can be computed efficiently using only the structure of the considered problem. In other words, syntactical symmetry is considered as a suffisient condition to hold semantic symmetry. An efficient search method for symmetry is given. Section 4 studies *syntactical dominance* which is a sufficent condition to semantic dominance and shows that syntactical dominants values of a CSP $\mathcal{P}$ can be identified as syntactical symmetrical values of a more constrained CSP $\acute{\mathcal{P}}$ obtained from $\mathcal{P}$. Section 5 concludes the work.

For simplicity we study binary CSP's, which involve only constraints between two variables. However, *dominance* remains available for non-binary CSP's; and non-binary CSP's can be transformed into binary ones (Rossi, Dhar and Petri[12]).

2 Semantic dominance and semantic symmetry

We are interested by two problems in CSP's : the problem of finding a solution (test of satisfiability) and the problem of findind all the solutions of the CSP. Thus two levels of semantic dominance resp. semantic symmetry are difined with respect to the two previous problems.

Definition 2.1 (Dominance for satisfiability) *A value b_i dominates an other value c_i for a CSP variable $v_i \in V$ for satisfiability (notation $b_i \succeq c_i$) iff [There is a solution of the CSP in which the value c_i participates $\Rightarrow$ there is a solution of the CSP in which the value b_i participates].*

In other words, the value c_i participates in a solution if the value b_i participates in a solution too; otherwise it does not. Thus dominance techniques complement the usual CSP inconsistency methods, which attempt to remove values that will not feet into solutions.

A domain value can dominate an other domain value not only for satisfiability (definition 2.1) but for the set of all solutions as too. Thus, if $sol(\mathcal{P})$ denotes the set of solutions of the CSP $\mathcal{P}$, then we define a second level of semantic dominance as follow:

Définition 2.2 (Dominance for all solutions) *A domain value b_i dominates an other value c_i for a CSP variable $v_i \in V$ for $sol(\mathcal{P})$ (notation $b_i \geq c_i$) if and only if all solution of the CSP in which c_i participates can be obtained by mapping some solutions of the CSP in which b_i participates.*

Thus if we are seeking all solutions of the CSP $\mathcal{P}$, dominant values for $sol(\mathcal{P})$ (definition 2.2) allow us to find a family of symmetrical solutions without duplication of effort, for each member of the family.

Remark 2.3 Dominant values for all solutions (definition 2.2) are also dominant values for satisfiability (definition 2.1).

Definition 2.4 *Symmetrical domain values for satisfiability resp. for all solutions are domain values dominatting each other for satisfiability resp. all solutions.*

Remark 2.5 1. Two domain values b_i and c_i for a CSP variable v_i are symmetrical for satisfiability (notation $b_i \approx c_i$) iff [c_i participate in a solution $\Leftrightarrow$ b_i participate in a solution];

2. They are symmetrical for all solutions (notation $b_i \simeq c_i$) iff each solution of the CSP in which b_i particpates can be mapped into a solution in which c_i participates, and vice-versa.

Example 2.6 (Graph coloring problem) *The problem consists in coloring the vertices so that no two vertices which are joined by an edge have the same color. The available colors (domain values) at each vertex are shown (figure 1).*

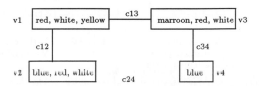

Figure 1: The graph coloring problem.

The *red* and *white* colors for vertex v_1 are two symmetrical domain values. Indeed, solutions in which one of them participates, can be obtained from the solutions in which the other value appears by permuting the values *red* and *white* for the variables v_1, v_2 and v_3. More precisely, in this example, both red_1 and $white_1$ participate in two solutions: (1) $\{red_1, white_2, white_3, blue_4\}$, and (2) $\{red_1, white_2, marroon_3, blue_4\}$ resp. (3) $\{white_1, red_2, red_3, blue_4\}$ and (4) $\{white_1, red_2, marroon_3, blue_4\}$, both $\{(1),(3)\}$ resp. $\{(2),(4)\}$ can be obtained from each other by the previous permutation. These are what we call symmetrical solutions. However, the value $yellow_1$ dominate both red_1 and $white_1$, since solutions in which red_1 resp. $white_1$ participate remains solutions when we substitute $yellow_1$ to red_1 resp. $white_1$.

On the other hand, Freuder introduced[6] the notion of interchangeability, where two domain values are interchangeable in some envronment, if they can be substituted for each other without any effects to the environment. Let us summarize the main definition.

Definition 2.7 *Two domain values b_i and c_i for a CSP variable $v_i \in V$ are fully interchangeable iff (1) every solution to the CSP which contains b_i remains a solution when c_i is substituted for b_i, (2) every solution to the CSP which contains c_i remains a solution when b_i is substituted for c_i.*

In other words the only difference in the sets of solutions involving b_i and c_i are b_i and c_i themselves.

Remark 2.8 Interchangeable values are particular symmetrical values for all solutions in which the mapping consists to permute the interchangeable values and still identity for the other values.

Example 2.9 *The values red_1 and $white_1$ of figure 1 are symmetrical but not interchangeable.*

Therefore, the notions of dominance and symmetry are more general than the principle of interchangeability. Thus eliminating dominated values can prune more great deal of effort from a backtrack search tree if such values are processed efficiently. We study in the next section syntactical symmetry resp. syntactical dominance of domain values which are sufficient conditions to semantic symmetry resp. semantic dominance and give an efficient method for search of symmetrical values and show that dominant values can be computed using this method.

3 Syntactical symmetry

Identifying semantic symmetry resp. semantic dominance as difined in the previous section is straightforward time consoming, as this requires solving the problem. This section studies syntactical symmetry which is more tractable computationally, thanks to the structure of the considered problem.

A permutation σ of domain values of a binary CSP $\mathcal{P} = (V, D, C, R)$ can be seen as: σ : $\cup_{i \in [1,n]} D_i \longrightarrow \cup_{i \in [1,n]} D_i$, such that $\sigma(d_i) \in D_i$, $\forall i \in [1, n]$ and $\forall d_i \in D_i$. The permutation σ have no influence on the sets $\{V, D, C\}$ of the CSP $\mathcal{P}$. However, it induces a permutation σ_t on the tuples in each relation $R_{ij} \in R$ and then a permutation σ_R [2] on the relations themselves.

A syntactical symmetry of a CSP $\mathcal{P} = (V, D, C, R)$ is a permutation of domain values that keeps the CSP P invariant (i.e. $\sigma_R(R_i) = R_i, \forall R_i \in R$). Formally:

Definition 3.1 (Syntactical symmetry) *A permutation σ is a syntactical symmetry of the CSP $\mathcal{P} = (V, D, C, R)$ iff $[\forall R_{ij} \in R, \ll d_i, d_j \gg \in tuples(R_{ij}) \Rightarrow \ll \sigma(d_i), \sigma(d_j) \gg \in tuples(R_{ij})]$.*

---

[2] Both σ_t resp. σ_R are natural generalizations for σ to tuples resp. relations.

Remark 3.2 A syntactical symmetry of a CSP is a domain value permutation σ such, $\sigma_R(R_i) = R_i$, $\forall R_i \in R$.

As the permutation σ have no influence on the sets $\{V,D,C\}$, the condition $\sigma_R(R_i) = R_i$, is suffisient for the CSP. $\mathcal{P}$ to be invariant under the permutation σ. We show in the sequel that such information is sufficient to handle semantic symmetry.

Remark 3.3 (1) The identity map (Id) is a syntactical symmetry, (2) the inverse map of a syntactical symmetry is also a syntactical symmetry, (3) the composition of syntactical symmetries is a syntactical symmetry.

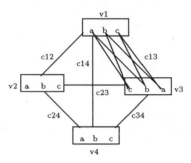

Figure 2: Pigeon-hole problem for 4 pigeons and 3 holes.

Example 3.4 (Pigeon-hole problem) *The problem consists in putting n pigeons in n − 1 holes such that each hole holds at most one pigeon. Take for instance 4 pigeons and 3 holes. The pigeons are represented by the set of variables the holes by the domain values, as it was shown in figure 2, the constraint c_{13} is given in its microstructure form showing the permitted tuples in the relation R_{13}.*

The permutation σ defined as: $\sigma(a_i) = (b_i)$, $\sigma(b_i) = (c_i)$, $\sigma(c_i) = (a_i)$, $\forall i \in [1,4]$ keeps the CSP invariant (i.e. $\sigma_R(R_i) = R_i$, $\forall i \in [1,4]$). Thus, it is a syntactical symmetry of the CSP.

Definition 3.5 *Two domain values b_i and c_i for a CSP variable $v_i \in V$ are syntactically symmetrical (notation $b_i \sim c_i$) if there exists a syntactical symmetry σ of the CSP $\mathcal{P}$ such that $\sigma(b_i) = c_i$.*

Remark 3.6 The relation ($\sim$) is a relation of equivalence.

Example 3.7 *In the privious example domain values a_1 and b_1 of the variable v_1 are syntactically symmetrical.*

Definition 3.8 *A set $\{a_1^1, a_1^2, \ldots, a_1^n\}$ of domain values form a cycle of symmetry in $\mathcal{P}$, if there exists a syntactical symmetry σ of $\mathcal{P}$ such that $\sigma(a_1^1) = a_1^2, \sigma(a_1^2) = a_1^3, \ldots, \sigma(a_1^{n-1}) = a_1^n, \sigma(a_1^n) = a_1^1$*

Example 3.9 *The sets of values $\{a_i, b_i, c_i\}$, $i \in [1,4]$ of the previous example forme four cycles of symmetry.*

All values in a cycle of symmetry are symmetrical two by two. Therefore, our method of search of symmetry will process a symmetry which gives for each domain, classes of values which are symmetrical together. Each classe will be identified by a cycle of symmetry. Before, describing the search method of symmetry, we will prove that syntactical symmetry is a sufficient condition for semantic symmetry.

Let I be a value assignment of the CSP $\mathcal{P}$, σ a syntactical symmetry of the CSP $\mathcal{P}$ and I/σ the value assignment obtained by substituting in I every domain value d_i of the CSP variable v_i by $\sigma(d_i)$, formally: $I/\sigma[v_i] = \sigma(I[v_i])$, $\forall i \in [1,n]$. Thus, the following property leads to get solutions form known solutions using symmetry:

Proposition 3.10 *I is a solution of $\mathcal{P}$ if and only if I/σ is a solution of $\mathcal{P}$*

Proof Suppose that I is a solution of $\mathcal{P}$ and R_{ij} the relations corresponding to the constraint c_{ij}. I is a solution of the CSP, thus I satisfies c_{ij}. Therefore, there exists a tuple $t_1 \in R_{ij}$ such that $t_1 \subset I$. As $\sigma_R(R_{ij}) = R_{ij}$ (σ is a syntactical symmetry), then $\sigma_t(t_1) = t_2 \in R_{ij}$. On other hand $t_2 \in I/\sigma$ (by definition of I/σ and the fact that $t_1 \in I$). Thus, I/σ satisfies c_{ij}, then I/σ is also a solution for the CSP $\mathcal{P}$ (QED). The converse can be proved in the same way as the first case.

Now we introduce the main property which lies syntactical symmetry and semantic symmetry.

Theorem 3.11 *If b_i and c_i are two syntactical symmetrical values of a CSP variable $v_i \in V$ ($b_i \sim c_i$) then b_i and c_i are semantic symmetrical values for all solutions of the CSP ($b_i \simeq c_i$).*

Proof We have to prove that each solution in which b_i participates can be mapped to an other solution in which c_i appears (definition 2.2) and vice-versa. The values b_i and c_i are syntactically symmetrical, then there exists a symmetry σ such that $\sigma(b_i) = c_i$. Suppose that b_i appears in a solution I of the CSP $\mathcal{P}$, then I/σ is a solution in which c_i appears (proposition 3.10). On other words the solution I is mapped into I/σ using the mapping σ (QED).

The converse can be proved in the same way as the first case.

Remark 3.12 Syntactical symmetrical values are also semantic symmetrical values.

On other hand, Freuder discuss neighborhood interchangeable values which are locally interchangeable values that can be processed efficientlly. Let us summerize the definition.

Definition 3.13 *Two values b_i and c_i are neighborhood interchangeable iff for every constraint $c_{ij} \in C$, $\{d/\ll b_i, d \gg \text{ satisfies } c_{ij}\} = \{d/\ll c_i, d \gg \text{ satisfies } c_{ij}\}$.*

Remark 3.14 Two domain values b_i and c_i of the CSP variable v_i are neighborhood interchangeable iff there exists a syntactical symmetry σ of the CSP, such that $\sigma(b_i) = c_i$, $\sigma(c_i) = b_i$ and still identity for other domain values.

See that neighborhood interchangeability is a very particular syntactical symmetry which can not exists frequently between domain values. Our approache is more general and will get more use. Bellow we give the search method for syntactical symmetry.

3.1 Search method for symmetry

Finding syntactical symmetrical values is equivalent to finding a syntactical symmetry σ of the CSP which lies them in a cycle. The symmetry σ partitiones domain values into classes of symmetrical value which are identified by the different cycles of the symmetry σ. To be syntactically symmetrical, values need to satisfy some necessary conditions:

Proposition 3.15 *Let $\lambda_{R_{ij}}(d_i)$ be the number of occurences of the value $d_i \in D_i$ in the relation R_{ij} and $tuples(R_{ij}^{d_i})$ the set of tuples of R_{ij} in which d_i appears, then to be syntactically symmetrical, values b_i and c_i must satisfy the following conditions:*

1. $\lambda_{R_{ij}}(b_i) = \lambda_{R_{ij}}(c_i)$, $\forall R_{ij} \in R$;

2. for each $d_j \in tuples(R_{ij}^{b_i})$, $\exists \acute{d_j} \in tuples(R_{ij}^{c_i})$ such that $\lambda_{R_{ij}}(d_j) = \lambda_{R_{ij}}(\acute{d_j})$, $\forall R_{ij} \in R$.

Proof The intuition of the two necessary conditions is that domain values must have the same number of occurences in the relations to be syntactically symmetrical[1].

The search method consists in three steps: (I) partitioning each domain w.r.t the previous necessary conditions into primary classes ($cl(d_i)$ denotes the class of d_i) of values which will be condidates for symmetry. (II) then process a permutation σ from the primary classes which keeps the CSP invariant. (III) finally deduce the classes of syntactical symmetrical values from the diferent cycles of the symmetry σ. Steps (I) and (II) are elementary operations, thus we will develope the step (II) which will give the complexity of the search method (figure 3).

A complexity bound for this algorithm can be found by assigning a worst case bound to each repeat loop. Given m relations, at most a values in each domain variable, we have the bound (the factors correspond to the repeat loops and the choose operation in topdown order):

$$\mathcal{O}(m * a * a^2) = \mathcal{O}(m.a^3)$$

procedure $symmetry(D_i \in D)$
Repeat for each $R_{ij} \in R$:
    Repeat for each $d_i \in D_i$, such that $\ll d_i, d_j \gg \in tuples(R_{ij})$:
        choose $\sigma(d_i) \in cl(d_i)$ and $\sigma(d_j) \in cl(d_j)$,
        such that $\ll \sigma(d_i), \sigma(d_j) \gg \in tuples(R_{ij})$

Figure 3: The search *symmetry* algorithm

Bellow we show how syntactical dominant values of a CSP $\mathcal{P}$ can be identified as syntacical symmetrical values of a more constrained CSP $\acute{\mathcal{P}}$ obtained from $\mathcal{P}$.

4 Syntactical dominance

Now we can give the definition of syntactical dominance and prove that it is a sufficient condition to semantic dominance.

Definition 4.1 *A CSP $\mathcal{P}$ is more constrained w.r.t a domain value b_i of a CSP variable $v_i \in V$ than an other CSP $\acute{\mathcal{P}}$ iff the only difference between $\mathcal{P}$ and $\acute{\mathcal{P}}$ is that the number of permitted tuples containing b_i for the constraints relating v_i to other variables in $\mathcal{P}$ is less than that one in $\acute{\mathcal{P}}$.*

Definition 4.2 *A domain value b_i of a CSP variable v_i dominates syntactically an other value c_i of the same variable of the CSP $\mathcal{P}$ iff b_i and c_i are syntacticaly symmetrical in a more constrained CSP $\acute{\mathcal{P}}$ w.r.t the value b_i of v_i.*

The CSP $\acute{\mathcal{P}}$ is obtained from $\mathcal{P}$ by carrying out some tuples containing b_i in the set of relation R of the CSP $\mathcal{P}$.

Example 4.3 *If we carry out both tuples $< yellow_1, red_2 >$ and $< yellow_1, red_3 >$ from the relations R_{12} respectivelly R_{13} corresponding to the constraints c_{12} and c_{13} of figure 1, we obtain a more constrained CSP w.r.t the value $yellow_1$ in which $yellow_1$ and red_1 are syntactically symmetrical. Thus, $yellow_1$ dominates red_1 in the former CSP.*

Now we give the sufficient condition for semantic dominance.

Theorem 4.4 *If b_i dominates syntactically c_i in a CSP $\mathcal{P}$, then b_i dominates c_i for all solutions in $\mathcal{P}$.*

Proof Suppose that b_i dominates syntactically c_i in the CSP $\mathcal{P}$, then there is a more constrained CSP $\acute{\mathcal{P}}$ w.r.t b_i in which b_i and c_i are syntactically symmetrical. As $b_i \sim c_i$ in $\acute{\mathcal{P}}$ then b_i and c_i are symmetrical for all solution in $\acute{\mathcal{P}}$ (theorme 3.11), in other words they are values dominatting each other in $\acute{\mathcal{P}}$. Since b_i has more chance to participate in solution of $\mathcal{P}$ than those of $\acute{\mathcal{P}}$ and $b_i \simeq c_i$ in $\acute{\mathcal{P}}$ then b_i will dominate c_i for all solution in $\mathcal{P}$.

Finding dominant values of a CSP $\mathcal{P}$ is equivalent to finding symmetrical values in a more constrained CSP $\acute{\mathcal{P}}$. The CSP $\mathcal{P}$ is obtained from $\acute{\mathcal{P}}$ by carrying out some tuples in which the dominant value participates so that in the resulting CSP $\acute{\mathcal{P}}$, the values satisfy the necessary conditions of symmetry. Therefore, the search method for symmetry defined in the previous section remains available for detecting dominant values.

A domain value b_i can dominates an other domain value c_i in$\mathcal{P}$ if the following conditions are hold.

Proposition 4.5 *Let $\lambda_{R_{ij}}(d_i)$ be the number of occurences of the value $d_i \in D_i$ in the relation R_{ij} and $tuples(R_{ij}^{d_i})$ the set of tuples of R_{ij} in which d_i appears, then the value b_i can dominate syntactically the values c_i if the following conditions hold:*

1. $\lambda_{R_{ij}}(b_i) \geq \lambda_{R_{ij}}(c_i)$, $\forall R_{ij} \in R$;

2. for each $d_j \in tuples(R_{ij}^{b_i})$, $\exists \acute{d}_j \in tuples(R_{ij}^{c_i})$ such that $\lambda_{R_{ij}}(d_j) \geq \lambda_{R_{ij}}(\acute{d}_j)$, $\forall R_{ij} \in R$.

As a consequence of the theorem 4.4 we give the following corollary :

Corollary 4.6 *If $\mathcal{P}_{v_i \leftarrow d_i}$ is the CSP $\mathcal{P}$ simplified by assignment of the variable v_i to the value d_i and $cl(d_i)$* [3] *denotes the classe of values of D_i dominated by d_i, then [$\mathcal{P}$ is satisfiable if and only if $\mathcal{P}_{v_i \leftarrow d_i}$ or $\mathcal{P}_{v_i \leftarrow \acute{d} \in \{D_i - cl(d_i)\}}$ is satisfiable].*

Proof It's a direct consequence of theorem 4.4.

This corollary expresses an important property that we use to make prune the search tree of a backtrack procedure. Indeed if d_i participates in no solutions of the CSP $\mathcal{P}$ and $d_i \geq \acute{d}_i$, then $\acute{d}_i$ will participate in no solutions too. Thus, we prune the sub-tree which corresponds to its assignment. Therefore, if there are n symmetrical domain values in $cl(d)$, then we can cut $n - 1$ branches in the search tree if one of the domain values in $cl(d)$ has already been identified that it paticipates in no solutions. Until now, we have studied dominance and symmetry between values of a same domain. However this notion can be extended to values of different domains in a natural way. Further investigation consists to detect and exploit such symmetries efficientlly and indicate what are the problems which are tractable using such information.

5 Conclusion

We have developed the formal concept of dominance and symmetry in constraint satisfaction problems, then various constraints satisfaction algorithms can be adapted to exploit such information. The principle of interchangeability is shown to be a particular case of symmetry. Further investigation will consist to extend the notions of dominance and symmetry to domain values of different variables and try to identify certain type of CSP's for which such symmetries get more use.

6 Acknowledgements

This paper is supported by the PRC-GDR Intelligence Artificielle, the project *BAHIA* and the MRE-INTER-PRC project *CLASSES POLYNOMIALES*

References

1. B. Benhamou. *Study of symmetry in constraint satisfaction problems.* Technical Report 1, Université de provence, 1994.

2. B. Benhamou and L. Sais. *Tractability through symmetries in propositional calculus.* Journal of Automated Reasoning (JAR), to apear.

3. B. Benhamou and L. Sais. *Theoretical study of symmetries in propositional calculus and application.* Eleventh International Conference on Automated Deduction, Saratoga Springs,NY, USA, 1992.

4. R. Dechter. *From local to global consistency.* Artificial Intelligence, **55**, pages 87–107, 1992.

5. E. Freuder. *Backtrack-free and backtrack bounded search.* In Kanal, Laveen and Kumar, Vipin, editors 1988, Search in Artificial Intelligence. Springer-Verlag, New York., 1988.

6. E. Freuder. *Eliminating interchangeable values in constraints satisfaction problems.* Proc AAAI-91, pages 227–233, 1991.

7. R. M. Haralik and G. L. Elliot. *Increasing tree search efficiency for constraint satisfaction problems.* Artificial Intelligence **14**, pages 263–313, 1980.

8. V. Kumar. *Algorithms for constraints satisfaction problems.* AI Magazine, pages 32–44, 1992.

9. A. Mackworth. *Consistency in networks of relations.* Artificial Intelligence **8**, pages 99–118, 1977.

10. A. Mackworth. *Constraint satisfaction.* In Stuart C. Shapiro, editor, Encyclopedia of Artificial Intelligence, pages 205–211, 1987.

11. B. Nadel. *Constraint satisfaction algorithms.* In Kanal, Laveen and Kumar, Vipin, editors 1988, Search in Artificial Intelligence. Springer-Verlag, New York.

12. D. Rossi and Petrie. *On the equivalence of constraint satisfaction problems.* Technical report, MCC Technical Report ACT-AI-**222**-89. MCC, Austin, Texas 78759, 1989.

---

[3] Symmetrical values with d_i are include in $cl(d_i)$.

Reasoning in Cardinality Boolean Constraints

Belaid Benhamou
Laboratoire d'Informatique de Marseille
URA CNRS 1787
UFR-MIM- Université de Provence,
3,Place Victor Hugo - F13331 Marseille cedex 3, France
phone number : 91.10.61.08
e-mail : Benhamou@gyptis.univ-mrs.fr

ABSTRACT

In this paper we use the cardinality to increase the expressiveness efficiency of propositional calculus and improve the efficiency of resolution methods. Hence to express propositional problems and logical constraints we use the pair formulas $(\rho, \mathcal{L})$ which mean that "at least ρ literals among those of a list $\mathcal{L}$ are true". This makes a generalization of propositional clauses which express only "One literal among those of the clause is true". Two cardinality proof procedures are developed in a former paper. In this one we study the SLRC method which is Sl-resolution procedure adapted with Cardinality. Good results are obtained on many known problems such as Schur's lemma, Queenes, Ramsey and Pigeon-hole when this method is augmented with the principle of symmetry.

Topic areas : Automated deduction, Representation formalisms, Constraint solving.

1 Introduction

Determining an appropriate language for the representation of knowledge, requires a good compromise between expressiveness of the language and efficiency of the resolution methods. With increased interest in theorem proving procedures, a collection of proof systems and constraint logic programming languages CLP[5,7,9] have been proposed to handle a variety of logical theories. The cardinality operator[8] is a new logical connective for constraint logic programming. It provides CLP users with a new way of combining (primitive) constraints to build non-primitive ones. It also implements the principle "infer simple constraints from difficult ones" which is actually the basic principle behind the design of CLP over Finite Domains, and would be appropriate to build non-primitive constraints as well.

Cardinality is well studied in[4]. In this paper we use the pair formulas to express more efficiently logic problems. A pair formula is a natural generalization for propositional clauses. Indeed the the pair $(\rho, \mathcal{L})$ means that "at least ρ literals among those of the list $\mathcal{L}$ are true", while a propositional clause express only "One literal is true among those of the clause". Thus a clause is a particulary pair formula $(\rho, \mathcal{L})$ in which $\rho = 1$ for example the clause $a \vee b \vee c$ can be seen as $(1, abc)$. In Section 2 we introduce the necessary terminology and notations. In Sections 3 we give the cardinality resolution proof system, which is complet and decidable. A linear proof for Pigeon-hole problem is found in this system while this is impossible in classical resolution.

In sections 4 we describe the method SLRC which is Sl-resolution[6] adapted to pair formulas. The property of symmetry[3] (section 5) is extended to pair formulas and used in SLRC to increase efficiency of the method. Finally we give computation times for the method SLRC with the advantage of symmetry on some known benchmarks.

2 Definition and notations

We shall assume some familiarities with the propositional calculus. A propositional variable is called a variable, and we distinguish it from a literal, which is a variable together with a parity-positive or negative. A formula means a well formed propositional formula using one of the binary connectives. The connectives of primary interest are: AND ($\wedge$), OR ($\vee$), NOT ($\neg$). The constants TRUE and FALSE will be represented by 1 and 0, respectively.

2.1 Syntax

A pair formula is a statement $(\rho, \mathcal{L})$ in which ρ is a positive integer and $\mathcal{L}$ a list of literals with eventual repetitions. The pair formula $(\rho, \mathcal{L})$ expresses the constraint "At least ρ literals among those of the list $\mathcal{L}$ are true" [1] . In the following we use pair instead of pair formula and let's $\mid \mathcal{L} \mid$ be the length of the list i.e the number of literals in $\mathcal{L}$.

Example 2.1 • $(1, abc)$ is logically equivalent to the clause $a \vee b \vee c$

• $(2, abc)$ is logically equivalent to the set of clauses $\{a \vee b, a \vee c, b \vee c\}$

• $(2, aabc)$ is logically equivalent to the set of clauses $\{a \vee a \vee b, a \vee a \vee c, a \vee b \vee c\}$ which is equivalent to $\{a \vee b, a \vee c\}$

It is interesting to note at this point that pairs are quite expressive. A conjunction of literals $\psi_1 \wedge \psi_2 \ldots \wedge \psi_n$ can be expressed by $(n, \psi_1 \psi_2 \ldots \psi_n)$, a disjunction $\psi_1 \vee \psi_2 \ldots \vee \psi_n$ by $(1, \psi_1 \psi_2 \ldots \psi_n)$ and a negation $\neg \psi$ by $(1, \neg \psi)$. In the sequel we prove that a pair $(\rho, \mathcal{L})$ represents $C_{|\mathcal{L}|}^{|\mathcal{L}|-\rho+1}$ of propositional clauses.

2.2 Semantics

A classical truth assignment I satisfies a pair $(\rho, \mathcal{L})$ if and only if at least ρ literals among those of $\mathcal{L}$ are assigned to the value true in I. It is obvious that a pair $(\rho, \mathcal{L})$ such that $\rho > \mid \mathcal{L} \mid$ is unsatisfiable (contradictory). On the other hand, each pair $(0, \mathcal{L})$ is a tautology. The assignment I satisfies a set S of pairs if it satisfies all of its pairs. Henceforth we will assume that the formulas are given in pair formula representation. We observe that in the case of sets containing only pairs of kind $(1, \mathcal{L})$ the definition of a truth assignment is the same as in propositional clauses.

Exemple 2.2 The truth assignment $I = \{a, \neg b, \neg c\}$ satisfies the paires $(1, abc)$ and $(2, ab\neg c)$, but does not satisfy the pair $(2, abc)$.

Definition 2.3 If $\mathcal{L}$ is a list of literals such that $\mid \mathcal{L} \mid = n$, and m an integer such that $m \leq n$ then $C_n^m\{\mathcal{L}\}$ denotes the set of propositional clauses obtained by considering all the disjunctions formed by the combinations of m literals among those of the list $\mathcal{L}$.

We are now able to show that all pair is equivalent to a set of propositional clauses.

Proposition 2.4 Let $c = (\alpha, \mathcal{L})$ be a pair such that $\mid \mathcal{L} \mid = \theta$ then we have the following logical equivalence :
$$c \equiv C_\theta^{\theta-\alpha+1}\{\mathcal{L}\}$$

Proof Let I be a model of c. Thus at least α literals among those of $\mathcal{L}$ are satisfied by I. In other words, I satisfies at most $\theta - \alpha$ literals among the negation literals of $\mathcal{L}$. This implies that I satisfies each clause of the set $C_\theta^{\theta-\alpha+1}\{\mathcal{L}\}$. This is so, because each clause of the set $C_\theta^{\theta-\alpha+1}\{\mathcal{L}\}$ contains exactly $\theta - \alpha + 1$ literals.

To prove the converse, we show that if $(\alpha, \mathcal{L})$ has no model then $C_\theta^{\theta-\alpha+1}\{\mathcal{L}\}$ has no model too. Suppose that $(\alpha, \mathcal{L})$ has no model, then any truth assignment I, satisfies less than α literals among those of $\mathcal{L}$ (at most $\alpha - 1$); That is, I satisfies more than $\theta - \alpha$ literals among the negation literals of $\mathcal{L}$ (at least $\theta - \alpha + 1$). It is not hard to see that the clause of $C_\theta^{\theta-\alpha+1}\{\mathcal{L}\}$ which is formed with the negations of the $\theta - \alpha + 1$ literals with the value true in I, is not satisfied by I. We conlude that I is

---

[1] Two additional cardinality formulas can be considered : "At most ρ literals among those of $\mathcal{L}$ are true", encoded by $(\rho, +, \mathcal{L})$ and " Exactly ρ literals among those of $\mathcal{L}$ are true", (notation is $(\rho, e, \mathcal{L})$), but in practice they can be expressed, using pairs.

not a model of $\mathcal{C}_{\theta}^{\theta-\alpha+1}\{\mathcal{L}\}$.

As a consequence of proposition 2.4, we obtain the following lemma.

Lemma 2.5 *If $S = \cup_{i=1,k}\{(\alpha_i, \mathcal{L}_i)/ \mid \mathcal{L}_i \mid= \theta_i\}$ is a set of k pairs, and S_p a set of propositional clauses, such that $S_p = \cup_{i=1,k}\mathcal{C}_{\theta_i}^{\theta_i-\alpha_i+1}\{\mathcal{L}_i\}$, then $S \equiv S_p$.*

The lemma is a direct consequence of the proposition 2.4. It is intersting to see that for each set S of pairs there exists an equivalent set S_p of propositional clauses and vice versa and the number of clauses in S_p is generally greater than the number of pairs in S.

A cardinality resolution proof system is given in[4]. Let us summerize the main rules and show a linear proof for the pigeon-hole problem.

3 Proof system

Let S be a set of pairs. We give two basic inference rules:

3.1 Resolution rule

Let $(\alpha, \ell_1\ell_2\ldots\ell_n.\mathcal{L})$ and $(\beta, \neg\ell_1\neg\ell_2\ldots\neg\ell_n.\acute{\mathcal{L}})$ be two pairs of the set S such that $n \geq 1$, then we can deduce the pair $(\alpha + \beta - n, \mathcal{L}.\acute{\mathcal{L}})$. This is,

$$\frac{(\alpha, \ell_1\ell_2\ldots\ell_n.\mathcal{L}), (\beta, \neg\ell_1\neg\ell_2\ldots\neg\ell_n.\acute{\mathcal{L}})}{(\alpha + \beta - n, \mathcal{L}.\acute{\mathcal{L}})}$$

Example 3.1 If $S = \{(2, abc), (1, \neg a\neg b)\}$, then a single application of the previous rule is enough to obtain the pair $(3 + 1 - 2, c) = (1, c)$.

However the previous rule is not sufficient to prove the unsatisfiability of the set $S = \{(2, aay), (2, \neg a\neg ax)\}$. To get a complete system, we need to introduce the following merging rule as it was done in classical resolution.

3.2 Merging rule

If $c = (\alpha, \ell^k \mathcal{L})^2$ is a consistent pair of S such that $\mid \ell^k \mathcal{L} \mid= \theta$ and k a positive integer, then for every sublist φ of $\mathcal{L}$ such that $\mid \varphi \mid= max\{0, \theta - \alpha + 1 - k\}$ we infer the pair $(1, \ell\varphi)$ and the pair $(max\{0, \alpha - k\}, \mathcal{L})$. This is ,

$$\frac{(\alpha, \ell^k\mathcal{L}), \forall\varphi \subseteq \mathcal{L} :\mid \varphi \mid= max\{0, \theta - \alpha + 1 - k\}}{(1, \ell\varphi), (max\{0, \alpha - k\}, \mathcal{L})}$$

Such a rule is missing in the proof system given for cardinality operator in[10]. Note that when $k \geq \theta - \alpha + 1$ the pair $(1, \ell)$ is deduced. This means that when the number of redundancy k of the literal ℓ is greater than or equal to $\theta - \alpha + 1$ we prove the literal ℓ. The number of pairs $(1, \ell\varphi)$ to be generated becomes smaller when $\theta - \alpha + 1$ gets close to zero. In general the number of pairs we generate is not important.
The proof of the previous example $S = \{(2, aay), (2, \neg a\neg ax)\}$ becomes now obvious. Indeed the pairs $(1, a)$ and $(1, \neg a)$ are infered by the merging rule. Applying the resolution rule on them we deduce the unsatisfiable pair $(1, \emptyset)$.
In the case of a pair $(1, \ell^k\mathcal{L})$, the rule has the same behavior as the merging rule in classic resolution.

Proposition 3.2 *Both previous rules are sound.*

Proof Due to the semantics defined before, the soundness of the previous rules becomes evident.

---

[2] ℓ^k means k times the literal ℓ

3.3   Subsumption rules

   To make the system decidable and more efficient, we have to add subsumption rules.

1. Let $(\alpha, \mathcal{L})$ and $(\beta, \acute{\mathcal{L}})$ be two satisfiable pairs of S such that $\beta \leq \alpha$ and $\mathcal{L} \subseteq \acute{\mathcal{L}}$, then the pair $(\alpha, \mathcal{L})$ subsumes the pair formula $(\beta, \acute{\mathcal{L}})$ in S.

   Example. $(3, a\ b\ c\ d)$ subsumes $(2, a\ b\ c\ d\ e)$

2. Let $(\alpha, \mathcal{L})$ and $(\beta, \acute{\mathcal{L}})$ be two satisfiable pairs of S such that $\beta \leq \alpha$, $\acute{\mathcal{L}} \subseteq \mathcal{L}$ and $\beta \leq \alpha - (|\mathcal{L}| - |\acute{\mathcal{L}}|)$, then the pair formula $(\alpha, \mathcal{L})$ subsumes the pair $(\beta, \acute{\mathcal{L}})$ in S.

   Example. $(2, a\ b\ c\ d)$ subsumes $(1, a\ b\ c)$

   It is well known that Pigeon-hole problem is exponential for classic resolution, in the following we give a linear proof for this problem showing the advantage of cardinality and the powerful of our proof system.

3.4   A linear proof for Pigeon-Hole problem

   The problem consists in putting n pigeons in $n - 1$ holes such that each hole holds at most one pigeon. We show here how cardinality leads to find a linear proof for Pigeon-hole problem. This problem is described with the following set of pairs.

1   $(1, p_{1(1)} p_{1(2)} \cdots p_{1(n-1)})$
2   $(1, p_{2(1)} p_{2(2)} \cdots p_{2(n-1)})$
$\vdots$

n $(1, p_{n(1)} p_{n(2)} \cdots p_{n(n-1)})$

n+1 $(n - 1, \neg p_{1(1)} \neg p_{2(1)} \cdots \neg p_{n(1)})$
n+2 $(n - 1, \neg p_{1(2)} \neg p_{2(2)} \cdots \neg p_{n(2)})$
$\vdots$

2n-1 $(n - 1, \neg p_{1(n-1)} \neg p_{2(n-1)} \cdots p_{n(n-1)})$

Note that $p_{i(j)}$ means that the the pigeon-hole j holds the pigeon i. The problem is expressed with only $2n - 1$ pairs, however the same problem requires $n + n(n - 1)^2/2$ propositional clauses.
One way to prove the unsatisfiability of the problem is to use a linear resolution method. It consist to apply at each step the resolution rule on the current resolvent and another pair of the remaining pair formulas. The proof is given by the following steps:

Proof   By application of the resolution rule on the formulas (1) and $(n + 1)$ we deduce the pair $(n - 1, p_{1(2)} \cdots p_{1(n-1)} \neg p_{2(1)} \cdots \neg p_{n(1)})$. We continue the resolution on the $n - 2$ first positive literals of the previous pair. Thus by $n - 2$ applications of the resolution rule we get the pair:
$((n - 1) + (n - 2)(n - 1) - (n - 2), \neg p_{2(1)} \cdots \neg p_{n(1)} \neg p_{2(2)} \cdots \neg p_{n(2)} \cdots \neg p_{2(n-1)} \cdots \neg p_{n(n-1)})$ in which only negative literals appear. It is obvious now that with $n-1$ applications of the resolution rule on the literals $\neg p_{2(1)} \neg p_{2(2)} \cdots \neg p_{2(n-1)}$ we obtain the pair $((n-1) + (n-2)(n-1) - (n-2) + (n-1)(n-2), \emptyset)$ which is identical to the unsatisfiable pair $(1, \emptyset)$. Therefore the unsatisfiability of the problem is shown using only $2n - 2$ applications of the resolution rule.

The method of Davis and Putname for cardinality constraints is studied in[4]. In the sequel we adapt the Sl-resolution method for the cardinality formalism.

4   The method SLRC

   The Sl-resolution algorithm for the propositional calculus is derived from J.A Robinson[13], D.W Lovland[12], R.A Kowalski[11]. It is considered as one of the best algorithm to decide satisfiability and unsatisiability of a set of clauses, since only resolvents between the curent resolvent and other clauses are computed. We define in smilar way the SLRC method. Resolvant pairs are computed only for a pair of S and the curent resolvent pair. The history of the resolvent is stored thank's to literals on which resolution is applied, we call them A-ancestors.

The method process a proof tree in which each node contains a pair and the coresponding set of A-ancestors under which the pair will be refuted. At the root the set of A-ancestors is empty. The number of branches that We can develope from a given node to refute a literal ℓ is at most equal to the number of pairs of S which contain $\neg\ell$. Bellow we give the SLRC procedure.

Let S be a set of pair formulas, A the set of A-ancestors and S_A the set S with consideration of the set A of A ancestors.

SLRC Procedure :

- Let $c = (\alpha, \mathcal{L})$ be a pair formula of S then c can be refuted in S_A if only if at least $\mid \mathcal{L} \mid -\alpha + 1$ literals of $\mathcal{L}$ are refuted in S_A.

- A literal p is refuted in S_A if and only if

1. Either $\neg p \in A$

2. Or $p \notin A$ and there exists a pair $c = (\beta, \neg p\acute{\mathcal{L}})$ such that $\mid \acute{\mathcal{L}} \cap A \mid < \beta$ which is refuted in $S_{A \cup \{p\}}$.

To refute a pair $c = (\alpha, \mathcal{L})$ in $SLRC$ we need to refute only $\mid \mathcal{L} \mid -\alpha + 1$ literals of $\mathcal{L}$, but to refute a clause in Sl-resolution we have to refute all literals in the clause. This is one of the advantages of cardinality.

A set S of pairs is contradictory if one of its pairs had been refuted with an empty set of A-ancesrtors, consistant otherwise.

Ameliorations can be envisaged to make the method more efficient as it was done in Sl-resolution. In the case of refutations occuring throughout the algorithm, cylinders without solutions may be stored and used later (B-ancestors). In the case that the algorithm fails to find a refutation tree, certain informations can be saved : the so called I-ancestors (I means : impasse). The set of pairs of the instance S satisfied by the set I of I-ancestors retained at a node is eliminated for a while if the corresponding literal is beeing refuted. Thus if we store the opposites of B-ancestors in the set B and the I-ancestors in the set I we get the the following variant for the SLRC method :

SLRC with B-ancestors and I-ancestors

- Let $c = (\alpha, \mathcal{L})$ be a pair formula of S then c can be refuted in S_A if only if at least $\mid \mathcal{L} \mid -\alpha + 1$ literals of $\mathcal{L}$ are refuted in S_A.

- A literal p is refuted in S_A if and only if

1. Either $\neg p \in A \cup B$

2. Or $p \notin A$ and there exists a pair $c = (\beta, \neg p\acute{\mathcal{L}})$ such that $\mid \acute{\mathcal{L}} \cap A \mid < \beta$, $\mid \acute{\mathcal{L}} \cap I \mid < \beta$ and $\mid \{x : x \in \acute{\mathcal{L}}, \neg x \in I\} \mid < \beta$ which is refuted in $S_{A \cup \{p\}}$.

It is obvious that this variant never takes more time and that there is a strict inclusion of calculation trees. It also takes every instance and, like Davis and Putnam procedure, gives a cylinder of solutions in the case of consistancy which is the set of I-ancestors.

Example 4.1 Take the Pigeon-hole problem for 3 pigeons and 2 holes. The problem is represented by the following set of pairs :

$$c_1 = (1, p_{11}p_{12})$$
$$c_2 = (1, p_{21}p_{22})$$
$$c_3 = (1, p_{31}p_{32})$$
$$c_4 = (2, \neg p_{11}\neg p_{21}\neg p_{31})$$
$$c_5 = (2, \neg p_{12}\neg p_{22}\neg p_{32})$$

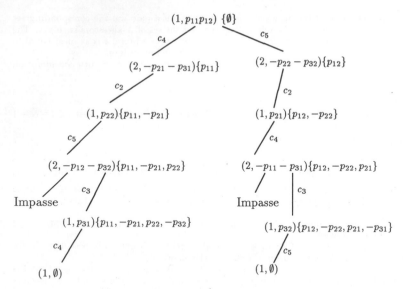

Figure 1: Refutation tree of the pair $(1, p_{11}p_{12})$

The refutation tree of the pair $(1, p_{11}p_{12})$ is shown in the figure (1). Each node of the search tree contains the curent pair to refute and the coresponding set of A-ansistors.

The pair $c_1 = (1, p_{11}p_{12})$ had been refuted under an empty set of A-ancestors. Thus the set of pairs is contradictory. In the following we show how symmetries can lead to improve the efficiency of the method.

5 Symmetries in cardinality formulas

Symmetries have been studied in[3,2] when the knowledge is expressed with sets of clauses given in conjunctive normal forme. Here we extend the principle of symmetry to pair formulas representation.

First of all, let us define the concepts of permutations and symmetry, and prove significant properties that will enable us to improve the proof algorithms.

If V is a set of propositional variables then a bijection map $\sigma : V \to V$ is called a permutation of variables. If S is a set of pairs, c a pair of S and σ a permutation of variables occuring in S, then $\sigma(c)$ is the pair obtained by applying σ to each variable of c and $\sigma(S) = \{\sigma(c)/c \in S\}$. A symmetry of S is apermutation of literals in S that keeps S invariant. Formally:

Definition 5.1 *A set P of literals is called complete if $\forall \ell \in P$; then $\neg \ell \in P$*

Definition 5.2 *Let P be a complete set of literals and S a set of pairs of which all literals are in P. Then a permutation σ defined on P ($\sigma : P \to P$) is called a symmetry of S if only if it satisfies the following conditions:*

1. $\forall \ell \in P, \sigma(\neg \ell) = \neg \sigma(\ell)$

2. $\sigma(S) = S$

Two literals (variables) ℓ and $\acute{\ell}$ are symmetrical in S (notation $\ell \sim \acute{\ell}$) if there exists a symmetry σ of S such that $\sigma(\ell) = \acute{\ell}$. A set $\{\ell_1, \ell_2, \ldots, \ell_n\}$ of literals is called a cycle of symmetry in S if there exists a symmetry σ defined on S, such that $\sigma(\ell_1) = \ell_2, \ldots \sigma(\ell_{n-1}) = \ell_n, \sigma(\ell_n) = \ell_1$.

Example 5.3 *Let $S = \{(2, abx), (2, bcy), (1, ac)\}$ be a set of pairs, then the permutation σ defined as follow : $\sigma(a) = c$, $\sigma(c) = a$, $\sigma(b) = b$, $\sigma(x) = y$, $\sigma(y) = x$ is a symmetry of S and the literals $a \sim c$, respectively $x \sim y$ are symmetrical.*

Remark 5.4 All the literals in a cycle of symmetry are symmetrical two by two.

Symmetrical literals are computed efficiently. Due to cardinality, detection of symmetries seems to be more efficient in pair formulas than in propositional clauses. Indeed, a new necessary condition for symmetry is added : two literals ℓ and ℓ' are condidats for symmetry in S if they have the same number of occurences in S and not only apear in pairs of the same length (same number of literals) but in pairs which have the same cardinality as wel. The method is not discribed here, it is the one given in[3] with the advantage of cardinality.

We give now the properties of symmetry. If I is a model of S and σ a symmetry, then we can get another model of S by applying σ on the literals which appear in I. Let I/σ be the truth assignment obtained by substituting every literal ℓ in I by $\sigma(\ell)$.

Proposition 5.5 *I is a model of S if and only if I/σ is a model of S.*

Proof Since S is unvariant under σ then σ transforms each model of S to an other model of S[1].

Proposition 5.6 *If ℓ and $\acute{\ell}$ are two symmetrical literals of S, then [ℓ participates in a model of S if only if $\acute{\ell}$ participates in a model of S].*

Proof Suppose that ℓ appears in a model of S, this means that there exists a model I of S such that $I[\ell] = 1$. On other hand $\ell \sim \acute{\ell}$, then there exists a symmetry σ of S such that $\sigma(\ell) = \acute{\ell}$. As $\ell \in I$, then $\sigma(\ell) = \acute{\ell} \in I/\sigma$ (by definition of I/σ). Or I/σ is a model of S (proposition 5.5), thus $\acute{\ell}$ appears in a model.
For the converse, let $\ell = \sigma^{-1}(\acute{\ell})$, then the proof is identical to the first case.

As a consequence we give the main theorem :

Theorem 5.7 *Let ℓ and ℓ' be two literals of S_A, A the set of A-ancestors. If $\ell \sim \ell'$ in S_A, then [ℓ is refuted in S_A if only if ℓ' is refuted in S_A].*

Proof Suppose tha ℓ had been refuted in S_A, then there is no model of S_A in which ℓ appears. As $\ell \sim \acute{\ell}$, then $\acute{\ell}$ can't participates to any model of S_A. Thus $\acute{\ell}$ is refuted in S_A. The converse can be proved in the same way.

This theorem expresses an important property that we use to make prune the search tree. Indeed if ℓ is refuted in S and $\ell \sim \ell'$, then ℓ' will be refuted in S by symmerty, thus we prune the sub-tree which corresponds to its refutation. Therefore, if there are n symmetrical literals we can cut $n - 1$ branches in the search tree if one of the literals has already been refuted. In the example 4.1 literals p_{11} and p_{12} are symmetrical, thus p_{12} can be refuted by symmetry, so we can prune in the search tree (figure 1) the sub-tree corresponding to its refutation.

A good strategy for the detection method of symmetries is to process all the literals which are symmetrical with the curent refuted literal. Such literals are refuted imediately by symmetry and considered as B-ancestors.

As a consequence of the previous theorem we give the following result:

Theorem 5.8 *Let ℓ and ℓ' be two literals of S_A, A the set of A-ancestors. If $\ell \sim \ell'$ in S_A, then [ℓ is in impasse in S_A if only if ℓ' is in impasse in S_A].*

The previous theorem leads to identify pairs which are not subject to refutation. Indeed symmetrical literals with literals proven in impasse are added to the set of I-ancestors, and the pairs which are satisfied by the I-ancestors are not considered for refutation.
The SLRC method increased with the advantage of symmetry (due to the results of both previous theorems) is applied to the following problems.

5.1 Benchmarks

- Queens. Placing N queens in $N \times N$ chessboard such that there is no couple of queens attacking each other.

- Erdös's theorem. Find the permutation σ of N first numbers such that for each 4-tuple $1 \leq i < j < k < l \leq N$ none of the two relations $\sigma(i) < \sigma(j) < \sigma(k) < \sigma(l)$ and $\sigma(l) < \sigma(k) < \sigma(j) < \sigma(i)$ is verified.
  This problem is modeled by creating for each couple (i,j) a variable $f_{i,j}$ which means $\sigma(i) < \sigma(j)$. The rules express the associativity of the relation $<$, and prohibit the misplaced 4-tuples.
  For $N \leq 9$ the problem admits solutions, beyond it doesn't.

- Schur's lemma: How to distribute N counters numbred from 1 to N into 3 boxes A, B, C in accordance with the following rules:
  1) A box can't contain both the counters numbered i and $2 * i$
  2) A box can't contain the counters numbered i, j and $i + j$
  This problem is modeled simply by creating one variable by counter and by box. For $N \leq 13$ the problem admits solutions, beyond it doesn't.

- Ramsey problem's: Color the edges of a complete graph on N vertices with three different colors such that no monochromatic triangle appears.
  For $N \leq 16$ the problem admits solutions, beyond it doesn't.

Problems	Size formula		SLRC+Sym	
	pairs	Variables	Steps	Times
Queens 8	50	64	37	0.26"
Queens 10	64	100	65	2.24"
Erdös 9	420	36	25	0.56"
Erdös 10	660	45	814	8.41"
Schur13	152	39	32	0.25"
Schur14	175	42	142	1.53"
Ramsey14	1274	273	192	3.82"
Ramsey15	1575	315	652	2'.53"
Ramsey16	1920	360	2957	4'.35"

Table 1: Schur's Lemma, Ramsey's problem, Erdös and Queens

Table (1) shows results obtained by SLRC with the advantage of symmetry for the previous problems. The programs are written in Pascal and run on a sparck server 410. Ofcours the CPU time for searching symmetries is included.

Number of pigeons	Size formula		SLRC+Sym	
	Pairs	Variables	Steps	Times
10	19	90	31	0.203"
15	29	210	101	0.970"
20	39	380	196	3.370"
25	49	600	460	9.970"
30	59	870	631	25.153"
35	69	1190	641	57.353"
40	79	1560	751	1'77"
45	89	1980	781	3'55"
50	99	2450	867	4'77"

Table 2: Pigeon hole problems

Table (2) contains results for Pigeon-hole problems. Pigeonhole and Ramsey problems are traited in[3] with only symmetries. Howover with the advantage of cardinality we get best times : with cardinality we solve Pigeon-hole untill 50 pigeons, while in[3] it is solved untill 30 pigeons. Note that the complexity of pigeon-hole problem, in number of elementary steps becomes linear and CPU time is not exponential, but proportional to n^2 (n is the number of variables). Without symmetries, the complexity of resolution for this problem becomes exponential when the number of pigeons is greater then eight.

6 Conclusion

In this paper, we have introduced the pair formulas to express problems in a more natural way and improve the efficiency of resolution methods in propositional calculus. The pair formulas have a simple semantic and let to get a generalization of the conjunctive normal form (CNF). A proof system which is at once complete and decidable is given. To reason about the statement "at least ρ literals are true among the literals of a list $\mathcal{L}$", the detection of symmetries seem to be less expensive in this formalism. Symmetries are applied to Sl-resolution with cadinality and satisfactory CPU times are obtained for different problems.

7 Acknowledgements

This paper is supported by the PRC-GDR Intelligence Artificielle, the project *BAHIA* and the MRE-INTER-PRC project *CLASSES POLYNOMIALES*

References

1. B. Benhamou. *Etude des symétries et de la cardinalité en calcul propositionnel : application aux algorithmes syntaxiques.* PhD thesis, LIUP, Université de Provence, Aix-Marseille 1, 1993.
2. B. Benhamou and L. Sais. *Tractability through symmetries in propositional calculus.* Journal of Automated Reasoning (JAR), to apear.
3. B. Benhamou and L. Sais. *Theoretical study of symmetries in propositional calculus and application.* Eleventh International Conference on Automated Deduction, Saratoga Springs,NY, USA, 1992.
4. B. Benhamou, L. Sais, and P. Siegel. *Two proof procedures for a cardinality based language.* in proceedings of STACS'94, Caen France.
5. A. Colmerauer. *An introduction to prolog III.* CACM, **4(28)**:412–418, 1990.
6. C. Cubbada and M. D. Mouseigne. *Variantes de l'algorithme de SL-Résolution avec retenue d'information.* PhD thesis, GIA Luminy (Marseille), 1988.
7. M. Dincbas, P. V. Hentenryck, H. Simonis, A. Aggoun, T. Grof, and F.Berthier. *The constraint logic programing language CHIP.* In the International Conference on Fifth Generation Computer Systems, Tokyo, Japon, December 1988.
8. P. V. Hentenryck and Y. Deville. *The cardinality operator: A new logical connective for constraint logic programming.* Technical report, CS Departement, Brown University, Technical Report, october, 1990.
9. J. Jaffar and J. L. Lassez. *Constraint logic programing.* POPL-87,Munich, FRG, January 1988.
10. J. Jaffar and S. Michaylov. *Methodology and implementation of a clp system.* In proceedings of fourth International Conference on Logic Programing, Melbourne,Australia, May 1987.
11. R. Kowalski and D. Kuehner. *Linear resolution with selection function.* Artificial Intelligence, **(2)**:227–260, 1971.
12. D. W. Loveland. *A linear format for resolution.* In Springer, editor, Lecture notes in computer science, **125**, 1970.
13. J. A. Robinson. *A machine-oriented logic based on the resolution principle.* **JACM, 12**, pages 23–81, 1965.

BOOLEAN CONSTRAINT PROPAGATION NETWORKS

GEORGI MARINOV   joro@sirma.bg

Sirma AI Ltd., 38A Hristo Botev Blvd, fl 4, apt 14, Sofia 1000, Bulgaria

VLADIMIR ALEXIEV[†]   vladimir@cs.ualberta.ca

Dept Comp Sci, 615 GSB, University of Alberta, Edmonton, AB T6G 2H1, Canada

YAVOR DJONEV   70751.2405@CompuServe.com

SIRMA International, 5-563 Riverdale Ave, Ottawa, ON K1S 1S3, Canada

ABSTRACT

This paper describes a particular inference mechanism which has been successfully used for the implementation of an expert system and a generic shell supporting consulting-type expert systems. The main features of Boolean Constraint Propagation Networks (BCPN) are: the inference flows in all directions, unlike inference modes of forward or backward chaining systems; all possible consequences of a fact are derived as soon as the user enters the fact, therefore the system is very interactive; if the user withdraws an assertion then all propositions depending on it are retracted; the inference architecture is simple and uniform. After a general description of BCPN we give an account of the problems encountered and the approaches we used to solve them. Some possible extensions of the mechanism and its applicability to various areas are also discussed. The current version of BCPN is written in C++ and took about one man-year to develop.

Keywords: constraint propagation, inference engine, knowledge-based system, expert system.

1. Introduction

Expert systems have been around for more than two decades now. There exist a vast variety of architectures for Knowledge-Based Systems, most of which have quite sophisticated and complex control strategies. This variety is motivated by the very different properties which application domains possess (for example backward chaining is probably suitable for a diagnosing ES but unsuitable for an automated design system). Below we describe the type of applications for which BCPN seems an appropriate inference mechanism.

A *consulting-type* ES possesses a large body of knowledge in a particular domain and tries to clarify a certain situation and interpret it according to that knowledge in collaboration with the user. For example many people experience difficulties interpreting taxation laws because of the large volume of these norms and they need

---

[†] Supported by a University of Alberta PhD Scholarship.

help for the task of filling tax returns. The knowledge is not very complex (typically inferences are not very deep) but the knowledge base consists of about 100,000 atomic facts. Such an expert system may interact either directly with the user on a personal computer or indirectly through a public service officer serving as a mediator. Another possible application domain is helping an air travel agent to find the best ticket fares, and so on.

Domains like these are characterized by the fact that it is not known a priori what kind of data the user may possess and therefore it is hard to predict the direction of the inference process. So it seems appropriate to assume that *every* direction is feasible and to give the initiative in the hands of the user. Furthermore, it is very useful to indicate to the user every inference as soon as it is made, so that s/he* knows where the problem-solving is going and can adjust his/her line of thought correspondingly. The user is never pressed for an answer: s/he simply states what s/he knows and sees relevant for the task.

The BCPN is constructed automatically by translation from a knowledge representation scheme that is convenient for the knowledge engineers to use to a network of objects. We do not address the issue of translation in this paper.

The rest of the paper is organized as follows. Section 2 describes the basic BCPN architecture and propagation process, the procedure for withdrawing previously stated propositions, the conflict resolution strategy and a goal propagation scheme. Section 3 describes certain problems we encountered with BCPN and some proposed solutions. Section 4 discusses two possible extensions to the basic BCPN architecture. Section 5 contains some concluding remarks and comparison with other well-known approaches.

2. Boolean Constraint Propagation Networks

This section gives a basic description of the BCPN and the inference process in BCPN. We leave some of the more sophisticated matters for subsequent sections.

2.1. The BCPN Architecture

A BCPN (in accordance with Winston[1]) is an undirected bipartite graph consisting of two alternating types of nodes: *propositions* represented by squares and *operations* or *gates* represented by ovals. A sample BCPN is shown on Fig. 1.

Every proposition corresponds to an atomic assertion (*e.g.* MaritalStatus= married) entered by the user (in which case it is called a *fact*) and/or inferred by the system. Propositions can be in one of the three states True, False and Unknown. Unlike *e.g.* Doyle's[2] approach, no Contradiction state is allowed because contradictions are not tolerated and are removed immediately (see Section 2.4). Operations bind the propositions and constrain the possible combinations of states. It is important to note that although the output pins of the gates are marked by arrows, the information can flow in all directions and not only along the arrow.

---

* S/he stands for he/she.

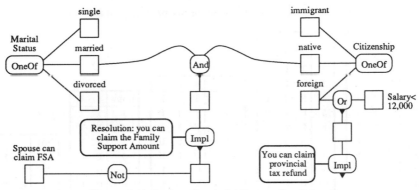

Figure 1: A Boolean Constraint Propagation Network

Impl (stands for *implication*) gates represent rules in the knowledge base. When the input proposition of a rule is established to T, the rule *fires* and an attached list of *resolutions* is printed and/or a list of *actions* is carried out. These resolutions/actions are not part of the BCPN itself (the logic part of the system) but of the Knowledge Base. KB and BCPN form two separate levels of the system and the inference is independent on the additional features of the KB objects. Every parameter and condition imposed on parameter values have a corresponding proposition but the KB objects have additional properties: set of allowed values, prompt, *etc.* On the other hand, there are intermediate propositions which do not correspond to any KB object and are not directly user-accessible (the ones which do not have a label on the figure). Such propositions are generated during the compilation of boolean expressions representing the relations between KB objects.

2.2. *Propagation of Boolean Values*

The inference process in BCPN is a process of *propagation*. When the user enters a new fact through the user interface, the corresponding proposition is changed and notifies all operations connected to it about the change. These operations check whether the change affects some of their other pins and if so, notify them appropriately. In turn these propositions change their values and repeat the procedure recursively. A "wave" of changing propositions forms and propagates through the network. In order to avoid this wave going back immediately to its initiator (something like a recoil) and to avoid infinite recursion, there is a flag in each proposition signifying whether it is under propagation. We should note that the user can set a proposition to U, that is to withdraw a fact stated earlier. For ease of understanding we explain this in the next section, though it uses basically the same propagation mechanism.

Table 1 shows all allowed value combinations for the gates. Of these only OneOf needs some explanation: it postulates that exactly one of its pins should be T (it is something like a multi-arity Not) and is used for parameters with mutually exclusive allowed values.

Table 1: The operations And, Or, OneOf, Impl, and Not.

And	a	b	c
1	T	T	T
2	T	F	F
3	T	U	U
4	F	T	F
5	F	F	F
6	F	U	F
7	U	T	U
8	U	F	F
9	U	U	U
10	U	U	F

Or	a	b	c
1	T	T	T
2	T	F	T
3	T	U	T
4	F	T	T
5	F	F	F
6	F	U	U
7	U	T	T
8	U	F	U
9	U	U	U
10	U	U	T

OneOf	a	b	c
1	T	F	F
2	F	T	F
3	F	F	T
4	F	U	U
5	U	F	U
6	U	U	F
7	U	U	U

Impl	a	b
1	T	T
2	F	T
3	F	F
4	F	U
5	U	T
6	U	U

Not	a	b
1	T	F
2	F	T
3	U	U

The last (tenth) lines of the And and Or tables do not represent a valid combination for a three-valued logic gate because if both inputs of a gate are in the third (U) state then so should be the output (which situation is already accounted for in line 9). But BCPN is different from Three Valued Logic: if the output of an And is established to F then BCPN cannot deduce anything better than U for either of the inputs. We just know that one of them must be F but we cannot tell which one. We will see later in Section 3.1 that these "illogical" situations cause problems. This is due to the fact that And and Or are not reversible operations: they lose information.

For efficiency reasons and to be able to easily increase the arity of operations, we have not implemented the gates using these tables but rather like explicit algorithms. For example the algorithm for And is like this: "If one of the inputs is F then set the output to F; if all inputs are T then set the output to T; if the output is T then set all inputs to T; if all pins except one have values, then set it to F" (the last two clauses propagate from output to input).

The propagation stops in a certain direction under one of the following conditions:

1. It enters a region of all-U propositions and has insufficient information to continue through this region.

2. It tries to set a proposition with a certain value but discovers that the proposition already has that same value.

3. It reaches a node that is already under propagation.

The first case is significant for large knowledge bases. Such KBs are naturally divided into modules (*topics*) which are loaded in memory as indivisible units. Propagation often will not pass the boundary of a topic because topics are linked weakly. In a typical consultation the user enters just a small amount of facts and only a small part of the KB and the underlying BCPN is activated. This is what makes the approach scalable.

2.3. Propagation of Unknown

The system supports withdrawal of previously stated assertions. All consequences of the cancelled fact should also be cancelled. To facilitate this, dependency information (*justifications*) is maintained, similar to Doyle's TMS.[2] First, all facts entered by the user get marked as such. Second, *arrows* which link propositions and operations are introduced and BCPN becomes a directed graph (Fig. 2).

There is an arrow from an operation to a proposition if the operation has set (or tried to set) that proposition's value; there is an arrow going the other way if the value of the proposition caused (or tried to cause) a change at some of the other pins of the gate. It is possible to have arrows going both ways in the case the user enters (confirms) already inferred data (*e.g.* the rightmost gate on Fig. 2).

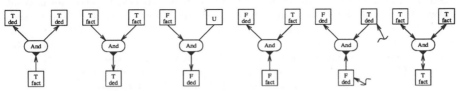

Figure 2: Some of the possible support states for And

An important design consideration for BCPN is that the order of presentation of facts should have no impact on the BCPN state, only the set of facts should. We paid particular attention to save this property and this is why the clauses (or tried to set) in the previous paragraph are there (see the second propagation-stopping condition in the previous subsection).

The dependency arrows can always be computed anew starting from the founding facts but it is more efficient to cache them explicitly.

When a proposition is to be set to U (that is, unset), it first checks whether it is a fact. If this is not so (it is *deduced*) then nothing happens, because even if the user says "I don't not know what this value is," the system knows it. If however it is a fact, then its "fact" flag is cleared. Then the proposition checks whether there are some propositions which support it (through neighboring operations) and who themselves are supported by still existing facts (they are "well-founded"). This is done by propagating the question "Are there any facts supporting you?" recursively. It would not be enough to check locally for outside support because there may be a loop of propositions supporting one another (circular support) which used to be justified by the withdrawn fact and now is to be broken. The same fact-gathering mechanism is used for conflict resolution, as described in the next subsection.

If there are no supporting facts then the proposition eventually becomes U and notifies all neighbor operations of the change. If some of them cease to support some of their other pins then they will propagate the wave of Us further.

This is a bit complicated. We considered the simpler approach to reset the network and restate all remaining facts anew. This is not obviously infeasible because all the propagation is localized in a small part of the network. But if the user has stated, say, 25 facts then s/he would have had to experience a 25 times bigger delay than the normal interaction delay, which may be intolerable.

2.4. Conflict Resolution

When the system or the user tries to change a proposition from a definite (non-U) state to the opposite state, a conflict situation occurs. It has to be resolved by withdrawing some of the clashing facts. The system cannot do this by itself because it does not know which of these are actually true / of higher priority. (Unlike ATMS[3], the system never makes assumptions itself.) What it can do is to present the user with the conflicting facts and ask him/her to choose. These facts are being collected starting from the point of conflict by (almost) the same support-collection algorithm described in the previous subsection. The difference is that here we need not only an answer to the question "Does anybody support you?" but the set of support itself. The set of support has and And/Or-tree structure: the Ts on the inputs of an And gate support the T on the output in a different manner then they would in an Or gate. Namely, in the And case the Ts are both needed, while in the Or case either one suffices. Therefore if one wishes to turn the output to U one will have to unset either of the inputs in the former case and both of them in the latter case.

This structure can be represented either by the traditional And/Or-tree or by putting different types of lines in the margin, like for a system of equations (Fig. 3). The latter would make the interface simpler, but if we want to avoid duplication of propositions (for example fact1 and fact3 might be the same proposition) then we will have to adopt the tree scheme and generalize it to an acyclic graph.

Figure 3: Alternative representations of And/Or structure

In either case, the user simply points which branch (or both) of an Or node s/he would like to cancel. The point of conflict corresponds to the root of the tree and is an Or node: one of the two "parties" supporting the two conflicting values should resign.

2.5. Goal Propagation

The goal of a consultation is to reach some conclusion. All possible conclusions (outcomes of a consultation) in the domain under consideration are known a priori: they are the resolutions attached to Impl operations (rules). Therefore it is possible to advise the user what (additional) information s/he should supply in order to reach certain conclusion(s). Namely, this is the And-Or tree of (yet not established) facts which would support a T in the input proposition of the Impl. Collecting this tree is different from the collection process for conflict resolution because the facts are not stated yet and therefore no support arrows exist. Fortunately such a structure can be generated based solely on the logical properties of the gates and the structure of the BCPN. The process stops at propositions which are linked to the higher level (KB) and thus accessible to the user. If the user does not know the value of such terminal proposition, s/he may opt to ask further what other propositions should be set to infer the value of the terminal proposition.

This "goal propagation" corresponds in some sense to backward propagation in traditional ES.

3. Problems with BCPN

In this section we describe the problems we have identified in BCPN and possible approaches for their solution.

3.1. Employing Constraint Satisfaction

The most important problem is that sometimes propagation alone is not sufficient to infer everything deducible. An example is given on Fig. 4 (this situation presents two Or gates in state 10 from Table 1). Propositions d and e say that $a \vee b = $ T and $b \vee c = $ T. The OneOf gate says that a and c cannot both be T. Thus, the only possibility is $b = $ T and $a = c = $ F. But this cannot be inferred by propagation of the two T values in d and e.

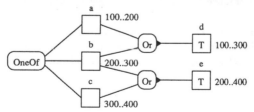

Figure 4: How to deduce that b=T from the given information?

This is not a purposely contrived configuration, it appears naturally when representing numeric values (see Section 4.2; do not pay attention to the numbers on the figure yet).

Therefore some other methods should be employed to amend this deficiency. They can be called *Constraint Satisfaction* (as opposed to Constraint Propagation). An enormous amount of research has been performed in this area in connection with Constraint Satisfaction Problems (CSP)[4-6] and Constraint Logic Programming (CLP).[7] The main problem is to localize the constrained configuration both spatially (in a small part of the BCPN) and temporally (at a certain moment in time).

Because of the large size of the network, standard backtracking approaches to CSP are inappropriate. Some approaches from CSP seem applicable, *e.g.* interchangeability,[8] articulation nodes.[9] Also relevant are approaches from CLP, *e.g.* arbitrary boolean expressions are supported and solved in Prolog III.[7,10] But the allowable systems of constraints in Prolog III are much smaller than the size of BCPN, and the scalability of that method is questionable.

An approach in the spirit of ATMS[3] would be the system to assume each one of T and F for a proposition and see whether both set some other proposition(s) to some definite values. However it is infeasible to trigger such tests before the constrained situation is localized, and the approach gives no hint in this respect.

We came up with a simple solution presented on Fig. 5. An auxiliary And gate is added during compilation which "injects" the correct value into b as soon as d and e are set to T. This solution eliminates the temporal localization problem and does not impose any changes to the inference mechanism. But it increases the size of the BCPN and furthermore it is not quite clear (yet) how to identify where such additional gates are needed (except for some standard configurations like intersected numeric intervals; see Section 4.2). In other words, the spatial localization problem remains.

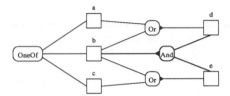

Figure 5: A simple solution: adding an And gate

We hope this is not very much of a problem because it occurs rarely and because it only concerns the completeness of the deduction but not its soundness. As a consolation, the strength of BCPN is in the propagation, not in the satisfaction.

3.2. BCPN Verification and Optimization

Typically BCPN contains a lot of redundancies: a proposition can be set from another proposition by many different (and sometimes implying each other) paths. Such redundancies are not immediately obvious to the knowledge engineers and they create a lot of unneeded links "just to be sure". A similar problem is a closed loop of propositions which imply each other. In this case they all can be reduced to a single node. A third related problem is a permanent conflict: two chains of propositions which would always imply opposite values at a certain node. This is an inconsistency in the KB which should be detected at compile time. Other things to check for are unconnected nodes, not fully connected operations, *etc.*

At runtime similar redundancies and inconsistencies are normally present and cause no harm because they are conditional upon a certain combination of "controlling" propositions. For example, if an input of an And (the "controlling" one) is T then the And transmits transparently and bidirectionally between its other input and its output which creates conditions for redundant/inconsistent loops. But static redundancies/inconsistencies should be detected by a preprocessing verifier and reported to the knowledge engineer. This program should also try to factor out common subnetworks. Its job may also include *introducing* redundancies to implement the solution mentioned in the previous subsection.

Currently we only implemented a simple common-subexpression eliminator which takes into account only some of the algebraic properties of the operations (commutativity, associativity) but not their logical properties.

4. Possible Extensions to BCPN

4.1. Temporal Reasoning

Temporal reasoning can be incorporated in BCPN with relative ease. One can attach to each proposition a history list holding its values from the past with time tags attached to them. It would be profitable to have distributed (nonuniform) time because typically only a small number of gates triggers at a given propagation cycle (which corresponds to an instant of the simulated time). This is similar to the approach adopted in modern electrical simulators where the time granularity is finer in the more active areas of the circuit and coarser in the passive ones. The user should be able to inspect and modify these history lists, though it would be more convenient for him/her to do so in a uniform manner (by setting the global time). If a user decides to "change the history" in some past moment then all history lists affected should be reevaluated from that moment onward. Hopefully this reevaluation will not have to go up to the present (at least not for all propositions) because the old and the changed histories may converge at an earlier point. More importantly, it will not spoil the aforementioned spatial locality of change.

The only real problem is to incorporate *rules* that access histories. Some language should be adopted for describing such temporal rules (*e.g.* "If your salary two years ago was $10,000 then ... ") and they are to be implemented in the inference engine. An obvious way to go without it is to define a separate parameter `Salary2YearsAgo`, but this is clumsy.

4.2. True Numeric Variables

Currently BCPN supports only numeric variables which are reduced to a set of ranges connected by `OneOf`. Now the problem from Section 3.1 (Fig. 4) appears naturally if there are two independent scales over which a numeric variable has some relevance. For we will have to intersect the two scales to get the atomic intervals a, b and c and then `Or` them to reconstruct the original intervals d and e. If the user has stated that the parameter is both between $100...300$ and $200...400$, then the program should be able to intersect d and e and deduce that the value is between $200...300$, that is in b.

5. Concluding Remarks

We described a simple but powerful inference architecture which is useful for building highly-interactive Knowledge-Based Systems in simply-structured yet very large domains.

In contrast to the TMS approach of Doyle,[2] the BCPN module provides not only truth maintenance (actually, justification maintenance), but also truth inference (propagation). The knowledge that the BCPN module has about logic gates allows it to optimize justification maintenance and use basically the same algorithms for both justification maintenance and propagation (the similarity of T/F-propagation and U-propagation mentioned in Section 2).

During our development we found that the standard constraint satisfaction approaches are unsuitable for BCPN due to its large size and relative sparseness of constrained situations.

An important property of BCPN is that since the density of connections does not depend on the KB size, the speed of the propagation (nodes/second) is independent on the KB size. Furthermore real KBs are "chunked" in a number of loosely connected parts so the average "free run" of the propagation is also independent on the KB size. This makes the propagation cycle and response times independent of the KB size, thus the approach is well-scalable.

BCPN is the base of the *Intelligent Workstation* project of *Sirma International*. The current version of BCPN is written in C++ and took some one man-year to develop.

Acknowledgements

Vesselin Kirov of Sirma AI participated actively in the development of Goal Directed Activation. One of the authors is grateful to the University of Alberta for providing the equipment to produce this paper.

References

1. P. Winston, *Artificial Intelligence*, 2nd ed., (Addison-Wesley, Reading, MA, 1984), ch. 4.
2. J. Doyle, A Truth Maintenance System, *Artificial Intelligence* **12** (1979) 231-272.
3. J. de Kleer, An Assumption-based TMS, *Artificial Intelligence* **28** (1986) 127-162.
4. A.K. Mackworth, J.A. Mulder and W.S. Havens, Hierarchical Arc Consistency: Exploiting Structured Domains in Constraint Satisfaction Problems, *Computational Intelligence* **1** (1985) 118-126.
5. E.C. Freuder, A Sufficient Condition for Backtrack-Free Search, *Journal of the ACM* **29(1)** (1982) 24-32.
6. I. Rivin and R. Zabih, An Algebraic Approach to Constraint Satisfaction Problems, *Proc. IJCAI'89*, 284-289.
7. A. Colmerauer, An Introduction to Prolog III, *Comm. of the ACM* **33** (1990) 69-90.
8. E.C. Freuder, Eliminating Interchangeable Values in Constraint Satisfaction Problems, *Proc. AAAI'91*, 227-233.
9. R. Dechter and J. Pearl, Network-Based Heuristics for Constraint Satisfaction Problems, *Artificial Intelligence* **34** (1988) 1-38.
10. W. Büttner and H. Simonis, Embedding Boolean Expressions into Logic Programming, *Journal of Symbolic Computation* **4(3)** (1987) 191-206.

AN ACCEPTOR FOR
ALLEN'S ORD-HORN SUBCLASS

Amar ISLI

LIPN - CNRS URA 1507, Institut Galilée, Université Paris XIII
Av. J.B. Clément, 93430 Villetaneuse, France
email: isli@lipn.univ-paris13.fr

Abstract

Allen's ORD-Horn subclass is very expressive (868 elements), and has the advantage of being tractable. It is a simple matter of enumerating it. However, testing whether an Allen's relation belongs to this subclass, especially when this has to be done for each constraint of an Allen's network, may take much time if we proceed by comparing the given relation to all of the 868 elements of the subclass. We propose in this paper a reasonable-size acceptor which accepts exactly the language consisting of this Allen's subclass. Another motivation of this work is that we strongly believe that the subclass can be used for designing an optimal backtrack algorithm for the consistency problem of full Interval Algebra.

1 Introduction

The minimal labeling problem (henceforth MLP) and the computationally equivalent consistency problem of an Allen's network have been shown NP-complete ([7, 8]). Allen ([1]) proposed the use of an approximate algorithm, known in the literature as a constraint propagation algorithm, which is an adaptation of Mackworth's path-consistency algorithm PC-2 ([4]). This approximate algorithm which has the advantage of being tractable does however not guarantee exactness in all cases.

Allen's propagation algorithm is exact for both of the consistency problem and the MLP of the convex part of Interval Algebra (IA) ([2, 6]). It is also exact for the consistency problem of the pointisable part of the algebra which is a strict superset of the convex part ([6, 3]).

van Beek ([6]) gave an $\mathcal{O}(n^4)$-algorithm for the MLP of Vilain and Kautz's Point Algebra (PA) ([7]), and proposed the use of this result to design a backtrack algorithm for the MLP of full IA.

Nebel and Bürckert ([5]) found a very large Allen's tractable subclass, called Ord-Horn Subclass. Path-consistency is sufficient for the consistency problem of this subclass. Moreover, since the subclass contains all Allen's atomic relations and that the consistency problem is tractable, it follows that the minimal labeling problem is also tractable for this subclass.

Ord-Horn Subclass is a maximal tractable subclass; that is, all tractable subclass contains at most as many relations. This makes sense to address the question of whether one can use this subclass to design an optimal backtrack algoritm for the consistency problem and the MLP of full IA.

In this paper, we propose a reasonable-size acceptor for Ord-Horn Subclass. Our motivation is twofold. First, testing whether an Allen's relation lies in Ord-Horn Subclass may take much time if we proceed by comparing it to each of the 868 elements of the subclass. The second motivation is that we believe that our result can be used to decompose an Allen's relation into a minimal disjuction of relations lying in Ord-Horn Subclass; that is, write an Allen's relation R as $R = \bigcup_{i=1}^{k} R_i$ such that R_i belongs to the subclass, for all $i = 1 \cdots k$, and k is minimal. If if happened that this is possible, this would give an optimal backtrack algorithm for full IA.

2   Allen's Interval Algebra

Allen's interval algebra consists of thirteen exclusive atomic relations that may exist between a pair of intervals (see Figure 1). The adjective "exclusive" means that a pair of intervals' configuration stands in one and only one Allen's atomic relation. For expressing that two intervals are allowed to stand in either of a given number of atomic relations, we use the set of these relations. For instance, interval I is before, equal to or after interval J is expressed as $I\{<,=,>\}J$. However, when a relation consists of a single atomic relation, we omit the braces in its set representation.

Allen defined two operations on his algebra: intersection and composition of relations. Intersection consists of computing a final relation R between two intervals I and J, knowing that both relations R_1 and R_2 hold between I and J. Namely, R consists of the set of atomic relations common to both R_1 and R_2. While composition, it consists of computing the relation between two intervals I and J implied by the relations linking each of I to a third interval, and this third interval to J. For instance, if interval I overlaps interval K, and interval K is started-by interval J, this implies that interval I contains, is finished-by or overlaps interval J.

The composition, $r_1 \times r_2$, of two atomic relations is given by a 13×13-matrix ([1]). In general, the composition, $R_1 \times R_2$, of two Allen's relations is given by the union $\bigcup_{r_1 \in R_1, r_2 \in R_2} r_1 \times r_2$.

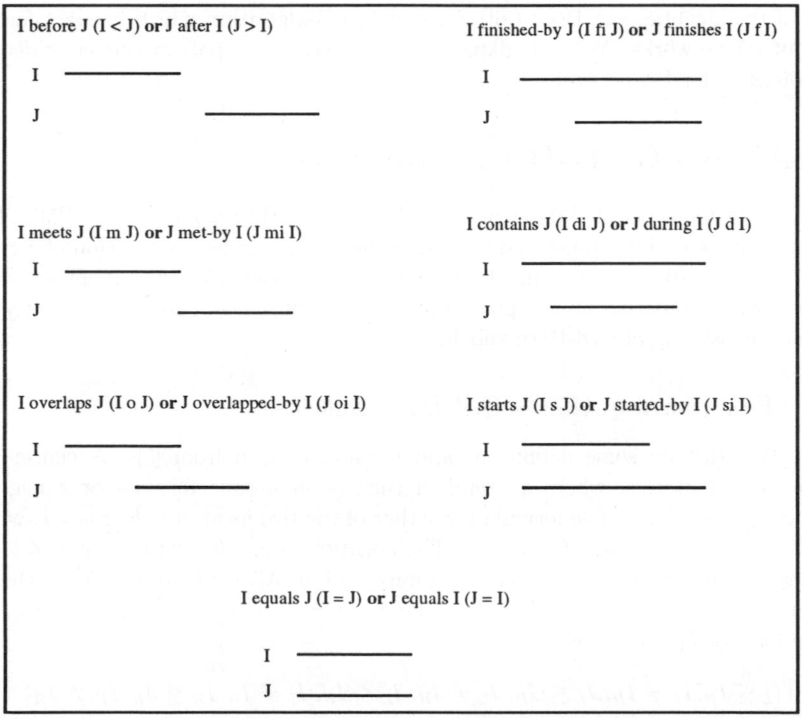

Figure 1: Allen's thirteen atomic relations.

3 Vilain and Kautz's Framework

Vilain and Kautz ([7]) considered the tractability of Allen's interval algebra ([1]). They showed that this algebra is NP-complete. They also defined a new temporal framework, which is "point algebra" (PA for short). PA contains three atomic relations, $<$, $>$ and $=$, that may exist between a pair of points, and PA-networks consist of binary temporal CSPs where the constraints are of the form $X\ R\ Y$, R being a qualitative relation, a subset of $\{<, >, =\}$, the set of the three atomic relations of the algebra. van Beek ([6]) gave an $\mathcal{O}(n^4)$-algorithm which is exact for the MLP of PA-networks. While Ladkin ([3]), he showed that path-consistency detects inconsistency for PA-networks.

4 Allen's ORD-Horn Subclass

For a more detailed description of Allen's Ord-Horn subclass, see ([5]). This subclass can be easily enumerated since it is the closure under intersection of a small set of Allen's relations containing 18 elements. It is precisely this 18-element set which will be used to construct an acceptor (a finite-state automaton) accepting exactly the language consisting of Ord-Horn subclass.

4.1 *Enumerating Allen's Ord-Horn Subclass*

We start by some definitions and notations taken from [5]. A clause is a disjunction of literals, where a literal in turn is an atomic formula or a negated atomic formula. An atomic formula has either of the two forms $a \leq b$ or $a = b$, where a and b denote endpoints of intervals. The negation of $a = b$ is written as $a \neq b$ and the negation of $a \leq b$ as $a \not\leq b$. The clause form of an Allen's relation IRJ is the set of clauses[1] over I's and J's endpoints' that is equivalent to IRJ. For instance, the clause form of $I\{d, o, s\}J$ is

$$\{I_L \leq I_R, I_L \neq I_R, J_L \leq J_R, J_L \neq J_R, J_L \leq I_R, J_L \neq I_R, I_R \leq J_R, I_R \neq J_R\}$$

where, for an interval I, I_L (resp. I_R) denotes its left (resp. right) endpoint. An Ord clause is a clause which does not contain negations of atoms of the form $a \leq b$; that is, such clauses only contain literals of either of the following forms:

$$a = b,\ a \leq b,\ a \neq b.$$

The Ord-clause form of an Allen's relation IRJ, written $\pi(IRJ)$, is the clause form of IRJ containing only Ord clauses.

---

[1] A set of clauses has the usual interpretation: it is a representation of the conjunction of its elements (clauses).

Number	Allen's relation	Ord-Horn form
0	$\{=,<,di,o,m,s,si,fi,\}$	$\{I_L \leq J_L\}$
1	$\{=,<,d,di,o,oi,m,mi,s,si,f,fi,\}$	$\{I_L \leq J_R\}$
2	$\{<,m,\}$	$\{I_R \leq J_L\}$
3	$\{=,<,d,o,m,s,f,fi,\}$	$\{I_R \leq J_R\}$
4	$\{=,>,d,oi,mi,s,si,f,\}$	$\{J_L \leq I_L\}$
5	$\{=,>,d,di,o,oi,m,mi,s,si,f,fi,\}$	$\{J_L \leq I_R\}$
6	$\{>,mi,\}$	$\{J_R \leq I_L\}$
7	$\{=,>,di,oi,mi,si,f,fi,\}$	$\{J_R \leq I_R\}$
8	$\{<,>,d,di,o,oi,m,mi,f,fi,\}$	$\{I_L \neq J_L\}$
9	$\{=,<,>,d,di,o,oi,m,s,si,f,fi,\}$	$\{I_L \neq J_R\}$
10	$\{=,<,>,d,di,o,oi,mi,s,si,f,fi,\}$	$\{I_R \neq J_L\}$
11	$\{<,>,d,di,o,oi,m,mi,s,si,\}$	$\{I_R \neq J_R\}$
12	$\{=,<,>,d,di,o,oi,m,mi,s,si,f,fi,\}$	$\{I_L \neq J_L \vee I_L \neq J_R\}$
13	$\{<,>,d,di,o,oi,m,mi,s,si,f,fi,\}$	$\{I_L \neq J_L \vee I_R \neq J_R\}$
14	$\{=,<,>,d,di,o,oi,m,mi,s,f,fi,\}$	$\{I_R \leq J_R \vee I_L \neq J_L\}$
15	$\{=,<,>,d,di,o,oi,m,mi,si,f,fi,\}$	$\{J_R \leq I_R \vee I_L \neq J_L\}$
16	$\{=,<,>,d,di,o,oi,m,mi,s,si,fi,\}$	$\{I_L \leq J_L \vee I_R \neq J_R\}$
17	$\{=,<,>,d,di,o,oi,m,mi,s,si,f,\}$	$\{J_L \leq I_L \vee I_R \neq J_R\}$

Figure 2: The set H of Allen's relations having an Ord-Horn form consisting of a single clause.

An Ord-Horn clause is an Ord-clause containing at most one positive literal, that is a literal of the form $a = b$ or $a \leq b$, and an arbitrary number of negative literals, that is literals of the form $a \neq b$.

An Allen's relation contains an Ord-Horn form if it contains a clause form containing only Ord-Horn clauses.

Allen's Ord-Horn subclass, call it $\mathcal{H}$ as in [5], is the set of Allen's relations having an Ord-Horn form. It is not difficult to see that $\mathcal{H}$ is the closure under intersection of the set, call it H, consisting of Allen's relations having an Ord-Horn form consisting of a single clause. The set H is depicted in Figure 2; it contains 18 elements.

5 An Acceptor For Allen's Ord-Horn Subclass

As already pointed to, we give in this section an acceptor accepting the language consisting of Allen's Ord-Horn subclass ([5]). The construction of the acceptor is straightforward from the method given above for enumerating the subclass. We start by giving some motivations of constructing an acceptor for Ord-Horn Subclass.

124

5.1 *Motivations*

Allen's Ord-Horn subclass contains 868 elements; this represents more than 10 percent of the full Interval Algebra (IA). Moreover, it has two advantages. The first is that it is tractable; that is, the consistency problem of an Allen's network restricted to this subclass is polynomial, and path-consistency is sufficient to solve it. The second is that since the consistency problem is tractable and that the subclass contains all Allen's atomic relations, it follows that the minimal labeling problem (MLP[2]) is also tractable. It follows that knowing whether an Allen's network lies in this subclass is important, since in the affirmative case we are ensured that path-consistency is sufficient for the consistency problem. However, if one has to compare each Allen's relation appearing in the network to all of the 868 elements of the subclass, this may take much time. While solving this membership problem using the acceptor we propose, it takes much less time since the acceptor size is reasonable. The second motivation of this work can be explained as follows. Ord-Horn subclass has been shown to be a maximal Allen's tractable subclass ([5]); that is, all Allen's tractable subclass contains at most as many relations. Moreover, it is the maximal subclass among the tractable subclasses containing all Allen's atomic relations. Hence the subclass is a good candidate for designing better backtrack algorithms than existing ones ([6]) for full IA. We conjecture that the work presented in this paper can be used to propose an algorithm decomposing an Allen's relation R into a minimal disjunction of elements from Ord-Horn subclass; that is, decomposing an Allen's relation into a disjunction $R = \bigcup_{i=1}^{k} R_i$ such that R_i belongs to the subclass, for all $i = 1 \cdots k$, and k is minimal. If it happened that this is true, this clearly would give an optimal backtrack algorithm for full IA.

5.2 *The Acceptor*

We now give the acceptor which straightforwardly follows from the method used for enumerating $\mathcal{H}$. The subclass $\mathcal{H}$ is the closure under intersection of H, the set of Allen's relations having an Ord-Horn form consisting of a single clause. The acceptor (see Figure 3) is a directed graph $A_{\mathcal{H}} = <H, E>$ defined as follows:

- the vertex set of $A_{\mathcal{H}}$ consists of the 18-element set H of Allen's relations having a one-clause Ord-Horn form, the closure of this set H under intersection giving, as already pointed to, Ord-Horn Subclass,

- the set of edges is as follows: a pair (A, B) of elements of H is an edge of $A_{\mathcal{H}}$ if and only if $(A \subset B$ and $(\forall C \ \neg(A \subset C \wedge C \subset B)))$.

---
[2]The problem of finding the minimal labels on edges of a network.

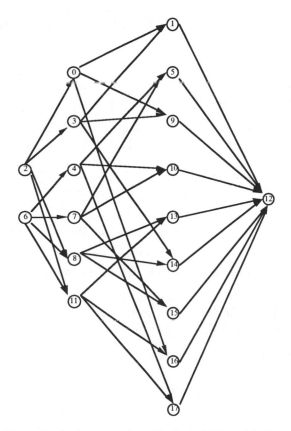

Figure 3: An acceptor for Allen's Ord-Horn Subclass.

A vertex of the directed graph, consisting of an element of H, is represented by its corresponding number shown in column 1 of Figure 2.

5.3   The Accepting Condition

We now give the accepting condition of our acceptor; that is, the condition for an Allen's relation to be accepted. For this purpose, let us denote by $p_1, p_2, \ldots, p_{24}$ the 24 3-edge paths of the acceptor (viewed as a directed graph). A path is represented by the sequence of its vertices. $p_1 = (2, 0, 1, 12), p_2 = (2, 0, 9, 12), \ldots, p_{24} = (6, 11, 17, 12)$. Testing whether an Allen's relation R is accepted is performed as follows:

- for each 3-edge path $p_i = (V_{i_1}, V_{i_2}, V_{i_3}, V_{i_4})$ $(i = 1, \ldots 24)$, compute the least index j_i $(j_i = 1 \cdots 4)$ verifying:

$$R \subseteq V_{i_{j_i}},$$

- then the relation R is accepted if and only if

$$R = \bigcap_{i=1}^{24} V_{i_{j_i}}.$$

5.4 *Simplifying The Acceptor*

The acceptor can be simplified as follows. For each vertex having $m > 1$ ingoing edges, drop $(m - 1)$ of these edges. The simplified form of the acceptor is given in Figure 4, and the accepting condition of an Allen's relation R by this final acceptor is as follows:

1. set S to A, the set of Allen's thirteen atomic relations: $S := A$;

2. for each path $p_i = (V_{i_1}, \cdots, V_{i_{n_i}})$, compute the least k, if any, belonging to $\{1, \cdots, n_i\}$ verifying $R \subseteq V_{i_k}$; and, in the case when such k exists, perform the following: $S := S \cap V_{i_k}$;

3. then the relation R is accepted if and only if $S = R$.

5.5 *Testing Whether An Allen's Relation Belongs to Ord-Horn Subclass*

The following theorem gives a necessary and sufficient condition for an Allen's relation to lie in Ord-Horn Subclass.

Theorem 1 *An Allen's relation lies in Ord-Horn Subclass if and only if it is accepted by the acceptor of Figure 4.*

Sketch of proof: If an Allen's relation is accepted then clearly it lies in Ord-Horn Subclass since it is equal to the intersection of Allen's relations having a one-clause Ord-Horn form. Suppose now that an Allen's relation R lies in Ord-Horn Subclass. Then $R = \bigcap_{i=1}^{k} R_i$, with R_i being an Allen's relation having a one-clause Ord-Horn form, for all $i = 1 \cdots k$. This clearly means that R_i belongs to the 18-element set H generating the whole Ord-Horn Subclass by closure under intersection. But the acceptor is constructed using H, and a set equal to the intersection of elements of H is accepted by this acceptor. ∎

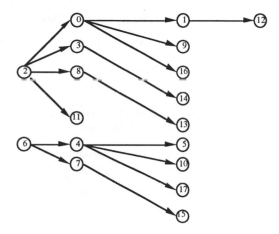

Figure 4: The simplified form of the acceptor for Allen's Ord-Horn Subclass.

6 Conclusion

We have been concerned in this paper with characterizing Allen's Ord-Horn Subclass ([5]) by giving an acceptor accepting exactly the language consisting of the elements of the subclass. Our motivation was twofold. First, the size of the subclass makes comptutationally hard to test whether a relation lies in the subclass, especially when this has to be done for each of the constraints appearing in a network. The second motivation is that since the subclass is a maximal tractable subclass ([5]), it makes sense to believe that the subclass can be used for designing an optimal backtrack algorithm for the full interval algebra; and we strongly believe that our result can be used for this purpose.

Ord-Horn Subclass has the advantage of being (1) tractable and (2) expressing a large class of problems. However, it only expresses qualitative information and suffers of its lack of expressing metric information. Our current interest is to address this problem of whether one can, without compromising tractability, extend the expressive power of the subclass by adding metric information such as "the distance separating objects A and B does not exceed 80 meters".

References

[1] **Allen, J.F.**, *Maintaining Knowledge About Temporal Intervals*, Communications of the ACM 26 (11) (1983) 832 − 843.

[2] **Granier, T.**, *Contribution à l'Etude du Temps Objectif dans le Raisonnement,*

Rapport LIFIA RR 716 − *I* − 73, Grenoble, France, (1988).

[3] **Ladkin, P.**, Unpublished manuscript, Kestrel Institute, Palo Alto, CA.

[4] **Mackworth, A.K.**, *Consistency in Networks of Relations*, Artificial Intelligence 8 (1977) 99 − 118.

[5] **Nebel, B. and Bürckert, H.J.**, *Reasoning about Temporal Relations: A Maximal Tractable Subclass of Allen' Interval Algebra.*

[6] **van Beek, P.**, *Exact and Approximate Reasoning about Qualitative Temporal Relations*, PhD thesis, University of Waterloo, Ontario, Canada, (1990).

[7] **Vilain, M. and Kautz, H.**, *Constraint Propagation Algorithms for Temporal Reasoning*, in Proceedings of the Fifth AAAI, Philadelphia, PA, (1986) 377−382.

[8] **Vilain, M., Kautz, H. and van Beek, P.**, *Constraint Propagation Algorithms for Temporal Reasoning: A Revised Report*, in D.S. Weld and J. de Kleer, eds., Readings in Qualitative Reasoning About Physical Systems, (1989) 373 − 381.

IV - MODAL LOGICS

RESOLUTION FOR WEAK MODAL LOGICS

STEPHANE DEMRI

LIFIA-IMAG, 46, Avenue Félix Viallet,

38031 Grenoble Cedex, France

ABSTRACT

We define modal resolution systems for the propositional weak modal logics C, CD, and CT. These systems are based on the Enjalbert and Fariñas Del Cerro's modal resolution systems with minor modifications. Roughly speaking, the axiom $\Sigma(\Diamond \perp, C) \to \perp$ is added if each disjunct of the clause C is a necessity formula ($\perp$ denotes the empty clause) and the simplification rule ($\Diamond \perp \approx \perp$) is deleted. Non clausal resolution systems are also presented for these weak modal logics. They are variants of Abadi and Manna's non clausal resolution systems. The new resolution systems are proved to be sound and refutationnally complete for these logics. The completeness proofs are inspired by the completeness proofs of the systems for normal modal logics with adequate modifications.

1 Introduction

Modal logics have shown to be a suitable tool for the formalization of numerous problems in the fields of Artificial Intelligence and Computer Science. In order to mechanize them, two approaches can be distinguished. The direct approach uses specific proof systems for modal logics. For example, resolution methods have modal versions (e.g. [4,1,3]). The translation approach roughly consists in translating non classical logics to (first-order, second-order ...) classical logic (e.g. [13,12,8]).

Among the non classical logics, weak* modal logics are of special interest since they do not admit in their axiomatic systems the necessitation rule† -see for example in [14] the so-called *regular* logics. If the operator $\Box$ is interpreted as a knowledge operator then the theoremhood of a formula does not entail that this fact is known. So, in the multiagent version of the weak modal logics C, CD, CT, CS4 and CS5 [14,6] the agents are not fully omniscient. That largely explains why these logics can be of special interest for Artificial Intelligence -see for example in [7,5] comprehensive studies about the knowledge operators. From the viewpoint of Automated Deduction, tableaux systems exists for these logics [6]. However there is a cruel lack since no resolution proof system has been defined for them.

The purpose of this paper is to define modal resolution systems for the propositional weak modal logics C, CD, CT (terminology used in [6]). The elegant resolution systems defined in [4] are modified for these logics. We emphasize that the systems in [4] can be

---

*For instance, the term 'weak' has been used in [11].

†If f is a theorem then $\Box f$ is a theorem.

naturally adapted to weak modal logics (it is not the least of their merits) and the results presented in [4] are used as much as possible in this work. Non clausal resolution systems are also presented for these logics. They use the systems defined in [1] for normal logics. In order to prove completeness the consistency properties defined in [6] are used. We therefore advice the reader to refer to [6] if needed. In that sense, this note *is not* self-contained. Along this note we shall very often refer to the works [1,4]. The reader is invited to compare the differences in the definitions and main results. Sometimes, the new definitions and the proofs of the propositions are presented to underline the differences with [1,4]. In that sense, the wish of the authors of [4] is partly fulfilled since even for weak modal logics *they have elaborated general techniques for establishing the completeness of decision procedures for modal logics.*

2 Weak Modal Logics

The source of the following definitions are [10,11,14]. We recall that the standard language for the propositional modal logics is the language of the propositional calculus with the additional unary operators $\square$ and $\Diamond$ (by definition $\Diamond A \equiv \neg\square\neg A$). Unlike the classical Kripke models [9], the models for the regular modal logics distinguish the *normal* worlds and the *queer* worlds.

Definition 2.1 *(Augmented Model) An augmented model is a 4-uple $\mathcal{M} = (W, Q, R, m)$ where W is a non-empty set of worlds, Q is subset of W (set of queer worlds), R is a binary relation on W called the accessibility relation and m is a function which assigns to each propositional variable p a subset $m(p)$ of W.*

Each world in $(W - Q)$ is said to be normal. Given a model $\mathcal{M}$, a world $w \in W$, and a formula A, the expression "w satisfies A in $\mathcal{M}$" ($\mathcal{M}, w \models A$) is defined as follows:
- $\mathcal{M}, w \models p$ iff $w \in m(p)$ for p a propositional variable,
- $\mathcal{M}, w \models \neg A$ iff not $\mathcal{M}, w \models A$,
- $\mathcal{M}, w \models A \wedge B$ iff $\mathcal{M}, w \models A$ and $\mathcal{M}, w \models B$,
- If $w \notin Q$, then $\mathcal{M}, w \models \square A$ iff $(\forall w' \in W, (wRw') \to (\mathcal{M}, w' \models A))$,
- If $w \in Q$, then $\mathcal{M}, w \models \Diamond A$.

A formula f is said to be *satisfiable* if there is an augmented model $\mathcal{M}$ and a world w in $\mathcal{M}$ such that $\mathcal{M}, w \models f$. A formula f is *valid in an augmented model* $\mathcal{M}$ iff for every world $w \in W$, $(\mathcal{M}, w \models f)$. A formula f is *valid* iff it is valid in every augmented model (noted $\models f$). When the operator '$\square$' is interpreted as an epistemic operator, the existence of queer worlds naturally entails that there are worlds where nothing is known and everything is believed.

The axiomatic system $C^\ddagger$ is defined as follows. An axiomatic system for the propositional calculus (resp. for the normal logic K [1]) can be the system below without the axiom scheme (4) and the regularity rule RR (resp. with the addition of the necessitation rule).

---

‡Without undesirable consequence for the sequel, it is assumed that a logic L is identified by an axiomatic system.

Axiom Schemes
(1) $A \Rightarrow (B \Rightarrow A)$; (2) $(A \Rightarrow (B \Rightarrow C)) \Rightarrow ((A \Rightarrow B) \Rightarrow (A \Rightarrow C))$
(3) $(\neg A \Rightarrow \neg B) \Rightarrow (B \Rightarrow A)$; (4) $\Box A \Rightarrow (\Box(A \Rightarrow B) \Rightarrow \Box B)$
Inference rules
MP (Modus Ponens) : $\frac{A \quad A \Rightarrow B}{B}$; RR (Regularity Rule): $\frac{A \Rightarrow B}{\Box A \Rightarrow \Box B}$

We write $\vdash_C A$ if A can be deduced by means of these axioms and inference rules.
Observe that if $\vdash_C A \Rightarrow B$ then $\vdash_C \Diamond A \Rightarrow \Diamond B$ [10].

Fact 2.2 [14] *A formula f is valid iff $\vdash_C f$.*

The systems considered in the present paper are the following:
• CD = C $\cup$ $\{\Box A \Rightarrow \Diamond A\}$, CT = C $\cup$ $\{\Box A \Rightarrow A\}$
• CS4 = CT $\cup$ $\{\Box A \Rightarrow \Box(\Box B \Rightarrow \Box A)\}$, CS5 = CS4 $\cup$ $\{\Box\top \Rightarrow (A \Rightarrow \Box\Diamond A)\}$
All these systems can be given a semantic interpretation in terms of augmented models.
As it is common for modal logics (e.g. [15]), each previously presented axiom scheme is
characterized by a property on the augmented models. Figure 1 recalls some properties
for augmented models. A formula f is said to be *P-valid* iff f is valid in any augmented
model satisfying the property P.

Notation	Name	Property
Refl	Reflexivity on normal worlds	$\forall w \in (W - Q), wRw$
Trans	Transitivity on normal worlds	$\forall x, y \in (W - Q), \forall z \in W(xRy) \wedge (yRz) \rightarrow (xRz)$
Sym	Symmetry on normal worlds	$\forall x, y \in (W - Q), (xRy) \rightarrow (yRx)$
Ideal	Idealization on normal worlds	$\forall x \in (W - Q), \exists y \in W, xRy$

Figure 1: Properties of Accessibility Relations

Fact 2.3 [14] *For any modal formula F, F is a theorem of CD (resp. CT, CS4, CS5)
iff F is Ideal-valid (resp. Refl, Refl+Trans, Refl+Sym+Trans).*

For any logic L in $\{C, CT, CD, CS4, CS5\}$, we use the standard definitions of *L-
satisfiability*, *L-validity* and *L-model* (e.g. CS4-valid stands for (Refl+Trans)-valid).

3 Clausal Resolution Systems

We use the definition of formulas in conjunctive normal form (CNF) and in disjunctive
normal form (DNF) defined in [4]. A modal formula is said to be in disjunctive normal
form (DNF) if it is a disjunction of the general form

$$L_1 \vee L_2 \vee \ldots \vee L_n \Box D_1 \vee \Box D_2 \vee \Box D_p \vee \Diamond A_1 \vee \Diamond A_2 \vee \ldots \vee \Diamond A_q$$

where the L_i's are literals, the D_i's are in DNF and the A_i's are in CNF. A formula
is in CNF if it is a conjunction of formulas in DNF. The symbol ',' is also used as a
conjunction operator. A *clause* is a modal formula in DNF.

Definition 3.1 *(Normal set of modal formulas, Necessity clause) A set of modal formulas is said to be normal iff it contains at least one necessity formula (of the form $\Box f$ or $\neg\Diamond f$). A necessity clause is a clause, different from the empty clause, such that each disjunct is a necessity formula.*

A necessity clause can only be satisfied in a normal world.

Proposition 3.2 *There is an effective procedure which, given any modal formula F, constructs a formula F' in CNF such that $\vdash_C F \Leftrightarrow F'$.*

The proof of this proposition is similar with the one for Proposition 1.3 in [4].

3.1 Resolution System for C

Like the system $\mathcal{R}K$ defined in [4], the system $\mathcal{R}C$ is composed of rules for computing resolvents, simplification rules and inference rules (by convention, the clausal resolution system for a logic L is noted $\mathcal{R}L$). The system $\mathcal{R}C$ is the system $\mathcal{R}K$ with the new axiom (A3) but without the simplification rule (S1):($\Diamond \perp \approx \perp$). Figure 2 presents the system $\mathcal{R}C$ (except the inference rules) with the notations used in [4]. Two relations are defined on clauses: C is a direct resolvent of A and B (noted $\Sigma(A, B) \rightarrow C$) and C is a direct resolvent of A (noted $\Gamma(A) \rightarrow C$). As in [4], the relation "A can be simplified in B" is noted $A \approx B$. It is the least congruence of the simplification rules (see Figure 2). For every formula F, there is a unique F' such that $F \approx F'$ and F' cannot be simplified further (F' normal form of F). We define $\Sigma(A, B) \Rightarrow C^{\S}$ (resp. $\Gamma(A) \Rightarrow C$) if there is some C' such that $\Sigma(A, B) \rightarrow C'$ holds (resp. $\Gamma(A) \rightarrow C'$) and C is the normal form of C'. The inference rules of $\mathcal{R}C$ are ($\frac{C}{D}$ if $\Gamma(C) \Rightarrow D$) and ($\frac{C_1, C_2}{D}$ if $\Sigma(C_1, C_2) \Rightarrow D$). We note $\vdash_{\mathcal{R}C}$ the deduction operator in $\mathcal{R}C$.

Simplification rules (S2) $\perp \vee D \approx D$; (S3) $\perp, E \approx \perp$; (S4) $(A \vee A \vee D) \approx (A \vee D)$

Axioms (A1) $\Sigma(p, \neg p) \rightarrow \perp$; (A2) $\Sigma(\perp, A) \rightarrow \perp$; (A3) $\Sigma(\Diamond \perp, C) \rightarrow \perp$ with C a necessity clause

Σ-rules $\vee - rule : \frac{\Sigma(A,B) \rightarrow C}{\Sigma(A \vee D_1, B \vee D_2) \rightarrow C \vee D_1 \vee D_2}$, $\Box\Diamond - rule : \frac{\Sigma(A,B) \rightarrow C}{\Sigma(\Box A, \Diamond(B,E)) \rightarrow \Diamond(B,C,E)}$

$\Box\Box - rule : \frac{\Sigma(A,B) \rightarrow C}{\Sigma(\Box A, \Box B) \rightarrow \Box C}$

Γ-rules $\Diamond - rule : \frac{\Sigma(A,B) \rightarrow C}{\Gamma(\Diamond(A,B,F)) \rightarrow \Diamond(A,B,C,F)}$; $\Diamond - rule2 : \frac{\Gamma(A) \rightarrow B}{\Gamma(\Diamond(A,F)) \rightarrow \Diamond(B,A,F)}$

$\vee - rule2 : \frac{\Gamma(A) \rightarrow B}{\Gamma(A \vee C) \rightarrow B \vee C}$; $\Box - rule : \frac{\Gamma(A) \rightarrow B}{\Gamma(\Box A) \rightarrow \Box B}$

A, B, C, D_1, D_2 denote clauses, E, F denote (possibly empty) sets of clauses and (A, E) denotes the result of appending the clause A to the set E. $\perp$ denotes the empty clause.

Figure 2: Resolution rules for $\mathcal{R}C$

Proposition 3.3 *(Soundness) (1) If $\Sigma(A, B) \rightarrow C$ then $\vdash_C A \wedge B \Rightarrow C$;*
(2)If $\Gamma(A) \rightarrow C$ then $\vdash_C A \Rightarrow C$; (3) If $S \vdash_{\mathcal{R}C} C$ then $\vdash_C S \Rightarrow C$

[§] From the context, '$\Rightarrow$' has to be understood either as a logical connective (implication) or as a derivation operator.

Proof: The proof is similar to the proof of Theorem 1 in [4] except that the following points must be established:

(i) If $\vdash_C A \Rightarrow B$ then $\vdash_C \Box A \Rightarrow \Box B$ (see the Regularity Rule) and if $\vdash_C A \Rightarrow B$ then $\vdash_C \Diamond A \Rightarrow \Diamond B$ (proof by an easy verification).

(ii) If $\Sigma(\Diamond \perp, C) \to C$ with C a necessity clause then $\vdash_C \Diamond \perp \wedge C \Rightarrow \perp$. The formula $\Diamond \perp \wedge C$ is C-unsatisfiable since $\Diamond \perp$ cannot be satisfied in any normal world and C cannot be satisfied in any queer world. Therefore $\Diamond \perp \wedge C \Rightarrow \perp$ is C-valid. Hence, from Fact 2.2, $\vdash_C \Diamond \perp \wedge C \Rightarrow \perp$. Q.E.D.

C-trees and Completeness We use the definition of trees defined in [4]. A tree is noted $(\mathcal{A}, \mathcal{T}, r)$ where $\mathcal{A}$ is the set of nodes, $\mathcal{T}$ is the binary relation on $\mathcal{A}$ and r is the root. In order to prove the completeness of $\mathcal{RC}$ we have to slightly modify the notion of K-trees [4].

Definition 3.4 *(C-tree) Let S be a set of clauses. A C-tree for S is a tree u whose nodes are sets of clauses such that (1) the root of u is S itself and (2) u is constructed by performing the operations 1 and 2 alternately until Operation 2 is inapplicable.*
Operation 1: *Repeat the following steps as long as possible:*
• *choose a leaf n of u and a clause C in n of the form $C_1 \vee C_2$,*
• *append two children to n, $(n - \{C\}) \cup \{C_1\}$ and $(n - \{C\}) \cup \{C_2\}$.*
Operation 2: *for each leave n of u*
• *if some propositional variable p, both p and $\neg p$ are in n, do nothing;*
• *otherwise we can write $n = \{L_1, \ldots, L_m, \Box A_1, \ldots, \Box A_k, \Diamond P_1, \ldots, \Diamond P_q\}$ -the L_i's are literals. If n is normal¶ ($k \geq 1$) then form the sets $n_i = \{P_i, A_1, \ldots, A_k\}$ for $i = 1, \ldots, q$ and append them as children of n. The n_i's are called the C-projections of n.*

The construction of a C-tree for a set of clauses always terminates. Moreover, a C-tree is said to be closed iff it satisfies the conditions for a K-tree to be closed [4]. Every node to which operation 1 has been applied is said to be of *type 1*. The others are of *type 2*.

Lemma 3.5 *If the set of clauses S has a nonclosed C-tree then S has a C-model.*

Proof: The proof is strongly inspired by the proof of Lemma 2.7 in [4]. However, a distinction must be operated in order to define the normal worlds and the queer worlds. A detailed proof is presented in order to convince the reader that the changes are very local. Let $u = (\mathcal{A}, \mathcal{T}, r)$ be a nonclosed C-tree for S. The trick of the proof is to build an augmented model from u. It can be easily seen by induction on the depth of u that there exists a subtree u' of u (in the sense of Definition 2.3 in [4]) such that (1) every node of u' is nonclosed, (2) every node of type 1 has exactly one descendant and (3) if w is of type 2, the children of w in u' are exactly the children of w in u.

Let ρ be the smallest equivalence relation containing the couples (w, w') of u' such that $w \mathcal{T} w'$ and w is of type 1. The equivalence class of w for this relation will be noted $|w|$. We define an augmented model $\mathcal{M} = (W, Q, R, m)$ such that (W, R) has a tree

---

¶See also the notion of normal branch defined in [6] p. 270.

structure:
- W is the set of equivalence classes of u' for ρ
- If $w' \in |w|$ and w' contains only literals or possibility formulas then $|w| \in Q$.
- for $|w|$ and $|w'|$ in W, $|w|R|w'|$ iff $|w| \neq |w'|$ and there are some $w_1 \in |w|$ and $w_1' \in |w'|$ such that $w_1 T w_1'$.
- $|w| \in m(p)$ iff $p \in w_1$ for some $w_1 \in |w|$

It can be shown by induction of the length of A that for every node w of u' and every A of w, $(\mathcal{M}, |w| \models A)$ holds. Only the case $A = \Diamond A_1$ is detailed here since the other cases are very similar with the proof of Fact 2.8 in [4] (for the case $A = \Box A_1$ the normality of $|w|$ has to be used).

There is a node w' of type 2 in $|w|$ such that $A \in w'$. Assume w' has a child. $|w|$ is normal and according to Operation 2, there is a child w'' of w' such that $A_1 \in w''$. By induction hypothesis, $\mathcal{M}, |w''| \models A_1$ and therefore $\mathcal{M}, |w'| \models \Diamond A_1$. Now assume w' has no child. $|w|$ is a queer world and therefore $\mathcal{M}, |w| \models \Diamond A_1$. As a consequence if r is the root of the tree, we have $\mathcal{M}, |r| \models S$ and $\mathcal{M}$ is a model for S. Q.E.D.

Lemma 3.6 *(Upward Lemma)*
(1) If $A_1, \ldots, A_n \vdash_{\mathcal{RC}} B$ then $\Box A_1, \ldots, \Box A_n \vdash_{\mathcal{RC}} \Box B$
(2) If $A_1, \ldots, A_n, Q_1, \ldots, Q_r \vdash_{\mathcal{RC}} B$ ($r \geq 1$, $n \geq 1$) and the proof uses at least one of the Q_i's then if $B \neq \bot$ then $\Box A_1, \ldots, \Box A_n, \Diamond(Q_1, \ldots, Q_r) \vdash_{\mathcal{RC}} \Diamond(B, Q_1, \ldots, Q_r, E)$ for some set E of clauses, otherwise $\Box A_1, \ldots, \Box A_n, \Diamond(Q_1, \ldots, Q_r) \vdash_{\mathcal{RC}} \bot$

Proof: The proof of (1) is identical with the proof of (i) of Lemma 2.9 in [4]. The first case of the proof of (2) - $B \neq \bot$ - is identical with the first case of the proof of (ii) of Lemma 2.9. If $B = \bot$, using the argument of (ii) we obtain that there exists a set E of clauses such that $\Box A_1, \ldots, \Box A_n, \Diamond(Q_1, \ldots, Q_r) \vdash_{\mathcal{RC}} \Diamond(\bot \wedge E)$. By using (A2), we get $\Box A_1, \ldots, \Box A_n, \Diamond(Q_1, \ldots, Q_r) \vdash_{\mathcal{RC}} \Diamond \bot$. By using (A3) we get $\Box A_1, \Diamond \bot \vdash_{\mathcal{RC}} \bot$. Q.E.D.

Corollary 3.7 *(Refutation)*
(1) If $A_1, \ldots, A_n, Q_1, \ldots, Q_r \vdash_{\mathcal{RC}} \bot$ ($n \geq 1$) then $\Box A_1, \ldots, \Box A_n, \Diamond(Q_1, \ldots, Q_r) \vdash_{\mathcal{RC}} \bot$.
(2) Let S be a set of clauses. If S has a refutable C-projection then S is refutable.

Proof: (1) Two cases have to be distinguished.
If $A_1, \ldots, A_n \vdash_{\mathcal{RC}} \bot$ then $\Box A_1, \ldots, \Box A_n \vdash_{\mathcal{RC}} \Box \bot$. By using the axiom (A2) and the $\Box\Diamond$-rule, $\Sigma(\Box \bot, \Diamond(Q_1, \ldots, Q_r)) \rightarrow \Diamond \bot$ holds. $\Sigma(\Box \bot, \Diamond \bot) \rightarrow \bot$ holds by using the axiom (A3). Hence $\Box A_1, \ldots, \Box A_n, \Diamond(Q_1, \ldots, Q_r) \vdash_{\mathcal{RC}} \bot$. Otherwise, if the proof of $\bot$ depends upon $Q_1, \ldots, Q_r$ then we apply Lemma 3.6(2).
(2) is an immediate consequence of (1). Q.E.D.

In Lemma 3.6 and Corollary 3.7 it is required that $n \geq 1$ whereas in the original results for $\mathcal{RK}$ in [4] n can be equal to zero (see Operation 2 in Definition 3.4).

Lemma 3.8 *In a C-tree, every closed node is $\mathcal{RC}$-refutable.*

The proof is identical to the proof of Lemma 2.11 in [4].

Proposition 3.9 *Any C-unsatisfiable set of clauses is $\mathcal{R}C$-refutable.*

Proof: Let S be an C-unsatisfiable set of clauses. By Lemma 3.5 its C-tree must be closed. By Lemma 3.8, its root S (closed) is $\mathcal{R}C$-refutable. Q.E.D.

3.2 Resolution for CD, CT

Figure 3 presents the additional rules[||] for the systems $\mathcal{R}CD = \mathcal{R}C \cup \{S_Q\}$, $\mathcal{R}T = \mathcal{R}CD \cup \{T-rule\}$ and $\mathcal{R}CS4 = (\mathcal{R}CT \cup \{S4\Box\Box - rule, S4\Box\Diamond - rule\})$. The rules S_Q,

---

$S_Q : (\Box \perp) \approx \perp$; $T-rule : \frac{\Sigma(A,B) \rightarrow C}{\Sigma(\Box A,B) \rightarrow C}$;

$S4\Box\Diamond\text{-rule:} \frac{\Sigma(\Box A,B) \rightarrow C}{\Sigma(\Box A, \Diamond(B,E)) \rightarrow \Diamond(B,C,E)}$ B, E contains a necessity clause

$S4\Box\Box - rule: \frac{\Sigma(\Box A,B) \rightarrow C}{\Sigma(\Box A, \Box B) \rightarrow \Box C}$ B is a necessity clause

Figure 3: Additional resolution rules for $\mathcal{R}CD$, $\mathcal{R}CT$, $\mathcal{R}CS4$

T-rule, S4$\Box\Diamond$-rule and S4$\Box\Box$rule have been defined in [4] but without the conditions on the necessity clauses.

Proposition 3.10 *Let L be a logic in $\{CD, CT\}$.*
(1) If $\Sigma(A, B) \rightarrow C$ then $\vdash_L A \wedge B \Rightarrow C$; (2) If $\Gamma(A) \rightarrow C$ then $\vdash_L A \Rightarrow C$
(Σ and Γ are defined according to the rules for each logic L)
(3) If $S \vdash_{\mathcal{R}L} C$ then $\vdash_L S \Rightarrow C$
(4) Any L-unsatisfiable set of clauses is $\mathcal{R}L$-refutable.

To prove this proposition, it is enough to combine the modifications of the previous section for the logic C with the modifications for Q, T in [4]. A preliminary version of this work stated the completeness and soundness of $\mathcal{R}CS4$. Until now, only the soundness has been proved. We conjecture the completeness of the system $\mathcal{R}CS4$ for CS4.

A resolution system for CS5 cannot be defined from a system for CT (as it has been done for RS5 with RT in [4]) since every CS5-formula is not equivalent to a formula without nesting of modal operators (for example $\nvdash_{CS5} \Box\Box A \Leftrightarrow \Box A$).

4 Non Clausal Resolution Systems

In [1], non clausal systems have been defined for first-order modal logics. One claim for non clausal resolution is that *the formulas do not need to be rephrased in unnatural and sometimes long clausal forms* [1]. In this section, we outline the definition of non clausal resolution systems for propositional logics C, CT, CD. We assume the reader familiar with [1] (for the non clausal resolution system for K) and with [6] (for the definition of *consistency property*). Herein, for brevity, the non clausal resolution system is detailed

---

[||]The new systems have the same inference rules than $\mathcal{R}C$ but they have different rules for computing resolvents and for simplification.

only for C. We note $\mathcal{NRK}$ the nonclausal resolution system defined in [1] for propositional logic K. We note $\mathcal{NRC} = (\mathcal{NRK} \backslash \{(\Diamond false \Rightarrow false)\} \cup \{(\mathcal{C}, \Diamond false \Rightarrow false)\}$ with $\mathcal{C}$ a necessity formula. Figure 4 presents the system $\mathcal{NRC}$. We recall that the

---

Simplification rules

$false \vee u \Rightarrow u$; $false, u \Rightarrow false$; $\mathcal{C}, \Diamond false \Rightarrow false$ with $\mathcal{C}$ a necessity formula (true-false simplification rules)

$\neg \Box u \Rightarrow \Diamond \neg u$; $\neg \Diamond u \Rightarrow \neg u$; $\neg(u \wedge v) \Rightarrow (\neg u \vee \neg v)$; $\neg(u \vee v) \Rightarrow (\neg u \wedge \neg v)$; $\neg \neg u \Rightarrow u$ (Negation rules)

$u, v \Rightarrow u$ (Weakening rule); $u, v_1 \vee \ldots \vee v_k \Rightarrow (u \wedge v_1) \vee \ldots \vee (u \wedge v_k)$ (distribution rule)

Inference rules

$A < u, \ldots, u >, B < u, \ldots, u > \rightarrow A < true > \vee B < false >$ (nonclausal resolution rule). The occurrences of u in A or B that are replaced by true or false, respectively, are not in the scope of any $\Box$ or $\Diamond$ in A or B.

$\Box u, \Diamond v \rightarrow \Diamond(u \wedge v)$

Figure 4: Resolution rules for $\mathcal{NRC}$

---

simplification rules replace formulas (use of the derivation symbol '$\Rightarrow$') whereas the inference rules add formulas (use of the derivation symbol '$\rightarrow$').

Proposition 4.1 $\mathcal{NRC}$ *is sound for the weak modal logic* C.

In the system $\mathcal{NRK}$ only the simplification rule ($\Diamond false \Rightarrow false$) is not sound for the weak modal logic C. Proof of Proposition 3.3 is sufficient to prove that $(\mathcal{C}, \Diamond false \Rightarrow false)$ with $\mathcal{C}$ a necessity formula, is sound for C.

Proposition 4.2 $\mathcal{NRC}$ *is complete for the weak modal logic* C.

Proof: Only differences with the proof of the completeness of $\mathcal{NRK}$ [1] are presented here. *Admissible* sets of sentences are defined as in [1] except that the system $\mathcal{NRC}$ is considered. More precisely, a set S of sentences is *admissible* (for C) if no finite conjunction of members of S can be refuted in $\mathcal{NRC}$. In order to show that admissibility is a *consistency property* (see [6] p. 282) if S is admissible then we have to check that if $\Diamond A \in S$ *and* S *is normal* then $S^{\sharp} \cup \{A\}$ is admissible. We recall that for the logic C, $S^{\sharp} = \{B \mid \Box B \in S\} \cup \{\neg B \mid \neg \Diamond B \in S\}$.

Assume $S^{\sharp} \cup \{A\}$ is not admissible. From the definition of *admissibility*, there is a finite sequence $\mathcal{S}$ of distinct elements of $S^{\sharp} \cup \{A\}$, namely, $B_1, \ldots B_k$, such that *false* can be derived from $\mathcal{S}$. If $A \notin \{B_1, \ldots B_k\}$ then after k applications of the rule $(\Box u, \Diamond v \rightarrow \Diamond(u \wedge v))$, the modal formula $\Diamond(B_1 \wedge \ldots \wedge B_k \wedge A)$ can be derived from $\Box B_1, \ldots, \Box B_k, \Diamond A$. From the hypothesis and with applications of the simplification rule $(u, false \Rightarrow false)$, $\Diamond false$ can be derived from $\Diamond(B_1 \wedge \ldots \wedge B_k \wedge A)$. The new simplification rule in $\mathcal{NRC}$ allows us to derive *false* (S is normal). So there is a finite sequence of distinct elements of S that can be refuted. Hence, S is not admissible. If $A \in \{B_1, \ldots B_k\}$ then a reasoning similar to the previous one can be used. Admissibility is a consistency property -other (non presented here) conditions also have to be checked- which entails that $\mathcal{NRC}$ is complete (see the full argument of this entailment in [1,6]). Q.E.D.

We define the nonclausal resolution system for CD (resp. CT) from the nonclausal resolution system for D (resp. T) [1] by deleting the simplification rule ($\Diamond false \Rightarrow false$) and by adding the simplification rule ($\mathcal{C}, \Diamond false \Rightarrow false$) with $\mathcal{C}$ a necessity formula. Soundness and completeness can be proved for these systems as it has been done for $\mathcal{NRC}$.

5 Conclusion

Clausal resolution systems for propositional weak modal logics have been defined from those defined in [4] for propositional normal modal logics. Minor but relevant modifications are provided to the original systems. Soundness and completeness have been proved. The techniques used in [4] have been used quite often, which confirms, once more, that they are general enough to handle a large class of propositional modal logics. The new proof systems can be easily implemented from an implementation of the systems for normal logics. Non clausal resolution systems have also been presented for these logics. They are variants of the systems defined in [1]. Completeness and soundness have also been proved. It should be noted that the clausal systems have more structural constraints on the applications of rules. However these constraints become an obvious asset from the viewpoint of Automated Deduction. We also conjecture that this work can be extended to the propositional logics CS4 and CS5 (see the system $\mathcal{RCS}4$ in Section 3.2).

Though only propositional logics have been considered in this work, we believe that the works in [12,8,3,1] can be extended to first-order weak modal logics. Furthermore, numerous complete strategies defined in [2] could be reasonably adapted to the modal resolution systems for weak modal logics. In other respects, every set of modal clauses containing clauses such that at least one disjunct is a possibility formula, is satisfiable in any queer world of any augmented model. Set of support strategies could therefore be adequate strategies for resolution systems for weak modal logics. However the completeness of the set of support strategy** remains an open question even for the resolution systems defined in [4]. These possibilities are presently under investigation.

Acknowledgment: The author wishes to express his thanks to Thierry Boy de la Tour for his useful comments and suggestions on earlier drafts of this paper.

References

1. M. Abadi and Z. Manna. Modal theorem proving. In J. H. Siekmann, editor, *CADE-8*, pages 172–189. Springer Verlag, LNCS 230, July 1986.

2. Y. Auffray, P. Enjalbert, and J-J. Herbrard. Strategies for modal resolution: results and problems. *Journal of Automated Reasoning*, 6:1–38, 1990.

**The proof for the completeness of the set of support strategy for the first-order classical logic presented in [16] cannot be straightforwardly adapted to the modal resolution systems. Similarly, though the subsumption strategy defined in [2] seems intuitively complete, the techniques used to prove the completeness of the subsumption for classical resolution cannot be used for the modal case. As noticed in [2], *the development of more powerful logical techniques* seems necessary.

3. M. Cialdea. Resolution for some first-order modal systems. *Theoretical Computer Science*, **85**:213–229, 1991.

4. P. Enjalbert and L. Fariñas del Cerro. Modal resolution in clausal form. *Theoretical Computer Science*, **65**:1–33, 1989.

5. R. Fagin, J. Halpern, and M. Vardi. A model-theoretic analysis of knowledge. *Journal of the Association for Computing Machinery*, **38**(2):382–428, April 1991.

6. M. C. Fitting. *Proof methods for modal and intuitionistic logics*. D. Reidel Publishing Co., 1983.

7. J. Y. Halpern and Y. Moses. A guide to the modal logics of knowledge and belief: preliminary draft. In *IJCAI-9*, pages 480–490, 1985.

8. A. Herzig. *Raisonnement automatique en logique modale et algorithmes d'unification*. PhD thesis, Université P. Sabatier, Toulouse, 1989.

9. S. Kripke. Semantical considerations on modal logics. *Modal and Many-valued logics, Acta Philosophica Fennica*, 1963.

10. S. Kripke. Semantical analysis of modal logic II: non-normal modal propositional calculi. In *Symposium on the Theory of Models, Amsterdam*, pages 206–220. North-Holland Publ. Co., 1965.

11. E. J. Lemmon. Algebraic semantics for modal logics I and II. *Journal of Symbolic Logic*, **31**(1-2):46–65, 191–208, June 1966.

12. H. Ohlbach. Optimized translation of multi modal logic into predicate logic. In A. Voronkov, editor, *LPAR'93*, pages 253–264. Springer-Verlag, LNAI 698, 1993.

13. E. Orlowska. Resolution systems and their applications I. *Fundamenta Informaticae*, **3**:253–268, 1979.

14. K. Segerberg. An essay in classical modal logic (three vols.). Technical Report Filofiska Studier nr 13, Uppsala Universitet, 1971.

15. J. van Benthem. Correspondence Theory. In D. M. Gabbay and F. Guenthner, editors, *Handbook of Philosophical Logic*, pages 167–247. D. Reidel Publishing Company, 1984.

16. L. Wos, G. Robinson, and D. Carson. Efficiency and completeness of the set of support strategy in theorem proving. *Journal of the Association for Computing Machinery*, **12**(4):536–541, 1965.

RELATIVE KNOWLEDGE AND BELIEF
SKL** PREFERRED MODEL FRAMES

MATIAS ALVARADO

e-mail matias@lsi.upc.es
Informatic Languages and Systems
Politecnique University of Catalonia
Pau Gargallo 5, 08028 Barcelona, Spain
Phone (34) (3) 401 69 94; Fax (34) (3) 401 70 14

ABSTRACT

Partial SKL^{**}-logic[2], based upon three valued logic of Kleene[8], provides a flexible framework to define, we hope in a suitable way, epistemic notions of **Knowledge, Belief, Aposteriori Knowledge** and the well related **Potential Knowledge**. Relations between these concepts are developed. The underling ideas in our definitions of knowledge and belief, are the same to those using the possible worlds semantics [5,6], but not yet the formalisation. Our definitions are constructive and recursive instead, and using the undefined truth value from SKL^{**}, it allows a not known or not believed status for a sentence.

1 Introduction

1.1 Possible Worlds Semantics and Logical Omniscience

For knowledge and belief, the possible world semantics has been attractive for its intuitive notion of making a discourse, not only of the *present* world but for any possible world[10]. The classical Kripke's possible worlds are sets of interpreted formulas, (*i.e.* sets of formulas and an arbitrary associeted interpretation). Worlds are related through an algebraical, usually reflexive, symmetric and/or transitive relation. If the true formulas in the actual world w_0 are also true in a world w, this last world is said to be possible from w_0 in the Kripkean model. However this is neihter a fair constructive nor *causal* relation and does not capture, in a sutiable way, the underling intuition to be *possible* or *conceivable* from the actual world.

Many logics of knowledge and belief that have used the semantics of possible worlds[6], consider the knowledge in the actual world w_0 as the true formulas in all the w_0-possible-worlds. If a formula φ is knowledge and ψ is a logical consequence of φ, then ψ is true in all the worlds in which φ does, and thus is knowledge too. So, all logical consequences of the initial knowledge is knowledge as well. This topic, known as *logical omniscience* is unintuitive to model *real* knowledge (belief) agents [13,17,20]. The logical omniscience agents should have unlimited time and informatic resources[17].

1.2 Possible Worlds: a New Proposal

The basic idea of our approach is inspired by the metaphor of an agent who *conceives* (or imagines) worlds which are possible in (or compatible with) the existing world, by means of a well-defined iterative process. This requires the existence of a *causal* relation between the agent's existing world and the world that he is capable of conceiving of on the basis of that world. Furthermore, it requires that possible worlds not be static, but the result of a dynamic process of creation and, therefore, dependent on the iterations which occur. In practice, these iterations will depend on the resources available. In accordance with the preceding, an agent's knowledge is conceptualised as a concept which is relative to the worlds which have been generated. This idea seems quite natural and adequately captures the intuition that knowledge is not static: it is being continually modified on the basis of experience. In relation to the reference world, the agent's knowledge in the nth iteration is constituted by those things which have been conceived of up to that iteration. In general, the total number of possible worlds can be finite or infinite.

For example, an agent can construct worlds by choosing from amongst distinct options which are presented to him. He can choose between getting married (P) and not getting married ($\neg P$). If he gets married, he must choose to have children (Q) or not to have them ($\neg Q$). If he does not get married, he has the option of working (R) or not ($\neg R$), etc.

In a general approach, each choice creates new possible worlds from the world in which the choice is made. This procedure for constructing worlds is highly intuitive and constitutes quite a natural conceptual model of how we, as human beings, go about defining our lives by *choosing from amongst possible options*. This idea is in accordance with that expressed in Kripke's work[10], in which it is observed that statements in possible worlds must be possible in the present world or consistent with the statements of that world.

The conceptual model presented can be formalised by considering worlds associated with partial —*not necessarily complete*[1]— interpretations related through a semantical *refinement* relation. The refinement is made interpreting a subset of undefined formulas in w_0. If the (actual) world w_0 is a set of formulas associated with a partial interpretation, we consider w possible or conceivable from w_0, if the set of true or false formulas in w_0 is a subset of the ones from w.

This is a more intuitive way making conceivable or possible a world w from a given w_0. Using partial interpretations, knowledge can be defined in accordance with the often real circunstance of incomplete actual information and limited resources. Whenever all the interpretation has been completed there is complete knowledge. But this is not a frequent case. The most of the times we have the ocurrence of partial knowledge, arising in the frequent situations with limited time and resources.

At this paper we explain the case of a single agent with a modal epistemic language $\mathcal{EL}$, in the partial three valued logic SKL**. The underground proof method is an extension of analytic tableaux. Moreover, the proposed procedure for to generat possible worlds is a iterative one. It can be based on classical rules for the expansion of analytic tableaux [19].

This paper is organized as follows, in section 2 a partial logic, namely the SKL**[2] is introduced. From this logic we outline our epistemic definitions in section 3, and a partial logic of knowledge and belief is developed with an example in section 4. Finally at section 5 we give paper conclusions.

2 SKL** Logic

In accordance with definitions of Langholm[12] for the Strong Kleene Logic, is defined the propositional language $\mathcal{L}$, consisting of a finite set of sentences p and the primitive connectives negation $\neg$ and disjunction $\vee$. From these are defined the conjunction $\wedge$ and implication $\rightarrow$ connectives in the classical way.

In order to define the language of SKL^{**} logic is added to $\mathcal{L}$ the *external negation* connective $\sim$, and from both negations are defined the nonprimitive connectives $L = \neg \sim$ and $M =\sim \neg^2$.

The semantical definitions for disjunction and negation connectives in the Strong Kleene Logic are given in Table 1 and 2, respectively. In Table 2 the semantical definitions of $\sim$, L and M in SKL^{**} are given.

Table 1

φ	ψ	$\varphi \vee \psi$
T	T	T
T	F	T
T	U	T
F	T	T
F	F	F
F	U	U
U	T	T
U	F	U
U	U	U

Table 2

φ	$\sim \varphi$	$\neg \varphi$	$\neg \sim \varphi \equiv L\varphi$	$\sim \neg \varphi \equiv M\varphi$
T	F	F	T	T
U	T	U	F	T
F	T	T	F	F

2.1 Partiality in SKL^{**}

Let $\mathcal{F}$ be the set of $\mathcal{L}$-formulas and i a valuation function from $\mathcal{F}$ to the $\{T, F, U\}$ set. The interpretation of T, F, U is **true, false** and **undetermined**. So, T and F

are determined values. The so called Degree-of-information (partial) order between the elements of $\{T, F, U\}$, is defined by $U \leq_i T$, $U \leq_i F$ and T, F are not comparable[2].

2.1.1 Definition (Partial interpretation)

A partial interpretation is a set $I = I^T \cup I^F \cup I^U$, so that I^T is the set of true formulas, I^F the set of false formulas and I^U the set of undefined formulas. When I^U is the empty set the interpretation is complete.

The informative order $\leq_i$ is extended on the set of partial interpretation Υ. Given an $I, I' \in \Upsilon$, $I \preceq_i I'$ is fulfilled if and only if $I^T \subseteq I'^T$, $I^F \subseteq I'^F$ and $I^U \supseteq I'^U$. The order $\preceq_i$ is a partial one on Υ.

The following formal structure taken from Doherty's work[2], provides a suitable framework in our intended definitions.

2.1.2 Definition (Model Frame)

A model frame is an ordered pair $\mathcal{M} = \langle \Upsilon, I \rangle$, where Υ is a (nonempty) set of interpretations and $I \in \Upsilon$ is the actual interpretation (*situation*). For any $I' \in \Upsilon$, we assume that $I \preceq_i I'$.

Notice that the initial interpretation I remaining fix through the succesive extension, constitutes an invariant and characterizes the model frame. The following definition of satisfaction is relative to a given model frame. This relativity is welcome in our aim to encourage the point of view considering knowledge and belief relative to actual information and context. So, the relativity at definning the capabilities of inference is imported from SKL**.

2.1.3 Definition (Satisfaction)

An interpretation $I \in \Upsilon$ in the model frame $\mathcal{M}$ satisfies a sentence $\varphi \in \mathcal{L}$, $I \models_{\mathcal{M}} \varphi$, if and only if $I(\varphi) = T$. Is said that the frame satisfies φ, $\mathcal{M} \models \varphi$, if every $I \in \Upsilon$ satisfies φ. For a set Γ such that any sentencence of Γ is satisfied by $\mathcal{M}$, is said that the frame $\mathcal{M}$ satisfies Γ, $\mathcal{M} \models \Gamma$

3 Knowledge and Belief in SKL^{**}

3.1 Context Relativity

At this section the notions of knowledge, belief and some related notions are defined. In SKL^{**}, definitions of satisfaction and entailment are relative to a given model frame $\mathcal{M}$. This relativity is manteined in our epistemic definitions: we propose that there is not *absolute* knowledge or belief, instead both are relative to the actual information and context.

A related point of view has been encouranged by Konolige[9], who defines agents of belief so that the set of agent's beliefs is the closed deduction from a initial set of premises and local (particular agent's) and efective inference rules. The Konolige's work is situated at the so called sentential approach[5].

More recently, Giunchiglia et al.[4] have defined non-omniscient context-based reasoning agents. They define the non-omniscience of agents of belief depending of several kinds of incompletness: language or basic facts or axioms or inference's rules, etc. The relatives agents' belief are defined from any one of these incompleteness. They contrast this agents respect the saturated or omniscient agents defined by possesing complete information and inference rules.

One of the more recent McCarthy's proposal[16] is intended with the formalization of **contexts**, defined through sets of information from which sentences are derived. Each context can be embedded in other one and conversely, each context is constituted by several contexts. McCarthy suggests some basic operations between contexts and provides motivations for its develope. In a cognitive sense he suggests to consider the individual mental states as *outer* contexts which provides the reasons (*pedegrees*) of each actual (*inner*) individual believe.

3.2 Knowledge K

The propositional language $\mathcal{L}$ is extended by adding the modal operators of **Knowledge** K, **Belief** B, **Potential Knowledge** K_p, and **Aposteriori Knowledge** K_{aps}. The language extended with these modal operators is called $\mathcal{EL}$ by epistemic language.

In some of the following definitions we take I' being a *direct succesor* of I. A direct succesor of I is a partial interpretation I' such that for any I'', $I \prec I'' \preceq I'$ then $I'' = I'$. In the satisfaction relation $I \models_{\mathcal{M}} \varphi$, whenever is clear the model frame $\mathcal{M}$ the subindex is ommited.

3.2.1 Definition (Knowledge)

A formula φ is knowledge in the model frame $\mathcal{M}$, $I \models_{\mathcal{M}} K(\varphi)$ if and only if,
1) $I \models_{\mathcal{M}} L(\varphi)$ or
2) $I \models_{\mathcal{M}} M(\varphi)$ and $I' \models_{\mathcal{M}} L(\varphi)$, $\forall I'$.

In 1) whenever the sentence φ is true at I, we can say that φ is *apriori* knowledge meanwhile the case 2) could be said the **Aposteriori Knowledge** $K_{aps}(\varphi)$. Depending on the context the distinction may be of interest. It is noted that the second condition subsumes the first one but not conversely. Thus, there are knowledge sentences $K(\varphi)$ that could be said factual *aposteriori* knowledge in I, regarding that φ is undefined at I but $L(\varphi)$ is satisfied at each I' (Fig. 1). They are considered knowledge in I too, although it has been *get on* latter.

Thus, eventually accepting the distinction between *apriori* and *aposteriori* knowledge, the knowledge could be consider the *summa* of them. The formal distinction is of interest to philosophical or epistemical approaches. In a context, the well known true sentences are the *apriori* knowledge. The true sentences arising at every possible world (situation) is the *aposteriori* knowledge. Inside our work the set of *apriori* knowledge sentences, are the initial true information.

There is some kind of defaults sentences about which we have special interest. They are the true sentences at all the direct succesors of I except at only one of them.

146

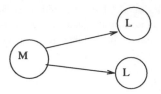

Figure 1: Aposteriori Knowledge

This are default sentences (or beliefs) that may be consider *nearly* knowledge. We emphasize them in the next subsection and analize its relation with the remaining default sentences.

3.3 Default, Belief and Potential Knowledge

Regard that the knowledge sentence $K_{aps}(\varphi)$, is a very *aposteriori* (factual) knowledge in I whenever both sentences $M(\varphi)$ and $\neg L(\varphi)$ are satisfied in I. The same condition must be satisfied by potential knowledge and belief. That means that φ is really undefiend at I. Whenever is true (or false) at the minimal interpretation of a model frame, it is *apriori* knowledge.

3.2.2 Definition (Belief) B

$I \models B(\varphi)$ iff $I \models M(\varphi)$, $\exists I'$, $I' \models L(\varphi)$ and $\forall I'$, $I' \models M(\varphi)$ (Fig. 2).

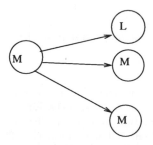

Figure 2: Belief

3.3.1 Definition (Potential Knowledge K_p)

$I \models K_p(\varphi)$ if and only if the following three conditions are satisfied.
1) $I \models M(\varphi)$,
2) Exists a direct succesor J of I, such that $J \models \neg L(\varphi)$
3) $\forall I'$, $I' \neq J$, $I' \models L(\varphi)$ (Fig. 3).

Formally, the definition of belief corresponds with default sentences from SKL**. The interpretation in epistemic context is very intuitive: a default conclusion, by its own

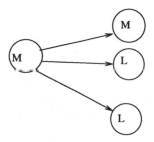

Figure 3: Potential Knowledge

character of *provisional,* it seems natural be consider belief. Conversely, a belief may be consider a default conclusion.

Now, we establishe the following relations between the above definitions. An interesting point is the condition that determine when potential knowledge turns up knowledge. $K_p(\varphi)$ turns up $K(\varphi)$ in I, when in the interpretation I', such that φ is undefined, φ turns up *aposteriori* knowledge $K_{aps}(\varphi)$. This is established in the following proposition.

3.3.2 Proposition
The $I \models K_p(\varphi)$ turns up $I \models K(\varphi)$ if and only if $I' \models K_{aps}(\varphi)$,
Demonstration
$I' \models K_{aps}(\varphi)$, thus $I' \models L(\varphi)$. So $I' \models K(\varphi)$.

From the unfulfillment of the hypotesis of K_{aps}, it follows that if eventually any succesor (direct or indirect) of I' satisfies $\neg\varphi$, then φ fails to be knowledge at I in this model frame. The arising of this fail —that could be interpreted as the refutation in the model frame $\mathcal{M}$ of φ — may suggest the change of model frame, or the suitable reception of the refutation against a *virtual* or *presumable* knowledge up to this step.

The semantical definitions of $\mathcal{EL}$-sentences involving the operators K, K_{aps}, K_p and B, and the distinction between them and the object or $\mathcal{L}$-sentences, makes to deal with situations such that a $\mathcal{L}$-sentence φ, can be argument of a $\mathcal{EL}$-sentence satisfied by an interpretation that satisfy $\neg\varphi$ also. This is an advantange attending the situation described in the previous paragraph: if some potential knowledge sentence does not turn up knowledge, this fact not disable the framework. The following is an obvious result.

3.3.3 Proposition

If $I \models K_p(\varphi)$, then $I \models B(\varphi)$

3.4 Recursivity and fulfillment of epistemic conditions

The definition of knowledge and potential knowledge are recursive: they appeal the satisfaction of the argument in all, or all in except one, of its direct succesors to decide if the argument sentence is knowledge or potential knowledge. Each succesor repeat the process. The same process is accomplished by belief. Whenever the conditions are satisfied stops the process and establishe if the sentence is knowledge, potential knowledge (a special case of belief) or belief. This is a constructive process, because the status of any sentence is determined up to the conditions are fulfilled. Never is determined without accomplished the punctual conditions.

On other hand, it is very useful that any operator can be applied to any sentence of a (direct or indirect) succesor of I. So that, for example, from $Kaps(\varphi)$ it may be established $L(\varphi)$ at any succesor of I. Related to local reasoning may be of interest the case of belief respect the succesor I' satisfying $L(\varphi)$, so that it implies $K(\varphi)$ in I'. That means that it is a local knowledge, altough this is not the case at everywhere.

4 Epistemic Entailment

To obtain the information that can follows from a initial given one, we are intended with the intuitive idea of fairly *what follows from what*. Its formalisation, the so called *entailment*, has been mainly realized by Shoham[18] and Makinson[14]. Entailment provides a suitable framework to model the getting conclusions from incomplete or imprecise information. The frequent situations involving incomplete information can be considered situations involving the minimal (actual) information from which it must be set up conclusions. At this sense it constitutes a formalism dealing with the presumible human mental act of jumpping to conclusions from the minimal plausible information and can be considered a semantical generalisation of McCarthy's Circumscription[15] and of Hintikka's Model Minimization[7]. The preferential entailment criteria given by Doherty[2] is adapted in our epistemic intend.

4.1 Definition (Preferred Model Frames)

Suppose $\mathcal{M} = \langle \Upsilon, I \rangle$, and $\mathcal{M}' = \langle \Upsilon', I' \rangle$, are two model frames satisfying a set of premises Γ. $\mathcal{M}$ is said to be preferred to $\mathcal{M}'$ if and only if is fulfilled any of the following conditions:

1) Satisfy the sentences in Γ using the minimal amount of information
2) If $I = I'$ prefer the frame that satisfy the minimal number of contraints defined by epistemic sentences
3) If $I = I'$ and the number of epistemic constraints are the same, is prefered the maximal number of interpretations.

4.2 Definition (Preferential Entailment)

Let Γ, Ψ be sets of senteces in $\mathcal{L}$. Γ preferentially entails Ψ, written $\Gamma \mid\approx \Psi$, if and only if, for all preferred models of Γ, written $\forall \mathcal{M} \in Pmod(\Gamma)$, $\mathcal{M} \models \Psi$. $Pmod(\Gamma)$ is the set of preferred model frames of Γ.

4.3 Example
The set Γ is the initial information. The subformulas appering in the succesives I_i, $i = 1, 2, 3, 4$ are the interpreted true formulas of refinament.

$$\Gamma = \{(P \to Q)^T, \ (Q \to R \vee S)^U, (R \to T)^U\}$$

$$I = \{Q\}$$

$$I_1 = \{Q, R \vee S\} \qquad\qquad I_1' = \{Q, R, R \vee S, T\}$$

$$I_2 = \{P, Q, R \vee S\} \qquad\qquad I_2' = \{Q, R, R \vee S, T, S\}$$

In I	B	K_p	K_{apr}	$K_{aps} \Rightarrow K$
1st iteration	R, T	R, T	Q	$R \vee S$
2nd iteration	P, S			

Let $\mathcal{M} = \{I, I_1, I_2\}$, $\mathcal{M}' = \{I, I_1', I_2'\}$. The set $\Psi = \{R \vee S\}$ is preferentially entailed by Γ. On the other hand, $\mathcal{M}$ is a preferred model frame with respect to $\mathcal{M}'$.

The $\mathcal{EL}$-formulas in the table are refered to I. In I_1, is satisfied $K_{aps}(\{P\})$ meanwhile in I_1' $K_{aps}(\{S\})$.

4.4 Proof method

The proof method given in Doherty's work [2] can be used in the obtaintion of the epistemic model frames of our enterprise. This proof method is an extension of Gentzen analytic tableaux. We can add our knowledge and belief conditions to the open branches containing the sentences of actual interest. So, the formalism we are using, based upon partial interpretations and model frames emphasizes the semantical entailment, but its proof method is realized by extending the powerful analytic tableaux method [3,9].

5 Conclusions

This paper emphasizes the relativity of knowledge and belief based upon the actual information. We propose epistemic and doxastic definitions based upon the SKL** partial logic. The formal definitions are recursive and constructive. The derivations capabilities are characterized by epistemic entailment. Our approach is closer to the characterization of actual information by contexts and that knowledge and belief depends of this ones.

Aknowledgments

The develope of this work has been benefitted from several interesting discussions with Lluís Godó and Carlos Sierra (CEAB), Ton Sales, Miguel Carrillo Ricardo Rodríguez and Javier Larrosa (LSI, UPC), and Gustavo Núñez (TII, México).

6 References

1. S. Blamey, *Partial Logic* In *Handbook of Philosophical Logic*, **III**. D. Gabbay, F. Guenthner, (Eds.) (Reidel Publishing Co, 1986).

2. P. Doherty, *A Three-Valued Approach to Non-Monotonic Reasoning.* Engineering Theses (Linköping, 1990).

3. Fitting Melving. *First-Order Modal Tableaux.* Journal of Automated Reasoning **4** (1988) pp. 191-213.

4. F. Giunchiglia, L. Serafini, F. Giunchiglia, M. Frixione, *Non-omniscient belief as context-based reasoning.* Proceedings of IJCAI (1993).

5. J. Halpern, and Y. Moses, *A Guide to Completeness and Complexity for Modal Logics of Knowledge and Belief.* Artificial Intelligence **54** (1992) pp. 319 - 379.

6. J. Hintikka, *Knowledge and Belief* (Cornell University Press 1962).

7. J. Hintikka, *Model Minimization - an Alternative to Circumscription.* Journal of Automated Reasoning **4** (1988) pp., 1-13.

8. S. Kleene, *Introduction to Metamathematical* (North Holland, Amsterdam, 1952).

9. K. Konolige, *A Deduction Model of Belief and its Logics* (Morgan Kaufmann, 1986).

10. S. Kripke, *A completness theorem in modal logic.* The Journal of Symbolic Logic. **24 - 1** (1959) pp. 1-14.

11. S. Kripke, *Semantical considerations on modal logic.* Acta Philosophica Fennica. **16** (1963), pp. 83-94.

12. T. Langholm, *Partiality, Truth and Modality.* CSLI Lectures Notes 15 (Stanford, 1988).

13. H. Levesque, *A logic of implicit and explicit belief.* Proceedings of the AAAI (1984).

14. D. Makinson, *General Theory of Cumulative Inference.* In M. Ginsburg, M. Reinfrank, E. Sandewall, (Eds.) Non-Nonotonic Reasoning, 2nd. International Workshop (Springer, 1988).

15. J. McCArthy, *Circumscription - A Form of Nonmonotonic Reasoning.* Artificial Intelligence (1986).

16. J. McCarthy, *Notes on formalizing context.* In Proceedings of IJCAI (1993).

17. G. Núñez, M. Alvarado, *Hacia una semántica realista de mundos posibles en lógica de creencias.* Reporte Interno del Laboratorio Nacional de Informática Avanzada (México, 1993).

18. Y. Shoham, *Reasoning About Change* (The MIT Press, 1988).

19. T. Sales, *How not to know it all.* Report de Recerca LSI-93-19-T, UPC (1993).

20. M. Vardi, *On epistemic logic and logical omniscience.* In Y. Halpern, (Ed.) Theoretical aspects of reasoning about knowledge (1986) pp. 293-305.

REASONING WITH INFORMATION SOURCES ORDERED BY TOPICS

LAURENCE CHOLVY

ONERA-CERT, 2 avenue Edouard Belin,
BP 4025, 31055 Toulouse, Cedex, FRANCE

and

ROBERT DEMOLOMBE

ONERA-CERT, 2 avenue Edouard Belin,
BP 4025, 31055 Toulouse, Cedex, FRANCE

ABSTRACT

This paper presents a logic for reasoning with information provided by several information sources. The main problem is that even if these sources are independently consistent, they might be contradictory. We introduce the notion of topic of information in order to gather information which concern the same subject. The logic defined here is a modal logic whose modalities allows us to express information about the relative reliability of the different sources, topic by topic. We show that when the orders of reliability are topic-compatible, then, our logic does not collapse even if the sources are contradictory.

1   Introduction

The main problem addressed in our paper is the problem of merging several information sources and more specifically, merging information sources which are contradictory. These sources may be databases which have been independently developped and which have to be federated[10] . They also may be belief sets of several agents which one wants to gather. For instance, this is the case when a police inspector queries different witnesses about a crime : he has to collect and to reason with the different accounts in order to find the clue. We assume that the different information sources share the same language, a propositional language, and reason in the same logic : the classical propositional logic. The main problem that may happen, even if each different source is consistent, is that they may be contradictory one each other. This problem has been studied under different names and different approaches. In[1,2] the authors address the problem of combination from a syntactical point of view, defining the combining on sets of formulas : two representations of the same theory that are syntactically different may behave in two different ways. In[8,4,5] the authors address the problem of "multi-source reasoning". The first paper describes the use of possibilistic logic and the last two papers adopt a model-based approach. From a theoretical point of view all these works try to find a solution to the problem of dealing with inconsistent information. Removing inconsistency requires to make choices, and they use extra-information and specific logics for that purpose. Notice that theses different approaches (formula-based, model-based ..) can be found in two related domains: database updates and belief revision[11,17,13,16,14,12]. A comparison between the problem of merging and the problem of updating will be given in the last section.

The main idea of our previous work[4,5] was to express the fact that, when merging different information sources, one often has an extra-information about the relative reliability of the sources. For instance, when federating databases, one may know that such a database is more reliable than such other, because it has been updated more recently. Ordering the different information sources according to their relative reliability allows to solve that problem of contradictions. We have defined two logics for reasoning with information provided by ordered sources corresponding to two different attitudes and are called "suspicious logic" and "trusting logic".

The purpose of this paper is to refine this previous work : indeed, until now, it has been supposed that there was only one order. The user, when merging the information sources, assumed that they were ordered according to their reliability. Here, we want to show that in fact, according to the topics of the data, the user may want to express several orders on the sources, which are then topics-dependent orders. The use of the notion of topics in combining knowledge-bases constitue the core of our paper. We focus on the extension of the trusting attitude. (An illustration of the trusting merging will be given in the next section).

Assumptions :

In this paper, we assume that the n information sources to be merged (we will also call them agents, knowledge bases, databases or more generaly bases) are satisfiable but not necessarily complete sets of literals of a propositional language L. We also will consider total orders on bases. Extensions of these assumptions are discussed in the last section.

2 Trusting merging with only one order : an example

The trusting attitude for combining ordered knowledge-bases consists in suspecting only the very information provided by a base which contradicts a more reliable base.

Let us take the exemple of a police inspector who gathers the accounts of two witnesses. Assume that the first witness, say Bill, said that he saw a black car, while the second, say John, said that he saw two men in a white car. Considering an order may reflect the fact that the inspector himself has some convinction (which can not be denied) or possesses some information which are true : for instance, he went to the meteorological station and he knows that the crime was committed on a foggy day. So he can assume that John is less reliable than Bill, since the latter was standing too far from the crime place and because of the fog, he could not see well. In this case, the inspector will consider that : inspector > Bill > John. The trusting attitude will lead the inspector to consider that the car was black and to reject the fact that it was white because this information contradicts an information provided by a more reliable agent. However, being trustful, the inspector will conclude that there were two men in this car, because this information does contradict nothing.

3 Topic-dependent orders

In this paper we aim to prove that considering only one order on the bases to be merged, is too restrictive. The following example will show that, in fact, one assumes as many orders as topics of data.

3.1 A motivating example

Let us come back to the example of the police inspector. Assume now that the two witnesses questionned by the inspector are a woman and a man. They both provide information about what they have seen. The woman says that she saw a girl, wearing a Chanel suit, jumping into a sport Wolkswagen car. The man says that he saw a girl wearing a dress. He assumed that she jumped into a car that he did not see but he heard that it was a diesel. The two accounts are contradictory : Did the girl wear a dress or a suit ? Was the car a sport car or not ? For solving these contradictions, the inspector may use the fact that, when speaking clothes, women are generally more expert than men ; and when speaking mechanics, men are generally more expert than women. This leads the inspector to assume two orders, depending on the two topics "clothes" and "mechanics" : the woman is more reliable than the man as regard to "clothes" and the man is more reliable than the woman as regard to "mechanics". Adopting a trusting attitude, the inspector will conclude that there was a girl, wearing a Chanel suit, jumping into a diesel car which was a Wolkswagen make.

3.2 Topics

The notion of topic has been investigated to characterize sets of sentences from the point of view of their meaning, independently of their truth values. For example, in the context of Cooperative Answering, topics can be used to extend an answer to other facts related to the same topic[7,3] . In the context of Knowledge Representation[15] , topics are used to represent all an agent believes about a given topic. It has also been used in the domain of updates[6] . In other works[18,9] the formal definition of the notion of "aboutness" is investigated in general. The purpose of this paper is not to define a logic for reasoning about the links between a sentence and a topic in general, but to define a logic that is based on source orders which depend on topics.

We assume that the underlying propositional language is associated to a finite number of topics which are sets of literals which agree on the following postulates :
- each literal of L belongs to a topic.
- topics may intersect.
- let l be a literal of L, let t be a topic: $(l \in t) \Longleftrightarrow (\neg\, l \in t)$.

3.3 Compatibility between orders and topics

The inspector example shows that it is useful to associate an order on the bases with any topic. The following definition defines a notion of compatibility between the topics and the associated orders.

Definition :
Let $t_1 \ldots t_m$ be the topics of L. Let $O_1 \ldots O_m$ be total orders on the bases, associated with the topics $t_1 \ldots t_m$. $O_1 \ldots O_m$ are $(t_1 \ldots t_m)$-compatible iff
$$\forall\, k = 1 \ldots m \,, \forall\, r = 1 \ldots m \quad t_k \cap t_r \neq \emptyset \implies O_k = O_r \,.$$

Intuitively, this definition characterizes orders which, in some sense, "agree on" the structure of the topics. According to topic-compatible orders, if a source is more reliable than another one, as regard to a topic, then it is also more reliable to this one, as regard to any sub-topic and any super-topic.

For instance, consider two topics "classical-music" and "baroque-music". The latter is included in the former. Consider two persons P1 and P2, providing you with information about baroque music and more generally about classical music. It is not realistic to assume that P1 is more reliable than P2 as regard to classical and that P2 is more reliable than P1 as regard to baroque. Indeed, if P1 is more reliable than P2 about classical music, he is also more reliable than P2 about baroque since any information which is about baroque music is also about classical music.

4 A trusting logic for reasoning on topic ordered sources

Notations :
Let us consider n databases to be merged. Let us note L the underlying propositional language and let $t_1 \ldots t_m$ be the topics on L.

If O denotes the total order $i_1 > i_2 > \ldots > i_p$, on some databases $i_1, i_2, \ldots, i_p$, and if i is another database, then $O > i$ will denote the order $i_1 > i_2 > \ldots > i_p > i$.

When associating an order with a topic, we will index this order by the topic 's index. So, O_k will be an order associated with the topic t_k.

O_Ω will denote a set of orders, $(O_1, \ldots, O_m)$, each of them being associated with a topic.

If O_Ω denotes a set of orders $(O_1, \ldots, O_m)$, then $O_{\Omega_k > i}$ will denote a set of orders $(O'_1, \ldots, O'_{k-1}, O_k > i, O'_{k+1}, \ldots, O'_m)$, where for any p different of k, O'_p is any order which extends the order O_p with database i. In other terms, i is considered as least reliable according to topic t_k, but i is inserted at any place in the order O_p, if p is different of k.

Let m be an interpretation of L, and t a topic of L, m | t will denote the set $\{l : l \in m$ and $l \in t \}$, i.e. m | t is the projection of m on topic t. Let us notice that, because topics are not necessarily disjoint, the set of m | t 's is not a partition of m.

Let E be a set of interpretations of L, and t be a topic of L, E | t will denote $\{ m | t : m \in E \}$.

4.1 The language of FT

The language L' of the logic FT we are going to define, is obtained from L by adding a finite number of modalities :

- B_{O_Ω}, where $O_\Omega = (O_1 \ldots O_m)$ such that the O_i's are total orders on subsets of $\{1 \ldots n\}$ which are $(t_1 \ldots t_m)$-compatibles.

Let $O_\Omega = (O_1 \ldots O_m)$ a set of total orders on k databases, which are topic-compatible. Then, $B_{O_\Omega}F$ will mean that F is true in the database obtained from merging the k databases according to the orders O_i.

Remark :

Let us notice that this general form of modalities allows us to represent the particular case where k=1. In this case, there is only one database, say i, to be merged. Thus, $O_1 = \ldots = O_m = \{i\}$. In this case, B_{O_Ω} will be noted B_i.

4.2 Semantics of the trusting merging with topic dependent orders

We first need to introduce the following definition : we will say that a set of interpretations of L "represents a database" iff E is the set of all the models of a given set of literals. More formally :

Definition :

Let E be a set of interpretations of L. Let PVAR be the set of the propositional variables of L. We define :

$dbE = \{l : \forall w\ (w \in E \Longrightarrow w \models l) \}$.

$PVAR(dbE) = \{p : (p \in PVAR)$ and $(p \in dbE$ or $\neg p \in dbE) \}$.

$\{p1 \ldots pm\} = PVAR \setminus PVAR(dbE)$.

$\overline{dbE} = \{ l_1 \ldots l_m : \forall i = 1 \ldots m, li = pi$ or $li = \neg pi \}$.

Then E "represents a database" iff $\forall l_1 \ldots l_m \in \overline{dbE}, \exists w \in E : w \models (l_1 \wedge \ldots \wedge l_m)$.

<u>Definition :</u>
An interpretation of FT, is a pair : $I = (W, r)$, where :

- W is the finite set of all the interpretations of the underlying propositional language L.

- $r =$ is a finite set of W subsets associated with the modalities B_{O_Ω} defined by :

  - if B_{O_Ω} is a modality of the form B_i, it is associated to a set noted M_i which is a non empty subset of W which "represents a database".
  - in any other case, if $O_\Omega = (O_1 \ldots O_m)$, the modality B_{O_Ω} is associated to M_{O_Ω} such that $M_{O_\Omega} = \{ s : s = s_1 \cup s_2 \cup \ldots \cup s_m$ and $s_1 \in M_1(O_1)$ and $\ldots$ and $s_m \in M_m(O_m) \}$ where :

    $M_k(O > i) = f_{k,i}(M_O)$ and
    $f_{k,i}(E) = \{ w : w \in E \mid t_k$ and $w \models L_{i,k,E} \}$ and
    $L_{i,k,E} = \{ l : l$ literal of topic t_k such that :
    $(\forall v \ (v \in M_i \mid t_k \implies v \models l))$ and $(\exists u \ (u \in E \mid t_k$ and $u \models l)) \}$

<u>Result 1 :</u>
Let us notice here that, since the considered orders are topic-compatible, if a literal belongs to an interpretation of one $M_i(O_i)$, then its negation cannot belong to an interpretation of another $M_j(O_j)$. This result is important because it guarantees that the sets of literals which are obtained by $\{ s : s = s_1 \cup s_2 \cup \ldots \cup s_m$ and $s_1 \in M_1(O_1)$ and $\ldots$ and $s_m \in M_m(O_m) \}$ are interpretations of L.

<u>Result 2 :</u>
We can also notice that, for any modality B_{O_Ω}, the set M_{O_Ω} is never empty. This guarantees that the database obtained by our trusting merging is not contradictory.

<u>Result 3 :</u>
For any modality B_{O_Ω}, we can prove that the associated set M_{O_Ω} "represents a database". This result ensures us that, when applying our trusting merging method to bases which are sets of literals, we obtain a base which is a set of literals.

<u>Definition</u> : Satisfaction of formulas :
Let F be a formula of L. Let F1 and F2 be formulas of L'. Let O_Ω be a set of total orders on a subset of $\{1..n\}$ which are topic-dependent. Let $M = (W,r)$ be an interpretation of FT and let $w \in W$.

$r,w \models_{FT} F$ iff $w \models F$
$r,w \models_{FT} B_{O_\Omega} F$ iff $\forall w' \ (w' \in M_{O_\Omega} \implies w' \models F)$
$r,w \models_{FT} \neg F1$ iff $r,w \not\models_{FT} F1)$
$r,w \models_{FT} F1 \wedge F2$ iff $r,w \models_{FT} F1$ and $r,w \models_{FT} F2$

<u>Definition :</u> Valid formulas in FT.

Let F be a formula of L'.

F is a valid formula in FT   iff $\forall\, M = (W,r), \forall\, w \in W$, $r,w \models_{FT} F$

4.3   Axiomatics

Axioms of FT are :

- (A0) Axioms of the propositional logic.

- (A1) $B_{O_\Omega} \neg F \rightarrow \neg B_{O_\Omega} F$

- (A2) $B_{O_\Omega} F \wedge B_{O_\Omega}(F \rightarrow G) \rightarrow B_{O_\Omega} G$

- (A3) $B_{O_\Omega} l \rightarrow B_{O_{\Omega_k > i}} l$ if l is a literal which belongs to topic k.

- (A4) $B_i l \wedge \neg B_{O_\Omega} \neg l \rightarrow B_{O_{\Omega_k > i}} l$ if l is a literal which belongs to topic t_k.

- (A5) $\neg B_{O_\Omega} l \wedge \neg B_i l \rightarrow \neg B_{O_{\Omega_k > i}} l$ if l is a literal which belongs to topic t_k.

- (A6) $B_{O_\Omega}(l1 \vee \ldots \vee lp) \rightarrow B_{O_\Omega} l1 \vee \ldots \vee B_{O_\Omega} lp$ where li's are non complementary literals.

Inferences rules of FT are :

- (Nec) $\vdash_{FT} F \Longrightarrow \vdash_{FT} B_{O_\Omega} F$ (if F is a propositional formula)

- (MP) $\vdash_{FT} F$ and $\vdash_{FT} (F \rightarrow G) \Longrightarrow \vdash_{FT} G$

(A3), (A4) and (A5) express the trusting attitude. They mean that :

- if a literal l, belonging to topic t_k, is true in the base obtained by merging some databases ordered with some orders, then it remains true if we merge a new database i considered as least reliable on topic t_k.

- if it is the case that a literal, belonging to topic t_k, is true in the database i and if its negation is not true in the base obtained by merging several database with orders O_Ω , then it remains true if we merge the new database i considered as least reliable on topic t_k.

- if l is a literal of a given topic t_k, which is true in a base obtained by merging several bases with another base i, considered as least reliable on topic t_k, then either l is true in the merging of these bases or l is true in database i.

(A6) expresses that when merging sets of literals, one gets sets of literals.

4.4 Propositions

Let us recall that the logic FT is introduced to modelize the trusting merging of databases which are sets of literals.

Let us note $\psi = \bigwedge_{i=1}^{n}(\bigwedge_{l\in bdi} B_i l \wedge \bigwedge_{bdi\not\ni c} \neg B_i c)$, where l is a literal and c a clause.

ψ expresses, for each database, the literals it believes and the clauses it does not believe. In other terms, ψ lists what each database "only believes".

We are interested in finding valid formulas of the form : $\psi \rightarrow B_{O_\Omega} F$, i.e finding formulas F which are true in the database obtained by merging several databases ordered by topic dependent orders O_Ω .

Result 4 :

Let F be a formula of L, and let O_Ω be a set of topic compatible orders on a subset of $\{1 .. n\}$. Then : $\models_{FT} (\psi \rightarrow B_{O_\Omega} F) \iff \vdash_{FT} (\psi \rightarrow B_{O_\Omega} F)$.

Sketch of proof :

This proof is based on the one we had made in the case when there was no topic and thus only one order on the sources.

We show the $(\Rightarrow)$ condition by showing that, for any formula F of L' we have : $\models_{FT} F \implies \vdash_{FT} F$. We first show this implication for all the axioms of FT. Then we show that the inference rules preserve that property.

We show the $(\Leftarrow)$ condition by induction on the length of the orders.

When the length is one, this means that there is only one base which is considered. Then, $B_{O_\Omega} = [\{i\} .. \{i\}]$. So $\models_{FT} (\psi \rightarrow B_{O_\Omega} F)$ implies that F is deducible from the base i. Thus, $(\psi \rightarrow B_{O_\Omega} F)$ is a theorem of FT.

When the length is greater than one, we make an induction on the form of F. First, we prove this condition for literals, then for disjunctions of literals, and finally, for conjunctions of disjunctions of literals.

Result 5 :

With the same assumptions : $\vdash_{FT} (\psi \rightarrow B_{O_\Omega} F)$ or $\vdash_{FT} (\psi \rightarrow \neg B_{O_\Omega} F)$.

Sketch of proof :

We prove it by induction of the form of F. In the case of literals, we make an induction on the length of the orders. Then we consider disjunctions of literals, then conjunctions of disjunctions of literals.

Result 6 :

In the particular case where there is only one topic, then :

$\vdash_{FT} (\psi \rightarrow B_O F)$ iff $\vdash_F (\psi \rightarrow B_O F)$

(where $\vdash_F$ was the symbol of deduction in the trusting logic with only one topic)

(The proof is obvious)

In other terms, the logic studied here is an extension of the logic previously defined.

4.5 An example

Let us come back to the police inspector example and define the language L whose propositions are : Chanel, suit, dress, sport, Wolkswagen, diesel (meanings are obvious). Two disjoint topics may be considered :
clothes = {Chanel, suit, dress } and mechanics = {sport, Wolkswagen, diesel } .

The two knowledge bases are :
woman = {Chanel, suit, ¬ dress, sport, Wolkswagen } and
man = {dress, ¬ suit, diesel, ¬ sport }

Let us consider ψ as before. Here are some deductions that the inspector can make (for readibility, the order indexes, representing topics, are forgotten : the first orders will concern the "clothes" topic and the second ones will concern the "mechanics" topic).

- $\vdash_{FT} (\psi \to B_{(woman \ woman)}$ (Chanel $\wedge$ suit)

  In other terms, when listening only to the woman, the inspector can deduce that the girl was wearing a Chanel suit.

- $\vdash_{FT} (\psi \to B_{(woman>man \ man>woman)}$ (Chanel $\wedge$ suit $\wedge \neg$ dress $\wedge$ diesel $\wedge \neg$ sport $\wedge$ Wolkswagen)

  In other terms, when considering that the woman is more reliable than the man when speaking clothes and that the man is more reliable than the woman when speaking mechanics, the inspector believes that there was a girl, wearing a Chanel suit (and not a dress) jumping into a diesel car (and not a sport-car) which was a Wolkswagen make.

- $\vdash_{FT} (\psi \to B_{(man>woman \ man>woman)}$ (dress $\wedge$ diesel $\wedge$ Wolkswagen)

  In other terms, if the inspector considers that the man is more reliable than the woman on every topic, then he believes that the girl who jumped into a diesel car Wolkswagen make was wearing a dress.

- $\vdash_{FT} (\psi \to (B_{(woman>man \ man>woman)}$ (suit) $\wedge$ $(B_{(man>woman \ man>woman)}$ (dress)

  In other terms, the inspector can deduce that the girl who was jumping into the car, was wearing a suit or a dress, depending on whether the woman is more reliable than the man on clothes or not.

5 Open questions

The work we have presented provides a contribution to three different kind of problems : reasoning about agents that "only believes" sets of literals, merging several information sources that have different levels of reliability, and refining levels of reliability by topics. However, there are still several open questions that are listed below :

- The first question one can ask concerns the fact that we have here considered total orders. Indeed, sometimes, one can not order the bases with total (topic dependent) orders but only with partial orders. We have recently shown a solution for the trusting logic with one order in the case of partial order. This solution consists in considering that a formula is true in the base obtained by merging several bases with a partial order if, by definition, it is true in any base obtained by merging these bases with any total order which extends the partial one. Such a solution can easily be applied in the present case of topic dependent orders.

- Few comments may be done on the notion of compatibility between orders and topics. The definition we give in section 3.3, does not take into account the content of the bases. It expresses that when two topics are not disjoint, the associated orders may be the same. However, this condition is not necessary if the bases do not provide us with literals which belong to the intersection of topics. This shows a way for refining the definition.

- As said in the introduction, two attitudes were defined for merging ordered sources. In this paper, we have focused on one of them, the trusting one, but the modification of this semantics to the suspicious merging with several orders is obvious. It leads, of course, to different merged base which express the fact that in each topic, the merging is supicious. For instance, if the inspector was suspicious, when considering that the man is more reliable than the woman about mechanics, it would not trust her when she says that the car was a Wolswagen make.

- Let us notice that the definition of interpretations of FT is based on a function $f_{k,i}$ which restricts a set of interpretations, $M(O_k)$, to the interpretations which satisfy all the literals of topic k which belong to any model of database i and which belong to almost one interpretation in $M(O_\Omega)$. We have shown that this function could be defined by : $f_{k,i}(E) = \bigcup_{m \in R(i)|t_k} Min(E \mid t_k, \leq_m)$, where $\leq_m$ is defined in[14] . So the link between information sources merging and updates is established : when there is only one topic, merging several databases ordered by $i_1 > ... > i_n$ according to the trusting attitude, comes to update the database i_n by the result of the update of database $i_{(n-1)}$ by ... i_1.

In other terms, updating database i by database j comes to trustfully merge database i and j, assuming that i is more reliable than j. The extension of merging to several topic dependent orders, gives an idea of how one could refine the definition of updates when there are several topics : indeed, when updating, the new information is generally considered as more reliable than the old one (except in the classical approach to database updates where the base is considered as more reliable than the new information). We could be more precise by considering topics and express that, according to such a topic, the new information is more reliable than the old one, but according to such other, it is less reliable.

- Finally, let us say that we are working on the extension of this work in the case where the bases are sets of clauses. We suggest to modify the semantics in two directions : the condition of sets which "represent a database" must be discarded, since it was introduced for our particular case of sets of literals. Furthermore, the definition of $f_{k,i}$ could be replaced by : $f_{k,i}(E) = \bigcup_{m \in R(i)|_{t_k}} Min(E \mid t_k, \leq_m)$. Defined in this way, trusting merging is still an extension of updating. For this extension, the axiomatics has to be modified and we could take inspiration of the work by Lakemayer[15] to represent the "only believes about" aspect of the problem.

Finally, let us say that a theorem prover is under development. It has been specified as a meta program. And it is implemented at the meta level of a PROLOG-like language. It is an extension of the theorem prover which we had defined previously in the case when there was no topic[5] .

References

1 J Minker C Baral, S. Kraus and V.S. Subrahmanian. Combining multiple knowledge bases. *IEEE Trans. on Knwledge and Data Engineering*, 3(2), 1991.

2 J Minker C Baral, S. Kraus and V.S. Subrahmanian. Combining knowledge bases consisting of first order theories. *Computational intelligence*, 8(1), 1992.

3 S. Cazalens and R. Demolombe. Intelligent access to data and knowledge bases via users' topics of interest. In *Proceedings of IFIP conference*, 1992.

4 L. Cholvy. A logical approach to multi-sources reasoning. In *Proceedings of the Applied Logic Conference*, University of Amsterdam, 1992.

5 L. Cholvy. Proving theorems in a multi-sources environment. In *Proceedings of IJCAI*, 1993.

6 L. Cholvy. Updates and topics of information. In *in proceedings of the IJCAI'93 workshop on Reasoning about action and change*, 1993.

7 F. Cuppens and R. Demolombe. Cooperative Answering: a methodology to provide intelligent access to Databases. In *EDS*, Tysons Corner, Virginia, 1988.

8 J. Lang D. Dubois and H. Prades. Dealing with multi-source information in possibilistic logic. In *Proceedings of ECAI*, 1992.

9 R.L. Epstein. *The Semantic Foundations of Logic, Volume1: Propositional Logic*. Kluwer Academic, 1990.

10 Y. Breitbart et al. Panel : interoperability in multidatabases : semantic and systems issues. In *Proc of VLDB*, 1991.

11 R. Fagin, J.D. Ullman, and M. Vardi. On the semantics of updates in databases. In *ACM TODS*, 1983.

12 L. Farinas and A. Herzig. Constructive minimal changes. In *Report IRIT*, 1992.

13 P. Gardenfors. *Knowledge in flux : modeling the dynamics of epistemic states.* The MIT Press, 1988.

14 H. Katsuno and A. Mendelzon. Propositional knowledge base revision and minmal change. *Artificial Intelligence*, 52, 1991.

15 G. Lakemeyer. All they know about. In *Proc. of the 11th National Conference on Artificial Intelligence (NCAI-93)*, 1993.

16 B. Nebel. A knowledge level analysis of belief revision. In *First conference on Principles ok knowledge representation and reasoning*, 1989.

17 J. Ullamn R. Fagin, G. Kupper and M. Vardi. Updating logical databases. *Advances in computing research*, 3, 1986.

18 R. Demolombe S. Cazalens and A. Jones. A logic for reasoning about is about. Technical report, ESPRIT Project MEDLAR, 1992.

UNRAVELLING NONDETERMINISM:
ON HAVING THE ABILITY TO CHOOSE
(EXTENDED ABSTRACT)

W. VAN DER HOEK

Department of Computer Science, Utrecht University, P.O. Box 80.089
3508 TB Utrecht, The Netherlands

B. VAN LINDER

Department of Computer Science, Utrecht University, P.O. Box 80.089
3508 TB Utrecht, The Netherlands

J.-J. CH. MEYER

Department of Computer Science, Utrecht University, P.O. Box 80.089
3508 TB Utrecht, The Netherlands

ABSTRACT

We demonstrate ways to incorporate nondeterminism in a system designed to formalize the reasoning of agents concerning their abilities, and the opportunities for and the results of the actions that they may perform. We distinguish two nondeterministic choice operators: one that expresses an internal choice, in which the agent decides what action to take, and one that expresses an external choice, which cannot be influenced by the agent. The presence of abilities in our system is the reason why the usual approaches towards nondeterminism cannot be used here. The semantics that we define for nondeterministic actions is based on the idea that composite actions are unravelled in the strings of atomic actions and tests that constitute them. With the techniques presented in this paper we show how the specific problems that occur when abilities for nondeterministic actions are considered can be solved.

1. Introduction

In order to formalize the behaviour of rational agents, we introduced in [1] a general framework in which the knowledge and abilities of agents, as well as the opportunities for and the results of their actions can be represented. Our framework is an expressive one, in which all of the notions that are necessary to formalize the reasoning of agents concerning the correctness and feasibility of their plans are incorporated. The actions that we considered in [1] are deterministic: the event that consists of some agent performing some action has a unique outcome. In this paper we consider a natural extension of the system of [1], given by the introduction of nondeterministic action constructors. These constructors combine two actions into a new one: the nondeterministic choice between the two actions. Due to the presence of abilities as a basic, independent notion, the usual approaches towards nondeterminism cannot be used in our framework.

The contents of the rest of this paper is as follows. In section 2 we give the intuition and the definitions of the formal system of [1]. In section 3 the intuition behind our approach towards nondeterminism is explained; furthermore it is shown on the basis of two canonical examples why the standard approach towards nondeterminism is not suitable for our goals. In section 4 we show how to incorporate internal nondeterminism into the system given in section 2. Section 5 contains the definitions used to incorporate external nondeterminism. Section 6 concludes this paper with a short summary.

Proofs are omitted; they can be found in [2].

2. Knowledge, abilities, opportunities and results

We use the system of [1] as a basis to build our treatment of nondeterminism upon. Nevertheless the way in which we deal with nondeterminism is dependent only on the class of actions under consideration, and does not depend essentially on any specific features of the system of [1].

Definition 2.1 The language $\mathcal{L}$, based on denumerable sets Π of propositional symbols and At of atomic actions and a finite set $\mathcal{A} = \{1, \ldots, n\}$ of agents, is defined by the following BNF:

$$\varphi ::= p \mid \neg\varphi \mid \varphi_1 \vee \varphi_2 \mid \mathbf{K}_i\varphi \mid {<}\mathrm{do}_i(\alpha){>}\varphi \mid \mathbf{A}_i\alpha$$

where α is from the class Ac given by:

$\alpha ::= a$	|	*atomic actions*
confirm φ	|	*confirmations*
$\alpha_1; \alpha_2$	|	*sequential composition*
if φ then α_1 else α_2 fi	|	*conditional composition*
while φ do α_1 od		*repetitive composition*

The constructs $\wedge$, $\rightarrow$ and $\leftrightarrow$ are defined in the usual way. Other additional constructs are introduced by definitional abbreviation:

tt	is	$p \vee \neg p$, for some $p \in \Pi$
ff	is	$\neg$**tt**
$[\mathrm{do}_i(\alpha)]\varphi$	is	$\neg {<}\mathrm{do}_i(\alpha){>}\neg\varphi$
skip	is	confirm **tt**
fail	is	confirm **ff**
α^0	is	skip
α^{n+1}	is	$\alpha; \alpha^n$

Remark 2.2 The formula $\mathbf{K}_i\varphi$ denotes that φ is knowledge of agent i, ${<}\mathrm{do}_i(\alpha){>}\varphi$ represents the fact that agent i has the opportunity to do α and that φ is achieved by doing so, $[\mathrm{do}_i(\alpha)]\varphi$ is noncommittal about the opportunity of the agent i to do α but states that should the opportunity arise, a state of affairs satisfying φ would result, and $\mathbf{A}_i\alpha$ denotes the fact that agent i has the ability to do α.

The action confirm φ is the analogon of the test actions from (propositional) dynamic logic (cf. [5]). These dynamic logic tests check for the truth of a certain formula:

if the formula holds, nothing happens, else the test action fails and the program aborts. As such these actions perform *confirmations*, or *verifications*, and do not model tests as looked upon by human beings (in [3] we formalized a more realistic, common sense notion of tests).

Definition 2.3 The class $\mathfrak{M}$ of Kripke models contains all $\mathcal{M} =< \mathcal{S}, \pi, \mathrm{R}, \mathrm{r}, \mathrm{c} >$ such that

1. $\mathcal{S}$ is a set of possible worlds, or states.
2. $\pi : \Pi \times \mathcal{S} \to \mathbf{bool}$ is a total function that assigns a truth value to propositional symbols in possible worlds.
3. $\mathrm{R} : \mathcal{A} \to \wp(\mathcal{S} \times \mathcal{S})$ yields the epistemic accessibility relations for a given agent.
4. $\mathrm{r} : \mathcal{A} \times At \to \mathcal{S} \to \wp(\mathcal{S})$ is such that $\mathrm{r}(i, a)(s)$ yields the (possibly empty) state transition in s caused by the event $\mathrm{do}_i(a)$. Without loss of generality, we assume that this function is such that for all atomic actions a it holds that $|\mathrm{r}(i, a)(s)| \leq 1$ for all i and s, i.e., these atomic events are *deterministic*.
5. $\mathrm{c} : \mathcal{A} \times At \to \mathcal{S} \to \mathbf{bool}$ is the capability function such that $\mathrm{c}(i, a)(s)$ indicates whether the agent i is capable of performing the action a in the possible world s.

Definition 2.4 Let $\mathcal{M} =< \mathcal{S}, \pi, \mathrm{R}, \mathrm{r}, \mathrm{c} >$ be some Kripke model from $\mathfrak{M}$. For propositional symbols, negated formulae, and disjunctions, $\mathcal{M}, s \models \varphi$ is inductively defined as usual. For the other clauses $\mathcal{M}, s \models \varphi$ is defined as follows:

$$\mathcal{M}, s \models \mathbf{K}_i\varphi \quad\quad\quad \Leftrightarrow \forall s'[(s, s') \in \mathrm{R}(i) \Rightarrow \mathcal{M}, s' \models \varphi]$$
$$\mathcal{M}, s \models <\mathrm{do}_i(\alpha)>\varphi \quad \Leftrightarrow \exists s'[s' \in \mathrm{r}(i, \alpha)(s) \,\&\, \mathcal{M}, s' \models \varphi]$$
$$\mathcal{M}, s \models \mathbf{A}_i\alpha \quad\quad\quad \Leftrightarrow \mathrm{c}(i, \alpha)(s) = 1$$

where $\mathrm{r} : \mathcal{A} \times Ac \to \mathcal{S} \to \wp(\mathcal{S})$ and $\mathrm{c} : \mathcal{A} \times Ac \to \mathcal{S} \to \mathbf{bool}$ are defined by:

$$\mathrm{r}(i, \mathtt{confirm}\ \varphi)(s) \quad = \{s\} \text{ if } \mathcal{M}, s \models \varphi$$
$$= \emptyset \text{ otherwise}$$
$$\mathrm{r}(i, \alpha_1; \alpha_2)(s) \quad\quad\quad = \mathrm{r}(i, \alpha_2)(\mathrm{r}(i, \alpha_1)(s))$$
$$\mathrm{r}(i, \mathtt{if}\ \varphi\ \mathtt{then}\ \alpha_1\ \mathtt{else}\ \alpha_2\ \mathtt{fi})(s) = \mathrm{r}(i, \alpha_1)(s) \text{ if } \mathcal{M}, s \models \varphi$$
$$= \mathrm{r}(i, \alpha_2)(s) \text{ otherwise}$$
$$\mathrm{r}(i, \mathtt{while}\ \varphi\ \mathtt{do}\ \alpha_1\ \mathtt{od})(s) \quad = \{s' \mid \exists k \in \mathbb{N} \exists s_0 \ldots \exists s_k \in \mathcal{S}[s_0 = s \,\&\, s_k = s' \,\&\,$$
$$\forall j < k[s_{j+1} \in \mathrm{r}(i, \mathtt{confirm}\ \varphi; \alpha_1)(s_j)] \,\&\,$$
$$\mathcal{M}, s' \models \neg\varphi]\}$$

where $\mathrm{r}(i, \alpha)(\mathcal{S}') \quad\quad\quad = \cup_{s' \in \mathcal{S}'} \mathrm{r}(i, \alpha)(s') \text{ for } \mathcal{S}' \subseteq \mathcal{S}$

and

$$\mathrm{c}(i, \mathtt{confirm}\ \varphi)(s) \quad\quad = 1 \text{ if } \mathcal{M}, s \models \varphi$$
$$= 0 \text{ otherwise}$$
$$\mathrm{c}(i, \alpha_1; \alpha_2)(s) \quad\quad\quad\quad = \mathrm{c}(i, \alpha_1)(s) \,\&\, \mathrm{c}(i, \alpha_2)(\mathrm{r}(i, \alpha_1)(s))$$
$$\mathrm{c}(i, \mathtt{if}\ \varphi\ \mathtt{then}\ \alpha_1\ \mathtt{else}\ \alpha_2\ \mathtt{fi})(s) = \mathrm{c}(i, \mathtt{confirm}\ \varphi; \alpha_1)(s) \text{ or}$$
$$\mathrm{c}(i, \mathtt{confirm}\ \neg\varphi; \alpha_2)(s)$$
$$\mathrm{c}(i, \mathtt{while}\ \varphi\ \mathtt{do}\ \alpha_1\ \mathtt{od})(s) \quad = 1 \text{ if } \exists k \in \mathbb{N}[\mathrm{c}(i, (\mathtt{confirm}\ \varphi; \alpha_1)^k;$$
$$\mathtt{confirm}\ \neg\varphi)(s) = 1]$$
$$= 0 \text{ otherwise}$$

where $c(i, \alpha)(S')$ $= \bigwedge_{s' \in S'} c(i, \alpha)(s')$ for $S' \subseteq S$

Satisfiability and validity are defined as usual. In order to keep our notation compact, singleton sets $\{s\}$, with $s \in S$, are usually denoted by s.

Remark 2.5 With regard to the abilities of agents, the motivation for the choices made in definition 2.4 is the following. An agent is capable of performing a sequential composition $\alpha_1; \alpha_2$ iff it is capable of performing α_1 and it is capable of executing α_2 after it has performed α_1. The definition of $c(i, \texttt{confirm } \varphi)(s)$ is based on the idea that an agent is able to get confirmation for a formula φ if and only if this formula holds, this in accordance with the ideas expressed in remark 2.2. An agent is capable of performing a conditional composition, if it is able to either get confirmation for the condition and thereafter perform the then-part, or it is able to confirm the negation of the condition and perform the else-part afterwards. Lastly, an agent is capable of performing a repetitive composition $\texttt{while } \varphi \texttt{ do } \alpha_1 \texttt{ od}$ iff it is able to perform the action $(\texttt{confirm } \varphi; \alpha_1)^k; \texttt{confirm } \neg\varphi$ for some $k \in \mathbb{N}$.

3. Internal versus external nondeterminism: Why the obvious approach will not do

Intuitively the meaning of a nondeterministic choice between the actions α_1 and α_2 is given by: 'choose one of α_1 and α_2, and perform the action that is chosen.' This intuitive description gives rise to two different implementations: one in which the actor makes the choice, another one in which the choice is made by some unspecified external environment. Following [6], the action in which the nondeterministic choice is made by the agent itself is called *internal*; if the external environment makes the choice, the action is called *external*. The notation used in this paper is also conform [6]: the internal nondeterministic choice between the actions α_1 and α_2 is denoted by $\alpha_1 \oplus \alpha_2$, the external nondeterministic choice is denoted by $\alpha_1 + \alpha_2$.

An important assumption that guides our treatment of internal and external nondeterminism, is that agents show an *angelic* behaviour, which means roughly speaking that it suffices that one of α_1 and α_2 has a pleasant property in order to conclude that $\alpha_1 \oplus \alpha_2$ has, and the external environment shows a *demonic* one, meaning that both α_1 and α_2 should meet some property in order to conclude that $\alpha_1 + \alpha_2$ does.

In [8] a semantics for events is given that deals with the concurrency operator $\cap$, which bears a close resemblance to our external nondeterministic choice $+$, and the nondeterministic choice operator $\cup$, which shows the same behaviour as our $\oplus$. One could be tempted to introduce nondeterminism into the system of [1] by using the approach of [8] for the semantics of events, and extending the semantics for abilities by adding the clauses

$$c(i, \alpha_1 \oplus \alpha_2)(s) = \mathbf{1} \Leftrightarrow c(i, \alpha_1)(s) = \mathbf{1} \text{ or } c(i, \alpha_2)(s) = \mathbf{1}$$

and

$$c(i, \alpha_1 + \alpha_2)(s) = \mathbf{1} \Leftrightarrow c(i, \alpha_1)(s) = \mathbf{1} \text{ and } c(i, \alpha_2)(s) = \mathbf{1}$$

to deal with internal and external nondeterminism respectively. However according to our intuition this semantics fails to satisfactory formalize the abilities of agents for *sequences* of actions. The following two examples make this point more clear.

Example 3.1 (Internal nondeterminism and sequential composition)
Consider the Kripke model $\mathcal{M} =< \mathcal{S}, \pi, \mathrm{R}, \mathrm{r}, \mathrm{c} >$ given by:

- $\mathcal{S} = \{s_0, s_1, s_2\}$, π is arbitrary, R is arbitrary.
- $\mathrm{r}(i, a_1)(s_0) = s_1$, $\mathrm{r}(i, a_2)(s_0) = s_2$.
- $\mathrm{c}(i, a_1)(s_0) = \mathbf{1} = \mathrm{c}(i, a_3)(s_1)$,
  $\mathrm{c}(i, a_2)(s_0) = \mathbf{0} = \mathrm{c}(i, a_3)(s_2)$.

Intuitively agent i is capable of $\alpha = (a_1 \oplus a_2); a_3$ in s_0: the agent itself makes the choice and s/he is able to do $a_1; a_3$. However should we use the semantics suggested above, in which the equivalence

$$[\mathrm{do}_i(\alpha_1 \oplus \alpha_2)]\varphi \leftrightarrow [\mathrm{do}_i(\alpha_1)]\varphi \wedge [\mathrm{do}_i(\alpha_2)]\varphi$$

defines the $\oplus$ for events, we would have to conclude that i is not capable of α:

1. $\mathcal{M}, s_0 \models \mathbf{A}_i(a_1 \oplus a_2)$ since $\mathcal{M}, s_0 \models \mathbf{A}_i a_1$,
2. $\mathcal{M}, s_0 \not\models [\mathrm{do}_i(a_1 \oplus a_2)]\mathbf{A}_i a_3$, since $\mathcal{M}, s_0 \not\models [\mathrm{do}_i(a_2)]\mathbf{A}_i a_3$,
3. hence $\mathcal{M}, s_0 \not\models \mathbf{A}_i(a_1 \oplus a_2) \wedge [\mathrm{do}_i(a_1 \oplus a_2)]\mathbf{A}_i a_3$, and thus $\mathcal{M}, s_0 \not\models \mathbf{A}_i \alpha$.

Example 3.2 (External nondeterminism and sequential composition)
Consider the Kripke model $\mathcal{M} =< \mathcal{S}, \pi, \mathrm{R}, \mathrm{r}, \mathrm{c} >$ given by:

- $\mathcal{S} = \{s_0, s_1, s_2\}$, π is arbitrary, R is arbitrary.
- $\mathrm{r}(i, a_1)(s_0) = s_1$, $\mathrm{r}(i, a_2)(s_0) = s_2$.
- $\mathrm{c}(i, a_1)(s_0) = \mathbf{1} = \mathrm{c}(i, a_2)(s_0)$,
  $\mathrm{c}(i, a_3)(s_1) = \mathbf{0}$, $\mathrm{c}(i, a_3)(s_2) = \mathbf{1}$.

Intuitively agent i is incapable of $\alpha = (a_1 + a_2); a_3$ in s_0: the agent has no influence on what sequence is chosen and s/he is unable to do $a_1; a_3$. Using the semantics of [8] for events would result in the equivalence

$$[\mathrm{do}_i(\alpha_1 + \alpha_2)]\varphi \leftrightarrow [\mathrm{do}_i(\alpha_1)]\varphi \vee [\mathrm{do}_i(\alpha_2)]\varphi$$

Using this equivalence in the approach suggested above, we have to conclude that the agent is capable of α in s_0:

1. $\mathcal{M}, s_0 \models \mathbf{A}_i(a_1 + a_2)$ since $\mathcal{M}, s_0 \models \mathbf{A}_i a_1$ and $\mathcal{M}, s_0 \models \mathbf{A}_i a_2$,
2. $\mathcal{M}, s_0 \models [\mathrm{do}_i(a_2)]\mathbf{A}_i a_3$, hence $\mathcal{M}, s_0 \models [\mathrm{do}_i(a_1 + a_2)]\mathbf{A}_i a_3$,
3. hence $\mathcal{M}, s_0 \models \mathbf{A}_i(a_1 + a_2) \wedge [\mathrm{do}_i(a_1 + a_2)]\mathbf{A}_i a_3$, and thus $\mathcal{M}, s_0 \models \mathbf{A}_i(a_1 + a_2); a_3$.

So we see that in both examples the naive approach does not work, neither for the case of internal nondeterminism, nor for the case of external nondeterminism. As the examples already suggest, in order to determine whether a composite (nondeterministic) action satisfies a certain property, the set of sequences of atomic actions that constitute the action has to be taken into account. Exactly this approach provides the foundation for the semantics that we propose in the following sections.

4. Introducing internal nondeterminism

Definition 4.1 The language $\mathcal{L}_I$ is an extension of the language $\mathcal{L}$. For the language $\mathcal{L}_I$ the class of actions Ac as given in definition 2.1 is extended by the clause $\alpha ::= \alpha_1 \oplus \alpha_2$, thus obtaining the class Ac_I of actions.

As touched upon in the examples of section 3, the unravelling of composite actions into the sequences of (atomic) actions that constitute them will be the basis of the semantics that we define. This unravelling is done using *finite computation sequences*, as defined in [5].

Definition 4.2 Let the language $\mathcal{L}_I$ be as given in definition 4.1. The class of basic actions Ac_b^I based on $\mathcal{L}_I$ is given by the following BNF, where a is a typical element of At and φ is a typical formula from $\mathcal{L}_I$.

$$\alpha ::= a \mid \texttt{confirm } \varphi \mid \alpha_1; \alpha_2$$

If some action α is either an atomic action a or some confirmation $\texttt{confirm } \varphi$, then α is called *semi-atomic*.

Definition 4.3 The function $CS : Ac_I \to \wp(Ac_b^I)$, yielding the finite computation sequences of a given action, is inductively defined as follows.

$$
\begin{aligned}
CS(a) &= \{a\} \\
CS(\texttt{confirm } \varphi) &= \{\texttt{confirm } \varphi\} \\
CS(\alpha_1; \alpha_2) &= \{\alpha_1'; \alpha_2' \mid \alpha_1' \in CS(\alpha_1), \alpha_2' \in CS(\alpha_2)\} \\
CS(\texttt{if } \varphi \texttt{ then } \alpha_1 \texttt{ else } \alpha_2 \texttt{ fi}) &= CS(\texttt{confirm } \varphi; \alpha_1) \cup CS(\texttt{confirm } \neg\varphi; \alpha_2) \\
CS(\texttt{while } \varphi \texttt{ do } \alpha_1 \texttt{ od}) &= \cup_{k=1}^{\infty} Seq_k(\texttt{while } \varphi \texttt{ do } \alpha_1 \texttt{ od}) \cup \{\texttt{confirm } \neg\varphi\} \\
CS(\alpha_1 \oplus \alpha_2) &= CS(\alpha_1) \cup CS(\alpha_2)
\end{aligned}
$$

where for $k \geq 1$

$$
Seq_k(\texttt{while } \varphi \texttt{ do } \alpha_1 \texttt{ od}) = \{(\texttt{confirm } \varphi; \alpha_1'); \ldots; (\texttt{confirm } \varphi; \alpha_k');
$$
$$
\texttt{confirm } \neg\varphi \mid
$$
$$
\alpha_j' \in CS(\alpha_1) \text{ for } j = 1, \ldots, k\}
$$

Definition 4.4 The relation $\models$ as given in 2.4 is modified as follows.

$$
\begin{aligned}
\mathcal{M}, s &\models <\texttt{do}_i(\alpha)>\varphi & \Leftrightarrow \exists\alpha' \in CS(\alpha)\exists s' \in \mathcal{S}[\mathbf{r}(i, \alpha')(s) = s' \,\&\, \mathcal{M}, s' \models \varphi] \\
\mathcal{M}, s &\models \mathbf{A}_i\alpha & \Leftrightarrow \exists\alpha' \in CS(\alpha)[\mathbf{c}(i, \alpha')(s) = 1]
\end{aligned}
$$

where $\mathbf{r} : \mathcal{A} \times Ac_b^I \to \mathcal{S} \to \wp(\mathcal{S})$ and $\mathbf{c} : \mathcal{A} \times Ac_b^I \to \mathcal{S} \to \textbf{bool}$ are defined by:

$$
\begin{aligned}
\mathbf{r}(i, \texttt{confirm } \varphi)(s) &= \{s\} \text{ if } \mathcal{M}, s \models \varphi \\
&= \emptyset \text{ if } \mathcal{M}, s \not\models \varphi \\
\mathbf{r}(i, \alpha_1; \alpha_2)(s) = s' &\Leftrightarrow \exists t \in \mathcal{S}[\mathbf{r}(i, \alpha_1)(s) = t \,\&\, \mathbf{r}(i, \alpha_2)(t) = s'] \\[6pt]
\mathbf{c}(i, \texttt{confirm } \varphi)(s) &= 1 \text{ if } \mathcal{M}, s \models \varphi \\
&= 0 \text{ if } \mathcal{M}, s \not\models \varphi \\
\mathbf{c}(i, \alpha_1; \alpha_2)(s) &= \mathbf{c}(i, \alpha_1)(s) \,\&\, \mathbf{c}(i, \alpha_2)(\mathbf{r}(i, \alpha_1)(s)) \\
\text{and } \mathbf{c}(i, \alpha)(\emptyset) &= 1
\end{aligned}
$$

Remark 4.5 When using the semantics for internal nondeterministic actions as defined in 4.4, it is indeed the case that an intuitively correct result is obtained in the model of example 3.1: since the agent is capable of performing $a_1; a_3$, which is one of the computation sequences constituting $(a_1 \oplus a_2); a_3$, we conclude that the agent is able to do $(a_1 \oplus a_2); a_3$.

Theorem 4.6 *For all agents* i, *actions* $\alpha_1, \alpha_2, \alpha_3 \in Ac_I$, *and for all formulae* $\varphi \in \mathcal{L}_I$ *we have:*

- $\models <\text{do}_i(\alpha_1 \oplus \alpha_2)> \varphi \leftrightarrow (<\text{do}_i(\alpha_1)> \varphi \vee <\text{do}_i(\alpha_2)> \varphi)$.
- $\models [\text{do}_i(\alpha_1 \oplus \alpha_2)]\varphi \leftrightarrow ([\text{do}_i(\alpha_1)]\varphi \wedge [\text{do}_i(\alpha_2)]\varphi)$.
- $\models \mathbf{A}_i(\alpha_1 \oplus \alpha_2) \leftrightarrow (\mathbf{A}_i\alpha_1 \vee \mathbf{A}_i\alpha_2)$.
- $\not\models \mathbf{A}_i(\alpha_1; \alpha_2) \rightarrow \mathbf{A}_i\alpha_1 \wedge [\text{do}_i(\alpha_1)]\mathbf{A}_i\alpha_2$.
- $\models \mathbf{A}_i\alpha_1 \wedge [\text{do}_i(\alpha_1)]\mathbf{A}_i\alpha_2 \rightarrow \mathbf{A}_i(\alpha_1; \alpha_2)$.
- $\models \mathbf{A}_i((\alpha_1 \oplus \alpha_2); \alpha_3) \leftrightarrow (\mathbf{A}_i(\alpha_1; \alpha_3) \vee \mathbf{A}_i(\alpha_2; \alpha_3))$.
- $\models \mathbf{A}_i(\alpha_1; (\alpha_2 \oplus \alpha_3) \leftrightarrow (\mathbf{A}_i(\alpha_1; \alpha_2) \vee \mathbf{A}_i(\alpha_1; \alpha_3))$.

5. Introducing external nondeterminism

The language $\mathcal{L}_E$ is defined in much the same way as $\mathcal{L}_I$; therefore definitions 4.1 and 4.2 can be repeated here, replacing $\mathcal{L}_I$ by $\mathcal{L}_E$, Ac_I by Ac_E, and $\oplus$ by $+$.

In the light of the remarks made in the previous sections, one could be tempted to modify definition 4.4 by replacing the existential quantification '$\exists \alpha' \in CS(\alpha)$' by a universal quantification '$\forall \alpha' \in CS(\alpha)$'. However this would not lead to intuitive results, as is shown in the following example.

Example 5.1 Consider the action $\alpha \stackrel{\text{def}}{=}$ if φ then skip else fail fi. Assume that the event $\text{do}_i(\alpha)$ occurs in a state s in which φ holds. Given the intuitive meaning of α one would expect the event $\text{do}_i(\alpha)$ to behave in s as the event $\text{do}_i(\text{skip})$ would. However, since $CS(\text{skip}) = \{\text{skip}\}$ and confirm $\neg\varphi$; fail $\in CS(\alpha)$, this is not the case: $\mathcal{M}, s \not\models <\text{do}_i(\alpha)> \text{tt}$ whereas $\mathcal{M}, s \models <\text{do}_i(\text{skip})> \text{tt}$.

To correctly deal with external nondeterminism, the *relevant* computation sequences of a given action, for a given agent in a given state, need somehow be singled out. We will call these relevant sequences the *finite computation runs* of the action, given an agent and a state. First some additional terminology is necessary.

Definition 5.2 For all agents i and actions α we define the event $\text{do}_i(\alpha)$ to be *voidly non-terminating* in a given state s if the event does not cause any state transition. For instance $\text{do}_i(\text{fail})$ is voidly non-terminating in all states s.

The event $\text{do}_i(\alpha)$ is defined to be *infinitely non-terminating* in a given state s if the event causes infinitely many state transitions. An example of an event that is infinitely non-terminating in all states s is $\text{do}_i(\text{while tt do skip od})$.

Since α may contain external nondeterministic choices, for $< \mathrm{do}_i(\alpha) > \varphi$ to hold it is demanded that no way of executing α exists such that a non-terminating event results. For $\mathbf{A}_i\alpha$ to hold it is necessary that no way of executing α exists such that an infinitely non-terminating event results: since people die and machines break down, agents cannot be expected to be able to perform actions that result in infinitely non-terminating events. For this reason the definition of finite computation runs is such that if some computation sequence of an action α results, for a given agent i in a given state s, in an infinitely non-terminating event, the set of finite computation runs of α for the agent and the state is equal to the singleton set $\{\texttt{fail}\}$; the action $\texttt{fail}$ is such that no agent is ever capable of doing it, and no end state results when performing it, and thus mirrors exactly the behaviour of infinitely nonterminating events. If none of the finite computation sequences of an action α results in an infinitely non-terminating event for i in s, the set of finite computation runs of α is defined inductively. In this inductive definition it is taken into account that, depending on the truth or falsity of the condition, only some of the finite computation sequences of a conditional or a repetitive composition are finite computation runs. Note that it is possible that agents are able to perform actions that would lead to voidly non-terminating events; it is therefore possible that actions resulting in a state s for an agent i in voidly non-terminating events still are relevant.

To check whether an action α, for a given agent i and a state s, can be executed in such a way that an infinitely non-terminating event results, the predicate *Term* is used. The definition of this predicate is a rather straightforward formalization of the idea that infinite events result in infinitely many state transitions. If we assume that execution of semi-atomic actions takes one execution cycle, then execution of an action that results in an infinitely non-terminating event takes more than k execution cycles, for all $k \in \mathbb{N}$. The function $|.|$ and the relation *Prefix* are used to make a concise definition of the termination predicate possible.

Definition 5.3 For $\alpha, \alpha', \alpha'', \beta, \gamma, \in Ac_b^E$ we define:
- The relation *Prefix* $\subseteq Ac_b^E \times Ac_b^E$ by:
    1. *Prefix*(α, α).
    2. if *Prefix*(α, β) then *Prefix*$(\alpha, \beta; \gamma)$.
    3. *Prefix*$(\alpha; \beta, \alpha; \gamma)$ iff *Prefix*(β, γ).
- The function $|.| : Ac_b^E \to \mathbb{N}$, denoting the norm of an action, by:
    $$|\alpha| \quad = 1 \text{ if } \alpha \text{ is semi-atomic}$$
    $$|\alpha; \beta| \quad = |\alpha| + |\beta|$$
- For all $n \in \mathbb{N}$, $|\alpha|_n$ by: $|\alpha|_n = \alpha' \Leftrightarrow Prefix(\alpha', \alpha)$ & $|\alpha'| = n$.
- The function *Term*, indicating termination of a given action, in a given state and for a given agent, by:
    $Term(i, \alpha, s) = \mathbf{0}$ if
    $\quad \forall k \exists n \geq k \exists \alpha' \exists \alpha'' [\alpha'' = |\alpha'|_n , \alpha' \in CS(\alpha) \text{ and } \mathbf{r}(i, \alpha'')(s) \neq \emptyset]$
    $Term(i, \alpha, s) = \mathbf{1}$ otherwise.

Definition 5.4 Let $\mathcal{M}$ be some Kripke model. The function $CS\ :\ Ac_E \to Ac_b^E$ is defined as in 4.3, where the clause for $\oplus$ is replaced by $CS(\alpha_1 + \alpha_2) = CS(\alpha_1) \cup CS(\alpha_2)$.

The function CR, denoting the *finite computation runs*, is defined by:

$$CR \qquad\qquad\qquad\qquad : \quad \mathcal{A} \times Ac_E \times S \to \wp(Ac_b^E)$$

$$CR(i, \alpha, s) \qquad\qquad\quad = \{\texttt{fail}\} \text{ if } Term(i, \alpha, s) = \mathbf{0}$$

else if $Term(i, \alpha, s) = \mathbf{1}$:

$$CR(i, a, s) \qquad\qquad\qquad = \{a\}$$

$$CR(i, \texttt{confirm } \varphi, s) \qquad = \{\texttt{confirm } \varphi\}$$

$$CR(i, \alpha_1; \alpha_2, s) \qquad\qquad = \{\alpha_1'; \alpha_2' \mid \alpha_1' \in CR(i, \alpha_1, s),$$
$$\alpha_2' \in CR(i, \alpha_2, \mathbf{r}(i, \alpha_1')(s))\}$$

$$CR(i, \texttt{if } \varphi \texttt{ then } \alpha_1 \texttt{ else } \alpha_2 \texttt{ fi}, s) = CR(i, \texttt{confirm } \varphi; \alpha_1, s) \text{ if } \mathcal{M}, s \models \varphi$$
$$= CR(i, \texttt{confirm } \neg\varphi; \alpha_2, s) \text{ if } \mathcal{M}, s \not\models \varphi$$

$$CR(i, \texttt{while } \varphi \texttt{ do } \alpha_1 \texttt{ od}, s) = \{\texttt{confirm } \neg\varphi\} \text{ if } \mathcal{M}, s \not\models \varphi$$
$$= \{\alpha' \in CS(\texttt{while } \varphi \texttt{ do } \alpha_1 \texttt{ od}) \mid$$
$$(\alpha' = (\texttt{confirm } \varphi; \gamma_1); \gamma),\ \gamma_1 \in CR(i, \alpha_1, s),$$
$$\gamma \in CR(i, \texttt{while } \varphi \texttt{ do } \alpha_1 \texttt{ od}, \mathbf{r}(i, \gamma_1)(s))\}$$
$$\text{if } \mathcal{M}, s \models \varphi$$

$$CR(i, \alpha_1 + \alpha_2, s) \qquad\quad = CR(i, \alpha_1, s) \cup CR(i, \alpha_2, s)$$
$$\text{and } CR(i, \alpha, \emptyset) \qquad\qquad = CS(\alpha)$$

The relation $\models$ as given in definition 2.4 is for events and abilities modified as follows:

$$\mathcal{M}, s \models <\mathrm{do}_i(\alpha)> \varphi \Leftrightarrow \forall \alpha' \in CR(i, \alpha, s) \exists s' \in S[\mathbf{r}(i, \alpha')(s) = s' \ \& \ \mathcal{M}, s' \models \varphi]$$
$$\mathcal{M}, s \models \mathbf{A}_i \alpha \qquad\quad \Leftrightarrow \forall \alpha' \in CR(i, \alpha, s)[\mathbf{c}(i, \alpha')(s) = 1]$$

where $\mathbf{r} : \mathcal{A} \times Ac_b^E \to S \to \wp(S)$ and $\mathbf{c} : \mathcal{A} \times Ac_b^E \to S \to \mathbf{bool}$ are defined in exactly the same way as their counterparts in definition 4.4.

Remark 5.5 The definition of finite computation runs indeed captures the intuition of *relevant* computation sequences: for events that are not infinitely non-terminating, the finite computation runs are exactly those finite computation sequences that may occur in actual executions of the events, and these are obviously the relevant ones.

Remark 5.6 The semantics given in 5.4 yields the correct result in example 3.2: since $a_1; a_3$ is a relevant computation sequence of $(a_1 + a_2); a_3$ for i in s, and the agent is not able to do $a_1; a_3$ in s, we conclude that s/he is not able to do $(a_1 + a_2); a_3$.

Theorem 5.7 *For all agents i, actions $\alpha_1, \alpha_2, \alpha_3 \in Ac_E$, and for all formulae $\varphi \in \mathcal{L}_E$ we have:*

- $\models <\mathrm{do}_i(\alpha_1 + \alpha_2)> \varphi \leftrightarrow (<\mathrm{do}_i(\alpha_1)> \varphi \wedge <\mathrm{do}_i(\alpha_2)> \varphi).$
- $\models [\mathrm{do}_i(\alpha_1 + \alpha_2)] \varphi \leftrightarrow ([\mathrm{do}_i(\alpha_1)] \varphi \vee [\mathrm{do}_i(\alpha_2)] \varphi).$
- $\models \mathbf{A}_i(\alpha_1 + \alpha_2) \leftrightarrow (\mathbf{A}_i \alpha_1 \wedge \mathbf{A}_i \alpha_2).$
- $\models \mathbf{A}_i(\alpha_1; \alpha_2) \to \mathbf{A}_i \alpha_1 \wedge [\mathrm{do}_i(\alpha_1)] \mathbf{A}_i \alpha_2.$

172

- $\not\models \mathbf{A}_i\alpha_1 \wedge [\mathrm{do}_i(\alpha_1)]\mathbf{A}_i\alpha_2 \to \mathbf{A}_i(\alpha_1;\alpha_2)$.
- $\models \mathbf{A}_i((\alpha_1+\alpha_2);\alpha_3) \leftrightarrow (\mathbf{A}_i(\alpha_1;\alpha_3) \wedge \mathbf{A}_i(\alpha_2;\alpha_3))$.
- $\models \mathbf{A}_i(\alpha_1;(\alpha_2+\alpha_3)) \leftrightarrow (\mathbf{A}_i(\alpha_1;\alpha_2) \wedge \mathbf{A}_i(\alpha_1;\alpha_3))$.

6. Conclusions

We have investigated ways to incorporate both internal and external nondeterministic actions in a system that formalizes the reasoning of agents on their abilities and the opportunities for and the results of the actions that they perform. To this end we defined the notions of finite computation sequences and finite computation runs: these are finite strings of atomic actions and tests. Our approach gives intuitively correct and desirable results for two canonical examples, and seems to be correct in general.

7. Acknowledgements

This research is partially supported by ESPRIT III BRA project No.6156 'DRUMS II', ESPRIT BRWG project No.8319 'MODELAGE', and the Vrije Universiteit Amsterdam; the third author is furthermore partially supported by the Katholieke Universiteit Nijmegen. Thanks are also due to the referees for their comments which helped improve this paper.

8. References

1. W. van der Hoek, B. van Linder, and J.-J. Ch. Meyer, *A Logic of Capabilities*, Technical Report IR-330 (Vrije Universiteit Amsterdam, July 1993). An extended abstract is to appear in the proceedings of LFCS'94.
2. W. van der Hoek, B. van Linder, and J.-J. Ch. Meyer, *Unravelling nondeterminism: On having the ability to choose*, Technical Report RUU-CS-93-30 (Utrecht University, September 1993).
3. B. van Linder, W. van der Hoek, and J.-J. Ch. Meyer, *Tests as epistemic updates*, Technical Report UU-CS-1994-08 (Utrecht University, January 1994). An extended abstract is to appear in the proceedings of ECAI'94.
4. J.Y. Halpern and Y.O. Moses, *A guide to completeness and complexity for modal logics of knowledge and belief*, Artificial Intelligence **54** (1992), pp. 319–379.
5. D. Kozen and J. Tiuryn, *Logics of programs*, in J. van Leeuwen, editor, Handbook of Theoretical Computer Science **B** (Elsevier, 1990), pp. 789–840.
6. J.-J. Ch. Meyer, *Free choice permissions and Ross's paradox: Internal vs external nondeterminism*, in P. Dekker and M. Stokhof, editors, Proc. 8th Amsterdam Colloquium (Universiteit van Amsterdam, 1992), pp. 367–380.
7. J.-J. Ch. Meyer and W. van der Hoek, *Epistemic logic for AI and computer science* (Cambridge University Press, 1994).
8. D. Peleg, *Concurrent dynamic logic*, Journal of the ACM **34(2)** (1987) pp. 450–479.

Representing Concurrency in a
State - Transition System

GERD GROSSE*

Fachgebiet Intellektik, TH Darmstadt, Alexanderstr. 10
64289 Darmstadt, Germany

ABSTRACT

In this paper we propose the representation of concurrent events and causality between events in modal logic. This approach differs from previous approaches in the following directions: first, events enjoy the same attention as states. In the same way as states can be viewed as models of the formulae describing the facts that hold in them we think of events as models of the formulae describing the subevents. Second, instead of postulating just one set of states as primitive objects we use two sets, a set of states and a set of events. In terms of modal logic, the universe then becomes a set of pairs in which one component is a state and the other is one of the events following the state. The connection between two subsequent pairs is expressed by an accessibility relation. This extension permits an elegant treatment of causality and simultaneity, which in turn are the corner stones of our theory of events.

1. Introduction

It is quite common to represent the behavior of dynamic systems by a sequence of states. These states are considered to be models of some set of logical formulae. Two subsequent states are connected by the occurrence of some event[1]. Syntactically each event is represented by a constant on the term level. Semantically, they are often identified by the pairs of states between which the event might happen (most obvious in dynamic logic [8,6]). Thus there is a strong asymmetry in handling states and events.

Recently, there has been a growing interest in forming a theory that allows for the concurrent execution of actions, e.g., Baral and Gelfond [1], Gelfond *etal.*[2], Georgeff [3], Große and Waldinger [4], and Lin and Shoham [7]. The handling of concurrent events is important since in any bigger domain a number of events happen at the same time. However, a proper treatment of concurrency has to solve the following difficulties: Starting from the axioms describing the effects of the atomic events

1. we want to derive the effects of a set of atomic events occurring in parallel. This point can be divided into the questions of what has changed after the simultaneous occurrence of a set of events and what remains unchanged.

---

*This research was supported by the German Research Council under grant no. HE 1170/5 - 1.
[1]We will use the term event as a generic term for actions and other changes

2. We do not want to be able to derive plans which are not executable. This might happen if our formalism cannot handle conflicts between actions.

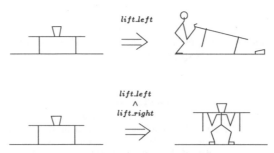

Figure 1: Lifting a table.

As a typical example see Figure 1. The first part of Figure 1 describes the single action of lifting the table on the left side. As an effect we would expect that the table is lifted on the left side and that the vase dropped down. The effect of lifting on the right side would be similar. However, lifting both sides of the table concurrently will lead to a state in which the vase has not dropped down (depicted in the second part of Figure 1). Thus the position of the vase is not affected and belongs therefore to the frame of the concurrent action. As we showed in Figure 1 the agent is able to lift the table simultaneously on both sides. Furthermore, suppose the agent were not as strong then our theory should somehow guarantee that we cannot form a plan in which the agent lifts the table on both sides simultaneously.

In this paper we propose a method for parallelizing events. We shall refer to this approach as "state event logic". The four main ideas are as follows: Firstly, much in the line of Lin and Shoham [7] we establish a symmetry of states and events. Analogously to the description of states by formulas over the set of primitive state symbols we describe events by formulas over a set of primitive event symbols. A possible description of the event happening in the first part of Figure 1 would be the formula $lift\_left \land \neg lift\_right$. Secondly, the effects of an event are divided into direct and indirect effects. Direct effects are effects which necessarily hold after the event (described by some event formula) has occurred. For instance, if we want to describe the effect of lifting the left side of the table we would state

> **If** $down\_left\_side$ **holds in a state and if** $lift\_left$ **holds in the event occurring in this state then** $\neg down\_left\_side$ **holds in the next state.**

The position of the vase or of the right-hand side of the table is not included in the postcondition, since they might depend on other properties of the event. In Figure 1 both events make $lift\_left$ true. However, the position of the vase is differently affected.

This representation of events is in contrast to the common description of events. There we have effect axioms in which we describe the effect of an event if it occurs in isolation. Here *lift_left* means all events for which the formula *lift_left* holds. Thus a conjunction like *lift_left* ∧ *lift_right* reduces the number of possible events to the ones which satisfy both conjuncts. The distinction between direct and indirect effects enables us to combine two (or more) effect axioms and to describe more specific events. The direct effect of such a resulting event is exactly the conjunction of the postconditions.

Secondly, we provide frame axioms which look similar to Schubert's explanation closure [5,9] , i.e., " if P is true in a state and the occurring event does not satisfy E, F or G, then P is true in the successor state". The combination of direct effects and this frame handling allows us to infer the propositions that change and the ones that persist as a result of some complex event.

Thirdly, indirect effects such as the dropping of the vase are treated as events. The movement of the vase cannot be seen as a direct effect of *lift_left* ∧ ¬*lift_right*. The vase falls if and only if the table is sloped, i.e., which is here a consequence of the direct effect of *lift_left*. This view results in the sequence of events as depicted in Figure 2. It

w_1 w_2 w_3

Figure 2: Lifting a table with a vase on top of it described by a sequence of lifting and falling.

could thus be formalized by

If   ¬*down_left_side* ∧ *down_right_side* ∧ *vase_on_table*   **holds in a state**
then   *vase_falls*   **holds in the event occurring in this state.**

Thus when we state that the vase will drop down we restrict the possible events happening in the given state to the models of *vase_falls*. It is clear that treating indirect effects as events implies that we have to provide effect axioms for them similar to the ones which we introduced for *lift_left*.

Finally, we want our formalism to handle the conflict problem properly. By regarding events as models of a set of subevents we can achieve that. If two subevents, say E and F, cannot occur in parallel then there exists no event which is a model of both. Thus, although we can form a statement "if event E and event F happen, then ...", no trouble arises. On the one hand, the statement is still true, because the precondition is false. On the other hand, the conclusion can never be used in a proof unless we satisfy the precondition. Consequently, we cannot build plans which are not executable.

2.   Propositional State Event Logic

In the following part we embed our formalism in modal logic K. The central difference is that we provide two sets for building the universe, a set of states W and a set of events E. The universe is a set $T \subseteq W \times E$. Each element of T is a pair which has a state and an event component as depicted in Figure 3. We provide two sorts of atomic

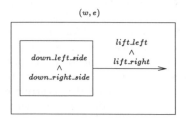

Figure 3: A pair consisting of the state w and the event e.

formulae, i.e., state and event formulae, to describe the respective components of pairs. Thus for the pair depicted in Figure 3 the formula

$$down\_left\_side \wedge down\_right\_side \wedge \; lift\_left \wedge lift\_right$$

holds, because $down\_left\_side \wedge down\_right\_side$ holds for the state component and $lift\_left \wedge lift\_right$ holds for the event component. The expressions of our language are built up from the two sorts of formulae by using the standard connectives. This is sufficient to describe pairs as depicted in Figure 3. The conjunction of two subevents means that the entire event is a model of both subevents, which we want to interpret as parallel occurrence. The disjunction of two subevents means that the entire event is a model of at least one of the two events. Finally the negation of a subevent means that the entire event is not a model of the respective event formula.

We are also free to build expressions combining both sorts. For instance, the formula

$$(down\_left\_side \wedge \neg down\_right\_side \wedge vase\_on\_table) \rightarrow vase\_falls$$

describes the union of the set of pairs for which antecedent and conclusion hold and the set of pairs which are not models of the antecedent. If we take this formula as an axiom we express that in every pair for which the antecedent holds the event formula $vase\_falls$ holds for the subsequent event.

In order to describe the course of the world we have to connect the pairs by an accessibility relation $R \subseteq T \times T$. Statements about subsequent pairs will be expressed by using a modal operator $\square$. The formula $\square\ p$ can be read as 'formula p holds in all next pairs'. $\square\ p$ is true in a pair (w, e), if p is true in all pairs $(w', e') \in T$ with $[(w, e), (w', e')] \in R$. In Figure 4 we show a relation between two pairs.

The transition between the two pairs in Figure 4 can be expressed by the formula

$$down\_left\_side \wedge down\_right\_side \wedge vase\_on\_table$$
$$\wedge\ lift\_left \wedge \neg lift\_right$$
$$\rightarrow$$
$$\square\ (\neg down\_left\_side \wedge down\_right\_side$$
$$\wedge\ vase\_on\_table \wedge\ vase\_falls)$$

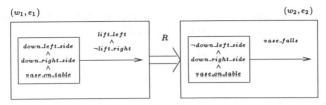

Figure 4: The accessibility relation R between two pairs.

This view on states and events is expressive enough to handle simultaneously oc-curring events, causality between events, and conflicting events. This we illustrate by an example in Section 3. But before that we set state event logic on a formal ground.

Syntax: We have two sets of symbols, Φ_0 and Π_0, standing for atomic state formulae and atomic event formulae. We use $s, t, \ldots$ to denote the elements of Φ_0, and $a, b, \ldots$ to denote the elements of Π_0.

The set of well-formed formulae Σ is defined as follows:

$$\Phi_0, \Pi_0 \subseteq \Sigma$$
$$\text{if } p, q \in \Sigma \text{ then } \neg p, p \vee q, \Box p \in \Sigma$$

We use $\wedge$, $\rightarrow$, $\leftrightarrow$ as abbreviations in the standard way. In addition, we abbreviate $\neg \Box \neg\, p$ to $\Diamond\, p$ as in modal logic.

Semantics: The structure underlying state event logic is basically adopted from modal logic K. Extending the universe to state event pairs implies that we also require two assignment functions, M_1 and M_2. M_1 assigns to each atomic state formula some subset of the set of states W. In addition, the mapping M_2 assigns to each atomic event formulae some subset of the set of events E. Based on these two mappings we will form a mapping M for assigning well-formed formulae to state event pairs. Finally we take the relation R to be a subset of $T \times T$. Thus we use the modal logic system to reason about the relation of state event pairs.

The semantics of state event logic logic is defined relative to a given structure $S\, =\, < W, E, T, R, M_1, M_2 >$. We postulate

1. a set of states W,

2. a set of events E,

3. a set of pairs $T \subseteq W \times E$,

4. a relation $R \subseteq T \times T$, and

5. two mappings M_1 and M_2:
$$M_1 : \Phi_0 \rightarrow 2^W$$
$$M_2 : \Pi_0 \rightarrow 2^E$$

Finally we need a mapping from the set of expressions Σ to the universe T. It can be inductively created with the mappings M_1 and M_2:

$$M : \Sigma \to 2^T$$

as follows

$M(p) = \{(w, e) \in T \mid \quad [p \in \Phi_0 \wedge w \in M_1(p)] \quad \vee \quad [p \in \Pi_0 \wedge e \in M_2(p)] \quad \}$

$M(\neg p) = T - M(p)$

$M(p \vee q) = M(p) \cup M(q)$

$M(\Box\, p) = \{(w, e) \in T \mid \quad \forall (w', e') \in T : \quad (w, e)R(w', e') \to (w', e') \in M(p) \quad \}$

The last equation asserts that $\Box\, p$ is true in those pairs (w, e) from which only pairs (w', e') are accessible such that p holds in (w', e').

The axiom system is the one of modal logic K:

PL.   All instances of tautologies of the propositional calculus

K. $\qquad\qquad\qquad \Box(p \to q) \to (\Box p \to \Box q)$

Inference rules:

$$\mathbf{RN} \quad \frac{p}{\Box p} \qquad\qquad \frac{p \qquad p \to q}{q} \quad \mathbf{MP}$$

Observe that a structure $\mathcal{S} = \ <W, E, T, R, M_1, M_2>\ $ of state event logic is logically identical to a structure $\mathcal{S}' = \ <T', R, M'>\ $ in normal modal logic K. The system K can be obtained by taking $\Phi_0 \cup \Pi_0$ as the set of atomic expressions. On the semantical side we postulate the universe T' in which each pair $(w, e) \in T$ of state-event logic is represented by a corresponding $t \in T'$. In addition we merge M_1 and M_2 to a mapping M'. We can state that a formula is a theorem in state event logic if and only if it is a theorem in its corresponding modal logic system (see long version for the proof). Consequently, propositional state event logic inherits the properties of modal logic.

The advantage of state event logic is that we can access the components of the state event pairs. Semantically, we can express that different events can follow the same state, i.e., $(w, e_1) \in T$ and $(w, e_2) \in T$. In the corresponding system K these two pairs would be represented by two different elements $t_1, t_2 \in T$ which had no relationship to each other. Moreover, the effort of separating the two different concepts of states and events from each other is comparatively small to the gain in clarification.

In the sequel we will make extensive use of the following theorem

R. $\qquad\qquad\qquad \Box(p \wedge q) \leftrightarrow (\Box p \wedge \Box q)$

3. Example

We now explain with an example how we can reason about the effects of simultaneously occurring events. This includes the changes caused by the events, the question of what remains unchanged, and our way of handling conflicting events. Finally we show an example proof constructed with our inference system.

The scenario in Figure 5 consists of a table which can be lifted on two sides by an agent. The goal of the agent is to lift the table on both sides. There are three ways for it to achieve the goal: first, it can lift on the left side and then on the right side expressed by the event sequence e_1 and e_2. Second, the agent might lift the right side first and then the left side, i.e., first e_2 and then e_1. And third, the agent is strong enough to lift on both sides simultaneously, which is represented by event e_3. Our agent cannot wait or lower the table.

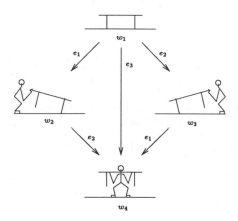

Figure 5: Simultaneous lifting of the table.

The atomic states and events will be described by the sets:

$$\Phi_0 = \{down\_left\_side, down\_right\_side\} \qquad \Pi_0 = \{lift\_left, lift\_right\}$$

In addition we provide a structure $S = (W, E, T, R, M_1, M_2)$ with

$$
\begin{aligned}
W &= \{w_1, w_2, w_3, w_4\} \\
E &= \{e_1, e_2, e_3, e_4\} \\
T &= \{(w_1, e_1), (w_1, e_2), (w_1, e_3), (w_2, e_2), (w_3, e_1), (w_4, e_4)\} \\
R &= \left\{
\begin{array}{l}
[(w_1, e_1), (w_2, e_2)] \quad, \quad [(w_1, e_2), (w_3, e_1)] \quad, \quad [(w_1, e_3), (w_4, e_4)] \,, \\
[(w_2, e_2), (w_4, e_4)], \\
[(w_3, e_1), (w_4, e_4)]
\end{array}
\right\}
\end{aligned}
$$

$$
\begin{aligned}
M_1(down\_left\_side) &= \{w_1, w_3\} \\
M_1(down\_right\_side) &= \{w_1, w_2\} \\
M_2(lift\_left) &= \{e_1, e_3\} \\
M_2(lift\_right) &= \{e_2, e_3\}
\end{aligned}
$$

Let us examine how we reason about the simultaneous occurrence of events and the conflict problem: We provide descriptions of the events in Figure 5 in the common fashion, a precondition implies a postcondition:

lift_left: $(down\_left\_side \wedge lift\_left) \rightarrow \Box(\neg down\_left\_side)$

lift_right: $(down\_right\_side \wedge lift\_right) \rightarrow \Box(\neg down\_right\_side)$

It is easy to see that our example is a model of these two sentences. An implication is true in each pair of the universe, if the conclusion is true in each pair which satisfies the antecedent.

By applying the tautologies of propositional calculus and the rule R of the given axiom system we can derive from these two sentences the formula:

$$
\begin{aligned}
&(down\_left\_side \wedge down\_right\_side \wedge lift\_left \wedge lift\_right) \\
&\quad \longrightarrow \Box \ (\neg down\_left\_side \wedge \neg down\_right\_side)
\end{aligned}
$$

It states that, if there exists a pair which satisfies the antecedent

$$down\_left\_side \wedge down\_right\_side \wedge lift\_left \wedge lift\_right$$

then the next pair will satisfy the conjunction of both postconditions

$$\Box \ (\neg down\_left\_side \wedge \neg down\_right\_side)$$

The conclusion that the next pair is a model of both postconditions is correct, because of the meaning of the $\Box$ operator. The single event descriptions express what necessarily happens after the event has occurred independently of other simultaneously occurring events.

The proper handling of conflicts is also a consequence of treating events on the predicate level. Consider the structure depicted in Figure 5 but without event e_3. Obviously this structure is also a model of both event descriptions. The derived sentence about the simultaneous occurrence is also correct. There is no pair in the structure which can satisfy the antecedent of the theorem. However, we cannot build up a plan in which the agent lifts on both sides in parallel, because then we would have to satisfy the antecedent.

In addition to describing the necessary effects caused by an event, we also want to express what remains unchanged. For instance, in Figure 5 we would like to express that the position of the right side of the table is not affected by lifting the left side. However, because of the simultaneity we cannot use a statement such as

$$(down\_right\_side \wedge lift\_left) \rightarrow \square \ down\_right\_side$$

Instead we will express persistence by sentences like

$$(down\_right\_side \wedge \neg lift\_right) \rightarrow \square \ down\_right\_side$$

This sentence makes a statement for the case that some event will not happen, i.e., if the table is on the ground on the right side and nobody lifts it there, then it will keep its position. This is essentially Schubert's explanation closure [5,9].

A further advantage is that we can combine frame axioms arbitrarily. For instance from the two sentences

$$(p \wedge a) \rightarrow \square \ p$$
$$(r \wedge \neg c) \rightarrow \square \ r$$

we can conclude by using rule R and the laws of propositional logic

$$(p \wedge a \wedge r \wedge \neg c) \rightarrow \square \ (p \wedge r)$$

Let us illustrate the theory by proving the following theorem:

$$(lift\_left \wedge \neg lift\_right \wedge down\_left\_side \wedge down\_right\_side)$$
$$\rightarrow$$
$$\square \ [lift\_right$$
$$\rightarrow$$
$$\square \ (\neg down\_left\_side \wedge \neg down\_right\_side)]$$

With respect to Figure 5 this sentence expresses that the occurrence of event e_1 followed by e_2 leads from state w_1 to w_7. The proof is as follows:

1.	$(down\_left\_side \wedge lift\_left) \rightarrow \square \ \neg down\_left\ side$	(Axiom)
2.	$(down\_right\_side \wedge \neg lift\_right) \rightarrow \square \ down\_right\_side$	(Axiom)
3.	$\square \ [(down\_right\_side \wedge lift\_right) \rightarrow \square \ \neg down\_right\_side]$	(Axiom,RN)

4.	$(down\_left\_side \wedge down\_right\_side \wedge lift\_left \wedge \neg lift\_right)$ $\rightarrow$ $\square \ \{\neg down\_left\_side \wedge down\_right\_side$ $\wedge \ [(down\_right\_side \wedge lift\_right) \rightarrow \square \ \neg down\_right\_side] \}$	(PL,R)

5.	$(down\_left\_side \wedge down\_right\_side \wedge lift\_left \wedge \neg lift\_right)$ $\rightarrow$ $\square \ \{(\neg down\_left\_side \wedge [lift\_right \rightarrow \square \ \neg down\_right\_side] \}$	(PL)

6.	$\square \ [\neg down\_left\_side \rightarrow \square \ \neg down\_left\_side]$	(Axiom,RN)

$$(down\_left\_side \land down\_right\_side \land lift\_left \land \neg lift\_right)$$

7. $$\Box \; [lift\_right \qquad\qquad\qquad \text{(PL)}$$
$$\to$$
$$\Box \; (\neg down\_left\_side \land \neg down\_right\_side) \,]$$

4. Acknowledgments

I would like to thank Johanna Wiesmet, Ute Sigmund and Hesham Khalil for many enlightening comments and improvements on previous versions of this paper.

5. References

1. C. Baral and M. Gelfond. *Representing Concurrent Actions in Extended Logic Programming.* In *International Joint Conference on Artificial Intelligence.* Morgan Kaufmann Publishers, Inc., 1993.

2. M. Gelfond, V. Lifschitz, and A. Rabinov. *What are the Limitations of the Situation Calculus.* In *Automated Reasoning — Essays in Honor of Woody Bledsoe,* p. 167–179, Kluwer Academic Publishers, 1991.

3. M. P. Georgeff. *Actions, Processes, and Causality.* In M. P. Georgeff and A. L. Lansky, editors, *Proceedings of the Workshop on Reasoning about Actions and Plans,* p. 99–122, 1986.

4. G. Große and R. Waldinger. *Towards a Theory of Simultaneous Actions.* In J. Hertzberg, editor, *Proceedings of the European Workshop on Planning,* p. 78–87, Springer LNAI 522, 1991.

5. A. Haas. *The Case for Domain-Specific Frame Axioms.* In F. Brown, editor, *Proceedings of the Workshop on The Frame Problem in Artificial Intelligence,* 1987.

6. D. Harel. *Dynamic Logic.* In F. Günthner D. Gabbay, editors, *Handbook of Philosophical Logic.* D. Reidel, 1984.

7. F. Lin and Y. Shoham. *Concurrent actions in the situation calculus.* In *Proceedings of the AAAI National Conference on Artificial Intelligence,* 1992.

8. V. R. Pratt. *Semantical Considerations on Floyd-Hoare Logic.* In *Proceedings of the 17th IEEE Symposium on Foundations of Computer Science,* 1976.

9. L. Schubert. *Monotonic Solution of The Frame Problem in The Situation Calculus.* In Jr. etal H.E. Kyberg, editor, *Knowledge Representation and Defeasible Reasoning,* pages 23–67. Kluwer Academic Publishers, 1990.

A BLACKBOARD APPROACH TO PARALLEL TEMPORAL TABLEAUX*

ROBERT JOHNSON

Department of Computing
Manchester Metropolitan University
Manchester, M1 5GD
United Kingdom

TEL: *(+44) 061-247-1536*
FAX: *(+44) 061-247-1483*
EMAIL: *robj@sun.com.mmu.ac.uk*

ABSTRACT

Before we can contemplate specifying, verifying and animating reactive systems using temporal logics the computational effectiveness of the reasoning process must be vastly improved. While parallel processing will not decrease the total amount of processing required to solve a problem, (in fact it usually increases it) it has the potential to solve the problem faster than sequential systems by distributing the load for for concurrent computation. We illustrate a mechanism by which we are able to harness the available potential of the tableau method for temporal logic, and give an account of an implementation that will permit us to selectively tailor the amount of parallelism for a particular physical architecture. Our approach builds a single, regulated, shared data structure with many concurrent processes acting on it.

1. Introduction

In order to port an existing algorithm to a parallel architecture a number of points must be addressed. Firstly, maximal parallelism must be identified in the algorithm, then a suitable process grain size must be determined, principally to suit the characteristics of the target architecture. The overheads involved with incorporating the parallelism must be deemed not to outweigh the potential benefits to be accrued. Finally, an efficient mapping between algorithmic processes and the target architecture must be constructed.

Temporal logics are used in order to facilitate reasoning about properties that change with time. Temporal logic formulas used in the modelling of large systems are correspondingly large, and require extensive computation for proof derivation. Thus,

---

*This research has been supported by SERC grant GR/J48979

184

a large amount of temporal information must be stored and manipulated during the proof process. Nevertheless, temporal logics have been used for modelling dynamic systems and reasoning about their domains. This reasoning inevitably requires proof procedures. The improved efficiency and effectiveness of these is our goal.

We are concerned with porting a variety of automated theorem proving techniques to novel parallel and distributed processing architectures. Here we shall restrict our discussion to the tableau method for linear, discrete propositional temporal logic.[4] We will not concern ourselves with possible topologies since the proposed approach is independent of any particular structure, however our design is based on a general message-passing architecture. It is currently being implemented using Strand88*.

Here we discuss our approach to the design and implementation of a parallel theorem prover for temporal logic. We give a semi-formal description of the original sequential algorithm, then suggest possible parallelisations. Some of these parallelisations maintain the structure of the original algorithm, others require a considerable restructuring of the approach. We then give specific algorithms that describe the function and interactions of a number of concurrent agents that collectively carry out the theorem proving operation. Finally we briefly consider the problem of load balancing across a network of processors.

1.1. Notation For Algorithm Specification

The notation we employ for the specification of algorithms seeks to present the fundamental processes of the algorithm in a semi-formal structure. Thus a specification may be used both for discussion and coding purposes, it being neither too rigorous for the former, nor too simplistic for the latter. Each statement is presented in the form:

$$<statement\ number>.<description>—\ Q_1, \ldots, Q_p : R_1, \ldots, R_q :: O_1, \ldots, O_r;$$

where $Q_i, 1 \leq i \leq p$ represent quantifications, $R_j, 1 \leq j \leq q$ represent restrictions on the quantifications, and $O_k, 1 \leq k \leq r$ represents the operations to be carried out. This is a coarse derivation of the schema employed in.[3] The restrictions component may have additional nested quantifications and further restrictions on them as required. The description and restriction components may however not always be required. Control of statement execution is provided by conventional loop and IF...THEN...ELSE type constructs. Simplified algorithms may dispense with much of the mathematical nomenclature, relying on the description to convey the function of each statement. Variables that are not temporal logic formulas (or sets of formulas) may in most cases alternatively be viewed as sets of formulas, or as pipes/channels/streams between processes, along which messages flow. It should be stressed that the notation is intended to be flexible and is designed as a vehicle for conveying the general semantics of an algorithm rather than for providing a full formal definition. Statements may be nested to describe more complex algorithmic functions. The statement numbers have no semantic relevance and are presented purely for reference purposes.

---

*Strand88 is a trademark of Strand Software Technologies Limited.[2]

2. Wolper's Sequential Algorithm For Temporal Tableau

The method described here is a non-analytic extension of the tableau method (described in[4]). The approach is essentially two-phased. Firstly, it involves constructing a digraph by applying tableau rules to the formulas stored at each node. Then the graph is reduced by the application of reduction rules that enable nodes of the graph to be discarded. If the root node is removed then the supplied formula may be deemed unsatisfiable. In the sequential case the graph reduction phase commences immediately the graph is fully constructed. The tableau expansion rules are given in .[4]

<u>Graph Construction</u>

1. Create node $N := (\{F\}, \emptyset)$ where F is the formula to be tested—
   $G := \{N_i\}$;

   WHILE $\exists g \in L_i, g$ is an unmarked, non-elementary formula, $N_i \in G$,
   $N_i = (L_i, \emptyset)$ DO

2. Apply tableau rule to $f - f \Rightarrow \{S_i\}$;

3. Build successor nodes (N_{s_i}) to N_i, and mark f as used —
   $\forall S_i :: N_{s_i} := (S_i \cup (L_i - \{f\}) \cup \{f^*\}, \emptyset)$ where f^* is f marked as used,
   $N_i' := (L_i, C_i \cup \{s_i\})$ (where s_i are the names of the successors),
   $G := (G - N_i) \cup \{N_i', N_{s_i}\}$;

4. If some N_j is a state then build prestate N_j' —
   $\forall N_j : N_j = (L_j, \emptyset)$,
   $\not\exists f \in L_j$ such that f is unmarked and non-elementary ::
   $N_{s_j} := (\{f \mid \bigcirc f \in L_j\}, \emptyset)$,
   $N_j' := (L_j, \{N_{s_j}\})$ (where N_{s_j} is a name),
   $G := (G - N_j) \cup \{N_j', N_{s_j}\}$;

END WHILE

<u>Graph Reduction</u>

REPEAT

5. Set flag to indicate that no graph reduction has occurred so far in this pass —
   $reducing := false$;

6. Delete contradictory nodes — $\forall N_i : N_i \in G, N_i = (L_i, c_i), f, \neg f \in L_i ::$
   $\forall N_j : N_j \in G, N_j = (L_j, c_j), N_i \in c_j ::$
   $N_j' := (L_j, c_j - \{N_i\})$ (where N_i is a name in the last two instances),
   $G := (G - (\{N_j\} \cup \{N_i\})) \cup \{N_j'\}$,
   $reducing := true$;

7. Delete nodes without successors — $\forall N_i : N_i \in G, N_i = (L_i, \emptyset)$ ::
$\forall N_j : N_j \in G, N_j = (L_j, c_j), N_i \in c_j$ ::
$N_j' := (L_j, c_j - \{N_i\})$ (where N_i is a name in the last two instances),
$G := (G - (\{N_j\} \cup \{N_i\})) \cup \{N_j'\}$,
$reducing := $ true;

8. Delete nodes in cycles where the prestate eventuality is unsatisfied —
$\forall cycle : cycle = \{N_i, N_i + 1, \ldots, N_j\}, cycle \subseteq G, N_j = (L_j, c_j), N_i \in c_j$ (where N_i is a name),
$\exists N_p : N_p \in cycle, N_p$ is a prestate, $i \leq p \leq j, N_p = (L_p, c_p), \Diamond f \in L_p$,
$\not\exists N_q : N_q \in cycle, N_q = (L_q, c_q), f \in L_q$ :: $G := G - N_p, reducing := $ true;

9. Delete nodes in cycles where the prestate $until(\mathcal{U})$ eventuality is unsatisfied —
$\forall cycle : cycle = \{N_i, N_i + 1, \ldots, N_j\}, cycle \subseteq G, N_j = (L_j, c_j), N_i \in c_j$ (where N_i is a name),
$\exists N_p : N_p \in cycle, N_p$ is a prestate, $i \leq p \leq j, N_p = (L_p, c_p), f_1 \mathcal{U} f_2 \in L_p$,
$\not\exists N_q : N_q \in cycle, N_q = (L_q, c_q), f_2 \in L_q$ :: $G := G - N_p$,
$reducing := $ true;

UNTIL $reducing = $ false

10. IF $G = \emptyset$ then F is unsatisfiable
ELSE formula F is satisfiable.

If the graph G is successfully reduced to nothing (i.e. we are able to remove the root node) then the supplied formula is unsatisfiable. Otherwise there exists an interpretation that will satisfy it.

3. Exploiting Control Parallelism

Given the above algorithms we are able to identify the opportunities for control parallelism in the algorithm as follows:

1. Partitioning during graph construction following β-rule application;

2. concurrently checking for duplicate state generation during graph construction;

3. deleting contradictory states;

4. deleting states without successors;

5. deleting states containing unsatisfiable eventualities, and within this:

    (a) concurrently searching graph for unsatisfiable eventualities,
    (b) concurrently applying graph deletion;

6. pipelining the entire procedure;

7. partitioning following α-rule application.

Note that contradictory nodes may be detected and deleted during the construction phase, thus avoiding redundant graph construction.

4. A Framework For Parallel Temporal Tableaux

Our design is implemented as a framework so that parallel options may be enforced or retracted enabling a range of configurations from maximal parallelism to sequential execution to be produced. This allows us to experiment with the process granularity and to tailor the system to suit the characteristics of a particular architecture.

Our implementation incorporates all of the parallel options given in with the exception of α-partitioning (option 7) which has not been implemented at present since the requisite level of preprocessing analysis suggests that the overheads associated with such an approach are relatively high.

The system is constructed using six communicating process agents: the director, process_supplier, preprocessor, constructor, checker, and searcher. The agents cooperate to build (and reduce) a digraph that is stored, under the control of the director, as a shared data structure, effectively a blackboard structure. Each different type of agent incorporates facilities for internal parallel computation to a lesser or greater degree. Additionally there exists scope for parallelism between the agents using partitioning and pipelining strategies.

For reasons of space the algorithms for each agent are presented in an abridged format (unabridged versions are also available). Given the shared blackboard data structure G some processes attempt to extend G through the application of tableau expansion rules; others try to clarify the graph structure, e.g. by detecting duplicate nodes; yet others attempt to prune the structure, e.g. by deleting contradictory nodes, deleting nodes with no successor, and deleting nodes with unsatisfiable eventualities. All these processes may proceed concurrently to exploit maximal parallelism. To a certain extent the model may be viewed as representing competition between the different processes where some are aiming at expansion, others at conciseness, and others still at the reduction of G.

During graph construction, all agents may be concurrently active. However, once the graph is completed, only the director and searcher will operate. Each agent may be allocated any number of processes on demand, as ultimately determined by the process_supplier. The process_supplier agent assesses the relative loadings of each processor and the level of activity of each agent with respect to the state of G before allocating a process.

4.1. The Director

The director agent is primarily responsible for the regulation of the graph G (the blackboard), and, through its subordinate agent, the process_supplier, for the allocation and mapping of processes to agents at the algorithmic level, and processes to processors at the physical level. During graph construction the director is ultimately responsible for adding nodes and edges to G. Similarly, during reduction, it acts upon the advice of the searcher as it systematically reduces G. In this algorithm we leave the process_supplier to operate independent of directorial control. However, since both the incoming process request stream and the outgoing process address stream pass through the director agent, control may easily be enforced if required. The abridged version of the director's algorithm is as follows.

1. state := construction;

2. Build initial *balance_set* (the set of relative processor loadings);

3. Spawn supplier sub-process to handle processor address requests for process distribution and pass to it both *balance_set* and the process request stream;

4. Pass initial node to constructor;

WHILE $\exists N \in G : N$ is active DO

5. Poll constructor for returned 'used' nodes N';

6. Pass N' to checker;

7. Terminate any constructor process that a checker identifies as having derived a duplicate node;

8. Update G with checker reports.

   (a) either $G := G \cup N'$

   (b) or update parent edge on existing $n \in G$ if a duplicate label;

9. IF N is a pre-state THEN pass it to a search process;

10. IF any searcher has a prestate P to delete THEN $G := G - \{P\}$;

END WHILE

11. state := reduction

REPEAT

12. IF $G \neq \emptyset$ THEN formula is valid ELSE

13. Poll search channels;

14. Delete any cycles from searchers - if dependent node then delete node - otherwise delete relevant edges;

15. IF any node has no successors THEN delete node;

16. Inform searchers of deletions

ENDIF

UNTIL no more deletions are possible

17. Formula is invalid.

4.2. The Process_Supplier

This agent receives a stream of process requests and operations information from the constructor via the director. It returns a stream of processor addresses while maintaining the relative processing loadings of *balance_set* so that the processor with the lightest load can be determined on each request.

WHILE *StreamIn* (the process request stream) not terminated DO
IF head item of *StreamIn* is a process request THEN

    1. Place address of processor with lightest load on *StreamOut*

ELSE

    2. Update process count to account for an expired process

ENDIF
ENDWHILE.

4.3. The Preprocessor

The preprocessor deals with the initial parsing of the supplied formula. It is responsible for inserting meta-information into the formulas and for applying a few syntactic manipulations such as the removal of double negations prior to commencing graph building. The preprocessor receives input from the user and returns it to the director. While the preprocessing operation may be pipelined so that processed formulas are passed to the director and on to the constructor in a piecemeal fashion, it should be noted that the complexity of the preprocessing phase is linear on the size of the formula, and is generally a relatively low cost procedure.

    1. Restructure formula;

    2. Insert meta-information into sub-formulas.

4.4. The Constructor

The constructor applies tableaux expansion rules to the formulas in a node to derive new successor nodes. It receives a node from another constructor as determined by the director then repeatedly returns derived nodes to the director (via the checker) until either a contradictory node is derived, no further rule applications may be made to the formulas in a node, or the constructor is instructed to terminate. The latter may occur if the formula has been identified as having derived a duplicate node and hence is pursuing a redundant computation. The constructor solicits the director for new processes when more than one successor node is derived. One successor is kept for expansion by the current processor while the other is expanded by the processor determined by the director. The granularity of each process is dictated by the frequency with which the constructor demands new processes.

WHILE not-terminated AND $\exists active - nodes$ DO

    1. Apply rule to active node N to derive new $active - node$ set $S = \{s1, ..., sn\}$;

    2. Mark N as used (N');

3. IF any $s \in S$ is contradictory THEN $S := S - \{s\}$, update child edge in N';

4. Place N' on G channel to director;

5. Spawn constructor process for some $s \in S, S := S - \{s\}$;

6. IF $s \neq \emptyset$ THEN $\forall s \in S$ spawn a new constructor process on the node dictated by Director process address channel;

END WHILE.

4.5. The Checker

This agent receives generated nodes from the constructor and searches the graph to determine whether or not they contain labels that are duplicated elsewhere. The checker may employ multiple subprocesses, each searching a subgraph to improve the efficiency of this operation. The efficiency of subgraph searching is of great importance since it is a relatively high cost operation in terms of processor time.

WHILE $state$=construction DO

1. IF $search - space$ is too large THEN partition it and spawn sub-processes to search partitions;

2. Poll director channel for incoming nodes N;

3. Pass N to all sub-checker processes (if they exist);

4. Check $search - space$ for duplicate label L;

5. IF any checker or sub-process finds a match THEN report 'found' on channel to director ELSE report unique;

END WHILE

6. Terminate process and all sub-processes.

4.6. The Searcher

The searcher agent is responsible for detecting unsatisfiable eventualities in any prestates that may occur in G. It does this by analysing G for strongly-connected components (cycles). Given that $\Diamond f$ occurs in a prestate N_p there must be a state N_i reachable from N_p that contains f, otherwise $\Diamond f$ is unsatisfiable and the director may be instructed to delete N_p from G. Similarly if f_2 does not appear in the cycle (which is detectable as a strongly-connected component of the graph) then formula $f_1 \, \mathcal{U} \, f_2$ (where $\mathcal{U}$ is the 'until' temporal operator) is unsatisfiable with the same operations resulting.

WHILE $state$=construction DO

1. Poll incoming channel for node N;

IF N is contradictory THEN

2. place its name on $Gdel$ channel (nodes to be deleted) and delete its local instance;

ELSE

3. Add N to each cycle that reaches it;

ENDIF

4. IF N satisfies eventuality e from pre-state P, and P reaches N THEN tag the cycle for e with a reference to N;

5. IF N is a prestate THEN for every eventuality $E \in N$ create a new cycle and add them to the set of cycles EV;

6. IF any cycle is subsumed by another THEN discard the subsumed cycle;

7. IF any cycle for e is strongly connected and e is unsatisfiable THEN delete the cycle for e, and IF the prestate P_e references no other cycles THEN place P_e on $Gdel$;

END WHILE

REPEAT

8. IF any cycle does not satisfy its respective e THEN delete the local instance of prestate P_e, place the name of P_e on $Gdel$, and remove cycles for any e in P_e from EV;

9. IF $d \in DN$ (nodes deleted by the director for having no successors) and d is tagged as satisfying e in a cycle THEN remove the tag;

UNTIL $EV = \emptyset$.

4.7. Incorporating Lemmata

Since we are dealing with a blackboard architecture incorporating lemmata is a straightforward task. The checker agent deals with the identification of duplicate labels in the graph which constitute cycles.

Theorem 1. (from Ben-Ari[1]) The structure created from a semantic tableau is a Hintikka structure.
Proof. Immediate by construction.

Theorem 2. Given subgraphs H_1 and H_2 generated respectively from nodes N_1 and N_2 which are labelled by the same set of formulas F, then H_1 and H_2 are Hintikka structures and $H_1 \equiv H_2$.
Proof. A corollary of the tableau soundness proof.

Assuming theorem 2 it follows that deriving any new node, N_2, that has an identical label to one (N_1) already existing in the G permits us to discard the new node (since the graph formed from the formulas in the label of a node represents a proof of the formulas and so constitutes a lemma), and simply redirect the parent of N_2 to inherit N_1 as successor node instead. Since it is necessary for us to search G for duplicates for the purpose of cycle identification anyway we incur no additional computational costs by incorporating lemmata. Additionally we benefit from reduced storage costs and the elimination of redundant duplicate computation.

5. The Problem Of Load Balancing

A distributed network of processors is likely to be less tolerant of high inter-process communication (IPC) levels than a physically localised network of message-passing nodes such as the KSR[†]. Therefore a schema based on a single distribution model and process grain size is probably inappropriate. An effective balance of parallelism may be determined by analysing the relative amounts of processing and IPC produced during test running. This will enable a suitable process grain-size to be predicted. Furthermore, profiling tools permit us to analyse the balance of process loadings across a network of nodes so that the most effective loading may be applied through the allocation of processors to pools available to particular agents, and the utilisation of the pools by each agent, under the control of the director. We shall consider a variety of load balancing techniques in future.

6. Conclusion

We have provided a semi-formal description of Wolper's algorithm[4] for temporal tableaux and have described the potential opportunities for parallelism exhibited by the general method. Moreover, we have described a system suitable for implementation on a parallel or distributed architecture. An important feature of the system is the incorporation of lemmata as an integral part of the approach. The implementation of this design will enable us to insert and retract parallel options in order to tailor the system to best exploit particular physical architectures through the analysis of typical relative processor loads and IPC levels.

References

1. M. Ben-Ari. *Mathematical Logic For Computer Science.* Prentice Hall. 1993.

2. I. Foster, S. Taylor. *Strand: New Concepts In Parallel Programming.* Prentice Hall. 1990.

3. F. Kurfeß *Parallelism In Logic.* Vieweg. 1991.

4. P. Wolper. *The Tableau Method For Temporal Logic: An Overview.* **Logique et Analyse vols 110-111** June-Sept 1985.

[†]Kendal Square Research machine.

V - REASONING ABOUT ACTION AND CHANGE

AN ANALYSIS OF SYSTEMATIC APPROACHES
TO REASONING ABOUT ACTIONS AND CHANGE

MICHAEL THIELSCHER

Intellektik, Informatik, TH Darmstadt
Alexanderstraße 10, D-64283 Darmstadt, Germany

ABSTRACT

Systematic approaches to reasoning about dynamical systems and causality provide a new view on how to proceed toward a general and uniform semantical framework which is independent from specific solutions to the frame problem, say. This direction of research enables to rigorously comparing known methodologies designed for reasoning about actions and change with respect to such a semantics.

Two actual systematic approaches, namely the Ego-World-Semantics[11,12] and the Action Description Language[5], are analyzed and compared in this paper. We present two equivalence results for ontological subclasses and elaborate the major differences. The ultimate aim of this analysis shall be a proposal about a combination of the two frameworks to obtain a powerful semantics which profits from the merits of both the Ego-World-Semantics as well as the Action Description Language.

1. Introduction

A key issue in Cognitive Science and Artificial Intelligence is to understand and model the ability of humans to reason about dynamical systems and causality. This kind of logical information processing is fundamental for prediction about effects of actions and events, for planning to achieve goals, for explaining observations, and many other intellectual capabilities. Automating this ability seems to be indispensable for creating autonomous robots and providing knowledge about everyday life for machines.

For more than 30 years research in this direction has focused on creating new or extending already existing specialized logical formalisms because classical logic, as it stands, seems to have difficulties — the technical *frame problem* — when used to express statements about non-static worlds. However, it has recently emerged that a more methodical and successful approach toward a general theory of actions and change consists in the development of an appropriate semantics first, instead of directly starting with a specific formalism.

Two independently developed, prominent systematic approaches to reasoning about actions and change are compared in this paper. Interpreting dynamical systems as a game between an active agent (the *ego*) and the reacting world is the basic notion underlying E. Sandewall's *Ego-World-Semantics* (EWS)[11,12]. The *Action Description Language* $\mathcal{A}$[5] is based on an elegant and natural way to describe the effects of actions. The main task of both approaches is to provide models given a complete description of actions and their effects along with a number of observations in certain situations.

Both systematic frameworks initiated a lot of further work, despite the fact that they were developed hardly two years ago, where several logics are assessed at their applicability to the semantics defined by the Ego-World-Semantics or the Action Description Language, respectively. The success of the two methodologies naturally raises the question whether they have a common ground. Nonetheless, this problem has not been investigated up to now.

The aim of this paper is to give a first answer to this question. Aside from the fact that the two approaches were developed with a similar intention, they share some fundamental assumptions:

- The approaches are systematic in the sense that they are based on a uniform semantics, and the key issue is to find a set of models given a number of action descriptions and a set of observations.
- The assumption of inertia is the overall principle stating that the value of a particular fact is static unless the fact is explicitly affected by an action.
- The concept of postdiction is supported, i.e. observations at some point of time can be used to derive additional information about situations before.
- Correct knowledge regarding the effects of actions is assumed, i.e. actions might have alternative, random effects but the set of possible effects is known.
- All actions which have been performed in a particular scenario are given.

In this paper, we fix the particular ontological subclass within the framework of the Ego-World-Semantics which is suitable for the Action Description Language and prove their equivalence. Furthermore, we use a recent extension of $\mathcal{A}$ regarding non-deterministic actions to obtain the analogous equivalence result for a more general ontological problem class. On the other hand, we elaborate an important feature supported by the Action Description Language but not by EWS.

The merits of our analysis are obvious: Firstly, once a logical system has been proved to be correct wrt some dialect of one of the two approaches, it is provably correct wrt the corresponding dialect of the other framework as well. Secondly, a clarification of the differences between both semantics yields a number of suggestions for improvements so that the two approaches can profit from the useful peculiarities of each other.

The paper is organized as follows. We give a brief introduction to the Action Description Language in Section 2 and the Ego-World-Semantics in Section 3, respectively. For more details, the reader should consult[5,13] and[11]. In addition, Section 2 includes a description of an extended version of the Action Description Language. Section 4 contains the main results of this paper: The respective ontological subclasses of EWS which are equivalent to $\mathcal{A}$ and its extension are fixed. Finally, a conclusion is given in Section 5.

2. The Action Description Language $\mathcal{A}$

Definition 1 A *domain* $\mathcal{D}$ is a tuple $(F, A, \mathcal{E}, \mathcal{V})$ where F and A are disjoint sets of symbols, called *fluent names* and *action names*, respectively, and $\mathcal{E}$ is a set of *effect propositions* of the form a causes f if $c_1, \ldots, c_m$ where $a \in A$ and $f, c_1, \ldots, c_m$ ($m \geq 0$) are *fluent literals*, i.e. elements of F possibly preceded by $\neg$. Furthermore, $\mathcal{V}$ is a set of *value propositions* of the form

$$f \text{ after } [a_1, \ldots, a_n] \tag{1}$$

where f is a fluent literal and $a_1, \ldots, a_n \in A$ ($n \geq 0$). In case $n = 0$, For.1 is usually written as initially f. ∎

Example 1. The *Yale Shooting scenario* describes a gun which might be loaded or not along with a turkey which is alive or dead. Three actions can be performed, viz. loading the gun, firing it which causes the turkey to drop dead provided the gun was loaded, and one action called waiting which is intended to have no effects at all. An instance of this scenario, called *Stanford Murder Mystery*, describes the reasoning process which has to be performed to conclude that the gun must have been loaded if the turkey was alive at the beginning and is observed to be dead after shooting and waiting. Let $\mathcal{D}_1$ denote the domain which consists of fluent names $F = \{loaded, alive\}$, action names $A = \{load, wait, shoot\}$, three effect propositions, namely

$$\begin{array}{lll} load \text{ causes } loaded & shoot \text{ causes } \neg alive \text{ if } loaded \\ & shoot \text{ causes } \neg loaded \end{array} \tag{2}$$

and two value propositions, namely

$$\text{initially } alive \quad \text{and} \quad \neg alive \text{ after } [shoot, wait]. \tag{3}$$

Definition 2 Given a domain $\mathcal{D} = (F, A, \mathcal{E}, \mathcal{V})$, a *situation* σ is a subset of F. For any $f \in F$, if $f \in \sigma$ (resp. $f \notin \sigma$) then f (resp. $\neg f$) is said to *hold* in σ. The *transition function* Φ maps an action name a and a situation σ into a situation $\Phi(a, \sigma)$ such that the following conditions are satisfied: For all $f \in F$,

1. if a causes f if $c_1, \ldots, c_m$ in $\mathcal{E}$ and each c_i holds in σ then $f \in \Phi(a, \sigma)$,
2. if a causes $\neg f$ if $c_1, \ldots, c_m$ in $\mathcal{E}$ and each c_i holds in σ then $f \notin \Phi(a, \sigma)$,
3. if $\mathcal{E}$ does not contain such effect propositions then $f \in \Phi(a, \sigma)$ iff $f \in \sigma$.

A pair (σ_0, Φ) is a *model* of $\mathcal{D}$ iff $\sigma_0 \subseteq F$, called the *initial* situation, Φ is the transition function determined by $\mathcal{E}$, and each member of $\mathcal{V}$ is true in (σ_0, Φ): A value proposition like For.1 is *true* in (σ_0, Φ) iff f holds in $\Phi([a_1, \ldots, a_n], \sigma_0)$, where $\Phi([a_1, \ldots, a_n], \sigma) := \Phi(a_n, \Phi(a_{n-1}, \ldots, \Phi(a_1, \sigma) \ldots))$. $\mathcal{D}$ is *consistent* if it has a model, and an arbitrary value proposition is *entailed* by $\mathcal{D}$ iff it is true in every model. ∎

Example 1 (continued). As regards $\mathcal{D}_1$, $\{alive\}$ is a situation where *alive* and $\neg loaded$ hold. The transition function Φ_1 determined by the propositions in For.2 is

$$\begin{array}{rcl} \Phi_1(load, \sigma) & = & \sigma \cup \{loaded\} \\ \Phi_1(shoot, \sigma) & = & \begin{cases} \sigma \setminus \{loaded, alive\}, & \text{if } loaded \in \sigma \\ \sigma, & \text{otherwise.} \end{cases} \\ \Phi_1(wait, \sigma) & = & \sigma \end{array} \tag{4}$$

Regarding the first value proposition in For.3, our domain $\mathcal{D}_1$ might have two models, viz. $(\{alive\}, \Phi_1)$ and $(\{alive, loaded\}, \Phi_1)$. However, following For.4 we find that $\Phi_1([shoot, wait], \{alive\}) = \Phi_1([wait], \{alive\}) = \{alive\}$, i.e. the former is not a model of the entire domain which requires $alive \notin \Phi_1([shoot, wait], \sigma_0)$ according to the second element in For.3. Hence, we conclude that initially $loaded$ is entailed by $\mathcal{D}_1$.

Example 1 is based on just a single sequence of actions, namely $[shoot, wait]$, which can be interpreted as the real development in this scenario. But, in addition to this, it is conceivable to consider two or more such sequences during the very same reasoning process which then can be regarded as a kind of hypothetical reasoning. This shall be illustrated by the following example, motivated by a scene in a Pierre Richard movie[10]:

Example 2. An additional fluent name $broken$ is introduced which describes the state of a vase. The action $shoot$ is replaced by the actions $shoot\text{-}at\text{-}pierre$ and $shoot\text{-}at\text{-}vase$, respectively, along with the effect propositions

$$shoot\text{-}at\text{-}pierre \quad \textbf{causes} \quad \neg alive \quad \textbf{if} \quad loaded$$
$$shoot\text{-}at\text{-}vase \quad \textbf{causes} \quad broken \quad \textbf{if} \quad loaded$$

and, as in For.2, $shoot\text{-}at\text{-}pierre$ **causes** $\neg loaded$ and $shoot\text{-}at\text{-}vase$ **causes** $\neg loaded$. Now, given the three value propositions

$$\textbf{initially } alive, \quad \textbf{initially } \neg broken, \quad broken \textbf{ after } [shoot\text{-}at\text{-}vase] \quad (5)$$

each model (σ_0, Φ) requires $loaded \in \sigma_0$ according to the second and third element of For.5. Hence, each model also supports $alive \notin \Phi([shoot\text{-}at\text{-}pierre], \sigma_0)$.

This example demonstrates how different developments of the world can be considered within a single model. As this kind of reasoning is not provided by the Ego-World-Semantics, we define the following restriction on $\mathcal{A}$:

Definition 3 $\mathcal{A}^1$ is as $\mathcal{A}$ except that the value propositions describing a particular domain are based on a single sequence of actions $[a_1, \ldots, a_n]$ ($n \geq 0$), i.e. each value proposition is of the form initially f or f after $[a_1, \ldots, a_k]$, $1 \leq k \leq n$. Furthermore, the transition function Φ determined by this domain is only defined in case of $\Phi([a_1, \ldots, a_k], \sigma_0)$ ($0 \leq k \leq n$). ■

The Action Description Language $\mathcal{A}$ was recently extended by integrating non-deterministic actions, i.e. actions with alternative randomized effects[13]:

Definition 4 A domain description in $\mathcal{A}_{ND}$ is as in Definition 1 except that $\mathcal{E}$ might contain *extended effect propositions* of the form

$$a \textbf{ alternatively causes } e_1, \ldots, e_k \textbf{ if } c_1, \ldots, c_m \quad (6)$$

where $a \in A$ and $e_1, \ldots, e_k, c_1, \ldots, c_m$ are fluent literals ($k \geq 0$, $m \geq 0$). ■

Example 3. To formalize the *Russian Turkey* scenario, $\mathcal{D}_1$ is augmented by a third action called $spin$ whose intended meaning is that its execution causes the gun to become randomly loaded or unloaded regardless of its state before. This can be expressed via the two extended effect propositions $spin$ **alternatively causes** $loaded$

and *spin* `alternatively causes` ¬*loaded*. Furthermore, let our modified domain $\mathcal{D}_3$ consist of a single value propositions, namely *alive* `after` [*load, spin, shoot*]. Due to the fact that the turkey is alive after shooting we intend to conclude that the gun became unloaded by spinning the gun.

To handle alternative effects, the notion of a transition function is replaced by a transition *relation* where two situations σ, σ' and an action name a are related iff σ' is a *possible* result of executing a in σ. In addition, a model includes an argument φ to determine, for this model, the choice of a particular alternative in any situation:

Definition 5 Given a domain $\mathcal{D} = (F, A, \mathcal{E}, \mathcal{V})$ in $\mathcal{A}_{ND}$, a *transition relation* Φ determined by $\mathcal{E}$ contains triples (σ, a, σ') such that the following conditions are satisfied: Let $\sigma, \sigma' \subseteq F$, and $a \in A$ then $(\sigma, a, \sigma') \in \Phi$ iff for all $f \in F$,

1. if a `causes` f `if` $c_1, \ldots, c_m$ in $\mathcal{E}$ and each c_i holds in σ then $f \in \sigma'$,
2. if a `causes` ¬f `if` $c_1, \ldots, c_m$ in $\mathcal{E}$ and each c_i holds in σ then $f \notin \sigma'$,
3. let the set

$$\left\{ \begin{array}{l} a \text{ \texttt{alternatively causes} } E_1 \text{ \texttt{if} } C_1 \\ \qquad\qquad\qquad\vdots \\ a \text{ \texttt{alternatively causes} } E_l \text{ \texttt{if} } C_l \end{array} \right\}$$

   contain all extended e-propositions such that $C_1, \ldots, C_l$ hold in σ [1] then we can choose a $\lambda \in \{1, \ldots, l\}$ such that all effects occurring in E_λ hold in σ', and
4. if neither f nor ¬f is forced to hold in σ' by 1., 2., or 3. then $f \in \sigma'$ iff $f \in \sigma$.

A triple $(\sigma_0, \Phi, \varphi)$ is a *model* of $\mathcal{D}$ iff $\sigma_0 \subseteq F$, Φ is a transition relation determined by $\mathcal{E}$, and φ is a total mapping form pairs $([a_1, \ldots, a_n], \sigma)$ into a situation such that for any sequence of actions $[a_1, \ldots, a_n]$ ($n \geq 0$) and situation σ the following holds:

1. $\varphi([\,], \sigma) = \sigma$ and
2. $(\varphi([a_1, \ldots, a_{n-1}], \sigma), a, \varphi([a_1, \ldots, a_n], \sigma)) \in \Phi$.

Furthermore, the members of $\mathcal{V}$ must be true in $(\sigma_0, \Phi, \varphi)$, i.e. for each For.1 $\in \mathcal{V}$, f holds in $\varphi([a_1, \ldots, a_n], \sigma_0)$. $\mathcal{D}$ is said to be *consistent* iff it admits a model. ∎

Example 3 (continued). The (extended) effect propositions of $\mathcal{D}_3$ determine a relation Φ_3 which is given by $(\sigma, a, \sigma') \in \Phi_3$ iff $\Phi_1(a, \sigma) = \sigma'$ if $a \in \{load, wait, shoot\}$ (c.f. For.4) and $(\sigma, spin, \sigma') \in \Phi$ iff $\sigma \setminus \{loaded\} = \sigma' \setminus \{loaded\}$, i.e. σ and σ' might differ on *loaded* but not elsewhere. Now, there are two different kinds of possible models $(\sigma_0, \Phi_3, \varphi)$ of $\mathcal{D}_3$: While in any case *loaded* $\in \varphi([load], \sigma_0)$, both *loaded* $\in \varphi([load, spin], \sigma_0)$ and *loaded* $\notin \varphi([load, spin], \sigma_0)$ have to be considered. However, only in the latter case *alive* $\in \varphi([load, spin, shoot], \sigma_0)$ is possible — provided *alive* $\in \sigma_0$. Hence, $\mathcal{D}_3$ entails ¬*loaded* `after` [*load, spin*].

Recently, a variety of logics designed for reasoning about actions have been proved to constitute a sound and complete encoding of $\mathcal{A}$, such as extended logic programs with two kinds of negation which use a special purpose semantics[4], an abductive logic programming approach[3], Reiter's approach[9], Baker's circumscription based approach[1] (both results established in[7]), and an approach based on equational logic programs[6,13]. The finally mentioned system has also been proved to be correct wrt $\mathcal{A}_{ND}$ [13].

---

[1] $C = c_1, \ldots, c_m$ is said to hold in a situation if all its fluent literals c_i's ($1 \leq i \leq m$) hold.

State r	$\texttt{Infl}(shoot, r)$	$\texttt{Trajs}(shoot, r)$
$\{loaded \hat{=} \texttt{false}, alive \hat{=} \texttt{false}\}$	$\{\}$	$\{\langle\rangle\}$
$\{loaded \hat{=} \texttt{false}, alive \hat{=} \texttt{true}\}$	$\{\}$	$\{\langle\rangle\}$
$\{loaded \hat{=} \texttt{true}, alive \hat{=} \texttt{false}\}$	$\{loaded\}$	$\{\langle loaded : \texttt{false}\rangle\}$
$\{loaded \hat{=} \texttt{true}, alive \hat{=} \texttt{true}\}$	$\{loaded, alive\}$	$\{\langle loaded : \texttt{false}, alive : \texttt{false}\rangle\}$

Figure 1: A trajectory description of *shoot* .

3. The Ego-World-Semantics

Due to the aim of this paper, when stating the formal definitions regarding EWS we concentrate on a restricted version of an ontological subclass called $\mathcal{K}$-*IbsA* .[2]

Definition 6   Let $\mathcal{F}$ be a set of symbols called *binary features* and A be a set of action names. A *state* r is a mapping from $\mathcal{F}$ into $\{\texttt{true}, \texttt{false}\}$. The effects of actions on states are described by means of a *trajectory table* which consists in a pair $(\texttt{Infl}, \texttt{Trajs})$ such that, for each action name $a \in A$ and state r , $\texttt{Infl}(a, r) \subseteq \mathcal{F}$ contains the features which are affected when executing a in r , and $\texttt{Trajs}(a, r)$ is a non-empty set of *trajectories* of the form $\langle f_1 : \nu_1, \ldots, f_m : \nu_m \rangle$ where $f_1, \ldots, f_m \in \texttt{Infl}(a, r)$ and $\nu_1, \ldots, \nu_m \in \{\texttt{true}, \texttt{false}\}$. A *possible result* of executing action a in state r is obtained by choosing a member of $\texttt{Trajs}(a, r)$ and executing its assignments in r . A *chronicle* is a triple $(\texttt{A}, \texttt{SCD}, \texttt{OBS})$ where $\texttt{A}$ is a formula representing a trajectory table,[3] the *schedule* SCD is a set $\{[0, 1]a_1, \ldots, [n-1, n]a_n\}$ where $a_1, \ldots, a_n \in A$ ($n \geq 0$), and OBS is a set of *observations* of the form $[\tau]f \hat{=} \nu$ where $0 \leq \tau \leq n$, $f \in \mathcal{F}$, and $\nu \in \{\texttt{true}, \texttt{false}\}$.   ∎

If each set $\texttt{Trajs}(a, r)$ contains a single element then the chronicle belongs to a subclass called $\mathcal{K}$-*IbsAd* where only deterministic actions (d) are considered.

Example 1 (reformulated).   Given the features $\mathcal{F}_1 = \{loaded, alive\}$, each set depicted in the leftmost column of Figure 1 represents a state. The entire table defines the effects of *shoot* : $\texttt{Infl}(shoot, r)$ contains the features which are affected when executing *shoot* in r . The trajectories in $\texttt{Trajs}(shoot, r)$ determine the resulting states by assuming that each assignment in the trajectory is performed while no other feature changes its value, e.g. executing *shoot* in $\{loaded \hat{=} \texttt{true}, alive \hat{=} \texttt{false}\}$ yields $\{loaded \hat{=} \texttt{false}, alive \hat{=} \texttt{false}\}$. To encode the Stanford Murder Mystery we use $\texttt{SCD}_1 = \{[0, 1]shoot, [1, 2]wait\}$ and $\texttt{OBS}_1 = \{[0]alive \hat{=} \texttt{true}, [2]alive \hat{=} \texttt{false}\}$. Let $\mathcal{J}_1$ denote this chronicle. Note that in any case $\texttt{Trajs}(shoot, r)$ contains only a single element as *shoot* is deterministic. In contrast, each $\texttt{Trajs}(spin, r)$ contains two

---

[2] I.e. we assume complete and accurate knowledge ($\mathcal{K}$), the world acts completely inertial (I), we consider alternative effects, depending on the situation where an action is executed (A), and we only consider binary features (b) and single-step actions (s) — see[11].

[3] For the purpose of our analysis it is not necessary to know how A is constructed given a trajectory table. The interested reader should consult[11].

State r	$\mathtt{Infl}(spin, r)$	$\mathtt{Trajs}(Spin, r)$
$\{loaded \hat{=} \mathtt{false}, alive \hat{=} \mathtt{false}\}$	$\{loaded\}$	$\{\langle loaded : \mathtt{true}\rangle, \langle\rangle\}$
$\{loaded \hat{=} \mathtt{false}, alive \hat{=} \mathtt{true}\}$	$\{loaded\}$	$\{\langle loaded : \mathtt{true}\rangle, \langle\rangle\}$
$\{loaded = \mathtt{true}, alive = \mathtt{false}\}$	$\{loaded\}$	$\{\langle\rangle, \langle loaded : \mathtt{false}\rangle\}$
$\{loaded \hat{=} \mathtt{true}, alive \hat{=} \mathtt{true}\}$	$\{loaded\}$	$\{\langle\rangle, \langle loaded : \mathtt{false}\rangle\}$

Figure 2: A trajectory description of the non-deterministic action $spin$.

trajectories — one where the gun becomes loaded and one where it becomes unloaded. Hence, $spin$ is non-deterministic (see Figure 2).

Models of a chronicle are obtained by interpreting a dynamically changing world as a game between an ego who initiates actions and the world which reacts according to the descriptions of effects:

Definition 7   A *timepoint* is a natural number or 0. Given a timepoint n, referred to as *now*, a *history* R is a mapping from timepoints $\{0, \ldots, n\}$ into the set of states. A *finite development* is a tuple $(\mathcal{B}, R, \mathcal{A}, \mathcal{C})$ where $\mathcal{B}$ is a set of timepoints with largest member n, R is a history, $\mathcal{A}$ is a set of actions which have been completed at time n, and $\mathcal{C}$ is a set of actions which have been started but are not completed at time n. Hence, elements in $\mathcal{A}$ are of the form (s, a, t) while elements in $\mathcal{C}$ are pairs (s, a), where $s < t \leq n$ are timepoints and a is an action name. If $\mathcal{J} = (\mathtt{A}, \mathtt{SCD}, \mathtt{OBS})$ is a chronicle then the set of intended models of $\mathcal{J}$, written $\mathcal{M}od(\mathcal{J})$, is a set of finite developments which are obtained as follows: Starting with the development $(\{0\}, R_0, \{\}, \{\})$ where R_0 maps timepoint 0 to an arbitrary initial state, the ego selects the first action according to $\mathtt{SCD}$ and adds it to the set of non-completed actions, i.e. the development changes to $(\{0\}, R_0, \{\}, \{(0, a_1)\})$. Afterwards, the world adds the next timepoint 1 to $\mathcal{B} = \{0\}$, executes a_1 in $R_0(0)$ by choosing one possible resulting state r_1 according to the trajectory table described by $\mathtt{A}$, and moves the action from $\mathcal{C}$ to $\mathcal{A}$. This yields the finite development $(\{0, 1\}, R_1, \{(0, a_1, 1)\}, \{\})$ where $R_1(0) = R_0(0)$ and $R_1(1) = r_1$. Then the ego selects the next element according to $\mathtt{SCD}$, the world reacts and so forth. The game ends after the ego has selected the final element of the schedule and the world has executed it. The final development $(\{0, \ldots, n\}, R_n, \mathcal{A}, \{\})$ is a member of $\mathcal{M}od(\mathcal{J})$ iff each observation $[\tau]f \hat{=} \nu$ in $\mathtt{OBS}$ is true in R_n, i.e. $R_n(\tau)(f) = \nu$. $\mathcal{J}$ is *consistent* iff $\mathcal{M}od(\mathcal{J})$ is non-empty. ∎

Example 1 (continued).   On the analogy of $\mathcal{D}_1$, we can find a single model of $\mathcal{J}_1$,[4] namely $(\{0, 1, 2\}, R_2, \{(0, shoot, 1), (1, wait, 2)\}, \{\})$ where $R_2(0)$ is the state $\{loaded \hat{=} \mathtt{true}, alive \hat{=} \mathtt{true}\}$ and $R_2(1) = R_2(2) = \{loaded \hat{=} \mathtt{false}, alive \hat{=} \mathtt{false}\}$.

This result obviously resembles the solution obtained by $\mathcal{A}$ and the value propositions in For.3. An analogous observation can be made by comparing Example 3 and

---

[4] Provided the effects of $wait$ are appropriately defined: For any state r, $\mathtt{Infl}(wait, r) = \{\}$ and $\mathtt{Trajs}(wait, r) = \{\langle\rangle\}$.

its encoding as a chronicle in the Ego-World-Semantics. In the following section, we formally compare the set of models of a domain description given in $\mathcal{A}$ or $\mathcal{A}_{ND}$, and the set of intended models of a corresponding chronicle.

4. Equivalence Results

Let σ be a situation based on a set of fluent names F and r a state based on a set of binary features $\mathcal{F}$ such that $F = \mathcal{F}$ then σ and r *coincide* iff for each $f \in F$ we find that $f \in \sigma$ iff $f \doteq \texttt{true}$ holds in r. For instance, $\{alive\}$ and $\{loaded \doteq \texttt{false}, alive \doteq \texttt{true}\}$ coincide. Given a situation σ, by r_σ we denote a state such that both coincide and vice versa, i.e. r and σ_r shall coincide as well.

Definition 8 Let $\mathcal{D} = (F, A, \mathcal{E}, \mathcal{V})$ be a consistent domain in $\mathcal{A}^1$. The *corresponding chronicle* $\mathcal{J}_\mathcal{D} = (\texttt{A}, \texttt{SCD}, \texttt{OBS})$ contains the features $\mathcal{F} = F$ and the action names A, and is constructed as follows: Let $\mathcal{D}$ be based on $[a_1, \ldots, a_n]$ ($n \geq 0$, see Definition 3) then $\texttt{SCD} = \{[0,1]a_1, \ldots, [n-1, n]a_n\}$. Furthermore, $\texttt{OBS}$ is obtained by translating each value proposition f after $[a_1, \ldots, a_k]$ in $\mathcal{V}$ into $[k]f \doteq \texttt{true}$ if f is a positive fluent literal and $[k]f \doteq \texttt{false}$ if f is negative ($0 \leq k \leq n$). Finally, $\texttt{A}$ describes a trajectory table $(\texttt{Infl}, \texttt{Trajs})$ which is generated as follows: Let Φ be the transition function determined by $\mathcal{E}$ then $\texttt{Infl}(a, r) = \{f \in F \mid f \in \sigma_r \not\Leftrightarrow f \in \Phi(a, \sigma_r)\}$ and

$$\texttt{Trajs}(a, r) = \langle f_1 : \nu_1, \ldots, f_k : \nu_k \rangle \tag{7}$$

where $a \in A$, r is a state, $\{f_1, \ldots, f_k\} = \texttt{Infl}(a, r)$ and $\nu_i = \texttt{true}$ if $f_i \in \Phi(a, \sigma_r)$ and $\nu_i \doteq \texttt{false}$ otherwise ($1 \leq i \leq k$).

Let $\mathcal{J} = (\texttt{A}, \texttt{SCD}, \texttt{OBS})$ be a consistent chronicle in $\mathcal{K}$-IbsAd based on features $\mathcal{F}$ and action names A. The corresponding domain $\mathcal{D}_\mathcal{J} = (F, A, \mathcal{E}, \mathcal{V})$, where $F = \mathcal{F}$, is constructed as follows: Let $\texttt{SCD} = \{[0,1]a_1, \ldots, [n-1, n]a_n\}$ then $\mathcal{V}$ is obtained by translating each observation $[k]f \doteq \texttt{true}$ in $\texttt{OBS}$ into f after $[a_1, \ldots, a_k]$ and each observation $[k]f \doteq \texttt{false}$ into $\neg f$ after $[a_1, \ldots, a_k]$ ($0 \leq k \leq n$). Finally, let $(\texttt{Infl}, \texttt{Trajs})$ be the trajectory table described by $\texttt{A}$. For each a, r and each assignment $f : \nu$ which is contained in $\texttt{Trajs}(a, r)$, $\mathcal{E}$ includes the effect proposition

$$a \text{ causes } e \text{ if } c_1, \ldots, c_m \tag{8}$$

where $e = f$ (resp. $e = \neg f$) if $\nu = \texttt{true}$ (resp. $\nu = \texttt{false}$) and $c_1, \ldots, c_m$ is an exact definition of the situation σ_r, i.e. $\{c_1, \ldots, c_m\} = \sigma_r \cup \{\neg f \mid f \in F \setminus \sigma_r\}$. ∎

Example 1 (continued). According to this definition, the value propositions in For.3 determine the two sets $\texttt{SCD}_1$ and $\texttt{OBS}_1$, respectively, and vice versa. Furthermore, the transition function For.4, applied to *shoot*, is translated into the table depicted in Figure 1. On the other hand, applying the second part of Definition 8 to this trajectory table yields a slightly different set of effect propositions, viz.

$$shoot \text{ causes } \neg loaded \text{ if } loaded, \neg alive$$
$$shoot \text{ causes } \neg loaded \text{ if } loaded, alive$$
$$shoot \text{ causes } \neg alive \text{ if } loaded, alive$$

but this is irrelevant for the equivalence result.

Lemma 9 *Let $\mathcal{D}$ be a consistent domain in $\mathcal{A}^1$ and $\mathcal{J}$ be a consistent chronicle in $\mathcal{K}$-IbsAd. If $\mathcal{J} = \mathcal{J}_\mathcal{D}$ or $\mathcal{D} = \mathcal{D}_\mathcal{J}$ then transition in $\mathcal{D}$ and $\mathcal{J}$ coincides.*

Proof (sketch): Let Φ be the transition function determined by the effect propositions of $\mathcal{D}$ then we have to show that for each action name a, situation σ, and state r', $\Phi(a, \sigma)$ and r' coincide iff r' is the result of executing a in state r_σ. In case $\mathcal{J} = \mathcal{J}_\mathcal{D}$ this follows from the fact that constructing the trajectory table of $\mathcal{J}$ via Definition 8 is based on Φ. In case $\mathcal{D} = \mathcal{D}_\mathcal{J}$ the claim follows from the fact that each assignment in the (single) trajectory of $\texttt{Trajs}(a, r_\sigma)$ is translated into an effect proposition which is applicable in σ but not elsewhere (c.f. For. 8). ∎

Let (σ_0, Φ) be a model of a domain in $\mathcal{A}^1$ which is based on the action sequence $[a_1, \ldots, a_n]$ and let $(\mathcal{B}, R, \mathcal{A}, \{\})$ be a finite development then they are said to *correspond* iff $\mathcal{B} = \{0, \ldots, n\}$, $\mathcal{A} = \{(0, a_1, 1), \ldots, (n-1, a_n, n)\}$, and $\Phi([a_1, \ldots, a_k], \sigma_0)$ and $R(k)$ coincide for each $k = 0, \ldots, n$.

Theorem 10 *Let $\mathcal{D}$ be a domain in $\mathcal{A}^1$ and $\mathcal{J}_\mathcal{D}$ be given via Definition 8. For each model of $\mathcal{D}$ there exists a corresponding member of $\mathcal{M}od(\mathcal{J}_\mathcal{D})$ and vice versa.*

Let $\mathcal{J}$ be a chronicle in $\mathcal{K}$-IbsAd and $\mathcal{D}_\mathcal{J}$ be given via Definition 8. For each member of $\mathcal{M}od(\mathcal{J})$ there exists a corresponding model of $\mathcal{D}_\mathcal{J}$ and vice versa.

Proof (sketch): Without value propositions the claim follows from Lemma 9, and a value proposition f $\texttt{after}$ $[a_1, \ldots, a_k]$ is true in (σ_0, Φ) if and only if the corresponding observation $[k]f \doteq \nu$ is true in the history of a corresponding finite development. ∎

On the analogy of Definition 8, domains in $\mathcal{A}^1_{ND}$, which forms a restriction on $\mathcal{A}_{ND}$ in the spirit of Definition 3, can be translated into chronicles in $\mathcal{K}$-IbsA and vice versa:

Definition 11 Let $\mathcal{D} = (F, A, \mathcal{E}, \mathcal{V})$ be a consistent domain in $\mathcal{A}^1_{ND}$. The corresponding chronicle $\mathcal{J}_\mathcal{D} = (\text{A}, \text{SCD}, \text{OBS})$ is constructed as in Definition 8 but the trajectory table is determined by the transition relation Φ of $\mathcal{D}$ as follows: If a is an action name and r a state then $f \in \texttt{Infl}(a, r)$ iff there is at least one σ' such that $(\sigma_r, a, \sigma') \in \Phi$ and the truth values of f regarding σ_r and σ' are different. Furthermore, each such σ' determines a trajectory in $\texttt{Trajs}(a, r)$ analogously to For.7.

Let $\mathcal{J} = (\text{A}, \text{SCD}, \text{OBS})$ be a consistent chronicle in $\mathcal{K}$-IbsA. The corresponding domain $\mathcal{D}_\mathcal{J}$ is constructed as in Definition 8 but the trajectory table determines a set of extended effect propositions as follows: If a is an action name and r a state then for each trajectory $\langle f_1 : \nu_1, \ldots, f_k : \nu_k \rangle \in \texttt{Trajs}(a, r)$, the extended effect proposition

$$a \text{ alternatively causes } e_1, \ldots, e_k \text{ if } c_1, \ldots, c_m$$

is generated, where $e_i = f_i$ (resp. $e_i = \neg f_i$) if $\nu_i = \texttt{true}$ (resp. $\nu_i = \texttt{false}$) and $c_1, \ldots, c_m$ is an exact definition of σ_r. ∎

Analogously to Lemma 9 we can prove that transition coincides in so far as if $(\sigma, a, \sigma') \in \Phi$ then $r_{\sigma'}$ is a possible result of executing a in r_σ and vice versa. Furthermore, let the correspondence relation between models be as before but it is required that $\varphi(k)$ and $R(k)$ coincide for any k, then Theorem 10 can be generalized to $\mathcal{A}^1_{ND}$ and $\mathcal{K}$-IbsA.

5. Conclusion

We have given a first answer to the question of how two prominent systematic approaches to reasoning about actions and change are related. We have fixed the respective ontological subclasses in the Ego-World-Semantics which are equivalent to the Action Description Language and an extension handling non-deterministic actions. On the other hand, we have elaborated a fundamental difference between the two frameworks.

An important consequence of this analysis should be a proposal about a combination of the two systems to profit from the merits of both. For example, the concept of hypothetical developments could be integrated into EWS. To this end, the notions of schedules and observations have to be generalized such that several schedules are considered and each observation is bound to a particular schedule. On the other hand, the expressive power of the language underlying E. Sandewall's framework as well as the complex methods to reasoning about time form valuable suggestions for extending $\mathcal{A}$.

Furthermore, future research effort should concentrate on continuation of our analysis concerning new developments in the two investigated frameworks like the recent extensions of $\mathcal{A}$ regarding concurrent actions[2] or actions with indirect effects[8].

References

1. A. B. Baker. Nonmonotonic reasoning in the framework of situation calculus. *Artificial Intelligence* **49**, p. 5–23, 1991.
2. C. Baral and M. Gelfond. Representing Concurrent Actions in Extended Logic Programming. In R. Bajcsy, ed., *Proc. of the IJCAI*, p. 866–871,1993.
3. M. Denecker and D. de Schreye. Representing Incomplete Knowledge in Abductive Logic Programming. In D. Miller, ed., *Proc. of the ILPS*, p. 147–163, 1993
4. P. M. Dung. Representing Actions in Logic Programming and its Applications in Database Updates. In D. S. Warren, ed., *Proc. of the ICLP*, p. 222–238, 1993.
5. M. Gelfond and V. Lifschitz. Representing Action and Change by Logic Programs. *Journal of Logic Programming* **17**, p. 301–321, 1993.
6. S. Hölldobler and M. Thielscher. Actions and Specificity. In D. Miller, ed., *Proc. of the ILPS*, p. 164–180, 1993.
7. G. N. Kartha. Soundness and Completeness Theorems for Three Formalizations of Actions. In R. Bajcsy, ed., *Proc. of the IJCAI*, p. 724–729, 1993.
8. G. N. Kartha and V. Lifschitz. Actions with Indirect Effects. In *Int. Conf. on Principles of Knowledge Representation and Reasoning*. Bonn, Germany, 1994.
9. R. Reiter. The frame problem in the situation calculus: A simple solution (sometimes) and a completeness result for goal regression. In V. Lifschitz, ed., *Artificial Intelligence and Mathematical Theory of Computation*, p. 359–380. Academic Press, 1991.
10. P. Richard etal. *À gauche en sortant de l'ascenseur*. Renn Productions, 1988.
11. E. Sandewall. Features and Fluents. Technical Report LiTH-IDA-R-92-30, Institutionen för datavetenskap, Linköping University, Sweden, 1992.
12. E. Sandewall. The range of applicability of nonmonotonic logics for the inertia problem. In R. Bajcsy, ed., *Proc. of the IJCAI*, p. 738–743, 1993.
13. M. Thielscher. Representing Actions in Equational Logic Programming. In P. Van Hentenryck, ed., *Proc. of the ICLP*, 1994.

COMPLEXITY RESULTS FOR STATE-VARIABLE PLANNING UNDER MIXED SYNTACTICAL AND STRUCTURAL RESTRICTIONS

PETER JONSSON

Department of Computer and Information Science
Linköping University, S-581 83 Linköping, Sweden
email: petej@ida.liu.se

and

CHRISTER BÄCKSTRÖM

Department of Computer and Information Science
Linköping University, S-581 83 Linköping, Sweden
email: cba@ida.liu.se

ABSTRACT

Most tractable planning problems reported in the literature have been defined by syntactical restrictions. To better exploit the inherent structure of problems, however, it is probably necessary to study also structural restrictions on the state-transition graph. We present an almost exhaustive map of complexity results for state-variable planning under all combinations of our previously analysed syntactical (P, U, B, S) and structural (I, A, O) restrictions, considering both optimal and non-optimal plan generation.

1 Introduction

Many planning problems in manufacturing and process industry are believed to be highly structured, thus allowing for efficient planning if exploiting this structure. However, a 'blind' domain-independent planner will most likely go on tour in an exponential search space even for tractable problems. Although heuristics may help a lot, they are often not based on a sufficiently thorough understanding of the underlying problem structure to guarantee efficiency and correctness. Further, we believe that if having such a deep understanding of the problem structure, it is better to use other methods than heuristics.

Some tractability results have been reported in the literature for restrictions on the propositional STRIPS formalism[7,9] and for restrictions on the related state-variable formalism SAS+.[5,6] These results are all based on essentially syntactic restrictions on the set of operators. Syntactic restrictions are very appealing to study, since, typically, they are easy to define and not very costly to test. However, to gain any deeper insight into what makes planning problems hard and easy respectively probably require that we study the structure of the problem, in particular the state-transition graph induced by the operators. Putting explicit restrictions on the state-transition graph must be done with great care, however, since this graph is typically of size exponential in the size of the planning problem instance, making it extremely costly to test arbitrary properties.

In a recent paper[13] we took an intermediate approach. Using the SAS$^+$ formalism we defined restrictions not on the whole state-transition graph, but on the domain-transition graph for each state variable in isolation. These can, hence, be tested in polynomial time. Although not being a substitute for restrictions on the whole state-transition graph, many interesting and useful properties of this graph can be indirectly exploited. In particular, we identified three structural restrictions (I, A and O) which together make planning tractable and properly generalize the tractable problems we have previously defined using syntactical restrictions. We also presented a polynomial-time, sound and complete algorithm for generating optimal plans under the new structural restrictions. Despite being structural, our restrictions can be tested in polynomial time. Further, this approach would not be very useful for a planning formalism based on propositional atoms, since the resulting two-vertex domain-transition graphs would not allow for much structure to exploit.

We have previously[6] presented a map over the complexity of planning for all combinations of the previously considered syntactical restrictions on SAS$^+$ planning. In this paper, we repeat this endeavour, taking also the new structural restrictions into account. We provide a map over the complexity of both optimal and non-optimal plan generation for all combinations of the restrictions, considering also mixed structural and syntactical restrictions. Hence, we augment our previous tractability result for the SAS*-IAO problem by also showing that it is a maximally tractable problem under the restrictions considered. (For reasons explained later in the paper, we actually study a restricted version of the SAS$^+$ formalism.)

2   The SAS$^+$ and SAS* formalisms

The SAS$^+$ formalism,[4,6] is a variant of propositional STRIPS, generalizing the atoms to multi-valued state variables. Furthermore, what is called a precondition in STRIPS is here divided into two conditions, the precondition and the prevailcondition. Variables which are required and changed by an operator go into the precondition and those which remain unchanged, but are required, go into the prevailcondition. We briefly recapitulate the SAS$^+$ formalism below, referring to Bäckström and Nebel[6] for further explanation.

Definition 2.1 *An instance of the SAS$^+$ planning problem is given by a tuple $\Pi = \langle \mathcal{V}, \mathcal{O}, s_0, s_* \rangle$ with components defined as follows:*

- *$\mathcal{V} = \{v_1, \ldots, v_m\}$ is a set of **state variables**. Each variable $v \in \mathcal{V}$ has an associated **domain** $\mathcal{D}_v$, which implicitly defines an **extended domain** $\mathcal{D}_v^+ = \mathcal{D}_v \cup \{u\}$, where u denotes the **undefined** value. Further, the **total state space** $\mathcal{S} = \mathcal{D}_{v_1} \times \ldots \times \mathcal{D}_{v_m}$ and the **partial state space** $\mathcal{S}^+ = \mathcal{D}_{v_1}^+ \times \ldots \times \mathcal{D}_{v_m}^+$ are implicitly defined. We write $s[v]$ to denote the value of the variable v in a state s.*

- $\mathcal{O}$ is a set of **operators** of the form $\langle b, e, f \rangle$, where $b, e, f \in \mathcal{S}^+$ denote the **pre-**, **post-** and **prevail-condition** respectively. Each operator $\langle b, e, f \rangle \in \mathcal{O}$ is subject to the following two restrictions

  (R1) for all $v \in \mathcal{V}$ if $b[v] \neq u$, then $b[v] \neq e[v] \neq u$,

  (R2) for all $v \in \mathcal{V}$, $e[v] = u$ or $f[v] = u$.

- $s_0 \in \mathcal{S}^+$ and $s_* \in \mathcal{S}^+$ denote the **initial state** and **goal state** respectively.

Restriction R1 essentially says that a state variable can never be made undefined, once made defined by some operator. Restriction R2 says that the pre- and prevail-conditions of an operator must never define the same variable.

We write $s \sqsubseteq t$ if the state s is subsumed (or satisfied) by state t, ie. if $s[v] = u$ or $s[v] = t[v]$. We extend this notion to whole states, defining

$$s \sqsubseteq t \quad \text{iff} \quad \text{for all } v \in \mathcal{V}, s[v] = u \text{ or } s[v] = t[v].$$

*If $o = \langle b, e, f \rangle$ is a SAS$^+$ operator, we write $b(o)$, $e(o)$ and $f(o)$ to denote b, e and f respectively. $\mathcal{O}^*$ denotes the set of operator sequences over $\mathcal{O}$ and the members of $\mathcal{O}^*$ are called **plans**. Given two states $s, t \in \mathcal{S}^+$, we define for all $v \in \mathcal{V}$,*

$$(s \oplus t)[v] = \begin{cases} t[v] & \text{if } t[v] \neq u, \\ s[v] & \text{otherwise.} \end{cases}$$

The ternary relation Valid $\subseteq \mathcal{O}^* \times \mathcal{S}^+ \times \mathcal{S}^+$ is defined recursively s.t. for arbitrary operator sequence $\langle o_1, \ldots, o_n \rangle \in \mathcal{O}^*$ and arbitrary states $s, t \in \mathcal{S}^+$, Valid$(\langle o_1, \ldots, o_n \rangle, s, t)$ iff either

1. *$n = 0$ and $t \sqsubseteq s$ or*

2. *$n > 0$, $b(o_1) \sqsubseteq s$, $f(o_1) \sqsubseteq s$ and Valid$(\langle o_2, \ldots, o_n \rangle, (s \oplus e(o_1)), t)$.*

*A plan $\langle o_1, \ldots, o_n \rangle \in \mathcal{O}^*$ **solves** Π iff Valid$(\langle o_1, \ldots, o_n \rangle, s_0, s_*)$.*

Finally, we define a restricted variant of the SAS$^+$ formalism.

Definition 2.2 *The SAS* problem is the SAS$^+$ problem restricted to instances $\langle \mathcal{V}, \mathcal{O}, s_0, s_* \rangle$ satisfying (1) $s_* \in \mathcal{S}$ and (2) for every operator $o \in \mathcal{O}$ and variable $v \in \mathcal{V}$, if $b(o)[v] = u$, then $e(o)[v] = u$*

3 Restrictions

In this section we define the various restrictions on SAS$^+$ planning to be analysed in the next section. We have previously presented both the syntactical ones (P, U, B and S)[5,6] and three of the structural ones (I, A and O).[13] In addition we present a new structural restriction, A$^+$. Before presenting the restrictions we must define some other concepts, however. Assume below that $\Pi = \langle \mathcal{V}, \mathcal{O}, s_0, s_* \rangle$ is a SAS$^+$ instance.

Definition 3.1 *An operator $o \in \mathcal{O}$ is **unary** iff there is exactly one $v \in \mathcal{V}$ s.t. $\mathsf{e}(o)[v] \neq \mathsf{u}$.*

Definition 3.2
*For each $v \in \mathcal{V}$ and $\mathcal{O}' \subseteq \mathcal{O}$, the set $\mathcal{R}_v^{\mathcal{O}'}$ of **requestable values** for $\mathcal{O}'$ is defined as $\mathcal{R}_v^{\mathcal{O}'} = \{\mathsf{f}(o)[v] \mid o \in \mathcal{O}'\} \cup \{\mathsf{b}(o)[v], \mathsf{e}(o)[v] \mid o \in \mathcal{O}'$ and o is non-unary $\} - \{\mathsf{u}\}$.*

Obviously, $\mathcal{R}_v^{\mathcal{O}} \subseteq \mathcal{D}_v$ for all $v \in \mathcal{V}$. For each state variable domain, we further define the graph of possible transitions for this domain, without taking the other domains into account, and the reachability graph for arbitrary subsets of the domain.

Definition 3.3 *For each $v \in \mathcal{V}$, we define the corresponding **domain transition graph** G_v as a directed labelled graph $G_v = \langle \mathcal{D}_v^+, \mathcal{T}_v \rangle$ with vertex set $\mathcal{D}_v^+$ and arc set $\mathcal{T}_v$ s.t. for all $x, y \in \mathcal{D}_v^+$ and $o \in \mathcal{O}$, $\langle x, o, y \rangle \in \mathcal{T}_v$ iff $\mathsf{b}(o)[v] = x$ and $\mathsf{e}(o)[v] = y \neq \mathsf{u}$. Further, for each $X \subseteq \mathcal{D}_v^+$ we define the **reachability graph** for X as a directed graph $G_v^X = \langle X, \mathcal{T}_X \rangle$ with vertex set X and arc set $\mathcal{T}_X$ s.t. for all $x, y \in X$ $\langle x, y \rangle \in \mathcal{T}_X$ iff there is a path from x to y in G_v.*

Alternatively, G_v^X can be viewed as the restriction to $X \subseteq \mathcal{D}_v^+$ of the transitive closure of G_v, but with unlabelled arcs. When speaking about a path in a domain-transition graph below, we will typically mean the sequence of labels, *ie.* operators, along this path. We say that a path in G_v is *via* a set $X \subseteq \mathcal{D}_v^+$ iff each member of X is visited along the path, possibly as the initial or final vertex.

Definition 3.4 *An operator $o \in \mathcal{O}$ is **irreplaceable** wrt. a variable $v \in \mathcal{V}$ iff removing an arc labelled with o in G_v splits some component of G_v into two components.*

In the remainder of this paper we will only be interested in SAS$^+$ instances satisfying combinations of the following restrictions.

Definition 3.5 *The SAS$^+$ instance Π is:*

(P) Post-unique *iff for all $o, o' \in \mathcal{O}$, if $\mathsf{e}(o)[v] = \mathsf{e}(o')[v] \neq \mathsf{u}$ for some $v \in \mathcal{V}$, then $o = o'$;*

(U) Unary *iff for all $o \in \mathcal{O}$, o is unary;*

(B) Binary *iff $|\mathcal{D}_v| = 2$ for all $v \in \mathcal{V}$,*

(S) Single-valued *iff there exists some state $s \in \mathcal{S}^+$ s.t. $\mathsf{f}(o) \sqsubseteq s$ for all $o \in \mathcal{O}$.*

(I) Interference-safe *iff every operator $o \in \mathcal{O}$ is either unary or irreplaceable wrt. every $v \in \mathcal{V}$ it affects.*

(A) Acyclic wrt. $\mathcal{R}^{\mathcal{O}}$ *iff $G_v^{\mathcal{R}_v^{\mathcal{O}}}$ is acyclic for each $v \in \mathcal{V}$.*

(A$^+$) Acyclic *iff G_v is acyclic for each $v \in \mathcal{V}$.*

(O) Prevail-order-preserving *iff for each $v \in \mathcal{V}$, whenever there are two $x, y \in \mathcal{D}_v^+$ s.t. G_v has a shortest path $\langle o_1, \ldots, o_m \rangle$ from x to y via some set $X \subseteq \mathcal{R}_v^O$ and it has any path $\langle o_1', \ldots, o_n' \rangle$ from x to y via some set $Y \subseteq \mathcal{R}_v^O$ s.t. $X \subseteq Y$, there exists some subsequence $\langle \ldots, o_{i_1}', \ldots, o_{i_m}', \ldots \rangle$ s.t. $\mathsf{f}(o_k) \sqsubseteq \mathsf{f}(o_{i_k}')$ for $1 \le k \le m$.*

From now on, we will consider the SAS* formalism instead of the SAS$^+$ formalism. One of the reasons for doing so, is that SAS$^+$ and SAS* are equally expressive formalisms under polynomial reductions. (See Bäckström[3, 2] for a discussion of expressiveness equivalences.) Another reason is that all previously described polynomial-time SAS$^+$ planners require that the problem instance satisfy both restriction I and A. This mixes badly with actions having u as precondition. For example, restriction I prevents the existence of a path in G_v from u to any state that is the precondition of a non-unary action and restriction A prevents the existence of two requestable values which are both reachable from u.

Many of the complexity results to be presented in the next section will carry over by inheritance, using the following subproblem relationships. (The proofs of theorems are omitted or only sketched. All proofs can be found in Jonsson and Bäckström.[12])

Lemma 3.6 *The following subproblem relations hold:*
1. $SAS^*\text{-}A^+ \subseteq SAS^*\text{-}A$ 2. $SAS^*\text{-}U \subseteq SAS^*\text{-}I$
3. $SAS^*\text{-}US \subseteq SAS^*\text{-}A$ 4. $SAS^*\text{-}P \subseteq SAS^*\text{-}O$
5. $SAS^*\text{-}PA \subseteq SAS^*\text{-}I$

Proof sketch: 1 and 2 are trivial. 3 follows from the fact that S and U in combination implies $|\mathcal{R}_v^O| \le 1$ for all $v \in \mathcal{V}$. Both 4 and 5 follow from analysing how post-uniqueness restricts the domain-transition graphs. $\square$

4   Complexity of plan generation

In this paper we will only discuss the plan generation problem (finding a solution). We will not consider the plan existence problem (deciding whether a solution exists), since we are ultimately interested in actually generating a solution.

Definition 4.1 *Given a SAS* instance Π, we have the following planning problems: The **plan generation problem (PG)** finds a solution for Π or answer that no solution exists. The **bounded plan generation problem (BPG)** takes an integer $k \ge 0$ as an additional parameter and finds a solution for Π of length k or shorter or answer that no plan of length k or shorter exists for Π.*

The complexity of the plan generation problems follows from the theorems in this section, Lemma 3.6 and inheritance. The tractability results appear in previous publications, as indicated below.

Theorem 4.2 BPG *is polynomial for SAS*-IAO.*[13]

Theorem 4.3 PG *is polynomial for SAS*-US.*[6]

For the intractability results we have to distinguish those problems that are inherently intractable, *ie.* can be proven to take exponential time, and those which are NP-equivalent, *ie.* intractable unless $P = NP$. Observe that we cannot use the term NP-complete since we consider the search problem (generating a solution) and not the decision problem (whether a solution exists). A search problem is NP-easy if it can be Turing reduced to some NP-complete problem, NP-hard if some NP-complete problem can be Turing reduced to it and NP-equivalent if it is both NP-easy and NP-hard. Loosely speaking, NP-equivalence is to search problems what NP-completeness is to decision problems. See Johnson[11] for formal details.

Theorem 4.4 *Optimal solutions are always polynomially bounded for (1) SAS*-A and (2) SAS*-IS.*

Proof sketch: We observe that for SAS*-A each requestable value is visited at most once in an optimal solution and, hence, (1) holds. For SAS*-IS we observe that cycles in a domain-transition graph can only contain unary operators. Hence, the proof of (2) is a simple extension to the proof that optimal SAS$^+$-US plans are of polynomial size.[6] □

Corollary 4.5 BPG *is NP-easy for SAS*-A and SAS*-IS.*

Theorem 4.6 PG *is NP-hard for SAS*-BSA$^+$O.*

Proof sketch: Proof by reduction from EXACT COVER BY 3-SETS. □

Theorem 4.7 BPG *is NP-hard for SAS*-UBSA$^+$.*

Proof sketch: Proof by reduction from MINIMUM COVER. □

Theorem 4.8 PG *is NP-hard for SAS*-BSIA$^+$ and SAS*-UBA$^+$.*

Proof sketch: Proof by reduction from 3-SATISFIABILITY. □

Theorem 4.9 *Both SAS*-PUB and SAS*-PBS have instances with exponentially sized optimal solutions[6] (and are thus inherently intractable).*

The complexity results are summarized in the lattice in Figure 1 which can be viewed as a three-dimensional cube. The figure is to be interpreted in the following way: The top-element of each diamond-shaped sublattice corresponds to a combination of restrictions on the SAS* problem defined by selecting at most one restriction from each of the sets $\{A^+, A\}$, $\{P, O\}$ and $\{U, I\}$. These restrictions are marked along the three axes in the figure, where "-" denotes that neither of the two restrictions on an axis applies. The other three points in each sublattice further specialize the top element by adding one or both of the restrictions B and S, as shown in the enlarged sublattice. As an example of how to interpret the lattice, the SAS*-SAO problem is indicated explicitly in the figure.

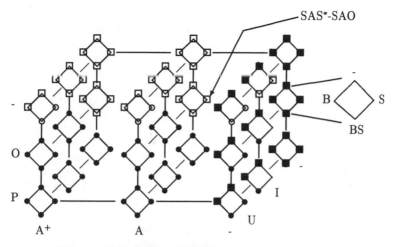

- • Polynomial for **PG** and **BPG**
- ○ Polynomial for **PG**, NP-equivalent for **BPG**
- □ NP-equivalent for **PG** and **BPG**
- ■ Inherently intractable.

Figure 1: Complexity of SAS* plan generation

The lattice presents complexity results for both bounded and unbounded plan generation as follow. Problems which are polynomial for both **PG** and **BPG** are marked with a filled dot, while those which are polynomial for **PG** but NP-equivalent for **BPG** are marked by an unfilled dot. The problems marked by an unfilled square are NP-equivalent for both **PG** and **BPG** and those marked with a filled square are inherently intractable for both **PG** and **BPG**. Unmarked positions denote problems whose complexity is unknown at present.

5 Discussion and conclusions

Not much research on structural restrictions on planning problems seems to be reported in the literature, although some exceptions can be found. Korf[14] has defined some subgoal dependency properties of planning problems modelled by state-variables, for instance serializability of subgoals. However, this property is PSPACE-complete to test,[8] but does not guarantee tractable planning. Mädler[15] extends Sacerdoti's[16] essentially syntactic state abstraction technique to *structural abstraction*, identifying bottle-neck states (*needle's eyes*) in the state-transition graph for a state-variable formalism. Smith and Peot[17] use an *operator graph* for preprocessing planning problem instances, identifying potential threats that can be safely postponed during planning—thus, pruning the search tree. The operator graph can be viewed as an abstraction of the full state-transition graph, containing all the information relevant to analysing threats. In addition to this, we have previously presented a polynomial-time algorithm for the SAS$^+$-IAO problem[13] and proven that this problem properly generalizes the previously studied syntactically defined tractable planning problems.

In this paper, we have extended this result by analysing the complexity of plan generation under all combinations of restrictions, considering both these new structural restrictions and the previously analysed syntactical ones. By the results in this paper, we can conclude that SAS*-IAO is maximally tractable under the structural restrictions I, A and O, thus being a structural counterpart of the result in Bäckström & Nebel[6] stating that SAS$^+$-PUS is the maximal tractable problem under the syntactical restrictions P, U, B and S. Obviously, this result holds for the SAS$^+$ case as well. Mixing syntactical and structural restrictions yield two problems, SAS*-SIO and SAS*-PSI, whose complexity we have not managed to show. Both problems seems to be of minor practical interest since the S restriction is very severe. Though, it is worth noticing that the SAS*-SIO class is incomparable wrt. expressive power with both the SAS*-PUS and the SAS*-IAO class. We have also shown SAS*-US (and consequently SAS$^+$-US) non-optimal plan generation cannot be further generalized with preserved tractability by replacing US with any combination of our studied syntactical or structural restrictions. By providing some additional hardness results, we have built a map over the complexity of planning for all combinations of both the syntactical and structural restrictions, considering both optimal and non-optimal plan generation.

6 Acknowledgements

This research was sponsored by *the Swedish Research Council for the Engineering Sciences (TFR)* under grants Dnr. 92-143 and Dnr. 93-00291.

References

[1] *Proc. 10th (US) Nat'l Conf. on Artif Intell. (AAAI-92)*, San José, CA, USA, July 1992.

[2] C. Bäckström. *Computational Complexity of Reasoning about Plans.* Doctoral dissertation, Linköping University, Linköping, Sweden, June 1992.

[3] C. Bäckström. Equivalence and tractability results for SAS$^+$ planning. In *Proc. 3rd Int'l Conf. on Principles of Knowledge Repr. and Reasoning (KR-92)*, pages 126–137, Cambridge, MA, USA, Oct. 1992.

[4] C. Bäckström and I. Klein. Parallel non-binary planning in polynomial time. In IJCAI,[10] pages 268–273.

[5] C. Bäckström and I. Klein. Planning in polynomial time: The SAS-PUBS class. *Comput. Intell.*, **7**(3):181–197, Aug. 1991.

[6] C. Bäckström and B. Nebel. Complexity results for SAS+ planning. In *Proc 13th Int'l Joint Conf. on Artif. Intell. (IJCAI-93)*, Chamberý, France, Aug.–Sept. 1991.

[7] T. Bylander. Complexity results for planning. In IJCAI,[10] pages 274–279.

[8] T. Bylander. Complexity results for serial decomposability. In AAAI,[1] pages 729–734.

[9] K. Erol, D. S. Nau, and V. S. Subrahmanian. On the complexity of domain-independent planning. In AAAI,[1] pages 381–386.

[10] *Proc 12th Int'l Joint Conf. on Artif. Intell. (IJCAI-91)*, Sydney, Australia, Aug. 1991.

[11] D. S. Johnson. A catalog of complexity classes. In J. van Leeuwen, editor, *Handbook of Theoretical Computer Science: Algorithms and Complexity*, volume A, chapter 2, pages 67–161. Elsevier, Amsterdam, 1990.

[12] P. Jonsson and C. Bäckström. Complexity results for state-variable planning under mixed syntactical and structural restrictions. Research report, Department of Computer and Information Science, Linköping University, 1994. In preparation.

[13] P. Jonsson and C. Bäckström. Tractable planning with state variables by exploiting structural restrictions. In *Proc. 12th (US) Nat'l Conf. on Artif. Intell. (AAAI-94)*, Seattle, WA, USA, July–Aug. 1994. To appear.

[14] R. E. Korf. Planning as search: A quantitative approach. *Artif. Intell.*, **33**:65–88, 1987.

[15] F. Mädler. Towards structural abstraction. In *Proc. 1st Int'l Conf. on Artif. Intell. Planning Sys. (AIPS-92)*, pages 163–171, College Park, MD, USA, June 1992.

[16] E. D. Sacerdoti. Planning in a hierarchy of abstraction spaces. *Artif. Intell.*, **5**(2):115–135, 1974.

[17] D. E. Smith and M. A. Peot. Postponing threats in partial-order planning. In *Proc. 11th (US) Nat'l Conf. on Artif Intell. (AAAI-93)*, pages 500–506, Washington, DC, USA, July 1993.

DEVIATION-PROOF PLANS IN MULTIAGENT ENVIRONMENTS

S. BRAINOV

Bulgarian Academy of Sciences
Institute of Mathematics
Bl. 8, Acad. G. Bonchev Str.
Sofia 1113, Bulgaria

ABSTRACT

Since in open multiagent environments agents cannot make binding commitments, agreements concluded between them are exposed to the risk of deviation. In this paper, a formal model of stability against deviations is proposed. According to this model, agents should negotiate over and agree on deviation-proof plans. When implementing deviation-proof plans, no single agent or group of agents could benefit more by not following the plan's execution. The model enables a group of agents to reject the plans which are not stable against deviations, thereby enhancing the coherence of the multiagent society. This model is independent of communication protocol and may be implemented in centralized as well as decentralized organizations.

In this paper, sufficient conditions for the stability of plans against deviations are defined. The question of existence of stable plans is considered. It shown that semi-cooperative situations exist, i.e. such situations in which cooperation is not stable, even though the situation is cooperative, the agent goals are consistent and there are no conficts.

The proposed model of deviation-proof plans is developed in the spirit of the theory of games and economic theory. It takes into account incentive and punitive mechanisms for regulation of multiagent interaction.

UPDATING KNOWLEDGE BASES
USING A PERSISTENT SET APPROACH

YAN ZHANG

Basser Department of Computer Science
University of Sydney
NSW 2006, Australia
Email: yan@cs.su.oz.au

and

NORMAN Y. FOO

Basser Department of Computer Science
University of Sydney
NSW 2006, Australia
Email: norman@cs.su.oz.au

Abstract

Propositional knowledge base updates have been widely studied recently. Katsuno and Mendelzon suggested eight postulates for characterizing the semantics of update where the principle of *minimal change* is embedded [5]. In this paper we propose a new method for knowledge base update called the *persistent set approach* (PSA). We examine the relations between the two different update semantics by investigating the satisfiability of Katsuno and Mendelzon's update postulates under our persistent update semantics. We then extend the PSA to represent preference information so that the preferred solution can be derived by the extended PSA.

1 Introduction

Propositional knowledge base updates have been widely studied recently [6; 2; 1; 3]. Katsuno and Mendelzon suggested eight postulates for characterizing the semantics of update where the principle of minimal change is embedded [5]. In this paper, we extend the work of Zhang and Foo described in [9], and propose a new method for knowledge base update called the *persistent set approach* (PSA). Although the basic motivations between the persistence principle and minimal change for representing update are quite different, we examine the relations between them by investigating the satisfiability of Katsuno and Mendelzon's update postulates under our persistent update semantics. We show that the persistence-based update operator satisfies their postulates (U1) – (U4), (U6) and (U8) but does not satisfy (U5) and (U7), from which we can see the essential distinction between the persistent update and the minimality-based update.

We then extend the PSA to represent preference information so that the preferred solution can be derived by the extended PSA.

The paper is organized as follows. We first review Katsuno-Mendelzon's update postulates in section 2. In section 3 we propose a *persistent set approach* for propositional knowledge base update. In section 4, we then examine the satisfiability of Katsuno-Mendelzon's update postulates under our persistent update semantics in detail. In section 5, we then extend the PSA in order to derive the preferred solution. The conclusion forms section 6.

2 Propositional Knowledge Base Update: Review

Let $\mathcal{L}$ be a finitary propositional language. We represent a *knowledge base* by a propositional formula ψ. A propositional formula ϕ is *complete* if ϕ is consistent and for any propositional formula μ, $\phi \models \mu$ or $\phi \models \neg\mu$. $Models(\psi)$ denotes the set of all models of ψ, i.e., all interpretations of $\mathcal{L}$ in which ψ is true.

The motivation of Katsuno and Mendelzon's proposal for update postulates is an observation on the difference between revision and update. Gardenfors *et al.* proposed a theory for belief revision, i.e., the AGM logic [4], in which there are some postulates that should be satisfied by any reasonable revision operator. Katsuno and Mendelzon revealed that the AGM postulates for revision are inappropriate for *update*, and then proposed eight postulates for characterizing the semantics of update. Let $\psi \diamond \mu$ denote the *update* of ψ by μ. Then Katsuno-Mendelzon's update postulates can be presented as follows [5]:

(U1) $\psi \diamond \mu$ implies μ.

(U2) If ψ implies μ then $\psi \diamond \mu \equiv \psi$.

(U3) If both ψ and μ are satisfiable then $\psi \diamond \mu$ is also satisfiable.

(U4) If $\psi_1 \equiv \psi_2$ and $\mu_1 \equiv \mu_2$ then $\psi_1 \diamond \mu_1 \equiv \psi_2 \diamond \mu_2$.

(U5) $(\psi \diamond \mu) \wedge \phi$ implies $\psi \diamond (\mu \wedge \phi)$.

(U6) If $\psi \diamond \mu_1$ implies μ_2 and $\psi \diamond \mu_2$ implies μ_1 then $\psi \diamond \mu_1 \equiv \psi \diamond \mu_2$.

(U7) If ψ is complete then $(\psi \diamond \mu_1) \wedge (\psi \diamond \mu_2)$ implies $\psi \diamond (\mu_1 \vee \mu_2)$.

(U8) $(\psi_1 \vee \psi_2) \diamond \mu \equiv (\psi_1 \diamond \mu) \vee (\psi_2 \diamond \mu)$.

Update operators satisfying these postulates can be characterized in terms of the following representation theorem. An *update assignment* is a function which assigns to each interpretation I a preorder $\leq_I$ over the set of interpretations of $\mathcal{L}$. We say that this assignment is *faithful* iff for any interpretation J, if $I \neq J$ then $I \leq_I J$ and $J \not\leq_I I$.

Theorem 1 [5] An update operator $\diamond$ satisfies (U1) – (U8) iff there exists a faithful assignment that maps each interpretation to a partial preorder $\leq_I$ such that:

$$Models(\psi \diamond \mu) = \bigcup_{I \in Models(\psi)} Min(Models(\mu), \leq_I),$$

where $Min(Models(\mu), \leq_I)$ means the set of elements of $Models(\mu)$ that are minimal under preorder $\leq_I$. $\square$

Katsuno-Mendelzon's update postulates characterize the update semantics for a class of update operators that are based on the principle of minimal change in knowledge base update. One of these update operators satisfying (U1) – (U8) is, for example, the *Possible Models Approach* (PMA) update operator [7], which is defined as follows. Let I, J be two interpretations of $\mathcal{L}$, and $Diff(I, J)$ the set of propositional letters that have different truth values in I and J respectively. $\psi \diamond_{pma} \mu$ means updating knowledge base ψ with μ under the PMA semantics. Then

$$Models(\psi \diamond_{pma} \mu) = \bigcup_{I \in Models(\psi)} Min(Models(\mu), \leq_{I,pma}),$$

where $J_1 \leq_{I,pma} J_2$ iff $Diff(I, J_1) \subseteq Diff(I, J_2)$. In other words, $Models(\psi \diamond_{pma} \mu)$ is the set of models of μ that are *minimally different* from I (or say "closest" to I)[1].

3 A Persistent Semantics for Update

In this section, we present a persistent semantics for propositional knowledge base update. We consider the occurrence of *domain constraints* in our problem domain. Let C be a consistent set of propositional formulas that represents all domain constraints of the world. Thus, for any knowledge base ψ, we require $\psi \models C$. Let I be an interpretation of $\mathcal{L}$. We say that I is a *state* of the world if $I \models C$. A knowledge base ψ can be treated as a *description* of the world, where $Models(\psi)$ is the set of *possible states* of the world with respect to ψ.

In our formalism, updating knowledge base ψ with μ is defined by updating all possible models of ψ with μ, and this is achieved by using the PSA as described next. We first give the definition of the persistent set as follows.

Definition 1 Let I be a state of the world, i.e., $I \models C$, μ a propositional formula and consistent with C. We define the *persistent set* of I with respect to μ, denoted as $\Delta(I, \mu)$, as follows:

1. $\Delta_0 = I - \{f \mid \{\mu\} \cup C \models \neg f\}$,

2. $\Delta_1 = \Delta_0 - \{f \mid$ there exists propositional letters $f_1, \cdots, f_n$, where f_i or $\neg f_i$ in I for each $i \in N = \{1, \cdots, n\}$, such that $\{\mu\} \cup C \models [\neg]f \vee \bigvee_{i \in N}[\neg]f_i$ but $C \not\models [\neg]f \vee \bigvee_{i \in N}[\neg]f_i$ and $\{\mu\} \cup C \not\models \bigvee_{i \in N}[\neg]f_i$, and for any proper subset M of N, $\{\mu\} \cup C \not\models [\neg]f \vee \bigvee_{j \in M}[\neg]f_j\}$,

3. $\Delta_i = \Delta_{i-1} - \{f_1, \cdots, f_k \mid$ there exists some subset $F \subseteq I - \Delta_{i-1}$ such that $(F \cup \Delta_{i-1} - \{f_1, \cdots, f_k\}) \cup C \models f_1 \wedge \cdots \wedge f_k$ but $(\Delta_{i-1} - \{f_1, \cdots, f_k\}) \cup C \not\models f_l$ where $1 \leq l \leq k\}$,

---

[1] Here, the Katsuno and Mendelzon definition is used to present the PMA in the form where domain constraints are ignored. If there exists a set of propositional formulas, C, to represent the domain constraints, we should require that for any knowledge base ψ, $\psi \models C$, and for any update operator $\diamond$, $S \in Models(\psi \diamond \mu)$ implies $S \models C$. This will be presented in the following section.

4. $\Delta(I,\mu) = \bigcap_{i=0}^{\infty} \Delta_i$.

The notation $[\neg]$ means that the negation sign $\neg$ may or may not appear. $\square$

This definition can be explained as follows. We propose a *persistence principle* for updating a state with a formula, which says that a fact *persists* if it is not *logically relevant* to those facts that *must* change or *may* be subject to change because of updating the state with a formula. We formalize this principle from the viewpoint of purely logical syntax and first order semantics.

Consider a state of the world I and a formula μ where μ is consistent with C. Obviously, after updating I with μ, a fact f in I *must* change if f is inconsistent with μ with respect to C, i.e., $\{\mu\} \cup C \models \neg f$. We call such a fact *non-persistent* with respect to μ (i.e., condition 1 in the above definition). On the other hand, suppose there exists some fact f where f or its negation $\neg f$ appears in a disjunction that is entailed by μ (or together with C)[2], we say that f is *indefinitely affected* by μ. The intuitive meaning of an indefinite effect is that after updating I with μ, the satisfaction of μ (together with C) in the resulting state may or may not cause a change of the truth value of f, but we do not know which is the case (i.e., condition 2). Moreover, for a fact f, if there exists a subset F of I in which some fact is non-persistent or indefinitely affected by μ, and f is entailed by F (or together with C), then f is *implicitly affected* by μ if there is no other justification for f, because after updating I with μ, f may lose its justification. In this case, it is incautious to assume that f persists (i.e., condition 3). We call those facts that are either implicitly or indefinitely affected by μ *mutable*. Finally, for a fact f, if for its every justification there exists some mutable fact in the justification, f is *mutable* (i.e., condition 3). Thus, a fact in I *must* persist if it is neither non-persistent nor mutable. We take all such facts to form the persistence set, as presented in the above definition (condition 4).

Theorem 2 [9] For any state of the world I and any propositional formula μ that is consistent with C, the persistent set $\Delta(I,\mu)$ is unique. $\square$

Definition 2 Let I be a state of the world, i.e., $I \models C$, and μ a propositional formula that is consistent with C. An interpretation I' of $\mathcal{L}$ is a *possible state* of the world resulting from updating I with μ, iff

1. $I' \models C$,

2. $I' \models \mu$, and

3. $\Delta(I,\mu) \subseteq I'$.

Denote the set of all possible states of the world resulting from updating I with μ as $Update(I,\mu)$. $\square$

---

[2]Of course, the disjunction should be non-trivial in our sense, i.e., $A \models B \vee C$, but $A \not\models B$ and $A \not\models C$.

Definition 3 Let ψ be a knowledge base, i.e., $\psi \models C$, μ a propositional formula. $\psi \diamond_{psa} \mu$ denotes the *persistent update* of ψ with μ^3, where

1. If ψ implies μ or ψ is inconsistent then $\psi \diamond_{psa} \mu \equiv \psi$, otherwise

2. $Models(\psi \diamond_{psa} \mu) = \bigcup_{I \in Models(\psi)} Update(I, \mu)$. $\square$

In the above Definition 3, condition 1 says that if ψ implies μ, then nothing is changed since the knowledge μ has been represented by knowledge base ψ; or if ψ is inconsistent, then any update can not change it into a consistent knowledge base. Condition 2 says that if ψ is consistent and does not imply μ, then ψ should be changed, and this change follows the persistence principle as defined previously. Obviously, our persistent update semantics differs from those based on the principle of minimal change. In our definitions for update, there is no similar representation for minimal change. The following example simply shows a difference between our method and those minimality-based approaches, for example, the PMA.

Example 1. Consider a propositional language $\mathcal{L}$ in which there are only two propositional letters $Ontable(Book)$ and $Ontable(Cup)$. Suppose the current knowledge base ψ is

$$\neg Ontable(Book) \wedge \neg Ontable(Cup),$$

that is, neither the book nor the cup is on the table at the moment. Assume the robot receives an instruction to put the book or cup on the table, i.e., updating ψ with μ, where $\mu \equiv Ontable(Book) \vee Ontable(Cup)$. Let us see how our method works for this example. Since ψ is complete, the only state of the current world is

$$\{\neg Ontable(Book), \neg Ontable(Cup)\}.$$

From the condition 2 of Definition 1, it is easy to see that both $\neg Ontable(Book)$ and $\neg Ontable(Cup)$ are mutable. Thus,

$$\psi \diamond_{psa} \mu \equiv Ontable(Book) \vee Ontable(Cup).$$

Applying the PMA, on the other hand, we have the following result:

$$\psi \diamond_{pma} \mu \equiv (\neg Ontable(Book) \wedge Ontable(Cup)) \vee (Ontable(Book) \wedge \neg Ontable(Cup)),$$

which says that after the update, either the book or cup is on the table, but not both. From our intuition, however, it seems that there is not enough *logical reason* to infer that *only one* of the book and the cup can be placed on the table after updating ψ with $Ontable(Book) \vee Ontable(Cup)$. This example reveals that the persistence principle is more conservative than the minimal change generally. $\square$

---

^{3}Here we only consider the *well-defined* update, that is, μ is consistent with C.

4 The Persistence-Based Update and KM Postulates

From the previous sections, we see that the basic motivations of the persistence-based update and minimality-based update are quite different. The relationship between them ican be examined by investigating the satisfiability of Katsuno-Mendelzon's update postulates under our persistent update semantics. We first give the main result of this section as follows.

Theorem 3 The persistence-based update operator $\diamond_{psa}$ satisfies Katsuno-Mendelzon's postulates (U1) – (U4), (U6) and (U8). □

Generally, (U5) and (U7) are not satisfied under the persistent semantics because the intuitive meanings of (U5) and (U7) are to force a minimal change for update while the persistent update does not follow this principle generally. However, if we change conditions of (U5) and (U7), we have the following result.

Theorem 4 The following properties hold:

(U5') If $\psi \diamond_{psa} \mu \models [\neg]\phi$ but $\psi \not\models \phi$, then $(\psi \diamond_{psa} \mu) \wedge \phi$ implies $\psi \diamond_{psa} (\mu \wedge \phi)$.
(U7') If $\psi \diamond_{psa} \mu_1 \models [\neg]\mu_2$ (or $\psi \diamond_{psa} \mu_2 \models [\neg]\mu_1$), then $(\psi \diamond_{psa} \mu_1) \wedge (\psi \diamond_{psa} \mu_2)$ implies $\psi \diamond_{psa} (\mu_1 \vee \mu_2)$. □

The above theorem effectively says that if there are no indefinite and implicit effects of update, the persistent update operator satisfies (U5) and (U7)[4]. Therefore, because Katsuno and Mendelzon's representation theorem (Theorem 1) says that any update operator satisfies (U1) – (U8) iff there exists a model-based minimality principle, it follows that indefinite and implicit effects of persistent update cannot be represented by any model-based minimality approach. This is the essential distinction between the persistent update and the minimality-based update.

5 Extending the PSA to Representing Preference

In the previous sections, we have presented the PSA and compared it with the minimality-based update approach. Generally, in knowledge base updates, our persistence principle is more conservative than the minimal change principle. This can be seen by Example 1 presented in section 3. However, on the other hand, sometimes, this conservative persistence principle may be unnecessarily weak. Let us consider the following example.

Example 2. Consider a simple blocks world, in which there are four propositional letters $Ontable(block1), Ontable(block2), Ontable(block3), Occupied(table)$ and one domain constraint C:

---

[4]Technically, this is illustrated by the proof of Theorem 4.

$Ontable(block1) \lor Ontable(block2) \lor Ontable(block3) \equiv Occupied(table).$

Let the current knowledge base be:

$\psi \equiv (Ontable(block1) \land Occupied(table) \land \neg Ontable(block2) \land \neg Ontable(block3)) \land C.$

Suppose the robot receives an order to move *block1* from the table. Then the robot updates its current knowledge base ψ with $\neg Ontable(block1)$. Using the PSA, since

$\{\neg Ontable(block1)\} \cup C \models Ontable(block2) \lor Ontable(block3) \lor \neg Occupied(table),$

$Occupied(table), \neg Ontable(block2)$ and $\neg Ontable(block3)$ are all mutable, thus, the resulting knowledge base is simply

$\psi \diamond_{psa} \neg Ontable(block1) \equiv \neg Ontable(block1) \land C.$

This result is quite weak because the truth values of $Ontable(blcok2)$, $Ontable(block3)$ and $Occupied(table)$ are all indefinite in the resulting knowledge base (eg., $block2$ or $block3$ may or may not "jump" on the table). From our intuition, however, moving $block1$ from the table should not affect the positions of $block2$ and $block3$ and the table should become unoccupied after $block1$ is moved out[5]. $\Box$

In order to avoid such undesired solution, we should have a way to combine the domain-dependent information into our approach so that the preferred result can be derived. The basic idea is described as follows. In applications, different facts may have different priorities of persistence. For instance, in Example 2, moving block1 may cause $block2$ or $block3$ to "jump" on the table; or $block2$ and $block3$ remain unchanged while the table becomes unoccupied. Obviously, if there is no other interference to this action, from our intuition, it is more likely that $block2$ and $block3$ remain unchanged while the table becomes unoccupied resulting from the action. On the other hand, in many applications, some fact(s) may *depend* on others. In other words, changing some fact(s) may cause other fact to change. For example, suppose we have constraint $Ontable(cup) \supset Occupied(table)$. If the cup is moved out from the table and there is no other object on the table, it seems reasonable to predict that $Occupied(table)$ is changed to $\neg Occupied(table)$. However, this preference is not expressed by the above constraint. Using the approach presented in section 3, we can only conclude that $Occupied(table)$ is mutable with respect to the update of moving out the cup. In order to combine these kinds of domain-dependent information into our persistence principle, we introduce different layers on all propositional letters.

Formally, all propositional letter of language $\mathcal{L}$ are divided into disjoint layers $1, \cdots, n$. For any letter f, let $L(f)$ denote the number of f's layer. Generally, for any two letters f_1 and f_2, if $L(f_1) > L(f_2)$, we will regard that f_1 is more *persistence-prioritized* than f_2, that is, (i) if both f_1 and f_2 are indefinitely affected by the update,

---

[5]If we apply the PMA to this example, on the other hand, we have the similar problem but the undesired possible results of PMA are less then that of PSA.

we will consider that f_2 is easier to change than f_1; (ii) if f_2 is supported by f_1, then changing f_1 will cause f_2 to change if f_2 has no other support set. We present the definition of the preferred persistent set as follows. Notice that we also need present the non-persistent set explicitly in order to define the preferred resulting state formally[6].

Definition 4 (Preferred persistent set) Let I be a state of the world, μ a propositional formula and consistent with C. We define the *preferred persistent set* of I based on the propositional letter layer, denoted as $\Delta_P(I, \mu)$, as follows.

1. $\Delta_0 = I - \{f \mid \{\mu\} \cup C \models \neg f\}$,

2. $\Delta_1 = \Delta_0 - \{f \mid$ there exists propositional letters $\{f_1, \cdots, f_k\} \subseteq I$ such that (i) $f \in \{f_1, \cdots, f_k\}$, and $\{\mu\} \cup C \models \bigvee_{i=1}^{k}[\neg]f_i$ where $C \not\models \bigvee_{i=1}^{k}[\neg]f_i$, (ii) for any proper subset M of $N = \{1, \cdots, k\}$, $\{\mu\} \cup C \not\models \bigvee_{j \in M}[\neg]f_j$, (iii) $L(f) = min\{L(f_1), \cdots, L(f_k)\}\}$,

3. $\Delta_i = \Delta_{i-1} - \{f_1, \cdots, f_k \mid$ (i) $\{\mu\} \cup C \not\models f_l$ for each $l \in \{1, \cdots, k\}$, (ii) there exists a *non-empty* minimal subset $F \subseteq I - \Delta_{i-1}$ such that $(F \cup \Delta_{i-1} - \{f_1, \cdots, f_k\}) \cup C \models f_l$ for each $l \in \{1, \cdots, k\}$, (iii) there exists some $f' \in F$, such that $L(f') > max\{L(f_1), \cdots, L(f_k)\}\}$,

4. Let $\Delta = \bigcap_{i=0}^{\infty} \Delta_i$. Then $\Delta_P(I, \mu) = \{f \mid f \in I$ and $\Delta \cup C \models f\}$. □

Definition 5 (Preferred non-persistent set) Under the same condition as above, the non-persistent set based on the propositional letter layer $\Delta_N(I, \mu)$ is defined as follows.

1. $\Delta'_0 = \{f \mid \{\mu\} \cup C \models \neg f\}$,

2. $\Delta'_i = \Delta'_{i-1} \cup \{f_1, \cdots, f_k \mid \{f_1, \cdots, f_k\} \subseteq I - \Delta'_{i-1} - \Delta_P(I, \mu)$ and (i) $\{\mu\} \cup C \not\models f_l$ for each $l \in \{1, \cdots, k\}$, (ii) there does not exist $f \in \Delta_P$ such that $\neg(\Delta'_{i-1} \cup \{f_1, \cdots, f_k\}) \cup C \models \neg f^7$, (iii) there exists a non-empty minimal subset $F \subseteq \Delta'_{i-1}$ such that $(F \cup I - \Delta'_{i-1} - \{f_1, \cdots, f_k\}) \cup C \models f_l$ for each $l \in \{1, \cdots, k\}$, (iv) there exists some $f' \in F$ such that $L(f') > max\{L(f_1), \cdots, L(f_k)\}\}^8$,

3. $\Delta_N(I, \mu) = \bigcup_{i=0}^{\infty} \Delta'_i$. □

Definition 6 (Preferred resulting state) An interpretation I' is a *preferred resulting state* of the world after updating I with μ, if

1. $I' \models C$,

---

[6]Because of the space limitation, here we omit explanations of the following definitions.

[7]$\neg \Delta = \{\neg f \mid f \in \Delta\}$.

[8]Conditions (i) and (ii) guarantee the consistency between the non-persistent set and the persistent set (e.g., a fact may be persistent or non-persistent, but not both). Conditions (iii) and (iv) say that fact f_l depends on one (or more) non-persistent fact(s) and at least one non-persistent fact's predicate layer is greater than f_l's.

2. $I' \models \mu$, and

3. $\Delta_P(I, \mu) \cup \neg \Delta_N(I, \mu) \subseteq I'$ [9].

We denote the set of all preferred resulting states as $Update_P(I, \mu)$. $\square$

Definition 7 Let ψ be knowledge base, μ a propositional formula and consistent with domain constraints C. $\psi \diamond_{ppsa} \mu$ denotes the *preferred persistent update* of ψ with μ, where

1. If ψ implies μ or ψ is inconsistent then $\psi \diamond_{ppsa} \mu \equiv \psi$, otherwise

2. $Models(\psi \diamond_{ppsa} \mu) = \bigcup_{I \in Models(\psi)} Update_P(I, \mu)$. $\square$

The following theorem represents the relation between $\diamond_{psa}$ and $\diamond_{ppsa}$.

Theorem 5 Let ψ be a knowledge base, μ a propositional formula and consistent with domain constraints. Then $\psi \diamond_{ppsa} \mu \models \psi \diamond_{psa} \mu$. $\square$

Example 2. Continued. Using the extended PSA described above, if we define $L(Ontable(block1)) = L(Ontable(block2)) = L(Ontable(block3)) = 2$ and $L(Occupied(table)) = 1$, then according to Definition 4 and 5, $\neg Ontable(block2)$ and $\neg Ontable(block3)$ are preferred persistent facts, while $Ontable(block1)$ and $Occupied(table)$ are preferred non-persistent facts. Thus, we have the following desired result:

$\psi \diamond_{ppsa} \neg Ontable(block1) \equiv (\neg Ontable(block1) \wedge \neg Ontable(block2) \wedge$
$\neg Ontable(block3) \wedge \neg Occupied(table)) \wedge C$. $\square$

6 Conclusion

We have proposed a persistent set approach (PSA) for knowledge base update, and shown the difference between the persistent update semantics and the minimality-based update semantics. We argued that according to Katsuno and Mendelzon's representation theorem, indefinite and implicit effects of update cannot be represented by any model-based minimality approach, while these kinds of effects have explicit representations in the PSA.

In order to derive the preferred solution in update, we extended the PSA to represent the preference information. The propositional letter layer introduced here is somewhat like Winslett's method of combining the predicate priority into the PMA (*Prioritized PMA – PPMA*) [8]. However, since the basic motivation of the PSA is different from that of the PMA, here we argue that the extended PSA can be applicable in more general problem domains than the PPMA [10].

---

[9] Recall that $\neg \Delta_N(I, \mu) = \{\neg f \mid f \in \Delta_N(I, \mu)\}$.

[10] This has been discussed in detail in our full paper.

We notice that the computation of the PSA, generally, is difficult. The key factor affecting the PSA's complexity is the computation of the persistent set. Our recent work has shown that, however, if the constraints are expressible as pure Horn clauses[11], the iterative phase of Definition 1 (where the fixed point is defined) has the complexity of the greatest fixed point of the corresponding program. In general, this is finite failure calculation for the ground atom that is being queried for the set Δ_i.

Acknowledgements

This research is supported in part by a grant from the Australian Research Council. The first author is supported by a SOPF scholarship from the Australian Government. Discussions with members of the Knowledge Systems Group of the University of Sydney have improved the presentation.

References

[1] T. S-C Chou and M. Winslett. Immortal: a model-based belief revision system. In J. Allen, R. Fikes, and E. Sandewall, editors, *Proceedings of the Second International Conference on Principles of Knowledge Representation and Reasoning (KR'91)*, pages 99–110. Morgan Kaufmann Publisher, Inc., 1991.

[2] M. Dalal. Investigations into a theory of knowledge base revision: Preliminary report. In *Proceedings of AAAI-88*, pages 475–479, 1988.

[3] A. del Val. Syntactic characterizations of belief change operators. In *Proceedings of Thirteenth International Joint Conference on Artificial Intelligence*, pages 540–545, Chembary, France, 1993. Morgan Kaufmann Publishers, Inc.

[4] P. Gardenfors. *Knowledge in Flux*. MIT Press, Cambridge, Massachusetts, 1988.

[5] H. Katsuno and A. O. Mendelzon. On the difference between updating a knowledge database and revising it. In *Proceedings of Second International Conference on Principles of Knowledge Representation and Reasoning*, 1991.

[6] A. Weber. Updating propositional formulas. In *Proceedings of the First International Expert Database Systems Conference*, pages 487–500, Charleston SC, 1986.

[7] M. Winslett. Reasoning about action using a possible models approach. In *Proceedings of AAAI-88*, pages 89–93, 1988.

[8] M. Winslett. Circumscriptive semantics for updating knowledge bases. *Annals of Mathematics and Artificial Intelligence*, 3:429–450, 1991.

[9] Y. Zhang and N.Y. Foo. Reasoning about persistence: a theory of actions. In *Proceedings of Thirteenth International Joint Conference on Artificial Intelligence*, pages 718–723, Chembary, France, 1993. Morgan Kaufmann Publishers, Inc.

---

[11]More generally, we consider this problem within a first order language.

Constructing Extensions with Matricial Resolution

MESSAOUDI Nadia*

Laboratoire d'Informatique de Marseille, URA CNRS 1787, Université Aix-Marseille II

Faculté des Sciences de Luminy, 163 Avenue de Luminy, case 901

13288 MARSEILLE Cedex FRANCE

e-mail : messaoudi@linda.cad.cea.fr

Abstract

When we've got a knowledge basis formalised with some logic, we want to be able to construct the set of conclusions which could be inferred from the set of facts describing the world at a given time. In the nonmonotonic logics, it's called constructing the extensions of the system. The principal difficulty faced with, is to find the methods with the least computational complexity. In this paper, we reduce the problem in the context of classical logic and default logics to a resolution of a system of linear equations. This reduction gives access to the resolution methods of the numerical calculus and its polynomial algorithms. Moreover, this approach can be extend to the multi-valued logics and at the present time we are implementing it for the Paradoxical Logic[2] for the developpement of several industrial projects.

1   Introduction

When we've got a knowledge basis formalised with some logic, and a set of facts describing the world at a given time, the problem is to find all the inferable conclusions of the system if some exists. This set is called the set of extensions of the system. To compute this one, we have to find the set(s) of formulae which can be inferred from the knowledge basis operating on a set of premisses (set of facts) by constructing the fixed-points for this operation. This method is used for non-monotonic logics of Mac-Dermott and as well for the default logics of Reiter[3] with the extensions of default theories.

In this paper, we transform the extension construction to a resolution problem of a system of linear equations in such a way to decrease the computing complexity of the

*This research is supported by a CEA-EDF project for the developpement of an expert system helping for nuclear fuel casing defaults diagnostic in nuclear reactors.

problem. The calculus become similar to a classical problem of numerical calculus from which we can borrow the methods (Gauss triangularisation, Choleski decomposition) and some heuristics.

First, we'll present this method of matricial resolution in the context of the classical bi-valued logic, then we'll adapt it to use it in the context of the default logics of Reiter. Finally, we will discuss the possible variations of this method and the perspectives in the context of several industrial projects.

2   Propositional calculus

A *literal* is a proposition x or it negation $\neg x$. A *clause* is a disjunction of a finite number of literals, this is to say a formula such as : $x_1 \vee x_2 \vee \ldots \vee x_n$. A *normal conjunctive form* is a conjunction of a finite number of clauses.

Theorem 1 *[5] Every formula admits a normal conjunctive form which is logically equivalent.*

Definition 1 *The propositional calculus formulae can be interpreted, this is to say, can receive a value of the domain of the semantic interpretation, for example $\{T, F\}$ for the classical bi-valued logic.*

Definition 2 *Let Literals $= \{a, b, c, \ldots\}$ the set of the literals of our knowledge basis. We'll add to the set $\{T, F\}$ the constant $\emptyset$ characterizing ignorence about a proposition or "lack of coefficient" (we'll see later what it means).*

3   Definition of the sets $\mathcal{A}$ et $\mathcal{M}$

Definition 3 *We introduce the operators $\odot$, $\oplus$ and $\asymp$ such as :*

1. $\odot : Literals \cup \{T, F, \emptyset\} \times Literals \cup \{T, F, \emptyset\} \longrightarrow Literals \cup \{T, F, \emptyset\}$
    Let $a \in Literals \cup \{T, F, \emptyset\}$,
    $a \odot T \asymp a$
    $F \odot F \asymp T$
    $a \odot \emptyset \asymp \emptyset$

2. $\oplus : Literals \cup \{T, F, \emptyset\} \times Literals \cup \{T, F, \emptyset\} \longrightarrow \{T, F, \emptyset\}$
    Let $a \in Literals \cup \{T, F, \emptyset\}$,
    $a \oplus T \asymp T$
    $a \oplus F \asymp a$
    $a \oplus \emptyset \asymp a$

The operators $\odot$ and $\oplus$ are commutative and associative.
The triplet $\{\{T, F, \emptyset\}, \odot, \oplus\}$ will be noted $\mathcal{A}$.

Definition 4 *Let M_A the set of the matrices $(n \times m)$ for n and m integers, with their coefficients in Literals $\cup \{T, F, \emptyset\}$, we define the operators $\bar{\odot}, \bar{\oplus}, \stackrel{\sim}{\asymp}$ such as :*

1. $\bar{\odot} : M_A \times M_A \longrightarrow M_A$
   Let A, $B \in M_A$ with $A = (a_{ij})_{i,j}$ and $B = (b_{ji})_{i,j}$ for $1 \leq i \leq n$ and $1 \leq j \leq m$

$$A \bar{\odot} B \stackrel{\sim}{\asymp} (\oplus_{k=1}^{m} a_{ik} \odot b_{kj})_{i,j}$$

2. $\bar{\oplus} : M_A \times M_A \longrightarrow M_A$
   Let A, $B \in M_A$ with $A = (a_{ij})_{i,j}$ and $B = (b_{ji})_{i,j}$ for $1 \leq i \leq n$ and $1 \leq j \leq m$.

$$A \bar{\oplus} B \stackrel{\sim}{\asymp} (a_{ik} \oplus b_{kj})_{i,j}$$

The triplet $\{M_A, \bar{\odot}, \bar{\oplus}\}$ will be noted $\mathcal{M}$.

Example 1 :

$$A = \begin{bmatrix} a & T \\ \emptyset & F \end{bmatrix} \quad B = \begin{bmatrix} b_1 & T \\ F & b_2 \end{bmatrix}$$

$$A \bar{\oplus} B \stackrel{\sim}{\asymp} \begin{bmatrix} a & T \\ \emptyset & F \end{bmatrix} \bar{\oplus} \begin{bmatrix} b_1 & T \\ F & b_2 \end{bmatrix} \stackrel{\sim}{\asymp} \begin{bmatrix} a \oplus b_1 & T \oplus T \\ \emptyset \oplus F & F \oplus b_2 \end{bmatrix}$$

$$A \bar{\odot} B \stackrel{\sim}{\asymp} \begin{bmatrix} a & T \\ \emptyset & F \end{bmatrix} \bar{\odot} \begin{bmatrix} b_1 & T \\ F & b_2 \end{bmatrix} \stackrel{\sim}{\asymp} \begin{bmatrix} a \odot b_1 \oplus T \odot F & a \odot T \oplus T \odot b_2 \\ \emptyset \odot b_1 \oplus F \odot F & \emptyset \odot T \oplus F \odot b_2 \end{bmatrix}$$

$$\stackrel{\sim}{\asymp} \begin{bmatrix} a \odot b_1 & a \oplus b_2 \\ T & F \odot b_2 \end{bmatrix}$$

4 Constructing extenstions in classical logic

Reasoning on knowledges, is to find the set of conclusions inferred from a set of formulae. This is the same as computing the fixed-point of the inference operator on the knowledge basis.

4.1. Rewriting the rules of the knowledge basis

From the **theorem 1**, with a set of rules, we can construct a set of clauses equivalent. We can rewrite each clause as the following way : $a \longrightarrow \vee_i b_i$ where a and $(b_i)_i$ are some literals. This rule can be rewrite in a new formalism using the operators already defined. Let n the cardinality of the set *Literals* for our knowledge basis, then $a \longrightarrow \vee_{i=1}^{n} b_i$ is rewritten in :

$$Value(a) \odot f \stackrel{\sim}{\asymp} Value(b_1) \odot x_1 \oplus Value(b_2) \odot x_2 \oplus \ldots \oplus Value(b_n) \odot x_n,$$

with $Value(b_k) = T$ if b_k, $Value(b_k) = F$ if $\neg b_k$, $Value(b_k) = \emptyset$ if $b_k \notin (b_i)_{i=1,\ldots,n}$,

(x_i) the unknown variable indicating possible conclusions, depending on the world at a given time and f the description of this world concerning a.

4.2. Rewriting the knowledge basis

For a knowledge basis constitued by the m rules :

$$\{a_1 \longrightarrow \vee_i b_{i,1},\ a_2 \longrightarrow \vee_i b_{i,2}, \ldots,\ a_m \longrightarrow \vee_i b_{i,m}\},$$

we rewrite each rule as explained before, and we obtain the following system :

$$\left\{ \begin{array}{l} Value(a_1) \odot f_1 \asymp Value(b_{1,1}) \odot x_1 \quad \oplus \quad Value(b_{2,1}) \odot x_2 \quad \oplus \quad \ldots \quad \oplus \quad Value(b_{n,1}) \odot x_n; \\ Value(a_2) \odot f_2 \asymp Value(b_{1,2}) \odot x_1 \quad \oplus \quad Value(b_{2,2}) \odot x_2 \quad \oplus \quad \ldots \quad \oplus \quad Value(b_{n,2}) \odot x_n; \\ \qquad \vdots \qquad\qquad\qquad\qquad \vdots \qquad\qquad\qquad\qquad \vdots \\ Value(a_m) \odot f_m \asymp Value(b_{1,m}) \odot x_1 \quad \oplus \quad Value(b_{2,m}) \odot x_2 \quad \oplus \quad \ldots \quad \oplus \quad Value(b_{n,m}) \odot x_n \end{array} \right\}$$

We can then copy the representation of a system of linear equations in order to obtain the construction of conclusions of an inference equivalent to resolution of the following matrices equation :

$$\begin{bmatrix} \emptyset & \emptyset & \ldots & Value(a_1) & \emptyset & \ldots & \emptyset \\ \emptyset & \ldots & Value(a_2) & \emptyset & \emptyset & \ldots & \emptyset \\ \vdots & & & \vdots & & & \vdots \\ \emptyset & \ldots & \emptyset & \emptyset & Value(a_m) & \ldots & \emptyset \end{bmatrix} \bar{\odot} \begin{bmatrix} f_1 \\ f_2 \\ \vdots \\ f_n \end{bmatrix}$$

$$\asymp \begin{bmatrix} Value(b_{1,1}) & Value(b_{2,1}) & Value(b_{3,1}) & \ldots & Value(b_{n,1}) \\ Value(b_{1,2}) & Value(b_{2,2}) & Value(b_{3,2}) & \ldots & Value(b_{n,2}) \\ \vdots & & \vdots & & \vdots \\ Value(b_{1,m}) & Value(b_{2,m}) & Value(b_{3,m}) & \ldots & Value(b_{n,m}) \end{bmatrix} \bar{\odot} \begin{bmatrix} f_1' \\ f_2' \\ \vdots \\ f_n' \end{bmatrix}$$

$$\Longleftrightarrow \quad M_G \bar{\odot} F \asymp M_D \bar{\odot} F'$$

$F = (f_1,\ f_2, \ldots,\ f_n)$ represents our basis of facts describing the considered world. $F' = (f_1',\ f_2', \ldots,\ f_n')$ the unknown variable represents an "intermediate extension", this is to say the conclusions of an inference from F.

What we had shown constitutes a stage of computing, the complete procedure is explained below.

Constructing extensions procedure :

Let F_0 the vector describing the basis of facts and $\{M_L, M_R\}$ the left and right matrices describing our knowledge basis. If the system $S = \{\{M_L, M_R\}, F\}$ admits at least one extension, then :

$$i = 0$$

Step 1 : Resolve $M_L \bar{\odot} F_i \gtrless M_R \bar{\odot} F_{i+1}$
If $F_i = F_{i+1}$ then go to Step 2
Else $i = i + 1$, go to Step 1.

Step 2 : F_i is an extension of the described system S.

Example 2 : Let the system of the following knowledge basis and basis of facts :

$$BK = \begin{cases} x & \longrightarrow & z \\ y & \longrightarrow & t \vee z \\ t \vee x & \longrightarrow & w \begin{cases} t & \longrightarrow & w \\ x & \longrightarrow & w \end{cases} \end{cases} \qquad BF = \{x, t\}.$$

The elements M_L, M_R, F_0 of the knowledge basis rewritten are the following :

$$M_L = \begin{bmatrix} x & y & z & t & w \\ T & \emptyset & \emptyset & \emptyset & \emptyset \\ \emptyset & T & \emptyset & \emptyset & \emptyset \\ \emptyset & \emptyset & \emptyset & T & \emptyset \\ T & \emptyset & \emptyset & \emptyset & \emptyset \end{bmatrix} \qquad M_R = \begin{bmatrix} x & y & z & t & w \\ \emptyset & \emptyset & T & \emptyset & \emptyset \\ \emptyset & \emptyset & T & T & \emptyset \\ \emptyset & \emptyset & \emptyset & \emptyset & T \\ \emptyset & \emptyset & \emptyset & \emptyset & T \end{bmatrix} \qquad F_0 = \begin{bmatrix} T \\ \emptyset \\ \emptyset \\ T \\ \emptyset \end{bmatrix}$$

Then, the system to resolve is :

$$\begin{bmatrix} T & \emptyset & \emptyset & \emptyset & \emptyset \\ \emptyset & T & \emptyset & \emptyset & \emptyset \\ \emptyset & \emptyset & \emptyset & T & \emptyset \\ T & \emptyset & \emptyset & \emptyset & \emptyset \end{bmatrix} \bar{\odot} \begin{bmatrix} T \\ \emptyset \\ \emptyset \\ T \\ \emptyset \end{bmatrix} \gtrless \begin{bmatrix} \emptyset & \emptyset & T & \emptyset & \emptyset \\ \emptyset & \emptyset & T & T & \emptyset \\ \emptyset & \emptyset & \emptyset & \emptyset & T \\ \emptyset & \emptyset & \emptyset & \emptyset & T \end{bmatrix} \bar{\odot} \begin{bmatrix} x \\ y \\ z \\ t \\ w \end{bmatrix}$$

$T \odot T \times T \odot z \implies z = T$
$\emptyset \times T \odot z \oplus T \odot t$ (we can't say anything)
$T \times T \odot w \implies w = T$

$$F_1 = \begin{bmatrix} T \\ \emptyset \\ T \\ T \\ T \end{bmatrix}$$

We apply the procedure one more time and we obtain :

$$F_2 \;=\; \begin{bmatrix} T \\ \emptyset \\ T \\ T \\ T \end{bmatrix}$$

$F_2 = F_1$, it's finished, the extension is $\{x,\ z,\ t,\ w\}$.

5 Adaptating the method for the default logics

5.1. An introduction to default logic

A *default theory*, $\Delta = (D, W)$ is constitued by a set of formulae, W, and a set of defaults, D. A default is an expression of the form :

$$\frac{A \ : \ B_1, \ldots, B_m}{W},$$

where A, B_i and W are called prerequised, justifications and consequent of the default respectively. If the prerequised is empty, it's a tautology. If $B = W \wedge C$ with C a formula, then the default will be called semi-normal. In a default, if the prerequised is known and the justifications are consistent (their negation is not provable) then the consequent can be inferred.

The defaults are nonmonotonic rules, since when we add a new information which denies the justifications of a default, we can invalidate some conclusions inferred before. The "theorems" of a default theory are not as easy to generate as those of a first order theory. What is inferred is determined from what is not inferred. To avoid this apparent circularity, the theorems of a default theory are defined by the construction of fixed-points. An extension, E, for a default theory $\Delta = (D, W)$ must have the following properties :

1. $W \subseteq E$,

2. $Th_L(E) = E$,

3. For each default
$$\frac{A \ : \ B_1, \ldots, \ B_m}{W} \in D,$$
   if $A \in E$, and $\neg B_1, \ldots, \ \neg B_m \notin E$, then $W \in E$.

These properties establish that E contains all the known facts, then E has to be closed for $\vdash$ (inference) and that the consequent of every default whose the prerequised is satisfied by E and whose the justifications are consistent with E, has to be in E. Reiter defines an extension for a closed default theory as a minimal fixed-point of an operator having the characteristics described before.

5.2.   Reasoning and default logic

An extension is a set of belief which are in some sense "justified" or "reasonable" in light of what is known about the world[1].

We remind that in a normal default, the consequent is equivalent to is justification. Each theory containing only normal defaults (normal theory) has at least on extension. But we can't assure the same property for the semi-normal default theories. For exemple the semi-normal default theory

$$W = \{ \, \},$$

$$D = \left\{ \tfrac{:A \wedge \neg B}{A}, \tfrac{:B \wedge \neg C}{B}, \tfrac{:C \wedge \neg A}{C} \right\}$$

has no extension. Though there is a large class of consistent semi-normal default theories which have at least one extension (this is to say, corresponding to a hierarchical knowledge such as there is no "cycle" of inference).

5.3.   Constructing extensions

We introduce two new values ε, $-\varepsilon$ to the domain $\{T, F, \emptyset\}$, characterising what is placed on justifications in the default. For exemple :

$\frac{A:B}{C}$ will be noted $(T \odot A) \odot (\varepsilon \odot B) \asymp T \odot C,$

$\frac{A:\neg B}{C}$ will be noted $(T \odot A) \odot ((-\varepsilon) \odot B) \asymp T \odot C$

The values ε and $-\varepsilon$ hold :

- $\varepsilon \odot \emptyset \asymp \emptyset, \, \varepsilon \odot T \asymp T, \, \varepsilon \odot F \asymp F,$

- $-\varepsilon \odot \emptyset \asymp \emptyset, \, -\varepsilon \odot T \asymp F, \, -\varepsilon \odot F \asymp T.$

Definition 5 *The triplet* $\{\{T, F, \emptyset, \, -\varepsilon, \varepsilon\}, \odot, \oplus\}$ *will be noted* $\mathcal{A}'$.
Let $M_{\mathcal{A}'}$, *the set of the matrices with their coefficients in* $\{T, F, \emptyset, -\varepsilon, \varepsilon\}, \{M_{\mathcal{A}'}, \bar{\odot}, \bar{\oplus}\}$ *will be noted* $\mathcal{M}'$.

As before, from a knowledge basis, constituted by a set of defaults D and a basis of facts W, we can establish a system of linear equations to resolve, to compute an intermediate extension W_i. And as the same way, we'll stop the calculus when $W_{i+1} = W_i$ and W_i will be an extension of our system.

Proposition 1 *There is a converging computation such that $W_n = W_{n+1}$ and $Th(W_n) = W_n$ if and only if W_n is an extension for the default theory (D, W).*

Proof : Let $W_n = W_{n+1}$, the fixed-point of the procedure presented above. To be an extension, W_n is required to have the following properties :

1. $W \subseteq W_n$, it's deduced from the construction of W_n,

2. $Th(W_n) = W_n$,
   $W_{n+1} \subset Th(W_{n+1})$ by definition,
   $$W_{n+1} = Th(W_n) \cup \{w \ / \ \left(\tfrac{\alpha:\beta}{w}\right) \in D, \ Value(\alpha) = \emptyset \tag{1}$$
   $$\text{or } (M_L)_\alpha \text{ and } Value(\beta) \neq -\epsilon\}$$
   $$W_{n+1} = W_n \Rightarrow Th(W_{n+1}) = Th(W_n) \tag{2}$$
   (1) and (2) induce $Th(W_{n+1}) \subset W_{n+1}$

3. for each default $\frac{A:B}{C} \in D$, if $A \in W_n$ and $\neg B \notin W_n$ then $C \in W_n$, we can deduce this from (1).

W_{n+1} is an extension, so we have :
$$W_{n+1} = Th(W_n) \cup \{w \ / \ \left(\tfrac{\alpha:\beta}{w}\right) \in D, \ Value(\alpha) = \emptyset \text{ or } (M_L)_\alpha \text{ and } Value(\beta) \neq -\epsilon\}$$
$$M_L \bar{\odot} W_n \succsim M_R \bar{\odot} W_{n+1},$$
we obtain for each line :
$$R \asymp w_1^{n+1} \odot a_{1,i} \oplus \ldots \oplus w_m^{n+1} a_{m,i}, \text{ and } w_j^{n+1} = w_j^n \text{ if } w_i^n \neq \emptyset, \tag{3}$$
if $R = \emptyset$, we can say anything more on the coefficients w_i^{n+1},
if $R = T, T = \oplus_k w_k^{n+1} \odot a_{k,i} \oplus \oplus_l w_l^n \odot a_{l,i}$

- $\oplus_l w_l^n \odot a_{l,i} = \emptyset$ or F then $T = \oplus_k w_k^{n+1} \odot a_{k,i}$, it means $\exists k_1 / w_{k_1}^{n+1} \odot a_{k_1,i} = T$, there are two solutions : first, $a_{k_1,i} = T$ and $w_{k_1}^{n+1} = T$ and $w_{k_1}^n = \emptyset$ (Cf (3)) $\Rightarrow Th(W_n) \subset Th(W_{n+1})$ strictly, it's impossible then W_n is not an extension, the second solution is $a_{k_1,i} = F$ and $w_{k_1}^{n+1} = F$ and $w_{k_1}^n = \emptyset$, we conclude in the same way.

- $\oplus_l w_l^n \odot a_{l,i} = T$ then $T = \oplus_k w_k^{n+1} \odot a_{k,i} \oplus T$ holds in any case, we have no more information on $w_k^{n+1}, \forall j \ w_j^{n+1} = w_j^n$.

Example 3 : Let $D = \left\{\frac{A:B}{B}, \frac{A:C}{C}, \frac{B:D}{D}, \frac{B:\neg D \wedge \neg C}{\neg D}\right\}$, and $W = \{A\}$.

$$
\begin{array}{cccc}
M_L & W_0 & M_R & W_1 \\
\begin{bmatrix} T & \varepsilon & \emptyset & \emptyset \\ T & \emptyset & \varepsilon & \emptyset \\ \emptyset & T & \emptyset & \varepsilon \\ \emptyset & T & -\varepsilon & -\varepsilon \end{bmatrix}
\bar{\odot}
\begin{bmatrix} T \\ \emptyset \\ \emptyset \\ \emptyset \end{bmatrix}
\succsim
\begin{bmatrix} \emptyset & T & \emptyset & \emptyset \\ \emptyset & \emptyset & T & \emptyset \\ \emptyset & \emptyset & \emptyset & T \\ \emptyset & \emptyset & \emptyset & F \end{bmatrix}
\bar{\odot}
\begin{bmatrix} A \\ B \\ C \\ D \end{bmatrix}
\end{array}
$$

$$T \asymp T \odot B \implies B = T,$$

$$T \asymp T \odot C \implies C = T,$$

$$\emptyset \asymp T \odot D \text{ (we can't say anything)},$$

$$\emptyset \asymp F \odot D.$$

$$F_1 = \begin{bmatrix} T \\ T \\ T \\ \emptyset \end{bmatrix}$$

We repeat the operation :

$$M_L \bar{\odot} F_1 \asymp M_R \bar{\odot} F_2$$

$$F_1 = \begin{bmatrix} T \\ T \\ T \\ T \end{bmatrix}$$

We repeat again $F_2 = F_3$.

6 Evolution of the knowledge basis

Two approaches can be considered :

- we don't take into account the evolution of the system we study, at each new basis of facts, we compute an extention but we don't add it to the knowledge basis. This approach can be interesting when we request only a diagnostic on the statement of the system,

- we take into account the evolution of the observed system, at each new basis of facts, we compute an extension and we add it to the knowledge basis. Then we have to make a revision of this one by the new information collected in the constructed extension.

In the context of our project, we choose the second approach. We use the formalism of the Pardoxical Logic[2] and the operation of revision that will be associated to it, will be the subject of a next article.

7 Complexity

The resolution of the equation $M_L \bar{\odot} F_i \asymp M_R \bar{\odot} F_{i+1}$ can be done by borrowing to the numerical calculus, polynomial algorithms such as Gauss method for the resolution of big linear systems. The complexity of this one being $\Theta\left(\frac{n^3}{3}\right)$ for a matrix $n \times n$, then let c the number of formulae and l the number of literals appearing in these formulae, it'll take at most $\min(c, l)$ stages of resolution or "triangularisation" of Gauss to compute an extension. The complexity will be roughly $\Theta\left(\min(c, l) \times \left(\frac{n^3}{3}\right)\right)$ for a matrix $n \times n$. But some heuristics can reduce this value[6][7].

8 Conclusions-Perspectives

In this paper, we presented our work concerning the bi-valued logic, but we can easily extend the method for multi-valued logics, that we are studying at the present time. The method is already implemented for the default logics presented previously, and now we extend the implementation to the Paradoxical Logic[2] which is a three-valued logic.

This is the logic we use to formalize the knowledge basis for the developpement of an expert system helping for nuclear fuel casing defaults diagnostic in nuclear reactors. This study is carried out in the CEA's center of Cadarache in France. This formalism is also used for a project developped by Arnaud Kohler at the ISL (French-German Research Institute, Saint-Louis, France).

References

[1] D.W. Etherington, *Formalizing Nonmonotonic Reasonning Systems,* 1987 Artificial Intelligence.

[2] A. Kohler, N. Messaoudi, *Modélisation de l'Incertain,* 1994 Congrès RFIA Paris.

[3] Léa Sombé, *Raisonnement sur des Informations Incomplètes,* 1989 teknea.

[4] C. Schwind, P. Siegel, *A Modal Logic for Hypothesis Theory,* 1993, in Fundamentals of Artificial Intelligence.

[5] A. Thayse et co-auteurs, *Approche logique de l'Intelligence Artificielle,* 1990 Dunod.

[6] Gene H.Golub, Gérard A.Meurant, *Résolution numérique des grands systèmes linéaires,* 1983 Eyrolles.

[7] C.Gueguen, *Matrices Proches de Toeplitz et Algorithmes Rapides,* Aussois 1981 Colloque Algorithmes Rapides pour le Traitement des Systèmes Dynamiques Linéaires.

VI - MACHINE LEARNING

DYNAMIC INDUCTION IN NETWORK OF RELATIONS

ZDRAVKO MARKOV

Institute of Informatics – Bulgarian Academy of Sciences

Acad.G.Bonchev St. Block 29A, 1113 Sofia, Bulgaria

Email: markov@iinf.bg

ABSTRACT

The paper presents a concept learning system, based on dynamic induction of relational definitions represented in function-free Prolog. The inductive process is dynamic in a sense that it takes place basically during the process of classification of new instances. In contrast to the majority of concept learning systems, where the primary goal is induction of a concept definition, our system infers directly missing data in a set of examples using an example-guided deductive inference. Given an incomplete data set, the system infers ground atoms and produces clauses justifying these inferences.

1. Introduction

Consider the following relational domain. B is a set of ground atoms, describing directional graph and explicitly specifying some paths in this graph.

$$B = \{link(a, b), link(b, c), link(c, d), link(c, e), path(a, b), path(a, c)\}$$

The set B is incomplete with respect to the *path* relation. Clearly, the missing relations T are

$$T = \{path(a, d), path(a, e), path(b, c), path(b, d), path(b, e), path(c, d), path(c, e)\}$$

Generally, two problems can be stated in this simple domain:

1. Given the set B, find a definition of the *path* relation, in some language. For example in Prolog this can be

```
path(X,Y):-link(X,Y)
path(X,Y):-link(X,Z),path(Z,Y)
```

Such a definition is important to be *correct* and *complete*. When we discuss these two properties we usually mean correctness and completeness w.r.t. $B \cup T$, i.e. the *intended* semantics of the problem domain.

2. Given the set B, infer the missing relations T (using the same intuition for the intended semantics of the problem domain).

A way to solve the second problem is by solving problem 1 first. Then B is a training set and T can be used as a test set, which can be possibly inferred from the hypothesis by deductive inference, thus solving the second problem. However, since the training set is incomplete, the created definition might happen to be incorrect or incomplete. For example, the system FOIL[5] faces major difficulties to find clauses for a predicate defined with incomplete set of positive examples (such as B). FOIL will classify all the unknown facts (T) as negative (using the Closed World Assumption) and will possibly build a definition trying to rule them out. Other systems (e.g. MIS[6] and GOLEM[2]) require explicit specification of the negative examples and thus the quality of the concept definition depend greatly on their proper choice.

Most of the efforts in inductive learning are focused towards building a possibly correct and complete concept definition, which later can be run on a standard deductive system. The objective here is to explicate the regularities found in large and complex data sets. However, this objective is pursued only theoretically. Most of the practical concept learners use simple data and create very simple definitions (for example, the predicates "append" and "member" in Prolog), which can be easily figured out by any student given very few examples. From the other hand, more complex data sets produce definitions, which though correct, can be hardly understood by humans. Many practical problems however, require classifications of unseen examples, rather than definitions of the classes they belong to. Whenever such definitions are built by the learning system, they can be used as explanations and justifications of the decisions made. (This approach is also pursued in the field of exemplar-based or case-based learning systems.)

Further in the paper we shall discuss the concept learning system DIRD (*Dynamic Induction of Relational Definitions*). The inductive process in DIRD is *dynamic* in a sense that it takes place basically during the process of classification of new instances. In contrast to the majority of concept learning systems, where the primary goal is induction of a concept definition, DIRD infers directly missing data in a set of examples using an example-guided deductive inference. Thus we overcome some of the problems mentioned above by solving directly problem 2 using positive examples only.

Given an incomplete data set, DIRD infers ground atoms and produces ground clauses justifying these inferences. The produced clauses can be easily generalized by variabalizations and reduction, and further used in the definition of the predicate, whose instances are the derived atoms. Thus the process of building a concept definition is a by-product of the system's operation. The focus of the approach is on the deductive inference, which uses extensively the set of examples and incorporates an inductive mechanism similar to FOIL's one.

The paper is organized as follows. In the next section we outline the approach. Section 3 discusses its computational complexity. A discussion of the performance of DIRD compared to the systems FOIL and GOLEM is given in Section 4.

2. Description of the approach

Consider problem 2 stated in Section 1 – given the set B, to find the set T. The basic idea to solve this problem is as follows. Consider for example, the atoms $link(a, b)$, $link(b, c)$, $path(a, c)$ from B as a ground instance of the clause $path(A, C)$: $- link(A, B)$, $link(B, C)$. Then using this clause and the set B as a database of facts, a missing atom – $path(c, e)$, can be inferred. Further, building various clauses variabalizing atoms from B, we can infer all the elements of T. The classical concept learning approaches pay attention basically on the problem of building clauses, using various heuristic or formal methods to induce correct clauses. In contrast, the basic idea of our approach is, firstly to build a generalization of all possible clauses by simple variabalization of the whole set B, and then to concentrate on the deductive inference of new atoms. Thus we come to the following algorithm:

Algorithm: *Dynamic Induction of Relational Definitions (DIRD).*
Step 1: *Building a network of relations.*
Let us denote the elements of B by $B_i, i = 1, 2, ..., 6$. Replace all constants occurring in B by variables (different constants by different variables), i.e. apply the *inverse substitution* $\theta^{-1} = \{a/A, b/B, c/C, d/D, e/E\}$ to B and obtain $P = B\theta^{-1}$. Denote the elements of P by $P_j, j = 1, 2, ..., 6$, i.e. $P_j = B_j\theta^{-1}, j = 1, ..., 6$.

$$P = \{link(A, B), link(B, C), link(C, D), link(C, E), path(A, B), path(A, C)\}$$

Step 2: *Example-guided deductive inference.*
At this step B plays the role of a database of ground facts and P is a generalized representation of all possible clauses built by variabalization of atoms from B.

Further in the algorithm we use the notion of *power of a substitution*, $PW(\theta)$, w.r.t. expressions $P = \{P_1, ..., P_n\}$ and $B = \{B_1, ..., B_n\}$, which we define as follows (similarly to the *power of a predicate*[4]). $PW(\theta)$ is equal to the number of $P_i\theta$, which cover elements from B, i.e. there exists a substitution σ, such that $P_i\theta\sigma \in B$.

For example, let $\theta = \{A/c, B/d\}$. Then $PW(\theta) = 2$, because the elements $link(b, B)$, $link(B, d) \in P\theta$ cover two elements of B – $link(b, c)$ and $link(c, d)$.

Let Q be an atom. The algorithm to check whether Q is derivable from $B \cup P$, is as follows:

1. Unify Q with some $P_i \in P$, i.e. find θ, such that $P_i\theta = Q$. If $PW(\theta) = 0$ w.r.t. P and B, then Q is *not derivable* from $B \cup P$, else go to 2.

2. For all $P_j \in P$ having variables substituted by θ ($vars(P_j) \cap vars(\theta) \neq \emptyset$) find a substitution θ_j, such that $P_j\theta_j = B_n$ with *maximum power*, where the maximum is taken for all $B_n \in B$. If this maximum is greater that zero then apply θ_j to P.

3. Replace θ with θ_j and repeat item 2 for all θ_j until the stopping condition in item 4 becomes true or there are no more substitutions applicable to elements of P (substitutions with power > 0).

4. *Q is successfully derived from* $B \cup P$ iff all non-variable arguments of Q occur within the set of all B_n found in item 2 – $\{B_{n_1}, ..., B_{n_k}\}$, and all variable arguments of Q are bound (obviously by terms occurring within the same set).

The algorithm is *determinate* and performs a *hill climbing* search. The only place for eventual backtracking is the initial choice of P_i to unify Q. Along with the prove whether Q is derivable from $B \cup P$, the algorithm produces a set of ground elements of B, which can play the role of a body of the clause used in the derivation. Thus the ground clause $Q : -B_{n_1}, ..., B_{n_k}$ is derived too. By simple variabalization and reduction this clause can be used for building a clause for defining the predicate whose instance is Q. All clauses of this predicate can be found easily by backtracking through all possible P_i's unifying Q (item 1 of the algorithm).

For example, the set of missing atoms T is inferred by the algorithm along with the following ground clauses:

```
1. path(a,d)  :- link(c,d),path(a,c)
2. path(a,e)  :- link(c,e),path(a,c)
3. path(b,c)  :- link(b,c),link(c,d)
4. path(b,c)  :- link(b,c),link(c,e)
5. path(b,d)  :- link(b,c),link(c,d)
6. path(b,e)  :- link(b,c),link(c,e)
7. path(c,d)  :- link(c,d)
8. path(c,e)  :- link(c,e)
```

When variabalized and reduced (removing the rightmost literals of clauses 3 and 4) all derived clauses are correct w.r.t. $B \cup T$. The standard definition of *path* shown in Section 1 can be build by clauses 1 and 7.

The described algorithm actually combines two techniques - the inductive learning algorithm similar to that of the system FOIL, and the usual resolution-based deductive inference. As in FOIL this is a *general-to-specific* search for a clause, however a ground instance of this clause is being built. At each step (item 2 of the algorithm) a new body literal is searched using an information gain measure (the power of the substitution) and when found this literal is promptly used in a resolution step. Thus its variables are bound and can further guide the search for new literals from the set of all possible literals P. This is the same idea used in FOIL to link each new literal to the clause body by *old variables* (variables occurring in the already found literals). In our case these are the bound variables in P.

The goal of the algorithm is to prove Q with minimal number of steps. By choosing a literal with maximum substitution power at each step, the currently built clause is guaranteed to have maximum power too (see next Section). This increases the probability that the specified goal Q will appear as an instance of the head of this clause (checked by the stopping condition in item 4).

The stopping condition (item 4) is actually based on the idea of restricting the search only to *generative clauses*[3], in which all variables in the head should also appear in the clause body.

3. Complexity of the algorithm

In this Section we shall show an upper bound of the complexity of the DIRD algorithm, based on the following terms:

- *Constant density* of a ground theory (set of ground atoms) introduced in an author's previous work[1] and defined as the number of occurrences of a constant in the set of atoms.

- *Power of a predicate* (used to estimate the complexity of FOIL's algorithm[4]), defined as the maximum number of correct instances of the predicate (instances belonging to the set of examples), when one of its variables is bound.

The upper bound of the computational complexity of DIRD is

$$(ConstantDensity * PredicatePower)^{MaxA*K}$$

where, $ConstantDensity$ is the maximum constant density of the set of examples, $PredicatePower$ is the maximum power of the predicates in the domain, $MaxA$ is the maximum arity of any predicate, and K is the length of the clause being learned (number of body literals).

When one variable within P is bound (item 2), then the term $ConstantDensity$ estimates the number of candidate literals P_j, and the term $PredicatePower$ – the number of B_n used to find a substitution with maximum power. To consider the case when all variables are bound by all possible θ_j's, the product of these two terms has to be raised to the power of the total number of variables in P. A lower estimate of this number is $MaxA * K$, i.e. the number of variables in the learned clause.

The complexity of the DIRD algorithm is similar to that of FOIL[5]. The exponential factors in both algorithms are the same. In difference to FOIL, the complexity of DIRD does not depend on the number of predicates. Therefore it is suitable for domains with large number of predicates and low constant and predicate density.

4. Empirical evaluation and discussion

This section discusses some empirical results achieved by DIRD in comparison with two advanced concept leaning systems – FOIL and GOLEM, which are typical instances of the two basic approaches to concept learning – *general-to-specific* and *specific-to-general* respectively.

Firstly, experiments were carried out in the *link and path* domain discussed in Section 1. With a *complete* set of examples $(B \cup T)$ FOIL derived the standard definition of *path* (shown in Section 1) in 10.7 seconds [1]

---

[1]The experiments were carried out on a Sun SPARCstation. The run times of FOIL in the experiments described further are substantially larger than these reported by Quinlan[5]. We think this might be due to the very inefficient Prolog implementation of FOIL, used in the experiments. DDIL is implemented in the author's NCL/Prolog system running on a Sun SPARCstation.

The same task given to GOLEM and DIRD was not easy to solve. GOLEM was very sensitive to the negative examples. With a complete set of negatives (generated by CWA as in FOIL), GOLEM produced 3 clauses including a ground fact and literals with constants in about 0.2 seconds. Using various sets of negatives, various definitions were produced ranging from a pure variable fact (the most general solution, given no negatives) to the set of foreground facts (the positive examples for *path*). All definitions were correct, however the standard definition of the predicate was never produced.

With the same complete set of examples DIRD produced only ground facts, i.e. the set of examples itself.

The task described in Section 1 (incomplete set of examples *B*) was solved by FOIL in 36 seconds, deriving quite a complex definition (including a clause with 4 literals), which covered none of the missing examples *S*.

GOLEM required about about 33ms. to infer just the two instances of *path* given in the examples (the set *B*). By carefully choosing the set of negatives both FOIL and GOLEM were able to derive almost correct definitions (covering the two instances of *path* in the examples and sometimes covering some of the instances in *T*, but *never* all of them). For these tasks GOLEM required from 0.2 to 0.5 seconds.

DIRD solved this problem in about 0.2 seconds for each clause and produced the clauses listed in Section 2.

The next experimental results are from the *family relationships* domain, used also by Quinlan to test FOIL[5]. We used only one of the isomorphic families, containing 56 examples over 12 individuals and 12 relationship types (*husband, wife, mother, father, daughter, son, brother, sister, uncle, aunt, nephew, niece*). The family tree is shown in Figure 1.

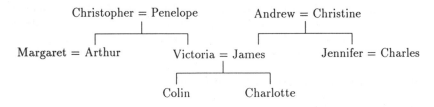

Figure 1. Family tree, where "=" means "married to".

The relation *father* was chosen as a target predicate. With a complete set of examples FOIL derived a definition in 92 seconds, GOLEM in 0.5 seconds and DIRD did not infer any sensible clause (only ground facts).

In the further experiments 1, 2, and 3 instances of *father* was successively removed from the training set. In all cases DIRD inferred correctly all missing instances. It also produced clauses similar to those inferred by FOIL and GOLEM, given complete sets of examples, in 2, 1.6 and 1 seconds respectively (for all clauses).

With 1 missing example of *father* FOIL required 160 seconds to build a definition which did not cover the same example. In two trials with two missing examples FOIL spend correspondingly 230 and 255 seconds. In one of the trials it inferred a clause covering one of the missing examples. Using a set with four missing examples in two trials FOIL required 84 and 121 seconds and derived clauses which did not cover any of the missing examples.

GOLEM required about 1 second in all 3 cases (1,2 and 3 missing examples) and produced definitions which covered all positives. The definitions varied very much with any small change in the set of negatives.

5. Conclusion

FOIL requires large sets of examples to built "good" clauses, since it uses an information-based heuristics. In most of the cases FOIL generates very concise and clear clauses.

Based on formal methods (*lgg*), GOLEM derives clauses, which are exactly as general as necessary to cover the positives and not to infer the negatives (therefore sometimes the derived clauses look a bit strange).

DIRD always derives correct atoms. However the clauses produced are proper only when it is given an *incomplete* set of examples. This is because its strategy is to *generate clauses with body literals with maximal predicate density* (predicate density is the number of the predicate's correct instances in the domain[4]). This means that all body literals should have more density than the head of the clause. If the head has a greater density than all possible literals, DIRD produces only ground facts (the head itself). Therefore to build proper clauses for a predicate we have to remove some of its instances and thus lower its density.

Generally the advantages of DIRD can be summarized as follows:

- No negative examples are required. The majority of concept learners are very sensitive to the choice of negative examples, since they prevent overgeneralization. Generally the negative examples can be easily generated by CWA, however this is not useful in case of incomplete training sets. From the other hand, the explicit specification of the negatives is difficult in complex domains.

- The algorithm performs particularly well on incomplete data sets. In these cases it derives useful explanations of its inferences (ground clauses), which can be used to build predicate definitions applicable to larger domains. For example, it infers the textbook definition of *path* given only two examples. Given the same task GOLEM produces more efficient clauses, but applicable only to the specific domain.

- DIRD performs better on domains with large number of predicates and few instances for each predicate, where the total number of examples is not critical. This was shown by the similar run times for the *link and path* domain with 6 examples and 2 predicates, and *family* domain with 56 examples and 12 predicates.

On the negative side the following can be pointed out:

- DIRD can build recursive definitions, but it cannot infer atoms recursively.

- The algorithm cannot make use of explicit negative examples.

- Further experiments are necessary to show the efficiency of the algorithm on large sets of examples.

6. References

1. Z. Markov, in Proceedings of the Third International Workshop on Inductive Logic Programming (ILP'93), ed. S. Muggleton (J. Stefan Institute, Ljubljana, Slovenia, 1993), 256-277.

2. S. Muggleton and C. Feng, in *Proceedings of the First Conference on Algorithmic Learning Theory* (Tokyo, Japan, Ohmsha, 1990).

3. S. Muggleton, *New Generation Computing* 8 (1991), 295-318, Ohmsha Ltd. and Springer-Verlag.

4. M. Pazzani and D. Kibler, *Machine Learning* 9 (1992), 57-94.

5. J.R. Quinlan, *Machine Learning* 5 (1990), 239-266.

6. E.Y. Shapiro, *Algorithmic Program Debugging* (MIT Press, Cambridge, MA, 1983).

Multiple Explanation-Based Learning Guided by the Candidate Elimination Algorithm

E. N. Smirnov

New Bulgarian University
54 Dr. G.M. Dimitrov Blvd.
1797 Sofia
Bulgaria

and

N. I. Nikolaev

Department of Computer Science
American University in Bulgaria
Blagoevgrad 2700
Bulgaria

nikolaev@aubg.bg

ABSTRACT

This paper proposes an approach to integration of the empirical and analytical learning strategies. The novel integration is a solution of the theory-based concept specialization problem of learning an unknown concept, considered a specialization of the goal concept, in the presence of its positive and negative examples. For guiding a multiple explanation-based learning process, the novel approach employs the candidate elimination algorithm. All the concept generalizations, which are analytically derived from the example explanations tree, are studied empirically by the boundary sets of the version space. The paper investigates the automatic production of problem-dependent operationality criteria by using the boundary sets of version space as dynamic boundaries of operationality for explanation-based learning.

1. Introduction

The combinations of empirical and analytical strategies[6] into integrated learning systems help to overcome the weaknesses of either strategy when considered alone. The empirical learning approaches in general do not use existing knowledge, and the analytical learning approaches require strong forms of knowledge.

The variety of symbolic methods for integrating the empirical and analytical strategies can be divided into three groups[13]. The first group of interleaved empirical and analytical learning, which includes OCCAM[9] and ML-SMART[1], uses the strategies in a mixed way. The second group employs analytical-after-empirical learning[5]. The latter explains the empirical regularities between the examples, in the context of available knowledge, for refining and searching for regularities' variants. The approaches in the third group perform analytical and then empirical learning IOE[2], and Combined analytical learning with incremental version space merging[3].

The IOE method has been developed as an approach to solving the theory-based concept specialization problem (TBCS). Given a domain theory, that defines a goal concept (GC), and a set of positive training examples of an unknown concept (SC), which is specialisation of GC, the TBCS task is to find a correct description of the concept SC. The IOE method uses domain theory to build an explanation from multiple positive examples, as in multiple explanation-based learning, and forms a description SC by an empirical technique over the explanation. The main shortcoming of the IOE is that it is not capable of learning from negative examples and therefore it could not be applied in real domains where negative experience exists.

Addressing the problem of building effective integrated learning systems, this paper presents a novel approach to integration of the empirical and analytical learning strategies called Multiple EBL guided by the Candidate Elimination Algorithm (MECEA). MECEA solves the TBCS problem which in addition to the above specification is to learn a conjunctive concept SC in the presence of its positive and negative examples. For guiding the multiple EBL process, the novel approach employs the candidate elimination algorithm (CEA)[7]. A distinctive characteristic of the novel approach is that the learning produces correct concepts in an incremental manner. It is demonstrated that different generalized concept descriptions can be extracted from the example explanations tree. These analytically derived concept generalizations are studied by the boundary sets of their version space[11]. When the boundary sets of version space are used as dynamic boundaries of operationality in EBL the operationality criteria are discovered automatically.

The presentation of MECEA begins with a description of the TBCS problem in section two. Section three offers the representation and ordering of the concepts. The fourth section presents the learning scenario, including the model for integrated learning by candidate elimination. In section five the boundary sets of the version space are studied as dynamic boundaries of operationality. Finally, an illustrative example is given and comparisons with related works are made.

2. The Theory-Based Concept Specialization Problem

The definition of theory-based concept specialization problem used in this paper is different from that of Flann and Dietterich because both the positive and the negative examples of the unknown concept SC to be learned are considered:

Given:
* *Goal concept*: A concept definition.
* *Domain theory*: A set of horn clauses to be used in explaining how the training examples are instances of the goal concept.
* *Training set*: A set of examples, which are positive examples of the concept GC, and are positive and negative examples of a concept under study (SC)
(SC *is considered a specialization of the goal concept GC*).

Determine: * *A necessary and sufficient conjunctive description of the concept SC* that is implied by the positive examples and not by the negative ones in the context of the domain theory.
* *Operationality criterion* over the concept descriptions which specifies how to form SC.

In this definition of TBSC it is supposed, first, that the goal concept is operational in the domain theory; second, that the set of examples is a correct set of examples of the goal concept and the concept SC; and third, that the domain theory is perfect for the goal concept and not perfect for the concept SC.

The presented definition can be reformulated into a definition closer to Mitchell's explanation-based generalization (EBG) problem[8]. The task is to find the necessary and sufficient conjunctive description of the goal concept in the presence of an incorrect goal concept description, overly general domain theory and correct positive, and negative examples of the goal concept.

3. Representation and Ordering of the Concepts

The proposed approach MECEA for solving the TBCS problem is unique in using the candidate elimination algorithm for guiding the multiple EBL process. It relies on the possibility of representing the candidate descriptions of SC by the boundary sets of the version space.

From an example explanation tree, produced by EBG, different generalized concept descriptions can be extracted. They are formed by different combinations of the subsets of domain theory rules necessary to derive the example generalization. These concept descriptions are conjunctions of predicates in the leaves of the trees (Fig. 1.).

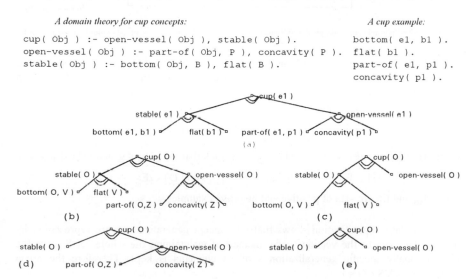

A domain theory for cup concepts:

```
cup( Obj ) :- open-vessel( Obj ), stable( Obj ).
open-vessel( Obj ) :- part-of( Obj, P ), concavity( P ).
stable( Obj ) :- bottom( Obj, B ), flat( B ).
```

A cup example:

```
bottom( e1, b1 ).
flat( b1 ).
part-of( e1, p1 ).
concavity( p1 ).
```

Fig. 1. Verification of a given example (a), in the context of a predefined domain theory,
which produces four different general explanations (b-e) of the cup concept

Definition 1 (*Concept Representation*): A concept is a conjunction of predicates being elements of different chains in the multiple example explanations tree starting from the root:

$$C = \{\, c = \cap\, p_{ij} \mid \forall\, p_{ij} \in H_i \,\}$$

where a chain H_i is each non empty subset of predicates such that $\forall\, p_{i1}, p_{i2} \in H_i$, one of the relations $p_{i1} \sqsupseteq p_{i2}$ or $p_{i2} \sqsupseteq p_{i1}$ holds. Here $\sqsupseteq$ is a relation partial ordering between the nodes in the explanations tree (it holds because of the character of the deductive entailment mechanism).

Concept descriptions constructed in this way are in a relation generalized concept partial ordering (GCPO) (Fig. 2), formalized as follows:

Definition 2 (*Generalized Concept Partial Ordering*): A concept c_2 is more general than or equally general to another concept c_1 : $c_1 \leq c_2$ in the context of domain theory DT, iff $DT \cup c_1 \vdash c_2$.

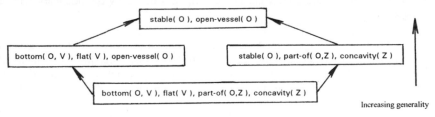

Fig. 2. GCPO of possible cup concepts descriptions which may be built with the use of the explanations from Fig. 1

It has been proven[11] that this partial ordering GCPO supports a well-structured space of concept descriptions, because the convexity and definitness conditions[4] for using boundary sets are satisfied. This makes it possible to maintain the concept generalizations according to the version space (VS) representation formalism:

$$VS \langle G, S \rangle = \{\, c \mid \exists\, s \in S \text{ and } g \in G \text{ such that: } s \leq c \leq g \,\}$$

where: $G = \{\, g \mid DT \cup E_n \not\vdash g \text{ and } DT \cup E_p \vdash g \text{ such that } \neg\exists\, g' : g \leq g' \text{ and } DT \cup E_n \not\vdash g' \,\}$

$S = \{\, s \mid DT \cup E_p \vdash s \text{ such that } \neg\exists\, s' : s' \leq s \text{ and } DT \cup E_p \vdash s' \,\}$

E_p and E_n are sets of positive and negative examples.

The latter specification shows that all concept generalizations are represented by the boundary sets of the version space. Instead of maintaining the whole set S, here the only maximally specific generalization s of its elements is kept. Therefore the novel formulation is VS $\langle G, s \rangle$.

4. The Learning Scenario

This is an algorithm for knowledge intensive learning with version space representation of the hypothetical concept descriptions guided by the candidate elimination algorithm. The algorithm is fully incremental and operates in the following way:

initialization:

G includes only one element which is the description of the goal concept.
s is the conjunction of the leaves' predicates from the explanation of the first positive example.
The global explanation tree GET = generalized explanation tree of the first positive example(ET)-this tree will be shared for all incremental steps and, because of supporting the partial ordering, determines the concept space between s and G ;

step 1:

Analytically derive for each subsequent training example an explanation tree:
the set G determines plausibly the operationality criteria for the negative examples ;
the description s determines plausibly the operationality criterion for the positive examples ;

step 2:

Update the version space VS<G,s> to a new one VS<G',s'>.

In case of a *positive example* e_p:

$G' = \{ g \in G \mid e_p \leq g \}$ / in case of $G' = \{\}$ the algorithm fails /
$s' = MSG_{DT}(s.e_p)$ such that $\forall g' \in G' : s' \leq g'$

In case of a *negative example* e_n:

$s' = s$ and $e_n \nleq s$ / in case of $e_n \leq s$ the algorithm fails /
$G' = \{ g' \in MGS_{DT}(G.e_n) \mid s' \leq g' \}$ / in fact MGS_{DT} produces sets G_g' /

A distinguishing characteristic of the novel algorithm is that the generalization and specialization operators are applied on the global explanation tree GET. The boundaries G and s are collected from predicates in the nodes of GET.

MSG_{DT} is the *generalization operator* which builds a maximally specific generalization given s and current postive example in the presence of domain theory. The generalization operator works by extracting predicates from the global tree GET. This presupposes imposing the generalized explanation tree of the current positive example on the tree GET. The merging of these two trees produces an AND/OR tree GET'. After that all subtrees in GET', rooted in a common OR bundle of possibly AND-related predicates from GET and possibly in AND-related predicates from the example explanation, are substituted by their root. The resulting tree GET" is a pruned version of the GET tree, and the conjunction of predicates in the GET" leaves is the maximal specific generalization. The resulting GET" will serve in the following incremental steps as the GET tree.

MGS_{DT} is the *specialization operator* which builds a set G_g' of maximally general specializations of g against the current negative example using the domain theory. This also supposes imposing the generalized explanation tree of the current negative example over the tree GET. Every element g' from G_g' is produced by replacing of each predicate p $\in$ g which is a root being a common OR bundle of possibly AND-related predicates from GET and possibly AND-related predicates from the negative example explanation. Every such predicate p is replaced by some of its descendants in the AND/OR subtree being in GET.

5. Boundary Sets as Boundaries of Operationality

The MECEA approach distinguishes by the capability of automatically discovering the operationality criteria of the concept SC to be learned by EBL. All the concept descriptions between the boundaries G and s, including s, determine the possible operationality criteria for SC. In this sense the search of concept descriptions also defines the search for accurate problem-dependent operationalities.

When a positive training example comes, it is analyzed in the context of the domain theory using an operationality criterion determined by the current maximally specific generalization s. Here the operationality can smoothly relax, allowing also predicates in tree nodes at equal depths as those in s to be considered. When a negative example comes, it is preanalyzed in the context in the same domain theory using operationality criteria determined by all descriptions immediately after those in the maximally general specializations G according GCPO. It is assumed that the possible explanations of the negative example have as criteria for operationality such descriptions of predicates that correspond to each g $\in$ G but differ in at least one predicate from a deeper level. Therefore, the analysis proceeds only until the most plausible predicates are found. Infertile analysis at greater depths is avoided.

The MECEA algorithm specifies that the performance of explanation derivation be guided by implicit requirements for operationality. Because the boundary sets of the version space are changed at every incremental step, dynamic boundaries of operationality are imposed. The dynamic variability of the operationality reflects the natural reformulation of the concept SC.

6. An Illustration

In order to reach a clear understanding of the integrated MECEA approach to learning, as well as to distinguish it from the related ones, let consider the following TBCS problem:

Given: * *Goal concept*:

```
cup( Obj ) :- liftable( Obj ), stable( Obj ), open-vessel( Obj ).
```

* *Domain theory*:

```
open-vessel( Obj ) :- cylindrical( Obj ), open-above( Obj ).
open-vessel( Obj ):-part-of(Obj,P),concavity( P ),upward-pointing( P ).
stable( Obj ) :- bottom( Obj, B ), flat( B ).
stable( Obj ) :- put-on( Obj, S ), support( S ).
liftable( Obj ) :- light( Obj ), has( Obj, H ), handle( H ).
liftable( Obj ) :- light( Obj ), made( Obj, M ), aluminum( M ).
```

* *Training set*: A set of positive and negative examples of a tea cup concept :

Tea-Cup1	Tea-Cup2	not-Tea-Cup3
has(e1, h1).	light(e2).	made(e3, m3).
handle(h1).	put-on(e2, s2).	light(e3).
bottom(e1, b1).	support(s2).	aluminum(m3).
flat(b1).	handle(h2).	flat(b3).
light(e1).	part-of(e2, p2).	bottom(e3, b3).
cylindrical(e1)	has(e2, h2).	open-above(e3).
open-above(e1).	concavity(p2).	cylindrical(e3).
	upward-pointing(p2).	

Determine: * *A necessary and sufficient conjunctive description of the tea cup concept* that is implied by the positive examples and not by the negative ones considered in the context of the domain theory.

The incremental steps in the learning process may be described in the following way. The global explanation tree GET is initialized to be the explanation tree of the first positive example:

$G - \{ ($ liftable(O), stable(O), open-vessel(O) $)_0 \}$
$S = \{$ light(O), has(O,X), handle(X), bottom(O,V), flat(V), cylindrical(O), open-above(O) $\}$

The assimilation of the example tea-*Cup2* produces a new set S and changes GET (Fig.3.).

$G = \{$ remains unchanged $\}$
$S - \{$ light(O), has(O,X), handle(X), stable(O), open-vessel(O) $\}$

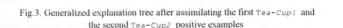

AND-related predicates ⎯⎯ new GET
OR bundle - - - explanations of the first and second examples

Tea Cup Concept Structure

Fig.3. Generalized explanation tree after assimilating the first Tea-*Cup1* and
the second Tea-*Cup2* positive examples

After assimilating the third example not-TeaCup3 GET is not changed (Fig.4.).

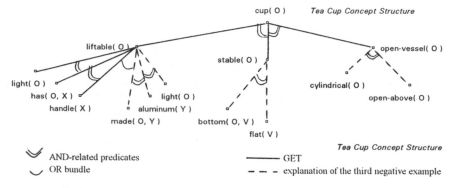

Fig. 4. Generalized explanation tree after assimilating the third example not-Tea-Cup3

Note, however, that only one specialization from three possible ones results because of the prunning of the GET:

$$G = \{(\text{light(O)}, \text{has(O,X)}, \text{handle(X)}, \text{stable(O)}, \text{open-vessel(O)})_1, \}$$
$$S = \{ \text{light(O)}, \text{has(O,X)}, \text{handle(X)}, \text{stable(O)}, \text{open-vessel(O)} \}$$

At the end focusing of the most general and most specific descriptions has resulted. That is why the learning terminates successfully at the following concept description:

```
tea-cup( O ) :-
      light( O ), has( O,X ), handle( X ), stable( O ), open-vessel( O ).
```

7. Comparisons and Relevance to Other Works

MECEA and IOE[2] are two approaches for solving the TBCS problem. The IOE method uses domain theory to build an explanation only from the positive examples and forms a definitions of SC by an empirical technique over the explanation. IOE and MECEA have the same advantage that an explicit domain theory can be exploited to aid learning, the dependence of the initial encoding of the domain theory is reduced, and the correct concepts can be learned from few positive examples. But the main shortcoming of the IOE is that it is not capable of learning from negative examples and therefore it could not be applied in real domains, where negative experience exists.

MECEA is very close to Hirsh's approach[3] for combining EBG and his incremental version space merging. His combination method uses EBG to generalize training examples before doing empirical learning. In contrast to MECEA, this approach syntactically performs the analytically derived generalized descriptions of the examples, while MECEA finds common structures of explanation trees of the positive examples against explanation trees of the negative ones. This suggests that MECEA presents more general form of learning.

8. Conclusion

A novel integrated algorithm called multiple EBL guided by the candidate elimination algorithm for machine learning, was presented in this paper. In its essence it is an analytical method driven by the empirical version space mechanism for constructing qualitative descriptions and achieves rapid focusing toward the final concept.

One of the advantages of MECEA is that it produces conjunctive concept descriptions in an incremental manner. It was demonstrated that the learning algorithm terminates at correct concepts when positive examples and negative examples are assimilated. A second advantage is that the boundary sets automatically determine the operationality criteria for analytical learning.

The MECEA integrated learning approach allows careless design of the domain theory, requires a small number of examples and few computation resources and constructs correct description for several unknown concepts SC.

Currently two additional models of integrated learning systems: for guiding multiple EBL by Incremental Non-Backtracking Focusing[12] and for guiding multiple EBL by Space Fragmenting[10] are under development. The first improves the time and space complexity of combined learning systems of this kind. The second builds disjunctive concept descriptions in the context of TBCS when the incompleteness and inconsistency conditions are satisfied.

Acknowledgments

The development of the MECEA approach and its implementation in a dialect of Common Lisp started at the Intelligent Systems Laboratory, ELSYM, University of Wales by a fellowship from The British Council, number BUL / 2233 / 89. The authors would like to thank to Haym Hirsh for his encouragement and valuable comments. The recent part of the work and the experiments were partially supported by a grant from the Bulgarian Ministry of Education, number MU-I-1/2. We thank Zdravko Markov from the Bulgarian Academy of Sciences who was kind to discuss the learning approach with us.

256

References

1. F. Bergadano and A. Giordana, *Guiding Induction with Domain Theories*, in Machine Learning: An Artificial Intelligence Approach, Y. Kodratoff and R.S. Michalski, eds. Vol. III (Morgan Kaufmann Publ., San Mateo, CA, 1990) pp. 474-492.

2. N.S. Flann and T.G. Dietterich, *A study of explanation- based methods for inductive learning*, Machine Learning, Vol. **4** (1989) pp.187-226.

3. H. Hirsh, *Combining Empirical and Analytical Learning with Version Spaces*, in Proc. Sixth Int. Workshop on Machine Learning, Ithaca, New York (1989) pp. 29-33.

4. H. Hirsh, *Theoretical Underpinnings of Version Spaces*, in Proc. Twelfth Int. Joint Conf. on Art. Intelligence, IJCAI-91, Sydney, Australia (1991) pp. 665-670.

5. M. Lebowitz, *The Utility of Similarity-Based Learning in a World Needing Explanation*, in Machine Learning: An Artificial Intelligence Approach, Y. Kodratoff and R.S. Michalski, eds., Vol. III, Morgan Kaufmann Publ., San Mateo, CA (1990) pp. 399-432.

6. R.S. Michalski, *Inferential Theory of Learning as a Conceptual Basis for Multistrategy Learning*, Machine Learning, Vol. **11**, N : 2 / 3 (1993) pp.111-151.

7. T. M. Mitchell, *Generalization as Search*, Artificial Intelligence, Vol. **18**, N: 2, (1982) pp.203-226.

8. T.M. Mitchell, R.M.Keller and S.T. Kedar-Cabelli, *Explanation- Based Generalization: A Unifying View*, Machine Learning, Vol. **1**, N: 1 (1986) pp.47-80.

9. M.J. Pazzani, *Integrated Learning with Incorrect and Incomplete Theories*, in Proc. Fifth Int. Conf. on Machine Learning, Ann Arbor, Michigan (1988) pp.291-297.

10. E.N. Smirnov, *Space Fragmenting: A Method For Disjunctive Concept Acquisition*, in Artificial Intelligence V- Methodology, Systems, Applications, B. du Boulay and V.Sgurev, eds., Elsevier Science Publ., North Holland (1992) pp.97-104.

11. E.N. Smirnov and N.I. Nikolaev, *Intelligent Tutoring by Knowledge Refinement with Version Space*, in Proc. Fourth Int. Conf. on Human Aspects of Advanced Manufacturing & Hybrid Automation, Manchester, UK (1994) (to appear).

12. B. Smith and P. Rosenbloom, *Incremental Non-Backtracking Focusing: A Polynomially Bounded Generalization Algorithm for Version Space*, in Proc. Tenth Nat. Conf. on Artificial Intelligence, AAAI-90 (1990) pp. 848-853.

13. S.B. Thrun and T.M. Mitchell, *Integrating Inductive Neural Network Learning and Explanation-Based Learning* (1993) (personal communication).

IMPROVEMENT OF KBS BEHAVIOR BY USING PROBLEM-SOLVING EXPERIENCE

GENNADY AGRE

Institute of Informatics - Bulgarian Academy of Sciences

Acad.G.Bonchev St. Block 29A, 1113 Sofia, Bulgaria

Email: agre@iinf.bg

ABSTRACT

The paper presents an approach for improving the behavior of "traditional" knowledge-based systems (KBS) by integration with a special-designed case-based reasoner. An abstract classification KBS with a simple rule-based architecture has been chosen as a test-bed for illustration of how the expert knowledge may be corrected by experience accumulated during the real use of the system. The structure of the correcting module is based on the general architecture of a case-based planner adapted for solving classification tasks. The organization of the system case memory is based on a vocabulary of possible problem solving failures which may be caused either by the original KBS or by the case-based reasoner.

1. Introduction

The recent experience in applying KBS in real domains have shown that the ability to solve difficult problems is tightly connected with the ability of the system to learn, since even the best domain theories are incomplete. So, the development of methods for improvement adaptability and overall robustness of the systems may be seen now as one of the most important challenges for AI researches[1]. Promising results in this direction are case-based methods for problem solving[2,3] and integrated learning architectures[4,1].

The problem addressed in the present paper is to develop methods that allow "traditional" knowledge-based systems (i.e. which were not originally constructed as case-based) to improve their problem solving behavior during their use in a real open environment. The problem requires to consider some additional issues:

- As the competent user (expert or knowledge engineer) is not available no explanations of the incompleteness or incorrectness of the system's knowledge could be expected. A possible "feedback" from the user (failure report) is very poor: it may contains the message that the system solution is wrong and what the "right" solution is.

- Very often the erroneous character of a system solution is detected after a given period of time. So it is practically impossible to extend the set of data describing this past situation to clarify a source of the failure.

- There is no guarantee that the right solution has been found in the same situation as the system inferred its wrong solution. Very often the source of a failure is that the system omitted to consider some problem features which have been later recognized as significant for the final decision.

Therefore, neither automatic inductive methods for knowledge refinement[5,6], nor methods of failure-driven explanation learning[7] or apprenticeship approaches[8,9] could be directly applied.

2. Assumptions About Knowledge Used

The main idea of improving a KBS behavior during its real use seems very simple. If the user reports that a decision produced by the system is wrong and the correct solution is known, the system should "simply" remember this "erroneous" situation. Then when a similar situation occurs in the future the system should apply this "user-supplied" remembered solution rather than one based on expert knowledge. If a correct solution is not known by the end-user too, the system should try to find another solution different from the remembered "erroneous" one.

As it is easy to see the realization of this idea crucially depends on the ability of the system to remember the solved problems (or cases) in appropriate manner as well as on the possibility to identify a current problem as similar to some of the remembered ones. This comes to the well-known problems of a proper selection of case representation, indexing scheme and similarity metrics which are fundamental in the case-based reasoning paradigm for problem solving[10]. Generally solutions of these problems are determined by the type of a task to be solved, the model of the problem domain used and the reasoning architecture of the system.

2.1. Task To Be Solved

Let us assume that the task to be solved by the original KBS is a classification task. Furthermore, we will assume that one of the existing generic models of this task (e.g.[11,12] etc.) is used. In all these models the diagnosis is considered as a hypothesis driven process. It starts with generating of a restricted set of possible solutions (so called "differential diagnosis") which are sequentially tested by comparing the expecting findings with observed ones. The hypothesis which is the best explanation of all observed findings is selected according some preference criteria.

2.2. Knowledge Representation

We will consider that domain knowledge is represented by nonprobabilistic rules.

For simplicity we will assume that the knowledge base contains only one type of rules:
$$RuleName : IF < conjunction\ of\ findings > THEN < diagnosis > .$$
Thus each diagnosis (or category to be classified) is represented as a set of disjunctive "exemplars" described by means of the corresponding rules. This is not a real restriction because in practice almost every base of rules can be represented in such a way. A finding is assertion describing if a given feature is present or absent, where a feature is attribute - value pair.

2.3. KBS Reasoning Architecture

We will assume that the system performs both backward and forward rule chaining as forward chaining is normally used for generation of a list of differential diagnoses and backward chaining - for testing of hypotheses. A hypothesis (diagnosis) is considered as confirmed if there is a satisfied rule having the diagnosis as conclusion. A hypothesis is considered as rejected if all rules leading to it failed. The system stops its operation either if a confirmed hypothesis has been found or all generated hypotheses have been tested and rejected. We also assume that the data base of the system contains all information obtained or inferred during the current problem solving session including problem features (findings) discovered and list of all tested hypotheses.

3. Memory Organization

3.1. A Case Structure

As many other researchers in CBR (e.g.[9,3] etc.) we represent a case as a single information structure. Using Prolog notation a case named CaseName may be represented as: $case(CaseName, List\_of\_Features, Solution)$, where every feature is an attribute-value pair. It should be mentioned that different cases may contain different number of different features. The solution is simply the result of classification - a category name. We did not include the explanation how the solution has been found because of two reasons. First, when so simple model of the domain is used an explanation is just the rule by which the solution was obtained (so called *solution rule*). And second, because we will use this "explanation" in the scheme of case indexing.

3.2. Indexing

3.2.1. Indexing of Success

The explicit goal of the classification task is to find correct classification of an object described by a set of its features. This goal may be further extended by an implicit goal - to reject all misclassifications which are possible (i.e. have some evidence) in the current case. The obvious result of this extension is using as indexes not only a solution of a case (the inferred diagnosis) but also all hypotheses which have been tested and rejected during solving the current problem.

Using the knowledge base refinement terminology[6], each solved by the KBS case may be indexed as *true positive (TP)* by the solution found and as *true negative (TN)* by each hypothesis rejected during problem solving. Furthermore, since one and the same classification can be inferred by means of different rules more detailed granularity of TP-type indexes is needed. So for this type of indexes the name of solution rule will be used along with the solution itself.

3.2.2. Indexing of Failure

TP- and TN-type indexes are used for indexing cases which have been success-fully solved by the original KBS with solutions confirmed by the user. However we are more interested in indexing of cases which have been *incorrectly* solved by the KBS since they are the source of possible improvement of the KBS behavior. It is obvious that the cause of inferring an incorrect solution is a natural candidate for indexing of the corresponding "erroneous" case. According to the rule-based representation of domain knowledge used possible failures may be classified as overgeneralization and overspecialization of some rules. Using the same terminology a case named $CaseName$ will be indexed as *false positive (FP)* by the rule $RuleName$ inferring the solution $Category$ if it satisfies the rule but real case solution differs from inferred one, i.e. $index('false\ positive', RuleName : Category, CaseName)$. We will index a case as *false negative (FN)* with respect to a given category which is its real solution if it has been tested and rejected as hypothesis by the original KBS. Since in general it is possible to have a failure which is caused by inappropriate use of the domain knowledge rather than by its incorrectness we should extend the failure vocabulary to cover this type of failures too. Such kind of failures may occur due to some deficiencies in, for example, the mechanism of formation of a list of differential diagnosis or because of erroneous termination of the process of hypotheses testing. A failed case will be indexed as *untested* with respect to its real solution if the solution has not been tested during problem solving session.

4. An Architecture of the Case-Based Reasoner

As mentioned in the previous section a solution of the problem of improving KBS behavior may be searched in integration of reasoning architecture of the existing KBS with a special designed case-based reasoner. The latter should correct "expert" solutions (i.e. produced by the KBS) according to the its accumulated experience. For this purpose the general architecture of a case-based planner proposed by Kristian Hammond[3] can be used with slight modifications.

4.1. The Analyzer

The Analyzer uses as input an information from KBS data base - problem features along with the problem solution and a list of rejected misclassifications. The first task of the Analyzer is to predict whether the current situation is potentially dangerous evaluating the possibility that the "expert" solution is wrong. The roles of the failure predictors are played by the name of the solution rule and by FP-type indexes connecting some of the expert rules with past cases which are the false positive examples of these rules.

4.1.1. Selection of Cases and Goal Value Hierarchy

When the current situation has been recognized as potentially dangerous the Analyzer tries to determine a set of past cases which are similar to the current situation as much as possible. All cases connected via FP-indexes with the solution rule form the initial set of candidates for similarity (we will further refer them as FP-cases).

With respect to their *real* solutions all FP-cases may be separated in two groups - "untested" and "false negative". A solved FP-case whose real solution was marked as untested is considered as similar enough to the current situation if the solution either has not already been rejected by the expert rules in the current situation or in the moment the KBS data base contains no data which "block" the possibility to infer the solution by the expert rules. When such "similar enough" past cases have been found their "untested" solutions become the main candidates for solving the current case. A solution proposed by an "untested" case is checked by means of the original KBS itself. If the proposed solution is rejected the corresponding past case is considered as irrelevant to the current situation and another "untested" candidate (if exists) is checked. When none of the "untested" solution has been confirmed the Analyzer "goes downhill" in the hierarchy trying to collect remindings to similar FN-cases.

If the KBS returns "confirmed" solution it is considered as *new expert* solution which overrides the previous one. But in order the solution to be accepted as the final one it should be tested against other system experiences again. In other words the Analyzer tries to correct this solution applying all described above reasoning to this *new elaborated* current situation. This "multilayer" analysis allows more intensive use of experience accumulated by the system.

4.1.2. Collecting Remindings

As already briefly discussed a FN-type index is created as a result of an explanation of past problem-solving failures and means that the real case solution was erroneously rejected by the expert rules. The general cause of this is overspecialization of one or more rules. So a given FN-case may be seen as similar enough if in the current situation the case solution has been rejected by the same overspecialized rule too. The process of index creation (learning) will be described in more detail in the description of the Repairer. Here we will use the information that FN-indexes are represented as: $index('false\ negative', Filter : RejectedCategory, Case)$, where $Filter$ has form of a conditional part of a rule. The filter reflects our current assumption about how the part of an unknown *correct* rule for classifying the category incorrectly rejected in the past case should look like.

The final set of the most similar past cases is formed by those FN-cases whose indexing filters are satisfied by the features of the current situation. It should be mentioned that during this process of "filtering" the description of the current situation may be enriched by acquiring new problem features from the user.

4.2. The Retriever

The task of the Retriever is to find the best match between the current situation and some case solved in the past. The set of candidates for matching is restricted by the indexes selected by the Analyzer. The result of matching process crucially depends on the similarity metrics which is generally based on the domain model used. The metrics determines relative importance of different case features. We can obtain an implicit information about feature importance by assuming that just that information was meant by the expert in determining the rule order in the knowledge base as well as the order of findings in the conditions. However, the problem is that this information has been already completely used by the original KBS. Furthermore, in the matching process the cases which have solutions *contradicting with the expert knowledge* are used. So it is naturally to assume that the contradictions are due to incorrect evaluation by the expert of the degree of importance of some problem features.

To avoid this problem we reduce the number of case features to be matched to the so called *relevant* features. A set of relevant case features depends on the real case solution and is determined as a set of all attributes which occur in the expert rules defining the corresponding case solution. In the current implementation of the Retriever a variant of the simple nearest neighbor algorithm[13] is used. The similarity between current situation and a case is evaluated as the ratio of the number of common relevant attribute values to the whole number of the relevant attributes used in matching. The algorithm is sequentially applied to the retrieved cases grouped according to their solutions. For each group only features from the correspondent set of relevant attributes are compared. The missing values of relevant attributes are acquired from the user. The case with the best similarity score is returned for each group and one of them with the highest score is selected as a best match case.

A group of past cases *confirming the expert solution* also takes part in matching as an "equal in rights" candidate for proposing a solution for the current problem. The group is formed by all past cases which are "true positive" in respect to the solution rule. The use of these cases allows to exploit more complete the experience accumulated by the system and to make more accurate the hypotheses about possible incorrectnesses in the expert knowledge. If the best cases from different group have the same similarity score they are matched against the current situation for the second time but now the similarity is determined on the base of all case attributes which are present in the current situation.

4.3. The Modifier

In contrast to planning or design tasks the structure of a module intended to modify a solution of a classification task is very simple. The Modifier decides whether the retrieved case solution or the expert one should be accepted. In the current implementation the conclusion is inferred based on a simple threshold scheme. The retrieved solution is preferred if the similarity score between the case and the current situation (counting off only relevant attributes) exceeds a given threshold. Otherwise the solution inferred by the expert rules is accepted as final solution of the whole (rule-based and case-based) system.

4.4. The Storer

When the final solution of the problem is found the current situation should be formed and stored as a new case in the system case memory. All features of a solved problem along with its final solution and identification name are stored as a single information structure in the case memory. The case is indexed by the final solution found, by the solution proposed by the expert rules and by all hypotheses rejected during searching the expert solution. If the final system solution differs from the expert one the case is indexed as "false positive" with respect to the expert solution rule and as "false negative" with respect to the solution found by the CB-reasoner. In this situation the FN-index of the current case inherits the corresponding "filter" from the retrieved case.

If the final system solution coincides with the expert one the case is indexed as "true positive" by the solution rule. In both situations the case is indexed as "true negative" by each hypothesis rejected during problem solving.

4.5. The Repairer

The main task of the Repairer is to repair the current model of the world used by the system after interacting with real environment. In the simplest case when the user confirms the system solution of a given case no changes in the "world" are needed. The Repairer just sends this confirmation to the Storer.

The explanation of a failure consists of two parts - first, why the erroneous solution has been inferred and second, why the right solution has not been found. The CB-reasoner may erroneously confirm the expert-based solution if either it could not find a similar enough past FP-indexed case proposing a solution different from the expert one or if the best matching past case was "true positive" i.e. confirming the erroneous solution. In all such situations the case should be re-indexed from the "true positive" example of the erroneous solution rule to the "false positive" one.

Further clarification of the source of the failure is done by analyzing the possible reasons for not finding the correct solution. For example, the failed case may describe the situation which has never been seen by the system before. That is the case when there are no "false positive" exceptions of the erroneous solution which real solutions are the same as the right solution of the failed case. In these situations the case should be re-indexed as "untested" or "false negative" with respect to the right solution.

Indexing of a case as "false negative" requires constructing of an indexing filter. In the current implementation the role of the filter is played by the longest satisfied part of the expert rule intended for inferring the right solution of the case.

The filters in the indexes may be overspecialized which automatically leads to rejecting some relevant past cases by the Analyzer. Such kind of errors can be recognized by comparing the indexing filter of the current case with the corresponding filters of past cases from the same FN-group. As a result all past cases with wrong indexing filter will be re-indexed by the new filter - that of the currently solved case.

5. Using Experience in Incomplete Situations

In the previous section the process of case-based correction of a solution *found* by the original KBS has been described. However improving KBS behavior is also needed when the system could not find any solution at all. Such kind of situations will be referred as *incomplete*.

One approach to use the described above CBR architecture in incomplete situations is to consider them as "complete" with the expert solution "unknown category". "Incomplete" cases successfully solved by the user will be indexed as "false positive" examples of such "expert solution". But that is not enough. When dealing with an incomplete situation it is naturally to try to find and apply experience in solving "complete" problems when the experience in solving incomplete situations has proved to be insufficient. This could be done based on the hypothesis that the real solution could not been found because the current case belongs to the class of "false negative" examples with respect to some of the suspected solutions (differential diagnoses) rejected during the diagnostic session.

A set of candidates for additional matching is formed by those "false negative" exceptions of the suspect solutions whose filters are satisfied by the current case. To decrease probability of misclassification, the set of candidates is enriched with cases in which the corresponding suspect solution was rejected correctly. These are cases indexed as "true negative" with respect to one of the solutions to be tested whose filters are also satisfied by the current case.

6. Remembering and Forgetting Cases

The problem what cases to forget is an open issue in case-based learning[14]. Evaluation of usefulness of a case is based on analyzing all possible situations in which the case may be fruitfully used in the future. Thus it is absolutely clear that all cases learned from failure should be remembered. The problem with remembering of cases learned from success is solved by consideration of the roles they could play in the case-based problem solving.

First, as "true positive" examples confirming a given expert solution they are used as balance for "false positive" ones in the case matching process. Thus the presence in the memory of some "false positive" exceptions of a given expert rule is the necessary sign that a "true positive" example of that rule is worth to be remembered. Second, as "true negative" examples they are used in the process of finding a solution in incomplete situations. Thus the presence of "false negative" exceptions of a category which is "linked" to the case through a "true negative" index is a "pro" argument to remember the case as well.

However in order to use a "true negative" case *fruitfully* some additional actions should be done before storing it in the system memory. First, to insure "quality" match of the case in the future, the current values for still unknown relevant (for the "truly rejected" category) attributes should be acquired from the user. The same holds for "true positive" cases in respect to the corresponding "false positive" ones. And second, to facilitate the Analyzer in selection of relevant "true negative" cases corresponding indexing filters should be created. This procedure is the same as for "false negative" indexes described in detail in "Analyzer" and "Repairer" Sections.

7. Conclusion and Future Trends

The described above approach for improvement of behavior of "traditional" KBS using their own problem-solving experience is implemented in Prolog for PCs and now is under testing. As a method for integration of rule-based reasoning with cases the approach may be considered as an extension of the architecture proposed in [15] towards the real use of the system, where the cases are used as different type exceptions of expert rules.

From the CBR point of view the approach may be seen as a version of a general case-based planner architecture for solving classification tasks. In contrast to planning where a failure in practice makes the CB-planner to change the assumptions what part of the available knowledge is important to solve particular type of planning problems, the repair of a classification failure requires changes in the expert knowledge. In order to do this during the process of real use of the system, hypotheses about incorrect portions of knowledge are constructed and then data allowing to clarify them by remembering such "useful" cases in its memory are purposely collected. In the future work we intend to integrate the approach with some inductive learning algorithm which use the collected cases for actual refinement of expert knowledge in cooperation with a competent user.

8. References

1. A. Aamodt, *Knowledge-intensive, integrated approach to problem solving and sustained learning* (Ph.D. Dissertation, University of Trondheim, May 1991).

2. J. L. Kolodner, *AI Magazine*, **91(2)** (1992) pp. 52-68.

3. K. Hammond, *Case-Based Planning: Viewing Planning as a Memory Task* (Academic Press, 1989).

4. E. Plaza, A. Aamodt, A. Ram, W. van de Velde, M. van Someren, in *Proc. of Machine Learning: ECML-93*, ed. P. B. Brazdil (Springer-Verlag, 1993) pp. 429-441.

5. J. R. Quinlan, in *Readings in knowledge acquisition and learning*, eds. B. G. Buchanan and D. C. Wilkins (Morgan Kaufmann Publishers, 1993) pp. 349-361.

6. A. Ginsberg, Sh. Weiss and P. Politakis, *Artificial Intelligence* **35** (1988) pp. 297-336.

7. D. C. Wilkins, in *Machine Learning: An Artificial Intelligence Approach vol. III*, eds. Y. Kodratoff and R. S. Michalski (Morgan Kaufmann Publ., 1990) pp. 493-514.

8. T. M. Mitchell, S. Mahadevan and L. I. Steinberg, in *Machine Learning: An Artificial Intelligence Approach vol. III*, eds. Y. Kodratoff and R. S. Michalski (Morgan Kaufmann Publ., 1990) pp. 271-301.

9. R. Bareiss, *PROTOS: A unified approach to concept representation, classification and learning* (Ph.D. Dissertation, University of Texas at Austin, Dep. of Comp. Sci., 1988).

10. Ch. K. Reisbeck and R.C. Schank, *Inside case-based reasoning* (Lawrence Erlbaun Ass., Hillsdale, New Jersey, 1989).

11. W. Clancey, *Artificial Intelligence* **27(3)** (1985) pp. 289-350.

12. R. S. Patil, in *Exploring Artificial Intelligence: Survey Talks from the National Conferences on Artificial Intelligence*, ed. H. E. Shobe (Morgan Kaufmann, San Mateo, CA, 1988) pp. 347-379.

13. T. M. Cover and P. E. Hart, *IEEE Transactions on Information Theory* **13** (1967) pp. 21-27.

14. J. Kolodner, in *Proceeding of a Workshop on Case-Based Reasoning*, (Pensacola Beach, Florida, 1989) pp. 1-13.

15. A. R. Golding and P. S. Rosenbloom, in *Proceedings of the National Conference on Artificial Intelligence* (Anaheim, MIT Press, 1991) pp. 22-27.

VII - OBJECT-ORIENTED KNOWLEDGE BASES

CLASSIFICATION OF COMPLEX OBJECTS IN A KNOWLEDGE-BASED DIAGNOSIS SYSTEM

DANIELLE ZIEBELIN

LIFIA IMAG projet SHERPA INRIA Rhône-Alpes - Université Joseph Fourier ,
46 avenue Félix Viallet F38031 Grenoble cedex 01, France
e-mail: Danielle.Ziebelin@imag.fr,

PETKO VALTCHEV

LIFIA IMAG - Université Joseph Fourier ,
e-mail: Petko.Valtchev@ufrima.fr,

IRENA IORDANOVA

Institute of Informatics, Bulgarian Academy of Science,
1113, Sofia, Bulgaria, e-mail: ari@iinf.bg

ANNICK VILA

Laboratoire d'EMG-EFSN CHU G B.P 217X
F38043 Grenoble cedex 9, France, e-mail: Annick.Vila@imag.fr.

ABSTRACT

When a human being doesn't know how to solve a new problem, one of the methods at his disposal consists in using problem-solving knowledge on known problems. This idea has been exploited by numerous researchers in artificial intelligence and revives the study of reasoning based on classification. In this paper, we examine various methods for classification based on an object-oriented knowledge representation formalism. We apply these methods to the domain of the Electromyographical (EMG) diagnosis elaboration. Since the specific domain knowledge is well structured, but heterogeneous, we use complex objects for its representation. This way, the diagnostic reasoning is modelled by the means of complex-object classification. In its turn, the classification uses some basic inference mechanisms associated with a specialisation relationship within complementary object hierarchies. Two basic models for the EMG diagnostic reasoning are studied and their advantages and drawbacks are pointed out.

Key words : Classification reasoning, object-based knowledge representation, complex objects, medical diagnosis.

1. Introduction

Nowadays, a variety of knowledge representation models are used for building knowledge-based systems. These models differ by their degree of declarativity and their suitability to the nature of both knowledge to be expressed. For instance, production rules constitute a declarative representation of knowledge and reasoning. They offer a simple means of problem solving know-how and are the most frequently used procedural method in knowledge-based systems. However, the descriptive knowledge in this model is spread across a set of rules, which makes it difficult to overview. In contrast, the object-oriented model offers a declarative, but also a structured expression of the knowledge. It has been inspired by the frame model proposed by Minsky[3]. Its fundamental idea is the use of a single syntactic unit - an object- to gather all the knowledge relative to a particular domain entity or a group of entities. In contrast, the reasoning processes are not explicitly represented. Instead, they are modelled in terms of inference mechanisms, offered by the system. Inheritance and classification are some of the inference mechanisms most commonly used for those purposes[1].

In the particular case of expert diagnostic systems, the choice of a representation formalism is generally domain-dependant. We found the object-oriented formalism to be especially suitable for medical diagnosis modelling as the recognition of the patient state resembles "a priori" the classification mechanism. When using such formalism, the set of patient state descriptions is represented in an object hierarchy. The heuristic reasoning consists in searching for one or several objects to represent a specific situation.

In the current paper, we discuss the application of the object formalism (combined a classification mechanism) to the domain of electromyographic medical diagnosis. We start with a brief presentation of the specific object model used (section 2). First, the two main types of objects - namely instances and classes, are described. Then, the associated set of inference mechanisms is given, with a special attention paid to the classification. At the end of the section 2, the complex objects and their classification are introduced. The third section deals with the modelling of electromyographical diagnostic reasoning. Initially, we propose a cognitive model for the so-called EMG process. Two different approaches to the implementation of that model, both using a classification mechanism, are studied next. In section 4 we conclude by underlying the benefits and limitations of both approaches presented.

2. Object-Based Knowledge Representation

The generic model of an object used may be considered to be a collection of features or attributes. Each attribute is represented by a slot, which is a kind of descriptor of a high abstraction level. The slots are described by sets of elementary characteristics, their facets. The facets are the "bricks" of the object structure. Generally, they define the semantics of the slot. An example of an object described by three slots is given below.

```
symptom
         kind-of                 =         object
         apparition-site         list-of   anatomy
         group-of-symptom        is-a      string
                                 domain    paresthesiæ, cramps,
                                           pain, palsy
```

A symptom is defined by the place it appears in apparition-site and the group-of-symptoms to which it belongs. The slot apparition-site is defined by the facet list-of, which gives the type and the number of values the slot can take (several values, in this case). The facet value anatomy is a reference to another object (describing the nerves and the muscles). Furthermore, the facet is-a defines the type of the slot group-of-symptoms. Its value is a string, which is a simple type. The facet domain restricts the range of its possible values.

The number and the types of the facets are fixed for a given formalism, while the set of attributes depends only on the application area. A particular object is completely defined by the totality of its slot values. Those values may be themselves objects or references to objects.

2.1 Classes and instances

There are two types of objects in the model we use: classes and instances. A class is the generic representation of a set of objects, while instances represent concrete entities of the domain. Classes are organised in a hierarchies, induced by the specialisation relationship. This relationship is equal to a set inclusion between super- and sub-classes. In the field of electromyographic diagnosis, the knowledge base is composed of several object hierarchies which represent the domain concepts like clinical signs, disease hypothesis, protocols of medical examinations, test results, electromyographic conclusion, etc.

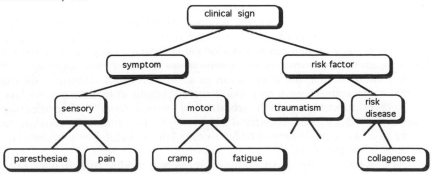

An EMG concept is represented by several classes, these classes are organised in a hierarchy, induced by the set inclusion relationship.

An instance is always associated with a particular class (instantiation relationship). The slots of a given class are intended to represent the common properties of its instances. The slot values of an instance have to satisfy the constraints settled by the description of the class it belongs to. The instances are completely defined by their name and slot values. An instance is linked to its class by the is-a slot, while a class is linked to its super-class by the ako (a-kind-of) slot .

```
{ symptom-Mr-Smith
                is-a                =     symptom
                apparition-site     =     median;
                group-of-symptoms   =     paresthesiae}
```

The symptom-Mr-Smith is an instance of the symptom class. Its slot values satisfy the constraints defined in that class.

Solving a diagnostic problem, consists in creating one or several instances, as description of the patient's state.

2.2 Value inferences

Concerning a given instance, the association with a specific class precedes its physical creation. When it is created, the instance may be only partially defined (some of its slots may have no values). The diagnostic problem resolution requires completion in order to clarify the situation as much as possible. Such completion may be performed in either a manual or an automatic manner. The former consists in asking the user or system some questions about the missing slot values, while the latter involves making some hypothesis or using computing subroutines. The tools for automatic value deduction are called inference mechanisms. Some of them, the most currently used, are listed below.

Inheritance and deduction by default are two inference mechanisms based on the specialisation relationship, i.e. they use the structural knowledge. The default inference may be applied when a pre-defined value for given slot is available. This value is contained in the default facet, which is considered when no other way to determine the slot value exists. Thanks to inheritance mechanism, each class transmits to its sub-classes its set of slots together with their facet values. Thus, the description of a sub-class may contain only the additional constraints, those who make it more specialised than its super-class. Inter-object relationships which are directly issued from the application domain are used by the procedural attachment mechanism. It consists in assigning to a slot a procedure in order to calculate its value (for a given class and its sub-classes possibly).

Classification is the most complex inference mechanism. It uses both structural and control knowledge, as well as other inference techniques. Its main purpose is to localise a given object within the class hierarchy as precisely as possible. Two kinds of classification may be distinguished with regard to the nature of the classified object : instance and class classification.

The classification of an instance starts from the class to which this instance has been attached and makes it descend as low as possible in the related hierarchy. At each step of the classification algorithm, the most possible completion of the instance is performed, each sub-class of the current class is assigned an instance-relevant status. If the instance satisfies all the constraints described by the slots of a sub-class, this class is said to be certain. The class is possible, if there is no stated contradiction between a class and an instance slot value, but the instance is incomplete. Finally, this class is impossible, if at least one contradiction has occurred.

The same process is repeated for each certain class until a hierarchy leaf is reached or no more certain classes are found.

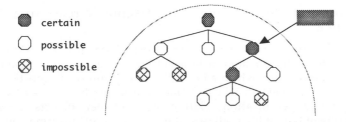

An example of classification is given where the impossible, possible and certain classes are shown. The instance remains attached to its instantiation class, unless the user needs to attach it to one of the certain classes

Class classification is not considered here since it is rarely used once the object hierarchies have been established.

2.3 Complex objects classification

In a large number of cases, several concepts, each one represented by a single hierarchy, are used to model the total amount of relevant knowledge[2]. In order to represent the interdependencies between those hierarchies, some object-valued slots have been introduced. Objects, whose descriptions contain slots of that kind, are called complex objects.

A complex object classification over a set of classes of a hierarchy requires some extensions to be brought to this above algorithm. To classify a complex object in its concept hierarchy, the algorithm attempts to classify each object-valued slot in its corresponding concept. One should note that the classification in the "secondary concepts" takes place only when required, and only towards specified classes. Since a complex object may reference another complex object, the classification may lead recursively to the partial classification of several objects in different concepts.

274

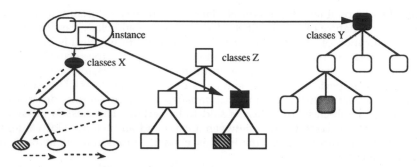

The instance to be classified within X hierarchy is a complex object which refers to two other objects. These objects belong to the hierarchies Y and Z and are also to be classified.

3 Modelling of electromyographic diagnostic reasoning through classification

When using an object-oriented formalism for knowledge-based diagnosis systems, three main categories of knowledge are to be distinguished. The domain knowledge, which allows the description of diagnostic concepts. The structural knowledge, which defines the object hierarchies by creating generalisation /specialisation relationships between objects. Finally, the control knowledge, which allows the selection of information for the resolution of the diagnostic problem. To identify the knowledge elements and their corresponding type is the initial stage of the whole modelling process. In order to facilitate such identification, we use a cognitive model described in the following subsection.

3.1 Cognitive model of the EMG diagnosis elaboration process

The EMG diagnosis process consists in finding the patient state among several known states. It starts by a preliminary description of that state in terms of clinical data. Those data evoke one or several disease hypothesis. One of them is chosen by the physician as the current hypothesis. Each hypothesis is itself associated with an examination protocol composed of several tests. The corresponding tests are carried out by the clinician and their results are interpreted. The set of interpretations is used to formulate an EMG conclusion which confirms or disproves the disease hypothesis. A complete scheme of the EMG cognitive model we have developed is given below.

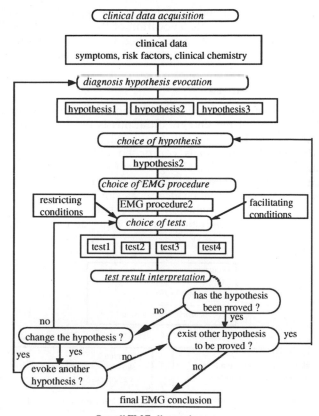

Overall EMG-diagnostic process.

According to that model, we have divided the EMG domain knowledge into six "basic" concepts : clinical data, disease hypothesis, medical examination protocols, tests, test results, EMG conclusion; and five "auxiliary" ones : symptoms, risk factors, clinical chemistry, topography and anatomy. The basic concepts are defined using the auxiliary ones. Each concept is represented by a class hierarchy in the knowledge-base. The objects of a basic hierarchy incorporate some auxiliary objects, and are therefore complex objects. Semantic links, directly derived from the above model are established between objects (of one or several hierarchies). Those links constitute the static aspect of the reasoning representation in the system. The complementary part consists of a set of inference mechanisms using links to gather the whole reasoning procedures. For instance, the formulation of symptom is modelled by the creation of one or several instances characterise the patient. Those instances can be incomplete, so in order to better describe better the patient's state a classification should be carried out within the symptom hierarchy. The specified instances should allow the evocation of the diseases hypothesis.

We have studied different approaches to the implementation of the EMG reasoning . Two of them are discussed in the following sub-sections.

3.2 *Reasoning by centralised class*

Knowledge centralisation is the basic idea of this approach. An additional hierarchy of all the known situations is used to model the solving process. In the case of EMG diagnosis, this hierarchy contains all possible patients conditions. A situation is composed of the complete information about the diagnosis process (data, all significant sub-results for each reasoning step and final conclusion). Thus, the classes of our "situation" hierarchy are defined using the six "basic" EMG concepts as slot domains (symptom, disease hypothesis, protocol, test, conclusions). The sub-classes of the root class situation represent distinct restrictions of the value domain of the considered slots.

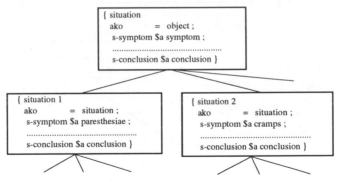

The sub classes situation1 and situation2 have been obtained through the s-symptom slot specialisation towards the root class situation. Similar specialisations, on different slots-concepts, have been used to build a complete hierarchy of all possible combinations .

The diagnosis elaboration process starts by creating a situation instance. In order to complete it, the complex object classification algorithm is used within the situation hierarchy. First, the s-symptom slot value is to be determined. So the second stage is a complex object classification in the symptom hierarchy (using the "auxiliary" hierarchies). Once the s-symptom value is provided, the situation instance may "descend" a level in its hierarchy. What follows is a similar process, on the s-hypothesis and s-protocol slots using the corresponding hierarchies (disease hypothesis and protocol). A specific protocol includes a set of tests, in the test hierarchy. At that level, the system stops until the test results (which are matter of a manual entry) are provided by the user. The classification goes on in the situation hierarchy, in order to detect the class which contains the combination of the entered results. The EMG conclusion should be directly available for the class found.

One of the main advantages of this approach is that it separates the domain knowledge into different concepts. The control knowledge is exclusively represented within the situation hierarchy. This allows reasoning modification while concept hierarchies remain unchanged. Nevertheless, the huge number of possible combinations, which is the case of the EMG diagnosis, results in an excessive size of the situation hierarchy. Its readability and, logically, maintainability is therefore very limited.

3.3 Association reasoning between classes

Another implementation approach consists in spreading the control knowledge over the six "basic" concept hierarchies. By doing so, instead of adding supplementary elements like the situation hierarchy which incorporates and hides the control knowledge, we use direct inter - class associations to model the semantic links previously mentioned. Those associations are expressed via procedural attachments to specific "link" slots in the class descriptions. The corresponding sub-routine creates an instance of the "target" class and classifies it in the appropriate hierarchy. The volume of information transmitted from one hierarchy to another increases gradually by classification chaining and leads to the addition of new slot values to the current instance.

One may notice that control is no longer assured solely by complex object classification, but by a sequence of instance creations and classifications performed on each of the different hierarchies.

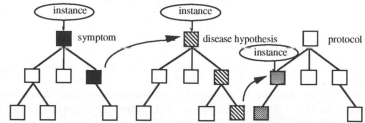

The first three steps of reasoning process are detailed. A single step is composed of instance creation, its classification within the corresponding hierarchy and procedural attachment to create a new instance in the next hierarchy.

The process of electromyographic diagnosis is carried out as follows: First, an instance of the symptom concept is created and classed. The "link" slot of the class found indicates a procedural method to call. As a result of its execution, an instance of disease hypothesis is created. A classification is made in the hypothesis hierarchy wherein the same operation sequence is performed and so on, until the appropriate set of tests is determined.

The results of the tests performed by the physician are introduced into the system in the form of `test result` values of the `test` instances. Then, an `EMG conclusion` instance is created and classified using the set of test results.

When speaking about the advantages of the current approach, the comprehensibility of the reasoning model built should be mentioned. This model seems to be very close to the human expert reasoning. It is, however more difficult to maintain, since different types of knowledge (control and domain) are mixed within the knowledge base.

4 Conclusion

Object-oriented formalism is particularly suitable for a diagnostic expert system, since it is convenient to describe the domain knowledge structuration. The associated classification mechanism provides effective means to represent the corresponding reasoning process. When the application domain requires the representation of several concepts and when knowledge involved is heterogeneous, several object hierarchies of different abstraction levels are usually built. In this particular situation, the complex object model is used to reflect the variety of inter-concept links.

We examined two different approaches to the implementation of the EMG reasoning model. Both of them use the complex object model with the classification mechanism. Nevertheless, they had different impacts on the realisation process and the utility of the concrete models obtained.

Concerning the first approach, its conceptual advantage is the perfect correspondence between a medical case and an object of the central hierarchy used. It makes the reasoning modelling highly comprehensive to the EMGer. From the developer viewpoint, the separation between the control knowledge, (incorporated into the central hierarchy), and the domain knowledge facilitates the further acquisition and explanation activities. On the other hand, performing a single global classification mechanism simplifies the implementation. A considerable problem arises, however, when this approach is applied to a complex domain like it is the case of the EMG diagnosis. Indeed, there are a large number of possible combinations, all of them explicitly represented in the central hierarchy. This implies an enormous central hierarchy, which is difficult to read and modify.

The second approach seemed to be of lower interest. It has been estimated as more complex to implement than the first one because of the inference mechanism switch used. Furthermore, control knowledge is mixed with the structural one in the knowledge base. This disturbs the eventual modifications and the maintenance. In despite of these drawbacks, this second approach has been better accepted by the physicians. The gradual use of different EMG concepts is shown to correspond to the consequent stages of the cognitive model. So, the resulting modelling should be closer to the human experts reasoning. Finally, we preferred this approach for the development of our own system.

Notwithstanding the differences the two approaches may show, there is a common feature of them which limits the global learning effect on the potential users -the EMGer novices. In fact, the reasoning process is to a great extent represented via inference mechanisms in the system, that means hidden for the user's eye. Therefore, our future researches in the domain considered will focus on the explicit reasoning representation in the knowledge base. Initial attempts to adapt the object formalism to this purpose have already been made.

Bibliography

1.   W. J. Clancey , *Heuristic classification*. Artificial Intelligence Journal vol.27, n°4, 1985, pp 289-350.

2.   Marino O., Rechenmann F., Uvietta P., *Multiple perspectives and classification mechanism in objet-oriented representation*. Proc. of ECAI' 90, Stockholm, Sweden, pp 425-430.

3.   Minsky M. *A framework for representing knowledge*, P.H. Winston ed. The psychology of computer Vision, McGrawHill 1975.

4.   Patel-Schneider P.F., *Practical, object-based knowledge representation for knowledge-based systems*. Information Systems Vol. 15 n°1, 1990, pp 9-19.

5.   Rousseau B., *Vers un environnement de résolution de problèmes en biométrie, apport des techniques de l'intelligence artificielle et de l'interaction graphique*. Thèse de doctorat, Université Claude Bernard, Lyon, 1988.

Knowledge and Demon Objects in GameTalk - Object Based Knowledge Representation in Distributed Environment

DIMITAR DIMITROV
Univ. of National & World Economy
Studentski grad, 1100 Sofia, Bulgaria

GALINA DIMITROVA
Faculty of Math. & Inf., Sofia University
5 James Bourchier Str., 1126 Sofia, Bulgaria
e-mail laso@bgcict.bitnet

ABSTRACT

This paper represents briefly the implementation of the knowledge and demon objects in GameTalk - a distributed object-oriented environment for business game simulation built on the basis of Smalltalk-80. Knowledge objects model experts' behavior in the environment. Demon objects facilitate the planing of game experiments. Both kinds of objects have in addition production rules and methods to interpret the rules. A different approach to compiling production rules through active objects is presented that makes it possible the phases of the interpreter work to be performed parallely. Knowledge objects can be active simultaneously and consult each other. Further advantage of the proposed approach is the possibility knowledge objects to receive messages from objects in other address spaces. From AI point of view knowledge objects can be treated as knowledge based systems in a distributed environment.

1. Introduction

GameTalk[2] is a distributed object-oriented tool intended for business game simulation implementations. It is a collection of objects which enable the direct representation of economic entities by active and passive objects, knowledge objects, demon objects, data objects and interaction objects.

Knowledge objects model experts' behavior in the environment. Demon objects facilitate planing of game experiments.

Recent development of the object-oriented approach permits its successfully application in languages and programming technology for creating distributed systems, data base systems, knowledge representation schemes, simulation facilities, software engineering etc. A variety of production systems have been developed using object-oriented programming systems: **Humble**[8] is an expert environment in **Smalltalk-80**[5] which follows **Emycin**; **Loops** combines many paradigms, it defines its own rules concerning the **Loops** classes. **Opus**[6] in **Smalltalk-80** follows the **OPS-5** approach, but provides more powerful describing facilities for language rules.

Knowledge objects in GameTalk are similar to **Opus'** objects, in addition GameTalk offers a different way of solving the problems in defining the rule language, and in describing the object structure; the working memory is organized using active objects; the phases of the interpreter work can be performed parally.

What follows is an overview of GameTalk (section 2), a description of the knowledge and the demon objects (section 3), a discussion of their implementation (section 4) and some conclusions (section 5).

2. GameTalk - General View

GameTalk is a distributed object-oriented environment for business game simulation implementations.

GameTalk is a collection of objects in the distributed object-oriented environment **Diprotalk**[7] (fig. 1). Every object has its own data, rules and behavior:

object = <slots, behavior, interpreter>.

The object is an independent unit of the system with its own life cycle and is processed concurrently with other objects. It is an instance of a certain class. Classes build a hierarchy with simple inheritance mechanism. Instances of a certain class have the same rules (methods) and the same data structure but different slot values. The behavior of the object depends on its rules, the arguments of its methods and its local state. Each object exists in the scope of a particular environment associated with a particular workstation. A communication subsystem is needed to provide for message exchange between objects of different environments.

According to the way objects interact with each other they are local or global. The local objects are known only in the environment they are in. The global objects can receive messages from objects of remote environments, too. Each global object has a unique name in the model. Message sending to global objects is hidden from the user through the virtual object space.

According to the way objects change their behavior they are active or passive [1,7]. Active objects change their behavior when they receive a message and their actions are performed parally. More than one active objects can exist in the model at the same time. Passive objects change their behavior after receiving certain messages which tell them the conditions have changed.

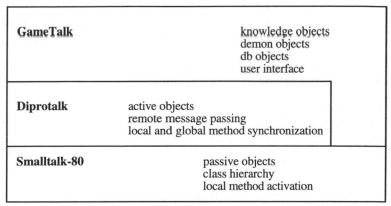

Fig. 1. Environment structure.

Except for the objects mentioned above there are objects in the system with special features concerning the modeling of business game entities: knowledge objects, demon objects, data objects and interaction objects. These objects interpret in a different way the messages they receive.

GameTalk is implemented in **SmalltalkV/286** and **Assembler** on LAN with **NetBios** interface. The business game **FAKT-3** is modeled using **Gametalk**.

3. Knowledge and Demon Objects

Knowledge and demon objects differ from the ordinary objects in being able in addition to define rules and interpret them.

3.1. Knowledge Objects

Knowledge objects are passive objects determining the expert behavior of the model.

A knowledge object has in addition three elements defined: data base (working memory), knowledge base (set of rules) and interpreter. The data base contains concrete data about the current state of the object. The knowledge base is a collection of production rules determining the expert behavior of the object. The interpreter is a special machine that interprets the messages received by the object and applies the appropriate rules to the current state of the object. The production rule has the structure:

IF <condition> **THEN** <action>

Objects from the virtual objects space can appear in the production definition, so that real parallelism can be achieved via all the phases of the interpreter work (matching, conflict resolution and action).

Knowledge objects can be viewed as expert systems being active simultaneously and able to consult each other.

3.2. Demon Objects

Demon objects are active objects. They determine the events that are important for further model performance and define the actions to be performed if these events happen. Demon objects have the following structure:

WHILE <condition> **DO** <action>

<action> is performed repeatedly while <condition> is true. <condition> defines the set of events being watched by the demon object, <action> - what to be done if those events happen. Global as well as local objects can be in rule definition. Rules can be inserted or deleted dynamically.

Demon objects describe the organizing structure of the system. They facilitate the way of maintaining and reconfiguring the system.

4. Knowledge and demon objects implementation

A new approach is proposed to implement both knowledge and demon objects using the facilities of the Diprotalk environment viz. capsulation, inheritance, active objects.

The **RuleObject** class determines the common behavior of both kinds of objects. Knowledge and demon objects are further specified in subclasses by defining additional slots and rules using the inheritance mechanism. Each knowledge object is represented by a subclass of the class **KnowledgeObject**. All demon objects are instances of the class **DemonObject**.

The new elements in the knowledge and demon objects (in addition to the Diprotalk objects) are the rules that need new language constructions to be defined. So a rule language has to be specified and a rule compiler to be written in addition to the Diprotalk compiler.

4.1. Rule Language

The proposed rule language (fig. 2.) is an extension of the Smalltalk language. The expressiveness of the rules depends on the characteristics of the matching primitives, which are determined by the generality level of the predicates in the left part and the actions in the right part of the rules.

rule	::=	*<rule name>*
		[*<rule comment>*]
		[*<rule variables>*]
		[*<rule condition>*]
		[*<rule action>*]
<rule name>	::=	<Diprotalk unary selector>
<rule comment>	::=	<Diprotalk comment>
<rule variables>	::=	'I'[*<variable declaration>*] ...'I'
<variable declaration>::=		<Diprotalk unarySelector>':'
		<Diprotalk unarySelector>
<rule condition>	::=	'{'*<rule predicate>* [*<rule predicate>*] ...'}'
<rule predicate>	::=	*<positive predicate>* I
		<negative predicate>
<positive predicate>	::=	<Diprotalk expression>
<negative predicate>	::=	'~'<positive predicate>
<rule action>	::=	**ifTrue:** '*<statement series>*
<statement series>	::=	'['<Diprotalk statement> [<Diprotalk statement>] ...']'

Fig. 2. Rule syntax.

The left side of the rule can contain positive or/and negative predicates. The positive predicates are Smalltalk statements and test if certain relations are true by sending messages with appropriate arguments to objects. The negative predicates test for absence of certain relations. Unexpected situations can arise when an working memory element is changed at the matching phase of the interpretation. Messages that can change working elements are controlled by the compiler using information about methods modifying objects in the working memory (Diprotalk extension).

A category is defined for each working variable. The category imposes a certain structure on the set of rules defined for an object. All the objects in the working memory are categorized, so it is possible to determine the method, corresponding to the message received, at compile time.

Methods can be performed concurrently. A matrix of dependencies is supported to maintain information about methods modifying objects slots.

4.2. Rule Compiler

The rules are defined in the knowledge and the demon objects by an application **RuleBrowser** which is functionally compatible with the application **ClassHierarchyBrowser** defining the **Diprotalk** classes.

The class **RuleCompiler** is a subclass of the class **Compiler** and represents the rule compiler. The rule compiler analyzes the rule according to the syntactic rules defined in section 4.1. If certain predicate is syntactically correct it is tested for messages which can change the working memory using information about object methods collected by the **Diprotalk** compiler in the matrix of dependencies. It is possible to determine the methods which correspond to messages in the predicates, because working elements are categorized.

The actual rule compilation follows. Each predicate (Smalltalk statement) is compiled in an instance of the class **CompiledMethod** using classes and methods of the Diprotalk compiler. Every predicate is considered to be independent of the rule containing it. Therefore only one instance of the method testing a certain predicate is needed if other rules have the same predicate. The predicate contains information about the rules whose part it is. This approach minimizes the number of the tests at the matching phase (see section 4.5.). An instance of the class **MethodDictionary** contains the compiled methods and is not user available. The right part of the rule is compiled in another method by analogy with the predicates' compilation.

So the compiled rule is represented by a set of compiled methods that implement the left and the right side of the rule. It is an instance of the class **CompiledProduction**. The compiled methods are put in the network used by the interpreter at the matching phase (section 4.3). Each node contains the name of the method performing the test. No parameter passing is needed, because the method contains all elements used at the matching phase. The approach uses most advantages of the Diprotalk virtual machine for direct access to slot values. In case the matching uses objects of the local memory of the knowledge objects (represented by slots) the access to them is optimized in contrast to the matching using index operations.

The compiler is implemented by a set of classes with specific compilation functions:

RuleCompiler defines the common protocol used by the other classes;

RuleCodeProcessor translates the rule into a set of byte codes known to the Diprotalk virtual machine;

RuleAnalyzer analyses syntactically the rule and displays error messages (if some);

RuleScanner separates the lexical elements of the rule and creates an instance of the appropriate subclass of the class **RuleLexeme**;

RuleLexeme defines the lexical elements of the rules in its subclasses.

4.3. Rules Network

The proposed implementation of the knowledge and demon objects is an adaptation of Forgy's Rete algorithm[3] and uses active objects. Unlike the associative memory in **OPS-5** the work memory elements are available through their addresses.

The network has a specific construction which enables every matching to be performed only once and concurrently using active objects. The parallelism of the matching phase is determined by the concrete implementation of the active objects. The recent **Diprotalk** implementation is pseudo-parallel within the framework of one workstation. Real parallelism is achieved in a distributed environment. The proposed algorithm called **ARete** (Actor **Rete**) can be implemented in an environment with real parallelism at object level (like in **Actor Machine**[1]), too.

The **ARete** network is built as a directed graph with four types of nodes: working element nodes, predicate nodes (positive and negative) and terminal nodes.

Terminal nodes represent the production rules. They are instances of the class **CompiledProduction** and contain the information needed for the complete test of the represented rule. Each condition part is decomposed in predicates.

Predicate nodes represent the positive and negative predicates and are instances of the classes **PositivePredicate** and **NegativePredicate**. Both types of nodes have the same structure and behavior except for the method value which returns the value of the evaluated predicate. Each node contains information about the rules having this predicate in their left part (in the slot **rules**) and information about the working elements taking part in the matching (in the slot **workObjects**).

Working element nodes represent the objects that take part in the predicates as message receiver or/and arguments. Only some objects in the system maintain the information needed for that role. Working element nodes are instances of the class **WCapsule**. They capsulate real objects in predicates in active objects with special features. The capsule is transparent to messages concerning the capsulated object. After the message is performed it is tested if that message has changed the status of the real object using a second definition of the **doesNotUnderstand:** method. If the state of the capsulated object is changed the interpreter is informed that the predicates containing this object as receiver and/or an argument must be evaluated once again. This option is provided by the matrix of dependencies in Diprotalk. The information about the predicates depending on that working element is in the slot **predicates** of the knowledge object. In addition, a unique time identifier is supplied for each working element that contains how long the element is in the working memory and is used at conflict resolution time.

4.4. Rule Interpreter

The interpreter interprets the current status using the rules and the working elements. It is an instance of the class **RuleInterpeter**. This class contains the common protocol of the interpreters used by the knowledge and demon objects.

4.5. Knowledge Objects

From AI point of view knowledge objects can be treated as object-oriented expert systems in Diprotalk environment. The proposed implementation follows the principles of the well known production system of **Forgy OPS-5**[3,4]. Knowledge objects in GameTalk have many common features with the objects in OPUS. There are some differences in the rule language definition, the objects' structure, the organization of the work memory.

Knowledge objects are defined in subclasses of the class **KnowledgeObject**.

The interpreter is an instance of the class **KnowledgeInterpreter** and performs forward chaining in three steps: matching, conflict resolution and action.

The interpreter starts its work when the knowledge object receives the message **infer**. According to the message **infer** each object can be in one of two modes. Modification of work elements while the object is not in interpretation mode doesn't activate reevaluating of the rules. The actions to be performed are remembered and performed after the message **infer** is sent. So a second testing of the rules is avoided.

At the matching phase the rules are selected whose left parts are satisfied by the current status of the working memory. Only those predicates of the rules in the working memory are tested which have been changed before the matching phase begins. Each working element has the slot **predicates** that contains a list of predicates to be tested if that element is modified. The receiver of a message that requires predicate evaluating is an active object so that the required tests can be performed parallely. If the evaluated predicate is true the rules with that predicate in their condition part are added to the set **addedRules** containing candidates for the conflict set. If it is false the corresponding rules are added to the set **removedRules** and deleted from **addedRules** and **conflictSet**. A rule can be added to **addedRules** if it is not in **removedRules**.

Next a rule from the conflict set is selected by an instance of the class **ConflictResolution**. The strategy is represented by an ordered set of predicates. In **GameTalk** it can be a knowledge object, too. This object returns a rule to be performed or a flag to indicate an impossible selection.

At the action phase the elementary actions of the selected rule are performed concurrently and can change the working memory. The actual modification of the working memory is performed by the updating methods, if it is caused by messages concerning appearance or disappearance of objects, or by the capsule WCapsule, if it is caused by messages modifying slots of working elements. After the action is performed the matching phase is started if there is no stop message (like **halt**).

Knowledge objects in GameTalk have all the features of the Diprotalk passive objects. They can receive sequences of goals in the form of messages. The result produced by the message performance can be used by other objects. It is possible for a number of knowledge objects to be active simultaneously and consult each other. Another advantage of the proposed implementation is that a knowledge object can receive messages from objects defined in other work stations. The parallel and distributed performance is hidden from the user.

4.6. Demon Objects

Demon objects recognize the events important for further system work. They define the actions to be performed if the events happen.

Each demon object is an instance of the class **DemonObject** and is defined by a production rule. There is no relationship between the rules defining demon objects, thus the production rules are mutually independent.

The rule interpreter is an instance of **DemonInterpreter**. Unlike the knowledge interpreter it performs all the rules with satisfied condition parts. Demon objects are in one status mode all the time. If some objects taking part in a rule change, the rule is evaluated again. No message is needed to activate a demon object.

290

5. Conclusion

Knowledge encapsulated as objects makes it possible to build hierarchical structures of knowledge objects. Thus each knowledge object in the hierarchy can encapsulate specific knowledge and the modularity of the knowledge represented in the system increases.

Unlike other similar tools[6,8], the production rules are realized by means of active objects in the system. The production definition can contain local objects as well as global objects. The latter makes it possible to achieve real parallelism in interpreter processing.

The results, achieved by knowledge objects, can be used by other objects, too. More than one knowledge object can be active at the same time; knowledge objects can consult each other. Knowledge structured in well known production systems can be used by the model.

6. References

1. G. Agha and C. Hewitt, *Concurrent Programming Using Actors*, in Object-Oriented Concurrent Programming, ed. A. Yonezawa and M. Tokoro (MIT Press, 1986).
2. D. Dimitrov, *GameTalk: A Tool for Distributed Business Game Simulation*, in Proceedings of ACMBUL-ISME'91 (Varna, 1991).
3. C. Forgy, *Rete: A fast Algorithm for the Many Pattern/Many Object Pattern Match Problem*, AI, No. 19 (1982).
4. C. Forgy, *The OPS-5 User's Manual*, Technical Report CMU-CS-81-135, Computer Science Department (Carnegie-Mellon University, 1981).
5. A. Goldberg and D. Robson, *Smalltalk-80: The Language and Its Implementation* (Addison-Wesley, 1983).
6. J. Laursen and R. Atkinson, *Opus: A Smalltalk Production System*, SIGPLAN Notices, vol 22, No 12 (Dec. 1987).
7. A. Petkov and Ts. Tsonev, *Diprotalk: a Tool for Object-oriented Design of Distributed Applications*, EUROMICRO Journal, Vol. 27 (North-Holland, 1989).
8. K. Piestol, *The Humble Reference Manual*, Xerox Special Inf. Systems (1986).

POLIMER CHARACTERISTIC DETERMINATION USING A BLACKBOARD MODEL

VIOREL NEGRU

Department of Computer Science, University of Timisoara,
4 V. Pârvan, 1900 Timisoara, ROMANIA,
Email : negruvio@roearn.ici.ac.ro

ABSTRACT

We present a novel architecture of a system for problem solving with the application for determining rheologic characteristics of the polymers. We use a blackboard model based on an object-centered representation. It can be used by the researcher for a better knowledge of polymer behavior on one hand, and to obtain characteristics necessary to modelling their putting in form, on the other hand. This system can serve as a base for the development of a problem solving environment. A minimal version has been realized on a SUN work station.

1. Introduction

The goal of polymeric rheometry is to correlate the behavior of polymers during the process of putting them in the form of functions that are easy to determine[2]. The laws describing the behavior of polymers are empirical or semi-empirical. For instance, to determine the viscosity the human expert follows the steps:

- takes measurements of samples;

- analyzes the measurements by approximating them with curves and applies corrections to them;

- validates the results by comparison with the expected form or with the existing data.

Besides his experience, the expert uses results obtained from the study of other polymers' behavior.

The existing programs, specialized or integrated, have difficulties adapting to the variety of situations and leave validation of intermediate and final results to the expert. They do not consider the imprecision and uncertainty of data, the existence of concurrent models, the use of incomplete and contradicting knowledge, knowledge that can come from several experts.

Our study refers to the formalization of the used knowledge types and to the proposal of an architecture for validating the results. The used domain knowledge refers to the evaluation of the measurements' precision, to existing physical phenomena and to the reasoning followed by the expert to obtain characteristics of the polymers.

The proposed expert system (**ALINA**) is a reflexive system[4], based on an object-centered representation of knowledge and on a blackboard architecture. This system is also a cooperating system[5] because it allows a system-user cooperation while solving the problem. It can be used by the researcher for a better knowledge of polymer behavior on one hand, and to obtain characteristics necessary to modelling their putting in form, on the other hand.

2. Architecture

Object-centered representation allows a good coupling between symbolic and numeric computing and combination between deep and surface knowledge[7] [9]. To achieve this we chose the **SMECI** expert system shell, which is written in **Le-LISP*** and contains an object language inspired by Minsky's frames, first order production rules and a deductive inference engine.

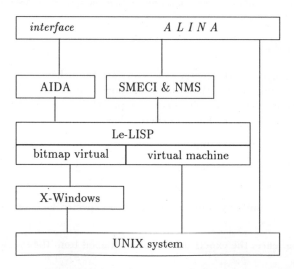

Figure 1: ALINA system environment

The reasoning develops according to the tasks tree and consists in creating a states tree. The management of this states tree allows the use of the notion of multiple worlds

---

*Le-LISP and SMECI are trademarks of INRIA and ILOG, Paris, France

and facilitates the work by the hypothetical reasoning. SMECI also has facilities of explaining the reasoning.

Due to the existence of several domain expertises, of concurrent interpretations and solutions, of a multiple point of view about solving the problem and of the possibility of modular and partial development of the system, we chose a blackboard model. The multi-specialist kernel (**NMS**)[4] is a blackboard model developed with SMECI.

NMS allows the decomposition of the knowledge base in modules called specialists. A specialist is a collection of reasoning units called tasks. The knowledge of a specialist is implemented as task trees, and thear structure is hidden from the other specialists. Specialists share information in a global database. Each specialist is capable of solving a subproblem or of determining the value of an object's field.

The cooperation between specialists takes place in the offer-call mode with or without competition. The specialists management is performed by a supervisor. The supervisor supports the request routing and metareasoning. NMS allows implementing nonmonotonic reasoning. Same data are considered as hypotheses that interest several specialists. When the the status of an hypothesis changes, the supervisor has to fire the concerned specilaists again.

The ALINA system environment is given in figure 1. The graphic user interface is built using the graphics interface generator **AIDA**[†].

3. Constructing the reasoning

Starting from assumptions relative to phenomena, the experts know *models* capable of representing these phenomena[11]. A problem is given by initial data (material, working assumptions), by the goal and by constraints on the result. Given a problem, we must build a reasoning that infers the measuring method, the current hypotheses, selection criteria, the behavior model, etc.

Several solving methods correspond to a given goal. A *method* can be compound or elementary. A particular case of elementary method is the user method by which the user is asked to solve information. A compound method can be split on one or more levels down to elementary methods.

An *elementary method* has a goal that can be satisfied by one or several computing procedures. Elementary methods refer to signal processing, corrections on measurements, regression functions, statistical processing, computing parameters, etc.

As a result of *constructing* the reasoning, we obtain a *construction graph* that will contain elementary methods. Applying selection criteria we determine a path in the construction graph (we obtain a sequence of elementary methods). In the next step, *the execution* step, we instantiate these methods. There are two situations:

- the solution has been found;

- constraints on data have not been respected (about the threshold, isolated points, non-physical behavior, error in a procedure, etc.)

[†]AIDA is a trademark of INRIA and ILOG, Paris, France

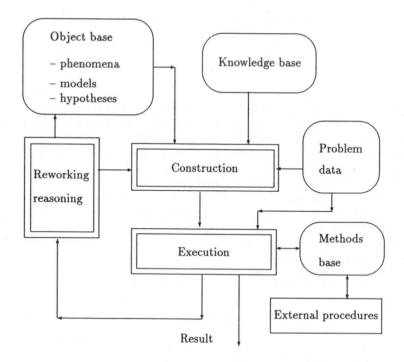

Figure 2: The mechanism for determining polymers characteristics

In the second case a *diagnostic* takes place and then the reasoning is started again. The partial reworking of the reasoning can be done by changing the values of same hypotheses, relaxing of some constraints, changing methods, selecting another model, etc.

The steps described above are given in figure 2. During the execution step we associate a *method-task* to each elementary method. The method-task is a specialization of the task notion of SMECI and represents an intelligent execution of a method[8]. It contains:

1. an external level of link with the domain;

2. an intermediate check level: conditions of application, constraints on entry parameters and on results;

3. and an interior level of interface with the computing procedure.

The coupling with computing procedures is done dynamically during the reasoning. Based on the input parameters, the required results and the goal given by the elementary method, there occurs the consultation of a *method base* which will return the computing procedures that meet these requirements. The computing procedures are stored in software libraries and are written in Lisp, C or Fortran. The methods tasks also handle the errors which may appear in these computing procedures.

4. The blackboard structure

The ALINA system consists of a global database (blackboard), a supervisor, several specialists and a user interface (figure 3). Information on the modelled domain and control is stored in the *blackboard*. Here the solution of the problem is developed in an incremental manner.

The control mechanism is ensured by the *supervisor*. He manages the specialists, unblocks the system and partially reworks the reasoning. For the control of the domain, the supervisor calls a *general specialist*. The general specialists calls the following specialists: *construction*, *execution* and *diagnosis*. This specialists correspond to the steps described in the previous section. This level of specialists allows a better knowledge base modularization and a hierarchical control.

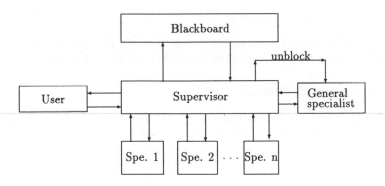

Figure 3: The blackboard model of the ALINA system

The next level of specialists include: measurement specialist, signal treatment specialist, statistical specialist, explanation specialist.

The *measurement* specialist gives: the properties of material, the conditions to make the measures and the measurement device. The *signal treatment* specialist determines the moment when the measurement process is stabilized, applies certain filters on the signal emitted by the measurement devices and obtains as a result a set of measurements which has associated an order of precision.

The *statistical* specialist determines the properties of the sets of measures while the *explanation* specialist is an extension of the SMECI explanation mechanism[6].

Our system allows the work in two modes:

- *user mode*, in which the user solves the problem and the system assists him;

- *system mode*, in which the system solves the problem and the user is able to intervene in order to modify hypotheses and validate results.

The interface made with AIDA allows the user to permanently visualize, (in the form of active objects) the experimental values, the regression functions, the advance of the reasoning, etc. A minimal version of the ALINA system has been realized on a work station SUN-4.

5. Conclusions

The ALINA system is a modular and reflexive system, which can be easy extended and gives also the possibility of introspection in order to be able to give pertinent explanations about the reasoning mode. To increase performances we need to:

- implement a control language at rule and task level[3];

- extend the inference engine to reason on uncertain and imprecise data;

- use the qualitative reasoning.

This system can serve as a base for the development of a problem solving environment, by making a conceptual model and creating tasks of a high level of abstractization[1] [9] [10].

6. Acknowledgements

I would like to thank Jean-Luc Wybo[‡] and Olivier Corby[§] for useful comments and discussions. I would like also to thank to the polymers domain experts Bruno Vergnes[‡]and Jean-Pierre Villemaire[‡]. Support for this work has come from the Office TEMPUS (Contract No. IMG-91-RO-0002) and ARMINES Paris (Contract No. 074120E 1 75231/1992).

References

1. B. Chandrasekaran. *Design problem solving. A task analysis.* AI Magazine, winter 1990, pages 59–71.

2. A. A. Collyer and D. W. Clegg. *Rheological measurement.* Elsevier Science Pbs., 1988.

3. O. Corby, F. Allez, and B. Neveau. *A multi-expert system for diagnosis and rehabilitation.* Transpn. Rea.-A, 24A(1), 1990, pages 53–57.

[‡]CEMEF, Ecole des Mines de Paris - Sophia Antipolis
[§]INRIA - Sophia Antipolis, France

4. O. Corby, S. Moisan, and B. Neveau. *Un formalisme pour le contrôle des règles d'inférence de systèmes experts.* In Actes des 9-èmes journées internationales sur les systèmes experts et leurs applications, Avignon, 1989, pages 307–316.

5. I. Delouis and J. P. Krivine. *Opérationnalisation du modèle conceptuel : vers une architecture permettant une meilleure coopération système - utilisateur.* In Actes des 12-èmes journées internationales sur les systèmes experts et leurs applications, Avignon, 1992, pages 165–176.

6. R. Dieng. *Coopération pour l'analyse d'un raisonnement.* In Actes de 9-èmes journées internationales sur les systèmes experts et leurs applications, Avignon, 1989, pages 319–333.

7. J. S. Kowalik and C. T. Kitzmiller, editors. *Coupling and numeric computing in expert systems.* Elsevier Science Pbs., 1988.

8. V. Negru. *Modélisation de connaissances en vue de la détermination des paramètres rhéologiques de matériaux polymères.* Technical report, Université de Nice - Sophia Antipolis, Ecole Nationale Superieure des Mines de Paris - Sophia Antipolis, 1992.

9. F. Rechenmann. *Modeling tasks and metods in a knowledge-based PDE solver.* *, 1991.

10. X. Tong and M. Tueni. *CARMEN - a Platform for building second generation expert systems.* In Actes de 10-èmes journées internationales sur les systèmes experts et leurs applications, Avignon, 1990.

11. J. L. Wybo. *Simulateur de phénomènes.* Technical report, Ecole Superieure des Mines de Paris - Sophia Antipolis, 1992.

VIII - HYBRID SYSTEMS

AN APPROACH TO EXTRACTION OF FUZZY PRODUCTION RULES FROM THE CONNECTIONIST COMPONENT OF A HYBRID EXPERT SYSTEM

HANS - ARNO JACOBSEN

Fakultät für Informatik Universität Karlsruhe (TH),
76131 Karlsruhe, Germany (s_jacobs@ira.uka.de)

and

IRENA IORDANOVA

Institute of Informatics, Bulgarian Academy of Science,
1113 Sofia, Bulgaria

ABSTRACT

The problem of knowledge transfer from one component of a hybrid expert system to another, i.e. how to combine knowledge from different representations, is central to the study of these systems. In symbolic-connectionist hybrid systems the extraction of rules from the connectionist component is important for the purpose of: 1) controlling and making explicit the knowledge encoded by the neural network; 2) refining the knowledge base in the logic component. This paper will outline the hybrid expert system SHADE, coupling a fuzzy logic module and a connectionist module. Various mechanisms for extracting fuzzy production rules will be described and discussed.

1. Introduction

In recent years hybrid systems are being used extensively by the research community for modeling expertise. The basic idea is to combine different knowledge representation schemes, decision making models and learning strategies in one complete system, as cooperative and interconnected components, with the ulterior motive of keeping the advantages of each. Above all, this hybrid approach is justified by considerations from cognitive psychology showing that human beings apply different problem solving strategies using different knowledge representations for various problems observed [1,10,6]. In this paper the discussion is limited to hybrid systems of the symbolic-connectionist type employing as representation and inference mechanisms a logic based approach (classical expert system) and a connectionist based approach (neural network). A closer look at these two paradigms justifies this hybridization by showing their complementary roles, such as the capability of the expert system to explain derived conclusions combined with the 'learning from example' capability of neural networks or the prototypical approach of learning undergone by the connectionist part in cooperation with

302

the rule based learning in the expert system part[10].

The possibility to exchange knowledge between the two principal knowledge representation modules gives further support for this approach. Knowledge extraction from the connectionist part, for example, in form of production rules, gives rise to a method to open up the black-box-like neural network and extract the represented information in a way readable and interpretable by a human expert but also reusable for further treatment and analysis by the system[11,12,13,14]. The knowledge extracted can then be compared explicitly with the knowledge expressed by experts in the rule base of the logic module. It can then also be used to automatically 'update' the rule base with new knowledge acquired by the neural network during classification-mode.

SHADE is such a symbolic-connectionist expert system which has been developed at LIFIA[1] [6,7,10]. The next paragraph will briefly present SHADE and summarize our reasons for replacing the logic module operating on the base of boolean logic by a module based on the concepts of fuzzy-logic. The application of fuzzy-logic in SHADE leads to a new mechanism of knowledge extraction: *Extraction of fuzzy production rules*. This new approach will be explained in detail and implications of its use will be outlined and discussed in the remainder of this paper.

2. The hybrid expert system SHADE

SHADE[2] is a particular application of its parent system SYNHESYS (Symbolic and Neural Hybrid Expert System Shell) which has also been developed at LIFIA[10]. The system is applied as a computer-aided-tool for diagnosing neuropathies based on analyses of EMG-data (electromyographic data) [7,9].

Its architecture is illustrated in figure 1. The system consists of two major modules

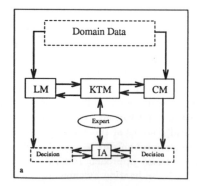 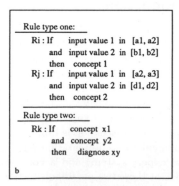

Figure 1: a) Architecture of SHADE and b) rule samples

for knowledge representation: A logic module (LM) and a connectionist module (CM).

---

[1] Laboratoire d'Informatique Fondamentale et d'Intelligence Artificielle, Grenoble, France
[2] Système Hybride d'Aide à la Decision en Electromyographie

Interaction between both modules is overseen by the interaction administrator (IA) also responsible for providing a final output diagnosis. The human expert has the possibility to interact in case of disagreement with the diagnosis provided by the system. All knowledge transfer is carried out by the knowledge transfer module (KTM) also giving the user the possibility of interaction.

Logic module: This module is a classical expert system applying forward and backward chaining over a rule base. The rule-based expert system NEUROP has been used to realize the LM [4,9]. The rule base consists of two types of rules. The first rule type maps numeric input vectors (e.g. measured nerve data from a patient) to semantic concepts. The second type uses these semantic concepts as premises from which the diagnosis is inferred.

Experimental application of SHADE has brought up some problems which led to the following questions:

- *Does the strict fashion of mapping numerical input values to semantic concepts, as described above in the rule samples, capture the reality?*

- *Is the strict decision made by the system for input values close to interval borders a good model for a human decision making process or would an expert considering other aspects decide differently?*

- *Is the concept of the system to infer always one single diagnosis a right model or couldn't a result consisting of several diagnosis with decreasing possibility of appearance be helpful?*

In order to answer these questions and to overcome the observed drawbacks we have introduced fuzzy logic concepts to the system NEUROP[4] and SHADE. This consisted mainly of replacing the strict interval borders by fuzzy regions as described in figure 2.

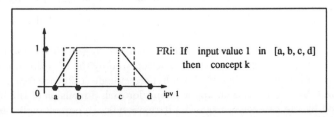

Figure 2: Replacing strict interval boundaries by fuzzy regions

The passage from numeric input values to fuzzy semantic values can now be described by *fuzzy-production-rules* also shown in figure 2. This modification gives rise to gradual membership which is extremely useful for a different interpretation of input vectors close to interval borders.

The introduction of fuzzy logic has not only contributed to answers to our questions from above but has also given us some new ideas for problems not specific to SHADE. A central question in the symbolic-connectionist approach is: *How can one interconnect the reasoning processes of a logic component and a connectionist component?* In the new context this question can be reformulated as: *How can one compare or find a connection between activation values of neurons produced by the neural network and degrees of truth inferred by the logic module?* The rest of this paper is devoted to this question.

Connectionist module: A protoype-based incremental neural network has proven to be the most appropriate for this hybrid approach [1,10]. The model is a feed forward network with one hidden layer representing the prototypical situations. In learning and recognition mode an input pattern (vector from $\Re^n$) is presented to the input layer. A similarity measure is calculated to all prototypical situations represented in the hidden layer and the most similar prototype determines the output category. The incremental aspect comes into play when a presented input pattern is too different from a situation learned so far. A new unit representing this situation will be created and added to the network. A more detailed description of the neural model can be found in [2,3].

3. Extraction of fuzzy production rules

Knowledge transfer from the connectionist module into the logic module (extraction of rules) and from the logic module into the connectionist module (compilation of rules) is restricted by the representation of knowledge in each module. Extraction of knowledge from the neural network, for example, has to deliver the information coded in the weights of the synaptic connections of neurons and distributed over the network in a form consistent with the form and syntax of knowledge represented in the logic module (production rules in our case).

3.1. From extraction of production rules to the extraction of fuzzy production rules.

In a previous version of SHADE the similarity measure mentioned above had been realised by the Euclidean distance which led to hyperspherical influence regions of neurons representing the prototypes. In order to extract knowledge interpretable by the logic module, the Euclidean distance had to be replaced by the max-distance leading to hyperrectangular influence regions [3,5]. Each hyperrectangle (influence region of neuron) is characterized by a lower and an upper bound for each dimension of the input space and is labeled by the category (diagnosis) it represents. Hyperrectangles are created, expanded and contracted during learning-mode and recognition-mode. The union of all hyperrectangles over the input space makes up all possible output categories. Influence regions of neurons are not disjoint and even regions of neurons representing different output categories may overlap. This is illustrated in the first part of figure 3.

The first approach to extraction of rules consisted in cutting hyperrectangles into disjoint pieces and extracting a production rule for every single piece, as described in figure 3 [5].

Whenever hyperrectangles (either representing the same output category or represent-

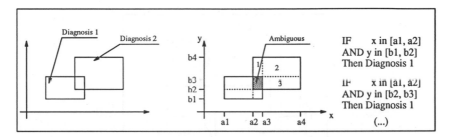

Figure 3: Extraction of production rules - classical approach.

ing different output categories) intersected this method led to a large number of mostly very specialized rules (regions represented by rules being to small). These specialized rules could not be used for further analysis neither by an automated approach nor by human experts. Moreover in the case where hyperrectangles representing different output categories intersected, overlapping regions could not be extracted at all (in figure marked as ambiguous regions) because this ambiguity would lead to inconsistencies in the rule base.

Geometric algorithms[5] applied to minimize the cutting up of hyperrectangles into disjoint regions could minimize the number of rules extracted (e.g. one rule for region 1 and region 2 plus one for region 3 ...) but solved neither the problem of specialization nor the problem of ambiguous regions.

Applying fuzzy logic concepts as described above led us to a new mechanism to extract knowledge from the connectionist module : *Extraction of fuzzy- production rules*. Each hyperrectangle is now uniquely represented by one production rule. Intersecting regions of different hyperrectangles (whether they represent the same output category or different output categories) are interpreted as fuzzy regions and input vectors in these regions belong with different degrees of membership to either hyperrectangle - as imposed by the fuzzy-logic-metaphor[3]. Figure 4 describes the above reflections more precisely. Obviously this method leads to a constant number of extracted rules (equal to the number of hyperrectangles representing output categories) and therefore a more manageable number of production rules. Also intersecting regions are no longer a problem since they have become fuzzy regions. Another advantage is that now all knowledge can be extracted and brought into a form interpretable by the logic module (before ambiguous regions had to remain unextracted).

A major problem which could not be solved entirely up to now is that there is no easy to exploit correspondence between the fuzzy regions extracted from the connectionist part and the fuzzy regions defined by the expert in the rule base of the logic module. Therefore the comparison of the knowledge represented in both modules has not become easier. The next section is devoted to a closer look at this problem.

Nevertheless this first approach made the control of knowledge in the neural network a

---

[3]This idea will be made clearer in the next subsection

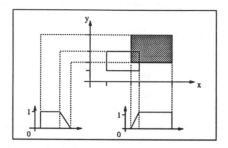

Figure 4: Extraction of fuzzy production rules.

lot easier to cope with. As outlined above the problem of specialization and extraction of ambiguous regions could be solved.

A solution to this correspondence problem will not only make it easier to compare knowledge obtained differently by both modules. It would also make it possible either to set up the fuzzy regions for the production rules automatically or fine-tune them over a long period of time. This is especially useful in an application domain with a lot of training data (examples) at hand but little structured expert knowledge.

3.2. Correspondence between activation of neurons and fuzzy operations

The principal objective of this section is to introduce an interpretation of the knowledge represented in the connectionist part of the system in terms of fuzzy-set theory. Secondly a more precise characterization of the fuzzy regions of intersecting hyperrectangles will be given.

The central idea is to interpret the hyperrectangles characterizing influence regions of neurons as fuzzy-sets over the input space with the normalized activation functions of neurons serving as membership functions.

In the terminology of fuzzy-set-theory[4] this means: The input space becomes the *referential set*, the normalized activation function becomes the *membership function* which determines the *membership grade* of an input vector to a particular hyperrectangle (fuzzy-set). The activation of a neuron is zero if the input vector does not belong to the hyperrectangle representing the influence region otherwise it is equal to one minus the distance of the given input vector from the center of the hyperrectangle. The most activated neuron wins the competition and determines the ouput category. For the reasons outlined above a correspondence between the activation function and the membership function of the corresponding fuzzy sets has to be established. This approach allows us to assign to every point in the input space a membership grade

---

[4]In fuzzy-set-theory a fuzzy set is characterized by a referential set, a membership function and a membership grade assigned to each element in the referential set by the membership function. Membership grades are often chosen from the unit interval, as we have done in our application. See e.g. [8].

to every hyperrectangle. These membership values are determined by the activation function values and represent thus the distance of an input vector to the center of the hyperrectangles (according to the distance measure used). In this interpretation the center of a hyperrectangle is the point of total membership in the fuzzy set representation. Points outside the influence regions of neurons are assigned membership grades zero. Membership functions are mappings from the input space to the unit interval. The above reasoning is expressed mathematically, as follows:

$$n \qquad \text{- dimension of input space,}$$

n	- dimension of input space,
$E_1 \times ... \times E_n$	- input space,
$X = (x_1, ..., , x_n)$	- given input vector,
$C_k = (c_{1_k}, ..., c_{n_k})$	- center of hyperrectangle k,
$d(.,.)$	- applied distance-metric (normalized),
$f_{\theta_k}(X) = 1 - d(X, C_k)$	- activation of neuron k, when X is presented as input vector.

Membership function : showing gradual membership of X to the hyperrectangle k:

$$\mu_{hyperrectangle_k}(X) \quad : \quad E_1 \times ... \times E_n \to [0,1]$$

$$\mu_{hyperrectangle_k}(X) \quad = \quad \begin{cases} 0 & \text{if } X \notin hyperrectangle_k \\ f_{\theta_k}(X) & \text{if } X \in hyperrectangle_k \end{cases}$$

Further analysis shows that it is possible to interpret a hyperrectangle not just as one single fuzzy set but as a composition of n fuzzy sets (n being the dimension of the input space): namely the fuzzy sets defined over its input values for each dimension of the input space. So that hyperrectangle k is defined in terms of its coordinate fuzzy sets I_{i_k} ($i = 1...., n$) for each input parameter i:

$$\mu_{I_{i_k}}(x_i) \quad : \quad E_i \to [0,1]$$

$$\mu_{I_{i_k}}(x_i) \quad = \quad \begin{cases} 0 & \text{if } x_i \notin I_{i_k} \\ 1 - d(x_i, c_{i_k}) & \text{if } x_i \in I_{i_k} \end{cases}$$

This decomposition of hyperrectangles in coordinate fuzzy sets of input vector components is illustrated in figure 5. The fact that only the center of the hyperrectangle is given total membership (due to the way neurons are activated) and the particular choice of the activation function of neurons determine the triangular and symmetric form of the fuzzy set representation. The discontinuities at the interval boundaries shown in figure 5 are caused by the definition of influence regions of neurons. Influence regions are not totally determined by the distance measure but depend also on threshold values associated with each neuron[5].

---

[5]Variable influence thresholds were introduced to the neural model to overcome miss-classifications due to either overgeneralization or undergeneralization [2,3]

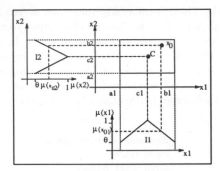

Figure 5: Representation of a hyperrectangle by a fuzzy set for each dimension.

Our intended goal was to extract the knowledge represented in the connectionist part in a way interpretable by the logic module. The decomposition introduced above gives rise to such an interpretation. The hyperrectangle can now be considered as the result of a fuzzy AND operation (realized by min) applied to their coordinate fuzzy sets. The same idea can be used to obtain the overall classification result over the whole input space. This is done by applying a fuzzy OR operation (realized by max) to the fuzzy set representations of the hyperrectangles. The above ideas are expressed mathematically as follows:

The distance : $\quad d(X, C_k) = max_{i \in \{1,...,n\}} \mid x_i - c_{i_k} \mid \qquad (X, C_k$ are normalized)

The activation function of neuron k:

$$
\begin{aligned}
f_{\theta_k}(X) &= 1 - d(X, C_k) \\
&= 1 - max_{i \in \{1,...,n\}} \mid x_i - c_{i_k} \mid \\
&= min_{i \in \{1,...,n\}}(1 - \mid x_i - c_{i_k} \mid)
\end{aligned}
$$

$\Rightarrow \forall X \in hyperrectangle_k :$

$$
\begin{aligned}
\mu_{hyperrectangle_k}(X) &= f_{\theta_k}(X) \\
&= min_{i \in \{1,...,n\}}(1 - \mid x_i - c_{i_k} \mid) \\
&= min_{i \in \{1,...,n\}}(f_{I_{i_k}}(x_i))
\end{aligned}
$$

$\mu_{hyperrectangle-of-winning-neuron}(X) = max\{\mu_{hyperrectangle_1}(X), ..., \mu_{hyperrectangle_m}(X)\}$
(where m is the overall number of hyperrectangles)

3.3. Discussion

The methods described in the paragraph 3.2 imposed the triangular and symmetric form of the membership functions. This form is in many situations too restrictive: For

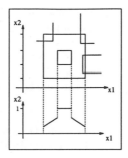

Figure 6: Extraction of production rules of quasi-trapezoidal form.

a compilation of rules (transfer of knowledge from the logic module to the connectionist module) or for a comparison of knowledge between both representations this specific form would restrict the knowledge being expressed by human experts in the rule base to this particular form. But our experiences with real data from the domain of application showed that for an appropriate modeling non-symmetric, trapezoidal forms had to be found.

The introduction of the concept of *winning regions* which had already been defined for the neural network [2] to our fuzzy representation of hyperrectangles gives rise to a *quasi-trapezoidal form*. A winning region is a subset of an influence region of a neuron defined by all the input vectors for which the particular neuron is always chosen as winning unit. Figure 6 illustrates this approach.

Another approach leading to a general, trapezoidal and non-symmetric membership function for the fuzzy sets, representing the knowledge extracted, can be realised by adapting the neural network to the new situation[6]. In the present implementation hyperrectangles are defined by two borders for each dimension of the input space. Replacing these two borders by four values [min, a, b,max] would make it possible to introduce the idea of fuzziness already in the neural network. The interval [a, b] are the winning regions (decisions are absolutely certain) described as above and the intervals [min, a], [b, max] describe fuzzy regions which can be shared with other hyperrectangles. These fuzzy regions are adapted independently by the dynamics of the neural model. Obviously this approach will change the dynamics of the present network and has to be further investigated.

4. Conclusion

Some approaches to extract fuzzy production rules from the connectionist part of a hybrid symbolic-connectionist system have been studied in this paper. It has been shown that this approach to extracting knowledge led to fewer rules extracted, as

---

[6]The neural network had at first been developed for a cooperation with a logic module operating only with boolean logic.

compared to a previous method applying boolean logic instead of fuzzy logic. The proposed approach is, therefore more useful for control of knowledge.

By interpreting influence regions of neurons as fuzzy sets over their input space, we have proposed a way to deal with the problem of knowledge correspondence. This problem needs further investigation, since a solution will make it possible to automatically fine tune fuzzy regions defined by experts in the rule base over a long period of time.

Acknowledgements

This study has been realized at LIFIA in Grenoble, France. The authors would like to thank Mr Arnaud Giacometti, who has developed the system SHADE, and Mr Bernard Amy, leader of the Neural Networks research group at LIFIA, for their helpful support and advice. The authors would like to thank also Mrs. Annick Vila, neurologist in the University Hospital of Grenoble, expert in the domain of Electromyography and author of the rule base used.

References

1. B. Amy, A. Giacometti, A. Gut, *Modèls connexionnistes de l'expertise*, Proc. of International Conference Neuro-Nimes, EC2 Nimes, France 1990, pp. 99-119.

2. A. Azcarraga, A. Giacometti, *A Prototype-Based Incremental Neural Network for Classification Tasks*, Proc. of International Conference Neuro-Nimes, EC2, Nimes, France 1991, pp. 121-134.

3. P. Broissiat, *Apprentissage par un réseau localiste et incrémental destiné à faire partie d'un système expert hybride*, D.E.A. d'Informatique, INPG 1991.

4. M. Dahou, *NEUROP, un système expert en électromyographie. Modèlisation de connaissances, mise au point et pré-évaluation du système*, D.E.A. de Génie Biologique et Médical, Université Claude Bernard-Lyon, Universitè Joseph-Fourier de Grenoble, 1992.

5. J.P. Duval, *Extraction de règles dans un système hybride. Mise en correspondance de connaissances*, D.E.A. d'Informatique, INPG 1991.

6. A. Giacometti, B. Amy, A. Grumbach, *Theory and experiments in connectionist AI : A tightly coupled hybrid system* , Proc. of ICANN'92 Artificial Neural Networks 2, Elsevier Science Publishers 1992.

7. A. Giacometti, I. Iordanova, B. Amy et al. *A Hybrid Approach in Computer-Aided Diagnosis in Electromyography*, Proc. of 14-th Annual International Conference of the IEEE Engineering in Machine and Biology Society part 3, 1992 pp. 1012 -1013.

8. G. J. Klir and T. A. Folger, *Fuzzy Sets Uncertainty and Information*, Prentice Hall, 1988.

9. V. Rialle, A Vila, Y. Besnard, *Heterogeneous knowledge representation using a finite automaton and first order logic : a case study in electromyography.*, Artificial Intelligence in Medicine 3 (2), 1991, pp. 65-74.

10. A. Giacometti, *Hybrid models for expertise*,(in french), French doctoral thesis, November 1992, Ecole National Supérieur des Télécommunications, Paris.

11. G. Towell, J. Shavlik, *Extracting Refined Rules from Knowledge-Based Neural Networks*, Machine Learning, **13**, 1993, 71-101.

12. C. Mcmillan, M. Mozer, P. Smolensky, *The Connectionist Scientist Game: Rule Extraction and Refinement in a Neural Network*, Proc. of the 13th Annual Conf. of the Cognitive Society. Hillsdale, NJ: Erlbaum, 1991, 424-430.

13. A. Konfe, B. Victorri, J.-P. Raysz, *Rule Extraction in Recurrent Connectionist networks* (in French). Proc. of Int. Conf. Neuro Nimes'90, EC2, Nanterre , France, 1990, 131-146.

14. L. Bochereau, P. Bourgine, *Implementation and Extraction of Semantical Features in a Neural Network: an Example from the First Annoncement in Bridge* (in French), Proc. of Int. Conf. Neuro Nimes'89 EC2, Nanterre, France, 1989, 125-142.

INTEGRATING DECISION TREES AND NEURAL NETWORKS

IRENA IVANOVA

INSTITUTE OF INFORMATICS - BAS, ACAD. G. BONCHEV STR., BL. 29A,

1113 SOFIA, BULGARIA, e-mail: irena@iinf.bg

ABSTRACT

This article describes TBNN, a multistrategy system that combines induction of decision trees with neural-nets learning paradigm. By mapping the tree to a neural network, which is then trained by backpropagation, the approach overcomes the shortcomings of both decision trees and neural nets. A successful application to the medical domain is reported.

1. Introduction

Neural Networks (NNs) are one of the actively pursued, general, and successful approaches to Machine Learning (ML). However, they have several well-known shortcomings, perhaps the most important of which is the *topology determination*, i.e. decision about the number of hidden units and layers, the way of connectivity, the initial weights and biases.

To get rid of this drawback Towell, Shavlik, and Noordewier[15], as well as Goodman et al.[7] analyze methods for the direct translation of production rules onto neural-net architectures; Sethi[14] describes a mechanism for the initialization of the NN by a decision-tree generating algorithm; Prem. et al.[10] use 'concept support technique', and Cios and Ning Liu[2] creates the net by means of an algorithm inspired by ID3.

Even though *decision trees (DTs)* are known to provide impressive classification performance they suffer from: 1) the *rigid ordering of the tests* in the internal tree-nodes and, in the case of numeric attributes, from 2) *the strict thresholds* imposed by the numeric/symbolic transformation. The latter inconvenience was pointed out by Quinlan[11] who alleviated this inconvenience by the technique of 'soft thresholding'.

This paper describes a multistrategy system TBNN (Tree-Based Neural Network), that combines DTs with neural backpropagation algorithm. By encoding the tree onto a neural net and subsequent training TBNN overcomes the above mentioned weaknesses of both NN and DTs. The application to a real-world problem in the domain of medicine shows that TBNN produces better results than DTs and randomly initialized NNs.

2. The System TBNN

The general outline of TBNN is summarized in Table 1. Since all attributes describing the examples in the domain are numeric, the decision-tree induction in step 1 is performed by the technique suggested by Fayyad and Irani[4]. The result is a binary tree such as the one depicted

Table 1. Overview of the of the TBNN algorithm

1. Run an algorithm capable of creating a DT from numerically described examples;
2. Translate the tree into a NN:
a) Each class is mapped to one output unit. Each interval imposed on the attribute value by the tests along the path from root to a leaf is mapped to one input unit; and each path is mapped to one hidden unit by connecting the respective input units (*regular links*);
b) Transform the original example description so that the new attributes give the membership of the original attributes into the respective intervals;
c) Apart from the regular links determined by the translation process in (a), provide *additional links* to make the net fully forward-connected;
d) Calculate initial biases and weights for the regular links so that the net encodes the tree as closely as possible. Set the weights along the additional links to small random values.
3. Train the network by the backpropagation algorithm.

in the part (A) of Figure 1. In the sequel, the tree-generating algorithm will be referred to as NID3 (Numeric ID3). The subsections below elaborate on steps 2 and 3.

2.1 Network Topology

Table 2. Correspondence between rules extracted from the DT and NN

Rules	Neural Net
intervals	input units
disjuncts	hidden units
classes	output units
dependencies	regular links

Let us illustrate the principle of TBNN's tree-to-net translation by the simple example depicted in Figure 1. The tree in (A) can be rewritten to the three formulae given in (B). The formulae in (B) are disjunctive normal forms, where atoms are the tests whether the given attribute values fall into the specified intervals. Denotation of the intervals by lower-case letters as indicated in (C) facilitates a more concise formulation of the logical expressions, as shown in (D). These are then simplified to (E) and immediately translated into the network topology in (F) using the correspondence given in Table 2. Regular links between hidden and output units are always positive while the regular links from input to alpha layer can be negative and positive in the case of negated and non-negated intervals, respectively. The dotted line stands for a negative regular connection; the solid line represent positive regular connections. Then, additional links (not shown in the picture) are provided so that each hidden unit is connected to each input and output units.

2.2 Input Transformation

The original attributes are translated to interval memberships values. Thus in the example from Figure 1, attribute *at1* from the tree in (A) is represented by the intervals *a* through *c* in the net in (F).

To get rid of the crisp interval boundaries, the following constraints on the resulting interval-membership function a_i are imposed: the largest value of a_i is in the middle of the interval and decreases towards the interval boundaries; the more distant the value is from the interval, the smaller the value of a_i.

A).

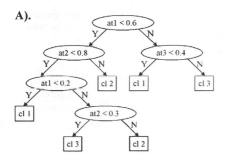

B). [(at1<0.6) ∧ (at2<0.8) ∧ (at1<0.2)] ∨
[(at1≥ 0.6) ∧ (at3<0.4)] =>cl 1

[(at1<0.6) ∧ (at2<0.8) ∧ (at1≥0.2) ∧ (at2≥0.3)] ∨
[(at1<0.6) ∧ (at2≥0.8)] =>cl 2

[(at1<0.6) ∧ (at2<0.8) ∧ (at1≥0.2) ∧ (at2<0.3)] ∨
[(at1≥0.6) ∧ (at3≥0.4)] =>cl 3

C).

0	a	0.2	b		0.6	c		1
0	d		0.3	e			0.8 f	1
0	g		0.4		h			1

D). $(\sim c \wedge \sim f \wedge a) \vee (c \wedge g)$ =>cl 1
$(\sim c \wedge \sim f \wedge \sim a \wedge \sim d) \vee (\sim c \wedge f)$ =>cl 2
$(\sim c \wedge \sim f \wedge \sim a \wedge d) \vee (c \wedge h)$ =>cl 3

E). $(\sim f \wedge a) \vee (c \wedge g)$ =>cl 1
$(b \wedge e) \vee (\sim c \wedge f)$ =>cl 2
$(b \wedge d) \vee (c \wedge h)$ =>cl 3

F).

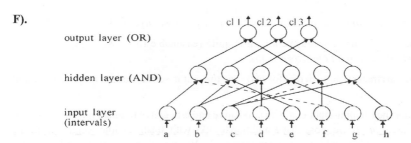

Figure 1. Tree-to-network mapping in TBNN

So, TBNN first determines the distance from the interval center:

$$v_i = \frac{R_i - 2|\mu_i - \chi_j|}{2R_i} \qquad (1)$$

where μ_i is the middle point of the i-th interval, R_i is the size of the interval, and χ_j is the actual value of the related attribute. Then, v_i is subjected to the function:

$$a_i = \frac{1}{1+e^{-h \cdot v_i}} \qquad (2)$$

where the parameter h is a positive constant. For very high values of h, (2) turns into step function; the smaller the values of h, the more 'fuzzy' the boundaries. Experiments indicate that good results are achieved for $h \in [6; 20]$. Note that a_i achieves its maximum when χ_j is in the middle of the interval; $a_i = 0.5$ when χ_j lies on the interval boundary; and $a_i \in (0;0.5)$ otherwise.

2.3 Initial Weights and Biases

As a transfer function for the hidden and output units, the *sigmoid function* has been chosen so that the output of the i-th unit is given by

$$o_i = \frac{1}{1+e^{-h.net_i}} \qquad (3)$$

where net_i is the overall input to the i-th unit as calculated by the formula

$$net_i = \sum_j w_{ji}.o_j - b_i \qquad (4)$$

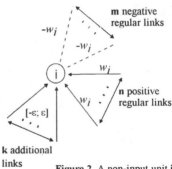

Figure 2. A non-input unit **i**

where j ranges over the units from the previous layer, w_{ji} is the weight attached to the link from j to i, and b_i is the bias of the i-th unit.

In the following definition, suppose that A_u and A_l are user-set constants, such that $0 \le A_l < A_u \le 1$.

Definition: *A unit is active if its output is $o_i > A_u$ and inactive if its output $o_i < A_l$.*

As the sigmoid function is symethric, it is quite reasonable to set $A_u = 1-A_l$, *and this is what we actually did in all our experiments.*

Let the parameter ψ be such that for $net_i = \psi$, the unit is active, and for $net_i = -\psi$, the unit is inactive.

Consider the i-th non-input unit with n positive and m negative regular links (note that for the output layer $m=0$). Suppose that k additional links with small random weights from the interval $[-\varepsilon; \varepsilon]$ have been added to the unit (Figure 2). Weights along positive regular links to the i-th hidden unit are set to $w_{i\alpha}$; weights along negative regular links to the i-th hidden unit are set to $-w_{i\alpha}$; weights to the i-th output unit are set to $w_{i\beta}$. Denote the biases by $b_{i\alpha}$ and $w_{i\beta}$, respectively.

If the *hidden layer* is to model the original conjunction of intervals in the presence of additional links, then the following three conditions must be satisfied:

a) The i-th hidden unit must be active if *all* positive regular inputs are active (even with the minimum value of A_u) while *all* negative regular inputs are inactive (even with the maximum value of A_l and if all additional links are maximally negative).

b) The i-th hidden unit must become inactive if *at least one* positive regular input is inactive (equal to A_l) and all other positive regular inputs have maximum values (equal to 1), even if *all* negative regular inputs are zero (and if the additional links provide maximally positive inputs).

c) The i-th hidden unit must be inactive if *all* positive regular inputs are maximally active (equal to A_u) and *at least* one negative regular input is active (equal to A_u), even if all other negative regular inputs are zero (and if the additional links provide maximally positive inputs).

These requirements are formally described as follows:

$$n.A_u.w_{i\alpha} + m.A_1.(-w_{i\alpha}) - k.\varepsilon - b_{i\alpha} \geq \psi$$

$$1.A_1.w_{i\alpha} + (n-1).1.w_{i\alpha} + m.0.(-w_{i\alpha}) + k.\varepsilon - b_{i\alpha} \leq -\psi$$

$$n.1.w_{i\alpha} + 1.A_u.(-w_{i\alpha}) + (m-1).0.(-w_{i\alpha}) + k.\varepsilon - b_{i\alpha} \leq -\psi \quad (5)$$

Turning these inequalities into equations and solving them for $w_{i\alpha}$ and $b_{i\alpha}$ we obtain (note that the last two inequalities in (4) are identical if $A_1 = 1 - A_u$):

$$w_{i\alpha} = \frac{2(\psi + k\varepsilon)}{A_u(n+m+1)-(n+m)}, \qquad b_{i\alpha} = (\psi + k\varepsilon)\frac{A_u(n+m-1)+(n-m)}{A_u(n+m+1)-(n+m)} \quad (6)$$

If the *output layer* is to model the original disjunction of leaves in the presence of additional links, then the following two conditions must be satisfied:

a) The *i*-th output unit must become active if *at least one* of the hidden units along the regular links is active (at least equal to A_u), even if all other regular links provide zero input (and if the additional links provide maximally negative inputs).

b) The *i*-th output unit must be inactive if *all* previous units along the regular links are inactive with the maximum value A_1 (even if the additional links are maximally positive).

These requirements can be formally described as follows:

$$1.A_u.w_{i\beta} + (n-1).0.w_{i\beta} - k.\varepsilon - b_{i\beta} \geq \psi$$

$$n.A_1.w_{i\beta} + k.\varepsilon - b_{i\beta} \leq -\psi \quad (7)$$

Turning these inequalities into equations, solving them for $w_{i\beta}$ and $b_{i\beta}$, and setting $A_1 = 1 - A_u$, we obtain:

$$w_{i\beta} = \frac{2(\psi + k\varepsilon)}{A_u(n+1)-n}, \qquad b_{i\beta} = (\psi + k\varepsilon)\frac{n - A_u(n-1)}{A_u(n+1)-1} \quad (8)$$

If the weights and biases are set to the values given by (6) and (8), the network will simulate the behavior of the original tree even in the presence of additional links.

2.4 Backpropagation

In the previous step, all positive regular input links and all negative regular input links to a specific unit are assigned the same weight. For the needs of further tuning by the backpropagation algorithm, the weights must be slightly perturbed by small random values.

TBNN uses the *backpropagation algorithm with momentum function* as described by Rumelhart and McClelland[12]. Even though many techniques have been published to speed up the learning process, to avoid local minima, and to achieve better classification accuracy, they are not implemented in the system. Otherwise, there is no garantee that the observed increased performance has really been achieved thanks to the original idea (and not by the plethora of tricks massed around it).

The only exception is the necessity to prevent the danger of *network overtraining*, which (as revealed by preliminary experiments) is a serious problem in our application domain. Therefore, the backpropagation part of TBNN includes a simple mechanism to avoid this phenomenon: the training examples are split into two subsets: one for the network training and one (smaller) for on-line testing. This second subset is called *training test set* (TTS). After each run through the training examples, the system tests the performance on TTS. The training stops when the classification accuracy on TTS declines, even if the mean square error on the real training set still improves.

3. Application Domain

Sleep classification is an important issue in medical diagnosis because some serious diseases, such as *epilepsy*, are accompanied by typical sleep disorders. Physicians measure a number of quantities (EEG, EMG, etc.) on sleeping subjects and then draw a *hypnogram* — a graph describing how the sleep stages changed throughout the night. An analysis of such a graph helps the doctor to determine the diagnosis. Unfortunately, to construct the hypnogram is a difficult task requiring several hours of hard work of a highly qualified specialist. Hence, a tool for automatic sleep classification is highly desirable. Another important application is in the research to the so called *sudden infant death syndrome* (SIDS) that appears almost exclusively in the REM sleep stage, when the baby is dreaming. Obviously, a system issuing an alarm whenever the REM-stage is detected will be very useful.

The data from which TBNN learns cannot be described by the same attributes as those available to the expert because experts often use 'linguistic' variables such as 'increased signal complexity.' Also, the expert has the advantage of substantial background knowledge that was not used for machine learning. Moreover, in our setting the learner does not see the evolution of the sleep stages because the original examples were permutated to make the learning task more general.

From the machine-learning perspective, the data can be characterized as follows. The data file contains 920 examples described by 15 numeric attributes normalized into theinterval [0;1]. The examples are classified by the expert into 7 classes. The attributes are noisy in the sense that they, on rare occasions (3 - 5%), acquire arbitrary values.

Much more noisy are the expert classifications. Kemp et al.[8] report that the agreement between six human classifiers does not exceed 75%, which is in accordance with our own experience. The results of TBNN can be evaluated as 'very good' if the classification accuracy reaches 80% — in that case, however, it already begins to copy the mistakes (and 'bad habits') of the given expert.

Finally, not all attributes used for learning were equally relevant and no information about their relevance was apriori available to the learner.

4. Experiments

TBNN was tested on two data files, obtained from the measurements and expert classifications on two different subjects, BR and KR. All numbers in Tables 3a, b, c give the percentage of correct classifications on unseen examples. For each subject and each method,

10 different splits of non-overlapping learning and testing examples were carried out.

Table 3a contains the results provided by TBNN and randomly initialized NN. For each of the 10-th permutations. In all cases of TBNN, NID3 was run on 200 examples to demonstrate that good performance can be achieved even if a small subset of examples is need for the network initialization. In BR22 and KR22, the same examples were used for backpropagation training; in BR24 and KR24 a superset of 400 examples were used for training. Testing was always performed on 320 examples. The column denoted by 'Binary TBNN' gives the results provided by TBNN but when the intervals were treated as binary variables, i.e. for each attribute, one of the respective input units received 1 and all other input units received 0. The column 'TBNN' contains the results achieved when the inputs were transformed by the equations (1) and (2). In both cases, the network was trained by the backpropagation algorithm. As for the topology of randomly initialized NN, the recommendation of Pfurtscheller, Flotzinger, and Matuschik[9] to use 10 hidden units was followed.

To prevent overtraining, the backpropagation algorithm always used 200 examples outside the learning and testing sets as the 'training test set'.

The averaged results from Table 3a are represented in Table 3b. They can be easily compared with the averaged results for various sizes of learning set achieved by NID3 that are given in Table 3c.

5. Discussion

The selection of the two subjects for the experiments was not arbitrary: BR always provided very good results, while KR has never been very successful, probably due to frequent mistakes in expert classifications (the data file KR was classified by a relatively junior specialist).

The mapping of the decision tree onto a neural net provides a flexible generalization that can be considered as an alternation to tree pruning. However, the usual generalization by pruning would not affect the original *ordering of the tests*. Hence, if several attributes possess comparable information contents (as is the case of our data), the fixed ordering of the tests may become an inconvenience. TBNN overcomes this shortcoming by putting all tests on the same level and finding the weights by the subsequent training. This provided some 4 - 5% performance gain over the decision tree (see 'Binary TBNN' in comparison with 'NID3-200 ex.'). On the other hand, Table 3a, b shows how the *softening of the intervals* by the input transformation led to dramatic performance gain (see 'Binary TBNN' against 'TBNN'). In the end, TBNN outperforms the original DTs by 12 - 13% and virtually reaches the natural limits achievable on these data.

In addition, note that using 400 examples to tune (by backpropagation) the structure provided by a tree generated from 200 examples provided significantly better results than NID3 run on the same 400 examples. Moreover, running TBNN on 200 examples yielded better results than running NID3 on 600 examples.

TBNN can be viewed as a method for *initialization of NNs* by DTs. The transformation procedure is defined by a one-to-one mapping between trees and nets. By integrating DTs and NNs, the system TBNN significantly outperforms randomly initialized NN in terms of

Table 3. The performance achieved in the domain of automatic sleep classification by different systems

A).

%		Pure NN		Binary TBNN		TBNN	
		BR22	BR24	BR22	BR24	BR22	BR24
BR	*p1*	59.38	64.36	75.63	78.44	87.50	93.13
	p2	52.18	55.63	76.25	79.06	79.38	85.94
	p3	59.06	63.75	75.94	76.56	80.94	83.44
	p4	56.56	59.38	69.69	70.63	73.44	83.13
	p5	53.44	60.63	81.88	84.69	85.94	91.25
	p6	54.69	58.13	76.25	73.75	77.82	82.81
	p7	57.50	62.81	72.81	80.93	78.44	83.75
	p8	52.81	59.06	74.38	74.69	78.13	83.44
	p9	56.25	57.19	72.81	73.44	80.00	81.88
	p10	55.31	57.50	75.94	77.50	85.63	86.56
		KR22	KR24	KR22	KR24	KR22	KR24
KR	*p1*	35.31	37.19	57.19	61.25	81.56	80.94
	p2	32.81	35.00	60.00	60.31	63.75	66.56
	p3	37.50	40.00	57.19	57.50	63.75	66.56
	p4	36.88	39.69	60.94	60.00	64.69	68.44
	p5	32.82	35.31	54.68	55.00	64.06	68.44
	p6	53.75	54.38	59.69	60.00	66.38	68.13
	p7	35.31	36.25	58.75	65.31	66.56	71.88
	p8	39.06	40.63	64.06	62.50	65.63	64.06
	p9	37.18	40.31	56.88	59.38	63.75	65.63
	p10	32.85	38.12	49.38	59.38	55.00	62.50

B).

%	Pure NN	Binary TBNN	TBNN
BR22	55.72 ± 2.4	75.16 ± 3.0	80.72 ± 4.2
BR24	59.84 ± 2.8	77.00 ± 3.9	85.50 ± 3.6
KR22	37.35 ± 5.7	57.90 ± 3.8	65.50 ± 6.2
KR24	39.69 ± 5.3	60.10 ± 2.6	68.30 ± 4.9

C).

%	NID3-200 ex.	NID3-400 ex.	NID3-600 ex.
BR	72.00 ± 2.5	74.60 ± 3.1	77.30 ± 3.0
KR	56.60 ± 3.8	62.10 ± 1.9	64.00 ± 1.6

classification accuracy. An important observation, not mentioned in Table 3, says that TBNN is very fast — while randomly started NN needed thousands of epochs to converge, the network obtained from the tree-to network translation converges in less than 30 epochs.

The relatively large standard deviations are caused by the fact that the decision tree has been built only from a small subset of examples. Due to the unequal representation of the classes, it sometimes happened that one or two classes were not found in the learning sample which caused certain performance degradation.

6. Related Research

Another method for translation of DT into NN has been described by Sethi (1990). In his approach, called *entropy nets*, each internal node of the tree is mapped to one first-hidden-layer unit whose task is to compare the attribute value to the threshold given by the respective node. Each leaf is mapped to one second-hidden-layer unit that performs the conjunction of the conditions along the path terminating at the leaf. Each class, understood as a disjunction of leaves sharing the same label, is represented by one output unit.

Three features distinguish TBNN from entropy nets: 1) the function of Sethi's first hidden layer is carried out by the attribute transformation in TBNN; 2) additional links are supplemented to make the network fully connected, thus providing more flexibility; and 3) the weights and biases are initialized to values ensuring that the fully connected net simulates the classification of the tree as closely as possible.

On the other hand TBNN can be viewed as an approach for integrating pre-existing symbolic knowledge into a network. There is a growing number of methods proposing rules-to-net mapping. Among them are: Gallant[6], Fu[3], Jones and Story[5], Towell et al[15], Sestito and Dillon[13], Berenji[1], Goodman et al.[7], Towell and Shavlik[16]. An good overview and detailed classification is given in Towell[17].

7. Future Work

While the current version of the TBNN has produced promising results, certain improvements can facilitate its future application to broader range of domains.

First, the system contains a few constants to be manually adjusted. Even though their number is smaller than in traditional randomly started NNs, they still represent certain clumsiness. As a rectification, the system should be able to perform a search through the space of parameter settings to fine-tune the performance without human interference.

Another extension receiving attention is the development of an incremental version of the system. The idea is to enable the system to find, one by one, those rules that contribute best to the classification accuracy.

Finally, methods for the automatic translation into symbolic rules of trained TBNN-initialized networks are being investigated.

8. Conclusions

This work demonstrates the promise of a multistrategy approach based on the combination of DTs and NNs. The system TBNN was successfully applied to sleep classification, which is an important issue in medical diagnosis.

The success of the system can be summarized as follows: 1) very good classification accuracy is obtained in comparison with randomly started NNs and DTs; 2) very few epochs are needed for convergence; and 3) the approach provides straightforward initialization of the neural net that saves a lot of improvisation.

The observed performance gain is achieved by overcoming the shortcomings of both DTs and NNs, namely: 1) by tree-to-net translation the system frees itself from the fixed ordering of the attribute-value tests; 2) using soft interval memberships TBNN escapes from the crisp thresholds limitations of the traditional DTs; and 3) the time for the network convergence is significantly reduced by proper setting of initial weights and biases as described in the paper.

There is one aspect of TBNN that was not discussed in this article - use of Prolog-like rules to initiate the net. In most applications, apriori domain knowledge is available, even though it might be incomplete and inconsistent. TBNN contains a module capable of translating

Prolog-like rules into disjunctive normal form and, if required, combining them with the rules provided by NID3. This capability has been omited since it would distract the reader from the main topic.

Acknowledgments

Part of the research was done when the author was with the Department of Medical Informatics at the Technical University in Graz, which provided the data. The visit was supported by the Austrian Ministry of Science and Research. Special thanks are due to Dr. M. Kubat who read earlier draft of this paper and suggested many improvements.

References

1. H.R. Berenji (1991). *Refinement of Approximately Reasoning-Based Controllers by Reinforcement Learning.* Proc. of the 8th Int. Machine Learning Workshop, 475—479.

2. K. Cios and N. Liu (1992). *A Machine-Learning Method for Generation of a NN Architecture: A Continuous ID3 Algorithm.* IEEE Transactions on NNs, **3**:280—290.

3. L.M. Fu (1989). *Integration of Neural Heuristics into Knowledge-Based Inference.* Connection Science, **1**:325—340.

4. U.M. Fayyad and K.B. Irani (1992). *On the Handling of Continuous-Valued Attributes in Decision Tree Generation.* Machine Learning, **8**:87—102.

5. M.A. Jones and G.A.Story (1989). *Inheritance Reasoning in Connectionist Network.* Proccedings of the International Conference on Neural Networks.

6. S. Gallant (1988). *Connectionist Expert Systems.* Commun. of the ACM, **31**:152—169

7. R.M. Goodman, C.M. Higgins, J.W. Miller, and P. Smyth (1992). *Rule-Based Neural Networks for Classification and Probability Estimation.* Neural Computation, **4**:781—804.

8. B. Kemp, E.W. Groneveld, A.J.M.W. Janssen, and J.M. Franzen (1987). *A Model-Based Monitor of Human Sleep Stages.* Biological Cybernetics, **57**:365—378.

9. G. Pfurtscheller, D. Flotzinger, and K. Matuschik (1992). *Sleep Classification in Infants Based on Artificial Neural Networks.* Biomedizinische Technik, **37**:122—130.

10. E. Prem, M. Mackinger, G. Dorffner, G. Porenta, and H. Sochor (1992). *Concept Support as a Method for Programming Neural Networks with Symbolic Knowledge.* Proceedings of the German Workshop on Artificial Intelligence, Springer Heildelberg.

11. J.R. Quinlan (1990). *Probabilistic Decision Trees.* In: Y.Kodratoff and R. Michalski (eds.): Machine Learning: An Artificial Intelligence Approach, 140—152.

12. D.E. Rumelhart and J.L. McClelland (1986). *PDP*, MIT Press, Cambridge, Vol. **1**.

13. S. Sestito and T. Dillon (1990). *The Use of Sub-symbolic Methods for the Automation of Knowledge Acquisition for Expert Systems.* Proc. of the Australian AI Conference, Perth.

14. I.K. Sethi (1990). *Entropy Nets: From DTs to NNs.* Proc.of the IEEE, 78:1605-1613.

15. G.G. Towell, J.W. Shavlik, and M.O. Noordewier (1990). *Refinement of Approximate Domain Theories by Knowledge-Based Neural Networks.* Proc. AAAI'90, 861—866.

16. G.G. Towell and J.W. Shavlik (1992) *Using Symbolic Learning to Improve Knowledge-Based Neural Networks.* Proc. AAAI'92, San Jose, 177—182.

17. G.G. Towell (1992). *Symbolic Knowledge and Neural Networks: Insertion, Refinement and Extraction.* PhD Thesis, University of Wisconsin - Madison.

FLEXIBILITY VERSUS EFFICIENCY:
THE DUAL ANSWER

BOICHO KOKINOV

Institute of Mathematics, Bulgarian Academy of Sciences
Bl.8, Acad. G. Bonchev Street, Sofia 1113, BULGARIA
E-mail: kokinov@bgearn.bitnet

ABSTRACT

A fundamental question that always arises in cognitive modeling is how to combine two contradictory constraints: the model should be as flexible as possible (to reflect human flexibility) and at the same time it should be maximally efficient. The decision proposed in this paper is the following. The space to be searched has to be restricted for computational reasons, but this restriction should not be done in advance. It should be dynamic and should reflect the particular situation encountered, i.e. it should reflect the dynamically evolving context. In this way making the computations context-sensitive they will be both flexible and efficient.

A multi-agent cognitive architecture is proposed consisting of hybrid (symbolic/connectionist) micro-agents. The behavior of the system at the macro level emerges from the collective behavior of the micro-agents. The symbolic computation performed by the system emerges from the symbolic micro computations performed by the agents, while their "power" or "rate" depends on their connectionist activation levels. The activation distribution over the agents reflects the particular context. This architecture allows for a greater flexibility of the cognitive system while at the same time decreasing the complexity of computation.

1. Introduction

A fundamental question that always arises in cognitive modeling is how to combine two contradictory constraints: the model should be as flexible as possible (to reflect human flexibility) and at the same time it should be maximally efficient. Each model is a trade-off between these two requirements.

The problem is that the greater flexibility makes the space to be explored larger therefore reduces the efficiency. Moreover, in most cases it makes the computation intractable. This problem is usually solved by restricting the problem space in advance in a way facilitating the search for the appropriate knowledge for completing the particular task or set of tasks the system is designed to accomplish. However, this restricts the system's flexibility: it makes the use of the model in other tasks (where the solution is outside the restricted problem space) impossible. In technical applications this is not a problem, because the most important feature there is efficiency, moreover, different systems could be designed for different cases. However, in cognitive modeling a single model of the cognitive process should be able to account for people's behavior under various circumstances.

Let's consider the following example. In an analogical reasoning task, relations from two subject domains should be put into correspondence. The set of possible pairings of relations is enormous large and it is impossible to search it in real time. That is why every model (proposed so far) restricts the search in a particular way. Thus Gentner[5,6] pairs only identical relations (this is a quite extreme restriction, but even in that case a large space of possible pairings remains, especially when the same relations are used several times in the problem description). This restriction, however, makes even the simple analogy between the following cases impossible: *on(vase, desk)* and *over(tablecloth, table)* - here, *o n* and *over* are not identical, but are semantically similar. Holyoak and Thagard[10, 15] solve the same problem allowing two relations which have an immediate common super-class to be paired - so, in the above example an immediate common super-class of *o n* and *over* might be *above*. However, even in this case a severe restriction is made: only relations with *immediate* common super-class are paired, e.g. *on(vase, desk)* and *supports(desk, computer)* cannot be put into correspondence using this mechanism, although humans will do it because both relations have a common super-class at a more abstract level. The restriction to *immediate* super-classes is made only for computational reasons, otherwise an exhaustive search is needed.

The decision proposed in this paper is the following. The space to be searched has to be restricted for computational reasons, but this restriction should not be done in advance. It should be dynamic and should reflect the particular situation encountered, i.e. it should reflect the dynamically evolving context. In this way making the computations context-sensitive they will be both flexible and efficient.

2. DUAL – A Context-Sensitive Multi-Agent Cognitive Architecture

DUAL is a multi-agent architecture, i.e. it consists of a large number of micro-agents, each of which represents some specific declarative and/or procedural knowledge. The agents are relatively simple - they do not have their own goals or reasoning mechanisms. They are some kind of specialized computational devices.

Each micro-agent is hybrid – it has a symbolic and a connectionist part called L-Brain and R-Brain, respectively. The symbolic part represents a piece of knowledge, while the connectionist part - its relevance to the current context. If, for example, the L-Brain of an agent represents the fact that "the Bulgarian state was established in 681" then the activation level established by its R-Brain represents its relevance to the current context and determines its accessibility at that moment. If, on the other hand, the L-Brain of an agent represents the procedural knowledge about a particular symbolic operation, such as marker passing or structure mapping, then the activation level established by its R-Brain determines whether this operation is allowed at that moment and what is its priority or rate. The former case allows only a small fraction of the knowledge base (KB) represented by the L-Brains of the agents to be searched at every particular moment and the latter case allows particular operations to be supported or suppressed depending on the context. This allows for a greater flexibility of the cognitive system while at the same time decreasing the complexity of computation.

All the micro-agents may act in parallel, but at each particular moment only the active agents are working together and competing or cooperating with each other. Moreover, every agent acts at its own rate (in an asynchronous manner) depending on its activation level. In this way the behavior of the system at the macro level emerges from the collective behavior of the micro-agents, i.e. the symbolic computation performed by the system emerges from the symbolic micro-computations performed by the micro-agents, where the particular set of agents taking part in the computation process as well as their competitive power depends on their activations which reflect the particular context.

Compared to other hybrid systems[1, 2, 4, 7, 8, 16], DUAL is hybrid at the micro level rather than at the macro level. That is, instead of having separate modules implemented according to the symbolic and connectionist paradigms each modeling a particular cognitive process (or a particular stage of it), it consists of a large set of small hybrid agents contributing to all cognitive processes. In this way both symbolic and connectionist aspects are considered important for every aspect of human cognition.

Compared to multi-agent systems such as the Blackboard architectures there are a number of differences:
• The agents themselves are part of the blackboard, i.e. there is no separation between data structures being placed on the blackboard and

agents acting on them and representing particular procedures. Instead, agents might by treated as data structures from other agents, while at the same time actively processing some other agents.

- The working memory is not a global base accessible for all agents, but instead every agent "sees" only a small fraction of the blackboard - the specific part connected with its functioning, i.e. there is only *local processing*: the agents are connected with each other (some of the links are permanent, others are dynamically created and removed) and every agent exchanges information only with its neighbors.
- All agents act in parallel, each of them at its own rate proportional to its activation level. This makes the computation context-dependent and allows competition between agents.

Another cognitive architecture close to DUAL is the one proposed by Hofstadter and his group[3, 9]. It is a multi-agent architecture with Codelets acting in parallel as agents over the blackboard (the Workspace consisting of data structures) and influenced by the activation levels of the nodes in a semantic network (called Slipnet). In this architecture, however, procedures and data structures are separated (in Coderack and Slipnet and Workspace, respectively) and different mechanisms ("urgencies", activation levels, and strengths) are used for their control. Agents are able to observe the whole Workspace and in this way they act as global processors. The parallel work of the Codelets is simulated by a stochastically constructed sequence of its running with probabilities corresponding to their "urgencies".

3. Internal Structure of DUAL Micro-Agents

Each DUAL agent consists of two highly interrelated processors – the L-Brain and the R-Brain. The L-Brain is designed according to the symbolic paradigm, whereas the R-Brain – according to the connectionist paradigm. The R-Brain of an agent acts as an power supply for the corresponding L-Brain. Thus, although all the L-Brains can potentially work in parallel, in each particular moment only a small fraction of them has the necessary energy supplied by the corresponding R-Brains for actual working. On the other hand, all the R-Brains are continuously working in parallel calculating the activation levels of the agents, i.e. their power supply.

3.1. L-Brains: The Symbolic Part of the Micro-Agents

The L-Brain of an agent represents a combination of declarative and procedural knowledge about a particular object/situation, a generic concept, or a given action. For this reason a frame-like representation scheme is used.

An example of a frame in the DUAL architecture is presented in Figure 1. The slot fillers are simply pointers to other frames or their slots and no special language is used for their description. The links between the agents correspond to these pointers and represent various semantic links. This leads to a highly distributed representation of the knowledge and keeps the symbolic processors quite simple.

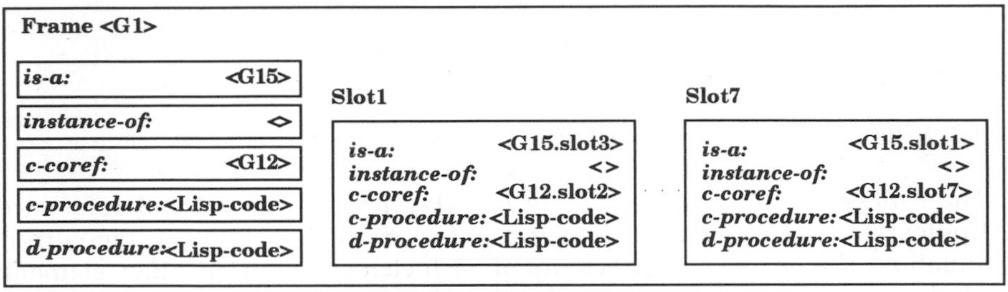

Figure 1.
An example of a frame in the DUAL architecture.

The *is-a* and *instance-of* links define the concept as a specialization of or as a particular instance of a class. Every two agents linked to each other by a *c-coref* link (short for "conceptual coreference") represent one and the same entity in the world possibly from two different points of view. This allows for multiple descriptions of one and the same object, concept, situation, etc. The *c-procedure* and *d-procedure* represent the procedural knowledge and correspond to "procedures to be called" and "demons", respectively.

The L-Brains are specialized symbolic processors (Figure 2). They have permanent memory for all outgoing links (pointers to other frames and labels of the semantic links) as well as temporary memory for markers (structures containing pointers to other, possibly non-neighboring nodes) and other local data. All L-Brains have the ability to receive and send markers and to differentiate links with different labels (e.g. to pass the markers only along links with specific label). In addition, the L-Brains of some agents are able to perform specific hard-wired programs (c- and d-procedures) corresponding to some possible actions of the cognitive system. Some examples of such specialized agents are the agents able to initiate a marker-passing process, the agents able to construct new agents (node constructors), the agents able to initiate a mapping between two descriptions, the agents able to establish local correspondence between two structures, etc.

Specialized symbolic processes: (c-procedures and d-procedures)	Common symbolic processes: (local marker-passing ability)
Temporary memory for its local data	Temporary memory for markers
Permanent memory for representing semantic links to other frames	

Figure 2.
The L-Brains of the agents.

3.2. R-Brains: The Connectionist Part of the Micro-Agents

The R-Brains of the micro-agents in DUAL represent context and relevance. Context is represented by the relevance factors of each agent to the current situation. The degree of connectivity of each element with all other elements of that situation is chosen as a particular measure of relevance and is represented by the activation level of the corresponding agent. Thus the activation level of the agent computed by its R-Brain within the connectionist aspect represents the relevance of the description corresponding to the agent within the symbolic aspect.

The links between the agents within the connectionist aspect have no labels and reflect only the strength of the associative relations between them, i.e. how often the two agents appear in the same context. All the links which have some semantic interpretation within the symbolic aspect are used also by the connectionist aspect ignoring their specific semantic interpretation. In addition the a-links (short for "associative links") represent arbitrary associations which are ignored by the symbolic aspect. They are not recognized by the symbolic processors and are used only by the connectionist aspect of the architecture.

Perception and system's goals are sources of activation. That is the R-Brains of agents corresponding to entities being perceived at the moment as well as of agents corresponding to the current goals of the cognitive system continuously emit activity.

The R-Brains are connectionist processors (Figure 3) calculating the activation values and outputs of the nodes on the basis of their input values and current activity running. They work in parallel in a discrete synchronous manner in order to simulate the continuous process of spreading activation. They have permanent memory for all outgoing links (pointers and weights) and temporary memory for their net input, activation value, previous activation level, and output. They have hard-wired programs calculating the activation and output functions as well as programs for weights learning.

Connectionist processes				
activation		output		learning
current net input	current activation level	previous activation level	current output	connection weights
Temporary memory				Permanent memory

Figure 3.
The R-Brains of the agents.

4. An Example of a Context-Sensitive Computation Performed by DUAL

Let us consider an example of performing context-sensitive computations which demonstrates the use of DUAL in a fragment of an analogy-making task. Let's have two simple propositions: *The pot is on the plate*, and *The immersion heater is immersed in the water*. A correspondence between *on* and *is immersed in* is being searched. This problem cannot be solved using the techniques of Gentner[5, 6] or Holyoak and Thagard[10, 15] as this two relations are neither identical nor have an immediate common superclass. So, to solve the problem we have to allow searching for common superclasses at any level. However, this leads to enormously enlarging the search space which will made the computations untractable. In DUAL this search is performed by a marker-passing mechanism, i.e. by a highly parallel process, but this is still not enough to reduce the search process to reasonable complexity. However, the marker-passing process is performed by the micro-agents and that is why only active agents can take part in the process. This reduces enormously the search space restricting it to the active part of the memory – the Working Memory (WM). The search within the WM is already a quite effective task. In this way DUAL combines the flexibility of being able to find common superclasses at any level of abstraction with the efficiency of searching only the currently active paths.

Moreover, if several paths are concurrently active and therefore several solutions are concurrently possible a natural criterion for preference exists in DUAL. Instead of using some fixed predefined criterion as "the shorter path", or "the path crossing nodes with lower fun outs", or any combination of these[7] a more flexible and more natural criterion is used – the more active path is selected as the path which is more relevant to the current context. It may happen that this is the shorter path (and probably this will occur more frequently), but it could also happen that this is the longer path (which may be a rare situation but allows interesting and deep analogies).

There is an additional flexibility in the system: its behavior becomes context-sensitive, i.e. in different contexts - different concepts will be active and therefore different paths will be followed by the markers (Figure 4) and as result different correspondences will be found. This is especially important in cognitive modeling as it is well-known that human cognition is context-sensitive[11, 12].

5. Conclusions

Models based on the DUAL architecture demonstrate high flexibility and variability in their behavior thereby reflecting the dynamic context-sensitive nature of human cognition. On the other hand they demonstrate high efficiency restricting all searches to small parts of the knowledge base.

The DUAL architecture has been used in modeling similarity judgements[13] and analogical reasoning[14].

6. Acknowledgments.

This research has been partially supported by the Bulgarian National Science Fund.

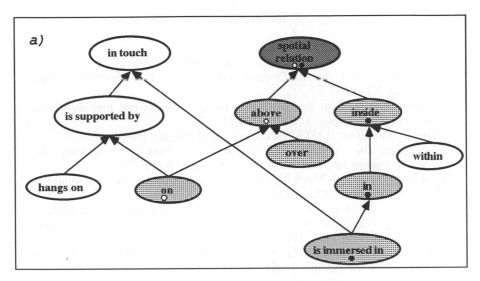

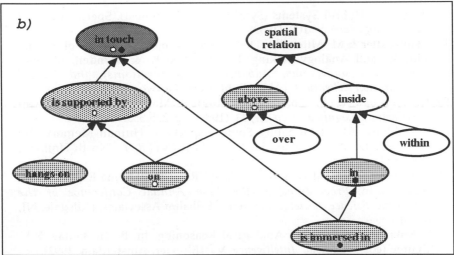

Figure 4.
Context-Sensitive Marker-Passing.
Depending on the particular memory state – the distribution of activity over the network
(presented by the filling patterns of the nodes) – different ways will be followed by the
markers (the white and black small circles) and consequently different correspondences will be
established.

7. References

1. J. Barnden & J. Pollack, *High-Level Connectionist Models, Advances in Connectionist and Neural Computation Theory,* **1,** (Ablex Publ. Corp., Norwood, NJ, 1991).
2. L. Bookman & R. Sun Special Issue: Integrating Neural and Symbolic Processes. *Connection Science,* **5(3&4)** (1993).
3. B. French, *Tabletop.* (PhD Thesis. Univ. of Michigan, 1991).
4. J. Dinsmore, *The Symbolic and Connectionist Paradigms: Closing the Gap.* (Lawrence Erlbaum Associates, Hillsdale, NJ, 1992)
5. D. Gentner, Structure-Mapping: A Theoretical Framework for Analogy, *Cognitive Science* **7(2),** (1983), pp. 155-170.
6. D. Gentner, The Mechanisms of Analogical Learning. In: S. Vosniadou & A. Ortony (eds.) *Similarity and Analogical Reasoning.* (Cambridge Univ. Press., New York, NY, 1989).
7. J. Hendler, Marker Passing over Microfeatures: Towards a Hybrid Symbolic/Connectionist Model. *Cognitive Science,* **13,** (1989). pp. 79-106.
8. J. Hendler, Hybrid Systems (Symbolic/Connectionist). Special Issue of *Connection Science,* **1(3),** (1989).
9. D. Hofstadter & M. Mitchell, The Copycat Project: A Model of Mental Fluidity and Analogy-Making. In: Holyoak, K. & Barnden, J. (eds.) *Analogical Connections, Advances in Connectionist and Neural Computation Theory,* 2, (Ablex Publ. Corp. Norwood, NJ, in press).
10. K. Holyoak & P. Thagard Analogical Mapping by Constraint Satisfaction. *Cognitive Science,* **13,** (1989), pp. 295-355.
11. B. Kokinov, About Modeling Some Aspects of Human Memory. In: Klix, Streitz, Waern, Wandke (eds.) *MACINTER II,* (North-Holland, Amsterdam, 1989).
12. B. Kokinov, Associative Memory-Based Reasoning: Some Experimental Results. In: *Proceedings of the 12th Annual Conference of the Cognitive Science Society,* (Lawrence Erlbaum Associates, Hillsdale, NJ, 1990).
13. B. Kokinov, Similarity in Analogical Reasoning. In: B. du Boulay & V. Sgurev (eds.) *Artificial Intelligence* V. (Elsevier, Amsterdam, 1992).
14. B. Kokinov, A Hybrid Model of Reasoning by Analogy. In: Holyoak, K. & Barnden, J. (eds.) *Analogical Connections, Advances in Connectionist and Neural Computation Theory,* 2, (Ablex Publ. Corp., Norwood, NJ, in press).
15. P. Thagard, K. Holyoak, G. Nelson, D. Gochfeld, Analog Retrieval by Constraint Satisfaction. *Artificial Intelligence,* **46,** (1990).pp. 259-310.
16. C. Thornton, Special Issue on Hybrid Models. *AISB Newsletter,* **78,** (1991).

IX - NATURAL LANGUAGE PROCESSING

SYNTACTIC TREES AND COMPACT REPRESENTATIONS IN NATURAL LANGUAGE PROCESSING

VINCENZO LOMBARDO

Dipartimento di Informatica Universita` di Torino
c.so Svizzera 185 - 10149 Torino - Italy
e-mail: vincenzo@di.unito.it

and

CRISTINA BARBERO

Centro di Scienze Cognitive
Universita' e Politecnico di Torino
via Lagrange, 3 - 10123 Torino - Italy
e-mail: cris@di.unito.it

ABSTRACT

The paper illustrates some advantages of the dependency approach in practical applications of NLP. We introduce a compact representation called a dependency graph, produced by an all-path left-to-right parser for a dependency grammar. The dependency graph keeps all the syntactic trees of a sentence in a single structure, thus allowing an economy of representation and an easier comparison between the alternative paths for the semantic processor. An algorithm for extracting all the legal syntactic trees from the dependency graph is finally presented.

1. Introduction

In NLP systems, practical parsers have to face two common difficulties that are caused by syntactic ambiguities. The first difficulty concerns the efficiency of the syntactic representation: the parses of a sentence may grow exponentially[1] and a parsing algorithm would take an exponential time only to enumerate all the possible parses. The second difficulty concerns the form of the representation that interfaces the parser and the semantic interpreter. The parse trees are presented one by one to the semantic component and some of them are interpreted, with the production of a semantic representation of its content, others are rejected because of the violation of the semantic constraints. Multiple syntactic trees and their interpretation as a whole do not allow the evaluation of the best local syntactic representation for a fragment of the sentence. These difficulties are greatly reduced via the introduction of a compact syntactic representation for the multitude of syntactic structures associated with a sentence. If the parser builds such a structure on line, the computation time is reduced and a large portion of memory is saved. Besides, in a compact structure the semantic processor could focus on the ambiguous points and compare some alternative readings for the same fragment.

334

Two recent practical parsers produce compact representations as output. Tomita[15] introduces the *shared-packed parse forest*, which exhibits subtree sharing and local packing. Subtree sharing avoids to produce the same parse for the same input fragment more than once; local packing produces a single non-terminal symbol even when it is "reduced" many times for the same input fragment. The empirical data show that subtree sharing and local packing allow to keep the limits of memory occupation in a logarithmic space. Seo and Simmons[11,12] propose a further simplification of the parse forest by introducing the *syntactic graph*. The syntactic graph, which is able to provide a focus on the local ambiguities, is computed via a three-step process: an all-path parser builds a parse forest (following Tomita's model), then the forest is translated into the syntactic graph, and, finally, an exclusion matrix is built to specify a grid of co-occurrence possibilities (within the same parse) for pairs of arcs. The construction of the exclusion matrix is based on intuitive principles, that have not been proved to be exhaustive.

The syntactic graph shares many similarities with a *dependency structure*, which is the result of a parsing algorithm with a dependency grammar. The peculiar difference between dependency and constituency syntax concerns the type of syntactic structure that is assigned to a sentence. According to dependency syntax, the structure is expressed in terms of the *head-modifier* (also called *dependency*) *relation* between pairs of words, a head and a modifier. This relation defines a *dependency tree*, whose root is a word that does not depend on any other word. In constituency syntax the type of representation is a *phrase structure tree*. A p.s. tree defines one of the possible decompositions of the sentence into smaller sequences of words, called phrases, down to one-word units. Figure 1 exemplifies the two structures associated with the sentence "The chef cooked a fish". Notice that the leftward or rightward orientation of arrows in the dependency tree of fig. 1a represents the ordering constraints: the modifiers that precede the head stand on its left, the modifiers that follow the head stand on its right.

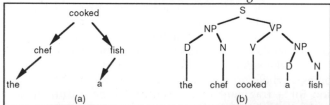

Figure 1. Syntactic structures for the sentence "The chef cooked a fish".

In spite of the little attention received in the past, a number of dependency formalisms, born both in the linguistics and the computational linguistics communities, witness the fertility of the ground and the variety of possible applications in NLP[3]. Besides, the expression of the syntactic constraints via a dependency approach seem to be well suited for many issues of current research in real NLP.

From the linguistic point of view, dependency theory offers a perspicuous treatment of free-word order constructs in natural languages. All natural languages exhibit free word order to a certain extent: topicalizations and extractions are very common in real texts even in configurational languages. Free ordered languages, like Slavonic languages[13], have been the traditional area of dependency syntax for decades: but the structural properties offered by head-modifiers representations are also advantageous for partially configurational languages, like Italian, where constituents order is highly free[10]. The impact of this characteristic on the assignment of grammatical relations and the consequent case analysis in NLP is particularly relevant: SVO is only the most common order, but all the other five permutations are admissible, also in written language[14]. The assignment of grammatical relations depends in most cases on semantic and pragmatic factors, and is therefore highly influenced by the underlying predicate-arguments structure of the sentence. The dependency structure reflects immediately the semantic representation because of the correspondence head-modifiers/predicate-arguments, thus simplifying the interpretation process[6].

Also the research in the area of "shallow parsing techniques" for tasks of information extraction from real texts[2,4] suggests that dependency-oriented formalisms can be useful in NLP. The traditional methods of language analysis produce an intractable number of interpretations when the hundreds of rules of a realistic grammar are applied to the 30-40 word long sentences that appear in actual texts. Weak methods focus on the meaningful predicate-arguments relations in a text, with the help of statistic information on word associations and a deep knowledge on a limited domain. The shallow(er) parsing techniques have revealed to be reliable and efficient enough to replace the traditional methods in the processing of real texts. The evident weaknesses are the possibility of producing gross analyses or taking misleading paths because of incompleteness of syntactic knowledge and the dependence of a method on a specific domain: it is convenient to integrate a weak method with a traditional approach[5]. Dependency-based approaches assign relation-based representations to a sentence: the integration of a weak method with a dependency parser is much more immediate than with a constituency parser, which must necessarily be followed by a phase of relation extraction, that navigates in an intricate forest of alternative constituent aggregations.

Compactness of the syntactic representation, treatment of free word order phenomena, immediate interaction with the semantic component, possibility of integration with shallow parsing techniques, are all important aspects of computational linguistics in dealing with real constructs in real languages for applications such as information retrieval and machine translation. Therefore, it is quite reasonable to think of dependency syntax as a useful approach to syntax in NLP. This paper proposes a *dependency graph* that is the result of a top-down all-path parsing algorithm for dependency grammars as a compact representation for a set of dependency trees. The next section describes the structure of the dependency graph; the parsing algorithm, with the mechanism for index assignment, is introduced in section 3. An algorithm for the enumeration of all the possible syntactic readings is finally presented. The paper is closed by some conclusions.

2. Structure of the dependency graph

A dependency structure expresses the dominance relations that exist for pairs of words in the sentence according to the constraints given by a dependency grammar: the nodes represent the words; the arcs express the relations. A *dependency grammar* is a quintuple $<S, C, W, L, T>$, where W is a finite set of symbols (words of a natural language; terminal symbols in constituency grammars), C is a set of syntactic categories (preterminals, in constituency terms), S is a non-empty set of root categories ($C \supseteq S$), L is a set of category assignment rules of the form X: $x_1, ..., x_n$, where $X \in C$, $x_1 \in W$, ..., $x_n \in W$, and T is a set of *dependency rules* of the form $X(Y_1 \ Y_2 \ ... \ Y_i \ \# \ Y_{i+1} \ ... \ Y_m)$, where $X \in C$, $Y_1 \in C$, ..., $Y_m \in C$, and # is a special symbol that does not belong to C. Each rule is associated with a category X, and enumerates the categories $Y_1, ..., Y_m$ that depend upon X in the order given by the rule, where X occupies the position of # (see fig. 2). In a dependency rule a modifier symbol Y can take the form Y*: as usual, this means that an indefinite number of Y's (zero or more) may appear in an application of the rule.

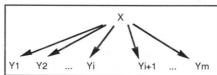

Figure 2 - A dependency rule.

An example grammar is G1=<{V}, {V, N, P, D}, {I, saw, a, man, in, the, park, with, telescope}, {V: saw, N: I, man, park, telescope, P: in, with, D: a, the}, T_1>, where the set of dependency rules T_1 is the following:
1. V(N #); 2. V(N # N P*); 3. V(N # P*);
4. N(#); 5. N(# P*); 6. N(D # P*);
7. P(# N); 8. D(#).
T_1 includes three rules for the root category V(erb), three rules for the category N(oun) and one rule for P(reposition) and D(eterminer), which is a leaf category (rule 8). A verb (V) can dominate one or two nouns and several prepositions (*). The subtree rooted in a noun (N) has no obligatory modifier (4), but, if present, the determiner precedes the noun (6) and the possibly multiple prepositional modifiers follows it (5-6).

Now let us define the dependency graph[9]. Each node n (see fig. 3) is a quadruple $<m, c, j, P>$, where m is the node name, c is the category of the node, j is the position in the input string of the leftmost word that belongs to the subtree rooted in the node, and P is a set that provides the path information, i.e.

information that relates this single node with the paths it belongs to. Each element of P is a triple $<i, w, s>$, where i is a set of indices identifying a path, w is the word in input associated with the node according to that path, and s is the state reached by the node in that path (see section 3). A node consists of several *versions*, each characterized by an element of P: each version represents the node in a different parsing path.

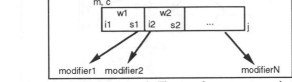

Figure 3. A node of the dependency graph. The arcs that connect a node to modifiers are also labelled with indices (not in the figure). The left-oriented arcs link modifiers that precede the head node; the right-oriented arcs link modifiers that follow the head.

Each arc of the dependency graph is a triple $<start, end, set\text{-}of\text{-}i>$, where *start* and *end* are nodes and *set-of-i* is a set of indices. The indices identify the node-version(s) of *start* (the governor) that are linked by this arc. In fact, both the arcs and the node-versions belong to one or more parses. It is the compatibility between the indices on the arc and the indices of one or more of the node-versions of *start* that specifies the correct co-occurrences. On the contrary, the entire *end* node (i.e. all of its possible versions) is part of the structure(s) identified by the arc. This is due to the overall strategy of the algorithm that is top-down. The various paths have to be kept distinct while expanding the graph in the top-down direction: indices that label the arcs can keep apart the several alternatives in the structure.

The indices are generated and inserted into the structure during the parsing process. An index consists of a pair of numbers: the first is a progressive number associated with each choice point encountered, the second identifies one alternative parse for that ambiguity. In other words, an index $i.j$ labels the j-th alternative of the i-th ambiguity. Indices are associated with node-versions and arcs: *a consistent structure cannot contain indices that have the same first element but differ for the second*. A substructure is labelled with an index i.j, if i.j is associated with the node-version that roots the substructure itself. The indices are originated and assigned for the first time in the points of non-determinism; then they are propagated when an extension of the structure is allowed only in the context given by a specific set of indices. In such a way the compatibility constraints span over long distances through the whole structure (see the next section).

In fig. 4 we report the dependency graph of the sentence "I saw a man in the park with a telescope". The example, chosen for its simplicity, does exhibit only attachment ambiguities and all the nodes have only one version. The index mechanism applies to this case with the same strategy of the general case, except that indices will never be assigned to node(version)s but only to arcs. The graph represents in a compact form the five trees that can be obtained according to the grammar G1 (fig. 5).

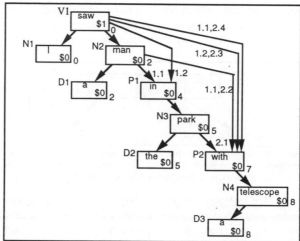

Figure 4. The dependency graph of the sentence "I saw a man in the park with a telescope".

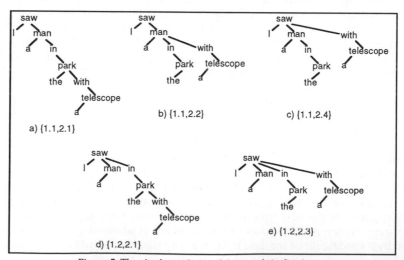

Figure 5. The single readings of the graph in fig. 4.

The two sets of indices 1.i and 2.j encode the attachment ambiguities for "in the park" and "with a telescope", respectively. The arcs <V1, P1, {1.2}> and <N1, P1, {1.1}> are incompatible, and the same holds for the set of arcs the connect the node P2 to the structure. At the bottom of each tree is the set of indices that identifies that structure. In section 4 we give an algorithm for the extraction of the single trees from the dependency graph.

3. The parsing strategy

The global strategy of the parsing algorithm is all-path, top-down, left-to-right, but a precomputation of the left corner information reduces the processing time. The left-corner information defines the pairs <partial tree structure, input category> that trigger the top-down guessing of a node. Skeletal (empty) nodes of a certain category, with neither a word nor modifiers, are "created" (a progressive number signals each new creation); then their form changes by finding first the left modifiers, then the word, and, finally, the right modifiers. A node evolves through a sequence of states. A state specifies 1) which modifiers have been found, 2) whether the head has been found, 3) whether the node can be considered as complete (final states). The parser executes two operations: *fill* and *crlink(Cat)*. The first of them "fills" a node with the current input word; the second one "creates" an empty node of category *Cat* and "links" it to a current node. The parsing algorithm[7] is outlined in fig. 6.

| Initialization |
for each root category Cat do generate the node-version <Cat$_1$, Cat, 0, {}, nil, 0>
If there is more than one root category then
   generate a set of indices {1.i} and assign each index 1.i to one node-version
| Body |
for each input word do
1 ---- Compute the set of current nodes
2 ----
 for each category Cat of the input word do
  for each current node-version of category C and state S do
   collect the operation(s) allowed for "<C, S> × Cat"
  if there is more than one operation then associate with each of them a new index
  Execute all the operations
3 ----
 for each category Cat of the input word do
  repeat until no more current node-versions
   for each current node-version of category C and state S do
    collect the operation(s) allowed for "<C, S> × Cat"
    if there is more than one operation then associate with each of them a new index
    Execute all operations
| Termination |
repeat until no more current node-versions
  take a node-version NV and remove it from the set of current node-versions
  if NV is complete and is a version of a root node then insert NV in ACCEPT-set
  else for each node-version NVfather that dominates NV through the arc A do
     augment the set of indices of NVfather with the indices in A
     make NVfather current
if ACCEPT-set is empty then REJECT else ACCEPT and RETURN(ACCEPT-set)

Figure 6. The parsing algorithm.

The algorithm begins by creating nodes of the root categories and specifying that they are the "current" nodes (initialization). The "body" is subdivided in three

parts:
1) The set of current node-versions is gathered by climbing the dependency graph from the nodes that were filled in the last step of the "for-each-input-word" loop (except for the initialization). A movement upward is allowed only when the node-version under examination is complete. In such a case, the parser can hypothesize the input word may be a dependant of its mother. The graph is climbed up until no further movement upward is possible. The arcs that are traversed while moving upward can be labelled with indices. Encountering an index while forming the set of current node-versions means that any new extension of the graph from upper nodes must be labelled with such an index. Any operation will take into account the new indices: a new expansion is compatible only with the substructures that enabled its construction.
2) All operations that are licensed by the grammar on the current node versions gathered above are collected. If more than one exists, a new set of indices which share the first component is generated in order to mark the different paths. The operations are executed and the set of indices associated with them are assigned to the new arcs (in case of CRLINK) and to the new node-version (in case of FILL).
3) In the third part, we must use the nodes just created to expand the graph until the input word has been consumed (used in a FILL) on all the paths. Since the different paths have already been kept apart in the expansion 2, now the generation of indices is required just in case more than one operation is executable from the same node version.

In the "termination" phase, the parsing algorithm makes all the possible climbings from the nodes that are current at the end of the analysis to the root nodes of the dependency graph, collecting, for each path individuated, all the indices found in the climbing (in the node-versions and in the arcs traversed). The variable ACCEPTset contains all the pairs <Root-node-version, Index-set> obtained in the termination phase: "Root-node-version" is the root node version reached in a given path, and "Index-set" is the set of indices collected during the climbing of that path. These sets of indices are exaustive (i.e. each of them includes all the indices for a path): in fact, as described above, all the indices collected while working on a left substructure belonging to a given path are passed to the right side to mark the substructures in the same path. Consequently, it is sufficient to climb the right frontier of the graph to collect automatically all the indices for a path. The legal combinations of indices, characterizing the possible syntactic readings, are so available in ACCEPTset at the end of the parsing analysis. The ACCEPTset returned for the dependency graph in fig. 4 is {<Root, {1.1, 2.1}>, <Root, {1.1, 2.2}>, <Root, {1.1, 2.4}>, <Root, {1.2, 2.1}>, <Root, {1.2, 2.3}>}, where Root is the node-version <V1, Verb, 0, {}, saw, $1>.

4. The enumeration algorithm

In order to verify that the dependency graph represents all and only the legal parses of the sentence, we illustrate an algorithm for enumerating all the possible syntactic readings compacted in the graph. The enumeration algorithm navigates in the graph given the pairs in ACCEPTset (each pair <Root-node-version, Index-set>, as we said, defines one and only one possible path): each tree is built starting from Root node version and collecting in the graph all the nodes and arcs with indices compatible to those in Index-set.

The Enumeration Algorithm

for each <Root-node-version, Index-set> in ACCEPTset do
    build-tree(Graph, Root-node-version, Index-set)

build-tree(Graph, Node-version, Index-set)
    /*Node-version=<Node, Category, Position, Indices, Word, State>
    build-node(Node-version)
for each Arc=<Node, Dnode, Arc-indices> in Position order and Compatible(Arc-indices, Index-set) do
    create-arc(Arc)
    identify Dnode-version=<Dnode, ..., Dindices, ...> such that Compatible(Dindices, Index-set)
    build-tree(Graph, Dnode-version, Index-set)

compatible(Local-indices, Index-set): boolean
    for each index i.j in Local-indices do
        if not(i.j in Index-set) then return(false)
    return(true)

An initial "for" loop calls the procedure "build-tree" (that has the task to build a possible syntactic tree) for each pair in ACCEPTset. The procedure "build-tree" is called recursively on the nodes of the graph belonging to the path which is currently followed. The first node to be built is the root node-version (the procedure "build-node" is called to construct this node); the arcs linking this node to its dependents are selected (in the order given by the Position of the dependent nodes), such that the indices associated to the arcs are compatible with Index-set. For each of these arcs, the procedure "create-arc" builds the arc in the tree, and the dependent node-version which is compatible with Index-set is identified. This dependent node-version is passed as an argument to the procedure "build-tree", that keeps on recursively the construction of the structure. Every check of compatibility between a set of indices local to a node or arc and the global set of indices Index-set is made by the procedure "compatible": all the indices "i.j" in Local-indices must also be in Index-set. It is easy to verify that the algorithm extracts from the graph in fig. 4 the trees in fig. 5.

5. Conclusions

The paper has presented a compact representation for the set of the dependency trees that are associated with a sentence. The numerical indices that distinguish the various trees are assigned without taking into account the properties of the structure itself and thus overcoming the difficulty[12] of finding out an exhaustive set of structural properties for the syntactic graph. An algorithm for the extraction of all the legal trees from the dependency graph has been

342

defined, in order to verify the results of the index mechanism and to provide a practical method for selecting interpretations from the compact representation.

This work explores the practical viability of dependency formalisms in NLP applications: the efficiency of the compact representation[7] and the neat coupling with the predicate-argument semantics[8] are very appealing in dealing with real texts. Many issues of current research in NLP seems to be well suited for a dependency approach: the treatment of free word order phenomena and the relationships with the shallow parsing techniques are more immediately concerned with a dependency rather than a constituency-oriented paradigm.

6. References

1. K. Church, R. Patil, *Coping with Syntactic Ambiguity or How to Put the Block in the Box on the Table*, **Computational Linguistics 8/3-4**, 1982, pp. 139-149.
2. K. Church, W. Gale, P. Hanks, D. Hindle, *Parsing, word associations, and predicate-argument relations*, in Proc. of the Int. Workshop on Parsing Tech., CMU, 1989.
3. R. A. Hudson, N. M. Fraser, *Inheritance in Word Grammar*, **Computational Linguistics 18/2**, June 1992, pp. 133-158.
4. P. S. Jacobs, *Parsing Run Amok: Relation-Driven Control for Text Analysis*, Proc. of AAAI 92, San Jose' (CA), 1992, pp. 315-321.
5. P. S. Jacobs, L. F. Rau, *Innovations in Text Interpretation*, **Artificial Intelligence 63**, 1993, pp.143-192.
6. L. Lesmo, V. Lombardo, *The Assignment of Grammatical Relations in Natural Language Processing*, Proceedings of (COLING 92), Nantes, 1992, pp. 1090-1094.
7. L. Lesmo, V. Lombardo, *Efficient Dependency Parsing.* submitted for publication, 1994.
8. V. Lombardo, *Incremental Dependency Parsing*, Proceedings of ACL 92, Newarc (DE), June 1992, pp. 291-293.
9. V. Lombardo, L. Lesmo, *A Compact Syntactic Representation*, to appear in MartinVide C. (editor), **Current Issues in Mathematical Linguistics**, Elsevier, 1993.
10. P. H. Matthews, **Syntax**, Cambridge University Press, 1981.
11. H. C. Rim, J. Seo, R. F. Simmons, *Transforming syntactic graphs into semantic graphs*, Proceedings of ACL 90, Pittsburgh (PA), June 1990, pp. 47-53.
12. J. Seo, R. F. Simmons, *Syntactic Graphs: A representation for the Union of All Ambiguous Parse Trees*, **Computational Linguistics 15**, 1989, pp. 19-32.
13. P. Sgall, E. Haijcova, J. Panevova, *The Meaning of the Sentence in its Semantic and Pragmatic Aspects*, D. Reidel Publishing Company (1986).
14. O. Stock, *Parsing with Flexibility, Dynamic Strategies, and Idioms in Mind*, **Computational Linguistics 15**, 1989, pp. 1-18.
15. M. Tomita, *An Efficient Augmented-Context-Free Parsing Algorithm*, **Computational Linguistics 13**, 1987, pp. 31-46.

STRUCTURING LEXICAL SEMANTICS INFORMATION IN A KNOWLEDGE EXTRACTION SYSTEM

FLORENCE PUGEAULT, PATRICK SAINT-DIZIER

IRIT-CNRS, Université Paul Sabatier, 118 route de Narbonne, 31062 Toulouse FRANCE

and

MARIE-GAELLE MONTEIL

EDF, DER, 1, avenue Gal de Gaulle, 92140 Clamart, FRANCE

ABSTRACT

In this paper, we present the different types of lexical semantics knowledge required for developing a system extracting knowledge from texts. In this system, we show how semantic information related to thematic roles, argument structure, predicate relevance, verb semantic classes and semantics of prepositions can be represented in a coherent and efficient way in order to guarantee an optimal use and access to lexical semantic information. We show how these types of data are related and how they interact. Finally, we show how a relation can be established between semantic forms and a variety of syntactic realizations.

1. Aims of the project

The aim of our project is to improve the quality of systems extracting knowledge from texts by introducing refined lexical semantics data. The output of the extraction is a partial semantic representation of these texts. The extracted knowledge must reflect the major aspects of the conceptual contents and organization of the text. Our project is applied to research projects descriptions (noted hereafter as RPD) where the annual work of researchers at the DER of EDF (Direction des Etudes et des Recherches, Electricité de France) is described in terms of research actions [2]. The extracted knowledge must be sufficiently accurate to allow for the realization of the following purposes:

(1) evaluation of the importance of the use of techniques, procedures and equipments,
(2) automatic distribution of documents in different services,
(3) interrogation, e.g. who does what and what kind of results are available,
(4) identification of relations of various types between projects,
(5) construction of synthesis of research activities on precise topics,
(6) creation of the 'history' of a project, evaluation of the advances of a project.

The linguistic analysis methods we have developed are designed to be as generic as possible and can indeed treat a large variety of texts.

About 2.000 RPD are available each year, each of about 120 words long. The total vocabulary is about 50.000 different words. Texts include fairly complex linguistic constructs. In addition to these texts, a thesaurus (encoding taxonomics, associative relations, and synonyms, in a broad sense) has been developed in the past years by a domain expert. The prototype we are developing is aimed at showing the feasability of the linguistic and computer techniques we have developed and at evaluating the costs and the techniques for extending the linguistic resources so that any RPD text can be treated properly.

In this document, we first present the general form of texts and identify the type of information which must be extracted. We then sketch out how the extraction of knowledge is organized, and next present in detail the different types of lexical semantics knowledge we consider, how they are organized and how they interact. In this work, we study in more depth the extraction of information under the form of predicate-argument and predicate-modifier structures, that we represent by means of set of refined thematic roles [10, 11, 12].

2. Semantic typology of the RPD texts

Let us first illustrate the type of text we are dealing with. Here is a standard text:

"Les mesures destructives (ou assimilables) posent toujours des problèmes concernant le faible nombre de données disponibles ou encore leur coût qui s'associe généralement à la nécessité d'une bonne précision. Il est donc nécessaire d'optimiser les campagnes de mesure pour mieux analyser les incertitudes de mesure, et, lorsque cela est possible, réduire les coûts induits. Ces problèmes sont d'autant plus difficiles à traiter que les paramètres en jeu ont des comportements non-linéaires. Il est donc nécessaire, au préalable, d'étudier les méthodes permettant de prendre en compte cette non-linéarité."

2.1 General organization of texts

A global study of these texts shows a great regularity in their overall organization. This is not, in fact, very surprising since they all have the same objective: to relate ongoing research. We have identified four major facets in most texts, called *articulations*. These articulations are not necessarily present altogether in a text. We have the following articulations:

- THEME, which characterizes the main purpose of the text. In this articulation, we have, for example, the topic of the text, and the domain on which engineers are investigating,
- MOTIVATIONS, which relate the main objectives, the needs, the goals and which explains the development of the current project.
- PROBLEMS, which correspond to the difficulties related to the current state of the art or to the limitations of certain equipments or methods.
- REALIZATIONS, which describe the different tasks required for the achievement of the project.

Articulations may be defined by one or more fragments of a sentence, by a whole sentence or by a set of sentences. They do not necessarily appear in the order they have been defined here. The decomposition of texts in articulations defines the **pragmatic level**. We view the articulations as defining semantic fields; articulation names can then be viewed as predicate names. The above text can be decomposed as follows:

[**theme** [les mesures destructives]],

[**motivations** [optimiser les campagnes de mesure pour mieux analyser les incertitudes de mesure, et, lorsque cela est possible, reduire les coûts induits.]],

[**problems** [[posent toujours des problemes concernant le faible nombre de données disponibles ou encore leur coût qui s'associe generalement à la necessité d'une bonne precision.], [problèmes sont d'autant plus difficiles à traiter que les paramètres en jeu ont des comportements non-linéaires.]],

[**realizations** [étudier les méthodes permettant de prendre en compte cette non-linéarité.]]].

Due to the size of this document, this pragmatic level will not be further investigated. More details about it can be found in [14].

2.2 Identification of knowledge to be extracted

Let us now concentrate on the nature of the semantic information which should be extracted by the system. We have identified three classes of information:

- *general nominal terms* (e.g. 'methods', 'data'), and *specific nominal terms* belonging to technical domains (e.g. terms denoting materials, products, methods, algorithms),
- *states or actions* in which these terms are involved,
- *general roles* played by these terms in actions or states.

Roughly speaking, the first class identifies arguments, the second class defines predicates, while the third one introduces the notion of semantic roles such as *thematic roles* [7, 8, 9, 10, 11, 12]. This latter level is of a crucial importance in knowledge extraction because it avoids making incorrect interpretations on the role of an argument with respect to the action or state being described [8]. This level is called the **linguistic level**.

The level of granularity we are considering in this project suggests us to group predicates with a close meaning into a class and to represent them by the same predicate name, viewed as a primitive term. For example, we have terms which express the notion of definition (e.g. define, specify, describe, identify, qualify, represent) or the notion of building (e.g. assemble, build, compile, develop, forge). However, for a relatively small number of classes, in particular for those classes of predicates which denote complex actions and for those which exhibit a high degree of incorporation [1] and where incorporated knowledge needs to be made more explicit, it is necessary to use a more conceptual type of representation. In this project, we want to explore the approach based on primitives of the Lexical Conceptual Structures (LCS) [11] which seems to match very well with the planned uses of the extracted knowledge on the one hand, and with the notion of thematic roles on the other hand.

Let us call this level the **conceptual level**. Since this level is relatively complex, we think that it is necessary to define different levels of granularity for the representations, so that users can adjust the granularity of the representations to the planned treatments. The determination of the level of granularity has obviously an impact on the efficiency of the system and on the complexity of the lexicon. This paper being mainly devoted to the linguistic level, we will not go into many details about that latter level.

3. The linguistic approach and the overall organization

Let us now introduce the way linguistic knowledge is organized in order to allow for an efficient and reliable extraction of knowledge. Fig 1below shows the different linguistic components of our linguistic system and summarizes the way they interact (dashed lines indicate hypothesis and relations we are currently investigating):

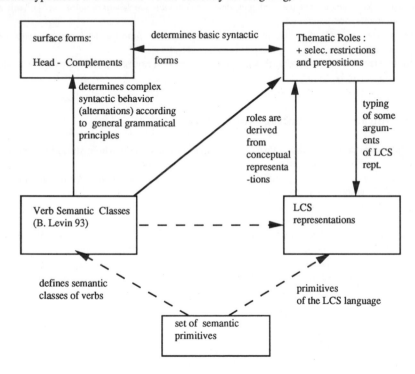

Fig. 1 The General Linguistic Organization

We consider a set of primitive elements (the lowest element), either general or related to our application domain, which includes notions such as being in contact with, being in a spatial motion, or being the cause of. This set of primitives is designed so that it corresponds to those needed for the definition of the semantic classes of verbs defined by [13]. Her approach shows that the syntactic behavior of a verb (and thus the different ways the arguments can be distributed and should be picked out by the parser and put at the right place in the semantic representation) essentially depends on the verb's semantic nature. This approach allows for a comprehensive treatment of predicate-argument structures because it complements the basic syntactic mappings realized from thematic roles specifications. Furthermore, this approach requires very economical lexical means since it removes a lot of idiosyncracies previously encoded in lexical entries.

We are reformulating B. Levin's work for a subset of verbs of French[4] relevant to our application. Although our study is quite general, we focus primarily on predicates found in applications. Our study includes determining the meaning of verbs, the meaning components that determine the syntactic behavior of these verbs, and the general grammatical principles that determine behavior. To these verb classes, we associate thematic grids, which describe the different possible thematic role distributions proper to that class.

From a different perspective, we also consider that a subset of the semantic primitives we have identified are those used in the LCS, which we use in a slightly simplified way, since we do not consider for our application its deepest refinements. The efficient use of LCS for practical applications has been shown in a number of works, including [5].

The novelty of our approach with respect to knowledge extraction can be summarized as follows:

(1) We have defined *three levels of knowledge representation* (pragmatic, linguistic and conceptual), which are *homogeneous*, expressed within a *single, incremental formalism*, incremental in the sense that (i) knowledge extracted at an outer level is refined at a deeper one, and (ii) the representations support *partial information*.

(2) We have defined simple *methods for extracting relevant terms* in texts, using a thesaurus.

(3) We show that the syntactic alternations given in Levin's work complement the basic syntactic forms generated from thematic roles, by refering to general grammatical principles. These semantic classes of verbs form *a very powerful tool for assigning correctly thematic roles* to predicate argument in a large number of syntactic forms.

(4) We are demonstrating that this approach can be implemented in an efficient way in spite of the complexity of lexical semantic knowledge. We also show that it requires lexical data which can be represented in a very economical way (saving thus a lot of time on lexical descriptions), and that this approach can be applied to large sets of texts.

4. The linguistic level

The input of this level is the set of fragments of texts extracted by the pragmatic level and labelled by an articulation name. We now want to represent information contained in these fragments by means of predicate-argument structures [8]. We will also consider predicate modifiers related to notions such as manner, instrument, and localization because they convey a significant portion of meaning. In this approach, there is a trade-off to settle between the quality of the extracted knowledge on the one hand and the linguistic description complexity on the other hand.

4.1 Identification of predicative terms

Predicative terms characterize states or actions. Verbs and prepositions are considered to be predicative terms. Nouns are slightly more difficult to treat. Nouns identified as heads of constructions with complements play the role of predicative terms. In this class we have nouns modified by noun complements which do not express possession (e.g. 'analysis' (in: 'analysis of the problem'), 'attempt', 'arrival') and those modified by small clauses. These nouns are often verb nominalizations, but we do not have any systematic way to detect them. We will not consider here adverbs and only a few important adjectives will be treated.

4.2 Identification of relevant predicates and arguments

The second aspect of the linguistic level is the identification of predicates and related arguments which are sufficiently relevant to be extracted. The degree of relevance of a term can be defined according to several criteria:

(1) *genericity*,

(2) *specialization*,

(3) *local importance*, where importance in a text is explicitly marked

Generic terms are identified by a global, manual analysis of texts, enriched by quasi-synonym terms obtained from a thesaurus. They form a finite set of terms, relatively small, which is stable and not updated. Specialized terms are obtained from the EDF thesaurus of electricity terms by extracting the most specialized terms, i.e. those which are at the lower levels in the hierarchies. From that point of view, proper nouns are often relevant terms. Notice that we do not consider *a priori* as relevant terms which appear frequently in texts: their meaning may indeed be empty.

4.3 Marking predicate arguments and predicate modifiers by means of thematic roles

The relationship between a predicate and one of its arguments can be represented by a thematic role. Thematic roles do confer a much stronger meaning to predicate structures, in particular when, as in our case, thematic roles have a relatively precise meaning.

Thematic roles can be defined in a more refined way than the usual definitions. From that perspective, our claim is that thematic roles can form the basis of a good and stable general descriptive semantics of predicate-argument relationships. Thematic roles have then a *conceptual dimension*, and not only a linguistic one. However, they must not be confused with the conceptual labels of the LCS. Thematic roles must remain general; they form a bridge between conceptual representations and syntax. They can be defined by means of clusters of properties organized in type hierarchies [6, 7].

We consider here an extended use of thematic roles assignment since roles are also assigned to predicate modifiers realized as prepositional phrases or as propositions in order to represent in a more explicit and uniform way essential arguments and modifiers, since they both play *a priori* an important role in the semantics of a proposition. Finally, we associate thematic roles with criteria that explain how these roles are realized in the syntax [14]. For that purpose, we introduce three main criteria:

(1) the semantic class of the predicative term; we consider here the semantic classes of verbs described in [13], which allow us to treat a large variety of syntactic forms, called alternations. Verbs of a given class have almost identical thematic distributions which are predictable from their semantics.

(2) the semantic type of the preposition, if any, which introduces the argument. The

semantic of prepositions allows us to restrict the number of possible thematic roles.
(3) the general semantic type of the head noun of the argument NP.

The general form of a semantic representation at this level introduces two functions for thematic roles:

(1) *an argument typing function*:
    predicate_name(..., role$_i$: {arg$_l$ }, ...)

(2) *a predicate modifier typing function*, where a predicate is marked by a thematic role:
    role$_j$: predicate_name(..., role$_k$: {arg$_k$ }, ...)   if the modifier is a predicate. The arg$_i$ are fragments of texts (NPs and PPs), which may be further analyzed in a similar way, if necessary. For example, a sentence such as:
    'John got injured by changing a wheel'   is represented by:
    injured(theme : {john}) ∧ causal theme : change(_ , theme : {wheel})).

If in an articulation, we only extract an NP, it is represented as an argument as follows:
    arg({ fragment of text corresponding to the NP }).
and no thematic role is assigned to it.

The result of the parse of our sample text is the following:
    [**articulation_name**, [extracted text from pragmatic level], partial predicate-arg representation]
The sample text given in section 2 is the represented as follows:
[[**theme** [les mesures destructives (ou assimilables)]
    arg: {mesures destructives}] ,
[**motivations** [optimiser les campagnes de mesure pour mieux connaitre, voire ameliorer, les incertitudes de mesure, et, lorsque cela est possible, reduire les coûts induits.]
    optimise(_ , Incremental beneficiary theme: {campagnes de mesure}) ∧
        goal: (analyze(_ , holistic theme: {incertitudes de mesure}) ∧
            reduce(_ , incremental victim theme:{coûts}))] ,
[**problems**   [[posent toujours des problemes concernant le faible nombre de donnees disponibles ou encore leur coût qui s'associe generalement à la necessité d'une bonne precision.] [problèmes sont d'autant plus difficiles à traiter que les parametres en jeu ont des comportements non-lineaires.]
    arg: ({faible nombre de données}, {coût}, {comportements non-linéaires})] ,
[**realizations** [étudier les méthodes permettant de prendre en compte cette non-linéarite.]
    study(_, general theme: {methods})]].

5. Representation of lexical semantics knowledge

We consider two levels of lexical semantics information: basic data, which are viewed as primitive, and complex data, formed out from the basic ones. Let us first present the basic data and the way they are organized.

Basic data include thematic roles, semantic hierarchies of prepositions, selectional restrictions and the semantic verb classes, as defined in [13].

Thematic roles are organized by means of hierarchies, leaves denote basic thematic concepts. Here are the hierarchies for agent and theme.

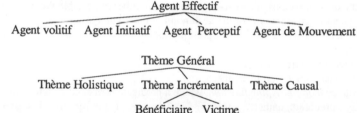

Agent Effectif

Agent volitif   Agent Initiatif   Agent Perceptif   Agent de Mouvement

Thème Général

Thème Holistique   Thème Incrémental   Thème Causal

Bénéficiaire   Victime

In the agent hierarchy, we distinguish agents initiating the action from those realizing, or doing the action via perception or movement. Among themes, we distinguish holistic themes where the theme (or object or patient) is not affected by the action, from incremental themes, which are affected by the action, positively (beneficiare) or negatively (victime). From thematic roles, we can defined thematic grids which describe the different possible thematic role assignments for a predicate. A thematic grid is a list of thematic roles which must all be assigned to different arguments of the predicate.

We have the same type of hierarchy form semantic classes of prepositions. Here are some samples:

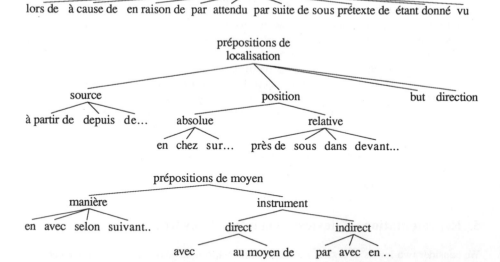

prépositions de cause

lors de   à cause de   en raison de   par   attendu   par suite de   sous prétexte de   étant donné   vu

prépositions de localisation

source   position   but   direction

à partir de   depuis   de...   absolue   relative

en   chez   sur...   près de   sous   dans   devant...

prépositions de moyen

manière   instrument

en   avec   selon   suivant..   direct   indirect

avec   au moyen de   par   avec   en ..

Leaves represent prepositions. These prepositions are directly related, semantically speaking to selectional restrictions. Selectional restrictions are directly based on the semantic fields definded in the thesaurus, to which we have added a few general types such as human, animate or technical_term.

We have then defined semantic verb classes. Verbs in a class all have the same syntactic behavior, and they have strong similarities in meaning. This allows us to associate with every verb class a set of thematic grids and a semantic representation. Here is a sample of these classes with thematic grids:

characterize verbs

arity 2: définir, déterminer, établir, étudier, organiser, détailler, préciser.

thematic grid [ae, th].

arity 3: identifier (par), spécifier (par), utiliser (pour).

thematic grids: [ae, th, mo], [ae, mo, but].

creation and transformation verbs

arity 2: procéder (à), simuler, effectuer, agir (sur), appliquer (à), compléter, développer, élaborer, concrétiser, produire,réaliser, travailler.

thematic grids: [ae, th], [ae, tib], [tg, tib].

arity 3: travailler (avec), construire

thematic grids: [ae, th], [ae, tib], [tg, tib].

with the following notations: ae: effective agent,   av: volitive agent,

tg: general theme,   th: holistic theme,   tc: causal theme

tib: incremental theme beneficiary,   tiv: incremental theme victim,

mo: means,   src: source,   pos: position, but: goal,   dir: direction.

Finally, here is a sample of the linguistic data which implement the thematic role assignemnt rules. they are based on the previous data presented here. Let us consider the agent role and its subclasses:

Effective Agent

verb classes: characterize, creation and transfo., continue, service, transfer of possession, searching, attaching, improve, forwarding, position, moving, etc.

semantic type of argument : human

examples: définir, représenter, créer, réaliser,continuer, poursuivre, aider, collaborer, donner, échanger, rechercher, résoudre, attacher, chaîner, améliorer, faciliter, diffuser, promouvoir, rester, mettre (sur), aller, venir, partir, etc.

Volitive agent

verb classes: volition, obligation

semantic type of argument: human

examples : vouloir, désirer, devoir, obliger, nécessiter.

Initiative agent

verb classes: allowing, decision

semantic type of argument: human or technical

examples: favoriser, permettre, conduire, décider, diriger, mener.

etc.

Conclusion

This document has summarized our approach to knowledge extraction from texts and the way lexical semantics knowledge is organized. We have shown how three levels of representation can be identified, which correspond to different levels of granularity in the extracted knowledge: pragmatic, linguistic and conceptual. These three levels form an

352

homogeneous representation, which is elaborated upon in an incremental way. A great care has also been devoted to limiting the amount of specific lexical knowledge needed for an application: the elaboration of general knowledge has been given priority in order to guarantee a better updating and re-usability of our methods and data, this is particularly the case for the lexicon. Our work can indeed be used for other types of texts having a quite similar external form. The two first levels are now implemented in Prolog using methods given in [15].

Acknowledgements
We are very grateful to Marie-Luce Herviou and Palmira Marrafa for discussions on this project. We also thank Martha Palmer and Bonnie Dorr for several discussions and for introducing us to B. Levin's work. This project is funded by the DER of EDF that we thank.

References

1. Baker, M. C., *Incorporation, A Theory of Grammatical Function Changing*, Chicago University Press, 1988.
2. Blosseville MJ, Hebrail G, Monteil MG, Penot N, *Automatic Document Classification: Natural Language Processing, Statistical Analysis and Expert System Used Together*, in proc. ACM SIGIR, Copenhaguen, June 1992.
3. Cruse, A., *Lexical Semantics*, Cambridge University Press, 1986.
4. Daubèze, S., *Mutations et classifications sémantiques de verbes du français*, research report IRIT, May 1994.
5. Dorr, B., *Machine Translation: a View from the Lexicon*, MIT Press, 1993.
6. Dowty, D., *On the Semantic Content of the Notion of Thematic Role*, in Properties, Types and Meaning, G. Cherchia, B. Partee, R. Turner (Edts), Kluwer Academic Press, 1989.
7. Dowty, D., *Thematic Proto-roles and Argument Selection,* Language, vol. 67-3, 1991.
8. Grimshaw, J., *Argument Structure*, MIT Press, 1990.
9. Jackendoff, R., *The Status of Thematic Relations in Linguistic Theory,* Linguistic Inquiry 18, pp. 369-411, 1987.
10. Jackendoff, R., *Conciousness and the Computational Mind,* MIT Press, 1987.
11. Jackendoff, R., *Semantic Structures*, MIT Press, 1990.
12. Katz, J. J., Fodor, J. A., *The Structure of a Semantic Theory*, in Language, issue 39, pp. 170-210, 1963.
13. Levin, B., *English Verb Classes and Alternations*, the University of Chicago Press, 1993.
14. Pugeault, F., Saint-Dizier, P., Monteil, M.G., *Knowledge extraction from texts: a method for extracting predicate-argument structures from texts*, in proceedings of Coling'94, Kyoto, 1994.
15. Saint-Dizier, P., *Advanced logic programming for language processing*, Academic Press, 1994.

THE BASIC PRINCIPLES OF A LOGICAL FRAME FOR
TIME MODELING IN NATURAL LANGUAGE

Paul AMBLARD

Department of Computer Science, University of Grenoble, LGI-IMAG BP 53X
F 38041 GRENOBLE Cedex 9 FRANCE

and

Edmundo PALACIOS

Department of Computer Science, University of Grenoble, LGI-IMAG BP 53X
F 38041 GRENOBLE Cedex 9 FRANCE

ABSTRACT

Our goal is to build a logical frame allowing the description of the timed meaning of a text, as a part of general natural language understanding. Two descriptions could be given by two different persons (or two different systems) and automatically checked for consistency between these two descriptions or for "internal" soudness of one of them. Our future system aims to allow verification of "good" understanding of temporal texts (education, specification, verification of translations,...)

This paper is a first presentation of the basic ideas supporting this frame, mainly a three scaled time. We intend *physical time, subjective time and narrative time* to be the basis of this frame. A second original point is the existence of different types of intervals to support linguistic features such as perfectivity and imperfectivity. The model then allows to deal with tense and aspect.

1. Introduction

Time is a component of general semantics of natural language. Any utterance contains references to time. A grammar showing the correspondences between form and substance must deal with expression of time. This remark applies to any kind of grammar, formal or not.

The field of modeling time in natural language has seen a lot of works. This field has mainly been investigated, with different goals, by linguists, logicians and computer scientists dealing with natural language processing or action representation.

1.1. Linguists' point of view

Linguists have analysed timed situation description either for one language, sometimes with a deep accuracy, or, more generally, by looking for a universal grammar of this timed part of Universal Grammar. Examples of analysis of the Bulgarian language system are [Gue90] [Lin85]. These works are often concentrated on tense and aspect expressed in verbs and adverbs.

Some works show an analysis of interaction between two sub-systems of the language : the tense/aspect system and, for instance, the system of topicality, discourse analysis, or definiteness [Kab84]. In the later, the author analyses the tense/aspect system of Bulgarian, compared to other Slavonic languages. He links the preservation of the aorist/imperfect distinction to the existence of an article in this language.

Several scholars have also studied relations between semantics and pragmatics of aspect (Meaning of one sentence or meaning of a sequence of sentences). Forsyth [For70 p 9-10] gives the role of the opposition perfective/imperfective in narrative sequences of sentences. This leads to analyse the meaning expressed by tense and aspect differently in isolated simple sentences, isolated complex when-sentences and in texts. The compositionality of meaning from a lower to a higher level is not yet fully established.

Works can be distinguished according to the purposes of the authors to be more or less formal in the grammar rules they give.

1.2. Logicians' point of view

Temporal logic deals with time, considered as a modality. Different works integrating time in logic are known. They are presented mainly in [ReU71]

The instanciation of this general idea for "natural" language appears in [Rei47]. Its main novelty was to introduce a "reference" time R as an intermediate object between physical time (event time E) and speech time S.

The model supporting the logic may be based on different "objects" either instants or intervals. The sets of instants (or intervals) can be organised by different algebraical or topological structures. This gives the temporal logic different deduction rules. The links between the model and the deduction rules are given by Kripke interpretation. The models give the logic more or less convenience to deal with temporality as it is expressed in natural language.

Some modal logics deal with parts of semantics such as "believe", "want", existence of agents... This is related to the so-called "modes" of natural language. But the exact boundary between mode and tense is very difficult to define from a linguistic point of view. The future is sometimes considered as a mode. We must avoid to map simply natural language modes to logic modalities. Galton [Gal87] gives three modal operators (perfect, progressive and prospective) in this field. They are part of his "logic of occurence".

1.3. Computational linguists' point of view

In formal description of general semantics, the timed part has often appeared to be the most easy (the least difficult !) component. Some rules can be given as the basics of automated Natural Language Understanding.

"(referring to an action not yet occurred) <=> (there is a future tense)"
"(describing the length of the action) <=> (there is a "time-length" adverb)"

This kind of rules seems to be programming rules. Computer scientists have tried to manage them from the beginning of artificial intelligence. [Bru72] and [FiC71] are examples of such pioneering works aiming to model the timed semantics of a text.

The problem of managing the aforementioned interaction between different sub-problems is a criterion to distinguish different computerised models. Discourse Representation Theory [Kam88] has been proposed to deal with discourse structure, pronominal anaphors and time. The model distinguishes events (instants) and situations (intervals). An implementation of a program dealing with the timed meaning of a text, SCARTT, is based on the model of DRT. [AsB92]
Other approaches are based on demonstrators in different logics. Hasle, [Has91], for example maps a temporal logic into Higher Order Logic to use the theorem demonstrator H.O.L.
A common lack of different tools is that aspectuality is not yet fully taken into account.

2. The proposed frame

The goal of this paper is to present basic ideas of a temporal logic to deal with aspectuality in sentences and in texts. Focus is put on the three times scales in section 2.1, their relations being investigated in 2.2. Section 2.3 contains two examples.

Our attempt is based on three simple basic ideas : the first idea is to use three scales of time, the second one, which is very common in this field, is to use a graphical description, at least in a first step. This description must then be translated into a formula. The third idea is to introduce different kinds of intervals, they correspond to perfective or imperfective expressions.
We present here the objects in a model for the temporal logic, not the syntax of the logic itself.

2.1. What about three times?

The first one is the physical time, the second one the subjective time, the third one the narrative time.

Physical time is the time of the events. It is fully ordered, dense. We do not refer to its begin or its end. It is generally described by the set R of real numbers. Bull [Bul60] gives a deep description of its properties. It allows to model the "true" world situations.

Narrative time is the time of the utterance, the discourse, the "text". Each "sentence" corresponds to a clock tick. This time is fully ordered, discrete. It has a beginning. We generally assume that it has an end. It can be described by (a part of) the set N of natural numbers. It allows to model "texts" as sequences of sentences.

The **subjective** time is the most complex one. It is related to "what the speakers wants to say". It correspond to Bull's "events inside man". It is partially ordered. Its elements are of different kinds. At least we use instants and intervals. We want it to have *"opaque"* and *"translucid"* intervals. The idea being that opaque intervals may not include any other interval, while translucid ones does. Translucid intervals are minimal for the inclusion relation. We are currently working on the formal definition and properties of modalities of a temporal logic to deal with this difference of intervals. In our figures, instants are represented by black boxes, intervals by rectangles, the brackets [ ] are for opaque intervals, the brackets] [for translucid intervals.

The subjective time may have some reference points (or intervals) strongly inspired by Reichenbach. Reference points are necessary to deal with backward references such as "It *had* occured". Many models have maintained this part of Reichenbach model. [Bru72] manages reference points and (at most 2) reference intervals.

2.2. Relations between the three times.

There is a "NOW" common to the three time scales. On the physical time, "now" is an instant. On the narrative one, "now" is generally the current sentence. In some special cases it may be a bigger unit, such as the full text itself. The subjective "now" could be given by the context of utterance. Some kinds of texts do not have a subjective "now". This occurs when the speakers does not involves him or herself in the text.

The full description of the different rules linking meaning and expression has to be made for each natural language. This task has already been done in a great number of publications by different scholars. Guentcheva, for example, dealt with Bulgarian, Bull with Spanish...

Our work may be described in three questions :
* what is "consistency" or soundness inside the subjective time ?
* what are the relations between the subjective time and the narrative time ?
* what are the relations between subjective time and physical time. ?

The relations between physical time and subjective time are established by composing two choices of the speaker. A first choice is the choice of "words" (atoms of meaning, member of an infinite lexical list). At this level the aktionsart, telicity,... are partially established. A second choice is the choice of "morphemes" (atoms of meaning, members of a finite grammatical list). At this level tense, mode and aspect are established.

The relation between subjective time and narrative time is currently a hot topic. It is a part of the general "Discourse Theory".[Kam88]. Some basic principles appear in [For70]

Compositionality of these relations with the information introduced by adverbs is not considered here. An interesting point of view is proposed by Anderson [And73, p41] The author considers the time of a "text" to be given only by the adverbs. He argues for the tense of the verb to be only a "concord" phenomenon.
The model presented here does not have special features to deal with complex sentences with, for example a "when" word connecting two "simple" clauses.

2.3. Examples.

Two detailed examples will made clearer the relations between these three times.

Example 1) Difference between perfective and imperfective
Comrie [Com76 p16] gives the difference of semantics between perfective and imperfective sentences referring to the fact that the speaker "sees the event" in a given way or not :
"Perfectivity indicates the view of a situation as a single whole, without distinction of the various separate phases that make up that situation; while imperfectivity pays essential attention to the internal structure to the situation."
We interpret this difference as a phenomenon of *subjective* time.

It represents a small "history" containing 3 sentences in Bulgarian. The first one is from [Lin85, p163]

(b1) kompozitorăt pišeše nova simfonija.
    The composer was writing a new symphony

(b2) kompozitorăt pisa pesen [i izleze (perfective aorist)]
The composer wrote a song [and went out.]
(b3) kompozitorăt šte napiše nova pesen.
The composer will write a new song
It is represented by Figure 1.

In sentence b1 we do not know if the situation had a beginning and an end. Perhaps it was not completed. Some events may occur while the situation is remaining. This is a full imperfective past. In Bulgarian, it is rendered by the imperfective imperfect: pišeše (We enforce here the imperfectivity by having the composer to work on a symphony instead of a song !). We translate it by an opaque interval.

Sentence b2 uses the Bulgarian imperfective aorist. This form is noted in [Gue90, p108] as occurring only in texts with a loose relation between the subjective "now" and the narrative "now" (our interpretation of the "registre du non-actualisé"). b2 refers to a past situation fully accomplished. The speakers wants to see it as having an internal part. It is also suggested by the drawing that the situation was completed. The completeness is enforced by the fact that another (perfective) process is described in the same sentence. It is a kind of intermediate between full perfective and full imperfective.

Sentence b3 contains a reference to a durative situation, not yet happening. The speaker puts focus on the fact that it is in the future, and wants to see it in a perfective way. These conditions lead to a perfective future. The interval representing the process has no internal structure in subjective time.
(The fact that the situation will "soon" occur could be taken into account by an inchoative form. We are not concerned here with this point which needs a metric on time)

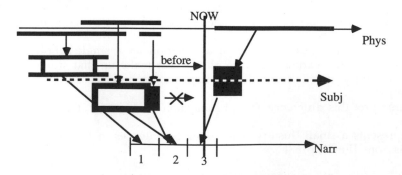

Figure 1 : Illustration of text < b1 b2 b3 >

Example 2) Relations between consecutive sentences.

The second example, inspired from [Ebe92] has the two kinds of units. We model them by opaque or translucid intervals. Eberle introduces relations between two consecutive items of discourse. An example, in English, of such a text could be given by the following one.

(e1) John decided to go to Paris.

(e2) He took his car.

(e3) It was raining.

(e4) He was tired.

(e5) He arrived in Paris late in the morning.

In this example item 2 is a "continuation" of item 1, item 3 and 4 are a "background" for item 2. Item 5, a continuation of item 2, stops the background introduced by item 3. This is represented by figure 2.

We observe here a relation, in the model, between a Bulgarian perfective aorist and an English non-progressive past, on one side, and, on the other side between a Bulgarian imperfective imperfect and an English progressive past.. We could probably add in the two categories the French passé simple and imparfait which are often quoted by Kamp.

Up to which point this comparison is valid is a question for linguists.

Eberle gives the rules of correspondence between

• on one side the kind of relation between two consecutive sentences (background, continuation), and,

• on the other side the tense, aspect and stativity of the two consecutive verbs.

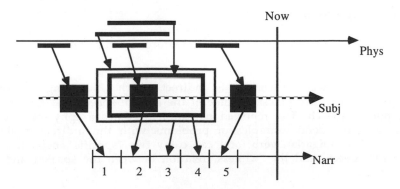

Figure 2 : Illustration of text <e1 e2 e3 e4 e5 >

It is possible to use the same graphical model to make clear the diversity of point of view between different researchers' approaches.

The attempt to translate some models with this kind of graphics shows that in some cases, there is only one "tick" of narrative clock. This occurs in attempts to model isolated sentences instead of texts.

The total /vs./ partial ordering of the subjective time appears also clearly. The theoretical framework used in [Gue90] is related to the existence or non existence of a "NOW" in the subjective time and to the more or less strong relations between the subjective now and the narrative now.

The approach of Kamp (the part devoted to time) is covered by the model. Kamp has two types of units in the subjective time : states and events.

2.4. What to do with the pictures ?

A picture, built from well established basic blocks, with well established rules, is equivalent to a formula A in the aimed temporal logic. The translation is easy to automatise at least from the drawing to the formula.

A more complex task is to code a text by a formula B. This task should be done by hand.

A typical use of this approach would be to ask a teacher of a foreign language to code texts, and to students to draw the history.

The establishment of comparison between formulas A and B will be our first implementation job. Two ways are considered : the use of a "standard" modal logic demonstrator, or the writing of a new theorem prover, dedicated to our logic.

3. Remaining problems

Our work is currently to investigate which features could be taken into account in a prototype.

The first one we want to work on is "indirect speech". A starting point is to consider two narrative times: the time of the current speech and the time of the reported speech. The reported narration becomes a "physical" event. Bulgarian gives good examples of problems with the indirect mode of narration. The Bulgarian verb form can carry two "specific" meanings: the "reported" speech, and the "witness" relation between the speaker and the reported fact.

A second point is related to the "lexical" meaning of the verb. Researchers working to build computerised dictionaries try to give an acute description of the "types" of verbs (activities, achievements, accomplishments or states). The word "Aktionsart" is often used to refer to this classification feature. One of the problems in automated extraction of Aktionsart from a text is that in some languages the difference is not given by the lexem of the verb but by the case of the "object" nominal phrase.

Estonian : (in the translation N,G,P mean nominative, genitive, partitive respectively, pikk, pika and pıkka, being the same adjective with the three cases)
üks   pikk   poiss   kirjutab ühe   pika   kirja
a(+N) tall(+N) boy(+N) writes a(+G) long(+G) letter(+G)
a tall boy writes a long letter . (The letter will be finished.)

üks   pikk   poiss   kirjutab üht   pikka   kirja
a(+N) tall(+N) boy(+N) writes a(+P) long(+P) letter(+P)
a tall boy writes a long letter . (We do not know if the letter will be finished.)

The "place" where this kind of information has to be written is difficult to establish : Must we have a dictionary with "kirjutama + G = to completely write; kirjutama + P = to write" ? Certainly not, because the same system is true for a lot a verbs. But not all. In Estonian, "aktionsart" is partly lexical (different kinds of verbs), partly syntactical (constraints exist), partly semantic (the speaker can choose) [Tau73]

The afore-presented frame could deal with different languages. The "availability" of some constructs in some language, and not in others, does not appear in our model. Some linguists use an approach where the meaning is not only in the elements "words, tense, cases" but, also, in the rule of choice amongst a set of available things. This structuralist approachis not present in our work.

4. Conclusion

This paper has shown an attempt to define a frame to deal with semantics of time in natural languages. The main new point is to establish a three tiers scale of time. The strong concentration of features on the "subjective time" makes this intermediate step very interesting.

5. Acknowledgements

The authors thank Märt PAIS, Petko VALTCHEV and anonymous referees for helpful comments.

6. References

[And73] : J. Anderson : *An essay concerning aspect*, Ed. Mouton, The Hague, 1973.

[AsB92] : N. Asher, M. Bras : *The temporal structure of french texts within segmented Discourse Representation Theory*, 4th Intl. Workshop "Semantics of time, space and Movement", Bonas, 4-8 september 1992, pp 203-217.

[Bru72] : B.C. Bruce : *A model for temporal references and its application in a question answering program.* Artificial intelligence, **vol 3**, N°1, 1972, pp 1-25.

[Bul60] : W.E. Bull : *Time, tense and the verb. A study in theoretical and applied linguistics, with particular attention to spanish.* Univ. of California, Publications in linguistics, **Vol. 19**, 1960.

[Com76] : B. Comrie : *Aspect*, Cambridge University Press, 1976.

[Ebe92] : K. Eberle : *Representing the temporal structure of a natural language text*, 15th Intl. conf. on computational linguistics, COLING 92, Nantes, 23-28 August 1992, pp 288-294.

[FiC71] : N . Findler, D. Chen : *On the problems of time, retrieval of temporal relations, causality and co-existence*, 2nd Intl. Joint Conf. on Artificial Intelligence, London, 1-3 september 1971, pp 531-545.

[For70] : J. Forsyth : *A grammar of aspect. Usage and meaning of the russian verb.* Cambridge University Press, 1970.

[Gal87] : A. Galton (ed) : *Temporal logics and their applications.* Academic Press, London, 1987.

[Gue90] : Z. Guentcheva : *Temps et aspect : l'exemple du bulgare contemporain*, Ed. CNRS, Paris, 1990.

[Has91] : P. Hasle : *Building a temporal logic for natural language understanding with the HOL-system*, 3rd Intl. Workshop on Natural Language Understanding and Logic Programming, Stockholm, 23-25 january 1991, pp 91-109.

[Kab84] : K. Kabakčiev : *The article and the aorist/imperfect distinction in Bulgarian : an analysis based on cross-language 'aspects' parallelisms.* Linguistica **22** (1984), pp 643-672.

[Kam88] : H. Kamp : *Discourse Representation Theory : What it is and where it ought to go?* Natural language at the computer, Heidelberg, February 25, 1988. Lecture Notes in Computer Science **N° 320**, Springer Verlag, pp 84-111.

[Lin85] : J. Lindstedt : *On the semantic of tense and aspect in Bulgarian.* Dissertation, Helsinki, 1985.

[Rei47]: H. Reichenbach : *Elements of symbolic logic*, (1st ed: MacMillan 1947), Ed The free press, New York, 1966.

[ReU71] : N. Rescher, A. Urquhart : *Temporal logic*, Springer Verlag, Wien, 1971.

[Tau73] V. Tauli : *Standard estonian grammar*, Uppsala, 1973-1983.

WHAT DO WE MEAN WHEN WE SAY TO THE LEFT OR TO THE RIGHT?
How to learn about space by building and exploring a microworld

Xavier BRIFFAULT & Michael ZOCK

LIMSI, Langage & Cognition, B.P. 133, 91403 Orsay Cedex / France
[briffault I zock] @limsi.fr

Abstract: The goal of this paper is to present the extension of a tutoring system in which the student learns to produce sentences in a foreign language (French, Arab, Russian). The extension deals with space. The user provides the conceptual input (he builds a scene) and the system produces the corresponding output (sentence). The rules for spatial expressions are meant to be learnt on the basis of correlations between input and output, that is, by varying the *nature*, the *position* and the *roles* of the objects composing the scene, and by listening to the corresponding outputs, the student is meant to discover what parameters govern linguistic form.

Keywords: natural language generation, locative expressions, knowledge representation, multimodality, visualization of metalanguage, tutoring system

1 Goal and motivation of the work

The goal of this paper is to present the extension of SWIM, a tutoring system designed to help people to learn foreign languages (sentence generation).[1] This extension deals with space, more precisely, it deals with the problem of how to express spatial information.[2] More precisely, we will show what parameters have to be taken into account when trying to generate such forms.

The problem of generating locative expressions can be stated in either of the following two ways: (a) given a scene, how can we describe the relative position of its composing elements or, (b) given this very same scene, what parameters control the generation of a specific locative expression? Dealing with this issue were are confronted with two problems: a linguistic problem: how to express spatial meaning (the relationship of meaning and form), and an interface problem (ergonomy): how to provide the language learner with an adequate tool ? Since the student is meant to learn the rules on the basis of correlations between input (meaning, scene) and output, how is he meant to convey this input: by using an abstract language (metalanguage, case-frame) like linguists do, or by using icons that allow the re-creation of a natural scene? We shall present in this paper elements of an answer to both of these questions.

2 Why are spatial prepositions hard to learn?

As we all know, even advanced learners of English sometimes find it difficult to decide which preposition to use: should one say "*on* the knee", "*over* the knee", or "*above* the knee", or conversely "*under* the clouds", "*beneath* the clouds" or "*below* the clouds"? There are situations where all three prepositions are correct, the difference of usage hinging on meaning and communicative goals. However, there can also be situations, where only one of these words can be used (e.g. *beneath* instead of *under/below*)

That prepositions are a delicate problem has to do, among other things, with the fact that they can't be predicted solely on semantic grounds. While the physical scene is a given (invariable), it can still be interpreted in various ways. According to whether we perceive an object as a point, line, 2-dimensional or 3-dimensional space, different prepositions will be needed. Other reasons of

---

[1]   SWIM, acronyme of See What I Mean, is a tutoring system for people learning a foreign language. Its scope is sentence generation. One of its main features is the fact the student asks the questions, — for example: How does one say <idea>?— and the system answers them. In doing so he learns the rules of the language on the basis of correlations between input and output: different inputs (meanings) yield different outputs (black box). In the most recent version the student can see not only what happens at the extremes (final output), but also what happens in between (intermediate levels). In other words, SWIM is both a black box, and a glass box. For more details see [17, 18, 10]

[2]   For reasons of "space" (limitations) we will discuss here only a subset of locative expressions: *projective prepositions* (to the left, to the right, over, under, in front of, behind, etc.). Other kind of prepositions will be discussed elsewhere (paper in progress).

complexity are the fact that the parameters governing usage are highly abstract,[3] and the fact that prepositions are often polysemic. For example, Quirk et al. (1986: 685) provide 8 different variations of sense for the preposition *over*:

POSITION:	A lamp hung over the door.
DESTINATION:	They threw a blanket over her.
PASSAGE:	They climbed over the wall.
ORIENTATION:	They live over the road. [on the far side of]
RESULTATIVE:	At last we were over the crest of the hill.
PERVASIVE [STATIC]:	Leaves lay thick (all) over the ground.
PERVASIVE [MOTION]:	They splashed water (all) over me.
ACCOMPANYING CIRCUMSTANCES:	We discussed it over a glass of wine.

3 Language and perception

Space and time are the major reference points for dealing with the complexities of the physical environment in which we live. As there are many ways of conceiving space, there are many ways to talk about it. We may refer to the *position*, relative *distance* or *dimension* of a static object. We may talk about the different positions of a moving object (starting point, path, destination), …

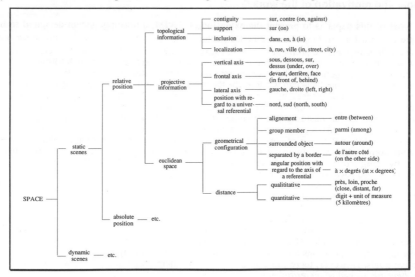

Table A

The ontology of space and their linguistic counterparts (resources) can be organized in the way described in table A here above.[4] These conceptualizations mediate between spatial configurations of percepts and language, that is, they describe states of the world at a given point in time (state) or over a stretch of time (event). While there are many ways to express spatial information (nouns,

---

3   How difficult it is for children to learn the relevant parameters has been demonstrated by Piaget [12]. He showed this in his *conservation tasks*, where children were asked to say whether or not the amount of water in two mugs was the same, or whether or not the amount of clay in two rope-like forms was the same. Young children attended to the *height*, yet ignored the *width* in the case of the water mugs , and they paid attention to the *length*, ignoring the *width* in the case of the clay ropes. Children also have problems with projective prepositions (confusing left with right, back to front, etc.) as they have difficulties in adopting another point of view (referential) than their own.

4   Please note, that many concepts can be expressed by various syntactic categories (nouns, verbs, adjectives, adverbes, prepositions). Our ontology is not definitive and shows only prototypical mappings.

verbs, adjective, adverbs, prepositional phrases), prepositions are by far the most frequently used means.

4 Spatial prepositions have only recently received serious consideration

Prepositions have been analyzed from various perspectives: *linguistics* [3, 5, 9, 16] *psychology* [11, 12], *artificial intelligence* [1, 2, 6, 7, 14, 15]. Most of the earlier work has strengthened the belief, that prepositions are easily understood. Let's take a look at the analysis of Quirk et al. [13]. According to these authors, the choice of a preposition depends on two factors (Fig.1): the way how the place is perceived [point, line, surface] and the type of process, or direction of the action [towards, away, touch, cross, parallel].

Though the representation is attractive from an ergonomic point of view, the underlying analysis is far from complete. It is underconstrained, thus allowing the production of incorrect forms, or not allowing the generation of an existing form.

Quirk's et al's analysis of locative prepositions is founded on geometric criteria. However, as Aurnague (1990) and Briffault (1991) have shown, these criteria are by no means sufficient, physical and functional criteria are also needed. Aurnague (1990) analyzes locative prepositions in terms of *contact* , *relative position*, etc. while Briffault (1991) relies on primitives such as *object's comparability* and *stabilization* .

Place seen as point		1) He went to Paris.
		2) He stayed at home.
		3) He came (away) from the theatre.
		4) I stayed away from the village.
Place seen as line		5) The ball rolled on to the goal-line.
		6) We turned off the main road.
		7) Memphis is on the Mississippi.
		8) Zanzibar is off the coast of Africa.
		9) They walked along the river bank.
		10) They drove across the border.
Place seen as surface		11) He fell onto the ground.
		12) He took the picture off the wall.
		13) There's a label on the bottle.
		14) That's a place off the map.
		15) We walked across the fields.
		16) He looked through the window.
Place seen as area		17) They crowded into the streets.
		18) We have a house in the city.
		19) He stayed out of the country.
		20) He flew out of the country.
		21) We went through the park.
Place seen as volume		22) The food is in the kitchen.
		23) I took the fruits out of the fridge.
		24) He ran into the house.
		25) He climbed out of the water.
		26) The wind blew throught the trees.

Fig. 1: locative prepositions

5 Projective prepositions

We will now present our analysis and model for a subclass of locative expressions in French (projective prepositions). *Projective prepositions* provide information concerning the relative or absolute position of a given object in a scene. The generation of such prepositions requires three kinds of information: choice of the located object (LO), choice of the object with regard to which the LO will be situated, i.e. the reference object (RO), and choice of a referential (REF), that is, choice of an object whose intrinsic axis provides a viewpoint.

> John is to my right.   (*LO* = John, *RO* = speaker, *REF* = speaker)
> John is to the left of Marvin.   (*LO* = John, *RO* = Marvin, *REF* = speaker)

In order to generate the preposition that expresses properly the spatial relation we have in mind, the following four problems have to be solved: (1) determination of the objects' intrinsic axis (problem 1); determination of the associations between a set of prepositions and the referential's intrinsic axis (problem 2)[5] ; choice of the preposition that fits well the purpose and describes best the situation or scene (problem 3); choice of the object serving as referential (problem 4). Only the first two problems will be discussed in this paper.

5.1 Determination of the objects' intrinsic axis (problem 1)

According to whether we are dealing with one-, two- or three-dimensional space we will need two, four, or six axes to locate another object (for examples see figure 2).

---

5   As we shall see, the association, hence the possible prepositions, may vary with the position of the referential.

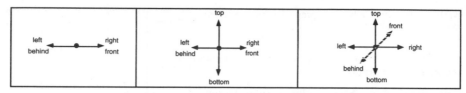

Fig.2 Reference for *one-, two* and *three dimensional space*

Herskowitz (1986), Vandeloise (1986) and Briffault (1992) have shown that the computation of the referentials' intrinsic axis requires the consideration of at least one of the following parameters: (a) *general orientation*, (b) *line of sight* (direction of the eyes), (c) *direction of movement*, (d) *similarity* with an object that has a clearly specified intrinsic referential (analogy "statue-human body").

Any object having an intrinsic axis can serve as referential. However, if different objects have different intrinsic referentials it is important to know how this intrinsic referential is determined. Briffault (1992) has built a taxonomy on the basis of the determination of the objects' intrinsic axis. Due to space limitations we will not present the results for all classified objects (leaves of the taxonomic tree, fig.3).

We will only discuss this problem with regard to persons. However, in order to appreciate the complexity, consider the following cases. For some vehicles (space shuttles) *in front of/above* and their correlates *behind/below* tend to be confusing. For others, the determination of the preposition is context-dependent: the front/rear of a train are obvious under normal circumstances. If the train runs, the *front* coincides with the direction of the train's destination. If it stands still, the extremes are signalled by a white/red light. The situation starts to get complex when you are at a train station with two tracks (or, worse, just one). The determination of the train's intrinsic axis depends on the knowledge of its destination, which in turn may depend on the hour of the train, etc.

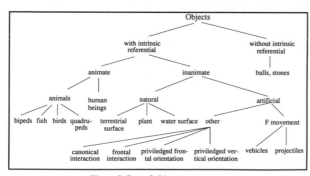

Figure 3: Part of object taxonomy

5.2 Determination of possible prepositions according to the referential's intrinsic axis (problem 2)

Prepositions may vary as a function of the referential and the referential's position (upright, horizontal, etc.). The semantics of a projective preposition depends on the projected position of the LO and the RO on the axis of the referential. For example, figure 4b can be described in various ways:

(a) LO1 is *behind* RO1

(b) LO2 is *in front of* RO1

(c) LO3 is *in front of* RO2

(d) LO4 is *behind* RO2.[6]

Note that the latter two cases are problematic in view of any simplistic definition of *in front of* and *behind*.

---

6   It would be also possible to talk about the objects *behind* or *in front of us* in terms of proximity: LO1 is *further away* than RO1 (instead of: LO1 is *behind* RO1), LO2 is is *closer* than RO1 (instead of: LO2 is *in front of* RO1).

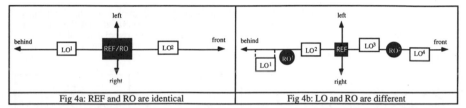

Fig 4a: REF and RO are identical	Fig 4b: LO and RO are different

By analyzing the examples given above we can see certain regularities concerning the use of *in front of /behind*: compare "b/c" for *in front of* , with "a/d" for *behind* . These regularities can be captured by a set of rules. The same kind of rules apply for all projective prepositions.

Rules for *<in front of/behind >*[7]

R1 & R2: The LO is {in front of/behind} the RO if the projection of the LO on the semi-axis in front /behind of the REF is {closer to /further away off} the projection of the REF than the projection of the RO.

figure 5a

There's a bird above me

Rules for <above/below> and <over/under>

We distinguish between two cases : (a) The LO and the RO do not touch and are not even close to each other (fig.5a, R3 & R4); (b) the two objects either touch each other, or are very close (fig. 5b - R5 & R6)

R3 & R4: The LO is said to be {above/below} the RO if the projection of the LO on the line of gravity is closer to the pole {high/low} than the projection of the RO.

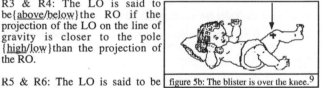

figure 5b: The blister is over the knee.[9]

R5 & R6: The LO is said to be {over/under} the RO if the projection of the LO on the canonic,[8] intrinsic, vertical axis of the REF is closer to the pole {high/low} than the projection of the RO.

These rules apply only for referentials in their canonical (usual) position. Put differently, prepositions may vary with the referential's position (horizontal, vertical, etc.). In the examples here below (Fig. 6) the LO serves also as REF, otherwise it would be hard to draw conclusions.

As one can see, the axes associated with the projective prepositions vary according to the position of the referential (compare fig 6a, 6c, 6d). Nevertheless, there are certain regularities: (6a) The vertical axis of gravity keeps its status of absolute reference, regardless of the position of the LO; (6b) *Left* and *right* are always associated with the front of either the REF or RO; (6c) The axes associated with the prepositions *in front of/behind* change according to the position of the referential (compare 6a, 6b, 6c).

These changes can be explained by physical (gravity) and anatomical laws (front side of body). Whenever the referential's intrinsic vertical axis (for humans, this is the line from head to feet) coincides with the axis of gravity there is no problem (figure 6a). If it does not coincide, that is, if

---

[7] Please note that this set of rules is incomplete: the rules are simplified for illustrative purposes. In particular, the problem of acceptability is not discussed here.

[8] *Canonic axis* here means "normal position". This feature is important, because, given the child's actual position, the blister is "under/below" his knee. Yet, in ordinary discourse one says: the blister is *over /above* his knee.

[9] According to what you want to focus on (*closeness* to the knee, *distance* from the ground), one says "The blister is over/above the knee" (blister = LO, knee = RO, leg = REF)

368

the person is not in an upright position (6b, 6c, 6d) there is a conflict: gravity imposing the usage of *over/under*, it is not obvious any more which preposition should be associated with the remaining axes. This conflict is solved in the following way: *in front of /behind* are associated with the body's front axis. In cases where this feature does not readily apply (see 6d), the choice is based on anatomical considerations.

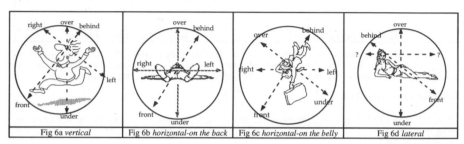

| Fig 6a *vertical* | Fig 6b *horizontal-on the back* | Fig 6c *horizontal-on the belly* | Fig 6d *lateral* |

The last case poses an additional problem. Suppose that the figure were lying laterally, having her head on a pillow. In this case we have no simple way (by using a preposition) to express the fact that something is behind her head or feet. In other circumstances we could use *in front of/behind* (person lying on the belly or the back), or *over/under* but both of these preposition pairs are taken already in this particular case (see figure 6d). The only way to fill this linguistic gap is to use a periphrastic expression like *over her head/under her feet*. Note, that in this case we introduce an additional RO (head/feet). This being so, we suggest to refine the rules offered here above for *in front/behind*:

Refinement of the rules for <in front/behind>

R9 & R10: The LO is {in front of/behind} the RO if the projection of the LO on the semi-axis contextually associated with the projective line {in front of/behind} the REF is {closer to/further away from} the projection of the REF than the projection of the RO.

The use of prepositions and their acceptability of usage depends not only on their meaning. Actually it depends to a large extent on the precise location of the LO and the RO. The further away these objects are from the ideal, or prototypical zone, that is, the closer they move to a neighbouring field, the more they get into "muddy waters": either the situation is undecidable (fuzzy zone), or the preposition gets in conflict with an alternative. The more one moves from the frontal position (Fig. 7a:white field ahead) to the left, the more it becomes necessary to replace the preposition "in front of" by "in front to the left" (FR-LE), or by "to the left in front" (LE-FR), "somehow to the left", "to the left", etc. Acceptability diminishes and ambiguity increases as one moves from the white zone towards the black zone.

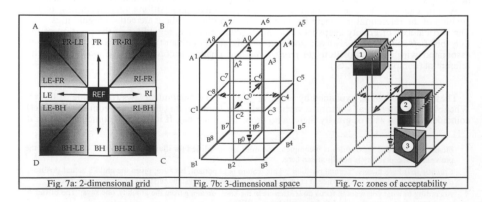

| Fig. 7a: 2-dimensional grid | Fig. 7b: 3-dimensional space | Fig. 7c: zones of acceptability |

The acceptability constraints of 2-dimensional space also hold for three-dimensional space (fig. 7b). By coding the majors point (left/right front/behind, etc.) at the upper, central and lower levels alphanumerically[10] and by specifying the frontal view (A6, C6, B6), one can define very precisely the correspondence between a preposition and a given point or zone. For example:

$$
\begin{aligned}
A0 &= \text{top center;} \\
B8 &= \text{bottom left;} \\
A6 &= \text{in front, above;} \\
A5 &= \text{above, in front, to the right,}
\end{aligned}
$$

Three things are worth mentioning: (a) some locations require more than one preposition (for example, A1, B1, A6), (b) some points do not really have a preposition at all (fuzzy zones, border line), (c) the acceptability of the prepositions varies with the closeness of the point to the ideal zone.

The subspaces contained in the big cube illustrate this (fig. 7c). Anything within the zone 1 can be expressed as "up to the left". The second zone delimits the space we usually associate with the preposition "to the right", whereas the third space shows what we mean when we say: "behind, on the bottom, to the right". The point B3 being the ideal spot.

6 Building an interface for the naive language user.

As we have seen, despite their apparent simplicity, projective prepositions are not simple at all. In this last section we will describe the philosophy underlying the interface that should allow the naive user to gain the necessary insights in order to produce correct spatial expressions (sentences composed of a locative preposition).[11]

One major problem that has to be solved is that of input. In what terms will the user communicate to the machine the message he wants to convey?[12] If we look at the work done by specialists [6, 11, 15], it appears that their metalanguage, though powerful, is far too complex. For example, in order to express such a *trivial* fact that two discrete objects are separated , Miller & Johnson Laird (1976: 62) offer the following definition : [Space $(x,y) \equiv$ Sept (x,y) & not $(\exists z)$ Betw (x, y, z)]. This is a simple case. Other situations such as, *two objects being next to each other* (adjacency) require three lines of definition (1976: 62). This being so, and the fact that even the most simple physical scenes require quite lengthy symbolic descriptions preclude this notation as a candidate for input in man-machine communication: these formulas are simply too heavy to handle.

6.1 Specification of the input

Since logical formulas are not the right approach, so what better alternative can we think of? Well, icons are a very natural way of communicating the same information in a much more elegant way. The idea is the following: the user specifies the input,— by choosing among a set of objects, and by locating them, he sets the scene,— and the system produces the corresponding output. However, choosing and placing different objects is not enough. As we have seen in section 5, we also need to know their respective roles: which of the two objects is the LO, which is the RO, which is the REF. We may also need to know who the speaker is. Finally, we need to specify the line of sight of the different objects (orientation), and the point of view (horizontal/vertical). Actually, the parameters *orientation* and *view* require both information on the three axis (x, y, z), each of them taking a value between zero and 360 degrees. The result of such a constructed scene is shown in figure 8.

---

10   A , B, C stand for the three planes *above, below, center* respectively. Even numbers represent the main directions of the intrinsic axis (in front/behind - left/right - top/bottom), odd numbers stand for diagonals; 0 represents the center.

11   Note, that we have the rules not only for projective, but for all major locative prepositions. These rules have been tested, but, the interface still remains to be built.

12   The solution to a similar problem (tense) has been discussed in [10].

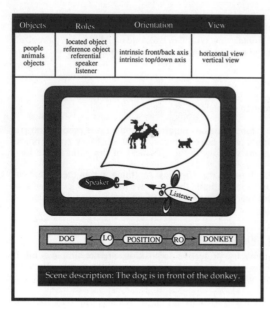

Objects	Roles	Orientation	View
people animals objects	located object reference object referential speaker listener	intrinsic front/back axis intrinsic top/down axis	horizontal view vertical view

Scene description: The dog is in front of the donkey.

Figure 8

6.2 A trial session with the future system : prepositions result from (a) the spatial configuration and (b) the point of view

In order to understand the functioning of the system let's imagine the following trial session. Given the scene described in figure 8 as input to the system, let us see what happens when we explore the so built microworld. As we have shown, the prepositions (or, more precisely, their computation) depend on factors such as (a) nature of the objects (intrinsic axis of the object), (b) relative position and (c) frame of reference, (d) what object will be the LO, the RO and the REF. As one can see in figure 9, changing any of these parameters may yield a change in the description of the scene, hence the preposition.

Let A, B, C, D be the elements of a scene (the nose shows the line of sight; S = speaker, L = listener). Let's now alternate the different parameters (LO, RO, REF) and see how the linguistic forms (locative descriptions) change accordingly.

Scene	LO	RO	REF	S	L	Description of the scene
	A	B	C	C	D	A is *behind* B.
	A	B	B	C	D	A is *to the right of* B.
	A	B	D	C	D	A is *to the left of* B.
	B	A	A	C	D	B is *to the left of* A.
	B	A	C	C	D	B is *in front of* A.
	B	A	D	C	D	B is *to the right of* A
	B	C	C	C	D	B is *in front of* me.
	B	D	D	C	D	B is *in front of you, to the right*.
						etc.

Figure 9

7 Conclusion:

In this paper we have presented the extension of a tutoring system, in which the student learns to express spatial information by building and exploring a microworld. He does so by building a scene. Once the user has provided the conceptual input (scene) the system produces the corresponding output (sentence). By varying the *nature*, the *position* and the *roles* of the objects composing the scene (input), and by watching the corresponding outputs, the student should be able to discover the relevant parameters governing linguistic form.

8 References:

[1]   Adorni, G., M. Dimanzo & F. Giunchiglia. *From descriptions to images: what reasonning in between.* ECAI 84. T. O'Shea (Ed.) Elsevier Science Publishers B.V. (North Holland), 1984.

[2]   André, E., et al. *Coping with the intrinsic and deictic uses of spatial prepositions.* Artificial Intelligence 2, 1987

[3]   Aurnague, M. *A cognitive approach to the semantics of space.* Cognitiva 90, 1990. 169-176.

[4]   Briffault, X. *Cognitive, semantic and linguistic aspects of space.* Ninth IASTED International Symposium Applied Informatics. Innsbruck, 1991, 228-231.

[5]   Herskowitz, A. *Language and spatial cognition.* Cambridge, Cambridge University Press, 1986.

[6]   Kalita, J. K. & N. I. Badler. *Interpreting prepositions physically.* AAAI-91. USA: 1991, 105-110.

[7]   Kuypers, B. *Modeling spatial knowledge.* Cognitive Science 2 , 1978, 129-163.

[9]   Leech, G. & J. Svartvik. *A communicative grammar of English.* 1979, Longman, London

[10] Ligozat, G. & M. Zock. *How to visualize time, tense and aspect.* COLING '92, Nantes, 1992

[11] Miller, G. & P. Johnson Laird. Language and perception. The Belknap Press, Harvard University Press, 1976

[12] Piaget J. & B. Inhelder. La structuration de l'espace chez l'enfant. Delachaux Niestlé

[13] Quirk, R., S. Greenbaum, G. Leech & J. Svartvik. *A comprehensive grammar of the English Language.* 1986, Longman, London

[14] Retz-Schmidt, G. *Various views on spatial prepositions.* AI Magazine 1988, 95-105.

[15] Schirra, J. *A contribution to reference semantics of spatial prepositions : the visualization problem and its solution in VITRA.* Universität des Saarlandes, Saarbrücken, 1990.

[16] Vandeloise, C. *L'espace en français.* Paris: Editions du Seuil, 1986.

[17] Zock, M. *SWIM or sink : the problem of communicating thought.* In, Swartz, M. & M. Yazdani (Eds.), Bridge to International Communication : Intelligent Tutoring Systems for Second Language Learning. 1991, New York: Springer

[18] Zock, M. & A. Laroui. *Visualizing results of choices in language generation : the use of intermediate structures.* Workshop on Natural Language Learning, IJCAI-91, Sidney, 1991

AN INDUCTIVE METHOD FOR AUTOMATED NATURAL LANGUAGE PARSER GENERATION

GREGERS KOCH

Department of Computer Science (DIKU), University of Copenhagen,
Universitetsparken 1, DK-2100 Copenhagen, Denmark,
E-mail: gregers@diku.dk

ABSTRACT

This paper comments on Johnson and Kay's 1990 proposal[3] for semantic abstraction in a definite clause grammar aimed at using the same rules to construct, among other things, predicate argument formulae in the style of Montague grammar and formulae similar to the discourse representations proposed by Hans Kamp[5,6]. Here is also presented an application of our system for performing a special kind of inductive inference sometimes called logico-semantic induction[7]. This system can be seen as a meta system producing automatically logical parsers (in the form of application-specific definite clause grammars) to perform translations as does Johnson and Kay's program. It is argued that instead of aiming at high degrees of abstraction, it makes much more sense to aim at simple application-specific programs produced automatically by meta systems, thus obtaining high degrees of concretization together with generality, simplicity, perspicuity, modifiability, and ease of use.

1 Semantic Abstraction

1.1 *Introduction to a System Using Semantic Abstraction*

Before discussing our own system, in this part of the paper we give a brief description of Johnson and Kay's way[3] of expressing syntactic rules that associate semantic formulae with strings. They show how the same rules construct predicate argument formulae in the style of Montague grammar[13], or representations similar to the discourse representations proposed by Hans Kamp[5,6]. The idea is that semantic representations are specified indirectly using semantic construction operators, which enforce a barrier between the grammar and the semantic representations themselves. Different operations can be associated with these operators and, depending on the set in force at a given time, the effect of interpreting the expression will be to construct a representation in one semantic formalism or another. The set of operators contains members corresponding to such notions as composition, conjunction, etc. The set is small and independent of the semantic formalism, but no claims are made for the general sufficiency. Not all of the constructors are relevant to all semantic theories and those not needed for a particular one are given degenerate definitions.

1.2 *A Grammar Using Abstraction*

The grammar generates simple transitive clauses and subject-relative clauses. It is based on the Montague-style grammars presented in Pereira and Shieber's book[12], and the treatments of agreement, Wh-dependencies, etc., presented there could also be incorporated, although be it with some difficulty.

```
:- op(950, xfy, ^).
:- op(300, xfy, =>).
parse(String,ExtSem) :-
   external(IntSem,ExtSem), s(IntSem,String,[]).
s(S) --> np(VP^S), vp(VP).
np(NP) --> det(N1^NP), n1(N1).
n1(N) --> n(N).
n1(X^S) --> n(X^S1), rc(X^S2), {conjoin(S1,S2,S)}.
vp(X^S) --> v(X^VP), np(VP^S).
rc(VP) --> [that], vp(VP).
v(X^Y^S) --> [Verb], {verb(Verb,X^Y^Pred), atom(Pred,S)}.
n(X^S) --> [Noun], {noun(Noun,X^Pred), new_index(X,S1),
                    atom(Pred,S2), compose(S1,S2,S)}.
det((X^Res)^(X^Scope)^S) --> [Det],
                    {determiner(Det,Res^Scope^S)}.
np((X^S1)^S) --> [Pronoun],
   {pronoun(Pronoun), accessible_index(X,S2), compose(S1,S2,S)}.

pronoun(it).
verb(beats, X^Y^beat(X,Y)).
verb(owns, X^Y^own(X,Y)).
noun(man, X^man(X)).
determiner(a, Res^Scope^S) :- conjoin(Res,Scope,S).
determiner(every, Res0^Scope^S) :-
   compose(S1, S2, S), subordinate(Res, ResName, S1),
   compose(Res0, Res1, Res), subordinate(Scope, ScopeName, Res1),
   atom(ResName => Scopename, S2).
```

It is somewhat more pedantically expressed than usual[1]. Following Pereira and Shieber, the semantics of VP and N are represented by terms of the form $X \hat{\ } S$, where X represents a referential index and S represents the semantics of a sentence. NP meanings are represented by terms of the form $VP \hat{\ } S$, where S represents a sentential meaning.

1.3 *An Application to Discourse Representation*

The representations built by the following constructors are inspired by Hans Kamp's[5,6] "box representations". A discourse representation "box" is represented by the list of items that constitute its contents. A representation is a difference-pair of the lists of the representations of the currently open boxes[4] (i.e. the current box and all superordinate boxes). In Prolog, we use the binary '-' operator to separate the two members of the pair.

```
atom(P,[B|Bs]-[[P|B]|Bs]).

compose(B0s-B1s,B1s-B2s,B0s-B2s).

conjoin(P1,P2,P) :- compose(P1,P2,P).

subordinate([[]|B0s]-[B|B1s],B,B0s-B1s).

new_index(Index,C) :- atom(i(Index),C).

accessible_index(Index,Bs-Bs) :- member(B,Bs), member(i(Index),B).

external([[]]-[S],S).
```

With these constructors, the parser yields the following semantic values for some test
sentences.

```
?- parse([a,man,owns,a,donkey],S).
S = [own(X,Y),donkey(Y),i(Y),man(X),i(X)]
```

This representation is true just in case there are two individuals X and Y, X is a man
and Y is a donkey, and X owns Y.

```
?- parse([every,man,owns,a,donkey],S).
S = [[man(X),i(X)] => [own(X,Y),donkey(Y),i(Y)]]
```

The representation is true just in case for all individuals X such that X is a man there
is an individual Y such that Y is a donkey and X owns Y.

```
?- parse([every,man,that,owns,a,donkey,beats,it],S).
S = [[own(X,Y),donkey(Y),i(Y),man(X),i(X)] => [beat(X,Y)]]
```

This representation is true just in case for all individuals X and Y such that X is a
man and Y a donkey and X owns Y, it is also true that X beats Y.

2 Logical Induction

2.1 *Introduction to a System Performing Logical Induction*

Here we present an application of our system for a kind of logical induction[7,9,10]. It deals
with the automated generation of logical parsers or translators.

A logical parser is a logical formula describing a translation process into some logical
notation. More precisely, we add the requirement to the meta system that the logical
description is capable of producing by deduction a feasible description of the translation
process. The translation takes place from a specified language fragment L, typically from
a fragment of a natural language like English or French, but a programming language like
Pascal may also be used. The target language of the translation is an appropriately chosen
logic Log1. As to the logical host language, the meta level translation takes place in one

logical language Log2, and the object level translation takes place in a possibly different logical language Log3. Here we shall confine ourselves to discussion of the situation where both logical host languages coincide with the Horn Clause Logic HCL. Other possibilities for Log2 and Log3 can certainly also be dealt with, but here we confine ourselves to Log2 = Log3 = HCL.

As target logic Log1 our system can accomodate virtually any possible logic, and this flexibility seems to be one of the really strong features of this approach. In that particular sense we may consider it a system with high semantic generality. In the style of Johnson & Kay[3] and as an illustration we can exemplify with a variant of Montague's intensional logic[11] or with a sort of discourse representation structures like Kamp and Reyle[6].

2.2 *The System*

Our meta program translates in seven steps for obtaining a so-called "logico-semantic induction"[7,8,11]. In this section I shall describe the method by means of an example. The method presupposes that a context-free grammar has been created, including a lexicon, and it performs semantic induction for a pair of text and semantic structure. The result of the induction is a definite clause grammar (DCG) corresponding to the grammar and it will be annotated with variables. Our example uses the following little grammar

```
s -> np vp
np -> det n
vp -> v np
```

The sample text is

```
"a horse eats an apple"
```

and the intended semantic structure is

```
a(x, horse(x), a(y, apple(y), eats(x,y)))
```

representing the predicate-logic formula
$\exists x[horse(x) \wedge \exists y[apple(y) \wedge eats(x,y)]]$
First step:
Reformulate the intended semantic structure into a functional tree structure where each functor has a label or a number attached.
Second step:
Create a syntax tree through parsing of the sample text in accordance with the grammar.
Third step:
Label the terminals of the syntax tree with the same labels or numbers as under step one in such a way that each functor in step one constitutes an element from the category of the syntax tree carrying the corresponding label. More precisely, make a connection from a numbered functor in the result structure to the lexical category in the syntax structure to which the word (lexical or syncategorimatic) belongs.
Fourth step:
Here we want to create one referential index (sometimes called a focus variable), for each noun phrase, and we shall construct a flow between the focus variable and certain

other constituents. The referential indices correspond to those variables (here x and y) being part of the semantic structure.

The aim is to obtain that during parsing the resulting DCG must create a variable (a referential index) as an identifier for one of the semantic objects occuring in the semantic structure (here horse, apple etc.).

Fifth step:

Here the lexical flow is constructed as a flow connecting each textual word with an element of the semantic structure. In the example a lexical flow connects the word "horse" with the arguments of the noun category.

Sixth step:

Each edge in the semantic structure of step one can be designated by the labels of the two ends of the edge. Connect the nodes with the same labels in the syntax tree through a flow following the edges of the syntax tree.

Seventh step:

In this step we control that the arity is the same for each occurrence of a functor and we control the consistency of the local flow. This means that each nonterminal function symbol has the same number of arguments in every occurrence, and these arguments are connected to the surrounding nodes in the same way for every occurrence of the same syntax rule.

In our example the method will give us the following DCG:

```
s(A) --> np(B,C,A),vp(B,C).
np(D,E,F) --> det(D,G,E,F), n(D,G).
vp(H,I) --> v(H,J,K), np(J,K,I).
```

2.3 *An Application to Discourse Representation*

Let us build upon the following little grammar

```
s -> np vp
np -> det n | det n rc | pron
vp -> v np
rc -> that vp
```

and let our system exploit the following pair of sample text and intended semantic representation

```
every man that owns a donkey beats it
```

$$[[i(x)\&man(x)\&i(y)\&donkey(y)\&own(x,y)] \Rightarrow [beat(x,y)]]$$

Then we get the following program generated automatically by means of our inductive meta system

```
s(Z) --> np(X,Y,Z),vp(X,Y).
np(X,Z,W) --> det(X,Y,Z,W),n(X,Y).
np(X,Z,W) --> det(X,Y,Z,W),n(X,U),rc(X,U,Y).
```

```
np(X,Y,Y) --> pron(X).
vp(X,W) --> v(X,Y,Z),np(Y,Z,W).
rc(X,Y,Z) --> that(Y,W,Z),vp(X,W).
det(X,Y,Z,[i(X)&Y]=>[Z]) --> [every].
det(X,Y,Z,i(X)&Y&Z) --> [a].
pron(X,pron(X)) --> [it].
n(X,man(X)) --> [man].
v(X,Y,own(X,Y)) --> [owns].
that(X,Y,X&Y) --> [that].
```

If we augment this program with a simple and commonplace pronoun resolution program, it seems to be a feasible translator into the relevant discourse representation, comparable to section 1.3. Notice that the construction of this part of the system is not
automated. We will have to maintain that such an automation would be beyond the
scope of present understanding of this problem area.

3   Discussion

In purely technical terms it is possible to follow Johnson and Kay's recommendation to
operate with one and only one parsing program, irrespective of which kind of analysis
you want. But as is apparent in the examples, the coupling to the individual applications
tends to be rather complicated, even in utterly simple cases as the one described in
section 1.3. So it seems to be far more practically sensible to work with a meta system
that for each individual application has the ability to produce automatically the intended
corresponding translator. How this can be done was described rather briefly in section
2.2. Furthermore, Johnson and Kay have the bad habit of expressing their programs in
an exceedingly abstract manner - understood quite literally as excessive use of lambda
abstraction. (It is tempting to draw the conclusion that they confuse abstraction and
generality).

It is considerably more pragmatically reasonable to avoid abstraction as far as possible
and so to speak to express matters in as concrete a form as possible. The method of
section 2.2 follows that principle. Any reader can convince himself that the resulting
parsing program becomes more comprehensible and easier modifiable in this way. So
in this respect we could be said to recommend semantic concreteness and generality in
contrast to semantic abstraction.

4   References

1. H. Abramson & V. Dahl, *Logic Grammar* (Springer-Verlag, Berlin, 1989).

2. C.G. Brown & G. Koch (eds.), *Natural Language Understanding and Logic Programming III* (North-Holland, Amsterdam, 1991).

3. M. Johnson & M. Kay, Semantic abstraction and anaphora, in *COLING Proceedings*
(1990) 17-27.

4. M. Johnson & E. Klein, Discourse, anaphora and parsing, in *COLING Proceedings*
(1986) 669-675.

5. H. Kamp, A theory of truth and semantic representation, in *Formal Methods in the Study of Language*, eds. J.A.G. Groenendijk et al. (Math. Centre, Amsterdam, 1981).

6. H. Kamp & U. Reyle, *From Discourse to Logic* (Kluwer Academic Publishers, Dordrecht, 1993).

7. G. Koch, Computational logico-semantic induction, in *Natural Language Understanding and Logic Programming II*, eds. V. Dahl and P. Saint-Dizier (North-Holland, Amsterdam, 1988) 107-134.

8. G. Koch, Linguistic data flow structures, in *Natural Language Understanding and Logic Programming III*, eds. C.G. Brown and G. Koch (North-Holland, Amsterdam, 1991) 293-308.

9. G. Koch, Data Flow Trees in Natural Language Interfaces, in *Advances in Information Modelling and Knowledge Bases*, eds. H. Jaakkola et al. (IOS, Amsterdam, 1991) 141-151.

10. G. Koch, Logics and Informatics in an Integrated Approach to Natural Language Database Interfaces, in *Information Modelling and Knowledge Bases III*, eds. S. Ohsuga et al. (IOS, Amsterdam, 1992) 602-616.

11. G. Koch, Montague's PTQ as a Case of Advanced Text Comprehension, in *Information Modelling and Knowledge Bases IV*, eds. H. Kangassalo et al. (IOS, Amsterdam, 1993) 377-387.

12. F. Pereira & S.M. Shieber, *Prolog and Natural Language Analysis* (Stanford University, 1987).

13. R.H. Thomason, *Formal Philosophy: Selected Papers of Richard Montague* (Yale University Press, London, 1974).

SUPPORTING FLEXIBILITY AND TRANSMUTABILITY: MULTI-AGENT PROCESSING AND ROLE-SWITCHING IN A PRAGMATICALLY ORIENTED DIALOG SYSTEM*

ALASSANE NDIAYE   ANTHONY JAMESON

Department of Computer Science, University of Saarbrücken
P.O. Box 151150, D-66041 Saarbrücken, Federal Republic of Germany
{ndiaye, jameson}@cs.uni-sb.de

ABSTRACT

Ways of achieving two desirable characteristics of pragmatically oriented dialog processing are discussed: (1) Flexible cooperation among the system's modules maximizes the system's exploitation of its knowledge and of its reasoning capabilities. (2) The ability to take either (or any) of the dialog roles in its domain enhances the system's ability to anticipate and interpret its dialog partner's reasoning and behavior. Ways of attaining these goals are being explored in the system PRACMA, which models noncooperative dialogs between a buyer and a seller. Attainment of the first goal is supported by the multi-agent architecture CHANNELS, which has been designed specifically for natural language systems. Two attempts to achieve the second goal are discussed which have been realized in two different modules of PRACMA: bidirectional, role-independent dialog planning operators; and Bayesian meta-networks for reasoning about the dialog partner's beliefs and evaluations.

1 Introduction

1.1 Issues

One key issue in developing natural language (NL) processing systems is how to find a suitable architecture that allows flexible interaction of the various modules within the system. For the NL system PRACMA [3, 10], we have integrated principles from cooperative distributed problem solving, multi-agent systems [4], and the object-oriented paradigm, to create a flexible architecture.

A second issue concerns suitable ways to make a pragmatically-oriented NL system *transmutable*, i.e. to enable it to take either of the two possible roles in a dialog. Transmutability has several advantages, one being that the system can better take into account the reasoning and the behavior of the human partner in the role it is not playing at the moment.

Possible answers concerning both issues have been realized within the NL system PRACMA. We first introduce this system and then present the CHANNELS architecture in Section 2 and our approaches to transmutability in Section 3.

---

*This research is being supported by the German Science Foundation in its Special Collaborative Research Program on Artificial Intelligence and Knowledge Based Systems SFB 314, Project N1, PRACMA.

1.2   The PRACMA System

Most natural language systems are restricted to cooperative dialogs. With the NL system PRACMA (**PR**ocessing **A**rguments between **C**ontroversially-**M**inded **A**ctors), we look deeper into the area of noncooperative dialog, which is widely represented in everyday situations. PRACMA models dialogs between a used-car owner and a potential buyer at a used-car market. The system has been designed to be transmutable, i.e. it is able to play the role of either the seller or the buyer.

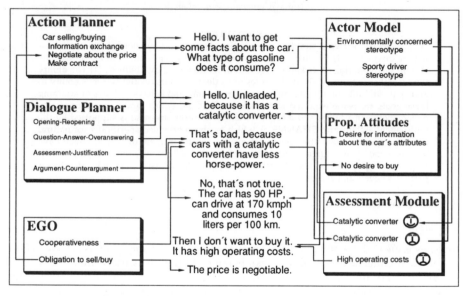

Figure 1: Schematic representation of PRACMA's processing

Figure 1 shows in the middle column an example dialog—originally in German—, surrounded by some of the processing components[1]. The arrows reflect their influence on the analysis and generation of specific dialog contributions.

Because of its primary concern with the pragmatic aspects of dialog (as opposed to syntactic and semantic aspects), PRACMA requires an architecture that allows each module to play various roles in the processing, at various stages of the processing. For example, an assessment of the buyer's interests can be used not only to determine an appropriate response to a buyer's question but also to determine the meaning of the question in the first place. The requirement of transmutability further increases the need for flexibility, as will be discussed below.

---

[1]Only the modules specifically needed to support the pragmatic processing are depicted.

2 Supporting Flexibility: The CHANNELS Architecture

2.1 Limitations of Some Existing NL Architectures with Respect to Pragmatic Processing

The design of the architecture of an AI system requires the decomposition of the system into modules; the specification of communication channels, communication protocols, and interaction languages between the modules; the specification of the data and control flow; and the design of the task and resource allocation strategies and the synchronization strategies[2].

Several architectures have been proposed to meet these requirements in the context of NL processing. But many of them do not optimally support flexible pragmatic processing. The *sequential* model, which specifies a fixed, unidirectional pre-ordered connection of the various modules (e.g., as realized in XTRA [2]), is inadequate because of the very limited possibilities for communication among the modules. The main disadvantage of the *hierarchic* model is the bottleneck caused by the central control module, which handles all communication between the modules. *Cascaded* (or *pipe-line*) architectures are often used in NL systems, especially for NL generation. They consist of a sequence of modules, where each module can communicate with the next as well as with the previous one. A cascaded architecture allows for incremental and parallel processing but still permits only restricted communication. In a *blackboard* architecture (e.g., HEARSAY-II [6]) the modules—the so-called *knowledge sources*—interact asynchronously via a global data structure, the blackboard. In many blackboard systems, a central control node allocates the resources and mediates between competing knowledge sources [19]. Often there is also a centralized scheduler and a blackboard monitor.

We have found many cases in which modules for pragmatic processing can best communicate directly with one another, independent of a predefined order or a central control mechanism. Accordingly, we have developed for PRACMA the multi-agent architecture CHANNELS (Cooperating Heterogeneous Agents for a Natural-Language System).

2.2 Agents and Messages

Each PRACMA module is modeled in CHANNELS as a (semi-)autonomous specialized problem solver, called an *agent*[3]. Each agent is characterized by, among other things, its acquaintances, its state, its skills (procedures associated with the object), and its agent model, which contains knowledge about the basic capabilities of the other agents. In addition, each agent has a table where pending messages are stored until they can be processed, as well as self-presenting capabilities[4].

There are two basic types of communication in multi-agent systems [5]: communication via a common shared data structure (e.g., a blackboard) and communication via message passing as realized in actor languages [1]. In CHANNELS, communica-

---

[2]The last point is optional while the others are necessary in each AI system.

[3]In this paper, *agent* refers to an active system module, while *actor* refers to a (human or simulated) participant in the PRACMA dialog situation.

[4]Each agent is able to present its current processing state, its results, and its communication links with other agents.

tion and interaction among the agents are achieved through a *communication-act-based protocol* which governs the exchange of messages. Each message is characterized by attributes including: the sender, the recipient(s), the type of communication act, the mode of communication (synchronous or asynchronous), the actual content of the message, and optionally the history of the message and the agents to whom the answer to the message's query should be forwarded[5].

The communication acts [18] we currently use (*inform, ask,* and *reply*) define the nature of the interaction among the agents. For instance, an *ask* requests the recipient(s) to send information back to the originator of the message, while an *inform* passes information from one module to another.

Messages communicate information between a sender agent and a receiver agent either *synchronously* or *asynchronously*. The communication is synchronous if the sender requires a response before continuing processing; until a response is received, it remains in the state *waiting*. With asynchronous communication, the sender can engage in further processing before receiving a response.

For each agent there is a state transition function that determines the next state depending on its previous state, on the communication act, and on the mode of the sent or received message. The agents run concurrently as simulated parallel processes and CHANNELS uses a scheduler and the history of the messages to manage synchronization.

2.3 Interlocking of Heterogeneous Architectures

The CHANNELS agents can vary in granularity and complexity from very simple modules to complex architectures[6]. It is therefore possible to incorporate in a single system agents with different local architectures. For instance, the analysis module in PRACMA is realized as a blackboard, while the generator we will use has a cascaded architecture. The interlocking of heterogeneous architectures enables the reuse of previously developed modules [20]. The agents need only to be enhanced by a layer supporting the communication and cooperation with the other agents within the overall system.

2.4 Related Work

As mentioned above, CHANNELS integrates principles from object-oriented concurrent languages like ABCL [21]. ABCL includes objects which are viewed as autonomous information processing agents interacting with other objects solely via message passing. There are three types of message passing: *past, now, future*; and three object modes: *active, waiting,* and *dormant*. The *past* type (send and don't wait) corresponds to the *inform* or *asynchronous ask* in CHANNELS, while the *now* type (send and wait) is analogous to our *synchronous ask*, and the *future* type (send, specify the return value and don't wait) is similar to our *asynchronous ask*, which is always followed by a *reply*.

---

[5]This last concept is analogous to the concept of *reply-to* continuation in object-oriented concurrent languages.

[6]"Flexible implementation support for DAI systems must provide ways of integrating heterogeneous problem-solvers of different granularity." [8, p. 94]

The utility of distributed NL processing based on cooperating agents is also demonstrated by CARAMEL [15, 16] and TALISMAN [17]. CARAMEL is an NL system with a multi-experts architecture. For task management and control it uses several blackboards, an agenda, and a supervisor. Recently, principles of actor systems have been introduced to provide additional flexibility [16]. TALISMAN is a multi-agent system for NL processing governed by linguistic laws. It manages communication between agents without appealing to a central control mechanism. The agents communicate and cooperate only via message passing, as in CHANNELS. It is not clear, however, how the approach based on linguistic laws might be generalized to pragmatic processing.

In [7], principles of a multi-agent architecture for NL processing are presented. The proposed framework features large-gained heterogeneous agents (*specialists*) which cooperate to solve an NL processing task; centralized control; and a combination of event-driven (bottom-up) and goal-driven (top-down) operation. In contrast to CHANNELS, all communication between the agents is mediated by a central *cooperation manager*; in this respect the architecture is similar to those discussed in Section 2.1.

3   Realizing Transmutability

The goal of enabling a system to take both roles within a dialog raises several issues: What are the benefits and costs of doing so? How can this be achieved efficiently and elegantly? These issues are discussed here with respect to two agents within PRACMA.

3.1   Dialog Planning Using Bidirectional Operators

PRACMA can model the dialog in Figure 1 taking the role of either the seller or the buyer. In both cases the same agents come into play, but each agent takes into account the role the system is currently taking. We discuss this transmutability using the DIALOG PLANNER agent as an example. This agent uses a hierarchical, incremental planner [13][7]. The plan operators have mostly been formulated *bidirectionally*. For instance, Figure 2 shows a part of a high-level plan operator[8]. It specifies three subgoals: to initialize the dialog, to negotiate about various aspects of the car, and to finish the dialog. The variables ?person1 and ?person2 hold information about the role (buyer or seller) that each dialog participant plays.

There are several advantages to using bidirectional dialog operators instead of two separate sets of operators, one for each role. First, the representation of the system's dialog planning knowledge is less redundant and more consistent with respect to the ways in which the two roles are handled. Moreover, it is ensured that any dialog strategy used by the system in one role can be coped with when the system takes the other role. But there are also disadvantages: A single bidirectional operator can be more complex and cumbersome than two corresponding unidirectional ones.

---

[7]Actually, there are two planning processes within PRACMA that interact when performing a dialog. A comparable approach is also proposed in [11].

[8]Each expression beginning with "(AM" represents an *ask*-message that the DIALOG PLANNER sends to the Actor Model, an agent which models the desires and beliefs of the actors in the language MOTEL [9].

Also, additional measures are required to do justice fully to the fact that the goals of the dialog partners conflict in part (e.g., that the invocation of a given operator may be desirable for one partner but undesirable for the other one). PRACMA's planning mechanisms are now being extended so as both to facilitate the writing of bidirectional operators and to increase the sophistication with which the DIALOG PLANNER uses them.

```
(define-plan-operator
  :NAME negotiation-dialog
  :GOAL
    (AM ((sb_facts am (:list (b believe all))
         (isa ?d dialog)(irole actor ?d ?person1)(irole counteractor ?d ?person2))))
  :PRECONDITIONS
    ((AM ((assert_ind (:list (b believe all)) ?d dialog)
          (assert_ind (:list (b believe all)) ?d ?person1 actor)
          (assert_ind (:list (b believe all)) ?d ?person2 counteractor)
          (sb_facts am (:list (b (believe ?person1)(b want all))
          (isa ?d dialog)(irole actor ?d ?person1)(irole counteractor ?d ?person2))))))
  :SUBGOALS
    ((AM ((sb_facts am (:list (b believe all))
          (isa ?init initialize)(irole actor ?init ?person1)
          (irole counteractor ?init ?person2)) *optional*))
     (AM ((sb_facts am (:list (b believe all))
          (isa ?n negotiate)(irole actor ?n ?person1)
          (irole counteractor ?n ?person2)(irole topic ?n ?negoitem))) *optional*)
     (AM ((sb_facts am (:list (b believe all))(isa ?f finish)
          (irole actor ?f ?person1)(irole counteractor ?f ?person2)))*optional*)))
  ...
```

Figure 2: A part of a top-level NEGOTIATION plan operator

3.2 Dialog Partner Modeling with Bayesian Meta-Networks

One advantage of transmutability is due to the fact that a dialog partner often tries to anticipate and reconstruct the reasoning performed by the other partner. A system should be better able to do this if it has the necessary knowledge and dialog strategies for taking the role of its partner.

In fact, one might think that, in the role of the seller S for example, PRACMA could simply invoke an instantiation of itself in the role of the buyer B as a subroutine, so as to model B's reasoning. Whether this simple conception is viable we will discuss here using an example from one part of PRACMA, the agent AXIOLOGIS, which reasons about the evaluation of various aspects of the car under discussion.

3.2.1 A Simple Network for B

The basic inference mechanism of AXIOLOGIS is the Bayesian belief network (see, e.g., [14]). The lower left-hand side of Figure 3 shows a small part of the network constructed by AXIOLOGIS when PRACMA is simulating the buyer B in a simple mode in which B takes all comments by S at face value. The node labeled HORSEPOWER represents B's *impression* about one aspect of the car which can play an important part in B's evaluation of the car, as illustrated in Figure 1, namely the horsepower (HP) of its motor. The first (left-hand) histogram shows that, although B does not know the HP precisely, he[9] has on the basis of previous experience with cars the indefinite expectation that the HP is around 150.[10] The node EVALUATION OF HP represents B's impression of how he would evaluate the HP if he knew its exact value. The initial impression for this node (depicted by the first histogram) arises through downward propagation as soon as the initial impression for HORSEPOWER has been formed.

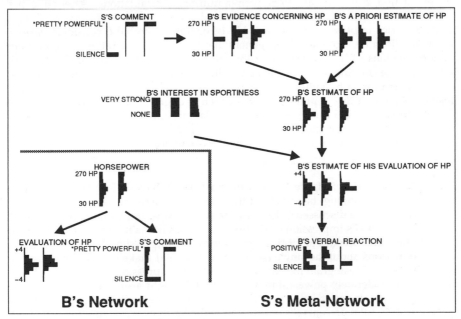

Figure 3: Illustration of the concept of a *Bayesian meta-network*

B's impression of the HP can be influenced by any comment S chooses to make about it. This dependency is represented by a parent-child link from HORSEPOWER to S'S COMMENT, because from the point of view of B, S's comment is probabilistically "caused" by the truth about HP. When S makes a comment about HP, B begins its updating of this part of its network using *upward propagation* according to the usual Bayesian principles, considering those HP values more probable that would have been most likely to cause the comment to be made.[11] The change in B's impression of the HP is then propagated downward to the variable EVALUATION OF HP. (These changes are shown in the second histogram for each node.)

When PRACMA is taking the role of S, it must reason about these types of probabilistic inference by B in order to anticipate B's reactions to what S says and to interpret B's behavior as reflecting B's underlying beliefs and interests.

---

[9]We arbitrarily use masculine pronouns to refer to B and feminine pronouns for S.

[10]This variable has nine possible values, each of which represents an interval such as "255–285 HP".

[11]The relationship between the meaning of a (vague) comment and the impression change it brings about in the listener is discussed in detail in [10].

3.2.2 Approach 1: Repeated Simulations

Since PRACMA can always construct a network for B, even when it is taking the role of S, it could use the network directly in order to simulate B. But even when performing an apparently simple subtask like anticipating how a given comment would affect B's evaluation, S would have to perform a number of simulations. After all, S has no precise information about most of the details of the network of a *specific* B, e.g., what B's prior impression of the car's HP is, or how desirable B considers various levels of HP to be. So S would in general have to consider a rather large number of combinations of hypotheses about the information in the nodes of B's network and about the conditional probabilities that link the nodes, running a simulation for each combination of hypotheses and making inferences on the basis of the collected results. Although this approach has an attractive degree of generality and may be feasible (especially if S can learn from its simulations and so minimize repetitions of them), there are advantages to an alternative approach which makes more explicit S's uncertainty about B's network, namely the use of *meta-networks*.

3.2.3 Approach 2: Meta-Networks

The right-hand side of Figure 3 shows the part of S's Bayesian meta-network that represents S's (changing) beliefs about the state of B's network. The three nodes in the top row will be discussed below. In the second row, the variable B'S ESTIMATE OF HP represents S's impression of B's impression of HP. As it would be impractical for S to take into account all of the various forms of impression that B might have, S simply reasons about the single *estimate* that B would make if asked to guess the car's HP. The first histogram for this node reflects the impression that B is most likely to expect a moderately powerful motor but that B might also have a considerably more optimistic or pessimistic expectation. Similarly, the node B'S ESTIMATE OF HIS EVALUATION OF HP represents S's impression of the best guess B would make if asked for a single evaluation of the car's HP.

The node B'S INTEREST IN SPORTINESS is a node in the meta-network that doesn't correspond to a node in B's network but rather represents S's uncertainty about B's evaluation criteria for different levels of HP. (In B's network, these criteria are reflected in the conditional probabilities linking the nodes HORSEPOWER and EVALUATION OF HP). Specifically, the meta-network is based on the assumption that B's evaluation of a given HP level is a multiplicative function of his interest in the general evaluation dimension of *sportiness*.

Given prior impressions of the variables in the nodes B'S INTEREST IN SPORTINESS and B'S ESTIMATE OF HP, S forms an impression of B'S ESTIMATE OF HIS EVALUATION OF HP using the same general propagation principles as those used in B's network—though of course the conditional probabilities that link the nodes in this meta-network are different from the ones linking the corresponding nodes in B's network. As the node B'S VERBAL REACTION shows, S can also go on to predict what type of utterance (if any) B might make reflecting his evaluation of the car's HP[12].

---

[12]The conditional probabilities used here were derived from an unpublished empirical study involving the role-playing of sales dialogs.

The top row of the meta-network shows that actually three nodes in all are needed to represent S's impressions of B's impression of the car's horsepower, if S wants to be able to *manipulate* B's impression by supplying B with relevant evidence. The three nodes B'S EVIDENCE CONCERNING HP, B'S A PRIORI ESTIMATE OF HP, and B'S ESTIMATE OF HP reflect the general principle that, for each node in a Bayesian network, to allow both upward and downward propagation it is necessary to store not just a single probability distribution representing a belief about the variable but also two independent distributions summarizing both the prior expectation for the variable and the relevant evidence due to observations[13]. So the top row of the meta-network reflects the fact that S cannot influence B's *a priori* impression about the car's HP but can provide B with specific *evidence* concerning this variable and thereby (within certain limits) influence B's overall impression of the HP. (The second histogram for each node shows S's impression for that node after S has made a positive, though vague comment: "The motor is pretty powerful".)

The example just mentioned involves *downward* propagation in S's meta-network for the purpose of anticipating the *upward* propagation that will occur within B's network. But of course S's own network can itself exhibit upward propagation. The third histogram for each node shows how S adapts her impressions of B if he produces an unexpectedly negative utterance about the car's HP (e.g., "The horsepower is a problem"). The only really obvious change is that B'S ESTIMATE OF HIS EVALUATION OF HP now seems very unlikely to be positive. Close inspection of the histograms higher up in the meta-network reveals that S distributes the "blame" for B's negative evaluation over several sources: B now appears slightly less interested in sportiness (B'S INTEREST IN SPORTINESS), his prior impression of the motor's power was perhaps more pessimistic than S originally suspected (B'S A PRIORI ESTIMATE OF HP), and he may have interpreted S's vague comment about the motor being "pretty powerful" relatively conservatively (B'S EVIDENCE CONCERNING HP).

In sum, meta-networks allow PRACMA to make some inferences about the dialog partner's processing which are intuitively familiar from everyday experience (though some have rarely, if ever, been handled by previous dialog systems), and to do this using a relatively explicit, straightforward representation[14]. But the approach raises a number of rather complex issues, and further investigation of these may lead to various changes in the form of PRACMA's meta-networks. For example, there are alternative ways of conceptualizing a meta-node such as B'S ESTIMATE OF HP; and it may prove unnecessary to represent the meaning of a comment explicitly with a meta-level node like B'S EVIDENCE CONCERNING HP.

References

[1] G. Agha. *The Structure and Semantics of Actor Languages.* In J. W. de Bakker, W. P. de Roever, and G. Rozenberg, (eds.), Foundations of Object-Oriented Languages, pp. 1–59. Springer, Berlin, 1991.

[2] J. Allgayer, R. Jansen-Winkeln, C. Reddig, and N. Reithinger. *Bidirectional Use of Knowledge in the*

---

[13]This information is in fact stored for each node in B's network, though only the overall probability distribution, which is derived from the two others, is depicted.

[14]In fact, S's meta-network in turn serves as a basis for a meta-meta-network that models the inferences of a sophisticated B; discussion of this would exceed the scope of the present paper.

Multi-Modal NL Access System XTRA. In Proc. of the Eleventh IJCAI, pp. 1492–1497, Detroit, MI, 1989.

[3] J. Allgayer, A. Kobsa, C. Reddig, and N. Reithinger. *PRACMA: Processing Arguments Between Controversially-Minded Agents.* In Proc. of the Fifth Rocky Mountain Conference on Artificial Intelligence: Pragmatics in Artificial Intelligence, pp. 63–68, Las Cruces, NM, 1990.

[4] A. Bond and L. Gasser. *Readings in Distributed Artificial Intelligence.* Morgan Kaufmann, San Mateo, CA. 1988

[5] A. Cawsey, J. R. Galliers, S. Reece, and K. Sparck Jones. *A Comparison of Architectures for Autonomous Multi-Agent Communication.* In Proc. of the Tenth ECAI, pp. 249–251, Vienna, 1992.

[6] L. D. Erman, F. Hayes-Roth, V. R. Lesser, and D. R. Reddy. *The HEARSAY-II Speech-Understanding System: Integrating Knowledge to Resolve Uncertainty.* In B. L. Webber and N. J. Nilsson, (eds.), Readings in Artificial Intelligence, pp. 349–389. Morgan Kaufmann, Los Altos, CA, 1981.

[7] D. Fum, G. Guida, and C. Tasso. *A Distributed Multi-Agent Architecture for Natural Language Processing.* In Proc. of the Twelfth COLING, pp. 812–814, Budapest, 1988.

[8] L. Gasser and J.-P. Briot. *Object-Based Concurrent Programming and Distributed Artificial Intelligence.* In N. M. Avouris and L. Gasser, (eds.), Distributed Artificial Intelligence: Theory and Praxis, pp. 81–107. Kluwer, Dordrecht, 1992.

[9] U. Hustadt and A. Nonnengart. *Modalities in Knowledge Representation.* In Proc. of the Sixth Australian Joint Conference on Artificial Intelligence, pp. 249–254, Sydney, 1993.

[10] B. Kipper and A. Jameson. *Semantics and Pragmatics of Vague Probability Expressions.* In Proc. of the 16th Annual Conference of the Cognitive Science Society, Atlanta, GA, 1994.

[11] L. Lambert and S. Carberry. *Using Linguistic, World, and Contextual Knowledge in a Plan Recognition Model of Dialogue.* In Proc. of the 14th COLING, pp. 310–316, Nantes, 1992.

[12] J. Laubsch and J. Nerbonne. *An Overview of $\mathcal{NLL}$.* Technical Report, HP Labs, 1991.

[13] J. D. Moore and C. L. Paris. *Planning Text for Advisory Dialogues.* In Proc. of the 27th Annual Meeting of the ACL, pp. 203–211, Vancouver, 1989.

[14] J. Pearl. *Probabilistic Reasoning in Intelligent Systems: Networks of Plausible Inference.* Morgan Kaufmann, San Mateo, CA, 1991. (Revised second printing).

[15] G. Sabah. *CARAMEL: A Computational Model of Natural Language Understanding Using a Parallel Implementation.* In Proc. of the Ninth ECAI, pp. 563–565, Stockholm, 1990.

[16] G. Sabah and X. Briffault. *CARAMEL: A Step Towards Reflection in Natural Language Understanding Systems.* In Proc. of the Fifth IEEE International Conference on Tools with AI, Boston, 1993.

[17] M.-H. Stefanini, A. Berrendonner, G. Lallich, and F. Oquendo. *TALISMAN: Un système multi-agents gouverné par des lois linguistiques pour le traitement de la langue naturelle.* In Proc. of the 14th COLING, Nantes, 1992.

[18] D. Vanderveken. *Meaning and Speech Acts.* Cambridge University Press, Cambridge, 1990.

[19] H. Velthuijsen. *The Nature and Applicability of the Blackboard Architecture.* Doctoral Dissertation, University of Maastricht, 1992.

[20] T. Wittig, (ed.). *ARCHON: An Architecture for Multi-Agent Systems.* Ellis Horwood, London, 1992.

[21] A. Yonezawa (ed.). *ABCL – An Object-Oriented Concurrent System,* The MIT Press, Cambridge, MA, 1990.

THE SUBLANGUAGE APPROACH:
A KEY TO REALISTIC NATURAL LANGUAGE PROCESSING

RUSLAN MITKOV

KAIST
Computer Science Department
373-1 Kusong-dong Yusong-gu
Taejon 305-701 KOREA
Email ruslan@cslab.kaist.ac.kr

ABSTRACT

The paper claims that the sublanguage approach is the only realistic approach in current Natural Language Processing (NLP) research and development. To start with, the key notion of "sublanguage" is presented from the viewpoint of various researchers. Next, some attractive properties of sublanguages with regards to NLP are discussed, followed by observations on the discourse structure differences in certain studied sublanguages. Finally, the paper will outline some sublanguage-based research and development in automatic abstracting, anaphora resolution and (discourse-oriented) machine translation.

1. What is a sublanguage?

One definition for a sublanguage is given by Kittredge[8] in which he defines a 'sublanguage' informally as any subsystem of a language which has the following properties:

- the language subsystem is used in reference to a particular domain of discourse, or family of related domains
- the set of sentences and texts in the language subsystem reflects the usage of some "community" of speakers, who are normally linked by common knowledge about the domain (facts, assumptions etc.) which goes beyond the common knowledge of speakers of the standard language
- the subsystem has all the "essential" properties of a linguistic subsystem, such as "consistency", "completeness", "economy of expression", and so forth
- the language system is maximal with respect to the domain, in the mathematical sense that no larger system has the same properties

Reference to a particular domain of discourse, or family of related domains is meant because the sublanguage can be made itself of other sublanguages. For example, we can refer to the sublanguage of "algebra", but we can speak also of the "sublanguage of mathematics". Though this definition is vague on a number of points, it has served successfully to indicate some of the important theoretical dimensions from which the sublanguage can be viewed.

Harris[6] gives a more mathematical definition: "certain proper subsets of the sentences of a language may be closed under some or all of the operations defined in the language and thus constitute sublanguage of it". In his theory, the important grammatical operations are mappings between sets of sentences. In essence, Harris' definition guarantees that a set of sentences will be considered a sublanguage only if it is grammatically complete and maximal with respect to the subject matter.

A problematic point in this definition may be the fact that sublanguages are mostly subsets of natural languages and on the latter it is not always easy to define certain language phenomena as "operations". Moreover, this definition does not tell us directly how to identify sublanguages, or how to determine their boundaries.

An interesting definition and an illustration of what sublanguage is, has been given by Baron[1]. He uses the notion of "linguistic core" (the "linguistic core" is supposed to be known by all recognized users of a particular language) to define the sublanguage as "precisely defined group of words and syntactic patterns whose meanings are agreed upon by a community of language users engaged in the same kinds of activity".

Among the researchers with prominent contribution to the theory of sublanguages are Harris[6], Raskin[20], Sager[22], Grishman[5], Lehrberger[11], Baron[1], Kittredge[8].

Some of the sublanguages in the real world that have been explored and have been used as major NLP/machine translation applications are: the sublanguage of weather (marine) bulletins[9], market reports[12], aircraft maintenance manuals[8], car advertisements[17].

2. Sublanguages and Natural Language Processing

Naturally occurring sublanguages demonstrate restrictions on the lexical, syntactic and semantic levels, which are beneficial for NLP. The recognition and exploitation of sublanguage patterns helps to reduce ambiguity of interpretation.

Adequate analysis of input text is crucial for successful natural language understanding and machine translation. If a source analyser is based on a sublanguage grammar, instead of a grammar of the whole language, then a significant gain in efficiency is possible.

There are a few factors which make the sublanguage-based natural language processing so attractive. Regarding the analysis, the parsing time is considerably shorter since sublanguage grammars are always smaller than the grammars of whole languages. Furthermore, the problem of structural and lexical ambiguity is greatly reduced, since many interpretations or analyses in the standard languages, are not valid for the respective sublanguages.

From our different studies we are now convinced that natural language processing can be realistically successful only within limited sublanguages. Yet there are certain further facts to be considered.

First, in a sublanguage, the rules for constructing meaningful sentences can be made much more precise than in language as a whole. These rules can be related in terms of word classes which are discovered by studying the distributional properties of words in texts.

Second, in a sublanguage the rules for constructing sentences may be quite different from (and even contrary to) the rules for sentences in the 'standard' sublanguage. The grammar of a standard natural language does not 'contain' the grammars of all its sublanguages, because some structures or operations exist only in particular sublanguages and have no role in a standard natural language grammar.

Third, sublanguages may be rather small (e.g., weather bulletins, car or house advertisements), or very large (e.g., texts in aircraft hydraulics or organic chemistry). What qualifies a variety of language as a sublanguage is not its size or complexity, but its adherence to systematic usage. The 'well-behaved' sublanguages of science and technology may use terminology from the everyday world, but this 'seepage' from general language is usually possible only in specific grammatical positions. We must admit that some sublanguages appear to be more systematic than others. It is in fact the degree of systematicity which will determine how appropriate a sublanguage is for automatic translation.

How should one select a specific sublanguage for a possible NLP application? Before picking a particular sublanguage for system design, it may be advisable to compare candidate sublanguages and estimate the computational tractability of the most likely choices. Methods for doing this are still experimental, but certain guidelines can be given.

The simplest measure of sublanguage size and complexity involves only its vocabulary. One can plot a curve of vocabulary growth against the number of running text words in a corpus which is considered representative of the sublanguage. To the extent that these curves flatten out after a certain point, one may assume that the sublanguage word usage is relatively constrained. From the slope of the curve and the maximal value of different words found in the largest corpus used, one can estimate the total size of the vocabulary.

Vocabulary growth curves are easy to compute and present only minor problems of methodology, but they do not give the accurate picture of sublanguage closure. What is more important than vocabulary growth is the degree of closure of the grammar itself. One attempt to measure grammatical closure[5] has used the number of grammatical production rules of a general English grammar which were applied in analysing a corpus of sublanguage texts. It would be still better to measure the specific sublanguage grammar rules (assuming that no other grammar exists) needed to account for a growing corpus. This requires rewriting the sublanguage grammar several times for a growing corpus, which is very hard work, but should give the most accurate prediction of sublanguage closure.

It seems that the most difficult tasks is to find an appropriate restricted sublanguage. One of the main reasons for the success of the TAUM-METEO operational machine translation system[7] (probably the best example of the sublanguage approach) is the excellent choice of the sublanguage (marine weather forecasts). Unfortunately, most subworlds are not as constrained with respect to vocabulary size, semantic ambiguity and syntactic diversity as repetitive weather forecasts.

3. Do all sublanguages across the natural languages exhibit the same discourse structure?

We should handle the sublanguages in applications like machine translation and multilingual text generation with caution. One should not expect identity of the discourse structure within the same sublanguages across the different natural languages.

We do not know any work which reports on parallel investigation of the sublanguage discourse structures and most of the multilingual generation systems assume indirectly their equivalence. As a result, most bilingual generators so far generate texts with identical or similar structure and not much attention has been paid to the fact that naturally occurring texts in different sublanguages with the same content do not necessarily have the same discourse organization structure. We found out that such texts have in many cases (sublanguages) different structures[16,17].

3.1 *The sublanguage of public weather forecasts*

The above argument holds for the sublanguage of public weather forecasts. Bourbeau et al.[2], describe bilingual generation (English and French) of marine weather forecasts. In marine weather forecasts the discourse organization rules for both English and French are practically identical. This is probably due the international conventions in marine forecasting and to its telegraphic style. Unfortunately, this is not the case in public weather forecasts. Public weather reports differ from country to country, from newspaper (radio/TV station) to newspaper (station). We studied many weather reports from English (The Independent) and French (Le Quotidien) newspapers (before that we had studied Bulgarian also texts) and came to the conclusion that weather report structures differ with the languages[16].

3.2 *Other sublanguages*

We have studied parallelly (for both English and Malay) the discourse structure of a few sublanguages, potential candidates for translation domains in a machine translation system[17]: the sublanguages of job vacancies, residential properties for sale, cars for sale and education advertisements from different newspapers in English (News Straits Times, Star) and Malay (Berita Harian, Utusan Malaysia). From our investigation we found out that discourse patterns across the sublanguages for English and Malay are not always identical and do not occur equally frequent.

4. Our sublanguage-based research and developments

We have been doing sublanguage-based research and developments at least in the following NLP areas: automatic abstraction, anaphora resolution and (discourse-oriented) machine translation. In this section we will present briefly our sublanguage-based work.

4.1 *Automatic abstraction*

We have developed and implemented a model for automatic abstraction of short summaries in the sublanguage of elementary geometry[18]. Unlike most of the automatic abstraction models which do not make use of knowledge of the domain (an therefore are hardly capable of differentiating the "important" from the other concepts in the area) and linguistic knowledge (the summaries obtained usually do not undergo any additional modifications and the uncontrolled linkage of the text picked up for summary may sometimes be unacceptable), our model relies on empirical, domain and linguistic knowledge, the latter enabling an additional treatment of the extracted text in order to obtain more coherent and natural text. Our approach is sublanguage-based: the knowledge (including most of the linguistic rules) incorporated is domain- and therefore sublanguage-dependent. The sublanguage of school geometry in Bulgarian has been chosen as a test language for our experiments.

The automatic abstractionpp model consists of separate, but flexibly interdependent empirical, domain and linguistic modules. The input text is analysed with respect to its empirically expected significance, domain importance and linguistic references by all the three modules in an interactive way. The rules of the empirical and domain modules suggest which text sequences are to be included in the preliminary summary and the linguistic module generates its final revised version. The described system is being used for producing short paragraph abstracts in the sublanguage of elementary (high school) geometry in Bulgarian.

4.2 *Anaphora resolution*

We have developed a sublanguage-based model for anaphora resolution in the sublanguage of computer science[18]. Special attention is paid to a new approach for tracking the center of a discourse segment, which plays an important role in proposing the most likely antecedent to the anaphor in case of ambiguity.

Given the complexity of the problem, we think that to secure a comparatively successful handling of anaphora resolution one should adhere to the following principles: 1) restriction to a domain (sublanguage) rather than focus on a particular natural language as a whole; 2) maximal use of linguistic information integrating it into a uniform architecture by means of partial theories. Some more recent treatments of anaphora[4, 21] do express the idea of "multi-level approach", or "distributed architecture", but their ideas (i) do not seem to capture enough discourse and heuristical knowledge and (ii) do not concentrate on and investigate a concrete domain, and thus risk being too general. We have tried nevertheless to incorporate some of their ideas into our own proposals.

Our anaphora resolution model is sublanguage-based (valid for the sublanguage of computer science) and integrates modules containing different types of knowledge - syntactic, semantic, domain, discourse and heuristical knowledge. All the modules share a common representation of the current discourse.

The syntactic module knows about the agreement of anaphors and antecedents in number, gender and person, checks c-command constraints, takes into consideration syntactic parallelism and topicalized noun phrases. The semantic module checks for semantic consistency between the anaphor and the possible antecedent, filters out semantically incompatible candidates and takes into account semantic parallelism.

The domain knowledge module is practically a knowledge base of the concepts of the domain considered and the discourse knowledge module knows how to track the center throughout a discourse segment. The heuristical knowledge module can sometimes be helpful in assigning the antecedent. It has a set of useful rules (e.g. the antecedent is to be located preferably in the current sentence or in the previous one) and can forestall certain impractical search procedures.

The syntactic and semantic modules usually filter the possible candidates and do not propose an antecedent (with the exception of syntactic and semantic parallelism). Usually the proposal for an antecedent comes from the domain, heuristical, and discourse modules. The latter plays an important role in tracking the center and proposes it in many cases as the most probable candidate for an antecedent.

4.2.1 *The need for discourse criteria and tracking center in the sublanguage of computer science*

Although the syntactic and semantic criteria for the selection of an antecedent are already very strong, they are not always sufficient, even in a limited sublanguage, to discriminate among a set of possible candidates. Moreover, they serve more as filters to eliminate unsuitable candidates than as proposers of the most likely candidate. Additional criteria are therefore needed. Usually the center of a sentence is the prime candidate for pronominal reference. Therefore, often the main problem which arises is the tracking of the center throughout a discourse segment. Certain ideas and algorithms for tracking center[3] have been proposed, provided that one knows the focus or center of the first sentence in the segment. However, they do not try to identify this center. Our approach determines the most probable center of the first sentence, and then tracks it all the way through the segment, correcting the proposed algorithm at each step.

Our approach is sublanguage-oriented and has been developed on the basis of an examination of numerous computer science texts. Extensive study in the sublanguage of computer science enabled us to formulate various rules for center selection or preference among the noun (verb) phrases of the sentences/clauses in a discourse segment.

On the bases of the concluded results, we proposed an artificial intelligence approach[18] to determine the probability of a noun (verb) phrase to be the center of a sentence. This approach, unlike the known other approaches, *allows* us to calculate this probability in every discourse sentence, *including* the first one and to propose the most probable center. Other existing approaches show how to track center, provided one knows the center of the first sentence in a discourse segment. This approach, combined with the algorithm for tracking the center[3], is expected to yield improved results.

4. 3 *Machine translation*

We have used a sublanguage-based approach also in a discourse-oriented English-Malay machine translation project[15] which takes into account the text organization rules of the target language. Most of the machine translation systems translate sentence-by-sentence and as a result the discourse structure of the output language is identical with that of the input language. As already stated however, in some sublanguages the discourse structures of the source and the target language are not identical. The mentioned project proposes a practical solution based on the recognition of the source paragraphs as schemata of rhetorical predicates (as defined in [13]) which are to be transformed into output schemata, characteristic of the discourse rules of the target sublanguage. Since machine translation can be successful only within a restricted domain, we have concentrated on studying different sublanguages for the needs of discourse-oriented machine translation and a few newspaper advertisement sublanguages have been studied.

The discourse-oriented English-Malay machine translation model performs "preliminary" translation by sentences, breaks up the sentences into propositions, recognizes each proposition as a rhetorical predicate of a discourse schema and before giving the output of the whole text (paragraph), arranges and coordinates the propositions within an overall organizational framework (schema) of the paragraph according to the organization rules of the target sublanguage[15].

4.3.1 *Sublanguages and schemata*

In the texts studied, we found out that schemata could not be always uniquely defined. There are sublanguages where more than one typical schema should be defined and consequently used. We examined numerous texts on the basis of which we defined "stable schemata"[15]. For translation from English into Malay, if more than one stable schema is available in the respective sublanguage, the stable schema, which is closest to the input of English text is chosen. For determining closeness, special metrics has been developed[17].

For the purpose of our study we have collected and studied 500 samples of English texts and the same number of Malay texts on job vacancies, 400 English and 300 Malay texts on residential properties for sale, 400 sample English texts and 450 sample Malay texts on cars for sale, and a total of 300 samples on education .

From our investigations on these sublanguages we drew three main conclusions:

1) The discourse patterns for English and Malay are not always identical and do not occur equally frequent
2) For some sublanguages there are more than one typical pattern
3) For some sublanguages there exists no stable schema

These conclusions are important for machine translation because in the second case there is no need for discourse transition rules and the translation should be undertaken sentence-by-sentence. Moreover, the conducted experiments justify undoubtedly the need of a sublanguage-based, discourse-oriented approach in machine translation since the studied sublanguages do not exhibit identical properties.

5. References

1. N. Baron, *Language, Sublanguage and the Promise of Machine Translation.*, Computers and Translation, Vol. 1, No.1, 1986
2. L. Bourbeau, D. Carcagno, E. Goldberg, R. Kittredge, A. Polguère, *Bilingual generation of weather forecasts in an operation environment*, Proceedings of COLING'90, Helsinki, 1990
3. S. Brennan, M. Fridman, C. Pollard, *A centering approach to pronouns*, Proceedings of the 25th Annual Meeting of the ACL, Stanford, CA, 1987
4. J. Carbonell, R. Brown, *Anaphora resolution: a multi-strategy approach.*, Proceedings of the 12. International Conference on Computational Linguistics COLING'88, Budapest, August, 1988
5. R. Grishman, T.N. Ngo, E. Marsh, L. Hirschman, *Automatic determination of sublanguage syntactic usage*, Proceedings of COLING'84, Stanford, California
6. Z. Harris, *Mathematical structures of language*, New York, Wiley-Interscience.

7. P. Isabelle, L. Bourbeau, *TAUM-AVIATION: Its technical features and some experimental results.* Computational Linguistics 11, 1985

8. R. Kittredge, *The significance of sublanguage for Machine Translation,* In Nirenburg S. (Ed): Machine Translation - Theoretical and methodological issues, Cambridge University Press, 1987

9. R. Kittredge, A. Polguère, *Synthesizing weather forecasts from formatted data,* Proceedings of COLING'86, Bonn, 1986

10. R. Kittredge, A. Polguère, *Dependency grammars for bilingual text generation: Inside FoG's stratificational models,* In Proceedings from the International Conference "Current Issues in Computational Linguistics", Penang, Malaysia, 10-14 June, 1991

11. J. Lehrberger, *Sublanguage analysis.* In: Grishman R., and Kittredge R. Analyzing language in restricted domains, Hillsdale, NJ, Lawrence Erlbaum Associates, 1986

12. K. Kukich, *Design of a knowledge-based report generator,* Proceeding of the 21st Annual meeting of the Association for computational linguistics, 1983

13. K. McKeown, *Text generation: using discourse strategies and focus constraints to generate natural language text.,* Cambridge university press, Cambridge, 1985

14. R. Mitkov, *Generating explanations of geometrical objects.* Computers and Artificial Intelligence, Vol.9, No.6, 1990

15. R. Mitkov, *Discourse-based approach in machine translation* From Proceedings of the International Symposium on Natural Language Understanding and Artificial Intelligence, Fukuoka, Japan, 13-15 July, 1992.

16. R. Mitkov, *Multilingual generation of public weather forecasts.* Proceedings of the SPICIS'92 (Singapore International Conference on Intelligent Systems) Conference, 28 September-1 October 1992, Singapore.

17. R. Mitkov, *Sublanguage schemata and their importance in machine translation.* Proceedings of the I International Conference on Mathematical Linguistics, Tarragona, 30-31 March, 1993.

18. R. Mitkov, *An integrated model for anaphora resolution,* Proceedings of the 15th International Conference on Computational Linguistics COLING'94, Kyoto, Japan, 5-9 August 1994

19. R. Mitkov, *Automatic Abstracting in a limited domain.* Proceedings of the Pacific Asia Conference on Formal and Computational Linguistics, Taipei, 30-31 August 1993

20. V. Raskin, *Towards a theory of sublanguages* (In Russian К теории языковых подсистем), Moscow, Moscow University Press, 1971

21. E. Rich, S. LuperFoy, *An architecture for anaphora resolution.* Proceedings of the Second Conference on Applied Natural Language Processing, Austin, Texas, 9-12 February 1988

22. N. Sager, *Syntactic formatting of science information.* In: AFIPS Proceedings, reprinted in Kittredge R. and Lehrberger J. Sublanguage: studies of language in restricted semantic domains, Berlin-New York, de Gruyter

AUTHOR INDEX